PORTLAND BOULDERING

SECOND EDITION

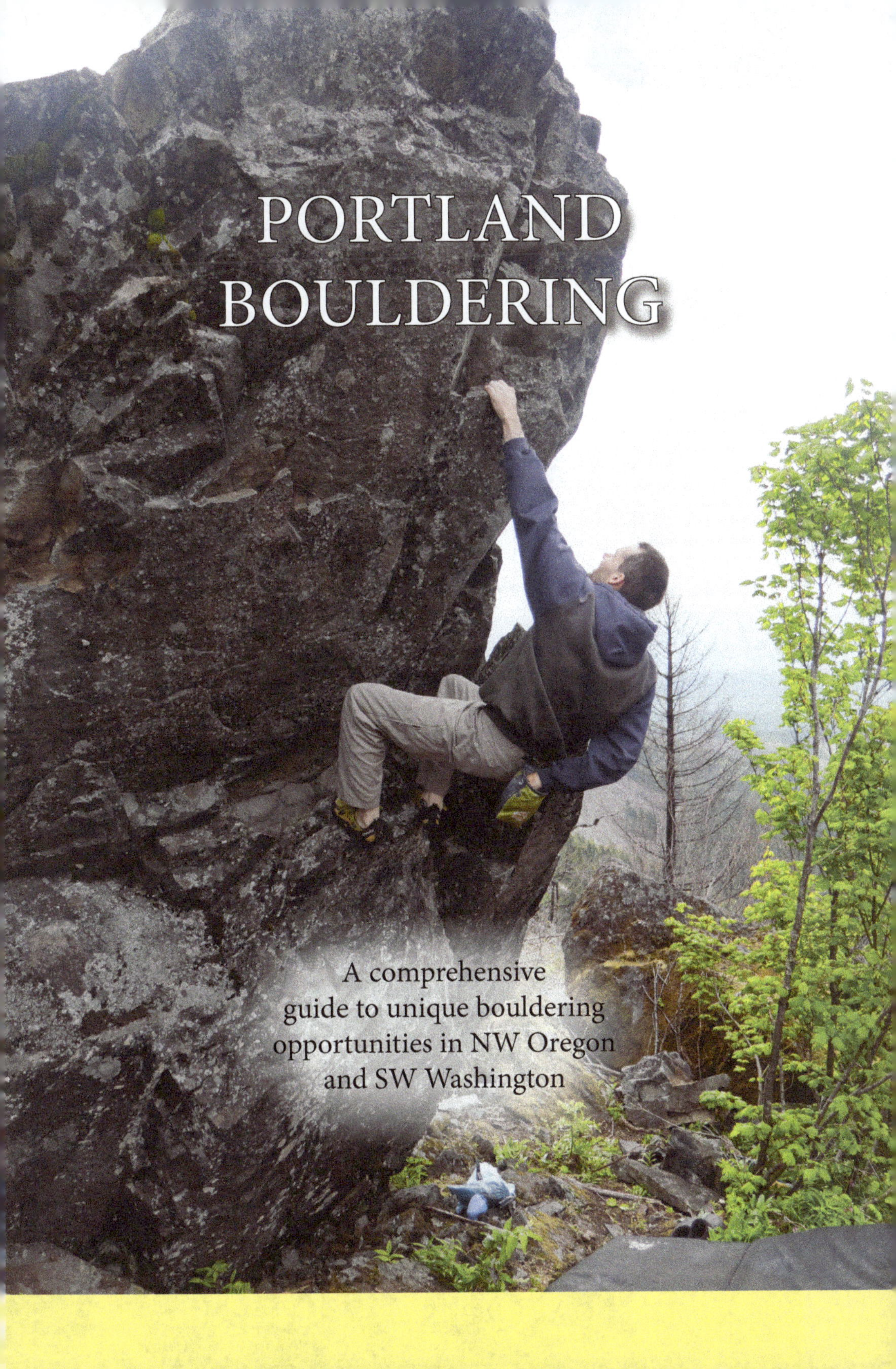

PORTLAND
BOULDERING

A comprehensive
guide to unique bouldering
opportunities in NW Oregon
and SW Washington

Portland Bouldering™
Copyright © 2019 East Wind Design

All rights reserved. No part of this book may be reproduced or transmitted in any form by any means, electronic or mechanical, including photocopying and recording, or by any information storage system, except as may be expressly permitted by the Copyright Act. Requests for permission must be made in writing to the publisher.

Book Design: East Wind Design
Technical Maps and Illustrations: East Wind Design

Cover Photograph: Bouldering at the *Empire*
Frontispiece images: *Larch Mtns, Empire, Larch, Empire, and High Rocks Boulders*

ISBN-13: 978-0-9997233-4-0
Library of Congress Card Number:
Portland Bouldering (PB2) v 2.2
Printed in the USA

PORTLAND BOULDERING

TABLE OF CONTENTS

DISCLAIMER

Rock climbing and bouldering contains certain inherent risks that may be dangerous to your health. The sole purpose of this book is to inform rock climbers of the many unique crag climbing opportunities available in and around our corner of Northwest Oregon. Before attempting any bouldering described in these pages you should first be proficient in the use of modern rock climbing and bouldering equipment.

This guidebook is not a substitute for personal insight, time-learned skills, or lessons taught by climbing instructors. There are no warranties, neither express nor implied, that this book contains accurate or reliable information. As the user of this or any guidebook, you assume full responsibility for your own safety. Because the sport is constantly evolving, the author cannot guarantee the accuracy of any of the information in this book, including the V-grades, location of routes, route names, route descriptions, or approach trails. No one can offer you any assurance against natural hazards such as lightning or other weather phenomena, loose or poor quality rock, or the risk of equipment failure. Consider with suspicion all fixed protection (such as bolts). Weathering, metal quality, and impact stress loading are some of the variants that can cause fixed gear to fail.

Only you can know the scope and the upper limit of your rock climbing abilities. Assess your prospective climb shrewdly, and make prudent decisions based on your strengths and weaknesses. If you have any doubt concerning your ability to safely ascend a climbing route today, then stop and consider a climb that is less difficult or dangerous.

This is not a how-to guide but rather a where-to book. This book explains where to rock climb, but you must honestly determine whether you have mastered the most important aspects of the sport before embarking on any rock climbing adventure.

Consult other climbers about the adventure or rock climb you are planning to embark upon. A skilled climber who knows the crag can give quality advice and insight as to proper gear placement as well as impart ideas about climbing technique and balance that will surely be beneficial to you.

Wisely seek assistance and attain good instruction from others such as a diligent climbing instructor who will teach you how to become a safe, intuitive climber.

Exercise good judgment as to where the climbing route ascends the cliff face, and learn to quickly perceive subtle variants you will likely encounter in route difficulty. Know your own strengths and weaknesses; develop a competent understanding of your route-finding abilities and safety skills, for these and the right equipment are your best protection against the hazards of climbing. Confidence and ability gained through many hours of physical and mental preparation are perhaps the most valuable skills you and your climbing partner will need when managing the degree of risk you both are willing to accept.

PREFACE

This edition of *Portland Bouldering* is the creative expression of several individuals who have brought considerable momentum to the sport of rock climbing and bouldering in this portion of the state. From a core group of persons came forth the primary portions of this little book, which began in younger years when various persons opted to collect their climbing and bouldering activity in a relative format from which to glean a concise storyline to build this book upon. Bringing their ideas and recommendations forward into this project gives it an essential value unmatched locally.

During your quest to tap into outdoor recreational sports, remember that our rock climbing and bouldering actions today impact and influence the future decisions of property owners and land managers alike. We are responsible for keeping ours a friendly, self-managed sport and for acting in full cooperation with land managers so that we will continue to be welcomed for generations to come.

By developing a perceptive, respectful awareness of the environment around us, from the peregrine falcon to *Sedum integrifolium*, we ultimately discover that we are entrusted with the keys to provide a legacy for tomorrow. Hopefully you will find the information bound within these pages both rewarding and fulfilling.

ACKNOWLEDGMENTS

The culmination of beta in this book exists primarily because of the shared knowledge and assistance of many friends and individuals. Thank you all for sharing your expertise about the exhilarating edge of this sport.

This guidebook is the end formulation of insight from all those boulderers who relish this sport and choose to maintain valued historical notes on the sport. Numerous tidbits of data exist in various small articles, but a major portion of the information is through close contact with friends and acquintances who have collected a rather impressive amount of bouldering information and data, each focused toward their relative prospective view of the sport.

Over many years various individuals provided expandable authoritative information, or climbing energy, or valued insight about various bouldering sites, persons not specifically referenced here, but who have collectively added to the wealth of knowledge of local bouldering in this region. Photo credits go to several individuals: Mr Abbott, Mr Fields, Mr Jones, etc.

Some of this regions most emphatic players in the game of bouldering are as follows:

From approximately 1990-2000: Mr Bernert, Mr Lyon, Mr Rall, Mr Pajunas, Mr Ryan, Mr Nakahira, Mr Schultz, Mr Chase, Mr Coleman, Mr Scales, Mr Abbott, Mr Alfers, Mr Hill, Mr Kester, etc. From about 2001-2019 onward: Mr Abbott, Mr Sowerby, Mr Polizzano, Mr Slayton, Mr Porter, Mr Davis, Mr Williams, Mr Vitt, Mr Crowder, Mr Cova, Mr Krossen, Mr Svenden, Mr Klesick, Mr Cousins, Mr Fields, Michael Brady, etc. The "etc" includes a vast number of additional individuals who did brief select new problems here and there.

A number of individuals were highly instrumental in sharing various crucial aspects of knowledge, ideas and energy that have helped to strengthen the quality and vibrant nature of this book. Those individuals are a virtual walking encyclopedia of superb detailed knowledge on multiple tangents of the sport in this region. Their wealth of local bouldering history, in-depth bouldering beta, extensive photography collection, as well as an express determination to continously explore unknown places to find the next hotspot crag or boulder site were instrumental in this project. Considerable portions of this book are reflective of that energetic personality and invaluable expertise. That information knowledge base yielded data that could be compiled accurately into a quality product that would satisfy the interest of all climbers in this region.

Altogether these people bring a life-time of broad-ranging highly valued climbing skills, indepth local climbing politics knowledge, and a profound interest in the various facets of rock climbing adventures in all its wild flavors. Within the various degrees of climbing, from rock climbing, bouldering to mountain climbing, their shared optimism to explore new crags and find new boulder sites is a unique creative energy that keeps this sport moving forward by promoting an increased wealth of publically accessible rock climbing areas, each person tackling unique ways to continually expand the sport in this region.

It's A Bouldering World

BOULDERING INTRO

Bouldering opportunities in Northwest Oregon and Southwest Washington

Portland Bouldering guidebook is a powerful detailed anthology, specifically focusing on the expansive wealth of bouldering opportunities and multi-faceted aspects of the bouldering world in a relatively minor region of the USA.

Encapsulated within this lengthy book you will find an in-depth analysis, a virtual encyclopedia, on the subject of bouldering around NW Oregon and SW Washington. The world of regional outdoor bouldering, centered around Portland, Oregon has been a rapidly changing game, bringing new opportunities for the quest seeking, nuance-driven boulderer who is determined to tap the latest cool problems found in the sport of bouldering. This section provides a power-packed analysis of numerous new and well established bouldering sites that are sure to spike your enthusiasm to a new high.

PB takes you on a grand tour through the core zones of interest (both popular and obscure sites) between Portland, The Dalles and south to Albany-Corvallis, capturing within this book the essential tools to play the game, as well as providing you with the primary reason to be part of this growing Northwest Oregon bouldering sport.

Today's boulderer can easily maintain 12-month continuity fitness levels throughout the year thanks to indoor sports gyms. Indoor sports bouldering gym facilities, first established in Portland in the early 1980's, are today quite numerous and very popular. Today these sports gyms provide quality indoor training and practice environs where dedicated individuals can build their skills base before venturing outdoors to the vast treasure of old and new bouldering sites this micro-region has to offer. This modern trend, mixing gym training sessions with an expansive wealth of new bouldering site options is a far cry from the limited choice of early era bouldering sites like Carver Boulders and BOGB. Indeed, year-round sports gyms have gradually, yet radically increased the appetite for people to step outdoors and explore this fascinating plethora of bouldering opportunities.

Considering the limitations that cold, rainy winter months have on this outdoor activity in western Oregon, it seems a bit odd that the activity has attained considerable increased value. Yet, using each good weather window, and tapping the sunny south-facing (or breezy) aspects of certain sites, you can extend your outdoor bouldering opportunities to virtual year-round sessions. Several mini sites such as Hamilton Boulders and Horsethief Butte offer year-round bouldering.

Portland has not been viewed as a primary bouldering haven in the 90's nor during the early part of this century. Yet with the latest additional string of quality new sites such as Hamilton Boulders, Alpenglow, and the Empire, a quality series of close proximity sites offer superb direct

Preston at *Empire Boulders*

opportunities for today's boulderer who no longer must endure long drives to Sisters Boulders.

So, mix a sweet combination of numerous city-based indoor bouldering gyms, numerous well-established (and new) bouldering sites with 3000+ total problems, stack on top of it Northwest Oregon's largest bouldering site (Lost Lake Boulders), toss into the mix about six months of great bouldering weather, and we may possibly have a nice comprehensive micro bouldering region after all (...maybe). So, grab your rock shoes and chalk bag and hit the road, and go visit some of the wealth found at Portland's best bouldering sites.

This analysis on the activity of bouldering around Northwest Oregon is purely introductory in scope, just one mere edge of the sport, and not a 'complete' discussion of it. Using Lost Lake Boulders as an example: it barely started seeing substantial sending activity in late 2013, yet when it is eventually fully tapped will easily qualify as the biggest bouldering site in this particular micro-

region. With all consideration toward all the numerous sites that compose regional bouldering in/near Northwest Oregon, certainly the sport of bouldering has essentially become its own stand-alone sport.

Outdoor recreation based sports in Oregon is increasingly popular, and growing community networks of sport enthusiests have made shared responsibility stewardship trends integral to their core group message, and have established relational goals in conjunction with local land managers in recent years. Ethical responsibility and an earnest desire to see more openness for climbing or bouldering helps frame citizen communication networks of stewardship based co-operation

GENERAL HISTORY

Prior to the advent of indoor sports bouldering and climbing gyms, enthusiasts frequented the stone wall formation at the top of Rocky Butte in the heart of east Portland for endurance training. The vertical short man-made walls offered thin edge problems, and long technical, pumpy traverses, a minor spot that in the past provided limited entertainment.

Bouldering in Portland, Oregon started gaining a form of brief value in the late 1980's (and early 90's) when several crag developers began unearthing a few mossy blocks at Carver Cliff. Several of the earliest stones developed were the Standard Overhang (V3), Darrell's Route (V4), Trask (V0), and T-face (V4), tagged by locals such as Lyon, Pajunas, and Nakahira. In the mid-90's the game did kickstart into high gear when Mr Rall and Mr Ryan developed the James Dean and Titlest Boulders in 1996 at Carver. Mr Pajunas, Schultz and Chase gradually tackled the Bonzai Boulder Cluster at Carver.

This mid-to-late 90's first major 'golden age' development wave at Carver Boulders progressed under the influential talents of several like-minded individuals and their connections at local indoor sports gyms. Mr Chase, Mr Coleman, Mr Lyon, and Mr Scales established a series of new power routes in the V6-V8 range (such as Gruel, Super Cool, Red Meat Man, Cedar, and Triangle Face).

The game of bouldering seemed to suit their style well. Through their connections at the indoor sports bouldering/climbing gyms the outdoor bouldering activism encouraged various acquaintances to add fuel to the flames of Carver's development phase. A broad range of persons who developed the first urban bouldering sites were Andy Coleman, Gary Rall, Mike Pajunas, Jered Bernert, Matt Slayton, Tom Scales, Greg Lyon, Curt Smith, Tymun Abbott, Brian Chase, Mr Alfers, Chris Hill (at Schwingus), and others. As interest grew for bouldering locally in the late 90's other players such as Pajunas sought out new sites like Magma Zone. Jason Kester and associates were even tapping the Meadow near Bulo in the late 90's.

In the end Carver became the trend setting bouldering site for Portland, even though the stones began to moss over the minute you walked back to your car. Carver was not gold, but it was the heart of Portland bouldering back-in-the-day, and continues to attract boulderers even today.

Because of Greg's avid perseverance within the game of bouldering it eventually presented a golden opportunity for him to compile the first known small booklet (Bouldering in Portland and the Columbia River Gorge, printed in 2000) about bouldering for Northwest Oregon. It covered a range of sites from Carver to Horsethief Butte and set the stage for future site development. His tiny booklet provided the incentive to expand the development of boulder problems at Carver further (Jered sent the first Portland V10 at Carver), but also gave reason for people to seek new haunts. It was through Jered's direct efforts to discover and tap into Bridge Of The Gods Boulders that the value of bouldering in this region proved there could be more quality bouldering opportunities further afield.

Those early years for Portland bouldering seem small and inscrutable when compared to national polarized sites like Bishop Boulders or Yosemite Boulders. In the lowly beginnings after a few hardy locals rolled the first 'carpet' of moss off from one of Carver's big stones, the bouldering concept in town morphed, deafeningly slow in the first few years, but once that initial vital wave of energy compounded, it eventually focused into a localized dedicated scene of its own.

A rather small yet diverse group of individuals crossed paths regularly in the process of boulder development in those days, yet some of those individuals seldom mixed even at the bouldering site. Mr Abbott, for example, along with his wife, cleaned, sent, and recorded his original Carver sends independently while in pursuit of wild forest games. For Tymun the bouldering methodology of crimp strength endurance suit his physique

Dave S. on *60° of Desperation*

well, so he has steadily absorbed the front edge of this sport ever since the late 90's. One may think of this as an African safari hunt, yet it was their enthusiasm for the hunt that set the future pattern for new bouldering sites in this region. Interactive timing, connections, and vision of each core group and its members seem to drive each phase of site development as the network of players widen with each new year.

Chris Hill (and friends) tackled the problems at the (Rocky Butte) Schwingus. That zone (popular back in those days) is a lowly dread bouldering hangout with certain unappealing nuances generally lacking long-term viability today. Mike Pajunas exclusively developed the Magma Zone, an obscure north-facing basalt outcrop east of Broughton Bluff that still rebuffs most interest.

At the turn of the 21st century, Jered Bernert and associates stepped beyond Carver to tap into the quality boulders at Bridge Of The Gods Boulders (BOGB). This long thin string of large andesite blocks provided a new source for additional entertainment.

The Beacon Boulders were sent as late as 1999-2000 by Greg Lyon and friends. Bulo Point was utilized by a mixture of Portlanders and Hood River locals, probably beginning in the 1970's, primarily for lead climbing (and TR'ing), and recently for bouldering. Near the city of The Dalles the crag called Horsethief Butte was likely initially tapped by bold young native Americans in moccasins, then more recently from the 1960's onward by a broad assortment of rock climbers who basically soloed or bouldered some of the obvious lines, before bouldering had terminology. Many persons have and still do find Horsethief Butte to be a great multi-season bouldering and climbing site, especially since the sport of bouldering has taken hold as a viable entity of its own.

Eventually, some of the early core individuals had (business or familial) life goal factors limiting their quest for new bouldering sites. It has been relatively easy to locate main corridor sites like Carver or BOGB, yet it entailed another methodology altogether in order to successfully locate and tap into that next level of the sport for regional bouldering. One method was day hiking (plus mushrooming), and lots of it, that solved part of this quest for new sites. The other method required a totally alien concept (till the advent of the Web), known as internet-based Earth geodetic satellite imagery.

During the 2001 season Mr Abbott (initially with family) and Mr Sowerby proceeded to tap the best of Three Corner Rock boulders. Over a few brief years they effectively tapped many of the quality lines there, including the discovery in late 2001 of one of this regions icon sites (Alpenglow Boulders). The qualitative characteristics of the environment at Alpenglow are virtually unsurpassed in this region. Considerable credit it given to Mr Abbott for the ongoing exploratory savvy that he has placed upon the sport of regional bouldering.

At Cascade (Locks) Boulders, Mr A solved the riddle on two minor boulders located along the Frontage Road near Herman Creek. The full extent of this area remained a mystery for many years until another life-long local [Mr O] explored the area a bit more thoroughly. Each deeper exploratory journey into this little wooded wonderland revealed even greater potential, which today exceeds 250+ problems.

The Garden (near Sweet Home) was heavily tapped over many, many years by various mid-valley locals, as well as further afield valley-*ites* from Portland and Eugene. The Druid Stones at Marys Peak were explored and tapped beginning in about 2010 through the collaborative efforts

of Paul Waters and associates, who bouldered and thoroughly documented the sites potential, bringing to full public light this unique little quality site on superb gabbro rock.

With exploratory zeal one local day hiker had delved extensively throughout this region, and over the years memorized many potential bouldery outcrops. Sometime after Mr O had met Mr A (and heard of his bouldering savvy), like a flash of insight it became obvious that many of those past observed locales now held value. A re-visit to Larch Mtn in southwest Washington proved the point; the place indeed had untapped high quality bouldering.

Larch Mtn Boulders were originally and extensively tapped by Mr O and Mr A starting in early 2011 at the main butte. From the Leavenworth Boulder cluster to the Wild West formation, and from the North Slope cluster to the East Bluff formation they tapped about 100+ lines. Several acquaintances pegged a small selection of additional choice lines. Spencer Williams tackled Cannonfire and other lines. In subsequent years, a handful of additional quality problems were added by a mix of individuals such as Mr Slayton, Mr Porter and various acquaintances who tapped power lines on the Obelisk stellae. Mr Davis sent the power line V7 on Bonanza Boulder on the east side of the Wild West bluff.

Mountaineering and day hiking on the slopes of Mt Hood revealed evidence of large stones just above tree line. The Timberline Boulders offered a plethora of problems that were known by very few Government Camp locals (who occasionally scrambled upon a few stones), but the site was primarily extensively tapped over a very broad span of years by Mr O starting in roughly the year 2003 and eventually was virtually tapped out by the year 2012.

The Hamilton Boulders (aka Horse Camp) were an intriguing discovery. This site was long known by a local due to hiking in the area, so he asked Mr W to tour the site, who in turn immediately informed his acquaintances at the gym, who in turn took an immediate avid interest in setting the site at the forefront of Portland bouldering. This site has now become highly valued for its quality friction problems, as well as its multi-season appeal. The sites mega players were Mr Vitt, Mr Crowder, Mr Cova, Mr Porter, Mr Slayton, including Mr Krossen and others. The arm length list of problems at this site still expands, mainly in the upper talus field.

Lost Lake Boulders received a brief initial wave of 40+ problems in 2013, and another 40+ by Mr A/Mr O very early in 2014. Also early in 2014 a diverse crew of people (such as Mr Crowder, Mr Porter, Mr. Vitt, Mr Cova, Mr Svenden, Mr Klesick, Michael Brady, and many, many others) quickly expanded the list of problems at LLB. Each team brought a new level of skill capabilities and extreme grades. Earlier bouldering history? It's probable the parking lot stones were explored lightly prior to 2013, but the remainder of the site was generally untapped. The locally famous LLB site will eventually yield 1000+ problems, so its history still unfolds steadily today.

This micro-regions' centerpiece — the Empire Boulders — was getting initial use from about 2012 onward. Only two persons were the primary site development stewards (Mr A and Mr O). They personally prepped and climbed the vast majority of problems (90%+), crafted the steep slope landings, enhanced the various network of paths, named many boulders and problems.

Larch Mtn Boulders

This place simply would not exist without their effort.

Spencer Williams took on a large task of compiling Jered's original Carver site beta/diagrams bringing a briefly sold quality Carver Bouldering guide to market in 2011.

To this day in Northwest Oregon, the wave for discovering new bouldering sites continues to progress. The game of bouldering in this region has forever changed in a productive, expansive way; new destinations, more characteristic diversity, with virtually endless quality and variety. This brief historical commentary on some of the active players at these new bouldering sites is just a short list, and in no way indicates the entire spectrum of players who were part of the total force within the movement. In essence, the gradual expanding niche sport of bouldering in this region attained much of its forward momentum as a non-import locals-only process.

After the 90's (and early 2000's) watershed era during which the initial roots of outdoor bouldering took hold in this region, it has steadily gained forward momentum ever since, and today is firmly planted in the soil of Northwest Oregon. The initial dynamic interplay between rock climbing and bouldering was well linked in the past, but today bouldering seems to ride its own wave. Thus, the interactive results we see today are tied inherently to a valuable combination of indoor bouldering gyms for year-round training continuity that is thoroughly blended with outdoor seasonal bouldering. This trend seems to effectively meet that all-important seasonal dash one must endure while chasing the prime 6-month seasonal weather window-of-opportunity in order to successfully tackle outdoor bouldering in this micro-region.

The top bouldering destinations in North America (such as Hueco Tanks, Joe's Valley, Rocky Mtn National Park, Yosemite, Bishop, Horsepens, and Squamish B.C.) will always predominate in your destination bouldering goals, but numerous lowly sites in Northwest Oregon yield viable 'en route' options when your on a road trip passing through this region to your next main goal.

CLIMATE

Western Oregon valleys and the snow laden High Cascade Range predominate in douglas fir, spruce and hemlock forests that are often wrapped in misty overcast or drizzly days. The Oregon climate west of the Cascade Range is predominantly wet six months of the year. Pacific marine air weather systems bring an abundance of rainfall that saturates the region, especially from late-October through May. Between the rainy weather patterns when sunshine prevails (May through October) outdoor bouldering recreation ensues in earnest. During this portion of the year mild marine air often mixes with inland Great Basin hot weather to bring a climber-friendly cycle that keeps the region quite comfortable.

During the summer months temperatures average in the seventies to mid-eighties (Fahrenheit) with occasional short peaks of blazing

At BOG Boulders

hot sunny days reaching the nineties in July and August (infrequently peaking near 100°F+).

On stifling hot days in July and August, but don't hide because your favorite bouldering site is a boilerplate. Instead go to high altitude stellar bouldering sites that offer ideal 'heat-escape' locales far better than the low elevation bouldering sites (such as Larch Mtn Boulders, Silver Star Mtn on Ed's Trail, Three Corner Rock Boulders, Timberline Boulders, Cooper Spur Boulders, Bulo Point, Lost Lake Boulders, or Rock Creek Boulders). Some folks are determined to crank only V-hard, so full sunshine bouldering may be too limiting on the hottest summer days, but for those who relish VB-V3 there is an unlimited plethora of stuff at all the higher altitude sites, with minimal to zero moss, and a general lack of mosquitoes (at breezy sites).

By late October, the Pacific marine air storm tracks become more active, usually bringing a consistent series of rain showers. The typical winter storm systems generate frequent cold, rainy days with average temperatures in the 35–50°F range. Average annual precipitation in the Willamette Valley near Portland is about 40 inches.

Nearby, in Central Oregon, the world class destination haven of Smith Rock and its surrounding environ offer a infinite variety of virtual year-round climbing and bouldering on welded tuff (at Smith), and an unlimited supply of lowly rimrock basalt formations scattered liberally across the arrid region in a mixed forest of pine and juniper.

In summation: If it is not raining and it's warm – go bouldering; if it's raining go to the eastside of the Cascade Mtn Range to various bouldering sites.

MOSSES AND LICHENS

The frequently cloudy, wet temperate climate in Northwest Oregon promotes an ideal spore germination and growth habitat for mosses and liverworts, especially in the lower elevation rain forests. While prevalent at all elevations, fungal lichens are also commonly found on rocky headlands, open forest settings, or alpine environs (such as the immense swath of large dark slate-blue leaf lichen covering Blacktop Behemoth at Timberline Boulders). The habitable environs, in conjunction with locale (exposed outcrops or forest enhanced), temperature, and weather elements, including elevation, proportionally effect the growth rate of mosses and lichens. As a general summary, you can anticipate considerable moss growth on the upper top side of boulders west of the Cascade Mountain range at low elevation bouldering sites, especially if it is enclosed in a heavily forested zone in the 10' to 2,500' elevation zone. Sunny low elevation south-facing rock slopes have less moss or lichen growth due to its summer season heat-baked zone qualities (like Hamilton Boulders). Bouldering sites situated on the eastern slopes of the mountain range (like Horsethief Butte) tend to be less moss/lichen festooned due to the generally sunnier semi-arid environs. From about the 3,000'-5,000' level, the percentage of moss growth on stone surfaces gradually declines (perhaps 50% less), being minimized primarily based on a set of variables ranging from locale, to aspect, forest cover, and elevation. Above 5,000' moss growth on stone surfaces declines still further to virtually zero, scoured by wind, snow and strong winter elements, but various hardy species of lichen tend to be more present.

At Boulder Mtn Boulders

BASIC GEOLOGY

                                    The *Hamilton Boulders*

Its a quirk, at least in the eye of a boulderer, that the greatest percentage of large stone clusters found in this region (of high quality and quantity) are composed of andesitic-basaltic rock characteristics. From a geological perspective, this is readily apparent, simply because most of the Pacific Rim volcanoes (from Japan, to the Alaskan archipelago, and from western Canada / western U.S., to the Andes mountain range of South America) actively expelled (in recent history and to this date) voluminous quantities of igneous lava, some of it being old lava flows with andesitic characteristics. Andesite rock, in essence, is water, gas content, bits of sediment, and a healthy dose of silica sprinkled in, all previously subducted by an oceanic plate, conveyor belt fashion down beneath the continental plate. These two plates rub and drag sediment material downward, in a process which heats and melts the rock, pooling into massive molten structures that, being lighter than the surrounding older congealed rock structure, rises slowly to the surface venting explosively as volcanic mountain peaks.

The results of this conjunctive igneous mix produce lighter colored silica-rich lava rock types (breccias, tuffs, andesites, dacites, and rhyolites) of volcanoclastics found along the entire Pacific Rim volcanic string. After long periods of erosional and chemical weathering processes, the resultant forested landscape revealed exposed clusters of large andesitic boulders (or short vertical escarpments), in surprisingly extensive quantities throughout the northern Oregon Cascade Mountain range.

Andesite is compositionally a mineral-rich plagioclause matrix, yielding a natural slightly gritty friction-friendly surface of superb quality, including occasional gaseous vesicle pockets, and parallel joint plains that create edges or ribbing for fingertips and foot holds. Many andesite, rhyolite, and dacite boulders originally congealed as larger bulky structures or bluffs, but were tumbled and survived the initial roll remaining relatively intact in variable sizes 7'-25' diameter (occasionally larger). Variables within the compositional matrix of andesite can be extensive and radical, even if just a short distance lay between two sites (i.e. Alpenglow and Super Heroes). One site may yield minute bits of pyroxene, feldspar, amphibole, biotite or some quartz, while another site will have ⅔" sized crystalline interstices in the plagioclase matrix.

Though andesite is the dominant and preferred bouldering stone in northern Oregon, it's not the only good quality rock available. Larch Mtn Boulders are composed of bullet hard, high-quality peripheral granodiorite, formed from a nearby subsurface batholithic intrusion. Marys Peak near Corvallis has beautiful high-quality gabbro rock, yielding superb friction-friendly bouldering. Near Broughton Bluff, the Magma Zone is basaltic (and slick-*ish*), which may be part of the reason locals tend to avoid this site. At low altitude sites moss and soil may lightly etch the surface of the stone, as well. Another example of smooth basaltic stone is at Horsethief Butte, but the semi-arid environs have given some of the surface aspects a friendly textured patina. Beacon Rock, being an old andesitic volcanic neck of a once very tall mountain, its andesite perimeter lava flows should theoretically still be visible as horizontal slices in the surrounding bedrock terrain, such as the bluff from which the primary string of Cascade Boulders originates.

INHERENT RISKS
Boulderers are like railroad train engineers, wrapped in centric steel-like tendinous muscle, on

a sports quest, and sometimes on a sophist quest. The game of bouldering is somewhat like mixing vodka and a race car, so if your not expecting to see a volatile reaction, guess again. Bouldering necessitates logical judgment skills, so consider carefully prior to delving heavily into the outdoor bouldering scene. Beware of the inherent risk of personal injury, especially if you are prodded on with guttural boosts from your bouldering partner. A mixed recipe of this sort sometimes presses beggarly for potentially serious consequences. You might prefer to live without thirteen steel pins holding your ankle together (one of the uglier risks of this sport). When you get high on an 18'-24' tall stone, well above that postage stamp sized crashpad, one mere slip and your 5-day week occupational reality show might end as an internal compression injury, or something far uglier. If your doing a quick send on an 18' hi-ball off the deck, be careful. There is no guarantee that your hands won't peal off first when plowing sideways across an overhung roof. The word 'crash'-pad should provide a clue. Face it, rock climbing is obviously inherently risky, while the bouldering game is a subtle degree beyond that.

BOULDERING DIKTATS AND POLITIKS

The game of bouldering has its share of superficial conflicts. Factional crews, often at odds with each other, still rend the local scene with an ongoing level of secrecy, all in a bid to be first or have a claim on infinity. Certain sites, such as Carver, do have a long history documented by various crew members (compiled by separate distinct sources). A pattern of rivalry repeats itself even today at various bouldering sites. A first is a first regardless of how mossy, when, or who, sent the line, even if an SS is scooped 1' further down into the talus. Some boulder problems have seen a 'first' ascent by different factions, given a present prevailing name that indicates nothing of the original earlier ascentionist. The Garden Boulders site has been utilized by multiple generations of boulderers, each sending 'anew' and naming the line something 'new', yielding overlapping names, and varied grading conventions.

In this sport there are three general types of climbers or boulderers:

A. Those who simply rock climb or boulder (the most friendly way to enjoy the sport!).

B. Those who arrive later, scratch a line, and rewrite it all.

C. Those who are frontier forging sport hunters.

It's this third group that intrigues, because they will diligently search, explore and inspect, tap and develop into the various crags and/or bouldering sites in this region. This 1% tends to be at the cutting edge bringing more outdoor sports climbing and bouldering sites within reach for the common public benefit.

Those who made the greatest impact regionally in bouldering are its long-vested local lifers who tend to tackle bouldering area development in-depth, then as if beckoned by that mysterious Siren call, went in search of, and found, then would tap into the next new crag or bouldering ground, often producing quality results that have added exponential assets to this regions sport, all by their hands striving above the ordinary call of duty.

This micro-regions' elusive bouldering sites are broadly distributed, but tend to be densely packed with an average of 20-90 boulder problems per site. The scattered boulder sites (or crags) are usually tree-shrouded, seldom of mega size (like the ultra long TLC crag, or the 1k LLB). Most are just small hidden quaint little pocket gems (by Oregonian standards). These bouldering sites offered tantalizing exploratory options for those dedicated resident hunters of the sport, not the fickle rush-job type that wastes the forest to snag a few lines, but those lifers who knew their own backcountry forest like a skilled mushroom hunter who knows the best spot to search for chanterelle mushrooms.

Climbing and bouldering tourism in this micro-region has steadily expanded because various dedicated individuals find solutions to override any non-civilisé muddy quagmire. This bouldering activity has an expanding array of multi-level broad-scoped personalities whose experience and knowledge help to make the activity as valued as it is today.

Sandbag ratings are hopefully at a minimum herein, but you may still encounter some old-school V-grades that will throw you off, yet through diligent site research our team has made lengthy efforts to either know or send many of the boulder problems in this book. In general the ratings aim for consistency on a per zone/area basis only.

Bouldering and rock climbing is an inherently dangerous activity and you could potentially get injured or die from either sport activity. Do not use this book as an instructional manual. Get proper training through a guide service or an educational class with a local outdoor organization. Learn the game gradually tutorially with associates who know how to keep you safe and alive and happy so you can go out bouldering again tomorrow.

Textual and visual errors may exist in this book. You assume responsibility for your own safety, not the book author, nor publisher.

If you have historical beta or development information that is missing from this book, and are inclined to share, or provide feedback, contact us via email with your info. We always aim to improve the accuracy of future book editions.

BOULDERING GRADE SCALE

Boulder problems use the well-known Verm or V-rating system. This effective grade comparison scale is designed to articulate a relational comparison involving short bursts of energy typical of concise boulder moves. Though it should relate to actual exact lead rock climbing grades it does not quite parallel, due in part to broad variables encountered in protection based roped climbing.

V-scale	YDS scale
VB	5.9 and under
V0	5.10a/b
V1	5.10c/d
V2	5.11a/b
V3	5.11c/d
V4	5.12-
V5	5.12b/c
V6	5.12+
V7	5.13-
V8	5.13b/c

V9	5.13+
V10	5.14a
V11	5.14b
V12	5.14c
V13	5.14d
V14	5.15a
V15	5.15b
V16	5.15c
V17	5.15d

Beta Nuances (Sit Start, Grades, etc)

In this bouldering book the V-scale grading units have meaning (sometimes subtle). VB means anything 5.9 and below. If it's shown as V2 (V4) the left rating is 'standing start' and the parenthesis is a 'sit start' rating. A single grade, like V2ss, is used if sit start is the common way its done, thus 'ss' is Sit Start. If no parenthesis grade follows the first grade then the listed grade is generally assumed to be sent as a standing start (typical for tall boulders).

Broadly listed ratings (such as V5-7 or V6-V9) are merely an approximation, but its probably within that range. And that type of graded problem may (or may not) be done. If done, it's usually narrowed to one single V-grade (but not always) or at the most two (V4/5) side by side grades.

A question mark '?' after the grade indicates an unknown rating (or possibly not yet seen an ascent). If the grade has a plus '+' symbol it's an open-ended grade assumed to be a minimum of that grade (or stouter); its a mere generic estimate not intended to indicate its final real difficulty. Any V-number may, theoretically, be off a bit. Lastly, some V-numerics on the topo are mere generic approximations, not implicatory of finality. What is not science is science fiction.

INFO SYMBOLS

A selection of boulder problem descriptions may have additional icons representative of other potential challenges found at that particular boulder or problem. The ⚠ symbol indicates our cutting edge of real high-ball problems at 17' (5-meters) and above. Tall problems below that range may still be spicy, but are not indicated in this guide. A jagged edge ⌂ symbol indicates a rocky or hard to protect landing (where extra crashpads and spotters are wise protocol).

Cody at Empire Boulders

0 MILES 50 100
0 KILOMETERS 50 100 150

Bouldering Sites & Groups:
10. Horsethief Butte
11. Silver Star Group
12. Beacon Group
13. Alpen Group
14. Stevenson Group
15. Empire
16. Cascade Locks Group
17. Mt Hood Group
18. Lost Lake Boulders
19. Fifteenmile Group
20. Jordan Group
21. Tygh Group
22. Clackamas Group
23. Santiam Boulders
24. Druid Stones
25. The Garden
26. Portland Urban Group

Silver Star Group:
• Larch Mtn
• Ed's Trail

Beacon Group:
• Beacon Boulders
• Hamilton

Alpen Group:
• Alpenglow
• Super Heroes
• 3-Corner Rock
• X Boulders

Stevenson Group:
• BOGB
• Rock Creek

Cascade Group:
• Cascade Boulders
• The Annex
• Herman

Mt Hood Group:
• Timberline
• Sandy River
• Boulder Mtn
• East Mosquito
• White River
• Enola B
• Mud Ridge
• Hunchback B
• Cooper Spur
• Eliot Boulders
• West Fork
• Lolo B
• Tamanawas
• Dee Flat
• Pinn Boulders

Fifteenmile Group:
• The Meadow
• Campfire Boulders
• Puma Boulders
• Muledeer Boulders
• Underhill Boulders
• Wolf Run Boulders
• Ponderosa Point
• Mars Boulders
• Bulo Point
• Highland

Jordan Group:
• Camp Friend
• Owl Hollow
• Quarry Boulders

Tygh Group:
• Tygh Boulders
• Ball Point
• Bonn
• Wamic
• Badger
• Swamp
• Boulder Lake

Clackamas Group:
• High Rocks
• Olallie
• Lemiti

Urban Group:
• Schwingus
• Carver
• Magma Zone

Columbia
Range
River
Range
Cascade
Coast
Mt St Helens
Washington
Oregon
Mt Hood
Mt Jefferson

Astoria
Longview
Vancouver
Portland
Salem
Albany
Corvallis
Newport
Detroit
Hood River
The Dalles
Madras
Sisters
Redmond

Bouldering Sites

PORTLAND BOULDERING

These extensive bouldering chapters are compiled based on primary sections of interest, utilizing easily recognizable zones, thus providing you a productive method for quick goal planning. The sections are: the Columbia Gorge sector, the Mt Hood Corridor sector (generally U.S. Hwy 26), the Hood River Valley sector (U.S. Hwy 35 including the West Fork Hood river), the Eastside Cascades sector (which cover Fifteenmile creek valley, Jordan creek valley, Tygh and Badger Creek valley sites), the Clackamas River sector, the Central-Southern Willamette sector, and finally a few miscellaneous bouldering sites in the urban Portland sector.

The Larch Mtn Boulders are included in the Gorge sector, though in reality it is located in the hill country about 30-minutes north of Camas, Washington. Its close proximity to Portland make it an ideal destination for quality bouldering, in some ways better than even Carver Boulders.

The Columbia Gorge sector has been further divided into the Western, Central, and Eastern sub-sections, so that based on weather conditions you may pick a goal based on seasonal climatic factors. The Central Gorge covers the bouldering sites in the general vicinity of Cascade Locks, OR / Stevenson, WA vicinity. The Willamette sector covers a broad area (though relatively few sites), from the Coast Range, to the Santiam River basins.

WESTERN COLUMBIA GORGE

LARCH MTN BOULDERS

High quality granodiorite bouldering on Larch Mountain surpasses all expectations, producing some of the finest bouldering opportunities in our region. Located a mere 23 miles from Portland, this quality site exceeds 100 boulder problems, ranging from VB-V7 (potential to V9+). Many hi-ball problems (12'-35' tall), stellar long rail traverses (4' tall x 25' long), overhangs, and techy vertical crimp lines, something for every degree of bouldering. The site is a combination of boulders and rocky outcrops spread over a large area, and in short time certain sections became quite popular, such as the Wild West Bluff formation. The site may eventually yield a minimum of 150+ boulder problems.

The rock has lightly weathered minimally abrasive surficial features that give it a rich texture from long-term weathering processes of the exposed rock surface. The result is ideal for crimps and smearing friction abilities with minimal moss or lichen.

The rock type reveals peripheral composition variables depending on specific locale, but general sam-

Abbott on *Locked & Loaded*

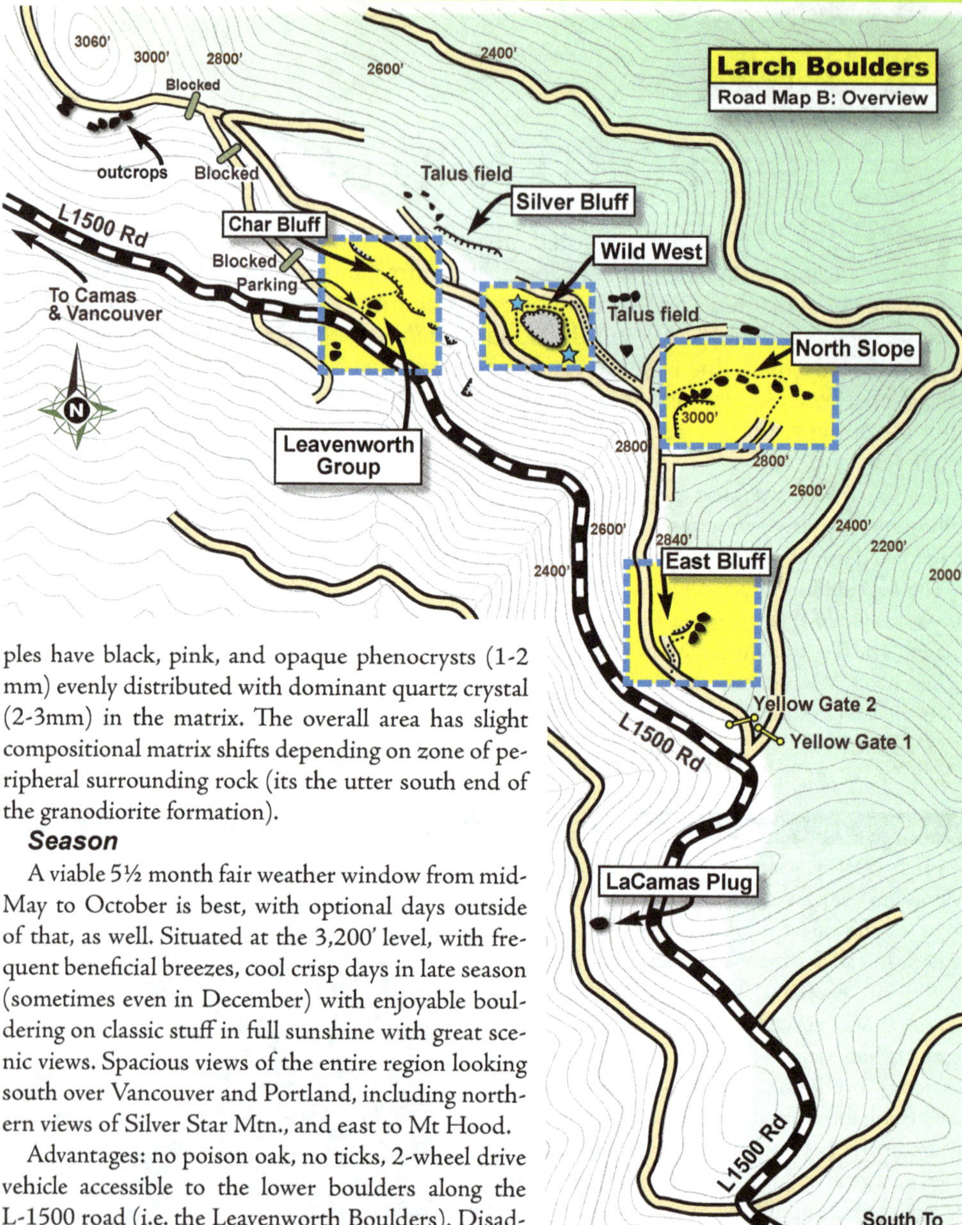

ples have black, pink, and opaque phenocrysts (1-2 mm) evenly distributed with dominant quartz crystal (2-3mm) in the matrix. The overall area has slight compositional matrix shifts depending on zone of peripheral surrounding rock (its the utter south end of the granodiorite formation).

Season

A viable 5½ month fair weather window from mid-May to October is best, with optional days outside of that, as well. Situated at the 3,200' level, with frequent beneficial breezes, cool crisp days in late season (sometimes even in December) with enjoyable bouldering on classic stuff in full sunshine with great scenic views. Spacious views of the entire region looking south over Vancouver and Portland, including northern views of Silver Star Mtn., and east to Mt Hood.

Advantages: no poison oak, no ticks, 2-wheel drive vehicle accessible to the lower boulders along the L-1500 road (i.e. the Leavenworth Boulders). Disadvantages: some areas may be used by target shooters (if you do not like the sound of cannon-fire in the distance you might want to boulder elsewhere); if gated its a ½ mile uphill trek past the yellow gate to the upper boulders. The mainline gravel road, though graded regularly, is a bit rough in spots.

Directions

From I-205 bridge drive east on State 14 highway to Camas, WA. At the signal light junction of 3rd avenue in Camas, drive northeast from Camas on state 500 road (passed Lacamas Lake). Turn right at NE 19th (at Fern Prairie store) and drive east 1 mile, and take a left at the "Y" and drive

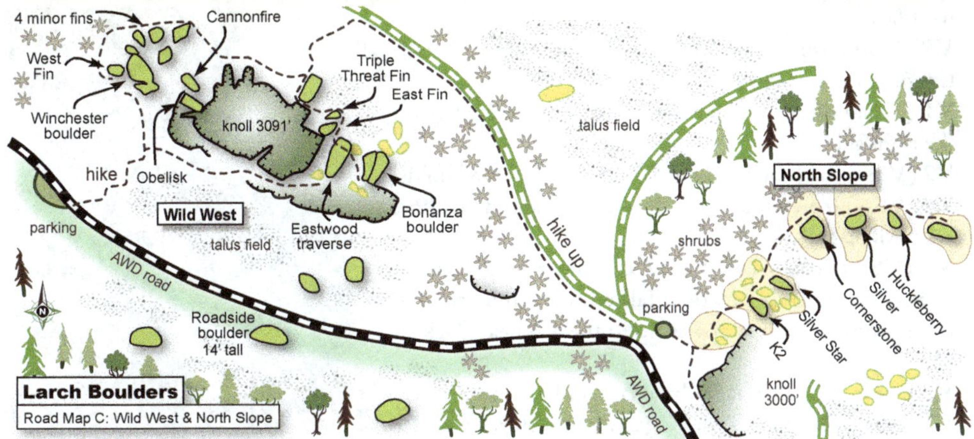

north uphill on 272nd. This winds north and east for 2 miles to a 3-way stop intersection. Turn north (left) on 292nd and drive one mile. Turn north onto Livingston Road and continue uphill for one mile till you reach L-1000 forest road which is gravel. Drive on L-1000 for 3-4 miles to a 4-way intersection. Turn right (east) uphill on gravel forest road L-1500 for one mile till it turns right and levels off (passing a yellow DNR gate on the left). Drive east along this generally level portion of the gravel road for one mile to an open area passing another common target shooting spot. Both the Leavenworth Boulder and Black Forest Boulder are located uphill above a secondary road, while the Eiger and Matterhorn stones are below the road.

To reach the Wild West Bluff formation at the upper knoll, continue east on L-1500 till you reach a saddle between two hills (at two closed roads with two yellow gates). Park here (near the yellow gate) and hike uphill ½ mile to the bluff. Scramble up the steep rocky slope to either the west side or east side of the butte. Road L-1500 is a bit rough but is 2WD viable.

Note: There are several alternate methods to reach Larch Boulders: via Hockinson (paved entirely to the 4-way interchange), or north from Camas past Fern Prairie store, or up the Washougal River a several miles turning left up onto Bear Prairie.

LEAVENWORTH GROUP

The **Leavenworth Boulder** is one of the premiere boulders at Larch Mtn., and its situated at the very first locale (when driving north from Camas) on the peak. Park on a dead-end side road directly below the boulders. Walk uphill one minute (80') to two massive boulders. The Black Forest Stone is the smaller boulder, and Leavenworth Stone is the giant 15' x 30' x 30' behemoth. The flowers are in full bloom in June-July. The path up is well established and lined with small rocks to keep you on course. This is the most convenient bouldering site at Larch Mtn for 2-wheel drive vehicle access. Plenty of powerful overhanging bouldering lines from juggy fun problems to delicate core intensive power crimp-fests. The Leavenworth Stone is considered to be the rare gem at Larch Mtn., of the type and quality found only once at the great bouldering sites. Beta L to R:

VB Crazy Get Down. A short juggy basic problem on

west face.

VB (V0ss) Terminate This. Its the fun warmup problem on a short arête prow.

V1 (V2ss) Super Cool. Start on the same arête but on the right side.

V2 (V3ss) Back In The Day. Great line with good holds.

V3 (V5ss) Iron Giant. The classic center south face line, a 12' tall hi-ball.

V7 (V8ss) Iron Clad. Upper core intensive. Start on Iron Giant aim up left, then fall onto the minute rock horn protrusion, then power up to the top near Back In The Day.

V8 Octagon is the quality hard core hi-ball line.

V5 (V6ss) Dragon's Tail. No jugs route. Start on under clings to thin crimps. Tough to see crimps, and the exit is thin and tricky. A 14' tall hi-ball.

V6 (V6ss) Scorpion King. Cool techy hi-ball line with a crucial right hand crimp up high.

VB (V0ss) Embers. on the east face of the block is a series of large steps. Just 'ss' extends line by starting low on left.

The traverses:

V3 Liquid Metal. An uphill rising traverse on the left (west) aspect of the rock formation.

V9 Leavenworth Traverse. Go from 'Terminate This' to the far rightmost route.

Black Forest Boulder

This stone is just below the Leavenworth Boulder and offers more of the same quality problems on high quality rock. Beta L to R:

VB is a minor down climb on the west end.

V1ss Soot. Just uphill of prow.

V1 Jungfrau. The overhung classic arête on the west end.

V3 The Great Escape. Start next and use the sloped face to two small divot holds to exit.

V0 (V0ss) Climbingruven. Start on small left-facing fins and finish up right on large appearing edges to a not so simple crux exit.

V1 (V3ss) Red Barron. Underclings to good hold and finish same as previous line.

VB (V1ss) Black Forest. A classic basic line with great holds.

VB Chocolate. Basic fun run.

V4 Black Forest Traverse. Start on the route #1 and fall into position on the arête, and continue across the south face of the boulder.

The Eiger and Matterhorn Boulders are located below the car parking spot at Leavenworth Boulder zone. Use the new bulldozer road grade that cuts down from the west to the cluster. The Eiger is 18' tall, and the Matterhorn has a

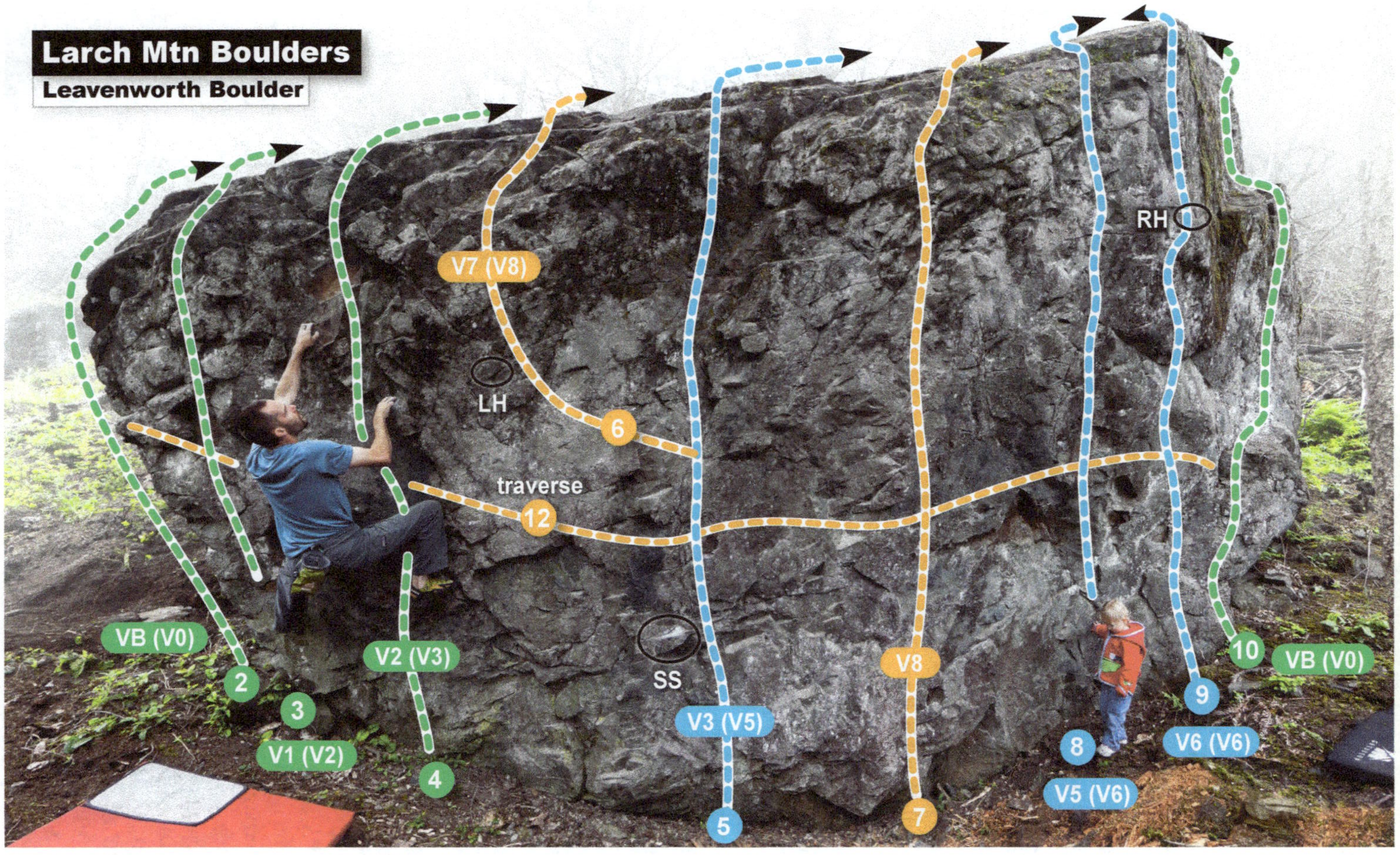
Larch Mtn Boulders
Leavenworth Boulder
V7 (V8)
RH
LH
6
traverse
12
VB (V0)
V2 (V3)
2
3
V1 (V2)
4
SS
V3 (V5)
5
V8
7
V5 (V6)
8
9
V6 (V6)
10
VB (V0)

short flat slightly hung face.

Matterhorn Boulder

VB Hot Butter. The left most line.

V1 Melting Hot. Start at the slight undercling.

V2 Sunburn. Move into it from left, then directly up.

V6 Where's da Shade. The center tall thin face.

V3 Summertime

V5 Rising Sun. Start low on right, and run left along the horizontal seam to far left end.

V0 Hot Tin Roof. This is the right most problem.

V7 Matterhorn Traverse entire face, avoid top lip.

Eiger Boulder

VB Titanic Ego. Left corner.

V1 Whymper's Wonder. Run tallest part of face.

V0 Collateral Damage. Up and right onto rib.

VB Rogue Nation. The rib.

VB Garbage Talk. East face.

Charcoal Bluff

Above the Leavenworth Boulders, a short walk (30 yards) up-hill, is a short cliff formation, with a slabby 25' wall about 80' wide viable for either TR options or solo VB/V0 runs. There is a 25' tall hi-ball, 5° overhung flat face with sharp crimp holds (V4?), and several other V4 problems just down to the right at a landing. A minor rocky outcrop (visible from road) 200' east of a tiny stream may offer 4-6 VB problems on a short 12' face.

EAST BLUFF FORMATION

A quality east-facing 15' tall by 30' wide bluff (this bluff is visible from the east Yellow Gate) with problems ranging from VB-V4 hi-ball lines. Below the wall 3-4 large boulders yield some minor bouldering. Walk horizontally to the right in the forest about 70' to reach the Halfway Slab (20' x 30' wide slab with four VB's). About 70' further right is the Great Northern Slab (50' wide x 30' tall, 50° slab) with about a dozen lines. Beta L to R.

VB War Zone. Far left crack and left face.

VB House of War. Start off top of pedestal.

V0 Pacific Pearl is a vertical thin crack.

Photos:
East Bluff, Huck Fin,
and East Fin (all at
Larch Mtn)

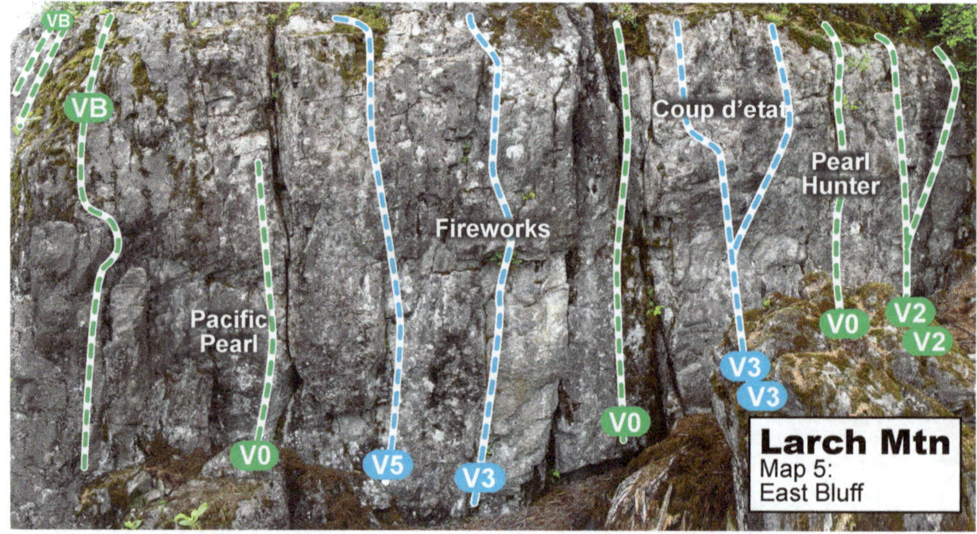

V5 Countdown. A thin powerful hung face.

V3 Fireworks. Techy hung face.

V0 Double Trouble. The double crack slot.

V3 Coup d'etat. Hung face (+ variation).

V0 Pearl Hunter is the hung seam.

V1 Frosted, and V2 Flakes. Hung face with two variations.

Two boulders below bluff (**VB SOS, V2 Loco Citato** (hung jugs), and next **VB Locus Minoris** (lower prow).

Great Northern Slab ⚠ 〰

V1+ left face shorty.

V2 Ad Infinitum. Crimps to slopers on face.

V0 Cold Kiss. short minor.

VB Slabrageous. A fun slab face near the prow (5.4).

VB Lost World. Start at the point and cruise face and corner up left (5.4). Or climb straight up

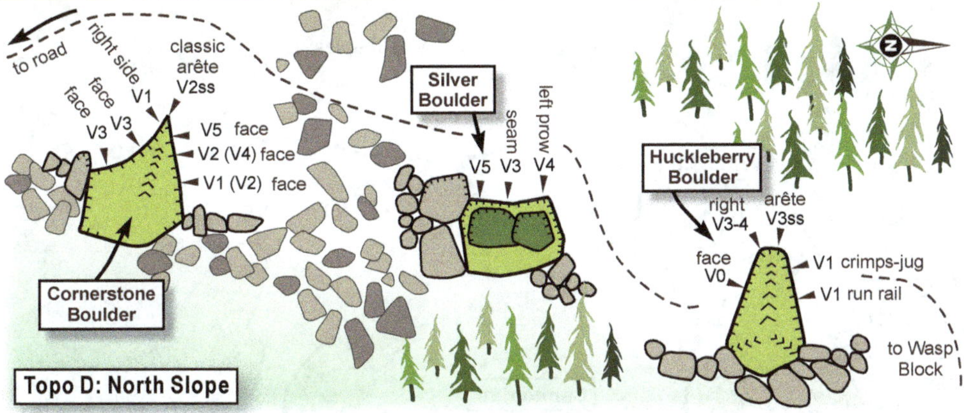

to top.

VB Hidden Treasure. Steep face immediately right of OW.

VB Great Northern Slab. Steep face.

VB the remainder of slab is quite basic.

NORTH SLOPE CLUSTER

At a flat landing walk east on a narrow trail, then descend north across the base of a talus slope. The site offers a series of five northward sloping talus fields separated by vine maple thickets. A good locale to escape from hot scorching temperatures of summer (even when it is 85°F boilerplate hot).

K2 Boulder

This trail side boulder (and next stone) is part of the initial talus slope visible from the road. There are several additional stones in this vicinity to tap. Beta R to L.

V2ss Locum Tenens. Right most line.

V2ss Locus Standi. Use the sloped nose.

V2ss Lorem Ipsum. Use the large incut jug hold to start then use crimps to finish.

V1ss Texas Wronghorn. Start low, grab a high right side pull, then high step.

V2ss Lucida Sidera. On the far left is a stout line that starts on a low sloper.

Silver Star boulder

One nice line, the Silver Star (V5). This is slightly up-hill of the previous boulder (great views of Silver Star). Start low, bear hug both arêtes, finish direct to top.

Cornerstone Boulder

A monster sized double faceted block with a large roomy crashpad landing zone. The block is about 14' tall with two main aspects and a prominent 130° overhanging arête. Beta L to R:

V1 (V2ss) Infinite Reality. Leftmost problem on crimps and slopers.

V2 face (V4ss) Cannibals Crowbars & Cocktails. A tech face with crimps. Catch the pinches on finishing rail, move up left and top out.

V5 Modus Operandi. On face immediately left of

Nathan on *Shooting Gallery*

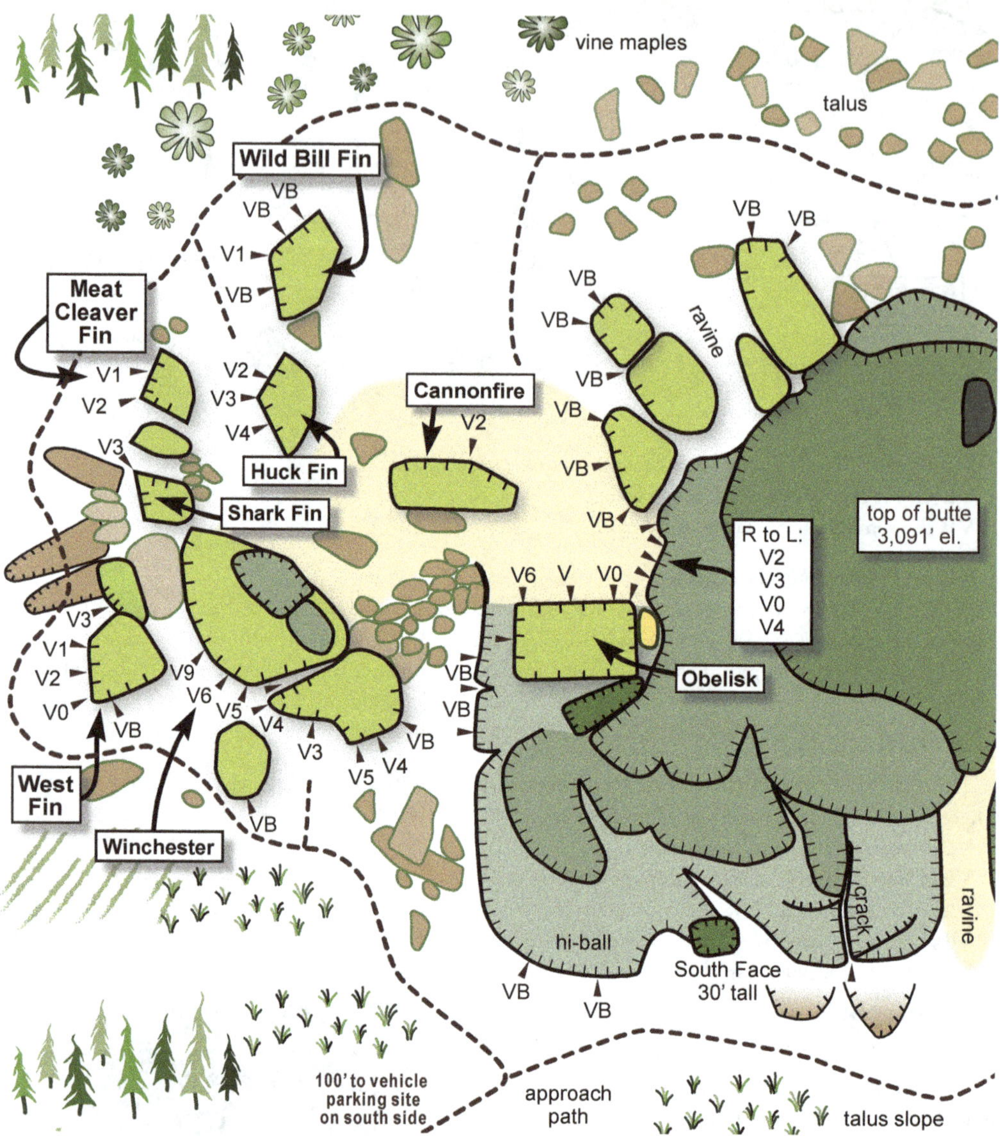

arête.

V1 (V2) Land Down Under. Ultra-classic super overhanging arête. Just 'ss' bump a long reach to a high left hold, then to ample holds on right side.

V1ss Illuminate This. Bump up 2-3 times to fat holds at seam, up left to arête, finish to top.

V3 Bad to the Bone. Corner and face (with variants) busting over small roof on right side.

V5 Cornerstone Traverse. Full traverse of both facets of the boulder.

Silver Boulder

Overhung north facing aspect offers some wild stuff. Beta left to right.

V4ss Lone Ranger. Just 'ss' left prow.

V3ss Hi Ho Silver. Punch past the overhang, then seam, aiming up right.

V5 Silver Bullet. Standing start to dicey mantle.

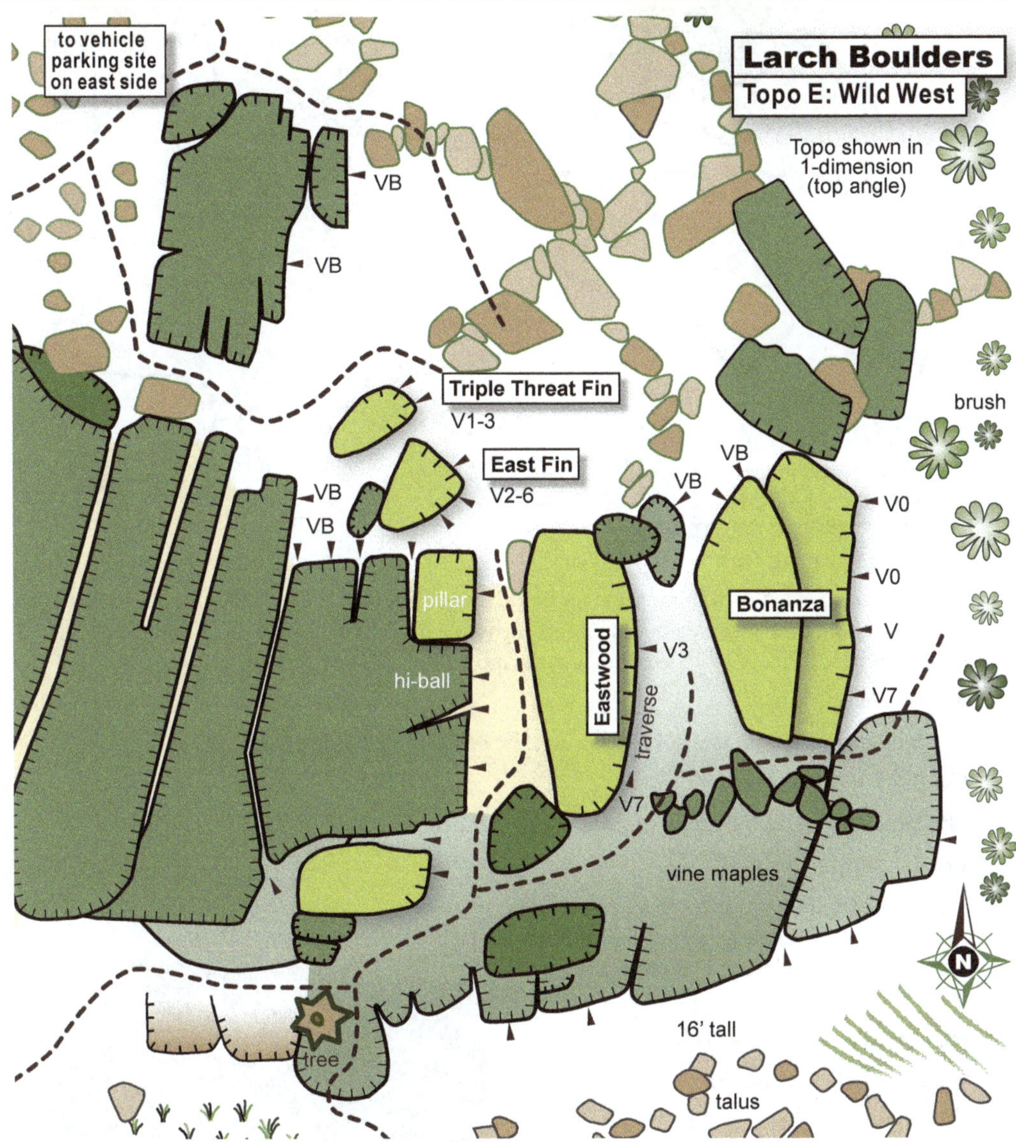

Huckleberry Boulder

This is a stellar 45° super-overhung rock fin. Beta is L to R:

V1 Bear Treats. Run the rail on the far left shaded side.

V1 Tom Sawyer. Crimps to a jug, then a tricky mantle onto that large jug.

V3ss Huckleberry Finn. Using crimps, angle up onto the left side of the 130° overhanging arête. Difficult to top out.

V4ss Doc Holliday. Virtually same as previous except bump up to jug high and right, then up and over the very nose of this 130° feature.

V0 A minor problem on the right face.

V4 Huckleberry Traverse. A very stout traverse of the entire face. Start on the right and swing along on the jugs and positive holds below the nose.

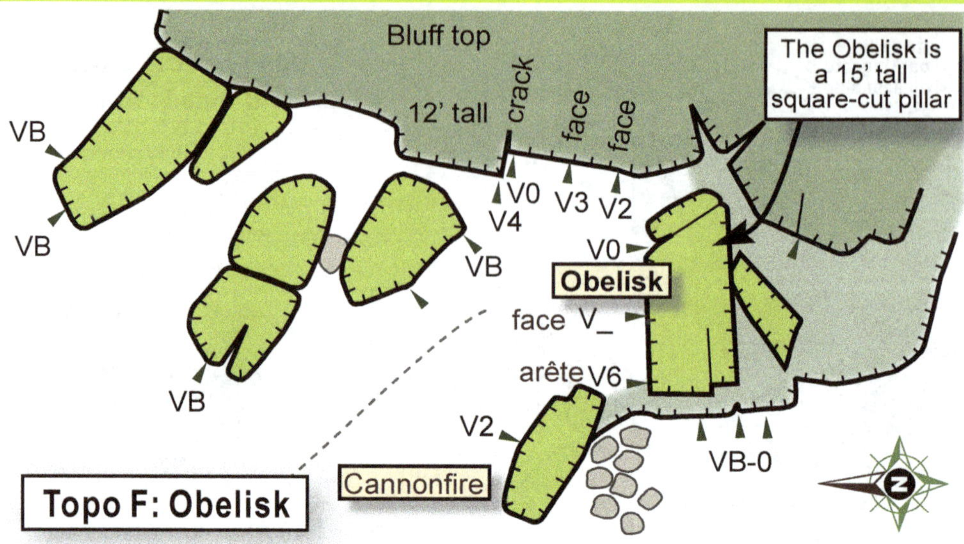

WILD WEST BLUFF

This is a steep sided rock butte great for bouldering, both on the west side and on the east side of the formation. The west side boulders encompass the four Minor Fins, the mega West Fin, and Bonanza Boulder. Plenty of varied lines and the most popular place for locals.

The Four Minor Fins:

A group of 4 minor boulders. Most are sit start problems; all well developed.

Wild Bill Fin (upper left)

This upper left stone offers four minor problems (Beta L to R: **VB, VB, V1ss, VB**).

Huck Fin (upper right)

This upper right stone offers three powerful 'ss' problems. Beta is left to right: (**V2ss Showdown, V3ss OK Corral, V4ss Most Wanted**) all sit start.

Meat Cleaver Fin (lower left)

The lower left stone. Sit start, reach, cross to jug, find the lip, top out (**V2ss**). The thin cleaver blade is long gone.

Shark Fin (lower right)

The lower right stone is a squat low overhung detached block held in place by stacked blocks (**V3ss Shark Fin**).

West Fin

Its the giant monster 18' fin, a very popular fin to warm-up on with ultra cool hi-ball status.

V3 Wrestling with 'Gators. Out from the cave on the left.

V1 Gun Runner. Is the left edge of the mon-

ster fin, with odd top out.

V2 Smith & Wesson. (can be rules by avoiding large right jug to make V3).

VB (VBss) Locked & Loaded. Ultra-classic line 'ss' low on right by wrapping your hands around the huge lower flake horn on either side, power up, then cross over to the super incut jug on the main fin, and finesse a final move to top out.

VB South Face. A brief run.

Winchester Boulder

The ultimate boulder hi-ball rock face at the Wild West knoll that offers a string of impressive powerful problems with enticing sequential madness. Beta Left to Right.

V9 Mag Seven. The ultimate power line at the knoll. Start at the crack, and power up left along the 25' long rising left leaning classic 20° overhanging prow. The ultra thin crux is at midpoint with a long reach to latch a flat jug, then continue on positive holds up leftward till you top out on the block on far upper left. **Magnum** variation exits right onto face.

V0 (V6ss) Winchester. ⚠ This is a 25' tall crack with slightly overhung standing start opening moves, then solid easy crack with jugs and steps on the upper half. The full Winchester sit starts under the 65° overhanging jam crack (V6), crank out with finger and foot jams, then up the entire route. The Slayton eliminate is **V7 Pistol Whipped**, and it starts just left of the crack and merges up into the crack. The FA was a standing onsite solo by Mr O and the full 'ss' by Mr A.

V5 Breach Loader. ⚠ Just right of the crack is an overhung start that lands in Winchester higher up.

V0 Gutter Ball is the chimney.

V3 (V4ss) Born on the Fifth of July. A superb line that begins 'ss' under an arête, power up the arête to finish on easy terrain. Immediately right of the deep chimney.

V3 Girls with Guns. Slightly hung scoop with tricky hi-ball move to top out.

V5 (Run For Cover?) Thin techy face on nose just right of scoop.

V4 (Surrender?) Seam crimps on steep face.

VB Low angle slab.

Cannonfire Boulder

Cannonfire V2ss is a large oblong boulder uphill from the Four Minor Fins just before you reach the Obelisk Stone. Sit start angled traverse problem. An ultra low direct eliminate is V4ss.

The Obelisk (aka Shoebox)

At the rim-top overlooking the West Cluster is a stunning four-sided stelae or stele shaped block perched on the edge on a

Abbott on *Eastwood Traverse*

15′ vertical drop. It is a stunning powerful looking block with bouldering on the north aspect. From L to R.

V0 ___. Left face.

V0 Pharoah. The north side jam crack. The face left of it is a V0.

V_ (?) North face is a thin techy face.

V6 Fortes Fortuna Adjuvat. This is the exposed vertical hi-ball northwest arête.

Directly below the Obelisk on the west side is a short 11′ tall bluff with 4 minor problems (range VB-V0) and a short jam crack.

Rimtop Face

Immediately uphill (east) of Obelisk is a short 12′ tall bluff. Beta from right to left as if departing from the Obelisk.

V2 ___ thin face on right.

V3 Right to Remain Silent. Central thin face.

V0 ___ the corner crack.

V4ss Meatish Sweetballs. Minor prow left of crack.

VB The nose on separate block on far left.

VB-V0 several more minor lines exist as the bluff trends downhill northward.

EAST SIDE (OF WILD WEST BLUFF)

A group of boulders, outcrops, and fins located on the east side of the butte formation.

East Fin

The exhilerating East Fin has three variant problems. This is a radically overhung 125° slice of rock, the primary 'Fin' on the east side.

V6ss East Fin. Sit start low on undercling, then mid-crimp, and long reach for lip.

V3 Straight Out Of Camas. Start mid-face on face holds, then catch the lip out right.

V2 Mobile Chunks of Liquid Carbon. The whole rail starting low on the right and run entire lip to far left.

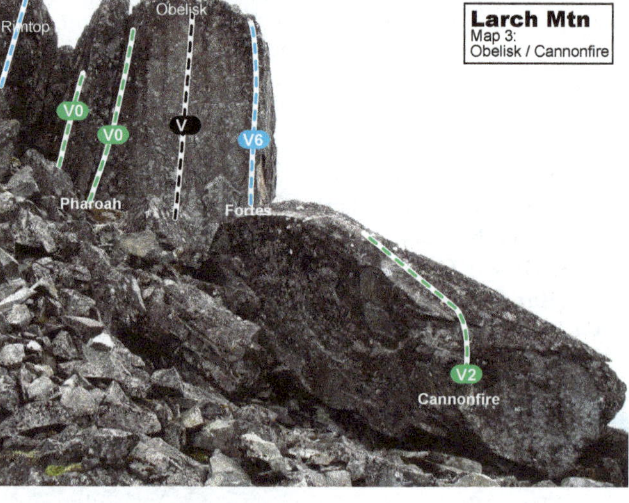

Triple Threat Fin

Just to the right of East Fin is this overhanging tall fin with jugs on the entire upper part. The standing start problem is V1 using the uppermost undercling. The triple undercling sit start is V3ss on a crack undercling on left outside and an inside right undercling, then proceed to the second and third undercling onward to the top.

The rocky rimtop formation behind the two primary fins offer five VB faces, corners, or offwidths (all are sent). As the bluff gets tall (left of East Fin) are several hi-ball lines (V0?).

Eastwood Boulder

Eastwood Traverse (V7ss). The locally famous traverse near the East Fin is a flat laying 25' long thin block of rock with a stellar hand-foot rail traverse. This is a premier attraction. The rail is an upside-down wrestling match, a horizontal traversing physical enduro power line 4' off the ground. The **Eastwood Direct (V4ss)** starts on a hollow flake and goes out the center overhang as a mantle.

Bonanza Boulder

A few yards downhill from the horizontal masterpiece is the Bonanza Boulder, a 17' hi-ball with 3 problems on a superb vertical face. Beta is listed L to R:

V7 Shooting Gallery rides the left arête and crescent moon undercling as high as you can (a right hand-heel match will help), then small face crimps and foot smears. FA Andy Davis.

V8+ (?) ______ is the extreme center line project.

V0 Jewel Heist is a long reach from a jug to a jug, mantle to a stance, then corner to top.

North Face Bluff

From the Wild West Bluff formation walk north to a rutted track and follow this west to its end. There is a north facing wall 15' tall by 45' long which may offer steep bouldering.

Roadside Boulder

One large 18' tall roadside block just under the access gravel road near a parking spot on the south side of the knoll (beta is Left to Rright): **V0 West Slab, V0 Slab Center, V1 Spooky Slab, V1 Broken Arrow, V0 NE Slab.** Nothing special; just tall.

Bulls Eye Boulders

This is a cluster of blocks just below the upper road, but in a near direct line from the lower target shooting site. Located on the last ridge before the upper road ends at a flat landing where the road cuts back hard to the north side. A closed 'dozer grade descends downhill to

the Leavenworth Boulder site. Andy D. sent the obvious horn (ala nearby shooters) at V0-1.

The region on the first and second knoll have a number of other outcrops and boulders, most necessitate considerable walking and are likely not to see much bouldering activity.

LaCamas Plug area

The area at the LaCamas Plug has minimal bouldering options nearby. Drive to Jones Creek Motocross parking area, then continue on L-1610 gravel road uphill to junction of L-1510 road. Go left (uphill) on L-1500 for ¾ mile, then take a left onto an unmarked graveled road, and follow this downhill for ¾ mile. Most of the options are plainly visible from the road. Walk 2 minutes uphill from the road.

SILVER STAR BOULDERS

Good quality andesitic-basaltic stones and outcrops perched along a high elevation (5,500' el) treeless alpine ridge crest alongside Ed's Trail on the northern slope of Silver Star Mtn east of Battleground, Washington. A fine selection of boulder problems; a few short 10'-14' lines with plenty of quality hi-ball lines up to 35' tall ranging from nice slabs, vertical face lines, to various finger/hand crack and offwidth systems. There are several superb gems. Magnificent scenery overlooking the entire Vancouver area with multiple mountain peaks visible and a colorful floral display in July. Some outcrops at Silver Star Mtn are too tall or fractured, so beware when

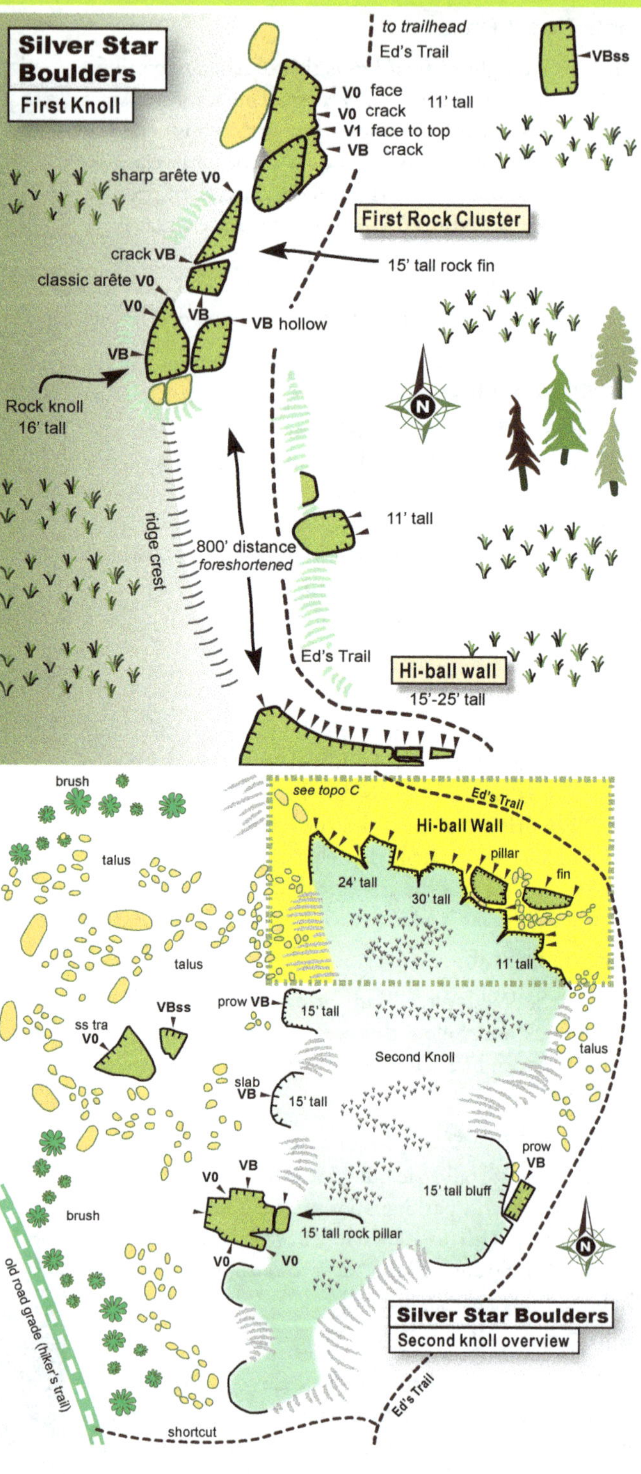

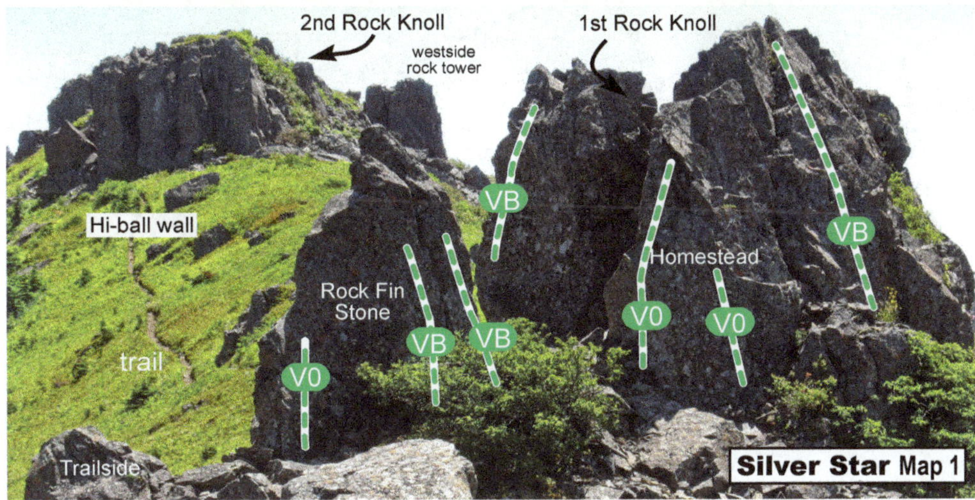

exploring. The site offers about 45+ possible problems from VB-V4, and 1-2 crashpads are recommended. The final 3 miles of gravel road are not maintained and require an AWD vehicle with high clearance. This hike (even if you do not boulder) is one of the best in this part of the state. **History:** A thorough exploration of various lines was done by Mr O in about 2013.

Directions

Drive I-205 north into Vancouver, Washington, and exit at Orchards onto State Route 500 road, continuing north on 117th Avenue (SR503 road) to Battleground. East on 219th (main road in town), north on 142nd, which curves for 4 miles to merge with Lucia Falls Road, which travels east along the Lewis River. Just before reaching Yacolt, drive east on Sunset Falls road, and continue east to Sunset Campground. Turn south on NF41 gravel road, drive south approximately two miles, then turn west on NF4109 one mile, then south on the unmaintained NF4109 road that climbs steeply up the forested north ridge to the parking site (there are alternated approach roads that might be used). Hike ½ mile up trail #180, then onto Ed's Trail (#180a) for ¼ mile to the first rocky knoll.

FIRST ROCK KNOLL 〽

First Rock Knoll Area is a set of two main outcrops, one is a well pronounced rock fin. This is the first viable stone outcrop along the trail for bouldering. There are a few other brief outcrops in this immediate vicinity that will be viable for bouldering. Beta starts at the north most problem (R to L).

Trailside Cluster (facing east)

V0 Trailside. Short face.
V0 Divided Loyalty. Crack through bulge
V1 Denial upon Denial. Taller part of face.
VB WMD. Vertical corner crack

Rock Fin (15' tall)

V0 Master of Bull. Sharp fun tall arête using the west side for full smears.
VB Political Eunuchs. Fat crack on west side.

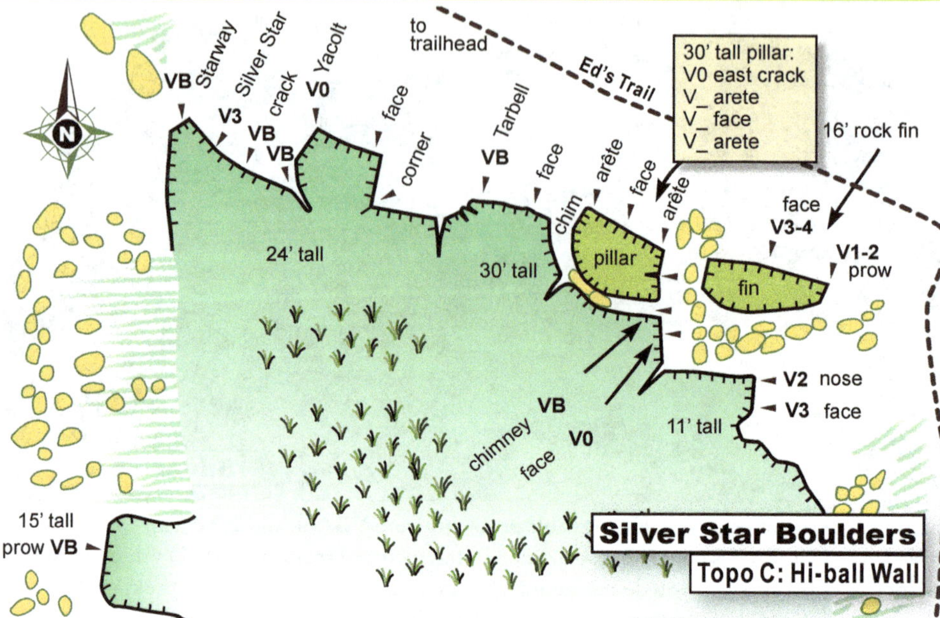

VB House of Cards. Descent on south aspect.

Homestead Boulder (15' tall)

This is the higher rock outcrop in the trailside cluster.

V0 Squatter's Rights. The classic short arête on north side.

V0 Mechanicus Ignoramus. Nice face to the right of arête.

VB Jugs. Basic run on west aspect.

VB Homestead. Around on the far east aspect is a tall but hollow problem.

SECOND ROCK KNOLL

This formation is about 800' further south along Ed's Trail is the Second Rock Knoll. Height ranges from 15' on the right, then is 30' tall in middle, then shorter 15'-20' options on the left side. Beta is R to L, starting on the minor west side sections, then the classic buttress (Starway), and proceeding left along the tall north facing aspect next to the trail.

Westside Rock Tower (15' tall)

V0 Abhoric Vacuum. Short south prow

V_ (?) Very tall south face.

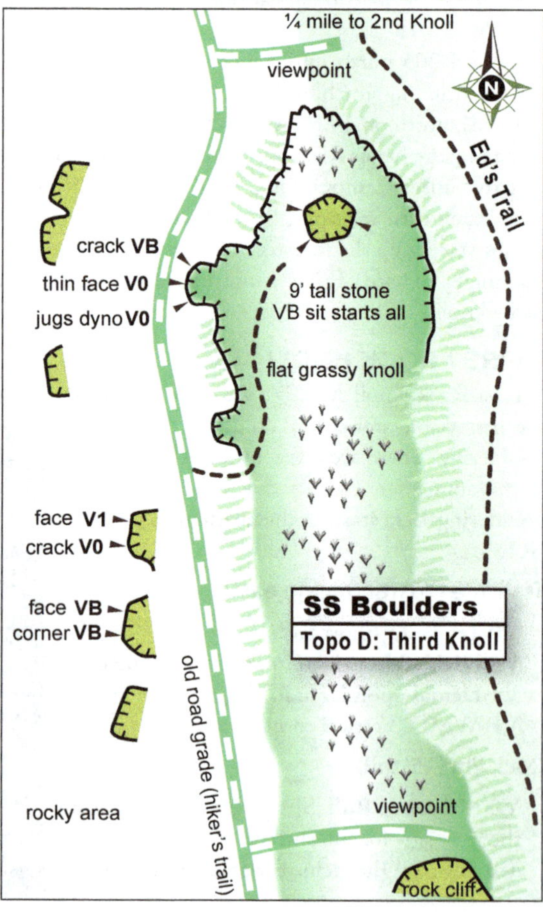

V0 ___. NW corner.

VB Boogerman. Basic north face run.

VB We Know. Nice 15′ slab (isolated outcrop).

VB Knowingly Unknowing. Nice 15′ prow (isolated outcrop).

V0ss Circumscribe. One big boulder in west talus, SS jug rail.

Hi-Ball Wall ⚠ ⋀⋀

VB Starway. Ultra-nice beautiful jug arête buttress line (25′ tall).

V4 Silver Star. Ultra-classic wave face with crimps.

VB Clutching Shadows. Crack with wedged block.

A deep moss step corner system used as the descent for nearby lines.

V0 Yacolt. Stellar arête line.

V_ (?) The face/arête direct.

V0-1 (?) Vertical hung crack corner system.

VB Tarbell. Fun, basic hi-ball on tall central face with big steps on steep face.

Next is a big fat chimney system, with a big pedestal rock formation to the left (35′ tall).

V_ (?) The incredible looking right arête.

V_ (?) Vertical face.

V_ (?) The incredible arête with numerous incut crimps and holds.

V0 Solidarity. Superb tall hand-jam crack facing east.

VB King Size Tyranny. Inner chimney (the left side of fat chimney system).

V0 Vanguard of the Proletariat. Tall face just left of the chimney.

V2 Canons of Logic. Short nose 11′ high (part way up rock slope behind Rock Flake).

V3 Mental Inertia. The vertical face direct on (avoids the easier nose to right).

Rock Flake ⋀⋀

A large narrow profiled Rock Flake stands 13′ tall and is independent from main formation.

V3-4 (?) Technical thin face.

V2-3 (?) Another stellar prow.

Walk south another 60′ to an east facing formation. Two problems (one done) depending on hollowness of rock formation.

VB Imperial Destiny. Nice fun 11′ tall jug run on

north prow.

THIRD ROCK KNOLL

The next minor options are at the Third Knoll, a flat, meadow area close in-between the old gravel road, and Ed's Trail. Some viable bouldering in low range, beware of some hollow rock below road.

Roadside Rock Nose

A brief set of problems alongside the old gravel road bed just below the Big Flat Stone.

VB A basic thin crack line on left.

V0 Skeletons in the Closet. Thin techy face line just left of next line.

V0 Something Exists. A brief cool roadside dyno jug run worth a tour.

A few yards uphill east of the roadside rock nose is a Big Flat Stone on the Third Knoll that is only setup with very stubby VB's using SS methods. Several outcrops just below the old road (see map) offer some bouldering, but use caution (rough talus, and hollow in spots). Offers lines from VB-V0 so far. Further south about 200' is the main prominent Fourth Knoll, a 50' tall rock bluff that is generally not conducive for bouldering.

The Silver Star Boulders zone has some future potential yet to be tapped, so a greater analysis of this entire boulder site will be detailed in future expanded editions of this guide.

Sam on *Mag7* (Larch Mtn)

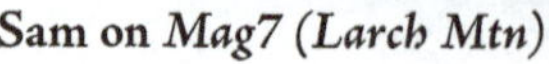

CENTRAL COLUMBIA GORGE (North Side)

BEACON ROCK BOULDERS

A small bouldering site at a convenient roadside locale, but less frequented these days due to other popular nearby options. Though situated in a windy portion of the Gorge the stones tend to dry out quickly after a rainstorm, even during the winter months. The site offers a virtual 12-month window of opportunity due to its low elevation (if the weather is dry). A powerful string of problems exist on friction-friendly andesite stone. Only two stones here are truly massive in size, one of which is in the North Forest, creased by the elusive and tenuous Minus Man (V8). Most blocks range in size up to 10'-11' tall, of which the North Forest has most of the large stones.

The entire cluster of stones that boulderers utilize today are huddled along the west side of Beacon Rock. The summit hikers trail straddles the talus slope providing easy access to most of the stones, but beware of considerable low growing poison oak throughout the area. The site is suitable for 1-2 crashpads. The site has good cell phone reception. A state park tourist parking fee is required when visiting this park. **Directions:** From Vancouver, Washington drive east on State Route 14 for 35 miles to Beacon Rock State Park.

NORTH FOREST

Chris Hill Boulder (1)

V3 Chris Hill's Arête. A large stone perched against the cliff in a low spot. Ascend the arête.

Diamond Block (2)

A short walk southward of CH boulder on the cliff scarp is a little overhung nook. A prominent diamond shaped block juts out from the wall at chest height. Several lines exist on this cube-like block. Climb down off right from top to exit.

Tooth Boulder (3)

V4 Sharp Tooth. A combination of pinches and slopers on west side.

V1 Overhang. Begins using the jug in the corner on east side. This same block has several additional variations V4-5.

Next Boulder (4)

V0 Corner, a **V1** Face, and a **V2** Mantle.

Slab Boulder (5)

V0 Slab Arête
V2 Thin Slab (rules: avoid the corners).
V2 Back Breaker. Layback the overhanging arête.

Minus Man Boulder (6)

V8 Minus Man. The site classic. Begin on the low crimpers in center of huge block.

V9-10 (?) Hi-ball on slightly overhung face right of MM.

V0 Fun with Rex. Ascends a tall groove. Hi-ball, poor landing.

V1 Minus Traverse starts on this stones far left end and cruise rightward up to top.

V1-V6+ The west overhung aspect of block can yield 3-4 more problems (some done?).

Two Uphill Boulders (7)

V3 South arête riding the east side and mantle up center.

V5ss East side face and up over.

V3 Hanging Around the House. Start at left arête, traverse right, and mantle up at horn.

V1ss One Move Two. A mini on the next tiny uphill boulder.

TALUS CLUSTER

Boulder in woods

V3ss Salad Days. Use opposing underclings on an isolated stone off right in forest ½ way from trail to next stone.

Tree Boulder

V1 Frontline Assembly. Begin on rounded hold, reach for side pull, mantel.

V3 Front Row Pimp Show. Begin with slopers in mid face, then directly up.

V3 Pumpin' Andesite. Begin on crimpers, ascend left face (rules: avoid left flake).

V5 Orbital Decay. Begin on jug (right of FA), traverse left to finish on PA.

Flat Boulder

V2ss Migration. SS low on column, traverse left along lip, then mantel.

V0 Mantle

Boulder [?]

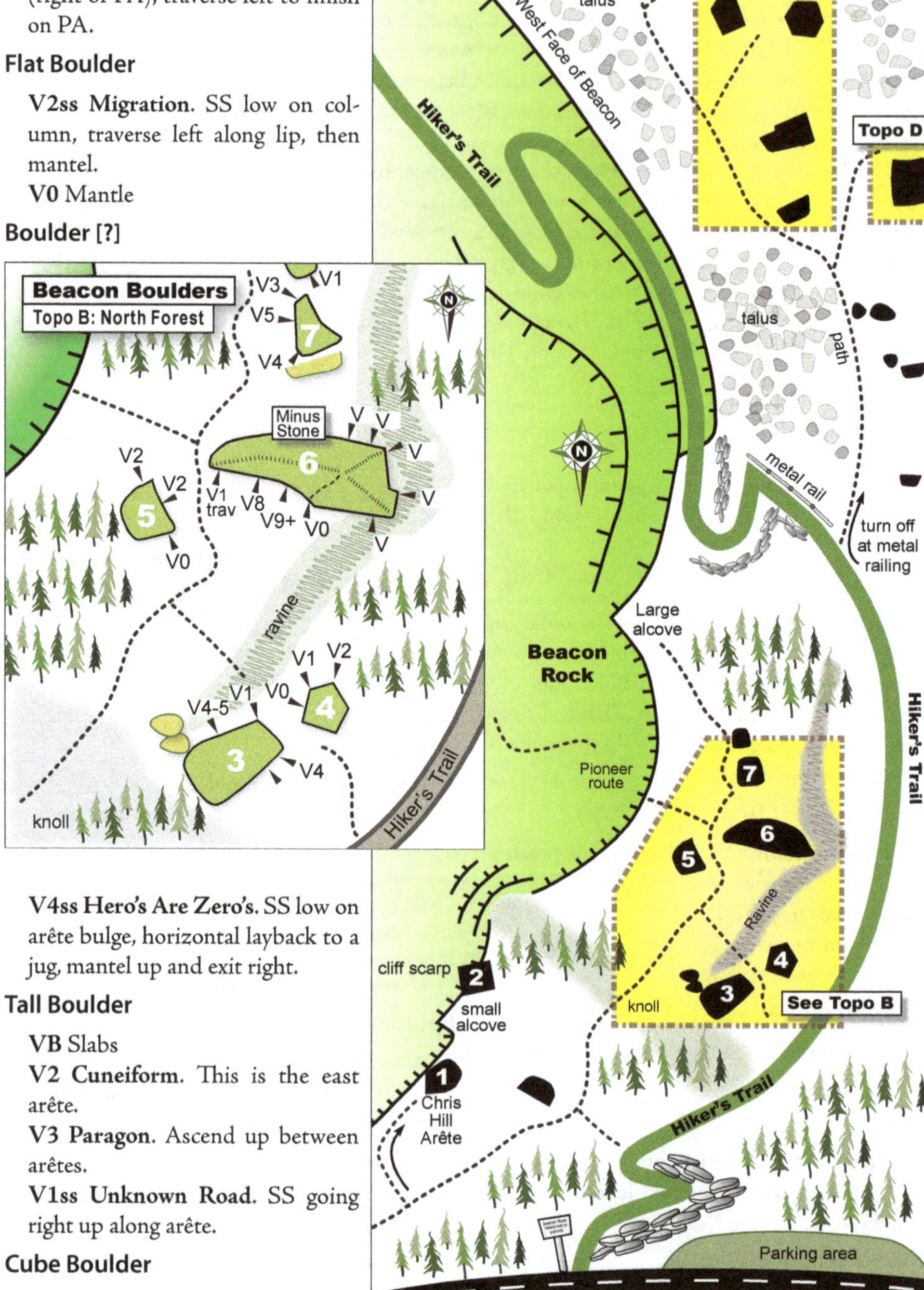

V4ss Hero's Are Zero's. SS low on arête bulge, horizontal layback to a jug, mantel up and exit right.

Tall Boulder

VB Slabs

V2 Cuneiform. This is the east arête.

V3 Paragon. Ascend up between arêtes.

V1ss Unknown Road. SS going right up along arête.

Cube Boulder

V0ss. Left edge.

V4ss. Low right going to left edge & up.

VB. Right edge.

Boulder X

V4 Train Spotting. The square face arête.

Roof Boulder

V2 Bucket Brigade. Begin on overhang, jug run to mantel.

V6 Begin on low crimps, then join BB.

V_ss Several powerful roof problems (untapped?).

Foxhole Boulder (Small)

V0-V1 Step Right Up is north side of small boulder.

V2 Foxhole. ⛰ Begin in the pit, ascend directly up, and exit right at the positive hold.

V4 Foxhole Atheist. ⛰ Same as Foxhole, ascend up and left, avoiding positive hold.

Boulder XX

V2 Trench Warfare. Begin in the pit, ascend the blunt arête to slab.

V1 Contribution.

Mega Man Boulder ⚠

The other great impressive Beacon Rock boulder well worth the visit is this 20' tall beast sitting in the forest just beyond the edge of the lower talus field (see topo). Beta R to L:

V0 _______ Southeast arête.

V3+ _______ Slightly hung south face.

V3+ _______ Slightly hung south face.

V0 _______ Southwest arête.

VB _______ Just left of previous arête is a fund run.

V1+ _______ Cruise an angled seam.

V0 _______ Face with small edges.

V1 _______ Go up near northwest arête on face.

VB _______ The northwest arête.

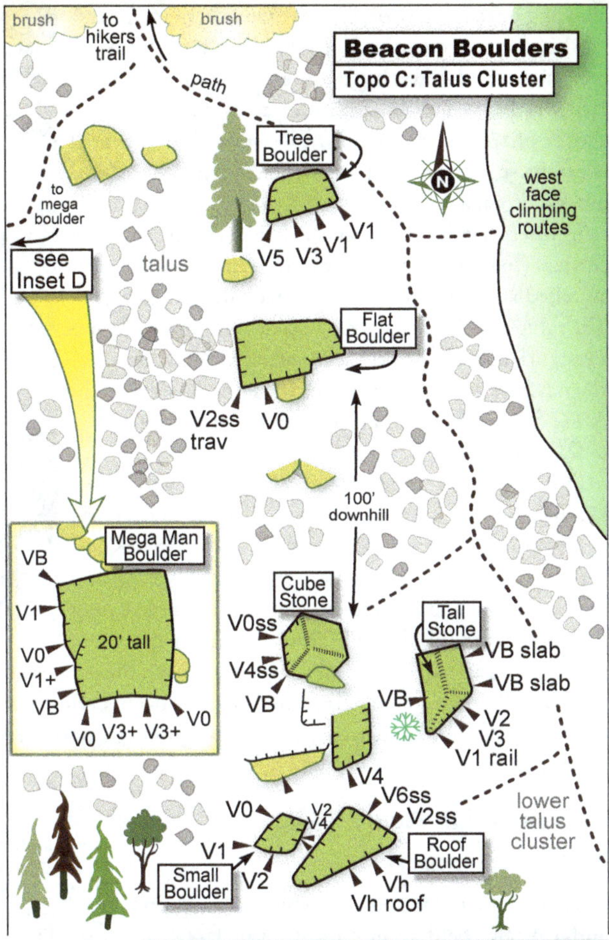

HAMILTON BOULDERS

Stellar compact arena of boulders in the midst of a complex south-facing talus field in a state park environment. The visible qualities being ideal, the Hamilton Boulders (aka Horse Camp) has become one of Portland's hotspot gems. And for good reason; it fits a trident combination difficult to match (low elevation, sunny locale, minimal moss), virtual year-round accessibility (except perhaps in July-Aug), and a powerful string of superb quality lines ranging from VB to V11. High quality andesite stone with ideal friction-ability, the site has appeal for its tightly packed core of large sized stones with considerable overhung aspects to swing like a chimp on. Andesite surficial texture of impeccable quality, retains a fine soft grit phenocryst matrix that offers superior grip and smear ops, allowing lines to be realistic regardless of its steepness.

The lower core cluster is a very short walk from the parking lot to the first big boulder. A decent path leads into the heart of an amphitheater, a closely packed cluster of stones (8'-14' tall). The entire boulder field is extensive, but does offer additional gems as isolated blocks, or small clusters (on difficult to negotiate terrain where agility is crucial). There are three main clusters (to date), but the entire talus field has been researched and some distant objectives are being tapped. The talus field is an open slope (with minor brush and substantial poison oak) so a savvy individual can generally navigate to the second and third tier clusters easily. A 1-2 crashpad minimum recommendation site.

Directions

Drive east on State Route 14 from Vancouver, Washington for 35 miles to Beacon Rock State Park. Turn left (north at the Ranger Office) on paved Kueffler Road, drive uphill 1 mile, turn right onto a gravel road and continue ¼ mile on this to the Horse Camp parking lot and hiking trail. This is an upper extension

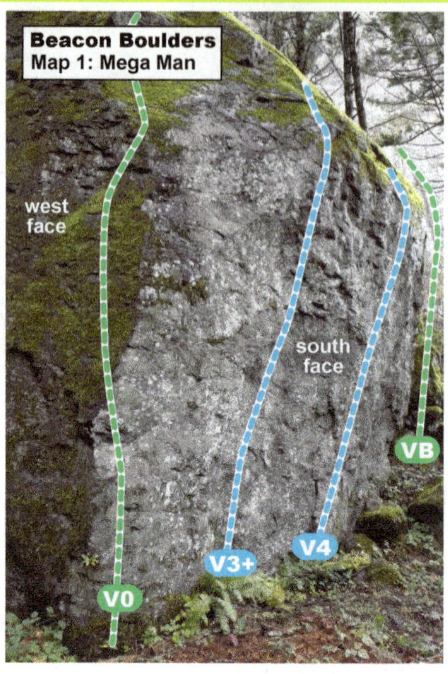

of the state park that is commonly used by both hikers and equestrians. Walk north past the white gate for 200', then follow a track left to the obvious talus field, following a cairn coordinated path to the core amphitheater. Extra pointers: good cell phone reception; it is a state park tourist fee required site.

Lower Talus Field

Boulder 1 (Sunspot)

The very first stone you see when you step up onto the talus field. Majestic tall sunny face.
V1 Freaky Flake. The left tall face
V7ss crimps on the right face

Boulder 2 (Low)

V4ss (left line), **V6ss** over and run rail

Boulder 3 (Giggles)

V0ss right, and a **V0ss** on the left

Boulder 4

V3 outer nose, and **V2** on left face

Boulder 5 (Yayo)

Beta is left to right:
V7ss Direct. Left direct on far left side
V6ss Chopin. Left side using sloped rail.
V3ss Prow. Use prow angle left to top
V2ss same as above but exit right to top
V1 slab right side of block

V2 slab right side of block
V5 traverse entire both aspects

Boulder 6 (Elephant)

V1ss far right at talus
V2ss Elephant. The right prow (VB stand)
V1ss Elephant Ear. Center slab
V1ss the left prow
VB far west side

Boulder 7 (Shorty)

V0ss left shorty
V2ss Shorty. Center-right shorty

Boulder 8 (Cave)

V2ss the pillar to the right of the cave
V7ss punch out the low cave
V1ss left side of cave
V2ss traverse lip of cave

Boulder 9 (Mcnugget)

It might be ultra short but its 'on-the-path' locale make is an obvious popular hit.
V4ss McNugget. Start on flat jug
V1ss low start on right

Boulder 10 (Stacked)

V1ss climb out of tiny pit up a shorty.
V0 Stacker. Go up the entire double stack.
V0 Rib Rail. Minor rib on right block

Boulder 11 (Big slab)

V0 left slab
V1 center slab
V0 right slab

Boulder 12 (Bruce Lee)

The Bruce Lee Boulder is often the destination stone of first choice. It sits in the very heart of the main talus amphitheater and provides some gem quality little bouldering problems.
V7ss East Arête. The classic east arête
V_ss (?) center up.
V5ss Enter The Dragon. Traverse left to right along east lip.
V5ss crimps south side only.
V8ss Fluid Like Water. Power up left side, then transition to right hung arête to finish Classic!
V3ss Kato. Face on hung large hold
V2ss Johnny Law. Far NW side

Boulder 13 (Frosty Flake) tall flake

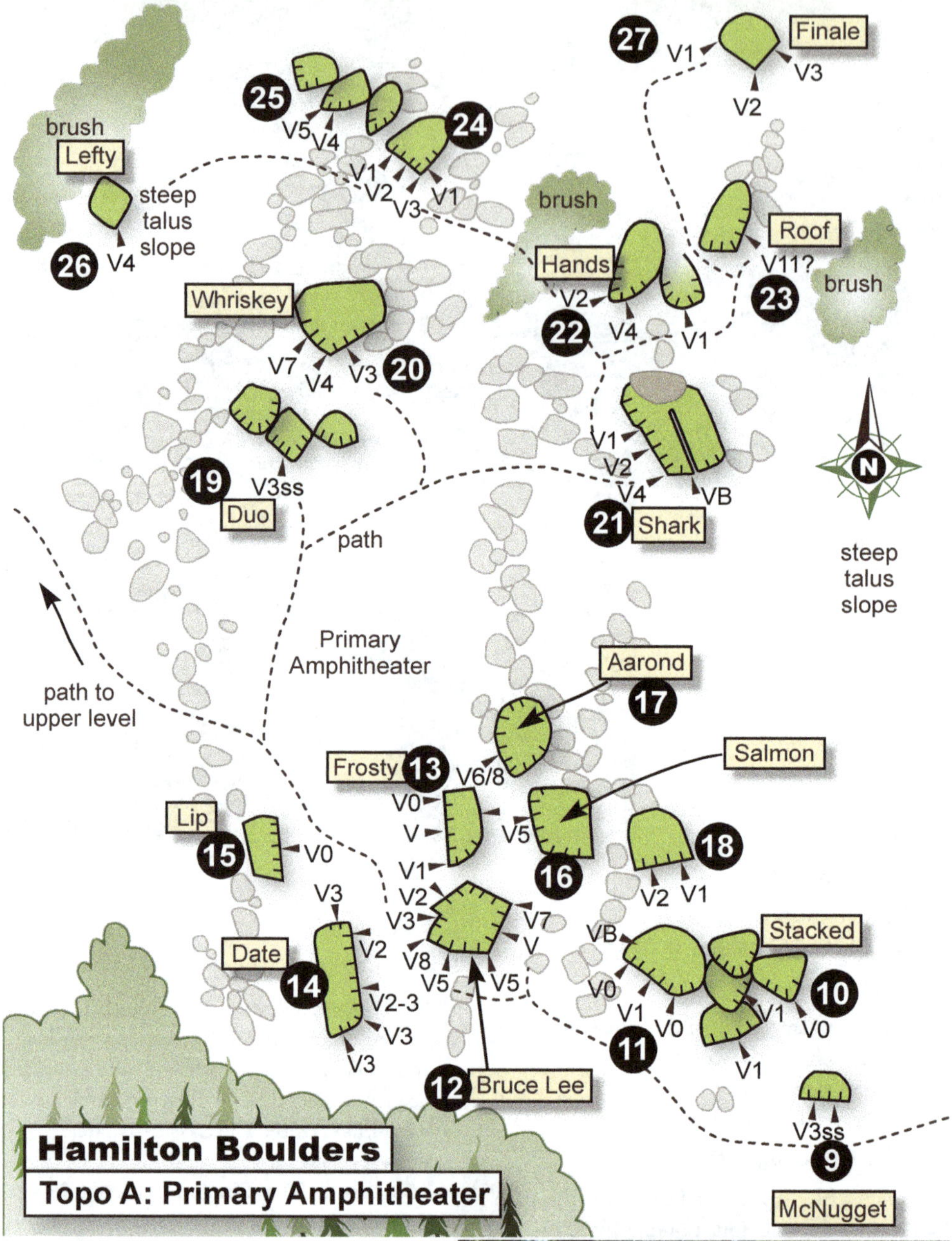

V1ss Frosty Flake. South prow of flake
V0 left to right traverse up over.
V_+ (?) middle west face

Boulder 14 (Date)

V3ss utter north side crimps
V2ss Cheap Date. Crimp up from low
start on main east side.

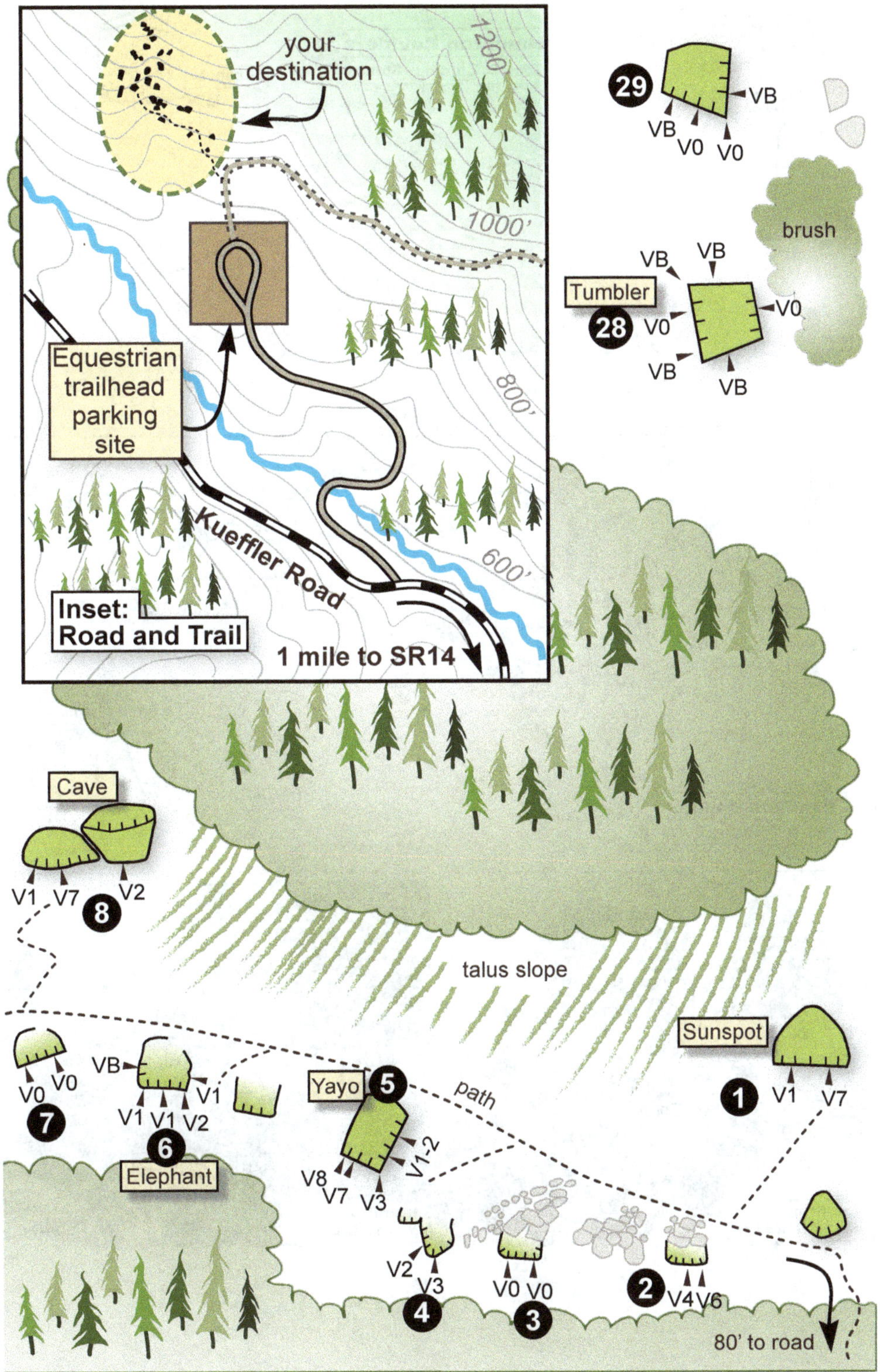
your destination
1200
1000'
Equestrian trailhead parking site
Kueffler Road
Inset: Road and Trail
1 mile to SR14
800'
600'
brush
29
VB
VB
V0
V0
Tumbler
28
VB
VB
V0
V0
VB
VB
Cave
V1
V7
V2
8
talus slope
Sunspot
1
V1
V7
VB
V0
V0
V0
V1
V1
V1
V2
7
6
Elephant
Yayo
5
path
V1-2
V8
V7
V3
V2
V3
V0
V0
4
3
2
V4
V6
80' to road

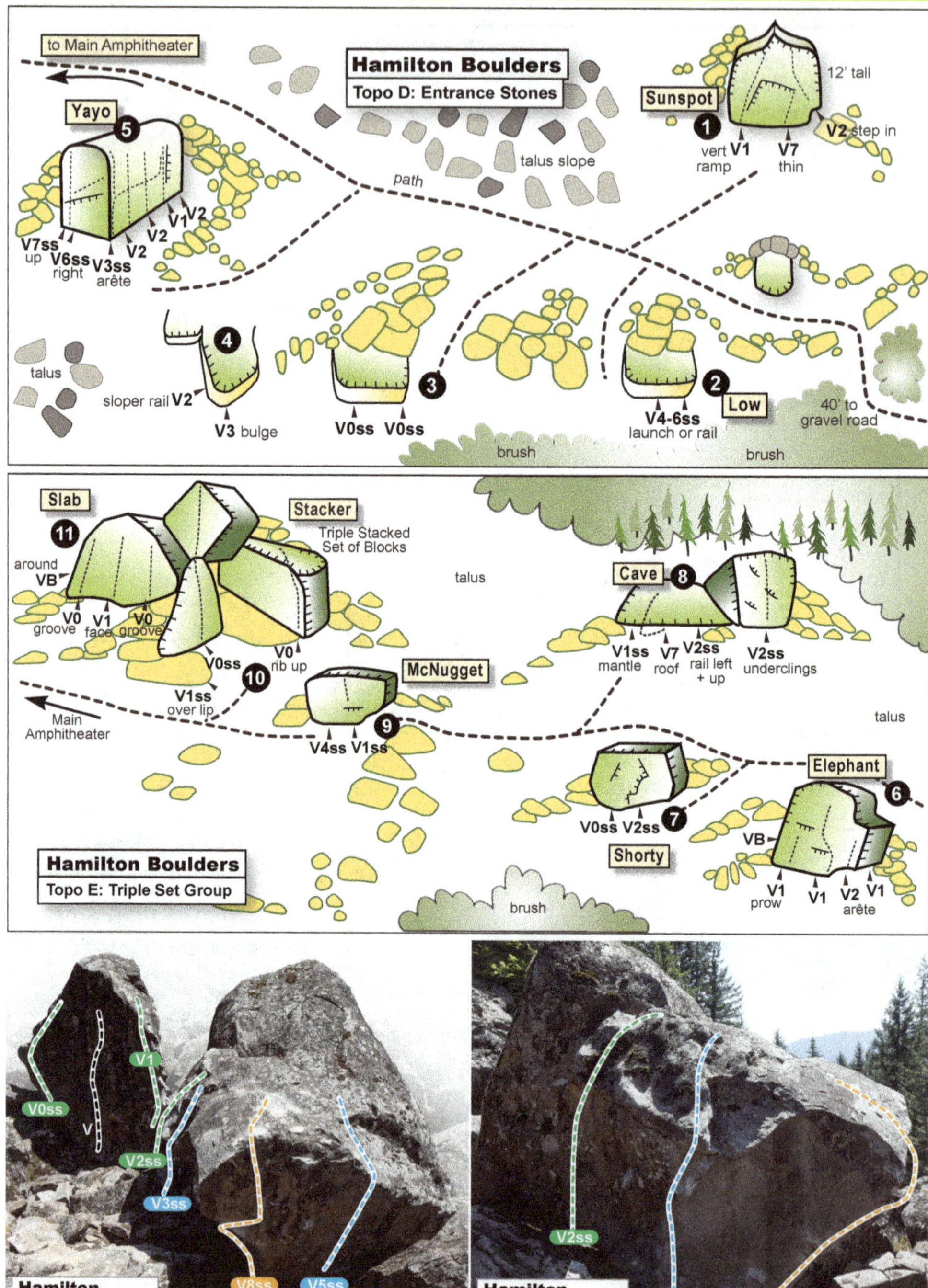
to Main Amphitheater
Hamilton Boulders
Topo D: Entrance Stones
Sunspot
1
12' tall
V2 step in
vert V1 V7
ramp thin
Yayo
5
talus slope
path
V1 V2
V7ss V2
up V6ss V2
right V3ss
arête
talus
4
sloper rail V2
V3 bulge
3
V0ss V0ss
2 Low
V4-6ss
launch or rail
40' to
gravel road
brush brush
Slab
11
Stacker
Triple Stacked
Set of Blocks
around
VB
talus
Cave
8
V0 V1 V0
groove face groove
V0ss
V0
rib up
V1ss
10
over lip
McNugget
V1ss V7 V2ss V2ss
mantle roof rail left underclings
+ up
Main
Amphitheater
9
V4ss V1ss
talus
Elephant
6
7
V0ss V2ss
Shorty
VB
V1 V1 V2 V1
prow arête
Hamilton Boulders
Topo E: Triple Set Group
brush

V1
V0ss
V
V2ss
V3ss
V8ss V5ss
Hamilton
Map 4a: Bruce Lee
V2ss
V3ss V8ss
Hamilton
Map 4b: Bruce Lee

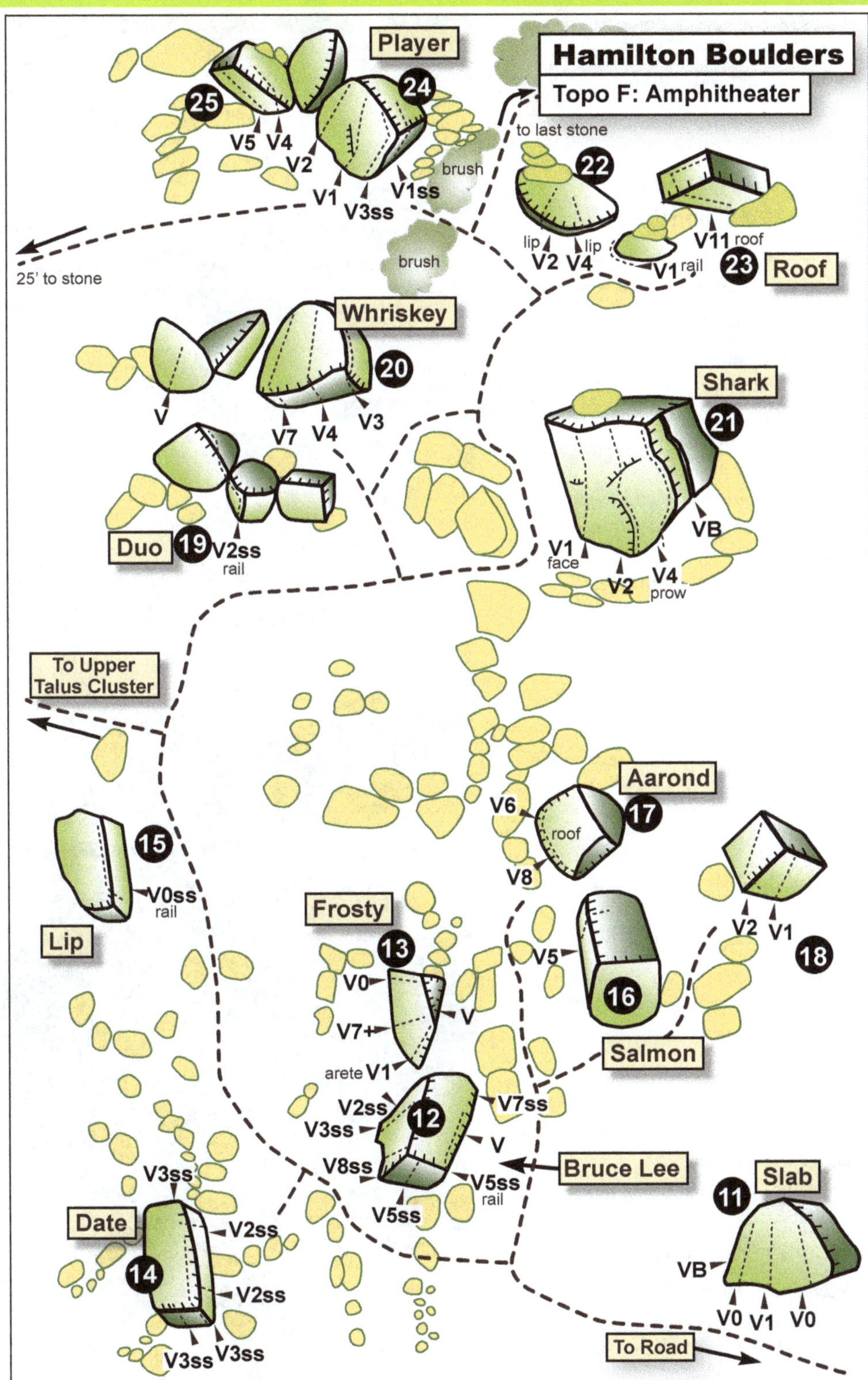
Player
Hamilton Boulders
Topo F: Amphitheater
to last stone
25
24
V5 V4
V2
V1
V1ss
V3ss
brush
22
brush
lip
lip
V2 V4
V11 roof
V1 rail
23 Roof
25' to stone
Whriskey
20
V
V7 V4 V3
Shark
21
Duo 19 V2ss
rail
V1
face
V2
V4
prow
VB
To Upper
Talus Cluster
Aarond
V6
17
roof
15
V8
V0ss
rail
Frosty
V5
V2 V1
Lip
13
V0
18
V
16
V7+
Salmon
arete V1
V7ss
V2ss
V3ss
12
V
V8ss
Bruce Lee
Slab
V3ss
V5ss
rail
11
Date
V2ss
V5ss
14
V2ss
VB
V3ss V3ss
V0 V1 V0
To Road

V2ss several variants on east aspect
V3ss lower leftmost hung point
V3ss far left side, up, and traverse lip right.

Boulder 15 (Lip)

V0 traverse left to right.

Boulder 16 (Salmon Cakes)

V5ss Salmon Cakes. Superb quality hung crimps problem well worth doing.

Boulder 17 (Aarond)

V6ss A-aron. Crawl into the far back side beneath this flake boulder. Begin on the back inner side of the overhang, foot force, grasp horizontal, reach outer lip and mantle it.
V8ss Aarond the World. Same start as previous, but power along the entire lip, then
mantle over at far south end.

Boulder 18

V2 left, and V1 on right.

Boulder 19 (Duo)

V2ss Begin on round incut rail on lower block, transition up onto second block.

Boulder 20 (Whrisky)

V7 Whrisky Left. Left side from under-cut
V4 Whiskey Business. Center from un-dercut base
V3ss Water to Whiskey. Right side out and over.
V_ (?) on a minor block 20' west.

Boulder 21 (Shark Tank)

A 12' tall vert face.
V1 left slab
V2 center, can split mid-height and go either way to exit.
V4 right slab but at nose
VB fat crack

Boulder 22 (Her Shirt)

V2ss Bad Touch. Left side as a heel hook
V4ss Her Shirt. Under going to the

right via incut jugs

Boulder

V1ss on a minor block to the right

Boulder 23 (Her Skirt Roof)

V11 (?) Toe hooks and long reaches under the roof to the lip then over it (project?)

Boulder 24 (Player)

V2ss Chocolate Thunder. Utter left side on bulge
V1ss center face crimps only
V3ss Vanilla. Round arête (V5 if cruise left)
V1ss Tug Job. Brief hung to jugs

Boulder 25 (Hands Down)

V5ss left underside
V4ss right underside

Boulder 26 (Lefty)

V4 short crimps face problem

Boulder 27

V1 left rounded nose
V2 center face on crimps
V3 right arête on crimps

Upper Talus Field

See the diagrams for specific details about the approach hike up to this zone. The illustration maps provide quick details on the existing tapped product. One of the superb gems in the upper field you may want to visit is Slashface Boulder. There is some potential yet to be tapped in the upper zone, some of it scattered a fair distance in various clusters. There are scattered thickets of poison oak to venture through just to reach the Midway Cluster and the Upper Talus Field, and that alone is enough of a detraction to keep some visitors at bay. Bouldering at the Lower Talus Field has enough quality problems suitable for most people.

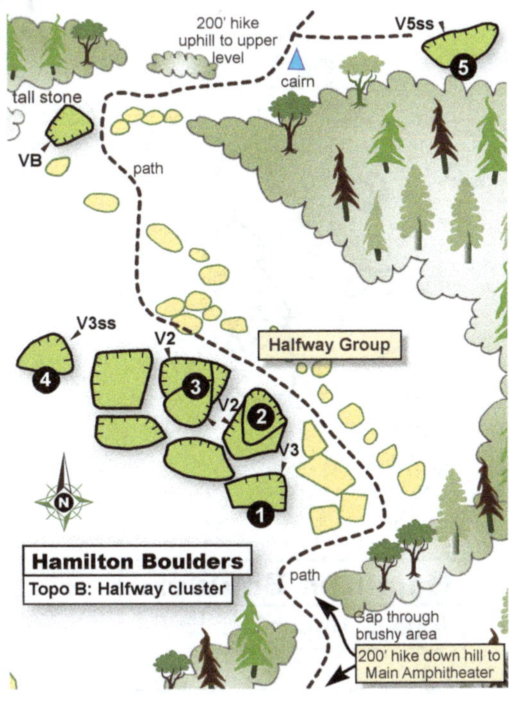

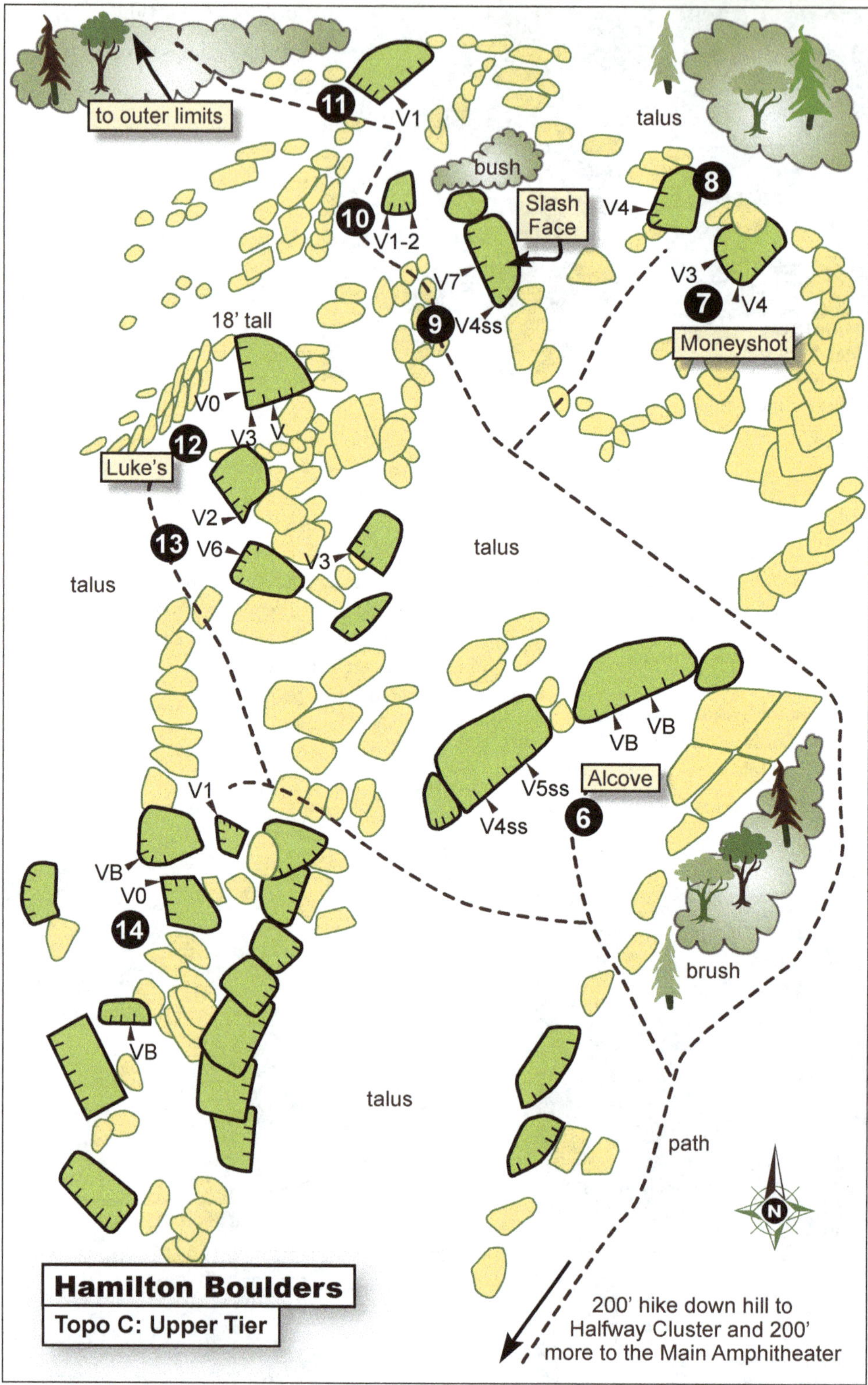

to outer limits
11
V1
talus
10
V1-2
bush
Slash
Face
8
V4
18' tall
V7
9
V4ss
V3
7
V4
Moneyshot
V0
12
V3 V
Luke's
V2
13
V6
V3
talus
talus
VB
VB
Alcove
V5ss
6
V4ss
V1
VB
V0
14
brush
VB
talus
path
N
Hamilton Boulders
Topo C: Upper Tier
200' hike down hill to
Halfway Cluster and 200'
more to the Main Amphitheater

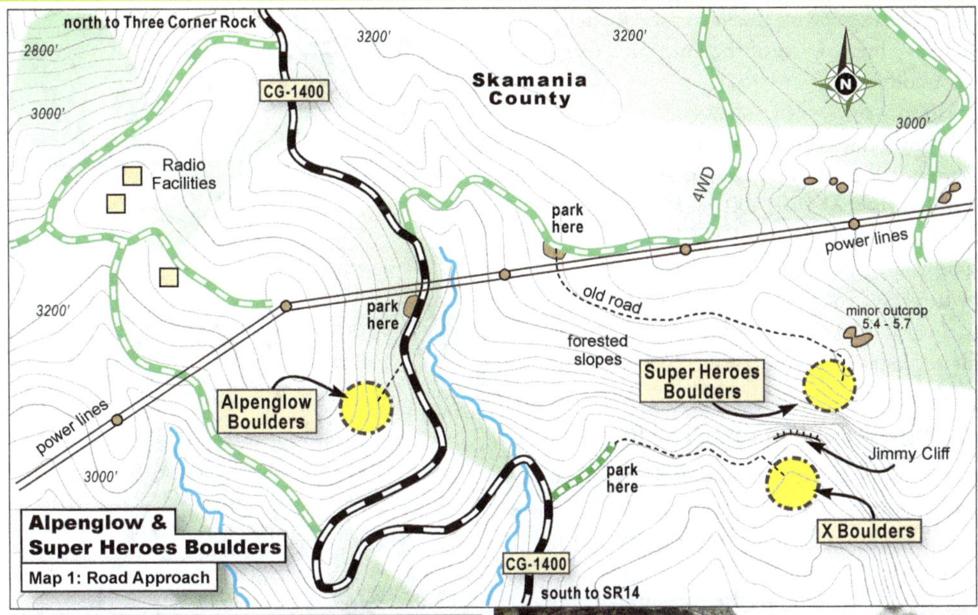

ALPENGLOW BOULDERS

Tymun on *Cathedral Arête*

Certainly noted for being one of Portland's finest bouldering areas Alpenglow holds a concentrated spectrum of VB-V10 problems situated on an open south-facing talus slope, surrounded by a fir forest with impeccable scenery, superb quality bouldering on stones ranging in size from 12'-18' tall, with the fattest stone measuring at nearly 35' in diameter. High altitude locale overlooking the Columbia Gorge on weather abrasion scoured stones ideal for chalk and send bouldering on about 50 problems and more than 6 traverses. The rock surface texture is slightly fine grain quality (no moss), natural divots, edges and smears, rippled textured surficial features, steep vertical faces (both thin techy and jug lines), super overhung aspects, dicey hi-ball lines, VB fun runs, arêtes and prows. All the quality you could ask for merged into a single core site offering the finest back-to-back list of classic boulder problems found in this region. This is 1-2 crashpad minimum recommended site.

History:

This site was specifically tapped by Mr Abbott (85% of all lines) and two close associates (Dave and Shane) starting way back in early 2002. As they returned late one October day from 3-Corner Rock bouldering they spied the Alpenglow cluster just above the tips of the trees. They parked and walked up and were impressed. But alas, the next day fall season rains began in earnest and neither were able to conquer the place until spring 2002. Aptly named Alpenglow Boulders after the quality sunset hues. Of the few leftover breadcrumbs (albeit some hefty stout ones) some were tagged in 2013-15 by 3-4 other locals.

Seasons:

Weather dependent conditional temperate variances exist at this site (it can get hot in July) based on the time of day, the season, if its a bright sunny windless day, or an overcast breezy afternoon.

Until you experience the flavor of Alpenglow you have missed one of the finest this region has to offer.

Directions

From State Route 14 at Beacon Rock, drive north on paved road Kueffler Road for 2 miles, then of NF1400 road for six miles till you reach the power lines. Park in a wide spot there, and walk 200' back down the main gravel road, then angle up slope (off-trail scramble) into the thick forest, aiming for a cluster of stones about 300' above the road.

Alpenglow Boulder (beta L to R)

This is the super big beast with a string of quality lines along its SE aspect.

V2 Mazama is the leftmost problem in a brief vertical scoop.

V1 Sunshine climbs the face immediately right of the previous problem.

VB Southside ⚠ A series of small sloped steps and edges leading up into a minor corner near the lip.

V1 Alpenglow ⚠ Classic hi-ball that tackles the tall section of the stone in the center of the face using a series of down sloping fat ramp rail edges, then delicately moves

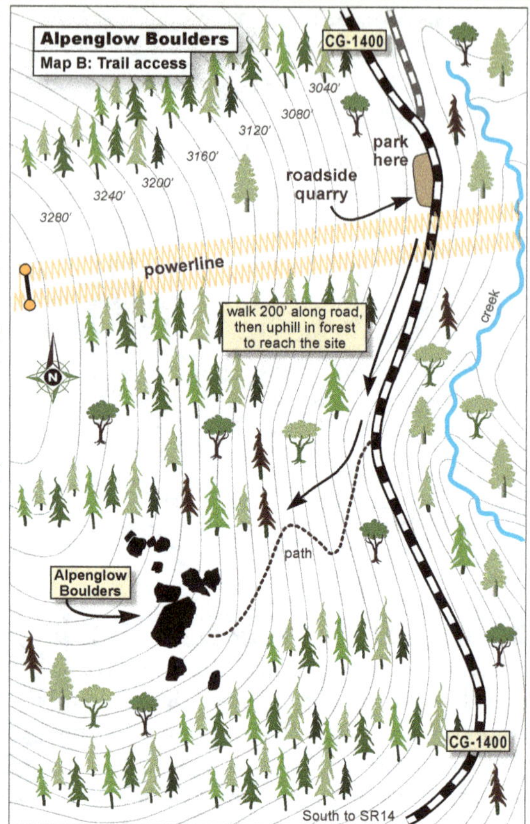

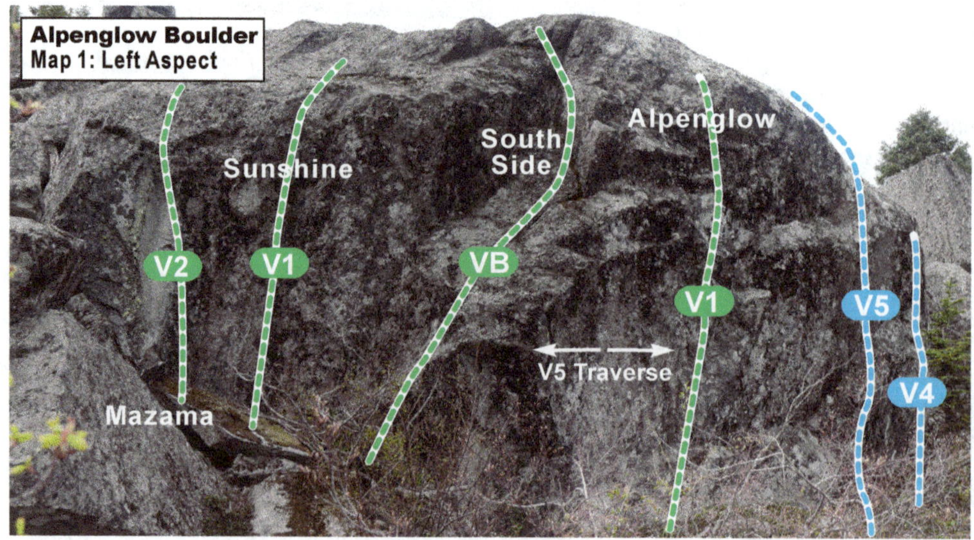

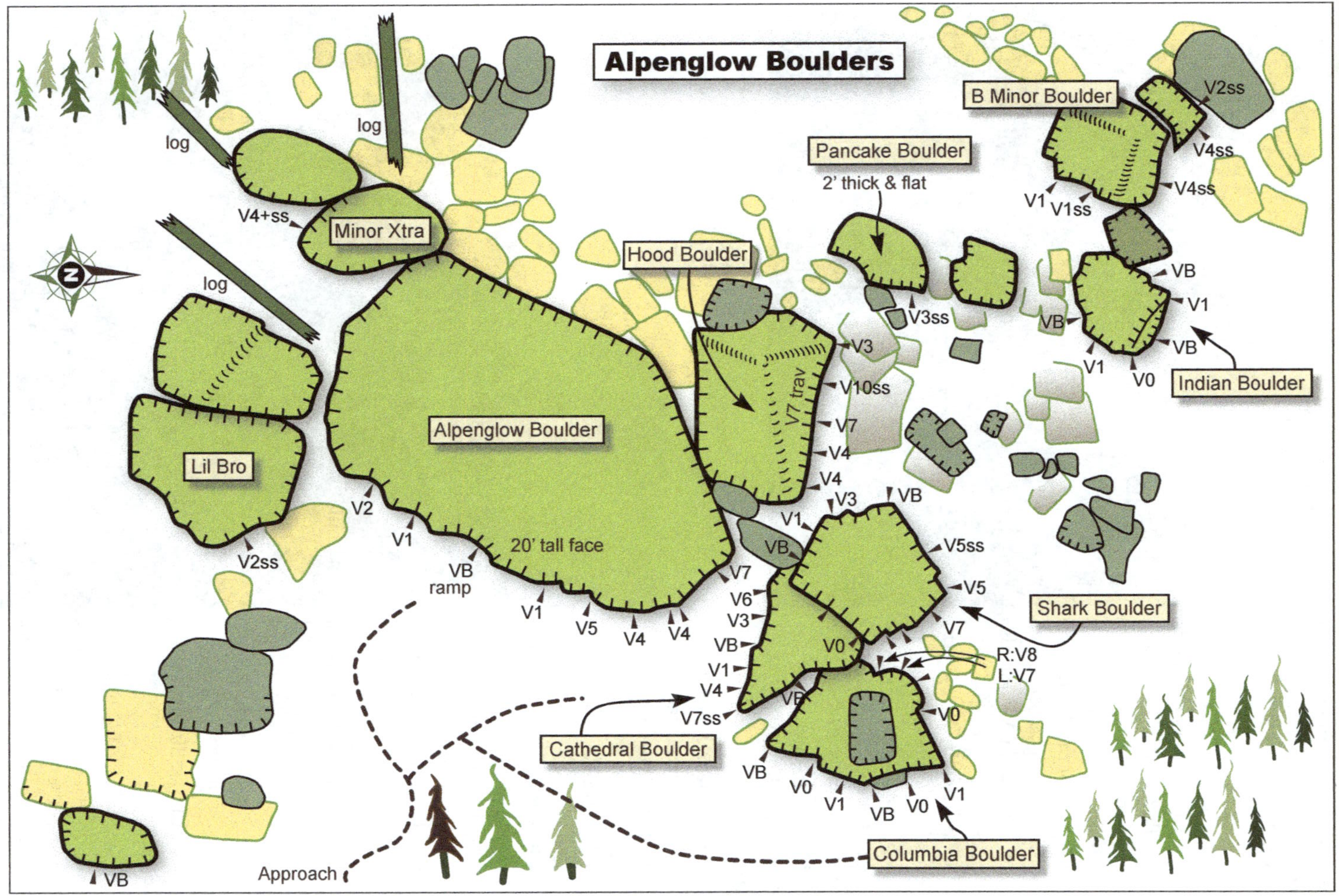
Alpenglow Boulders
B Minor Boulder
V2ss
V4ss
V4ss
V1 V1ss
Pancake Boulder
2' thick & flat
VB
V1
VB
V1
V0
Indian Boulder
V3ss
Hood Boulder
V3
V10ss
V7 trav
V7
V4
V4
V3
VB
V1
VB
V5ss
V5
V7
Shark Boulder
V0
R:V8
L:V7
V0
log
log
Minor Xtra
V4+ss
log
Alpenglow Boulder
Lil Bro
V2
V1
20' tall face
V2ss
VB
ramp
V1
V5
V4
V4
V7
V6
V3
VB
V1
V4
V7ss
VB
Cathedral Boulder
VB
V0
V1
VB
V0
V1
Columbia Boulder
Approach
VB

past the high rounded bulge onto the slab.

V5 The Spur. ⚠ Tackles a slight bulge using two down sloping fat rails (behind tree).

V4 Ice Feathers is pockets, sidepulls on slight hung double nose feature.

V4 Sunspot is crimps to a slight notch at the lip, then follow the seam past the notch onto top slab (a V5 var also merges).

V7ss Bring It On is a techy crimp line on the far right.

V5 Alpenglow Traverse is a traverse of the entire base of this boulder (exclude the rightmost V7ss).

Cathedral Boulder (beta L to R)

V6 Cathedral is rounded slopers, starts far left at nook (plus an ending V6 var).

V3ss Heather. Minor short scoop.

VBss Bear Grass. Minor short groove.

V1ss Lip of Light. Face.

V4ss Cathedral Arête is the classic quality overhung nose. A must-do for everyone!

V7 Cathedral Traverse (R to L). Quality powerful traverse beginning at lowest point and cruising up left along entire lip.

Columbia Boulder (beta L to R)

This is a tall square-ish stone with a smaller block perched on top of it. The east face aspect is a tall hi-ball slab, while the shorter uphill sec-

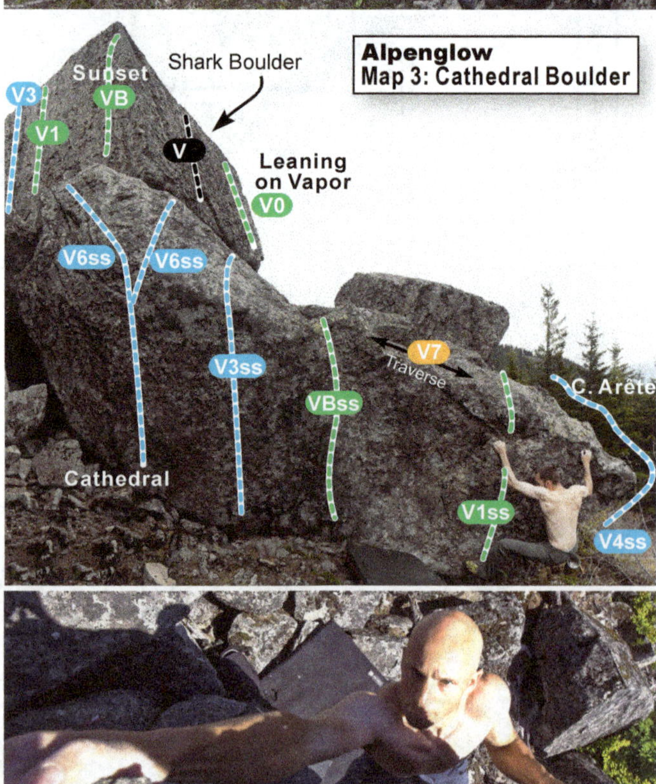

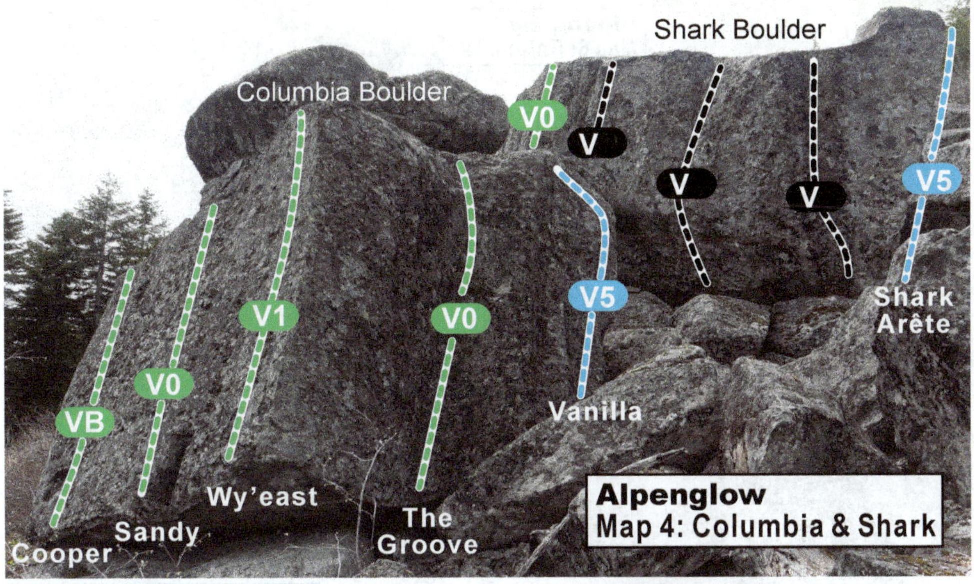

tion is tucked in a nook.

VB Modus Operandi. March up steps, groove and minor prow on left.

V0 (V1ss) Mea Culpa. Use the giant gas pocket.

V1 Ex Nihilo Nihil Fit. Start at overhang using a leftward slanting seam.

VB Cooper. Starts on base stone, step onto an incut gas pocket, then up slab on small pockets.

V0 Sandy. The right part of slab starting at a slight notch, then cruise the small pockets on the face.

V1 Wy'east Arête. The classic sharp profiled arête.

V0 The Groove. An obvious minor and commonly climbed groove.

V5ss Vanilla. A short hung rounded face (using left arête).

V7ss Don The Armoire. Hung powerful crimps face tucked in the small nook.

V8ss Don't Sweat The Technique. Powerful overhung problem deep in nook (left hand uses

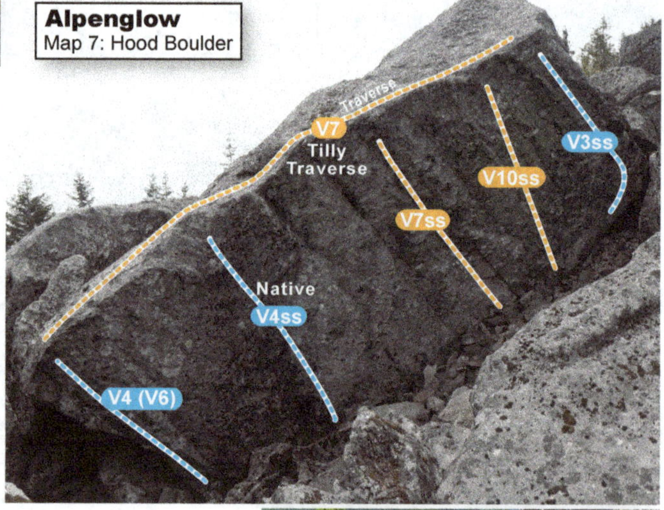

hung rail).

Shark Boulder

The high perched stone that is stacked on part of the Cathedral Stone. The first problem listed is the basic line on the southwest aspect (going clockwise [R to L]).

VB Sunset. Sent by standing on *Cathedral Stone*, make one move up, mantle onto summit.

V1ss Northern Lights. Slight vertical seam on flat face.

V3ss Edge of Life. Use right hand on sharp fin.

VB brief jug mantle.

VB the descent.

V5ss+ (?) ____ tucked in further right of Shark Fin Arête [block in the way].

V5 Shark Fin Arête. The super cool classic problem that ascends the prominent sharp profiled arête. A must-do classic problem!

V7 (?) ____ start on left side of arête, go up left to flat

Shane on *Tilly's Traverse*

Tymun at Alpenglow Boulders

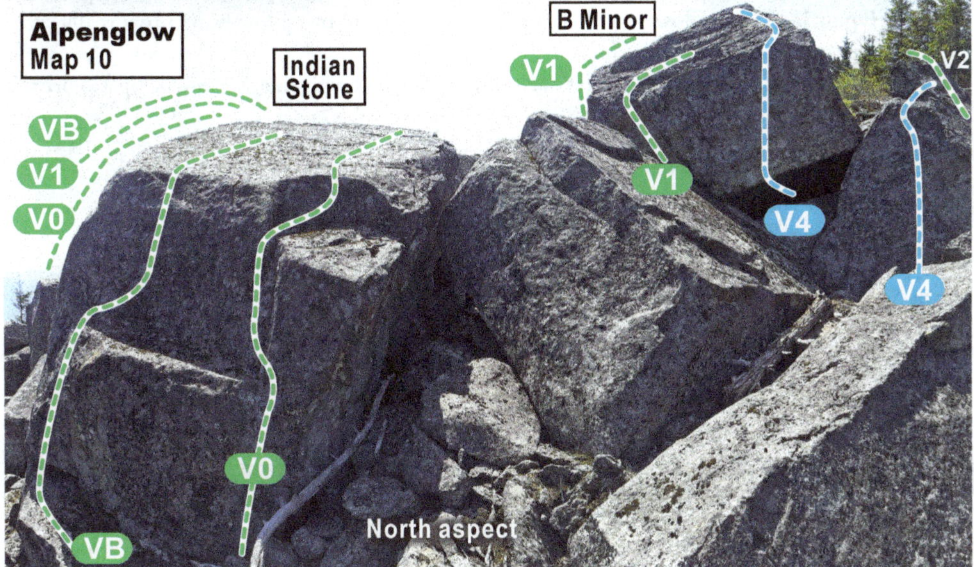

lip.

V7 (?) ____ a hung groove.

V8 (?) ____ a hung groove.

V0 Leaning on Vapor. Stand on *Columbia Stone*, do a high step one-move up onto this problem (with a friend guarding your backside).

V8-9ss+ (?) ____ the overhung east aspect.

Hood Boulder

A quality stone with impeccable problems, and a common spot to boulder in the shade at Alpenglow.

V4 (V6ss) Fait Accompli. Start low and power up the rib.

V4ss The Native. Start slow and end on groove.

V7ss (Shattered?). Low sidepull to crimps.

V10+ss (?) _____ thin face on right half of stone.

V3ss Columbine. Rounded right nose.

V7 Tilly Jane Traverse. Quality and very powerful slopers rail traverse (aka Tilly's Traverse). Begin on leftmost route down low and run rightward up along the entire lip.

Pancake Boulder

V3ss Pancake. A minor flat 2' thick block with a very low traverse.

Indian Boulder

Some fun problems. Beta is left to right:

VB Teepee. Climb scoop with right hand on fin.

V1ss Indian Scout. Left hand on fin going up face.

V0ss Peace Pipe. A minor rounded face.

VB Palamino. On the north aspect is a series of steps.

V0ss Bring Your Bow. A minor point and the rightmost problem.

B Minor Boulder

A brief set of very short problems (see map).

V1ss Nolens Volens. SS ultra low, catch lip and up. On SE aspect.

V1ss Hypnotic. SS ultra low, face hold, grab lip, and up (all using low hung prow really). On the SE aspect.

V4ss Lost & Found. Under the lowest part of the stone on north side. SS low, using a short rail and get up.

C Minor Boulder

Another set of brief short problems (see map).

V4ss Raison d'etat. On its outer steep aspect is this low crimpy SS problem.

V2ss Hypnosis. Minor last problem one on back uphill side.

Minor Xtra

And way over on the SW upper side of the Alpenglow Boulder is a brief block that's got just enough height to yield a minor SS problem.

V4ss Alpen Xtra. SS low and crimp an overhang to the lip and over the top.

SUPER HERO BOULDERS

A high quality, high elevation site overlooking the scenic breadth of the majestic Columbia Gorge, SHB encompasses a unique assortment of problems on naturally wind and weather abra-

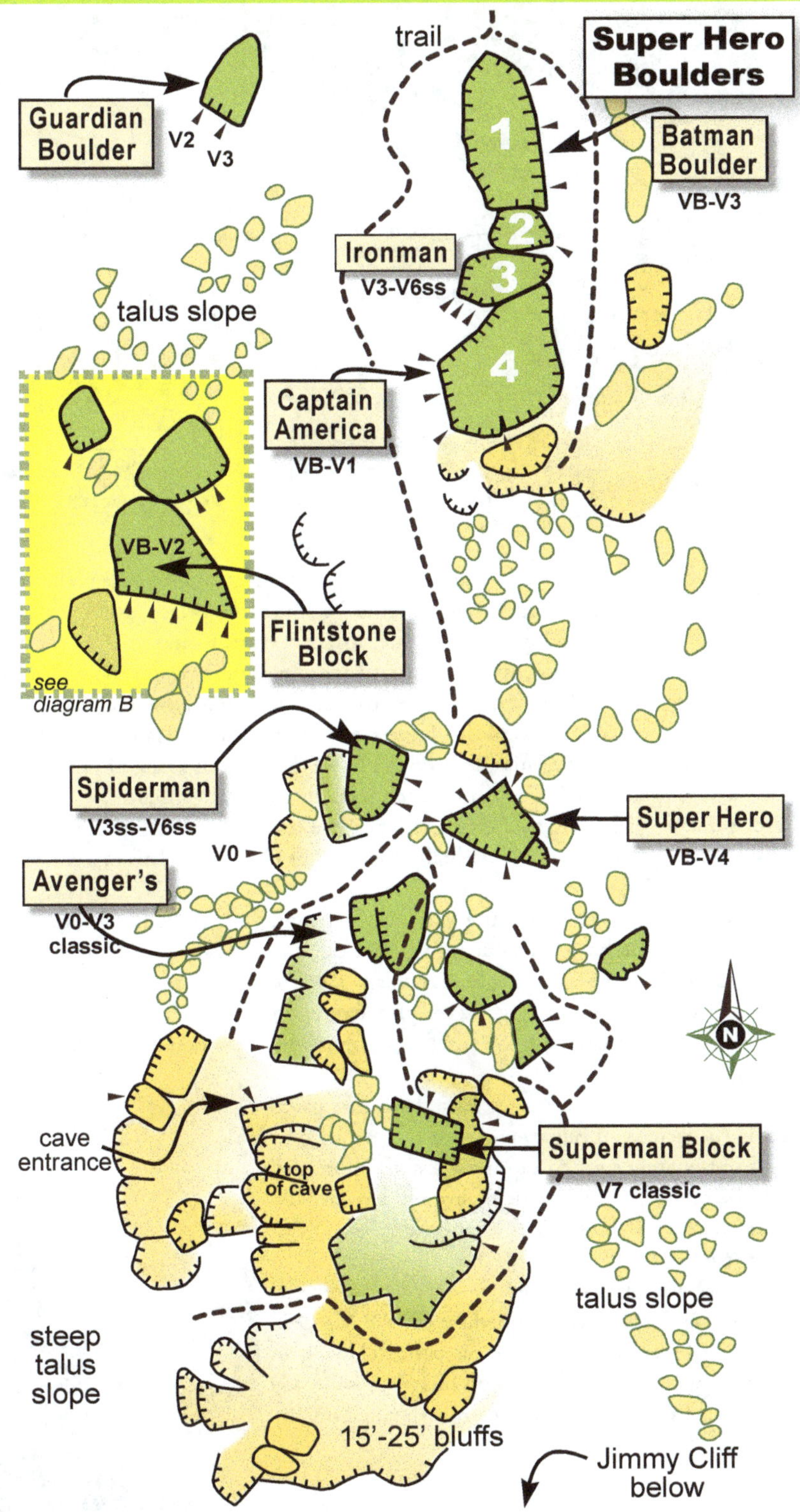
Super Hero Boulders
trail
1
2
3
4
Batman Boulder
VB-V3
Guardian Boulder
V2
V3
Ironman
V3-V6ss
Captain America
VB-V1
talus slope
see diagram B
VB-V2
Flintstone Block
Spiderman
V3ss-V6ss
V0
Super Hero
VB-V4
Avenger's
V0-V3
classic
cave entrance
top of cave
Superman Block
V7 classic
talus slope
N
steep talus slope
15'-25' bluffs
Jimmy Cliff below

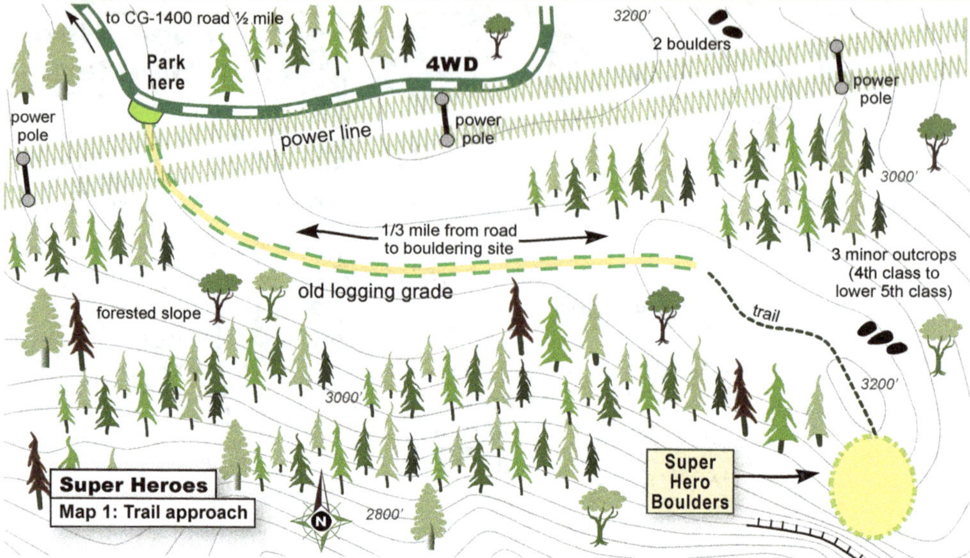

sion scoured andesite that has formed intriguing surficial etchings in the rock, such as wobbles and undulations that create excellent finger holds. Yet the rock surface also has a slight greasy feeling due the the wind scoured loss of crystalline surface texture. Compact site on a sunny south-facing talus slope with limited potential, but offers superb naturally clean problems ranging from VB to V7, mostly on blocks of moderate size (9'-15' tall) with some long lengthwise laying stones. Stellar sweeping panoramic views of the western Gorge. The site is a talus slope that descends steeply to the top of Jimmy Cliff. This site is quite photographic with a mix of gray rock, light green vine maple foliage (golden red in autumn), dark green fir trees and jet blue sky.

Rock quality yields unusual characteristics like natural pockets, divots, and knobs, all a mere quirk of nature. The site may eventually yield V9 or close to it. This is a 1-2 crashpad minimum recommended site.

Expect conditional temperature variances depending on the time of day, season, and type of weather. It may be hot on windless days, but due to its locale on the top of a ridge, it generally receives a steady breeze. Visiting here requires good foot agility, as the rock scree is rough and a bit loose in places. Extra pointers: good cell phone reception, caught from the towers down by the river. Season is best from late May to early November, if the snow does not block road access (elevation 3,200').

In a few years expect a greater string of future problems in the vicinity of Superman Stone. There are over a half-dozen stones yet to tap into, a steep short wall yet to be tapped, including an elusive hidden cave-*like* recess where a few lines will be established.

History:

This site was briefly tapped by Abbott & Sowerby (in 2003), and extensively tapped by Mr A/ Mr O in 2013 (Mr A also opened the access path following an old logging grade) so the history on this place is already a well established fact, yet there are still some quality

Tymun on *Beam of Light* (*Super Hero*)

leftover breadcrumbs that will expand the V-range.

Directions

This site involves some adventure, with a healthy walk. From State Route 14 at Beacon Rock, drive north on paved road Kueffler Road for 2 miles, then on NF1400 road for six miles. When you reach the power lines, turn right onto a very rough power line access road, and drive ½ mile (use GPS) and park exactly where the map indicates. Then walk an old grade into the forest, and follow the old logging grade ¼ mile out along the forested ridge to the very end, then on a faint trail, then descend down onto the boulder covered scree slope.

Batman Boulder

This horizontal laying stone offers a nice fun string of options on the east face. Beta is R to L (upper to lower).

V0ss Zoroaster. Uppermost line on right using jugs on slight hung start.

V3ss Batman. Starts on rail, catch large knob, then up.

V2ss Tabula rasa. Start on rail, catch long flake, then up.

VB Gitgone. Lowest point on stone.

The two traverses:

V0 Obon. High traverse with feet on horizontal rail crack.

V4 Batman Traverse. Low traverse on horizontal rail crack, catch knob, end on last line.

Ironman Boulder

Four problems, all powerful sit

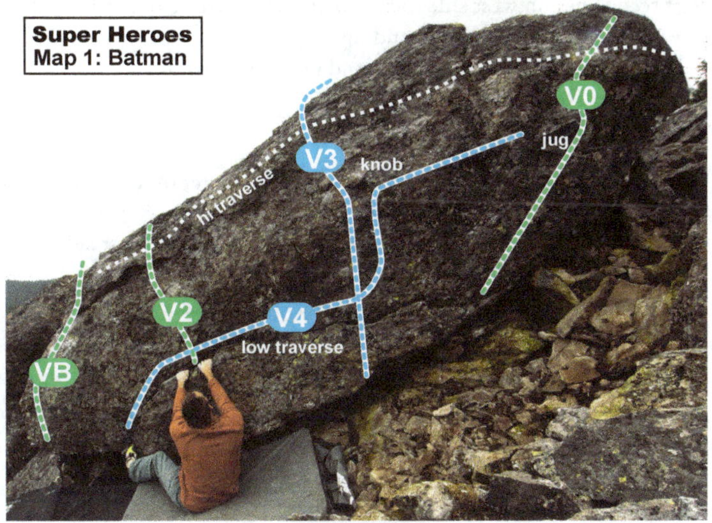

start techy lines on west side tucked between the third and fourth stone downhill from path.

V3ss Lex Talionis. On left and up

V6ss Ironman traverses left around prow and up

V5ss Lex Rex. Straight up on right

Captain America Boulder (15' tall)

A west facing aspect with several tall lines. A cluster of four stones downhill from trail (this being the fourth). Beta L to R (upper to lower).

V1 Captain America. Rounded minor nose on upper west side.

V0 Code of Valour. obvious left leaning crack.

V0 Labyrinthine Literati is the classic knobby arête.

VB Flights of Fancy is the crack slab on south side.

Super Hero Boulder

This superb stone has a water hole pocket on the summit. The entire stone is well featured with a 360° circuit of problems. Beta starts at the VB descent on north side.

VB The NE face descent.

V0 Sphere of Influence. The north arête.

V2-3+ _____ West hung face.

VB Oasis. Mega-classic arête and a treat for everyone.

V1 Oasis Direct. Start on lower block, smear initial edge with right foot, catch horizontal crack, then run the knob-fest arête on second upper block to top.

V4 Super Hero. A techy line in the middle section of face on lower block on south slab.

V2 The Verge. The easier right variant of the same south slab.

VB Virtue or Vice. At very southeast foot of this tall rock slab start on another protruding stone, pull the lip (crack nearby) and run knob rib to top.

Spiderman Boulder

This is immediately west of Oasis Stone

V6ss Spiderman. The traverse is a classic crimp and smear traverse line.

V3ss, V3ss, V5ss There are three vertical crimp SS problems (**Libra, Loco, & Locus**).

Superman Boulder

V7ss Superman. The ultra-classic at the site. Sit under the belly of the big beast, start on positive incut pockets, and power out the north side of block using stellar incut pockets, and jugs.

Avenger's Boulder (15' tall)

You likely set your pack on top of this boulder without realizing the gem under your feet. Beta is L to R.

V3ss Persona moralis. Shorty on left side.

V2ss Avenger's line tackles the hung left prow straight on by SS.

V0ss Beam Of Light. Incut jugs traverse that travels left across entire overhung face, then up left side to top out. Considered to be an ultra-classic for this site.

VBss Beam Me Up. Same start as previous, but go directly up.

Flintstone's Boulder (11' tall by 18' wide)

The popular angled warmup slab with numerous fun variants. Beta is R to L.

V0ss Barney's Arête smears up the right fin of the boulder.

V2 Popeye. Runs up face and over flake.

VB Fred's Favorite. Waltz up the middle ramp.

VB Blondie. Basic face.

VB Dino's Dilemma. Basic face.
VB Bliss. Basic face.
V1 Zorro goes up a thin face exiting left
V0 Green Lantern is the far left rounded nose.
V1 Flintstone's Traverse.

Justice League Boulder (right)

Located just up right of Flintstones Boulder.
V3ss Justice. Out left.
V3ss League. Out right.

Wonder Woman Boulder (feft)

V4ss Wonder Woman. Shorty. Its just uphill left of Flintstones Boulder.

Guardian Boulder (12′ tall)

At the top of the west talus slope is this isolated stone.
V2 X-men
V3 Guardian

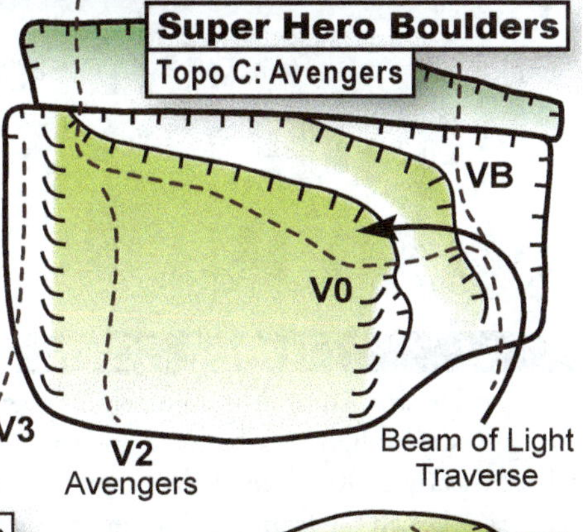

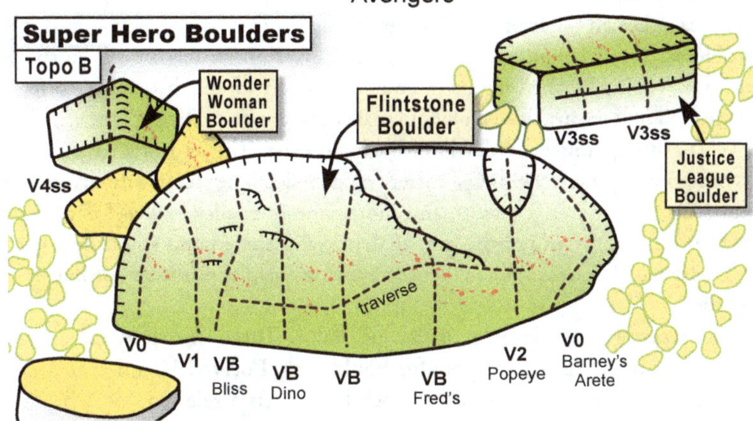

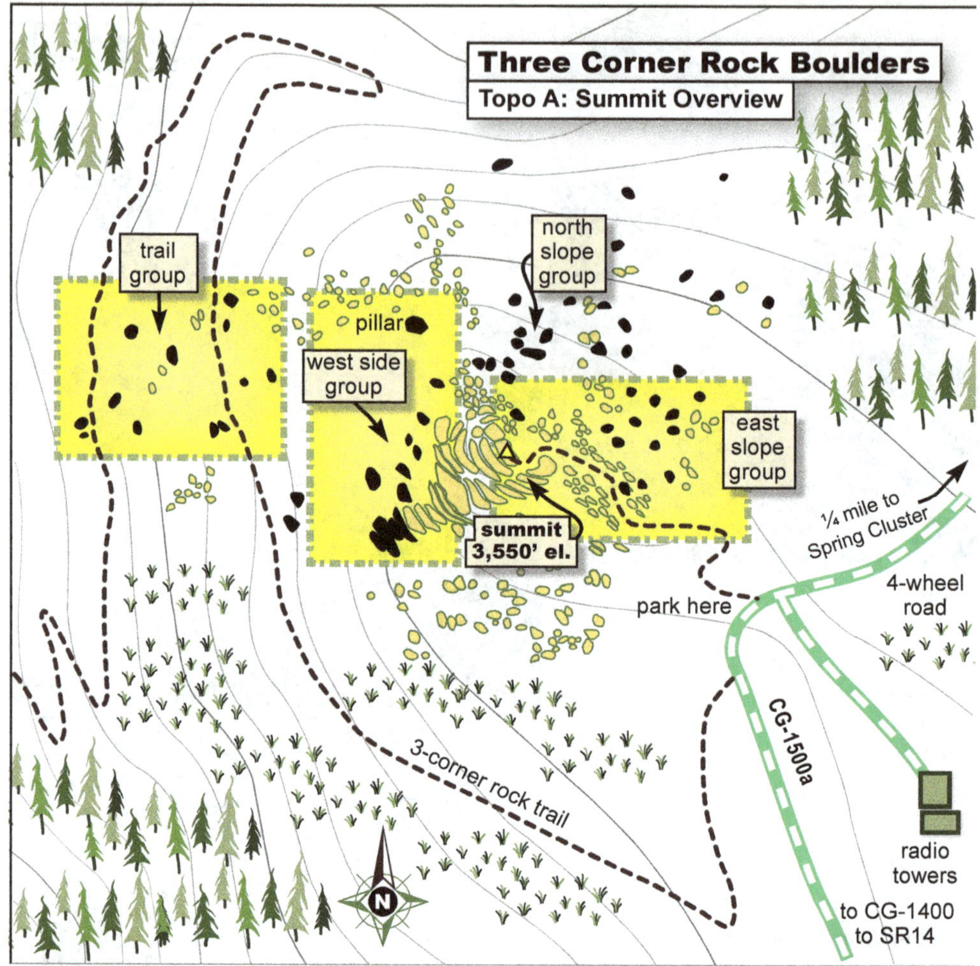

THREE CORNER ROCK BOULDERS

This ridge crest summit is an extensive region with tremendous variable opportunity for bouldering on superb light-gray colored andesite boulders and outcrops. Initially realized for its potential in the early 2000's, a small team rapidly developed a stunning selection of problems throughout the area. Though far from tapped out, in those initial years they logged upwards of 90+ boulder problems. This high altitude (3,400') site has a limited season due to snow. Imagine raging mosquitoes droning by the billions in your ears. Even so, this broad area offers superb bouldering on stones scoured naturally clean by the seasonal elements. The present string of problems range from VB-V8, though much harder lines likely do exist. The andesite rock textural nuances are similar to other nearby sites, yielding a variety of slab face lines, techy smooth smear dances, arêtes, round palmy desperadoes, overhangs, and more. The rock slickness feel is due to the radical chemical/mechanical weathering of the gray matrix being etched and smoothed, giving the surface its slick or greasy feel that necessitates focused effort for grip and smears (primarily on exposed west-facing aspects).

The west slope bouldering cluster just below Three Corner Rock summit, and a minor hi-ball short rock fin are popular spots for bouldering. Located ¼ mile southeast of the summit communication towers is a 12'-20' tall rock bluff with a selection of VB-V1 lines (off-trail walk to get there) on columnar blocks with prows and corners (a plethora of rounded holds and features). The third common site is 'The Spring Cluster' located ¼ mile east of the summit near a 4-wheel road, where a minor string of boulders along the tail-end of a stubby 11' tall bluff tucked in a fir forest offer quality challenges. If venturing along the north slope below the summit of Three Corner Rock beware of the risky 25'-35' deep gaps around the large blocks. There may be viable lines there, but it is high risk due to the nature of the cavernous gaps below the stones, and a mere misstep just scrambling across the blocks could end in disaster.

Brief History of Bouldering at 3CR

Mr Abbott started bouldering at Three Corner Rock in 2001 beginning low along the westside trail by sending lines on each stone encountered on the hike uphill, including the **V7 Autumn Splendor** line, a sheer trailside stone. As he hiked further uphill he reached the open slopes and tapped some lines. But at this point he realized he needed to bring in more guns to share the routes to get 'er done. So he contacted Mr Sowerby, and the two of them tapped many common lines around the summit massif, then tapped various other spots such as the cliff band to the southeast. They even spent one overnight weekend car camping there, bouldering on a multi-day effort. It was during one of those last-of-the-season October 2001 road trips while departing from Three Corner Rock that they spied the Alpenglow Boulders barely showing above the tree tops. They quickly hiked up to the stones and realized its stunning quality. Yet the Fall rains and snows arrived that week and kept them from tapping that site until the Spring of 2002. Altogether, Tymun and Dave sent many of the common lines at Three Corner Rock. A team of three persons (Tymun, Dave and Shane) were the prime individuals who sent 90% of the lines at Alpenglow Boulders in 2002-2004. At the Three Corner Rock bouldering site, the team used a simplified grading system while bouldering there because it was convenient, required minimal thought, and since there was no cleaning involved, it also allowed for a speedy send and quick move over to the next problem. That fast rating system was: easy (VB-V2), medium (V3-V6), hard (V7+).

The rock compositional matrix is a uniform fine-grained phenocryst andesite with noticeable weathering, generally no moss, and minimal lichens (near cracks or north-facing aspects). Peripheral deformation variances in rock structure exists based on proximity to the magma vent summit massif in some cases producing substantial small gaseous

Sam Elmore at Three Corner Rock

Dave on Pandora's

Abbott at 3-Corner Rock

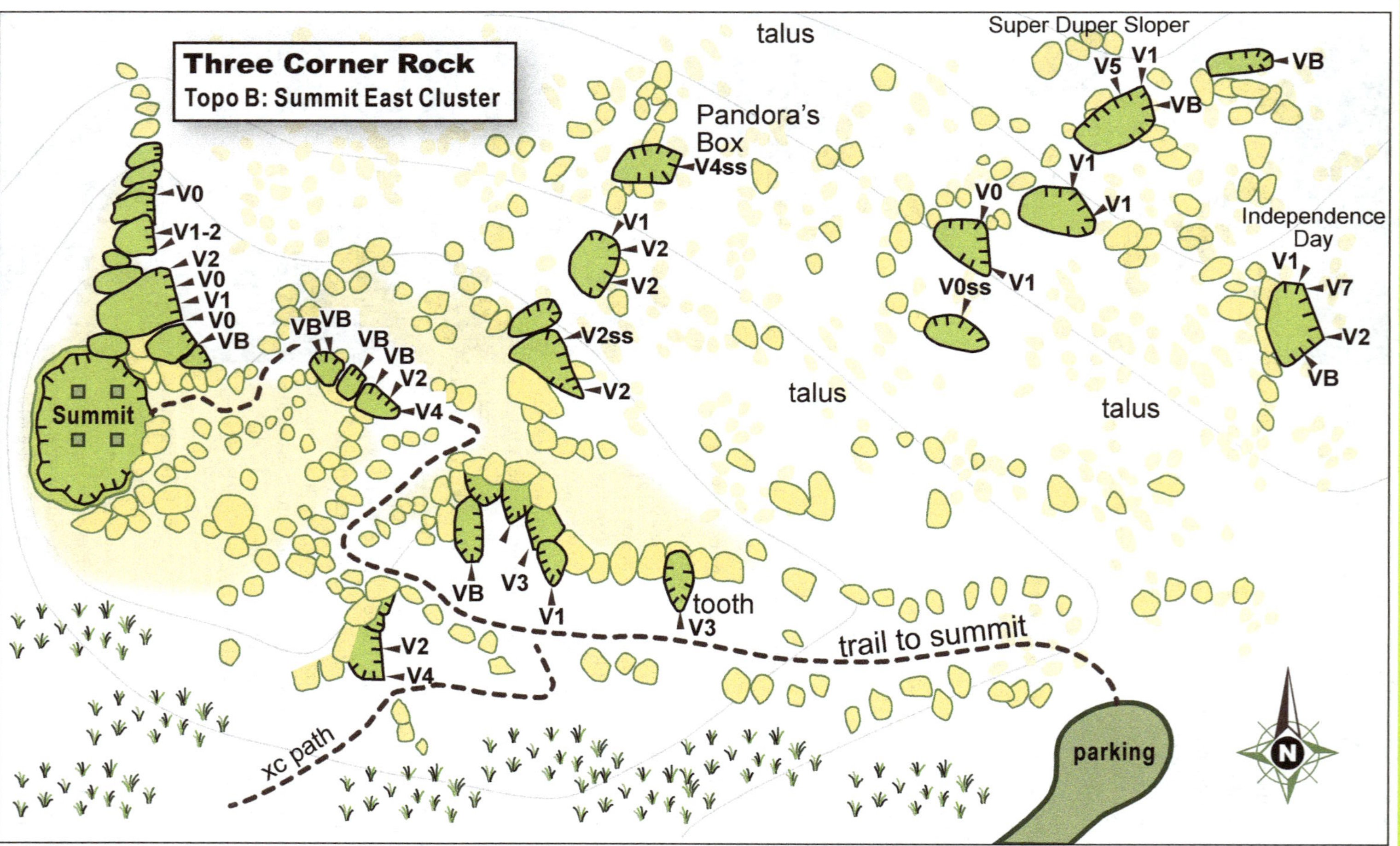
Three Corner Rock
Topo B: Summit East Cluster
talus
Super Duper Sloper
Pandora's Box
V4ss
V5
V1
VB
VB
V1
V0
V1
V1
Independence Day
V1
V7
V2
VB
V0ss
V1
V0
V1-2
V2
V0
V1
V0
VB
Summit
VB VB
VB
VB
V2
V4
V2
V2ss
talus
V2
talus
VB
V3
V1
tooth
V3
V2
V4
trail to summit
xc path
parking
N

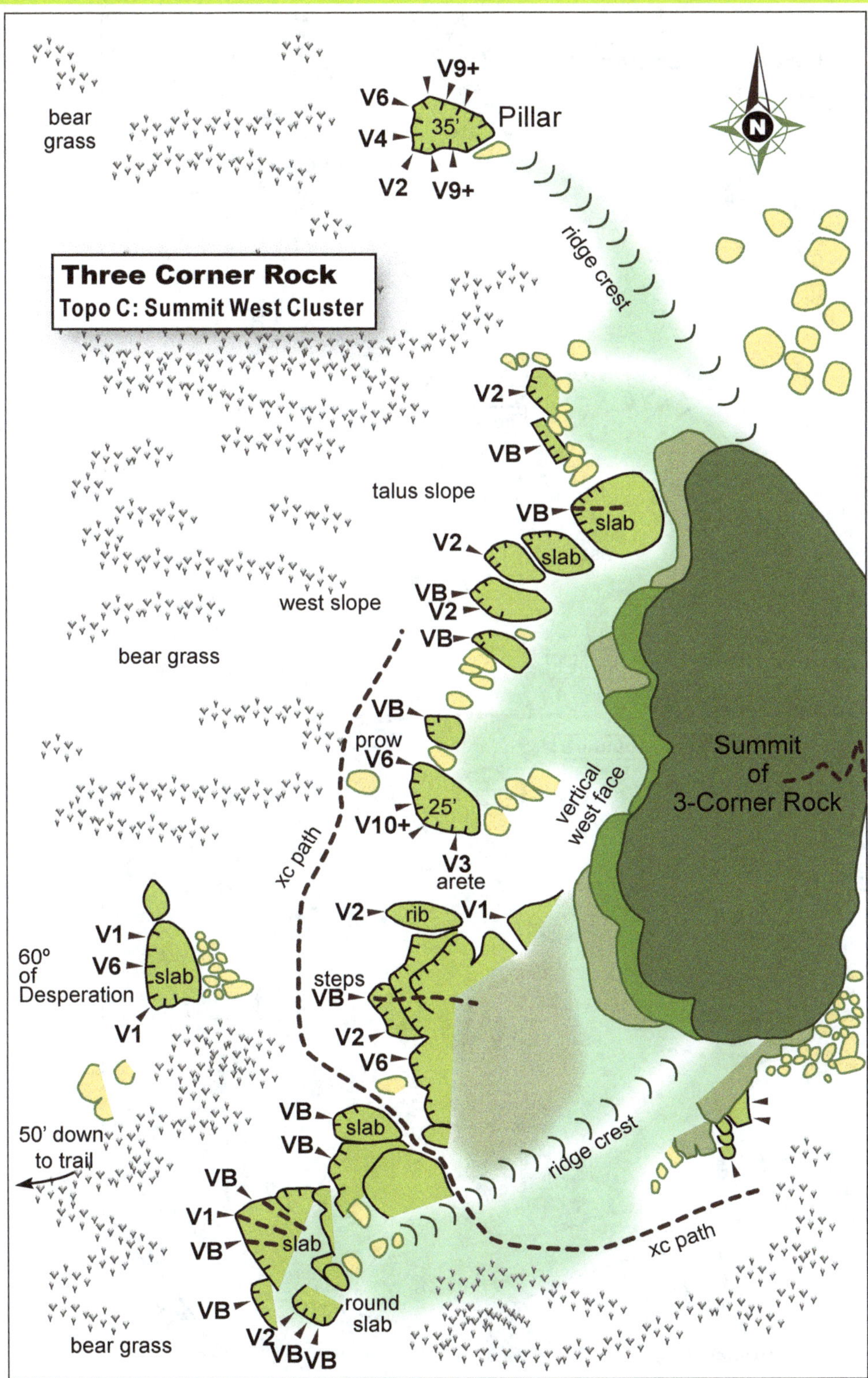

Three Corner Rock
Topo C: Summit West Cluster
bear grass
bear grass
bear grass
V9+
V6
V4
35'
Pillar
V2
V9+
ridge crest
talus slope
west slope
V2
VB
VB
slab
V2
slab
VB
V2
VB
VB
prow
V6
25'
V10+
V3
arete
vertical west face
Summit of 3-Corner Rock
V2
rib
V1
60°
of
Desperation
V1
V6
slab
V1
steps
VB
V2
V6
VB
slab
VB
50' down
to trail
VB
V1
VB
slab
VB
round
slab
V2
VB VB
ridge crest
xc path
xc path
N

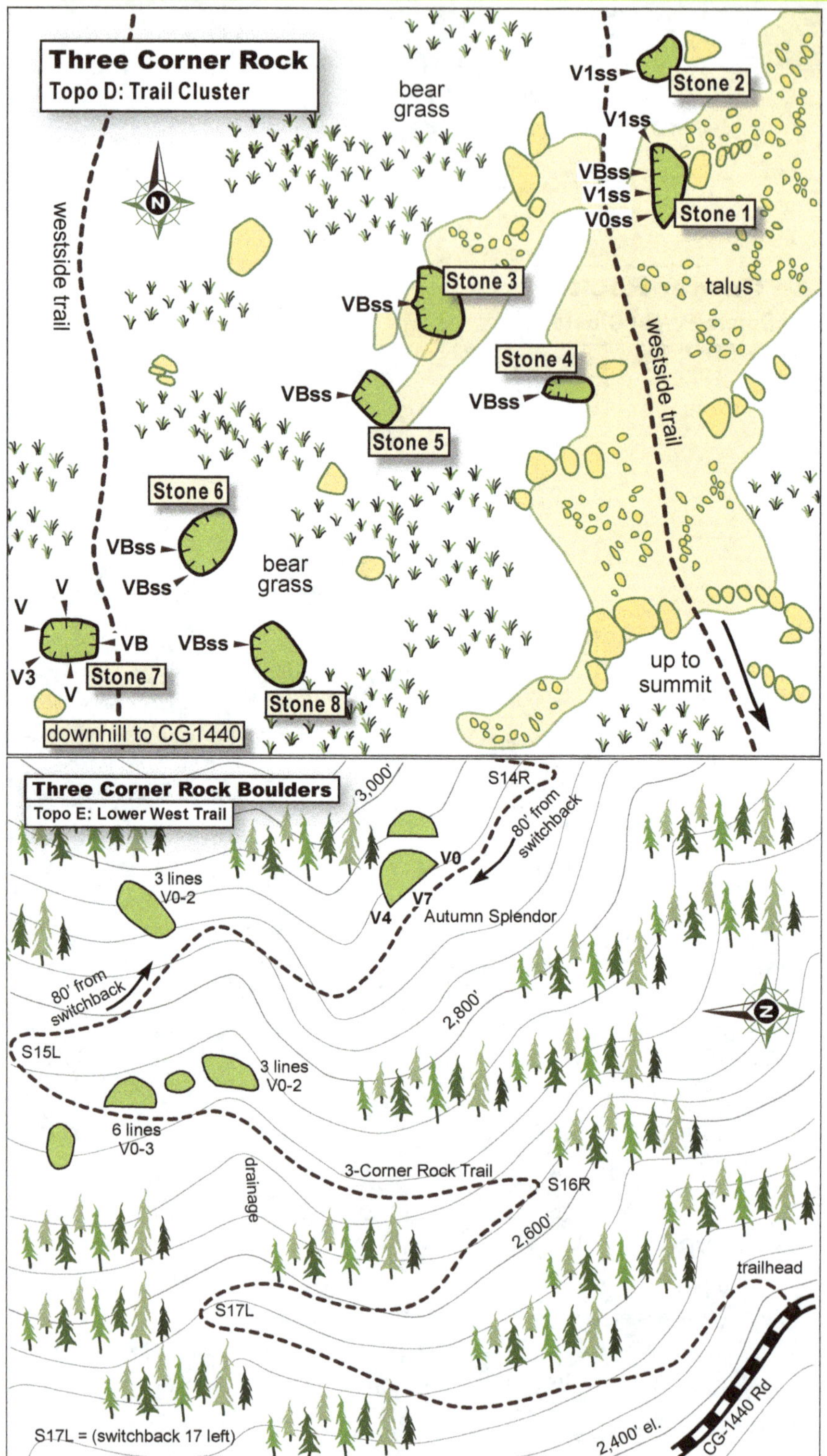
Three Corner Rock
Topo D: Trail Cluster
bear grass
V1ss
Stone 2
V1ss
VBss
V1ss
V0ss
Stone 1
westside trail
N
talus
Stone 3
VBss
Stone 4
VBss
VBss
Stone 5
westside trail
Stone 6
VBss
VBss
bear grass
V
V
V
VB
VBss
V3
Stone 7
V
Stone 8
up to summit
downhill to CG1440

Three Corner Rock Boulders
Topo E: Lower West Trail
3,000'
S14R
80' from switchback
V0
3 lines
V0-2
V7
V4   Autumn Splendor
80' from switchback
Z
S15L
2,800'
3 lines
V0-2
6 lines
V0-3
3-Corner Rock Trail
drainage
S16R
2,600'
trailhead
S17L
CG-1440 Rd
S17L = (switchback 17 left)
2,400' el.

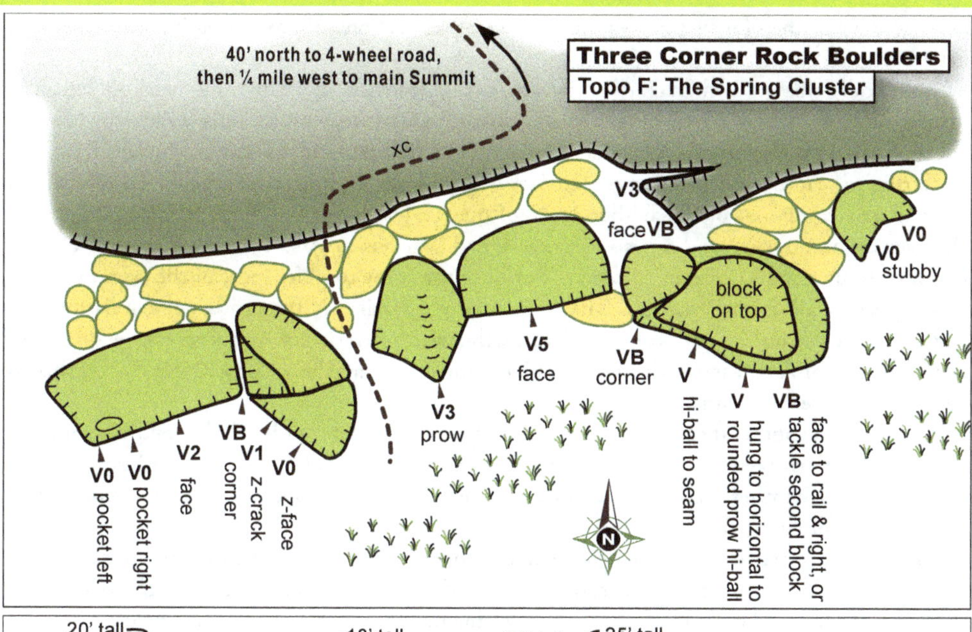

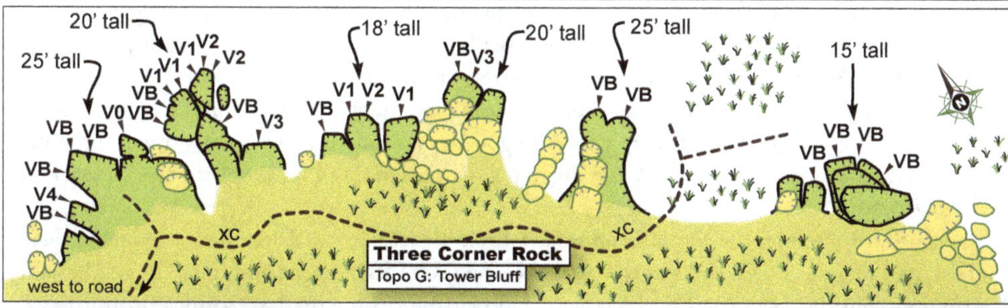

Dave on *Independence Day*

Dave on *60° of Desperation*

pockets, some with colorful silica variances, and other sections of stone yielding a rougher grit matrix.

Geologically, this site is characteristically similar to Alpenglow and Super Heroes Boulders. The textural nuances change based on the chemical/mechanical decompositional weathering factors and the structural integrity of the crystalline matrix at that particular locale in the lava flow. The rock structure is uniformly blended gray to dark gray andesite, some gas pocket elongation is woven into a matrix composed of a rich abundance of quartz, feldspar, amphibole, all very minute and wherever exposed facing west is also well weathered. Various original formation features tend to offer numerous crimps (crisp or softened), but once the stone tumbles most of the crimp features tend to become a bit more rounded. The main summit massif is in the process of exfoliation, initially as a steep vertical 25'-40' broken rock mass, then as a scattering of stones across a wide area of open slope downhill and across the hikers trail. For most areas at Three Corner Rock 1-2 crashpads are a minimum recommendation.

The rock bluff southeast of the communication towers is basaltic with a dark toned platy matrix, minute feldspar, pyroxene and other rich ferromagnesian minerals (1-2mm), a smooth rock texture overall but a bit weather etched on exposed surfaces. The upper slope of this minor bluff hold a majestic stand of young spruce trees.

Seasonal access ranges from June through October, though snow patches may limit early approach. Overcast cloudy weather days, or windy conditions may limit availability. The main summit area is treeless and exposed to the weather elements. The steep, narrow one-lane gravel road is frequently used by logging trucks so use caution while driving up the road. Even though the site is at high-altitude mid-summer can be quite hot during the day if a westerly breeze is lacking.

Extra pointers: bring your camera to capture a scenic moment at sunset; floral scenery abounds from July to August. The landings are generally good as is, and an extra crashpad will often take care of the minor terrain variances. Avoid digging any base landings; its simply not necessary here.

Directions:

The south main road is the common approach. From Beacon Rock, drive north on Kueffler Road 2 miles, then on gravel CG-1400 to the gate, then on CG-1500a to the summit. The road quality deteriorates considerably (AWD vehicle with high clearance) for the last 2 miles (from the gate onward), or park the car and walk to the summit.

The super classics at Three Corner Rock are: **Super Duper Sloper, 60° of Desperation, Independence Day, Autumn Splendor**, and **Pandora's Box**. Where's the easier classics?

There is no long detailed breath-taking beta list for this site, though Abbott and Sowerby climbed an estimated 70+ bouldering lines. This extensive quantity includes the summit area, and the 'tower rock bluff' formation to the southeast ¼ mile. Getting actual problems named (years later) was like raising the Titanic. So, if the mood strikes you and you git an itch, throw a name at an unnamed line while your there (now yur famous). The diagrams do mirror most of the known boulder problem ratings that the A-team could verify. And the few famous 5-star named gem routes are also placed on the topo diagram. The site still has considerable potential if your into tapping new territory such as the minor pinnacle on the NW slope.

The Spring Cluster (9'-14' tall)

This is about 40' from the road, and has quality, variety, and technicality. There are five independent blocks with numerous lines, and a few lines on the actual rounded escarpment. A quality spot to boulder at. Beta is from left to right.

V0ss Peril and Passion. Ascend the face left of big natural pocket.

V0ss Sponge. Ascend the face right of big natural pocket.

V2 H$_2$O. Steep face in middle.

VBss Dark Vader. Inside corner where the two big blocks abut against each other.

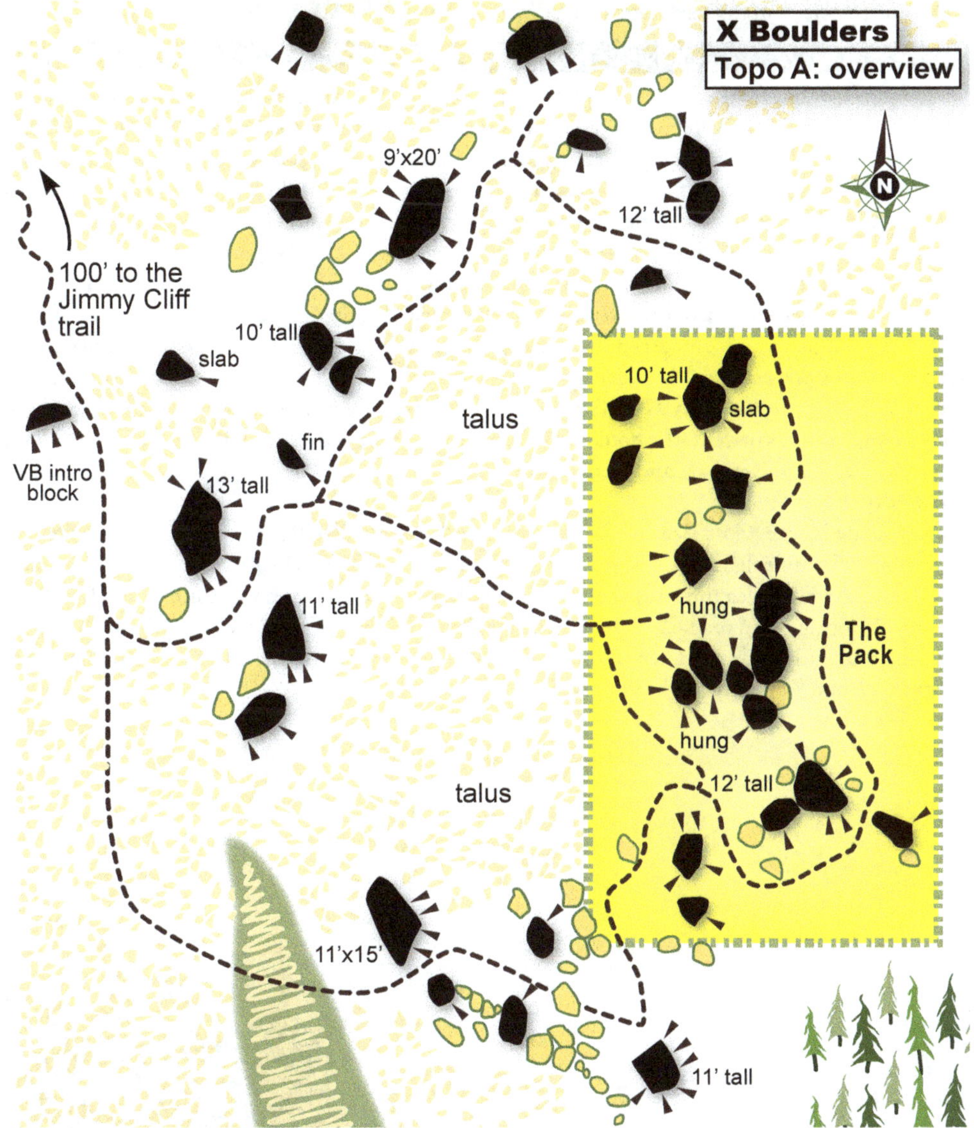

V1 Z-crack. A block sits on top of a lower block.

V0 The Measure of Man. Start up the rail of crack, then face to top.

V4 Mineral Water. The entire traverse from the pocket on left to inside corner.

V3 Artesian. The quality prow on the third stone.

V5 Flood Control. The steep face on the fourth stone.

This section is apparent based on its big upper block stacked on a lower block.

VB Don't Mess with Texas. A corner and crack combo.

V_ (?) ___ Hi-ball face to seam. A big upper block stacked on a lower block.

V_ (?) ___ Hi-ball starts hung to horizontal crack, then up rounded prow.

VB Limited Infinity. Face to horizontal rail, then exit up right on ledge.

V_ (?) ____ The same as above, except it tackles the scoop on the top block.

V0 and **V0** on the farthest east block are two short overhung variants side by side.

A minor isolated stone north across the dirt road yields (V0, V1, V2 traverse).

X BOULDERS

A unique, complex packed core of quality large blocks on a south-facing sunny talus slope below the infamous Jimmy Cliff. The site offers numerous smooth basaltic stones (with no noticable phenocrysts in a deep gray matrix) that originated from the lower portion of the lava flow. Many stones (with a grittier andesitic plagioclase matrix) originated from the upper portion of the lava flow, tumbled down to intermingle into the complex. Rock nuances: crimps, smooth faces, sharp ribs, long overhung power lines, and VB slabs. Estimated to be 100+ potential problems in one primary condensed area in the initial 300' of talus slope. Only agile footed persons with diligent scrambling abilities should venture here initially, because the site has considerable jagged smaller debris where injury can be incurred. Seasonally, the snow may linger at this elevation until early-May, but a lengthy season of bouldering can be attained until November. Expect it to be hot in mid-summer, and on windless days. Two to three crashpads are wise, but in time the landings will likely be adjusted. As of 2016 the boulders were virtually untapped. Conveniently close to Portland (1 hour drive), no poison oak, and scenic views.

Directions:

From State Route 14 at Beacon Rock, drive north on Kueffler Road (set your odometer and drive exactly 5.1 miles). This road (at 2 miles) turns to gravel on CG1400 road. Stay on this main gravel road. At 5.1 miles the road veers left abruptly, but you will turn right into a small pullout onto an old logging skid road. Park here or drive a short distance along the skid road and park at its end. The trail initially drops down to the east but becomes very apparent on a nice path that walks mostly horizontally east to the bluff in ¼ mile.

ROCK CREEK BOULDERS

The 'Forest Cluster' is an extensive list of power lines on quality stone. The Riverside Cluster is a small but quality hangout ideal for hot summer days when the creek flow drops to minimal levels. Boulders range from 10'-16' tall. The site beckons the serious minded sportster, well-honed with upper-end bouldering skills. If you are seeking V-ratings mostly in the V2-V7 range, get a ramble in your jeepster, and double-deck yourself with crashpads and go for a drive...in the heat of the summer, of course. The site yields stout power lines on rounded andesite boulders with surface nuances that often yielding focused smears. Mostly flat base landings (1-2 crashpads). A superb traverse line exists (V7), and a classic V4 rib rail. Extra pointers: no cell phone coverage; viable season is July-August (perhaps September); mosquito hour starts early in the evening, so do not stay too late.

This (river & roadside) site was heavily tapped by Mr A, Mr O, and Mr Bishop (and other close friends) so the history on this place is well known.

Directions

Drive time to reach the site is 1½ hours from Portland. Drive east of Vancouver, Washington on State Route 14 to Stevenson, WA. Drive past Skamania Lodge, take the next left uphill, to the northwest side of town, then turn left on Red Bluff Road, and go ½ mile to a road split, then take the right split onto CG-2000 road. This road follows alongside Rock Creek. At 8½ miles the road turns sharply left to cross another small bridge (CG2060 goes right to Rock Creek Wall). But you must continue on the main gravel CG-2000 forest road for another ½ mile and park alongside the road overlooking the obvious big stone in the creek below.

CREEKSIDE CLUSTER

Metamorphosis Stone

V4 Joybean. ⚠ This is the ultra-classic 2" wide flake rail on west aspect of the stone. The opening move crux is a crimp and foot smear, then ascends the narrow rail flake. This line is the very reason folks come here.

V6+ (?) Mythology. Stick the slopers, then palm over onto slab. Project.

V5+ (?) Superstition. Palm the slopers and mantle over. Project.

V7ss Metamorphosis is the ultra-classic heel hooking rail traverse on east side on block. SS low on left, run the rail, then hard pumpy topout at far right end.

V3 Crown Prince. A mantle over at the mid part.

V5 Checkmate. Do just the top out on the far right.

Benchmark Stone (11' tall)

V4 (V8) King. Standing start using obvious low pocket. SS is kissing the pocket.

V2 Queen. A rib corner on left with incuts.

V5 Bishop. Odd rounded upside down nose.

Creekside Stone (11' tall)

V4 Chess Game. Start on left rounded rail, cruise to top. Goes blank part way up.

V7 Knight. Send a thin sequence on the right side of block.

Tymun at Rock Creek

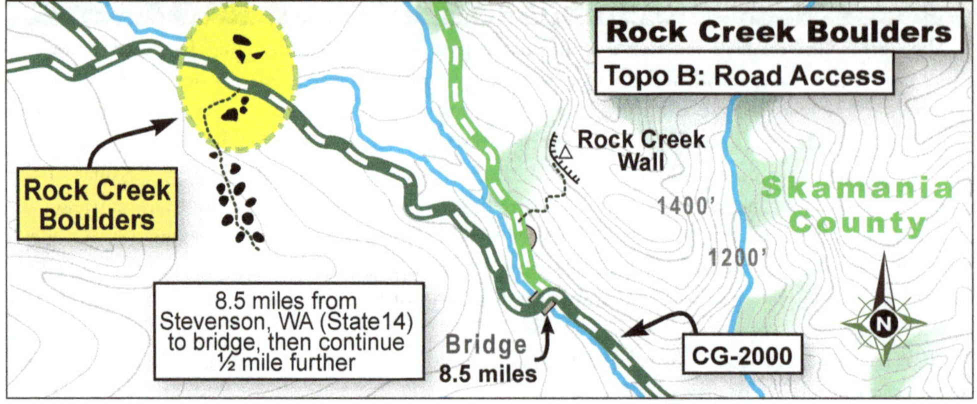

Boulder 4

V0 Fish Bait. A brief sloped problem to the east of Metamorphosis about 15' walk. **Boulder 5** has not been tapped (pool of water).

ROADSIDE CLUSTER

Woodside Stone (25' tall)

On the southwest side of the road in a dense brushy thicket are a minor set of stones: This is the really tall one.

VB Fishing for Fish. Starts on left, jugs all the way, waltz up easy holds to stand. Go right on ramp, or up left to top out.

V0-1 (?) There may be one other possible line on this.

Stone Soup Boulder (12' tall)

V0 Wasp. A brief excursion between the two stones.

V4 Hornet. Thin tech face line.

V6 Rock of Gibraltar. Thinner techy line on point.

VB Stone Soup. One move, as low

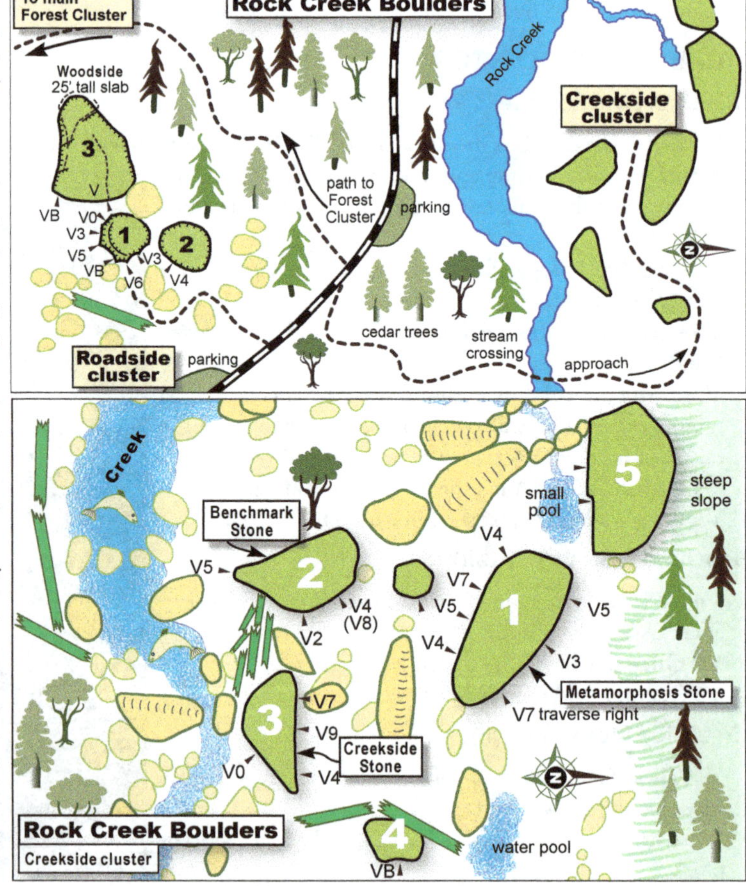

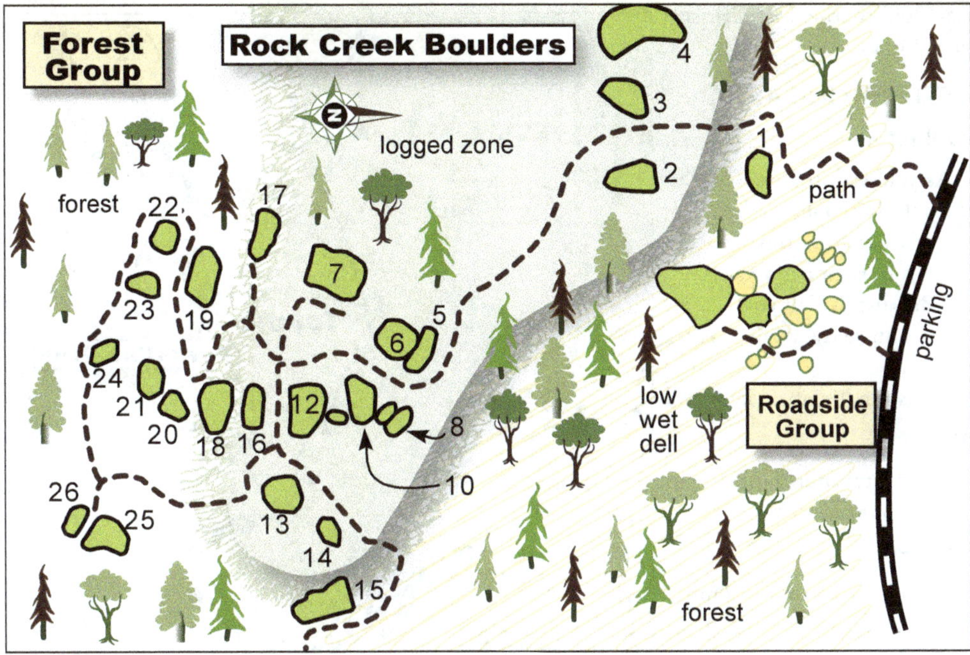

as possible on pinchy rib.

V6 Power Rail. Standing start in pit under block, and power up onto pinchy rib with left. SS would be much harder.

V3 Yellowjacket. Tackle the minor corner with nice holds.

FOREST CLUSTER

See diagram for boulder details and path details (no beta); projects in process.

BRIDGE OF THE GODS BOULDERS

When it came time to explore beyond the confines of Carver way back in the day, the locals delved into the Gorge and tapped these boulders. The BOGB is set in a extensive talus field with a long thin band of quality andesite blocks, ranging in height from 9' – 16' tall, and a few taller ones. The talus field originated from Table Mtn to the north, and sloughed off into the Columbia River long ago.

There are two popular areas, the Lower Powerline area, and the Dome (or Knoll) area one mile up a rough gravel road. The common established areas are good destinations during the cool weather months from May-Oct (but virtually year-round when its sunny). BOGB is a south-facing site in the rainiest part of the Gorge, but strong prevailing wind patterns can dry out the stones in 1-2 days in winter. One to two crashpads are the minimum recommendation. Considerable loose, jagged talus limits future exploratory interest to the boulders near the road. The area is infested with substantial poison oak growth, surrounded by forested sections and brushy ravines. Rock type nuances: the andesite stones yield powerful overhangs, techy crimper lines, traverse smear-fests, on a light grain crystalline phenocryst matrix that gives the problems a quality sticky appeal.

Directions

Drive I-84 to Cascade Locks (or State Route 14), cross the bridge into Washington. Ashes Lake is just to the east of the bridge. Take the paved road that wraps around the northwest side of the lake, then drive up a steep gravel road en route to the quarry at Blue Lake, but when you reach the first set of power line towers, turn onto a minor dirt road, and park here (see map). A path wanders east 200' to the first primary cluster of blocks.

POWERLINE AREA

Boulder A

As you walk the path east to reach the big cool popular boulder you pass this tiny creature off to your right a few yards.

V3ss just the left rib

V4ss angle right using center crimps

VBss run the rib up leftward.

Boulder B

VBss ultra shorty

V3ss ultra shorty.

Boulder C

A nice sized stone immediately south of the big mega boulder.

V4 nose

V4 nose to face

V3 slab on the right

Boulder D (Big Boulder)

This is a very common spot to visit at BOGB because of convenience and quality lines. Beta starts on the SE side at the stout line.

V6 All Right Jury. Southeast prow and face.

V8 All White Jury. Hung south face, crimps up right into previous line.

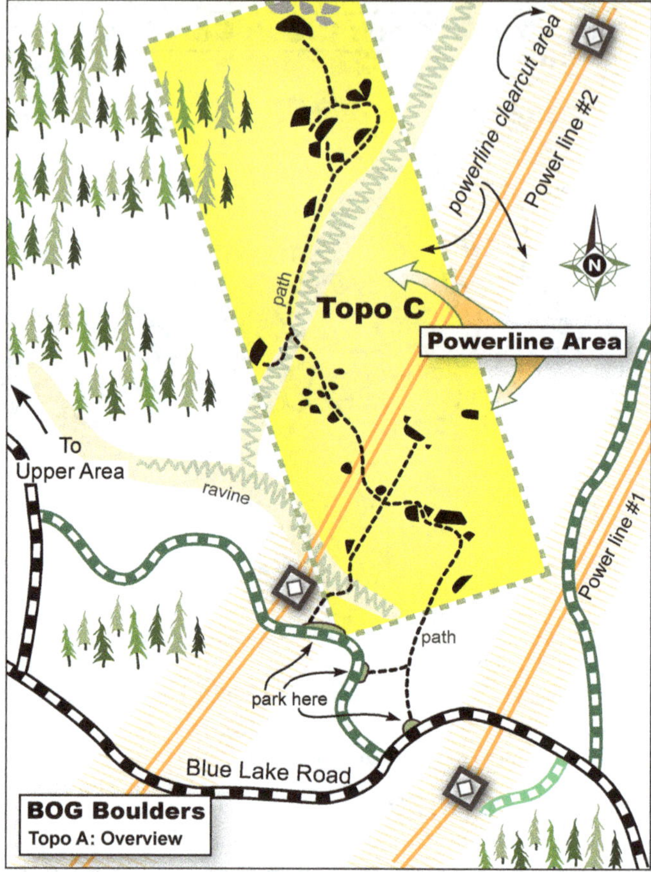

V5 El Percy. South nose starting on jug horn.

V6 Roller Skates. Thin face on west aspect.

V3 Itchy & Scratchy. Thin seam - west side.

V2 Land Down Under. Slabby face on west

side
V0 north nose
V4 **Tsunam.** Short north face

Boulder E

V4ss very low on west bulge.
V5ss hung crimps on south aspect.
V0 on east side slab.

Boulder F

A prominent and enticing overhung flat south face.

V5 on far right to lip.

V7ss on hung face make a long reach up right along rail. Quality line.

V3ss start on hung face but break up left onto easy slab.

V0ss low start using left edges.

Boulder G

V3ss very short.

Boulder H

V2ss shorty

Boulder xx

VBss on another block to left.

Boulder I

A long stone lacking height, but offering several sit start problems.

V7+ the entire traverse
V1ss on left getting over lip.
V2ss in middle & get over lip.
V3ss on the right & over lip.

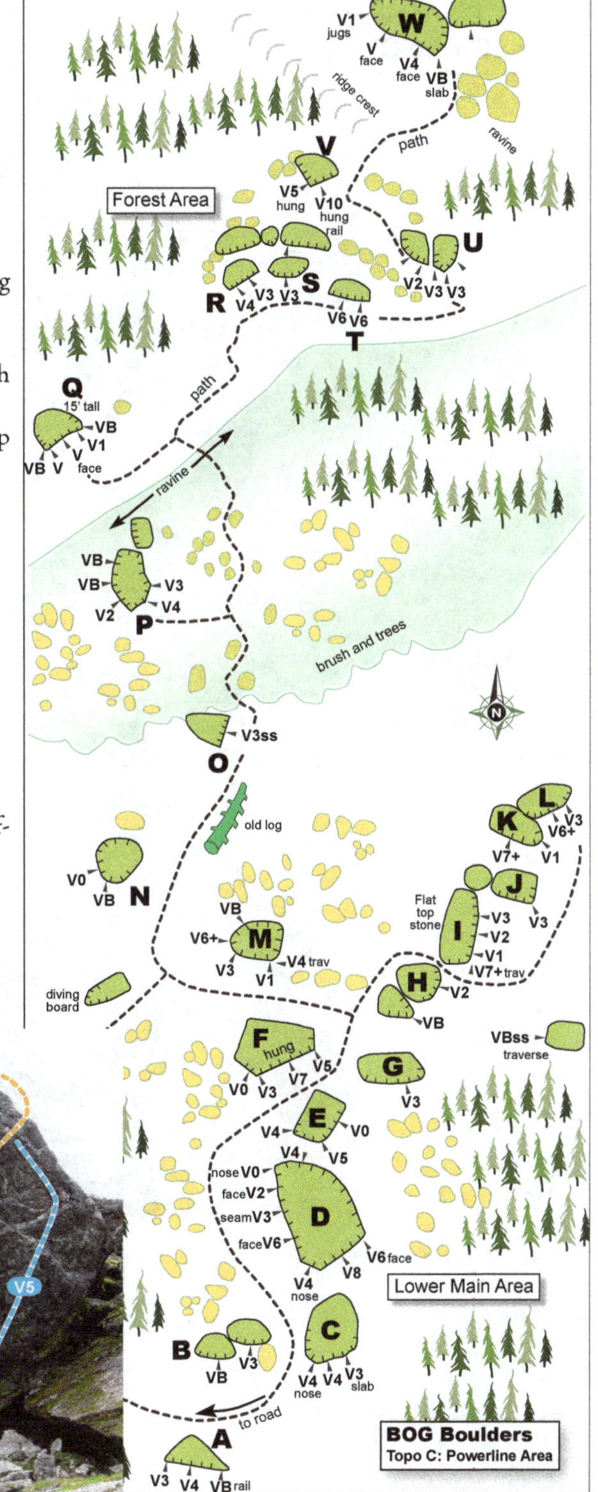

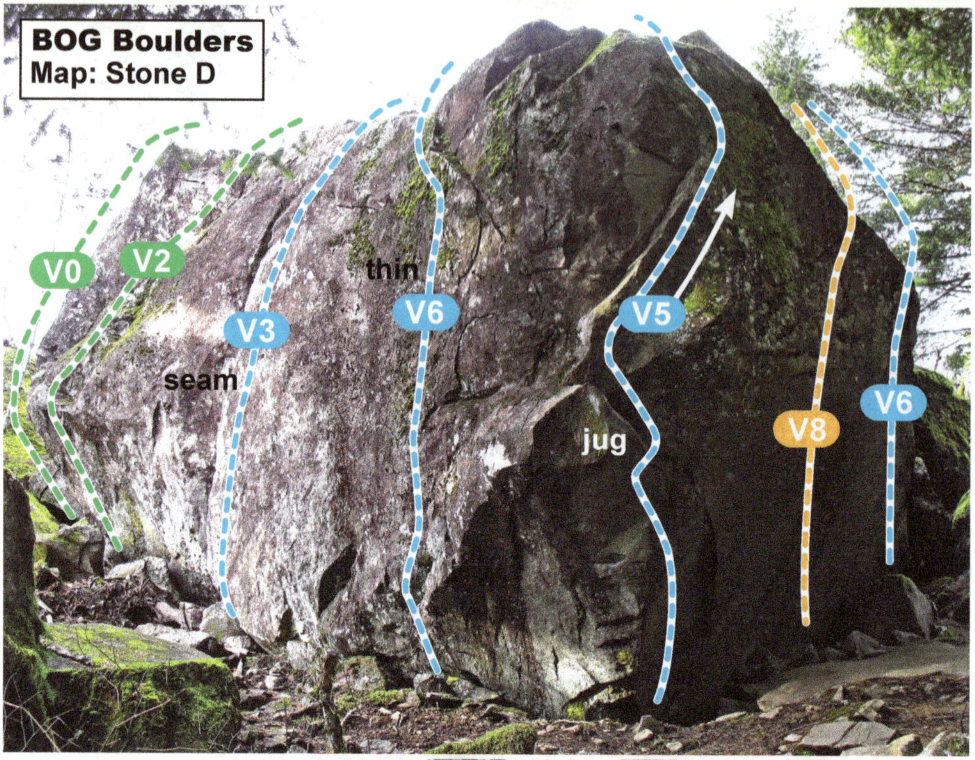

Boulder J

V3ss sit start in low spot and pull over lip and up rib.

Boulder K

V7+ on left side
V1 the nose.

Boulder L

V6+ on left
V3 on right.

Boulder M

Quality time boulder always a favorite to hit.

V4ss Traverse entire lip leftward and then top out.
V1 Positive holds bump up along incut rail, moving left and over lip.
V3 Low crimps on south aspect.
V6+ Sit start just the hung west nose.
VB NW face

Boulder N

V0ss sit start minor.
VBss ultra minor.

Boulder O

Right on the path so its a popular problem to experience. Quite short but quality.

V3ss crimps on the hung east face.

Boulder P

Large stone just west of the path with fun lines. Beta R to L.

V3ss East hung aspect near center; power up right onto the slab.

V4ss Begin on east face, use left on rib, power up to hight point and top out.

And on the west side....

V2 Slab run starting at an undercling.

VB center slab

VB The west side slab on far left.

Boulder Q

A quality boulder with a hi-ball south aspect (and poison oak). Where the path splits, go left for 100′ to reach this boulder. Beta is L to R.

VB Do brief face just left of nose.

V_ Left nose but with left hand on left rib.

V_ The powerful center face exiting high right.

V1 Right face using good small edges.

VB Far right on brief round nose.

Boulder R

A triangular shaped stone on the path.

V4ss on hung left face using lip then move left onto slab.

V3ss hung smears, sloped crimps to start, and catch rib, exit right onto the slab.

Boulder S

V3 a minor problem.

Boulder T

V6 smooth hung face with slight foot smears and dicey crimps (left hand on rib). Top slab is often mossy.

V6 hung crimps, then crimps on mossy slab, and tough to exit up onto the slab..

Boulder U

A split block that is roughly shaped like a big heart. Beta is R to L.

V_ far right rib.

V3 the center flat nose using crimps.

V3 climb crimps on the vertical face (where the two blocks split apart).

V2 the rib on the left block.

V_ (?) just the left face of the left block.

Boulder V

Poison oak infested base but several powerful lines.

V10ss right face starting low on powerful overhung slopers/crimps, move up to a sloper rail, then cruise left along rail to top point.

V5ss start low on left hung face using reachy

crimps and jugs.

Boulder W ⚠

From the last boulder, walk north uphill briefly and then downhill into a ravine choked with mossy boulders to this massive tall beast. Beta is Right to Left.

VB long cool southeast prow slab

V4 the vertical direct face.

V_ (?) Another powerful potential face.

V1 steep jug run on the left.

THE UPPER AREA

The Upper Area has perhaps the finest double set of leaning pillars in this region perfectly designed for ultra cool quality bouldering. These two stones are White and Lotus Boulders. A visit here is a must-do on everyone's hit list. You're not on-the-top till you have played on these pillars.

To reach the Upper Area drive up a rough gravel road (past the natural gas pipeline) one mile (toward Mosley Lakes), then turn right onto a cul-de-sac road and park at its end (see map). A rough path scrambles down slope (from the parking spot) and across a talus zone to the lower end of a minor wooded knoll.

Trail Boulder (#1)

The first substantial boulder you see alongside the path. It's in a cold low trough and well worth doing all the fun lines. Beta is R to L.

VB Fun fat jugs going up the south end.

V0 (**V2ss**) Hung fat crack on south facing section.

V3 Begins same as next, but use mid face crimp to catch high lip, then power over lip to top.

V0 The prominent overhung, yet quality and enjoyable wide crack (west facing). Use primarily the sharp right edge of the wide crack.

V1 The far left north aspect, by running up right along a round rib on crimps.

Short Nose Boulder (#2)

A few yards to the south of Trail Boulder is this well hung low forest pig.

V5-6ss (?) Sit low under it and power rounded features over the bulge nose.

Bouncer Boulder (#3)

V11 Yojimbo. Start low in center, power up left over slightly hung sloped lip.

V5ss The Bouncer. Start low on rail in center of face, move up right over bulge, commit to thin crimps.

White Boulder (#4)

Walk right along a path around the corner about 30' to two parallel free-standing pillars. The White Boulder is the left leaning pillar.

V3 prow on NW aspect of the pillar.

V7 (V11ss) Rodeo. Classic hung left arête.

V6 White Lines is the impressive right arête of same block that angles up leftward.

V2 Grey Lines. Slabby face between pillars.

Lotus Boulder (#5)

This boulder is the right leaning pillar.

V10 Lotus Throne (left arête). Toss to a side-pull, then series of left-handed slaps up the arête.

V8ss Upsetter is the classic right arête. Start low on the arête and arc up leftward to top.

V2 Springtime. Smears on the east slab.

V0 the northwest outer corner.

This next set of stones are tucked behind (north of) the White / Lotus Boulders. To reach stone set #6 walk between White/Lotus. To reach stone set #7 walk around the left side of White to access it.

Boulders #6a & #6b

V2ss Ballrog Low start at lip with jug, move up onto face (on #6a stone).

V3 Log Jam The taller unit on the right (#6b stone).

Boulders #7a & #7b

Two options; range **V2** to **V4** (one can be done as 'ss').

Boulder 8

Beta is from L to R.

V0 tall crack, **VB** crack, **VB** crack.

Boulder (xx)

V1 All Prime. Minor shorty about 20' south of Lotus Stone.

Boulder (xx)

V0 crack, **VB** face, **VB** crack, **VB** crack.

Boulder (xx)

Minor rock finger on the path.

V3 Climb overhanging rock finger.

V0 On right side of stone.

V0 Mummy. The rightmost problem.

Boulder (#9)

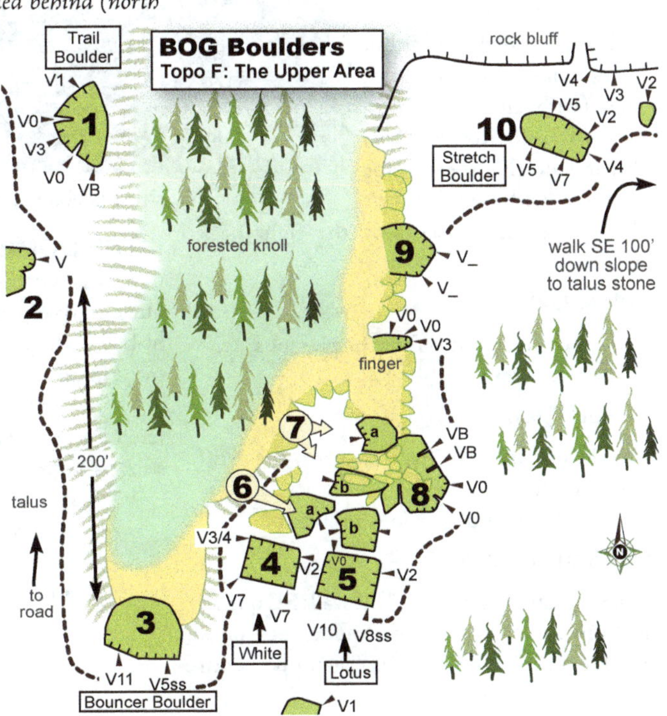

Untapped tall overhung big block on path. Poor landing.

Stretch Arm Boulder (#10)

From the previous boulder, walk a short distance eastward to the final tall stone.

V5ss One Move Wonder. Southwest face reaching up left to catch rib then cruise up rib to top.

V7ss Stretch Murphy. South face crimps using the seam and the face moving up leftward.

V5ss Four Star Arête. Tackles the vertical east arête straight on. Classic.

V2 on the north aspect but using some of the same east nose (with left hand).

V5 (V7ss) Stretch Arm Strong north aspect using an arête (with right hand).

V7ss Lightning uses only the right back prow.

Boulder (xx)

Minor boulder just NE of the previous
V2ss The Wave

The Rock Bluff

V4 High Arête Hi-ball arete on the bluff (**V5** optional direct).
V3 To the right of previous problem.

Talus Boulder (#11)

This last stone is about a 100' walk SE downhill from the Stretch Arm Boulder out on a large talus field. The stone is flat topped with

short problems, choked with poison oak.

THE DOME

This is a compact boulder zone with a large hung scarp of rock bluff, yet most problems are hi-ball status. Located uphill close to the forested knoll.

History goes back to the early days when Jered Bernert discovered and tapped a few lines such as Vato Loco.

V7 Vato Loco Incut powerful line on the right portion of the bluff.

Some additional V4 - V7 problems do exist here, and most are hi-ball.

EMPIRE BOULDERS

The Empire Boulders is certainly the gem quality site Portlander's have been long awaiting to see. Packed into a remarkably compact zone of about 700' square with a wide variety of sizable boulders that are loaded with every rating possible from VB to V-insane (including hi-ball lines) the Empire is truly destined to become a locally popular, highly favored site.

For those folks who prefer nationally famous places like Buttermilk Boulders (or any global bouldering site) this little site is quite good. For those who live in this micro-region this site is a cool gem that seemingly fits a miniaturized version of one of those ultra-stellar destination bouldering places. When compared to other bouldering sites in this region few compare with the sheer magnitude of the technical nature, quality, and difficulty found at this one bouldering site.

Empire's combined total number of problems on the boulders and on the bluff outcrop exceeds 300 problems (90%+ of it tapped by just two persons). The height of many boulders are in that spice and dice range where several crashpads stacked minimize the jump-off gambit.

The bouldering ratings are suitably broad for both entry level boulderers and skilled experts, with plenty of warm-up lines VB-V4, a lesser string of mid-level power lines V5-V8, followed with a select upper string of V9-V12+ futuristic lines. All the boulders tumbled long ago from a minor cliff band just above the dense stone cluster. The bluff offers a plethora of power problems (some substantially overhung) with beastly lines trending upward to 25' tall.

Empire Boulders is easily reached by a convenient paved road to a parking pullout spot (there are residential dwellings nearby so think low-key non-noise environment) and a short path.

Bring more than one crashpad, especially if you plan to do anything hi-ball. Bring a chalkbag for your waist especially if you are there on a warm summer day doing hi-ball lines. When the moss regrows you may need to apply a brush to some lines a bit, though many overhung lines will not see much regrowth. Fir needles become a slight nuisance in the spring season so consider bringing a small whisk broom to knock off the excess needles. Certain 18'-27' hi-ball boulders and outcrops have a top anchor (or nearby tree) if you desire a top-rope.

History

Empire is ultra secluded in a forest grotto. It's discovery would have been impossible except for the sleuthing skill of a local mushroom hunter. Therefore, considerable appreciation goes to our close friend Mr. B who stumbled upon this site long ago and kept it secret for many years. He eventually revealed it to Mr O, who, after an additional several years elapsed invited Mr A to the site so that he could get that renewed spark for bouldering. His comment pretty much sums it up, "...I've been waiting a life-time for a place like this near home base." So this exclusive team tapped into the site even more heavily in 2015-2018. These two folks are the highly valued primary site development stewards at this site (as well as many of this regions other sites). Yet there are some un-tapped lines at EB (albeit hi-ball and extreme power lines). The V9-V12+ lines, though stunning, tend to be few in totality (no more easy sugar cookies).

Stepping briefly back into a historical time frame, it can be noted that for many years Bridge of the Gods Boulders were thought to be charting the next golden age of Port-land bouldering. Then, along came a string of gems such as Alpenglow and Three Corner Rock to shake up the scene (if you were part of that inner circle). Then along came Lost Lake Boulders which in its own way is an earth shak-ing site for this region. Yet all of these places missed just a few minor details; ultra compact site, hi-ball lines with natural soil landings, summer time bouldering in a forested scene (imagine boiling hot days at Hamilton Boulders), gargantuan stone beasts, easily accessible boulders from a paved county road, superb quality stone textural nuances,

and virtual all-year bouldering. With a few days of dry weather in the winter this site may be viable even in the winter months. This lengthy combination of unique factors make Empire Boulders this micro-regions prime bouldering site.

In this northwest USA micro-region the boulder size does not necessarily equate to quality boulder problems, but this compact site offers a surprise, in that even the tall V0 sketch lines are crimp/smear adventure spicy problems that can satisfy even the most ardent chalk warrior. So just how big is the biggest stone here? The Roman Boulder is a triangular shaped beast that logs in at 36' x 34' x 28' girth, and 19' tall on its east aspect. OK...super wow! Surprisingly, this yields a rare single massive stone that is both easily accessible and of a quality composition ideal for bouldering (within a short drive of Portland). The tallest single stone is 27' tall (Inca Boulder). The tallest part of the cliff outcrop is over 25' tall.

Rock type and rock surface nuances

The bluff formation and boulders are broadly classed as a pyroclastic or volcanoclastic rock de-posit, and was likely laid down under rapid volcanic processes that enhanced the stratified layering effect with heat compaction under pressure. The strata is duo-tone gray welded lithic (e.g. solidi-fied) ignimbrite-*like* ash bed. The strata contains vesicular pockets, small scooped out spheroidal surface weathered divots, distinct internal stratified banding, including considerable embedded

fragments of basaltic rock chips of various small sizes, and limited quantities of various scattered minerals such as quartz.

The rock textural nuances are very amenable for bouldering, and offer a well textured friction-friendly surface, some large angular flat aspects, substantial overhung sections, considerable gas pockets of variable sizes (usually rounded but sometimes incut) from micro to 7", small embedded basaltic nubbin protrusions (up to 5") welded into a gray ground mass.

Pesks and other Nuisances

Yes, there are some. Poison oak exists in very limited spotty places, varieties of flies, horseflies, mosquitoes, spiders, etc., pretty much all the typical things one might find in the forest except gorillas. The flying pests are active primarily in early summer but relatively inactive on cool cloudy or breezy days. Evenings will bring out the mosquitoes. Hornets are a difficult encounter (they give no advance warning) and nests may exist in the general vicinity (use caution when marching off trail). Moss and various dust lichens occur mainly on less traveled boulder problems. And did we forget to mention the bears. If you are bouldering silently for considerable periods, bears may wander unexpectedly through the bouldering area (sing a little jingle if you are there alone).

Advantages

The site is shaded all year by tall Douglas fir trees, so summer time is quite viable here, even in July so long as there is a breeze. It's a low elevation (1050') site so it seldom gets snowed in, but it can be damp in the winter months, therefore its seasonally viable 12-months of the year *when* its dry. On boiling hot summer days (90°F or higher) that lack a breeze the humidity factor tends to limit your ability to crank V-hard. Contrary to most bouldering sites in this region the Empire Boulders do offer parameters highly favorable to *family-friendly* bouldering outings (approach, some low angle boulders, non-rocky terrain). Cell phone reception is good. Additionally, the site is on US Forest Service managed land.

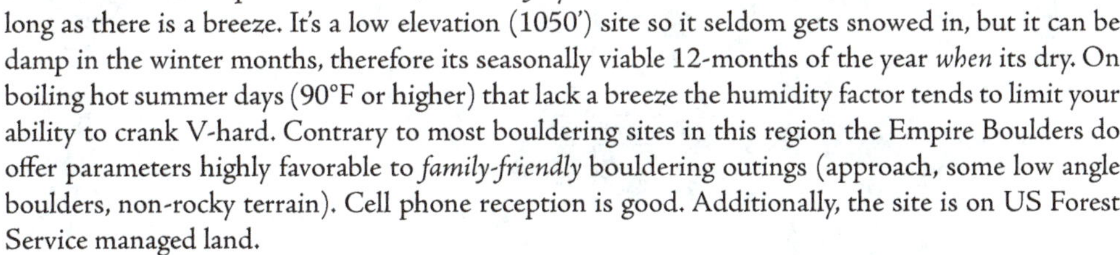

Site Variety

This is a viable multi-use site offering fall season bouldering, mushrooming, and perhaps minor top-roping. Power is always needed for the crimpy stout lines, but a sustained level of endurance and steady focus is beneficial for the lower grade hi-ball lines. For the low-ball fanatic there are plenty of short lines and traverses to tweak your tips.

Grades

The boulders yield a suitable range of difficulties conducive to most persons in this sport. The total problems here exceed the 300 goal post. The most common grade of course is V0-V3 (40%); the next most common is VB (30%) [anything 5.0-5.9]; a lesser group of V4-V8 (20%); and only a smattering of extreme V9-V14 problems (10%).

Naming convention of boulders

The ideological naming conventions seen at the Empire Boulders are generally attained from obsolete empires, emperors, dynasties, or autocracies from the various imperialism's of centuries past. And due to a friendly local bear population we dedicated a few stones to the furry black creatures, too. Part of the outcrop bluff formation is broadly named the Great Wall of China with correlating dynasties (or prominent regional features) to pinpoint each specific smaller outcrops. All this and more at a curiously fascinating bouldering site spiked by a wealth of history.

Stewardship

There are residential dwellings nearby along the primary paved road, so common etiquette is required for long-term viability of this site. Enjoy the quiet forested appeal of the site. Avoid using boombox stereos, keep pets in control (i.e. leashed), use the established path network, bury your pooh in a distant location, etc. You might limit smoking here (a LNG pipeline is located nearby) for everyone's safety. The vine maples around the boulders keep the poison oak from growing too easily, so keeping as much undergrowth growing is vital. The site steward is Mr A; he frequently boulders here with friends, and he often emphasizes site values, promotes safety, user discretion, and courteous interaction. If you send a new line (a rare day here indeed) provide your latest project 'send' info to him, and be of valuable service to this site by assisting the 'caretakers' in various stewardship opportunities at this site.

Path Access

A brief 500' long path gently ascends an open forested slope passing several smaller stones en route to the Roman Boulder. When you reach this big stone the path splits four ways. A prominent deer path ventures NW to the Greek-Persian stones, a NE path trends past Russian stones en route to the bluff, an east path (past Napolean stones) leads direct to Babylon-Inca stones. Some

of the forest near the boulders is a tangle of low brush, wind fall, and minor poison oak.

Site Orientation

This site is encompassed by a long east-west randomly outcropping short bluff. Below this bluff formation the entire group of boulders are found concentrated into generally four primary areas; the initial trail cluster (the Bear Cluster), the central cluster (the Roman Boulder), the upper west cluster (the Greek Boulder), and the east cluster (at the massive Inca Boulder). The site is nicely wrapped in a deep forest canopy of fir trees.

Camping arrangements

Timberlake Campground and RV Park is located less than one mile down the road, and it offers quality seasonal camping arrangements for those travelers who are on a road bouldering tour of the US west coast region. Another quality seasonal campground is located at the Skamania county baseball park (east end of park). This county park and campground offers riverside access and free shower facilities. The county campground is open from May 1st – Oct 31st . With two very nearby quality camping facilities, do not camp at the bouldering site, nor at the end of the paved road at the parking spot.

Amenities

The nearest large grocery store is located in Stevenson, Washington, though a good tiny mart exists at Home Valley (⅛ mile east of Berge Road junction) for basic items. Stevenson also has a variety of shops and fast food arrangements, and is the county seat for administration and emergency services.

Directions

Drive east from Portland, Oregon on I-84 freeway. At Cascade Locks cross the Bridge of the Gods bridge. From the north end of the bridge on State Route 14 continue east (passing Stevenson, WA) for 8.3 miles. When you enter the small community of Home Valley turn left (north) onto Berge Road and drive uphill for 3.6 miles to the end of the paved road and park alongside the paved road, or park on a dirt side spur [*see map*] (do not block the private driveway, nor the USFS road). Walk uphill on a narrow path for about 500' to reach the first boulders. Anticipate about 1¼ hours drive time from Portland-Vancouver.

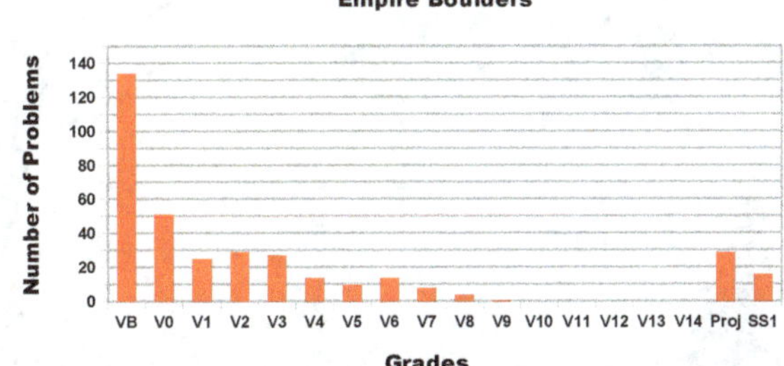

BEAR CLUSTER

The Bear Cluster is the first series of six boulders that range in height from disgustingly short to invitingly

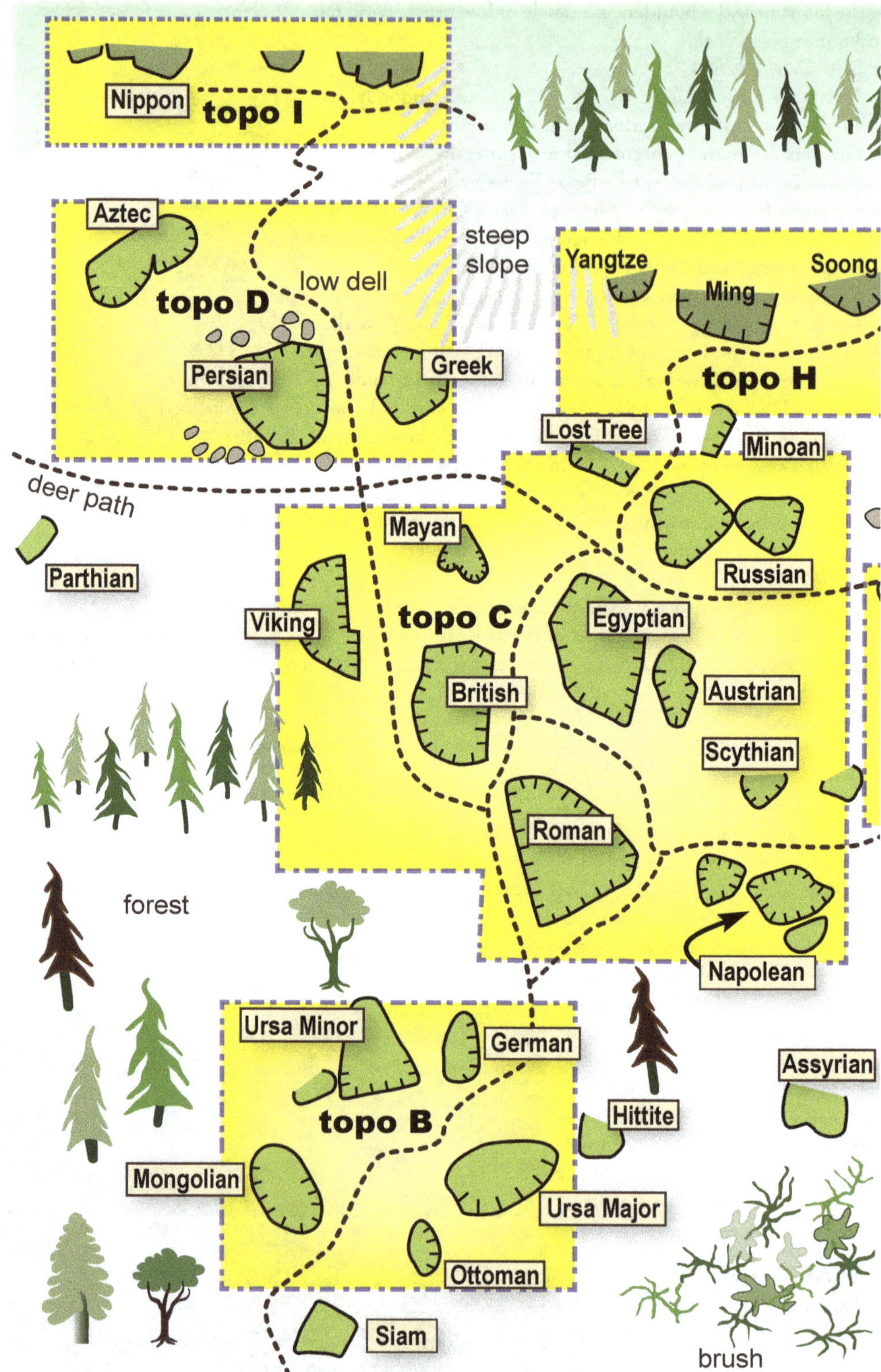
Nippon
topo I
Aztec
topo D
low dell
steep slope
Persian
Greek
Yangtze
Ming
Soong
topo H
Lost Tree
Minoan
deer path
Parthian
Mayan
Russian
Viking
topo C
Egyptian
British
Austrian
Scythian
Roman
Napolean
forest
Ursa Minor
German
Assyrian
topo B
Hittite
Mongolian
Ursa Major
Ottoman
Siam
brush

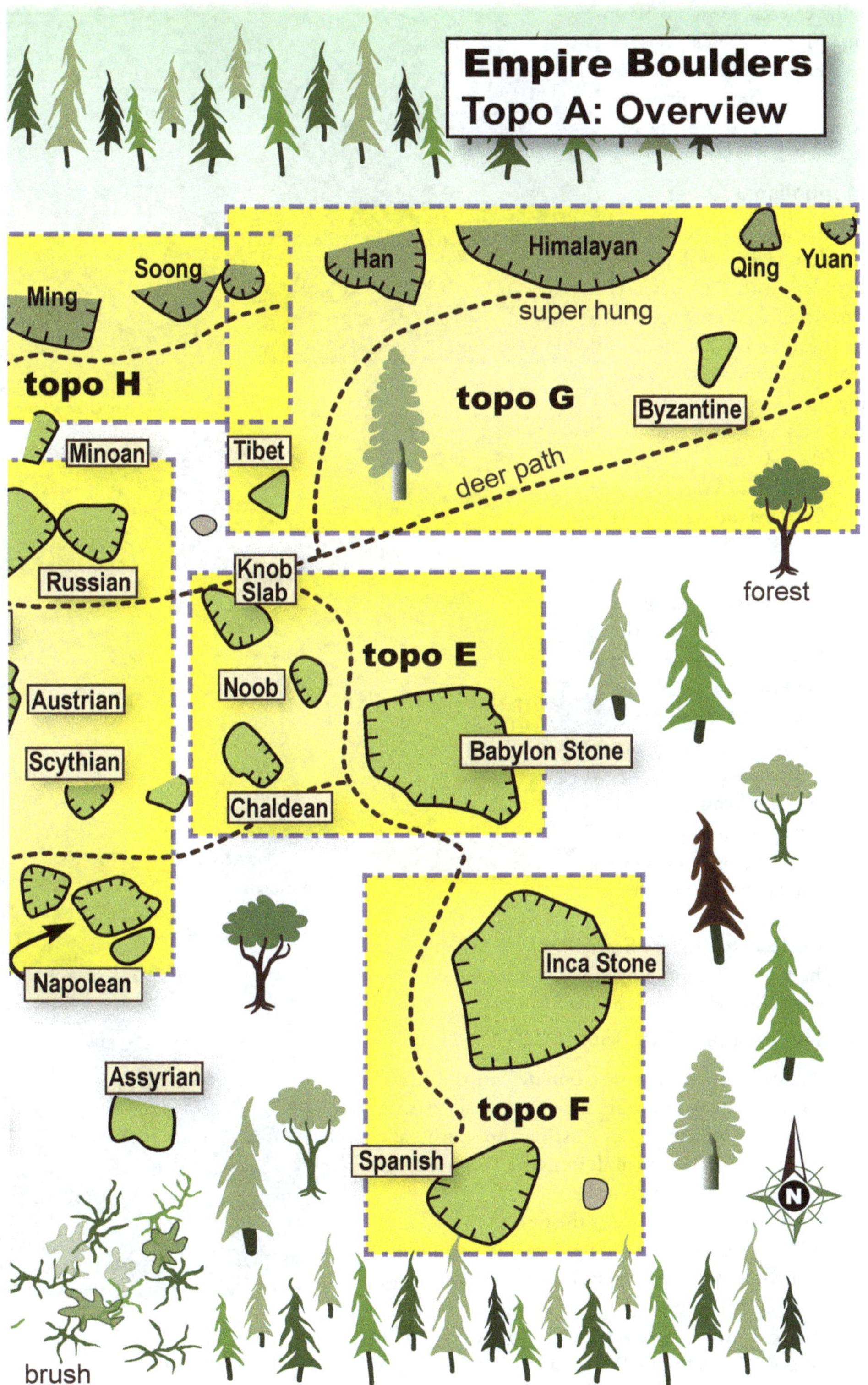
Empire Boulders
Topo A: Overview
Ming
Soong
Han
Himalayan
Qing
Yuan
super hung
topo H
topo G
Byzantine
Minoan
Tibet
deer path
Russian
Knob
Slab
topo E
Noob
Austrian
Babylon Stone
Scythian
Chaldean
Napolean
Inca Stone
Assyrian
topo F
Spanish
forest
brush
N

tall, yet each seems to have quantitative gems certain to wet your palette. So, let's begin this famous site tour with our first stone, the Pax Mongolia.

Mongolian Boulder

This is the initial minor low laying oval-shaped boulder with an obvious sloped lip wrapping around its south aspect. Its the first stone you encounter walking up the path en route to the main area. Beta L to R:

VB Ultima Ratio Regum (aka War).

V0ss Mandate from Heaven. Brief small crimps over lip.

VB (V3ss) Khublai Khan. Fat hold mantle. SS adds a long lunge.

V3ss Hwacha. Crimps at the lip, and a tough deadpoint to reach crimps on the slab face above.

V6ss The Scourge. Start on two sloper edges, use lip moving right up over the very point of overhang.

V4ss Genghis Khan. Start very low on left pocket and right side pull, then lunge for the jug, and power mantle over the lip yield a superb line.

Siam Boulder (aka Thai Boulder)

Technically, this is the first boulder on the hike uphill, though due to its low profile its easy to walk past it without realizing that a few lines exist on the southeast aspect. It's situated about 30' downhill from the Mongolian Boulder just east of the trail. Beta L to R:

V1ss Siamese Twin. Left of the fir tree.

VB White Elephant. Brief flat face just right of fir tree.

V0 Little Buddha. Also just right of tree (very close to left VB) more on the point.

VB Red Curry (short vertical scoop). **VB King and I** (short vertical face). **VB Angkor Wat** (east point). **VB Sticky Rice** (traverse north slab). **VB Kneejerk** (north point).

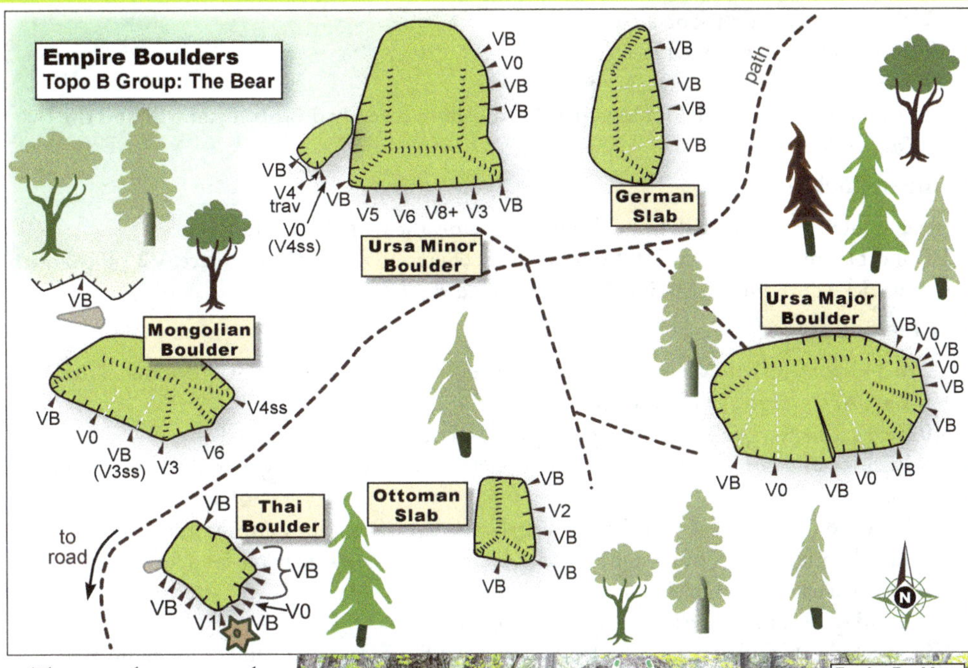

The south aspect has four very short family/kid friendly **VB's** (2 smear, 2 mantle).

Ursa Minor Boulder

The next substantial sized boulder on the hike uphill. Its a superb 13' tall trail-side stone that has a vertical south-facing aspect with a treasure of serious problems on it. The first beta is for the independent round low blob on the far left. Beta L to R:

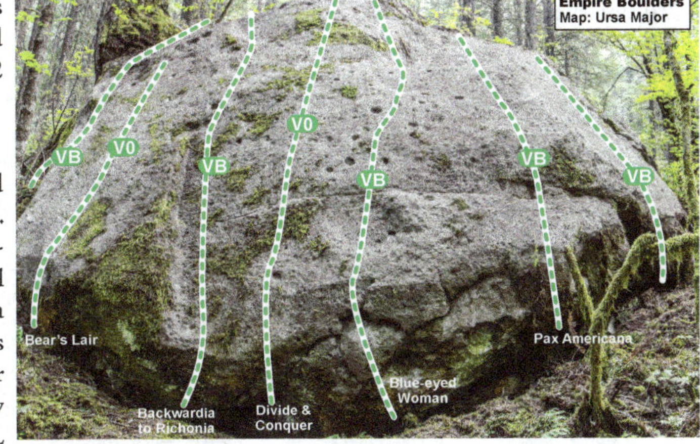

    VB & V0 Bear Rug. Several minor variants on left. No cookies.

    V4ss Bear Claw. Traverse from left all the way right into V0 and up over.

    V0 (V4ss) Chubby Huckster. SS low left dish & crimp, bump. Standing is one move less.

...On the main vertical south face of main boulder (beta L to R):

    VB Pocket Rocket. Use the obvious natural pocket on nose.

    V5 Bear Minimum. Left face using a sloped pocket and reaches for more sloped holds.

    V6 Big For Your Boots. Center power line – pinches, balance, dead-point reaches.

    V8-9 Three Bears. Power line in center of face cruising a partial seam (project).

    V3 Bearly There. Skinny face on the right with surprisingly subtle holds.

    VB Bear Facts. Right nose doing one-two move.

...And on the east side of this same large stone:

    VB a brief face left of crack (some family-friendly stuff).

VB Bear Bait is the crack on slab.

V0 Bearvilla. Thin rounded face on slab.

VB Grin & Bear It. Low angle ramp.

While standing on the path looking up at Ursa Minor, directly downhill you will find the two following boulders.

Ottoman Boulder

Small minor east-facing slab located about 25' below the path. Beta L to R:
VB short leftmost low angle. **VB Stairway** steps & jugs on nose. **VB** short face. **V2 LP** is a quality yet tricky pure smear slab line. **VB** short round right face.

Ursa Major Boulder

Large 24' tall stone with a substantial south-facing slab. Located 30' below path. Beta L to R:

VB Lost Art is a brief line below the big fir tree.

V0 Bear's Lair is a quality skinny opening crux section on a long slab.

VB Backwardia-to-Richonia. ⚠ The prominent double sloped troughs create a popular hi-ball fun run.

V0 Divide & Conquer. ⚠ Tackles the hi-ball face and has a skinny crux at mid-height.

VB Left-handed Blue-eyed Woman Series of prominent pockets make for a fine fun run.

VB Pax Americana is a minor blunt rib.

VB Bondage is a minor series of edges and steps on the far right.

V0 Spoofed. Quality east prow (rules by staying on face) starts left hand on sidepull.

VB Eulachon. East steps to smear slab (plus variation).

V0 Git Lost. One move face onto slab.

VB Pax Europa. Low angle slab.

Hittite Boulder

A brief ultra low boulder a few steps east of previous boulder. Four lines (L to R). **VB Kitty** (face), **VB Cool Cat** (one-move crack), **VB Dog** (slab), **VB Pony** (one-move onto right slab).

German Boulder

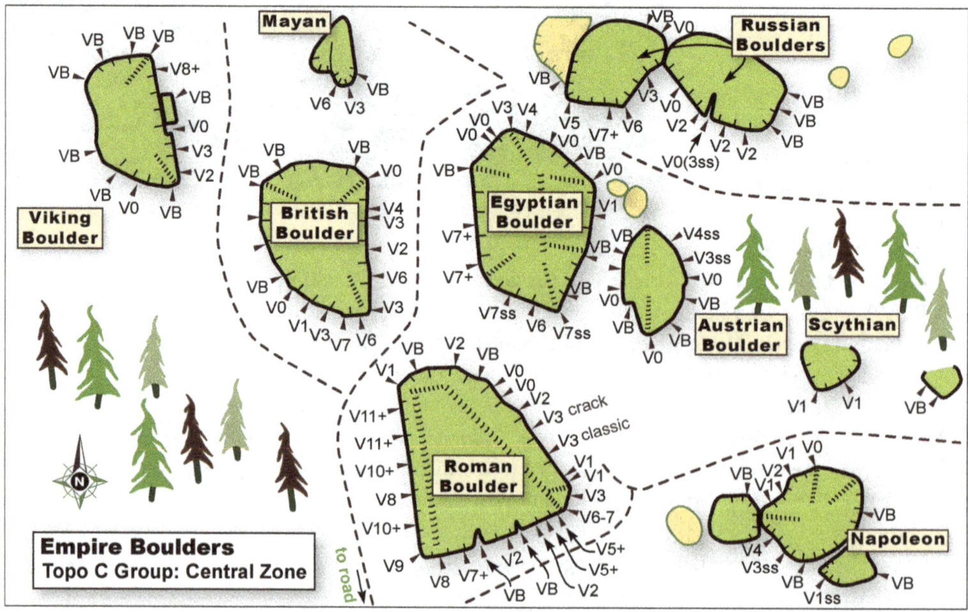

This is the minor trail-side low angle eastern-facing slab stone. All 4 problems are VB (including a cross all routes variation). A quality family and kid friendly slab. Beta L to R:

VB Eagle Claw is a left slanted groove.

VB Gothic Art is the shorter central face.

VB Boar's Tusk is the taller central face.

VB Berlin and the right rib.

CENTRAL BOULDER CLUSTER

This concentrated and popular spot entails four massive boulders and four smaller stones, primarily wrapped around the famous Roman Stone. Its the area where you will likely hike to first in order to get a quick taste of the power, punch and quality this little site has to offer. The primary approach path splits from this cluster of stones, one path traveling northwest (to the upper west grotto), one path travels northeast (up to the deer path), and a brief path travels southeast to a small set of two minor stones.

Roman Boulder

This is the prominent really big boulder you encounter when the trail lands at a compact cluster of boulders. The Roman Boulder is the *tour-d-force* at EB with everything from mundane to absolutely extraordinaire. This large stone offers a host of quality 360° bouldering. There are several top anchors if you prefer to rope it. The path directions to reach the remaining stones in the area are coordinated from this major stone. Beta starts at the north point and is described clockwise:

VB Empirical Dreams is the north point fun run and often used as the down climb. This is the *first* line established on the Roman Stone and at the Empire.

V2-3 Etruscan. Several short enjoyable variants on a slight overhang (all end the same on next VB).

VB Via Appia goes up easy steps; viable as a down climb.

The next six are 18' hi-ball lines.

V0 The Empire. ⚠ Classic. First half of seam then right face. Start up the leftward angling seam till you reach mid-height, then aim up right on smears.

V0 Rome. ⚠ Ultra classic full angled seam. Start at a large pocket on a slight bulge at seam, then go leftward up the seam to the top.

V2 Centurion. ⚠ This starts at the crack, pulls the initial bulge using a large pocket then angles up right crossing Rome and finish on The Empire (or finish on the Rome route).

V3 Gladiator. ⚠ The prominent center crack. Crimps till the crack widens at mid-height, then balanced movement to finish. Crack can be lead with small stoppers and cams.

V0 Gladiator Var. ⚠ Start same as Gladiator crack but bust up right as an ending variant.

V3 Aqueduct. ⚠ Ultra classic at Empire. Tiny crimpy pocket moves to attain large mid-face pockets, then dicey moves to finish. Way to go Mr A!

V1 Colosseum. ⚠ Crux opener move to sloped stance, then calm reach up left to jug, then jug again.

V1 Colosseum Direct. ⚠ The same crux opener move to sloped stance, then reach up right to catch a rail and a big flat jug.

V3 Damascus Steel ⚠ is a superb tall 17' hi-ball line using an inner scoop of the overhung southeast prow utilizing good crimps and holds (if merged right with Colosseum its V2).

V6/7 Caesar. ⚠ The same tall tall prow, but utilizing blunt overhung prow-like feature on the left. A classic problem well worth doing!

...the next set are all on the south aspect of this boulder.

V5-7 Vesuvius. Short vertical face with skinny skinny smears (project).

V5 Via Delarosa. Start with two small pockets, one for each hand.

V1
V1
V3
V1
V1
V3
V3
V1
V0
V0
Rome
Empire
Via
Appia
V2
VB
VB
Centurian
V2
Empirical
Dreams
Etruscan
Damascus
Steel
Colloseum
Aquaduct
Gladiator
Empire Boulders
Map: Roman (east)

V9
V8
V7+
VB
V2
VB
V2
Nero
V5
V6+
V6
Cobblestone
Gladius
Architect
Empire Boulders
Map: Roman (south)

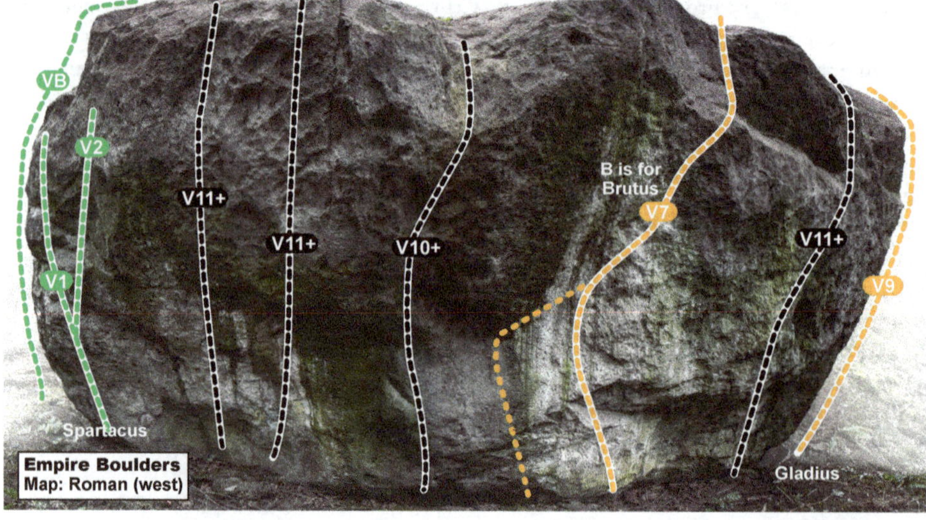
VB
V2
V11+
V11+
V10+
B is for
Brutus
V7
V11+
V9
V1
Spartacus
Empire Boulders
Map: Roman (west)
Gladius

V2 Nero. Thin short face with a few pockets.

VB Preston's Nemesis. Corner-*ish* nuance.

V2 Cobblestone. Everything on short face with pockets.

VB The Scramble. The walk up and walk down.

V7-8 Prima Facie. Thin crimps just left of the down scramble. Project.

V8 Architect. The right aspect of prominent overhung prow on tiny crimps & slopers.

Six futuristic lines exist on main west aspect of Roman Stone (not counting the two end lines)....and these six problems are:

V9 Gladius. Overhung technical round arête prow. Crimps to catch high sloper. A powerful variation (V9*ish*) starts near Architect, then moves up left and merges at the sloped jug on Gladius.

V11+Imperialist. Tech face to sloper rail then into slight groove (project).

V7 (V8ss) B is for Brutus. Overhung technical face. Standing start on high crimp and pop for sloped jug. The 'ss' uses a left low undercling.

V10+ _____ Tiny crimps and undercling pocket to knob on rail, and into groove at top.

V11+ _____ Overhung face with marginal crimp features.

V11+ _____ Another overhung face with marginal crimp features.

V1 Spartacus. Minor squeeze shorty just right of the standard north point *Empirical Dreams* line. As rated V1 Sparticus Left, and V2 Sparticus Right.

British Boulder

The Anglo-Saxon boulder has a broad rounded prow on the south end, and a slightly overhung flat face on the east side. Beta L to R starting on the far west face:

VB Left Coast. A brief move and mantle (+ minor var).

VB The Real and The Ideal. Go up a brief round rib (use or avoid pocket).

VB Boulderville. Basic slab run just right of rib.

VBss Cosmic Order. Low bulge mantle onto easy slab.

VBss England. Reach high and grab giant pocket and pull over.

V0 Balance of Power. Undercling pinch, high right smear, move up left to giant 4" pocket.

V1 British Isles. Start on same undercling pinch, high right smear, but move up right directly over the bulge.

V3 Mini Cooper. Overhung face using crimps directly up a seam. Start low on a good right hand crimp and a small left hand crimp.

V7 (V7ss) Notre Dame. Start left hand side pull and right hand on good right side pull. Substantially overhung bulge with tenuous reach. The 'ss' uses the undercling.

V6 (V7ss) Quasimodo. Hung prow. Start under bulge, power to flat crimp.

...And on the east face of this same boulder:

V3 Bulldog. The right side of an overhung prow starts by using underclings and a knob hold to reach better holds.

V6 Crusade. Powerful slightly hung thin face. Start with low right hand crimp pinch and dyno for the high sloper.

V2 King Arthur. Start at center of boulder below two under clings and climb straight up to the top.

V3 Excalibur uses two small undercling sidepulls, but exit left using natural rail and committing

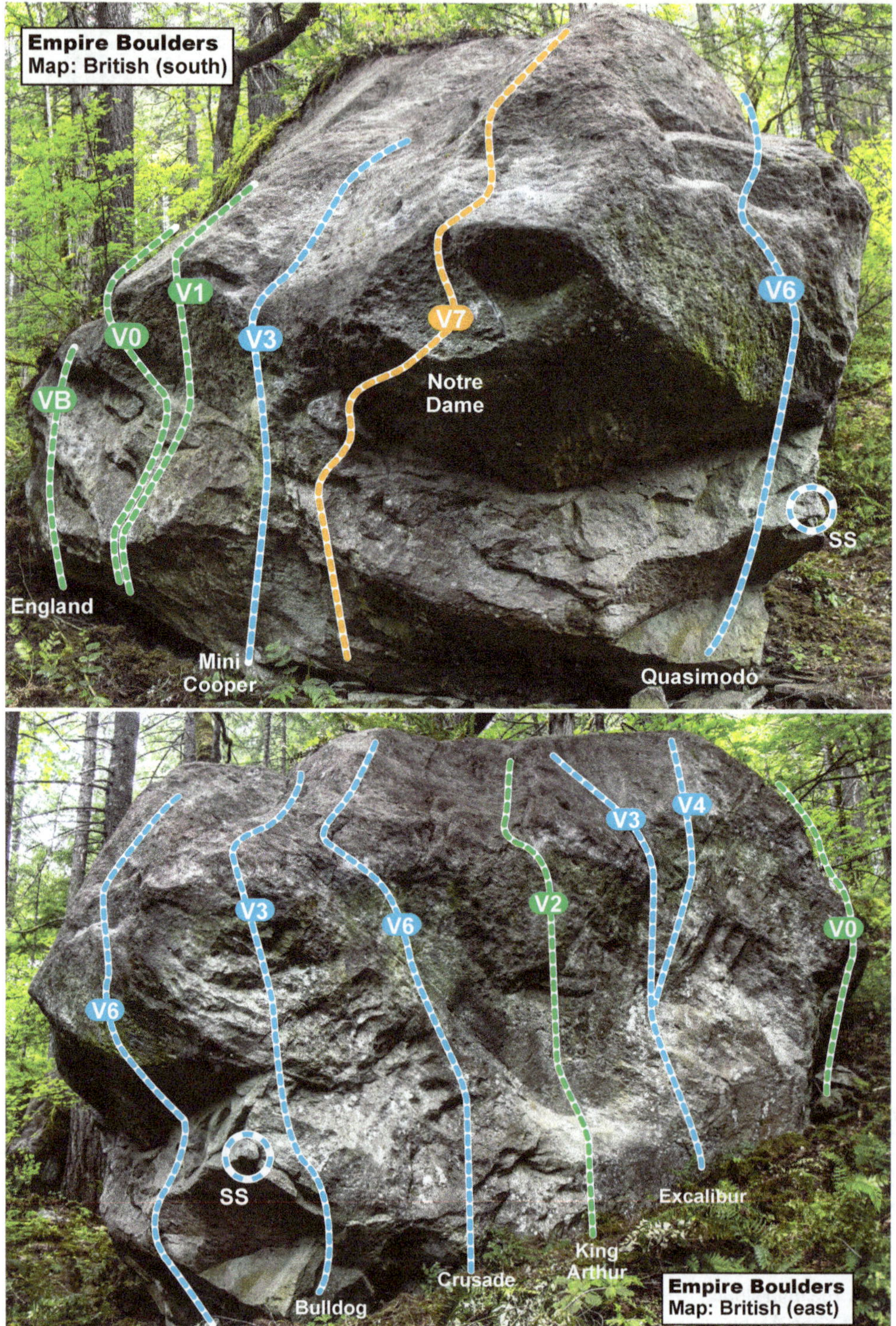
Empire Boulders
Map: British (south)
V1
V0
VB
V3
V7
Notre
Dame
V6
SS
England
Mini
Cooper
Quasimodo
V3
V4
V3
V6
V2
V0
V6
SS
Excalibur
Crusade
King
Arthur
Bulldog
Quasimodo
Empire Boulders
Map: British (east)

top out.

V4 Excalibur (direct). Start same as previous using the two small undercling side-pulls but continue directly up a blank section with a few reachy high pockets.

V0 Badge of Honor. Seam going over bulge.

VB Fabric of Deceit. Face going over bulge.

Viking Boulder

Immediately NW of Roman Stone is the Anglo-saxon Stone, and another 25' NW is the Viking Stone which has a sheer east face about 16' tall. Beta L to R:

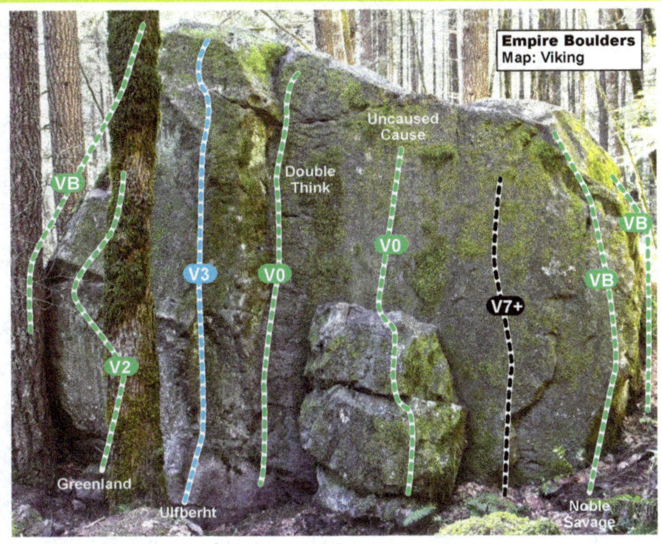

VB Raven's of Odin. West face angled slab.

VB False Peace. Brief moves going up left onto slab.

V0 Force Majeure. Smears on face with small sloper holds.

VB Tectonic Shift. Obvious step prow next to tree.

V2 Greenland. Vertical face between two trees. Crimps to jug rail, then a side pull.

V3 Ulfberht. Minor prow with long committing reaches.

V0 Doublethink. Vertical corner that steps up onto the stacked blocks, then several minor moves in the right facing corner to top out.

VB Uncaused Cause. Get onto stacked block, then mantle face above.

V8-9[?] ___ A skinny face with improbable holdless features maybe.

VB Noble Savage. The minor face at NE nose.

VB Cultural Suicide. Minor short face merging left.

VB Standard Bearer. Minor short rounded north face.

Mayan Stone

A minor short slanted hung prow-like stone a few yards uphill from Brit Stone with a few intriguing lines on it.

VB Chai Frappuccino. The east side shorty.

V3ss Sclerotic Stagnant Superstate. Crimp prow, move up right onto slab.

V6 Downtown Funky Stuff. Crimps & palm on left side of prow to lip and mantle exit.

Egyptian Boulder

About 30' northeast of the Roman Boulder is the Egyptian Boulder, a tall, yet roughly pyramidal shaped beast with a long slab on its west aspect with a slight overhang to start each problem. Beta runs clockwise starting with the easy lines on the east side:

VB Cheops. The basic up/down line on east side.

VB Hatshepsut. Another basic up/down line on east side.

V8ss Chi Jin Yu. Full under prow utilizing incut holds, power out and up. Ends at head height by merging into the previous VB. This is right of fir tree.

V6 Ancesters Protect Me. Left of fir tree. Start on smooth face, utilize a sidepull undercling to make a long reach.

V7ss Only God Forgives. SS low on left in hung nook, cruise several incut holds rightward, then up using a slight crimp and a very long reach over a round bulge.

V7+ _______ A variation starting the same as previous line but exits up left (project).

V6-8ss (?) ___ on round overhung nose is a crux sequence using a small knob.

V6-8ss (?) ___ power crimps getting over the bulge, then easy slab.

VB Hieroglyph. Easy steps up onto the slab, then run the center of the easy slab.

V0 Sand of the Sahara. Use the crack with your left hand to surmount the bulge.

V0 Sphinx. The crack straight on.

V3 Valley of the Kings. Using the crack with your right hand, move left along the lip, around to north aspect, then surmount the north side of the hung prow.

V4 King Tut. Cool direct start with long reach on north aspect of hung prow.

V0 Pounding Sand. Climb up using the 7" diameter pocket.

VB Giza. Face-crack next to a detached flake.

V0 State Of DeNile. East prow (and large crack of detached block).

V1 Pharaoh. Quality face with small crux crimps (rules avoid crack on right).

V6 The Nile. The north side traverse (starts on Sphinx problem going left).

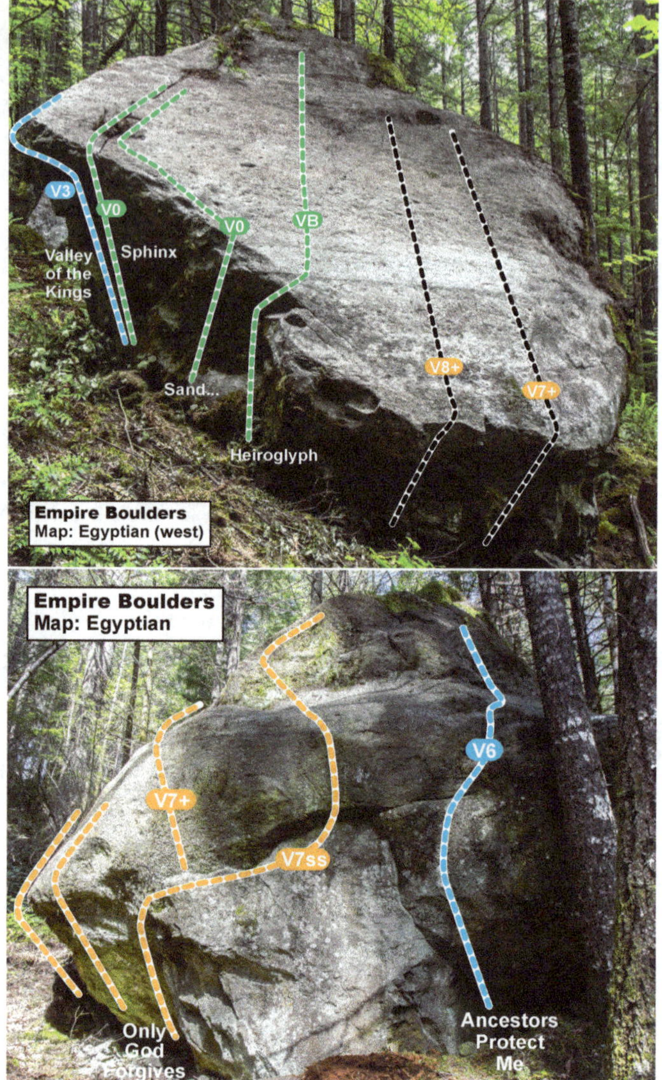

Austrian Stone

A minor block on the immediate east side of the Egyptian Stone. Beta L to R:

VB short kids slab on west aspect.

VB Alps. Short face crack with incuts on west aspect.

V0 All Things Nice is a brief vertical face on west aspect.

VB Symphony. Steep corner steps on the west side.

V0 Last Waltz. High step getting onto the south nose.

VB One Move. Short one move face on east aspect.

VB Globalize Me. East ramp.

V0 (V2ss) Renaissance. Brief face on east side starting with hand in the pocket.

V3ss Tic Tac. Good quality line utilizing a series of sloper crimps and a slap finish.

V4ss Little Red Monster. A series of short right facing sidepulls on east side.

Russian Boulders

Uphill NE of Egyptian Boulder is this double set of stones. Beta L to R (starting on left stone):

VB Urals. A short move far left side.

V7ss Kremlin. Outer left overhung nose above block. Pinch and good edge.

V7-8 Vodka Queen. A hard send on the overhung face using an insipient seam (project).

V6 Natasha. The first V6 established at the site. Start on the left block on its inner aspect on two small gaston's, then up short overhung face on small sloped holds. Gets a V7ss if you start on the round point then goes up right to merge and finish.

V3 Czar. Scooped face using left undercling pinch and high reach to catch small crimps.

...And on the right boulder:

VB Volga. Deep wedge slot of both blocks.

V0 Mockba (aka Moscow). Vertical short flat face on the right block.

V2 Ikon. Use jutting prow just left of deep overhung OW crack.

V0 (V3ss) Gulag. The OW crack itself is a viable challenge.

V2 Caviar. Start about 4' right of crack very low, traverse left upward on positive lip holds (this start is **V3** now that the foot flake is missing). A popular alternate is to begin 'ss' with right

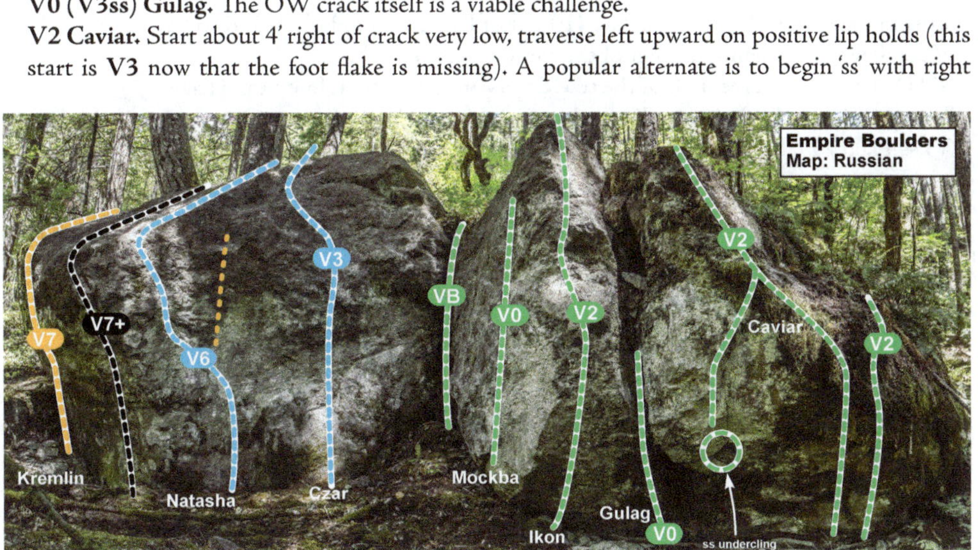

hand on under cling and left hand in the OW, then punch up right into Caviar.

V2 Russian Bear. Start same as previous line, but mantle right over onto slab.

VBss Dr Zhivago (left edge of crack) [on far east side].

VBss Politburo (crack) [on far east side].

V0 Siberia. A nice crimp smear line [on north side of boulder].

VB Russophobia. Basic short run [on north side of boulder].

Minoan Boulder

A brief low boulder just uphill from Russian Boulders.

VB King Crossis. Basic low traverse.

VB Scrapheap of History. A minor face with a big fir above it (15' NE of Minoan Stone).

Lost Tree Boulder

Brief boulder with short vertical face (10' left of Russian Boulder). Beta R to L:

V1ss Sleepy Salamander. Right of the tree on rounded face.

V0 (V4ss) John Deere. Left of the tree. Starts on crimps with foot near a flake.

V2ss Minimum Bark. Undercling right, reach high with left.

V2ss Flakey Flake. Brief crimps. Leftmost shorty.

Napoleon Boulders (aka French Boulders)

About 35' southeast of the Roman Stone is this a triple set of short boulders sitting low in a bowl. Beta L to R on the north side:

VB Arch De Triumph. A minor move left onto stance, then up face crimps.

V1 The 1812 Overture tackles a vertical nose straight on for a top out finagle.

V2 Esprit de Corps. Start in scoop, move up to catch the obvious flat rail, go straight up.

V1 Boreas Rising. Start in the scoop, catch the obvious flat rail, then exit up right.

VBss Last Waltz is the low minor step on a short west stone.

On the south side of the same big boulder (L to R):

V3ss Revolution (the direct start).

V3ss Waterloo. Start low on right, cruise leftward and up rounded prow, hand wrap and bounce up the rounded nose. The classic line on this boulder.

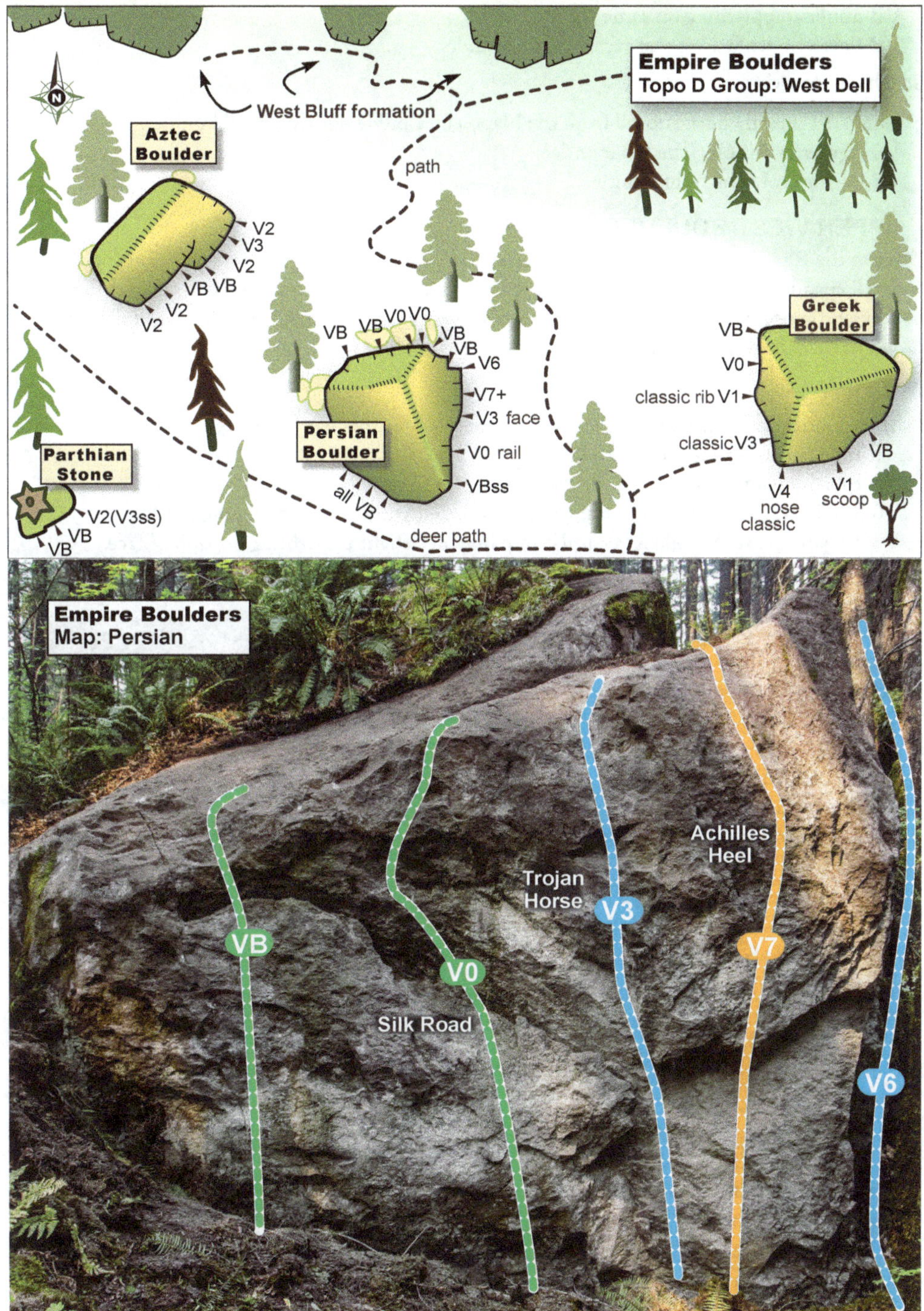

VB Trampling March of Power. Minor move, starts at slot.

And...on another small stone which is on the south side of the big boulder:

V1ss Mr Cool. Fun hung warmup arête. Start low cruising incut jugs up leftward onto arête.

VB minor steppy thing on same stone.
VB Paris. Short face on east face of main boulder.

Scythian Boulder

About 20' directly north uphill from the Napoleon Boulders is this small boulder.
V0 Agnostic Babble. The left mantle.
V0 Pagan Idol. The right mantle.

UPPER WEST BOULDER CLUSTER

From the Russian Boulders a deer path extends uphill westward to a low dell or trough, where you will encounter three large boulders. The west cliff formation outcrops perch above this minor dell like little political sentinels glaring down at your slow progress. The narrower tall east-most proud stone is the Greek Stone.

Persian Boulder

This giant boulder has an excellent vertical east face with superb quality problems. The north aspect has some fun runs. Beta L to R:
VB Boar's Head. Minor short mantle.
V0 Silk Road. A great quality fun run up a steep, slightly hung left angling rail.
V3 Trojan Horse. Excellent vertical crimp line on a slightly overhung portion of face.
V7+ Achilles Heel. A tech climb which starts at a series of six minute pockets in a seam, but branches up right. Its also feasible to make a variation utilizing the pockets up leftward.
V6 Ante Bellum. The 16' tall prow with a tree close at your backside.

The following are on the north aspect of this boulder:

VB Idle Dreams. The sloped corner steps.
VB Masters & Slaves. Off the top of the smaller block.
V0 Rattling Sabers. Quality line that starts low in an trough between two stones. Climb a slightly hung scoop, and transition onto flat right face at mid-height, catch top lip, and mantle out. A minor variant runs left out of the scoop.
V0 Laka Educayshun. Start same as previous line and transcends up

right to a large pocket (crossing over next line) and continues on face up rightward to top of stone.

VB All Hat 'n No Cowboy. Step off the top of the large flat block into a large foot pocket, then pull onto the top lip.

VB Genie. A minor steep face with a variety of crimps and edges make a nice fun run. Last line on utter northwest side.

And...on the south aspect (of Persian) is some family friendly short slab stuff. **VB Diva** (left nose), **VB Double-dip** (scoop), **VB High5** (seam smear), **VB Deep-Six** (bulge smear).

Greek Boulder

This is the taller stone in the upper west trough with a solid string of high quality problems. Beta is L to R:

VB Mossophobia. The down climb.

V0 Croton. Thin face with a reachy move.

V1 Imperial Ambition. ⚠ Superb line that starts low in center and prances up a minor rib using various angled crimps and small edges (16' tall). Super classic.

V3 Alexander the Great. ⚠ Three pocket start up a steep face. Ultra-classic line.

V4 Zeus. Powerful line that starts on two pinches (left & right) and moves up into a scoop aiming for the obvious fin up high on the prow. A tech classic not to be missed.

V1 Gatekeepers. Scoop-seam and mantle onto sloped finish.

VB Drunk on War. Minor edges.

Aztec Boulder

About 35' west of the double hitter boulders in the low dell is this last sole remaining challenger, a squat unit with a nice spat of brief lines on it. Beta L to R:

V2 Aztec. Leftmost mantle problem.

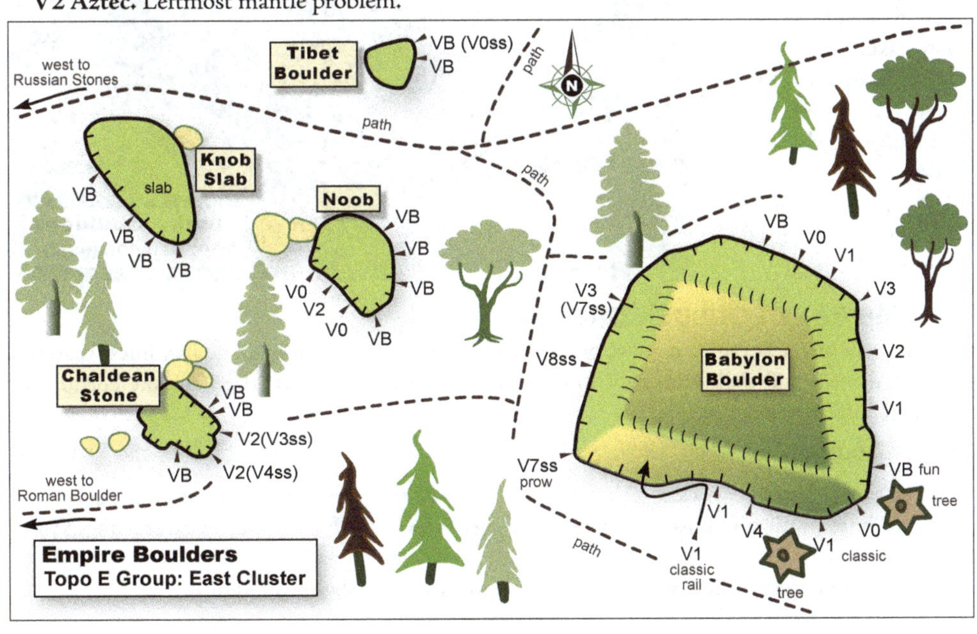

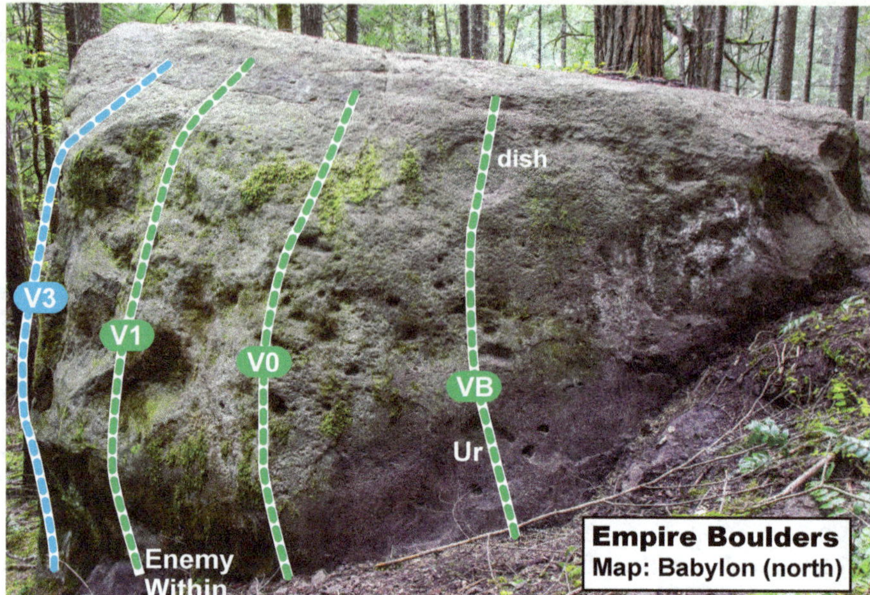

V2 Beast. Mantle.

VB Fault Line. Grab rounded hung prominence and move up obvious crack rightward.

VB Sombrero. Just right of the same crack slither up (just left of a tree).

V2 Total Depravity. Right side of tree at hollow flake.

V3 Utopian Visionaire. Crimps on rounded bulge reaching for a pocket.

V2 Sanity Awakening. Use crimps on rounded bulge on far right.

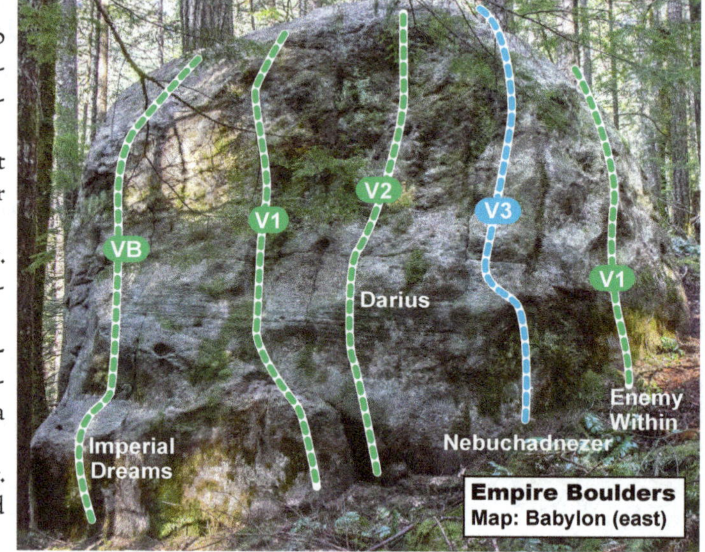

LOWER EAST BOULDER GROUP

In the east cluster are three massive boulders with a broad variety of high quality lines (easy and stout). A short uphill walk leads to the tallest and most overhung part (the V-insane portion) of the actual bluff formation.

Babylon Boulder ⚠

As the trail proceeds eastward it descends gradually to this very massive stone. A fine spectrum of quality lines await for those who like lower spectrum stuff. Beta is clockwise starting on the north side.

VB Ur. A fun quality short string of pockets leading up to a slight round dish.

V0 Graveyard of Empires. Obvious string of small pockets ending with sloper crimps. A minor variation exists between this and the previous).

V1 Enemy Within. Several nice jugs ending with a few skinny crimps.

V3 Nebuchadnezer. Start up a seam, smearing and crimps will get you a fair high hold, then a series of tricky thin crimps crux at the top give you a quality hi-ball finale.

V2 Darius. Initial starter

move, and crux cross-over gets you into the slight groove to several nice pockets, then ends with a flat topped finale.

V1 Xerxes. Initial step, then steepens to vertical dicey thin face at the top.

VB Imperial Dreams. Start on the immediate right side of the large fir tree, grab a large obvious pocket, and dash up the easy terrain to a brief vertical crux move. Fun run hi-ball.

V0 Tower of Babel. Start on the immediate left side of a large tree, and dance up numerous holds. Where it steepens, a series of large pockets await with a minor crux move. Fun run hi-ball.

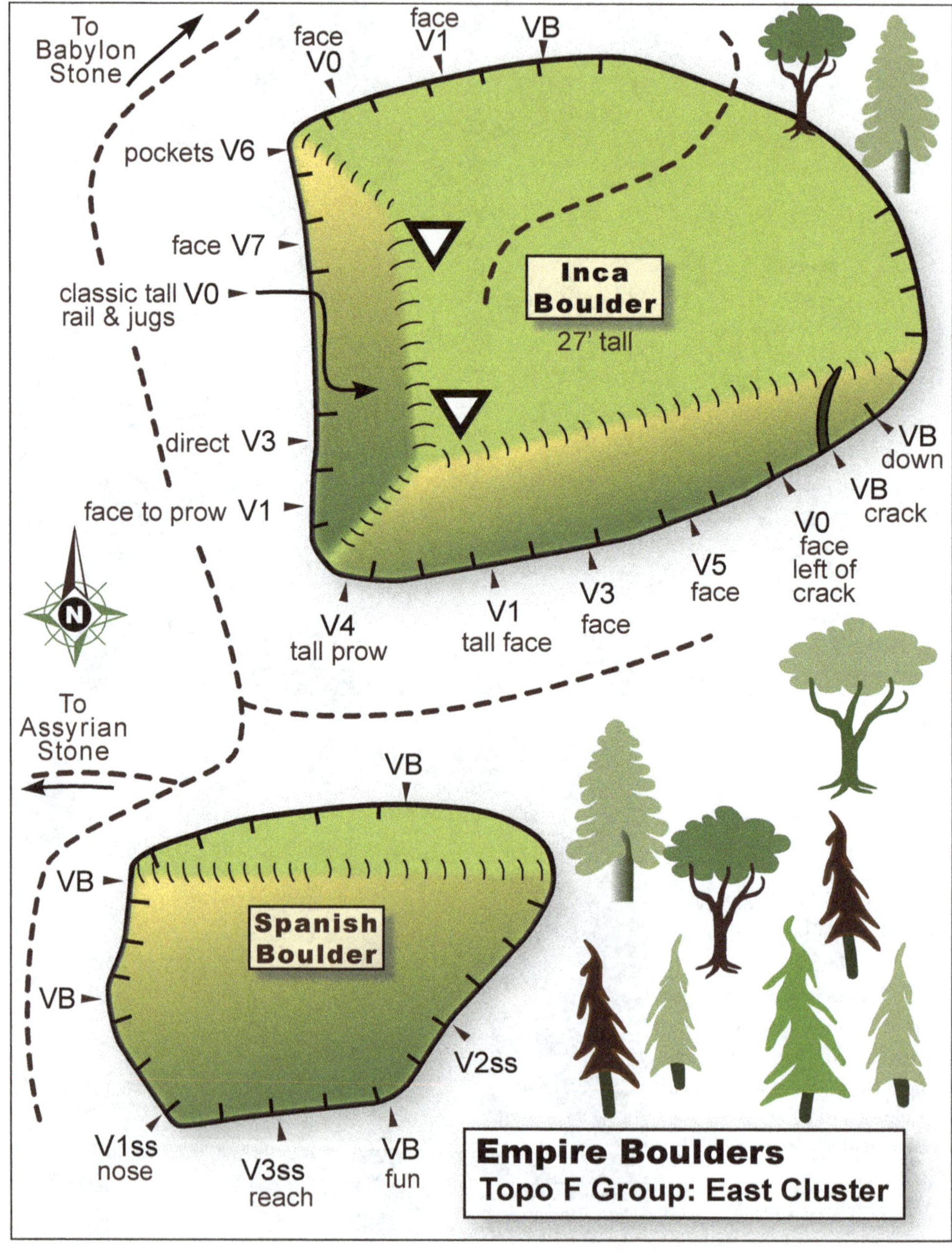

Located between the two trees. This is the right of two cool tall problems.

V1 Seventh Wonder. A superb hi-ball problem on a vertical face with several big pockets on its upper portion. Located between the two same trees.

V4 Fiery Furnace. A right angling corner-ish seam, that gets vertical and very dicey at the last portion of the problem. Crux is last move.

V1 Spice and Dice. Start low in center of face (same as for next line), move up left a few moves along the rail system, then bolt straight up using a series of small crimps on a vertical face. Better holds to exit.

V1 The Emperor. The ultra-classic line at EB. Start low in the center of face and run the rail monkey style up leftward,

then at a bulge of rock crimp directly up the slightly overhung face on small holds. A perfect climb!

V7ss Widowmaker. The powerful reachy super overhung west prow. Another (V7+) variant is to run the classic rail leftward into this super overhung prow problem.

V8ss Enemy Within. Thin rounded pockets and scoops on short overhung face.

V3 Tigris. Next to the tree trunk is a brief power move with a sloped top out.

Inca Boulder

The tallest (tumbled) boulder at Empire, logging in at a wildly majestic 27′ tall on its west aspect. The beta is L to R:

VB Stone Stairs. Basic set of steps.

V1 Native Soul. Quality short sequence of moves using two small slopers.

V0 At The Table Or On The Menu. A brief rounded face next to a fir tree.

V6 Pyramid. ⚠ Tall face loaded with tiny pockets and knobs ending left on an arête on upper portion.

V7 High Priestess. ⚠ Tall face (start same as next) that goes up through a slightly hung scoop to a high crux exiting left. Direct top out is harder.

V0 (5.10-) Machu Pichu. ⚠ Premier central route on the tall west face. Crux opening move to jugs, and crux exit move.

V3 (?) Directissimo. ⚠ Vertical direct merges into other route.

V1 (5.10+) Imperial Hubris. ⚠ Vertical face with nice pockets; merge onto arête.

V5 (5.12b) Blood Sacrifice. ⚠ Long arête with low crux.

V1 (5.10c) Pulmonary Edema. ⚠ Superb route on tall south face. Go up arched seam, then up steep slab on better holds.

V3 (5.11c) Manco Capac. ⚠ Crux opening move is a single small inclusion, finish on small holds. [An Inca ruler.]

V5 (5.12c) Bleeding Edge. Thin opening moves to a slight hung rounded lip. Dicey crux slopers above lip.

V0 Nowhere Fast. Start of small holds on left side of crack system (rules left of crack for all holds). At stance make a crux move to small pocket up right.

VB Ibex. Fat crack system.

VB Fen Fu. Down step.

Spanish Boulder

Just a few yards to the south of the Inca Boulder is the Spanish Boulder. Though squat-like with a broad slab top-out, the south aspect does offer several nice lines. Beta L to R:

VB Hobgoblin. Seam on north side.

VB Spaniard. Round ramp.

VB Galleon. Minor scoop.

V1 Columbus. Bulge at nose.

V3 Doobloon. A bulge with a scoop that refutes the less than diligent. A variation exists between this and next.

VB Realm of Uncertainty. Vertical fun run using positive holds on center of the stone.

V2 Mandolin. A nice string of moves that makes a high step onto the slab finish.

Assyrian Boulder

About 50′ directly west of the Spanish Boulder is this extremely low obscure flat stone. Beta from L to R.

V2ss Blackball. Left bulge (rules: avoid seam).

V0ss Unthinkable Thinkster. Up just the seam (rules: seam only).

VB Imperial Umpires. Mere high step.

V0ss Fastball. Low start using several incut small pockets (rules: just the pockets).

The next three minor boulders (Knob, Noob, Chaldean) are located just west of the Babylon Stone about 35′ distance.

Knob Slab

A low angle 12′ slab with a liberal dose of knobs, located next to the main east-west deer path.

VB Pork Bellies (5.0-5.3) all four variations on Knob Slab.

Noob Boulder

An inconsequential argumentative uncooperative tiny stone (like

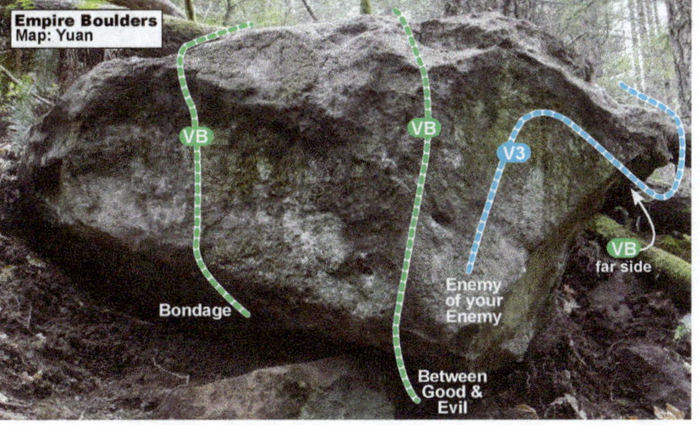

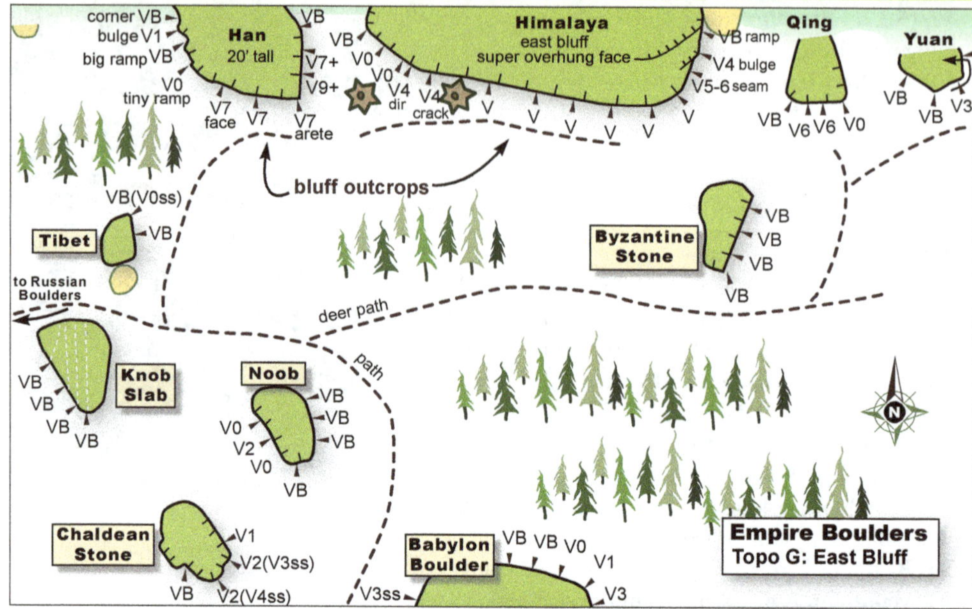

some people we know).

V0 Noob. Squnched tightly left of the next unit.

V2 Motherland pockets (left-right), high step right, top slopers.

V0 Fatherland the high step south side.

VB All Noob. South and east side ramps, & two short kids east side lines.

Chaldean Boulder

Directly west of Babylon Stone about 30' is this stone with a brief SS overhang. Beta is from R to L:

VBss Noob. Squnchable kids line on right.

VB (V1ss) Just Do It. Short crimps line.

V2 (V3ss) Whiskey & Whine. Start on right side, latch rounded nose, get up.

V2 (V4ss) Crocodile Tears. Start low on two finger slopers, left foot way out left, launch to fix on bulge jug, get up over.

Hittite Boulder

Minor blob between Chaldean and Scythian stones.

VB Schmoo.

VB Whangdoodle.

Tibet Boulder

A very minor small rounded stone above Knob Slab and just above the main east-west path.

VB (V0ss) Broken Spear. Standing jug mantle, or SS crimps below jug.

VB War 'n Peace. A one move smear left of the previous line.

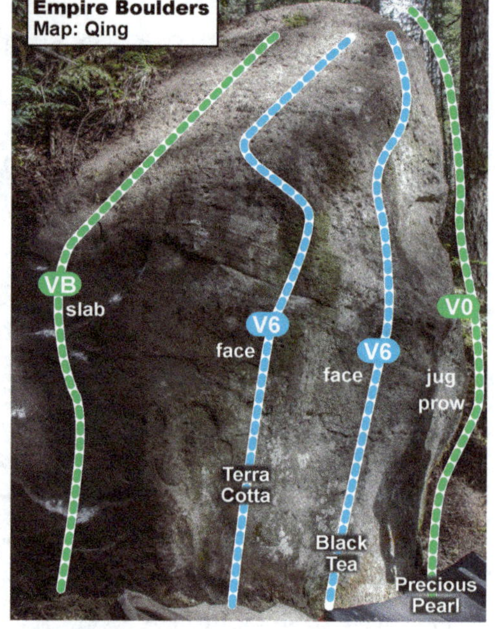

Byzantine Boulder

Just north of the Babylon Boulder, walk the deer path for 80' to this minor 10' tall stone. The south side is flat faced and offers four possible brief odd lines.

VB Iconoclast. The left nose.

VB Byzantine. Run the rail uphill from L to R ending high on rightmost VB.

VB Tetragram. Midway step-in.

VB Constantinople. Direct on taller portion (rules out any big foot hold).

GREAT WALL OF CHINA

This refers to portions of the bluff outcrops that protrude from a steep hillside. The Great Wall offers an exhilerating and extensive selection of serious hi-ball lines, some classic lines, and possibly even the stoutest mega overhung face at the Empire Boulders. Each specific outcrop is given a Chinese dynastic reference name to parallel the major dynasties. The outcrops are described from right to left (east end to west end).

Yuan Dynasty Boulder

At the utter east end of the outcrops (beyond even the Qing) is a tipsy little spec of stone. This is the Yuan Stone with a very minor set of lines. Beta L to R.

VBss Bondage. Start on left side low, mantle up over.
VBss Between Good and Evil. Start low at pockets on center point, mantle over.
V3ss Enemy of your enemy. Just right of previous, run right horizontally around the hung prow, and mantle over far right side. Quality problem.
V0ss Gutless Wonder. Start low, mantle far east side.
And another 150' further to the east is a VB minor on an isolated tiny kids block.

Qing Dynasty Boulder (Manchu)

Beta is R to L:
V0 Precious Pearl. Fun quality vertical layback rib with opening crux move (rules avoid big flat stance part way up on right).
V6 Black Tea. Powerful and thin. Right sidepull crimp, send middle part of face via left sloped crest.
V6 Terra Cotta. Start on obvious fat flat hold on left, go up to small divots high on left face.
VB Polished Jade. Slab on left.

Himalaya Face ⚠

Incredible super overhung face about 25' tall at its center. It offers about 5 futuristic potential problems, some pushing the edge (V10-12+). Beta is Right to Left (east to west end).
VB Lucky You. Basic rightmost low-angle ramp.
V5 Flying Pigs. Brief bulge mantle onto slab.
V4 (V7ss+) Divine Fury. Crimps at a seam. Powerful 'ss' under entire.

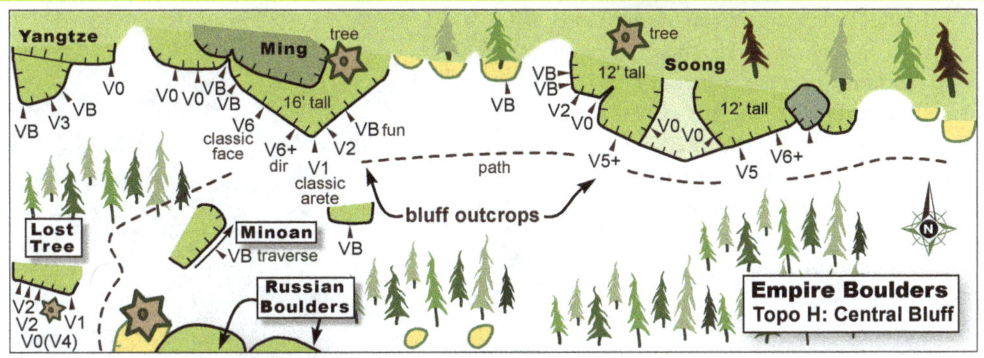

V_ (?) ____ the super hung face.

V_ (?) ____ the super hung face.

V_ (?) ____ the super hung face.

V_ (?) ____ the super hung face.

V_ (?) ____ the super hung face.

V4 The Sword. Tall cool thin finger crack (project).

V4 Unreal Unperson. Direct using smears and a long reach to catch two pockets.

V0 Logic. Brief smear and crimps on rightward angling seam.

V0ss Szechuan. Crimp reach, pull, attain top lip, mantle over, done.

VB Manchu. Leftmost basic crimp fun nose. And the get down method.

Han Dynasty Boulder ⚠

Prominent bluff with two main aspects with impressive 25' sharp arête. Beta R to L:

VB Yes No Maybe. Basic groove next to a tree (east aspect).

V7+ (?) _____ vertical crimps east face; the higher line.

V9+ (?) _____ vertical powerful thin crimps on east face.

V7 Red Dragon. The ultra classic arête and one of the great reasons to be here.

V7 Automation. Delicate face crimps to mid-stance, then techy moves up vertical face.

V7 The Empress. Thin crimps, crux onto sloped stance, then crux exit at top lip.

VB Jade. Right angled tiny ramp [landing #3] to a block pinch, then high step up left into the crack corner system (the nextVB to finish). The V0 variant starts on landing #2. V3 is the direct finish.

VB Shanghai. Fun hi-ball corner with large pockets, crack-*ish* nuance, and bulge at top.

V1 Loaded Dice. Go up easy steps to a right hand pocket, then over short bulge to top out.

VB Cobwebs. Very short minor groove.

Soong Dynasty Boulder

A unique double-set of overhung outcrops with a flat ledge squnched between each outcrop. Several quality lines exist on both. Beta is R to L (starting at the east outcrop):

V6-9 (?) ____ super hung east face.

V5 Mass Production. Fine opening jugs to start and powerful crimps to finish.

V0 Rampart Right. Short face off high landing.

...on the west outcrop:

V0 Rampart Left. The other short face off high flat landing.

V5+ (?) Mirabile Visu. Powerful hung techy crimp fest (project).

V0 White Tiger short hung crack.

V2 Jade Gate quality crimps. Start at the V0 crack, go up left face to next VB.

VB & VB (one move problems). **VB** rounder stone (to left).

Ming Boulder

Just uphill northward about 30' from the Russian Boulders is this tall 17' high outcrop with numerous stellar lines. Beta is from R to L:

VB I Am Not Your Guru. Cruise up incut sidepulls and slopers on vertical face (right side of outcrop). The *first* boulder problem es-

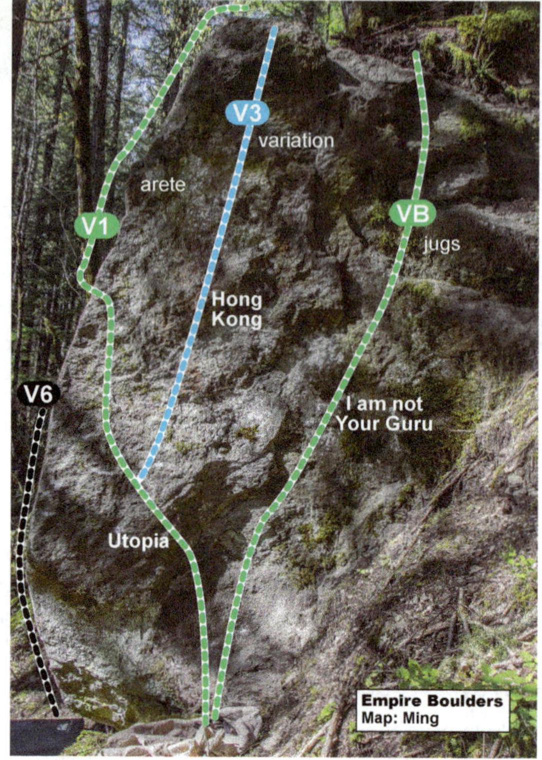

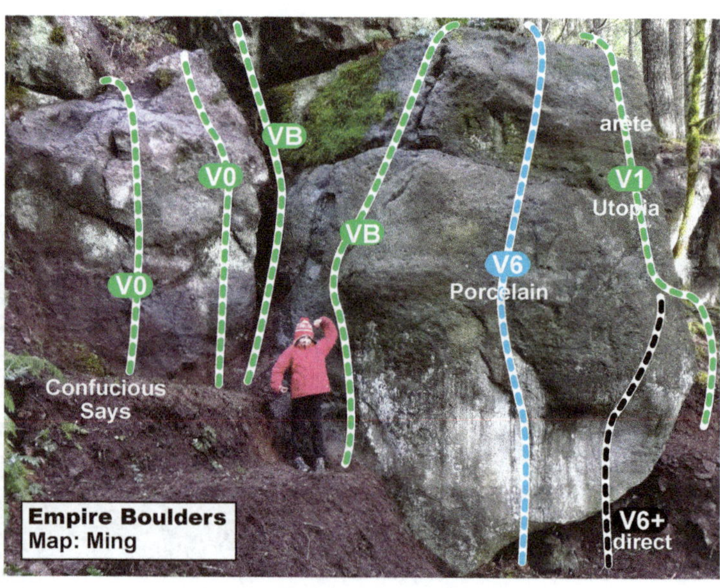

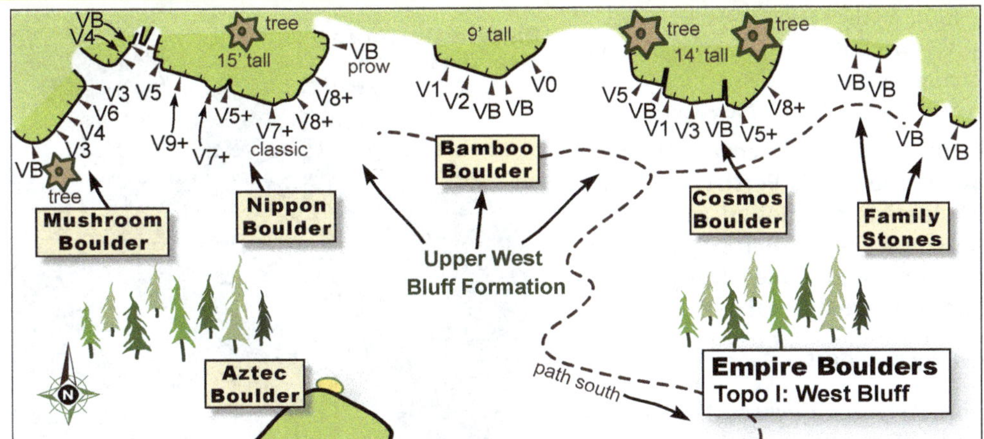

tablished on the bluff outcrops.

V2 Hong Kong. Stay on the right side of arête all the way (left hand on arête).

V1 Utopia. ⚠ Classic arête. Cruise up east side, transfer to arêtes left side at tiny mid-height stance, then dicey crux move to top. Exit left before crux is V0.

V6-7 (?) Mittimus. ⚠ Hung scoop face that merges into the upper arête of previous line (project).

V6 Porcelain. ⚠ Ultra classic face and serious hi-ball. Begin in a slight overhung scoop and utilize tiny pockets, small knobs and slopers. Way to go Mr A!

VB Royal Blood. Left side aspect using curved seams (fun run).

VB Huckypuk. The fat offwidth.

V0 Fuzzy Thinking. Crimps face just left of OW.

V0 Confucious Says. Seam on a short face.

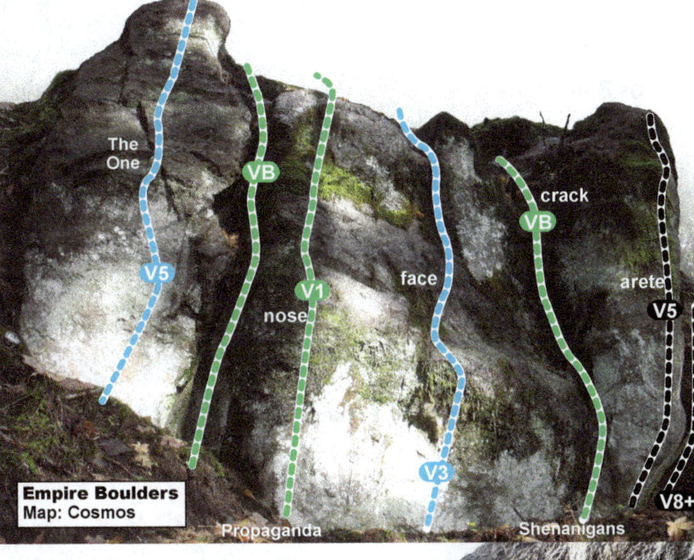

Yangtze Slab

A low angle slab with a midway landing, then a brief vertical second tier (kind of like a multi-pitch climb). Just uphill from Lone Tree Boulder. Beta is from L to R:

VB WhoWhatWhy. A basic initial crux smear move, then a slab run. Step right at dirt landing to tackle a V0 finalé on the next shorty tier.

V3 Dirt Bag. Start low on right at odd crimp maneuver.

VB Boorish Crack. No cookies.

In the upper west cove (about 40' above the Greek, Persian and Aztec Boulder) is a series of minor bluff outcrops. These outcrops yield some fun runs, and some ultra powerful lines that are the real deal.

Family Boulders

Three very tiny stones with a few basic brief **VB**'s for kids to dash up (with parental control) all located to the east of the next boulder.

Cosmos Boulder

A fairly tall (14' high) outcrop with a vertical east prow. Beta is from R to L:

V8+ (?) ____ (right face).

V6 Globalism. Cool hung right arête on crimps and top out slopers (project).

VB Shenanigans (right crack).

V3ss Copore Sano. SS begins below jug, power over bulge, chill, then over top lip.

V1ss Propaganda. Nice hung minor arête (right side of OW) with crimps to stance, then over top lip on crimps.

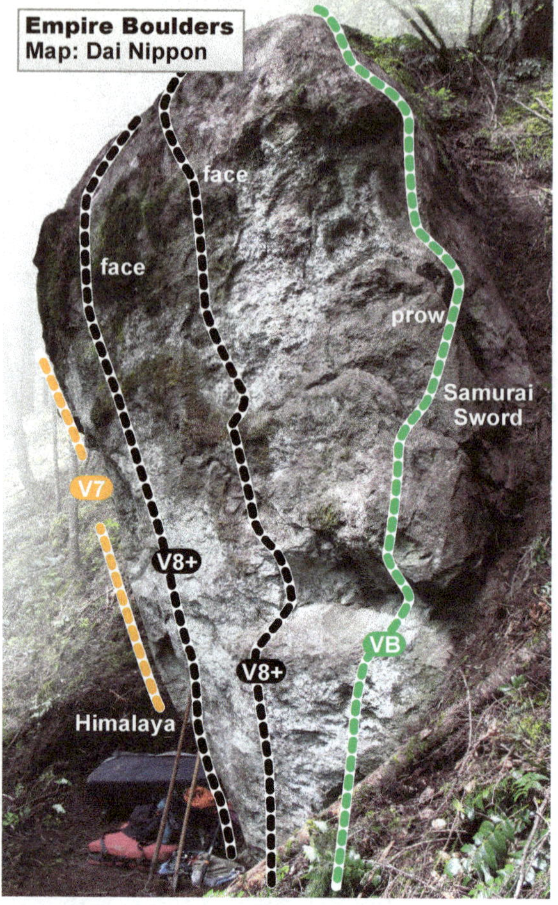

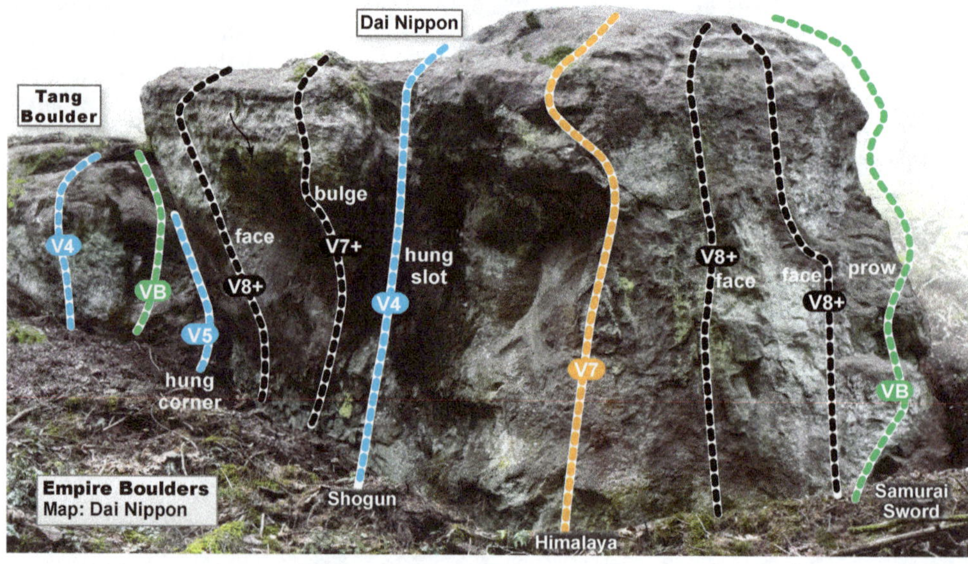

VB Cosmos. The left fat OW crack.

V5ss The One. Tricky setup and powerful crimps on this fine quality face line.

Bamboo Boulder

Midway between the two major stones is this minor shorty stone. Beta R to L.

V0ss Far East. Low minor one move two on far right.

VB Nine Yak Tails. Outer crack one move wonder using crack and steps.

VB Bamboo. Left start on face ending in the crack.

V2ss Kim Chi. Crimpy short face.

V1ss Serpent. Short crimpy face.

Dai Nippon (Japanese) Boulder

Impressive 16' tall outcrop with a serious overhang, and a fine string of ultra-wild lines. The beta is from R to L:

VB Samurai Sword. ⚠ Cool warmup on hi-ball east prow.

V8+ Yamamoto. ⚠ Flat face on right aspect (starts powerful, then gets more so). Project.

V8+ Fujiyama (aka Fuji). ⚠ Start on jugs, quickly morph to extreme sloper crimps. Project.

V7 Himalaya. ⚠ Classic powerful hung prow just right of slot. Power flat crimps to lip, trend up left then over.

V5 Shogun. Overhung fat slot full on.

V7+ (?) Rising Sun. The jutting overhung nose just left of slot. Project.

V8+ss (?) Real Mojo. Technical hung crimp face (left hand uses edge of dihedral) (project).

V5 Velocity. Far west overhung short dihedral corner. Classic, deceptive, powerful.

V5 L'il Kicker. Minor shorty tucked on far left.

Tang Boulder

VB Intellectual Idiots. Minor short seam (rightmost line).
V4 Emperor's Clothes. Crimps over bulge (project).

Mushroom Boulder

The final westmost bluff outcrop at Empire. A shorty 9' tall stone, with a few punchy odd minor problems. Cheers to the mushroom man! Beta R to L.
V2 (V3ss) Forest Frenzy. Minor round short face on right.
V6 Spore. Power crimps on face.
V4 Express. Flat short crimps face.
V3 Panda Bear. Make a move, catch the nob, reposition balance, mantle slowly. Phew!
VBss Chantrelle. Ultra shorty on far left.

Parthian Boulder

A tiny tiny stone located about 100' southwest of the Persian/Aztec boulders. Beta R to L.
V2 (V3ss) Square Peg Round Hole. Crimp rounded shorty rounded nose.
VBss Red Herring. Center line.
VBss Zero. Leftmost line.

And at that final tiny boulder we wrap up the entire discussion about the Empire Boulders. So how's that for a power packed group of boulder problems (VB to V-insane), all of it stacked majestically into one single impressive bouldering zone that close to Portland, Oregon?
Totally cool....

CENTRAL COLUMBIA GORGE (South Side)

CASCADE LOCKS BOULDERS

Does a secluded quality bouldering site composed of andesite boulders close to Portland sound reasonable? Near Cascade Locks is a plethora of good boulders composed of enjoyable tumbled andesite stones scattered broadly in a forested setting. The roadside cluster was tapped long ago by Mr A, but in recent years teams have explored much of this extensive complex, from the Herman Creek trail to a wooded knoll south of Anderson Point. Encompassing an area about 2 miles long the primary groups are scattered in random forested strings across the extensive area at virtually the same elevation (200' to 500' el), and are the tumbled remnants of an old cliff scarp immediately south of Herman Campground. From the Herman Group (Arcade & Tabletop), to the Talus Cluster (west, east, castle, & spring), the Orchard Group, and to the Annex Group (and Labyrinth) its all compiled together under one main section, the Cascade Locks Boulders.

The Cascade Boulders are enveloped within a secluded forest of tall Douglas firs filtering the light, often touched by a cool waft of breeze even on hot days (humid days are rare). The entire area is an open forested setting where a buildup of forest duff (except south of the powerlines) has made many landings user friendly. The size of the stones range from 8'-14' tall, but several 20' horizontal beasts laying on their side do exist, as well.

One to two crashpads minimum recommendation. Rock type nuances are diverse, composed of andesite with a quality fine surface grit in a gray matrix that offers good friction-ability. Some boulders have pockets, slight edges (crisp or soft), long rail traverses, and plenty of substantially overhung aspects. Cell phone reception is good. Minimal poison oak in a few spots, but the fir trees keep most of it at bay.

Though it's a forested north-facing setting, the site, besides being in a very rainy portion of the Columbia Gorge, is a breezy zone. So, when the rains stop, the boulders dry out fairly quickly in 1-2 days in winter. Typical season for warm weather bouldering is a 6-month seasonal window from May-October, but in essence is a fully viable 12- month bouldering site. The door to adventure here is virtually unlimited.

History

The Cascades Boulders saw extensive development by Mr A and Mr O (2009-2012), and a continued resurgence of activity after the late 2017 Gorge fire burned up all the moss. Other teams (Slayton, Porter, Vit, Firestone, etc) did fill in a fair portion of the gaps, adding quality to the Arcade, West Talus, and Spring Cluster. The bouldering zone attained its broad all encompassing name, not from the mountain range, but from the nearby town, Cascade Locks.

Directions

Drive I-84 freeway to Cascade Locks, then drive east on old Hwy 30 past City Hall (duck beneath the I-84 freeway). From a stop sign, continue on Frontage Road (travels on immediate south side of I-84) past Herman Creek Campground to the stop sign at exit #48 (this is a westbound I-84 exit only), then turn east on Wyeth Road for ¼ mile, and park on the south shoulder at a metal gate for access road NF 2800-022. Walk past the metal gate south on a forested lane to reach the

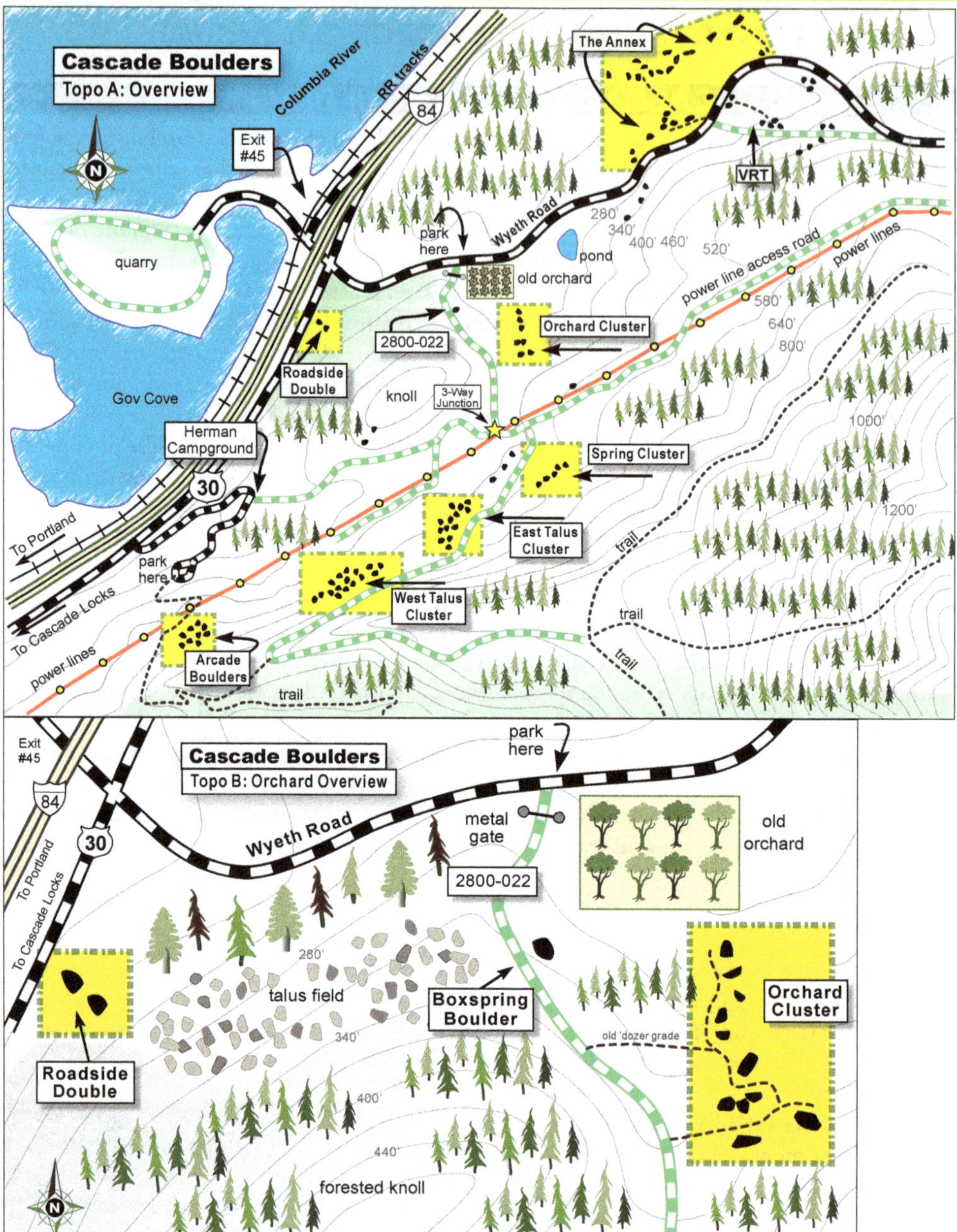

boulder clusters.

From the parking spot the nearest boulder (Boxspring) is about a 3-minute walk from Wyeth road, and the Orchard Cluster is about a 5-minute walk (about 1,056').

Several Circuits

The following beta list will take you on several tours and will describe each cluster en-route. The first circuit tour is from the gate south on the dirt road to the Orchard Cluster. The second circuit tour continues further south on the road to the Newt Boulder, the Spring Cluster, then west past

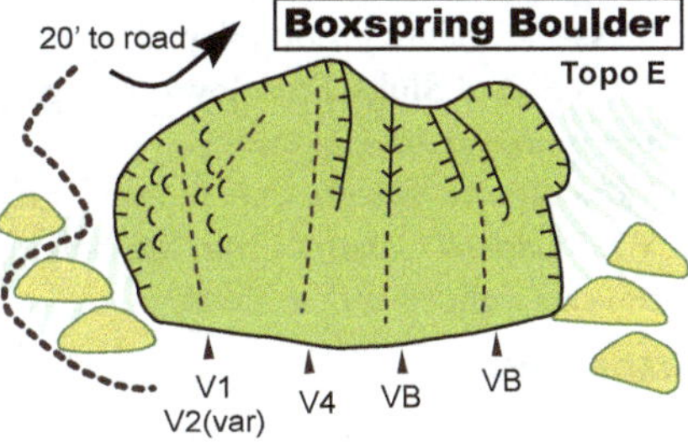

the Castle onward to the East Talus Cluster, over to Big Kahuna set, and last to the Oligarch Boulder set at the Green Ravine area.

The third circuit tour is taking the west powerline access road to Powerline Boulders, then along the west road (past Surge Protector) to Burger Boulder, up to Cascade Boulder, then along the entire West Talus Cluster (which includes all nearby Forest Clusters).

First Circuit Tour

Start walking south on NF 2800-022 past the metal gate (an old pear orchard is east of path). As the old dirt road starts up an incline, the Boxspring Boulder is a few yards off the trail on the left (facing east) below the dirt road.

Boxspring Boulder

V1ss Jump on the Bed. SS and up knobby face (V2 variation).
V4ss Queen size. SS, over bulge, and up the prow.
V1 King size. Right of prow, over bulge via groove.
VB Pillow Fight. Far right over bulge.

ORCHARD GROUP

From the metal road gate walk south uphill for 1,056' on the dirt road until it levels off. The Orchard Cluster is left (east) 60' on a minor flat wooded knoll (about 5-minutes walk from the metal gate).

Blackcap Boulder

V2ss Jam n' Jars. Up left face.
V4 Black Raspberry. Low start, tech up into corner under second lip, then use rib to top.
V4 Thorn in my side. Low start onto the low bulge, pinch rib, then up the rib to top.
V5 Raspberry Gnosh. Far right, lay low on crimps,

On Blackberry Boulder

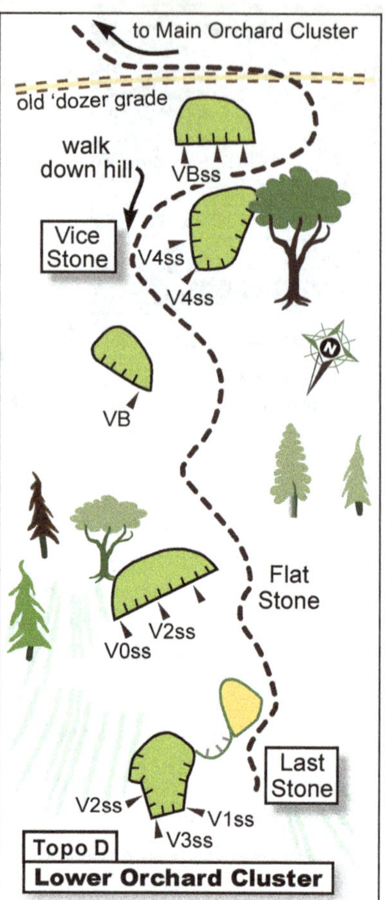

then move left along slopers to catch rib, then up top.

Banana Boulder

V7ss+ (?) Slight groove, slap, thug thing.
V3ss Salted Slugs. Start low on bulging rounded point, and power mantle up on top.
V0ss Drama Queen. One mover far right side.
V5ss Lapsus Calami. From the bulging rounded point traverse right to end of block.

Grape Cluster

V1ss Lege Artis. SS mono pocket, one move.
V2 Fruit Leather. Steep slab face with a low groove.
VB Green Apple Envy. The double stacked block on the right, start as SS, bump up to jug on upper block.
V5 Green Tea. Thin tech face on right.

Potato Boulder

V3 Idaho Spud. Left side next to tree.
V3 Yukon Gold. Bulge to slab, giant pocket.
V3 French Fry. Nose bulge to big pocket.
V1 Potato Cakes. Right side route.

The following are a minor string of stones in the lowest part of the Orchard Cluster.
Stubby Stoner Boulder: VBss, VBss, VBss, SS all or bail.
Vice Boulder: V4 Cheap Shot (left), **V4 The Vice** (right next to maple tree).
Wander down slope a bit further to two more small stones:
Second Class Citizen Boulder: V0ss, V2ss. All on a very short flat vertical face.
Last Boulder: V2, V3, & V1. The lowest and last stone in the series.

Second Circuit Tour

Back on the main gravel access road continue walking south 200' to a 4-way road junction under the power lines (that run east-west). Walk east along the powerline access road (200'+) to a crest,

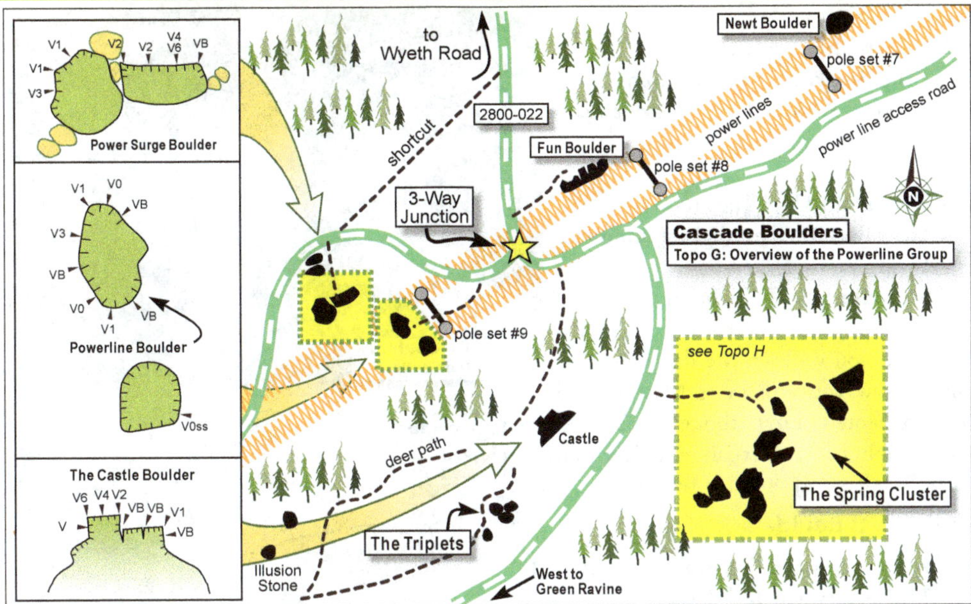

step left down slope to the Newt boulder.

Newt Boulder

VB Heatwave. On far left.

V0 Lizard. Steep face.

V4ss Salamander. Bump over the overhang then up slab.

V4ss Gravity. Bump up to arête then to top.

VB Cool Shade. Vertical face on far right with nice holds.

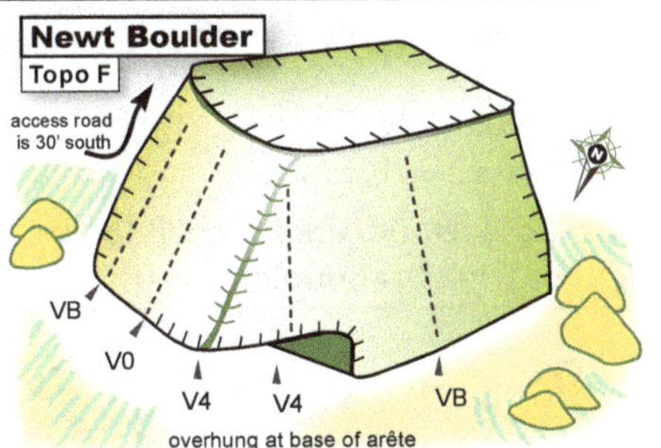

From the 4-way road junction proceed walking south on NF 2800-022 a short distance (crossing a tiny water rivulet), then step left and follow a brief faint path to The Spring Boulders, a nice cluster of blocks that still may yield additional potential problems. This cluster is just uphill and south of the dirt access road.

The Spring Cluster

Yields about a 20+ problems ranging from VB to V7, some as SS (see diagram for beta). Convenient access.

The Castle

Back again at the 4-day junction, proceed directly ahead southwest into the forest to The Castle. Beta

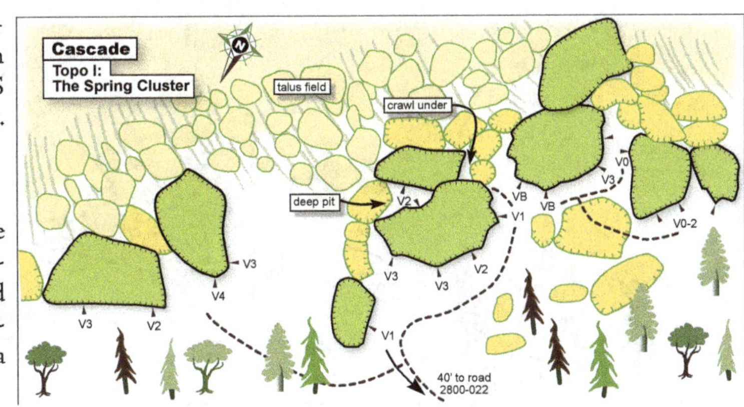

is left to right.

VB Secret Service. Left face.
V1 Big Break. Nice vertical arête.
VB Forest Monkeys. The obvious jam crack.
VB corner
V2 Keystone Cop. The arête
V4 Double-07. The slightly hung face with crimps
V6 Goldfinger. The right arête.

Now, if you walk on the flats west to a minor draw you will meet Mystery and Illusion Stones. First, though let's walk slightly uphill 150' west-ish on a deer trail to the Triplets and the Moe Boulder.

The Triplets Boulders

V3 Three Stooges. Vertical east arête.
V2 Silver Screen. Tech face.
V5 Silent Film. Bulge with thin, marginal crimps.
V0 Technicolor.
VB descent on back side.

Moe Boulder (located uphill to the right of Triplets about 20')

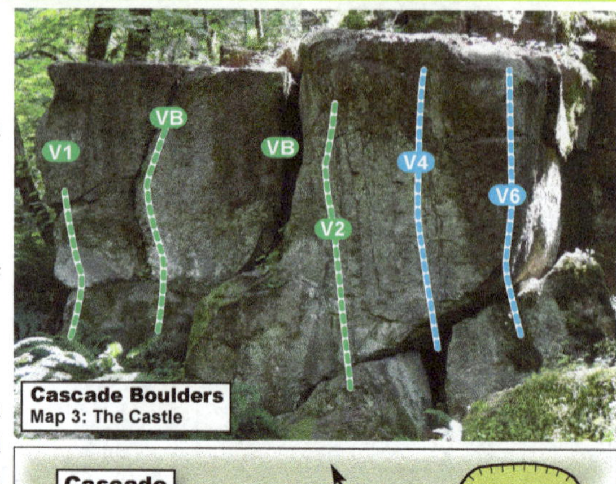

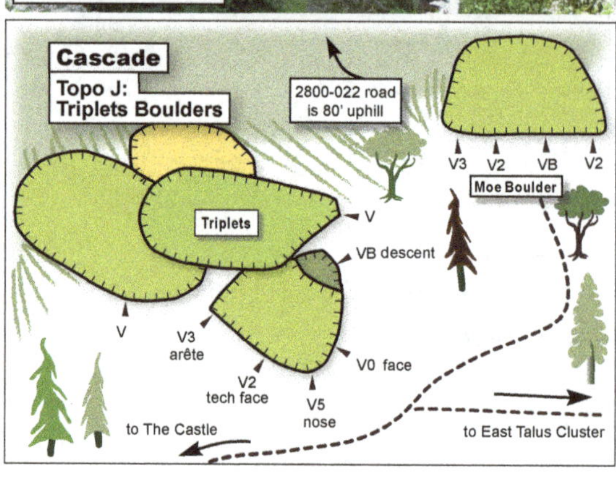

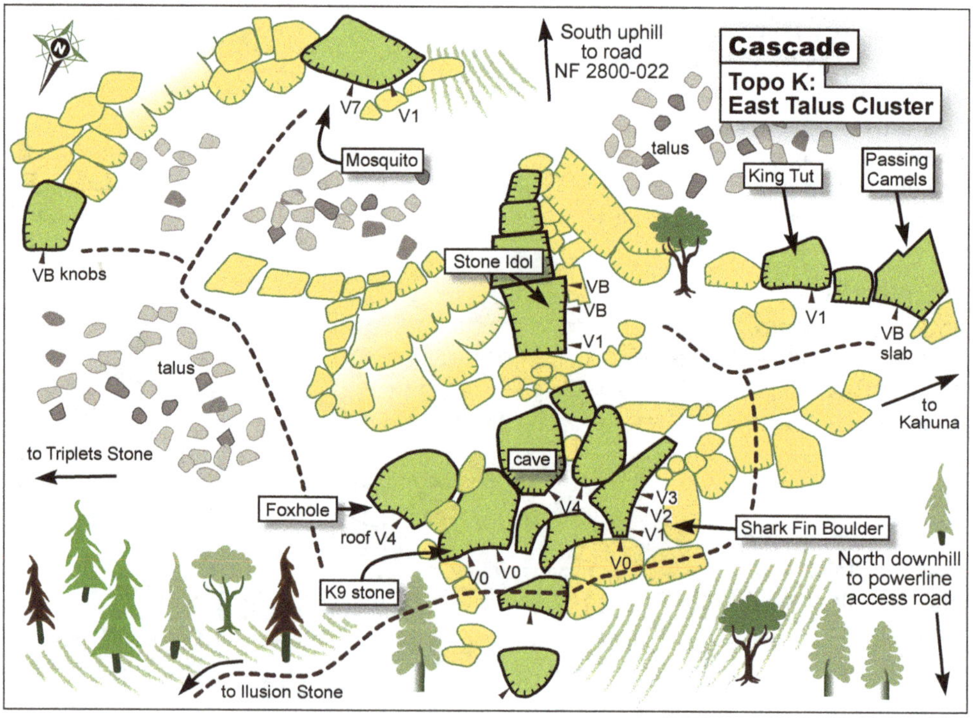

V3 **North face** (plus a variant), plus...**V2, VB, V2.**

Walking west from the Triplets about 100' dumps you in a minor low draw with a Mystery Stone and Illusion Stone (one nice problem **V1 Super Nova** is on Illusion Stone.

EAST TALUS GROUP

Now walk 80' angling uphill from Illusion to the East Talus Group. This complex cluster yields a dozen big stones up to 14' tall, all located near a single tall fir tree.

K9 Boulder (13' tall)

V0 K-9. Classic. Start low on right, and angle up left to incut jugs, then to top.
V0 Culture Shock. Cool. Start low at same spot, and dance up the thinner face to the right.

Shark Fin Boulder

V0 Shark Fin. SS tackles the fin straight on.
V1ss Aqua Mining. SS using the fin with your left, focus on the face straight up.
V2 Great White. SS and work face up to right.
V3 Hammerhead. Traverse entire face right, top out.

Six Boulders

V4ss Foxhole Boulder. Roof and a brief traverse.
V3 & V4 Cave Boulder. Has two problems.
VB (& V3) Sloped Boulder (downhill from K9 stone).
VB & V0ss Bowing to Stone Idols is 11' tall with a nice vertical west face (+variations).
V2ss King Tut Boulder. A shorty.
VB Passing Camels. Tall smear slab with variations.

Mosquito Boulder (80' to the south)

V7 Jungle Juice. Start low, power up left on crimps, over sloping bulge to top.
V1 Mosquito Eater. Face move up right onto slab.

Now walk west across the open talus field to the far upper west end. There you will find the biggest monsters in the park (Kahuna, Crown Jewel, and another beast).

Big Kahuna Boulder (35' long x 15' wide)

V6 Squeezebox. Tucked in a very narrow slot on far right.
V1 Kahuna. Directly mantle onto the top dish left of high point.
V0 Goats of Corruption. Direct mantle onto another sloped dish.
V2ss Grand Strategy. Start low on left and run the rail lip rightward to V1 and up.
V5+ (?) Kahuna Traverse. Either half rail (north end or west end). The full rail has ob-

Cascade - East Talus
Topo 4: Stone Idols

stacle, though it might yield V6+ if obstacle does not hinder.

Crown Jewel Boulder

Just uphill a few yards is a long block with a low rail.

V2ss Crown Jewel. Up short flake and mantle.

V2 Laid Back is the traverse (and the 'diving platform' V1 is at lower right end of stone).

Broken Beast

Big broken beast stone immediately west of CJ is about 35' long, but broken.

VB crack n' up.

V4 (?) full lip traverse from the crack n' up start, going left along lip.

GREEN RAVINE GROUP

Just over the rock knoll about 80' from Crown Jewel, tucked in a minor ravine (immediately below the NF 2800-022 road that leads to Herman Creek Trail) is another final string of boulders, the Green Ravine Group. This spot is the upper edge of the long East Talus Field where it finally encounters the dirt access road. To reach the Green Ravine Group it is easiest to walk NF 2800-022 from the power lines (past The Spring Cluster) over to this point, then descend a few yards directly to the boulders, which sits at the edge of the dirt road. This locale is .7 mile from the paved road (.3 mile from the power lines). This section has a string of good quality problems.

Oligarch Boulder

Beta is counterclockwise starting with the descent line on the west side.

VB Global March. west slab.

V1 Something Wonky This Way Coming.

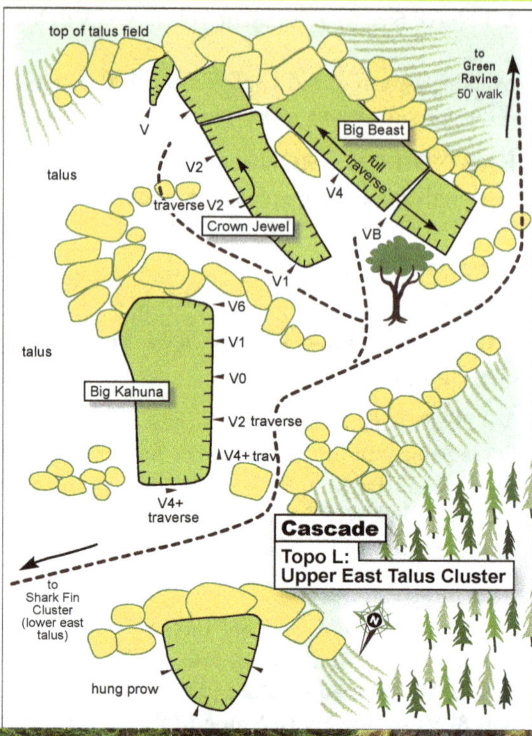

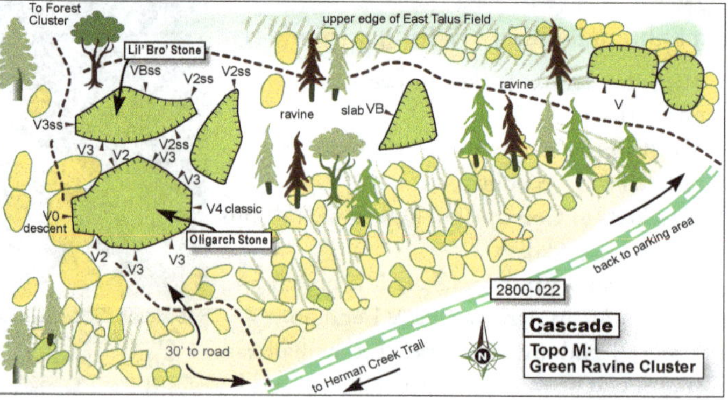

Slight groove corner on south side.

V3 Thin Ice. Thin tech crimps up flat vertical face on south side straight up.

V3 Shonky World Gone Wonky. Tech opener move, reach up right, catch lip, fast mantle to slab.

V6 Spy. Ultra-classic. SS low on holds under lip, catch lip, high step into position, lean forward and while using momentum slap for a pocket in the middle on top. Yowza!

V3 Throw 'Em Down. Start down left on face, catch round lip, move up right along lip, then mantle onto slab.

V3 Secret Service. Straight up the minor vertical rib feature on north side.

V4 FBI. Steep slab 'n jus' smears on NW side.

V1 Private Eye. Slightly left of descent on steep slab.

Lil' Bro' Boulder

V3ss Stone Cold. Left of west nose.

V4ss Deadpoint President. The west nose

V4ss A Jackson. Just right of west nose.

V2ss Six Feet Under. Deep pit on SE side.

VBss __. Left of tree.

V0ss Foot Locker. On east nose.

Note: A third boulder has minor V0ss-V3ss. Several blocks in the ravine to the east have also been sent (VB).

EAST FOREST GROUP

Just west of the previous stones tucked in an extensive forest are a selection of large boulders and a few tiny stones near a talus zone square between Cabbage Boulder and Oligarch Stone. These boulders will be detailed in future edi-

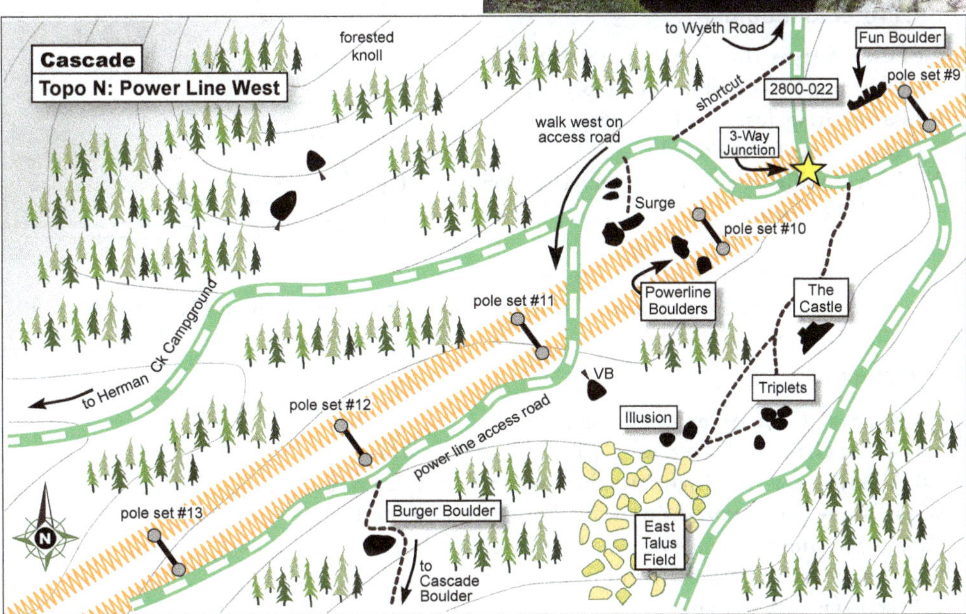

tions.

Clockwork Boulder V0-V5ss [6 lines].
Diamond Boulder V0-V5ss [4 lines].
Cape Boulder V1-V4ss [3 lines].
So, that completes the second circuit tour.

THIRD CIRCUIT TOUR

This third tour begins at the 4-way junction where NF 2800-022 goes beneath the power lines. Walk west 100′ to power pole set #9. Immediately beyond the poles are two large stones.

Powerline Boulder

VB Power Plant. South sunny side rounded prow.
V1 High Voltage
V0 Generator
VB Steps n' Jugs
V3ss Lightning Bolt (the seam)
V1 Amp'd tackles just right of the north nose.
V0 Solar tackles the north side nose straight on.
VB Power Outage. A minor slab.
V2 entire traverse. Phew...all on a boulder the size of a cow. Moooving on to better things.

Go back a few yards east to the access road. This road veers north into the forest and 'U' turns shortly back out again under the powerlines further west. Walk this until you can tuck into the forest anywhere and aim for two boulders tucked in the middle of this 'U'.

Surge Protector Boulder

V4 Power Surge. Thin face, crimp & side pulls.
V6 Lightning Strike. Thin face, sloper & side pulls.
V2 Power Strip. Just left of the arête.
V2 Short Fuse. Arête on right.
Blackout Boulder is next door and has **V1** on left, **V1** middle, **V3** on right.

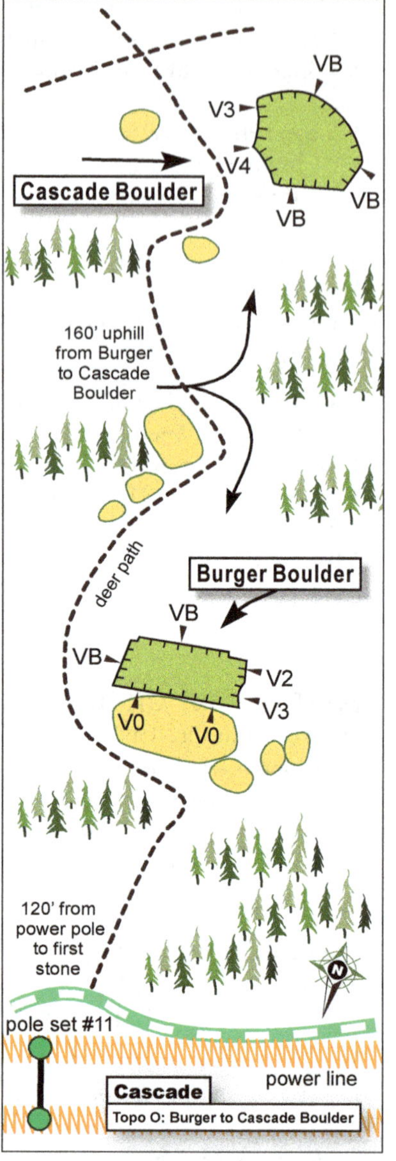

Continue west on the powerline access road west to the next pole set #11. From power pole set #11 walk southwest into forest about 150′ to reach the first boulder in this string.

Burger Boulder

VB Runner's Edge. Arête on left end of flat face.
V0 (V1ss) Great Wall Left. use the left part of the flat face.
V0 (V2ss) Great Wall Right. use the right part of the flat face.
V3ss Torque Convertor. the prow on the right end of the flat face.
V2ss Eight Ounce. the scoop immediately right of the prow.
V2 Mono's On My Mind w/o pocket (V3 w/pocket).
VB get down back side anywhere.

V4 Great Wall Traverse. Start on Mono's line, traverse to first line.

From Burger Boulder hike south 180' uphill on a deer path to the next boulder.

WEST FOREST GROUP

Cascade Boulder

This is the 'first' official boulder tapped in this entire region at the Cascade Boulders zone (beyond the two initial roadside stones).

VB Grease. dance up rightward on slopers and smears (NE side).

V4 BLT. Classic tech smears and pinches up center nose of east face (traverse in low makes V5). Variations exist.

V3 Milkshake. dance up the left side from the center of the east face.

VB First Base. descent south or west side.

A few yards south of Cascade Boulder is a 4-way path junction for several deer trails. North (downhill) goes to Burger Boulder. East rambles (500') over to the East Talus Cluster passing some extra blocks (East Forest Group). South leads to Cabbage Boulder, the Proud Pedestal, and the Classic Rail in the West Talus field. Walking west leads to the Pocket Boul-

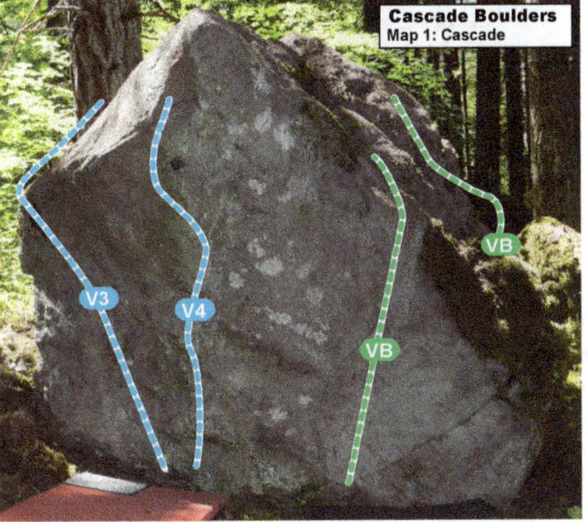

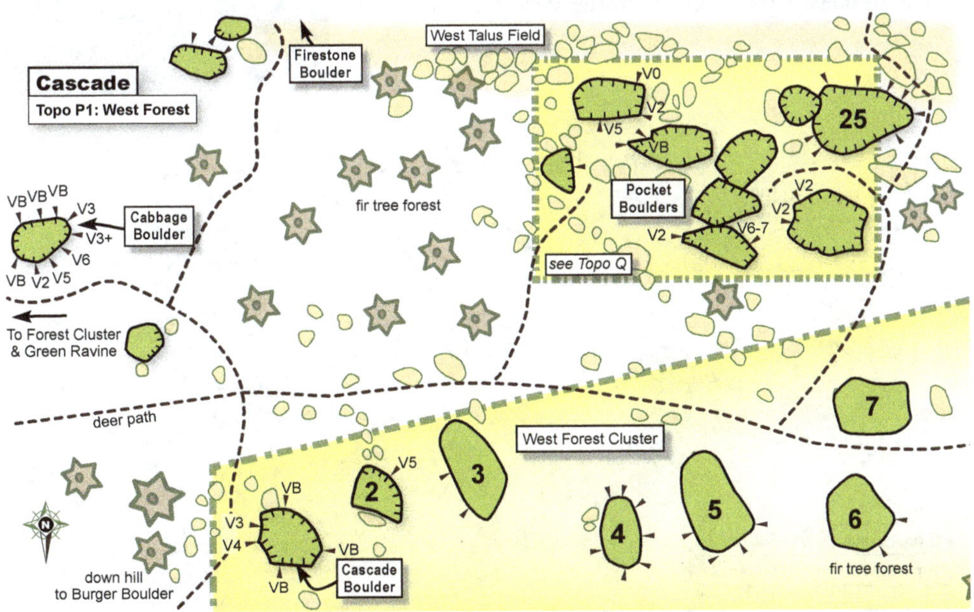

ders, then way over to Iceberg Hole (all a part of West Talus Cluster). The zone from Cascade Boulder westward in the forest is the West Forest Group and will be detailed in future editions of the book.

Cabbage Boulder

Starting with the cabbage-meister, walk a mere 80' on the south trail to a round cannonball with a cone-*ish* point & 360° problems. Difficult problems are due to its slightly overhung nature on the lower half and lack of foot holds and limited crimps. The south side is a slab.

VB Speaking with Forked Tongue. The obvious knobby face to the prow.

V2 Razor Cut. Scoop at your knee, go up rounded nose on north side.

V5 Ignoramus. Several small crimps, long reach to a tiny rail, then to top edges.

V6 Ringworm. grip the sliver flake, tuck and reach.

V3+ Kimchi. Rounded west side.

V3 Cafe Suavé. Lw on round aspect using slight dish.

VB Metastasis. south slab left side.

VB Me2. South slab center.

VB Me Me. South slab right side.

OK, enough here. Follow a continuing faint path south 50' more to one section of the West Talus Cluster. This section will be broken into batches that fit convenient pathways to three popular sections: Classic Rail area, the Pocket Boulders, and

On the classic Rail Traverse

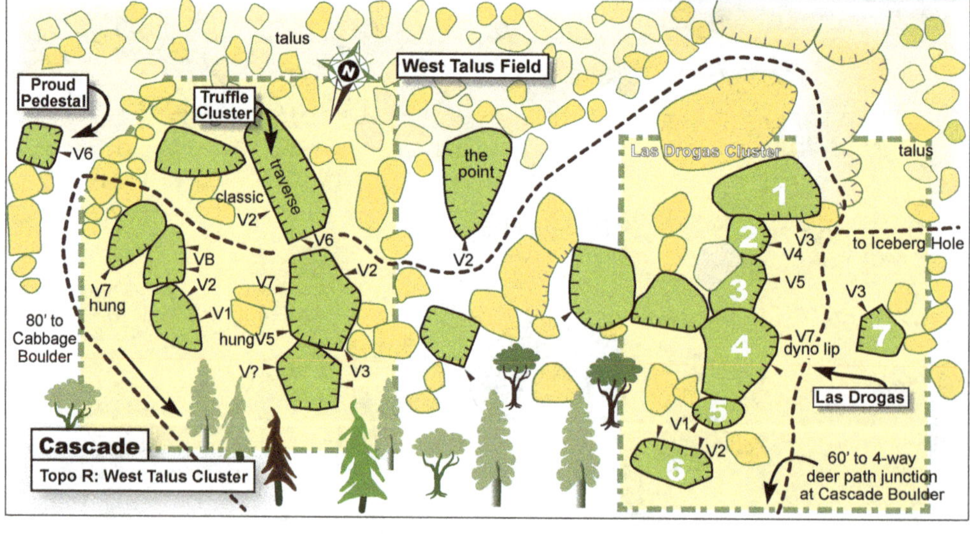

Iceberg Hole area (see diagram). First stop is:

WEST TALUS GROUP

Truffle Cluster

V6ss Power pedestal is a tall smooth west facing aspect of an isolated stone. V2 (V4ss) right exit.

V4ss The Tooth begins underneath and goes out to lip.

V2 (V6ss) Truffle Shuffle. The V2 is just doing the lip traverse. V6ss starts low on end at far right side, use both left/right ribs, catch lip, turn corner, and traverse the entire long crisp rail leftward. Direct begins low at end on sharp pinches, launch up to catch the rail then run left.

The entire Truffle Cluster group offers numerous problems ranging from VB to V7+ on a half dozen large boulders.

V2 The Point is a brief overhung lip.

A brief walk further west in the talus brings you to...

Las Drogas Boulder

Continuing westward in the talus field you quickly reach this compact little alcove.

Beta L to R on four stones: **V2ss Slick Shoes** (on 1st stone), **V3 Las Drogas** classic dyno (on 2nd stone) starts low then super dyno to lip and mantle over. **V2ss Rocky Road** (3rd stone), **V3ss Skeleton Keys** (4th stone).

On the backside of the Las Drogas dyno bloc is a tiny nook with several problems on two stones. VB (V1ss) is the north block. The south block is V2, V7ss, and V?.

Just west of Las Drogas dyno is a minor tall block: **V2 Pincers of Power** hung face, and V0 east

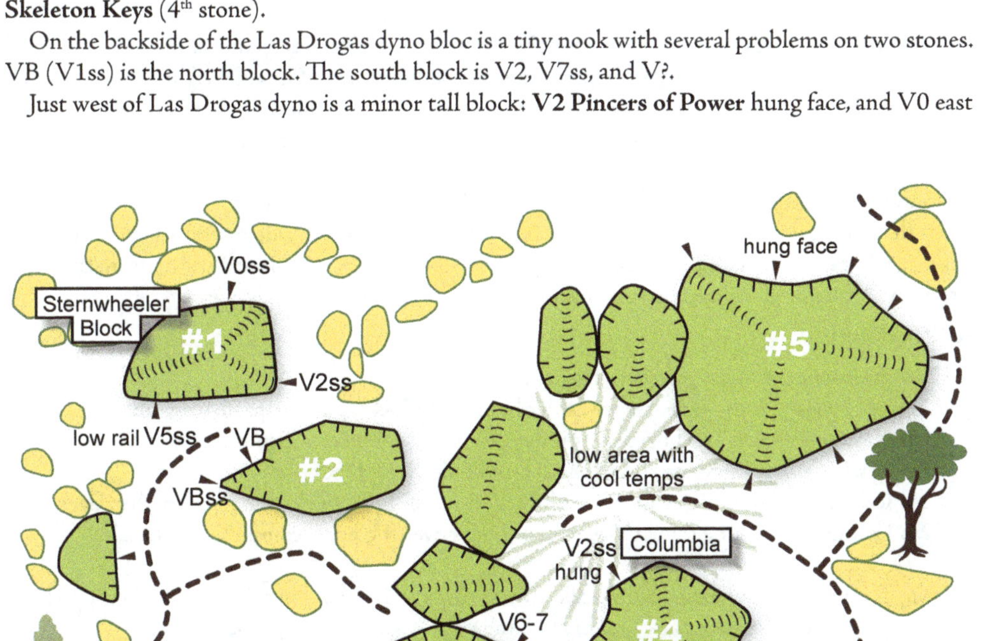

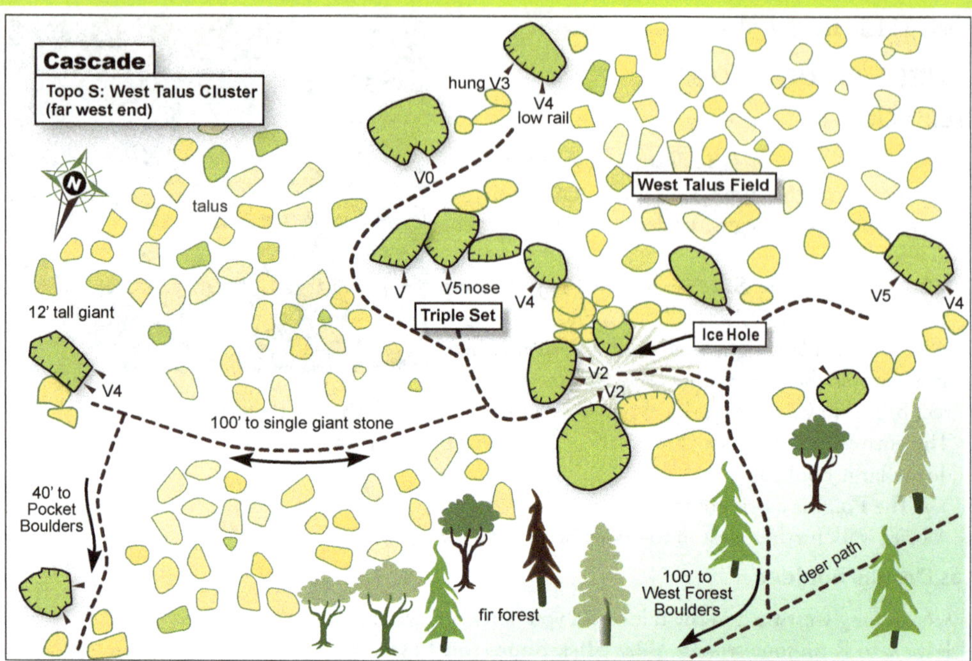

point.

From the dyno boulder walk north into the forest to the deer path (lands a few yards west of Cabbage Bloc). From the 4-way deer path junction walking west. On your right (25' west from Cascade Boulder) you will pass a low oblong donut shaped block called Cookie Boulder.

V5ss Some Like It Wet. Start low on right and run the round slopers up left.

Continue west on the deer path a few more yards, then turn south (left) and enter a low area called the Pocket Boulders. Its about 75' west of the real **Cascade Boulder**, and this small zone offers a tightly packed string of seven large blocks. This low area has cool air wafting up from the deep pits around the boulders keeping this cluster comfortable even on summer days.

Pocket Boulders

V5ss Sternwheeler. Low rail on (#1 block) east end.
V2ss Lex Artis. On the same sternwheeler block (#1 block), punch up the west rib.
V6-7ss Perseverance. The business boulder (#3 block). Start low, crimps, slap, catch, sloper.
V2ss Lex Loci. The opposite end of the same perseverance block, up a low prow.
V2ss Icebox. On Columbia Block (#4 block). SS under lip, move right along lip, then over.
V2ss Columbia is on the same block, and bounces over the lip, then up the south slab.

From the Pocket Boulders cluster walk around the big Bertha stone (VB-V4), then up slope onto the talus a few yards to one other big (12' tall) stone with several problems (V2-3).

Wrapping this section up...we proceed back to the deer path. Walk west along the deer path in the forest for approximately 100', then turn left (south) and enter onto the talus slope at the Iceberg Hole. This area offers perhaps 10-12 problems, scattered across 8 large boulders (see map), ranging from V2-V5 approx. This is the utter west end of the West Talus boulder field. So, there you have

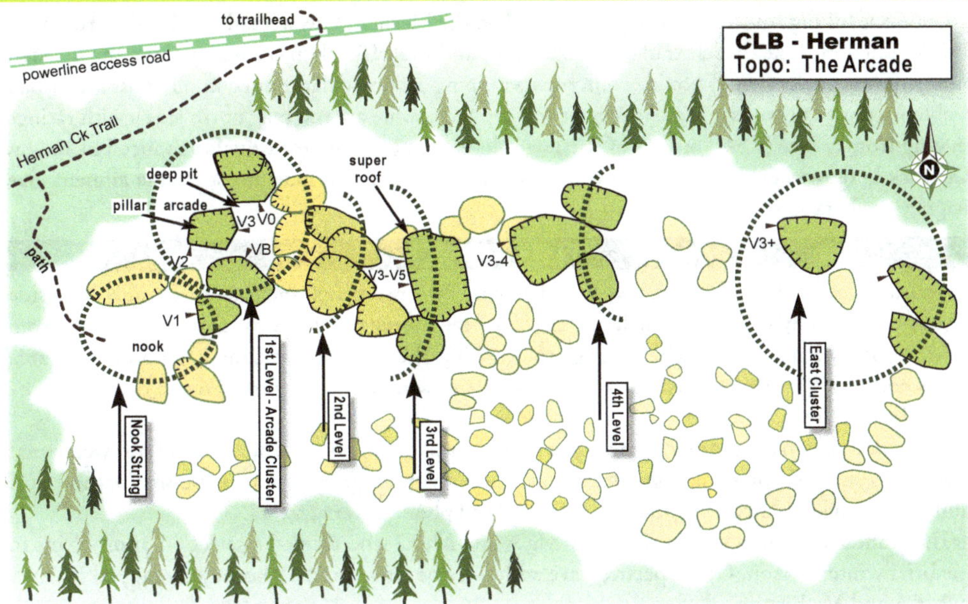

it — the official **Cascade Boulders** *tour-de-force* circuit.

HERMAN BOULDERS

Arcade Boulders

A minor, minimally used site alongside the Herman Creek Trail called the Arcade. Convenient access, but limited potential. Drive I-84 to Cascade Locks, then drive old Hwy 30 past Oxbow fish hatchery to Herman Creek Campground. Park at the day use area, and walk up the hikers trail ¼ mile, past the power lines, then step left to a cluster of large stones.

The diagram details "strings" as tiers or levels: the initial entrance nook level, the arcade deep pit level, and so on, with each succeeding higher level of stacked boulders (2, 3, 4, etc). Problems range from V0 to V7 approximately (see diagram). The Arcade Cluster was tapped by Mr Slayton and associates.

Tabletop Group

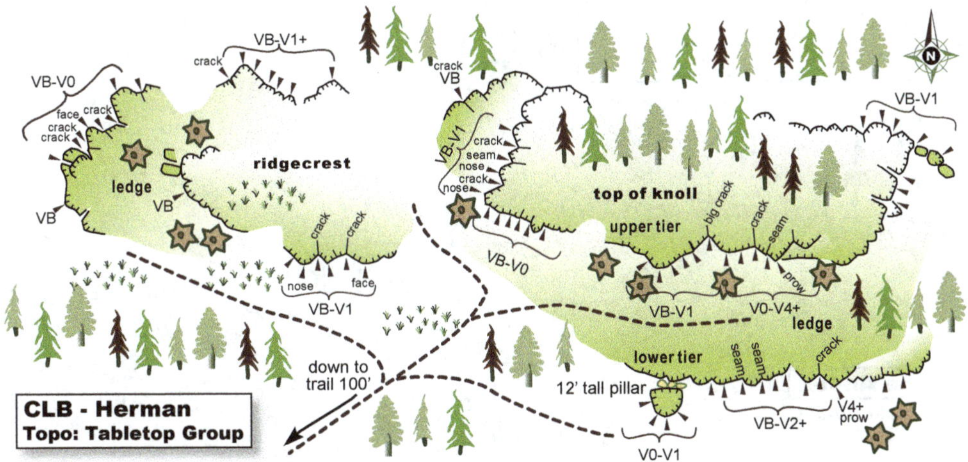

Continue hiking south (past the power lines) on the Herman Creek Trail. In ¼ mile it reaches a trail 'Y' junction. Take the left trail (Herman Trail) and walk 100' then cut left uphill to the forested butte. Here is a selection of boulder outcrops wrapping around a flat topped knoll, most are hi-ball problems, unusually mossy (considering it was tapped), some are too tall (north side), with ratings ranging from VB to V6+ (mostly of the lower level ratings). The rock quality is nice but mossy. The rock knoll was explored briefly by an unknown with a mysterious mossophobia ailment. See diagram for beta estimates.

THE ANNEX

An extension of the Cascade Locks Boulders with 50+ problems, and easily accessible alongside Wyeth Road. Many stones are small in size (8'-10' tall average). Problems range in difficulty from VB-V4 (SS yields slightly higher ratings to V6-*ish*). The open forest zone has minor Mahonia plants and fern growth, but generally is windswept in winter and easy to navigate because of the lack of brushy areas.

A circuit tour can be done by following various deer paths. Rock type nuances are soft weathered edges with some slight surface grit texture, and minor moss growth. Extras points: natural duff landings, a single crashpad viable zone, and good cell phone coverage.

The Annex was initially tapped first by Mr A and Mr O who tackled a selection of problems in one brief winter season. Other parties have added to the sites variety (thoroughly tapped in 2018 by Mr A and Mr Bishop).

Directions

Drive I-84 to Cascade Locks, then drive old U.S. Hwy 30 past Oxbow fish hatchery (past Herman Creek Campground) to exit #45, then turn east on old U.S. Hwy 30 (Wyeth Road) and drive for .7 mile, and park alongside the main road (at a spur dirt road) across from the boulders. Walk north 80' into the forest on a deer path.

Bouldermania Stone

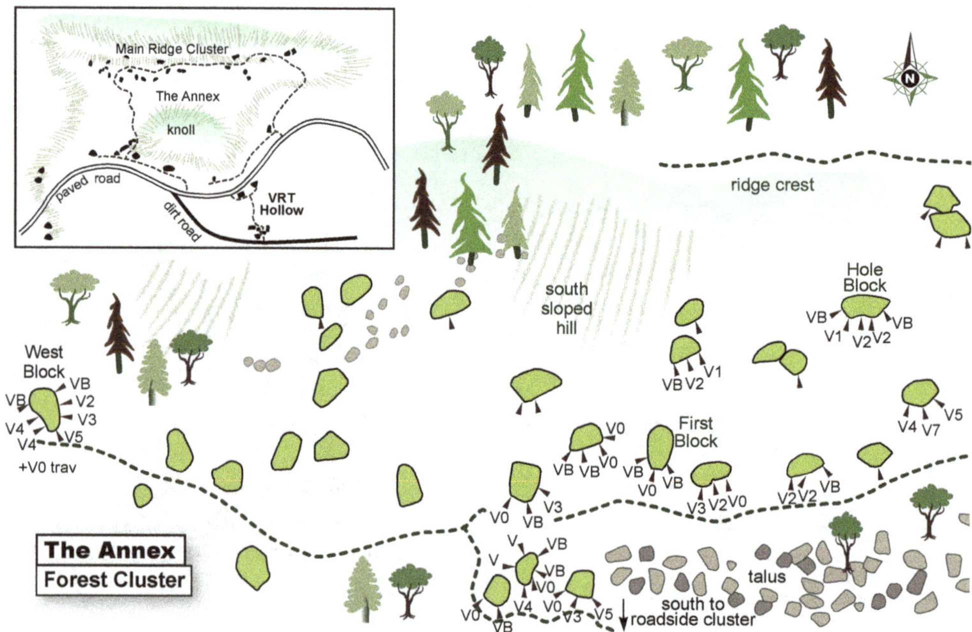

This is the closest stone to the road.

V0ss Nesting Instinct. Low and up, a bounce move, on far left.

V4ss Bouldermania. Classic problem.

V3+ Credentialed Ignorance. Standing and power over bulge

V3 (V7ss) Divine Spark Within. Power bulge on right.

V2ss Salesmen, Vultures, and Warriors. Undercling start (on far right).

First Block

The first boulder problems ever done at the Annex.

VB E=MC² The left side.

V0 Rudderless Shipload of Fools Bound For Nowhere. The nose.

VB Cowboy Capitalist. The right side.

Go Stone has several quality short SS problems on hung aspect. **Beast Stone**, located along the ridge crest at the far east end is the largest stone at the Annex (VB to V1 options).

VRT HOLLOW

Just across Wyeth road on its south side a minor foot path descends to several roadside boulders, and a path continues south to the next series of boulders.

Ghost Boulder (L to R) (#A)

V0ss Stars, V4 Thumb Tac's (traverse), VB (V4) Oh Maria (nose), V6 Waste Some Time, V2ss She

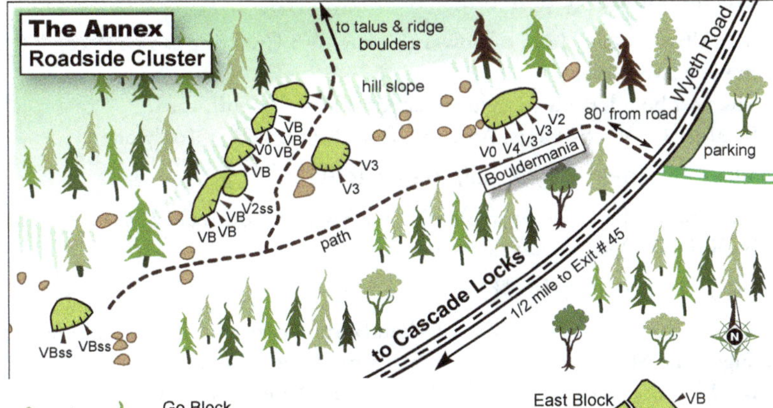

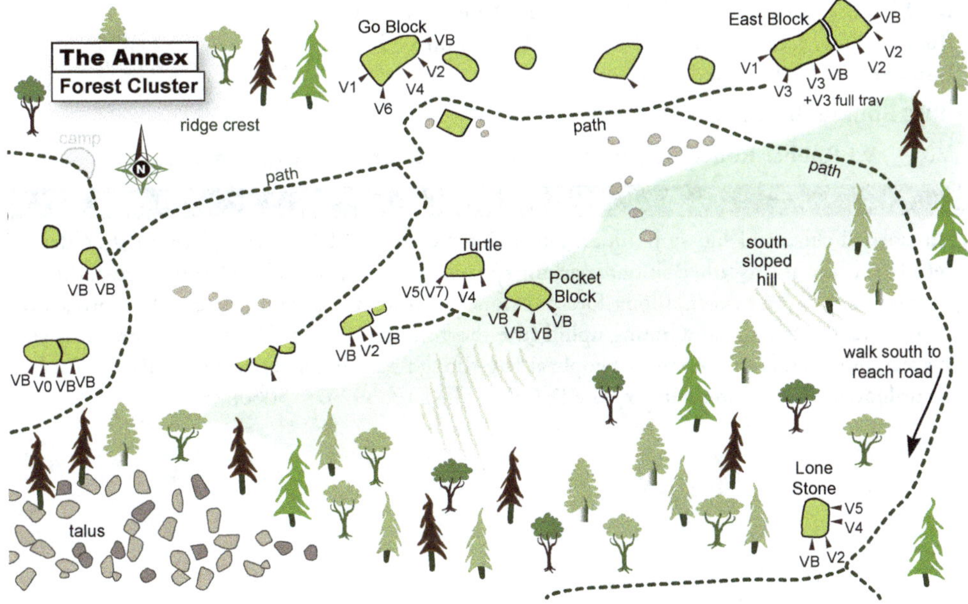

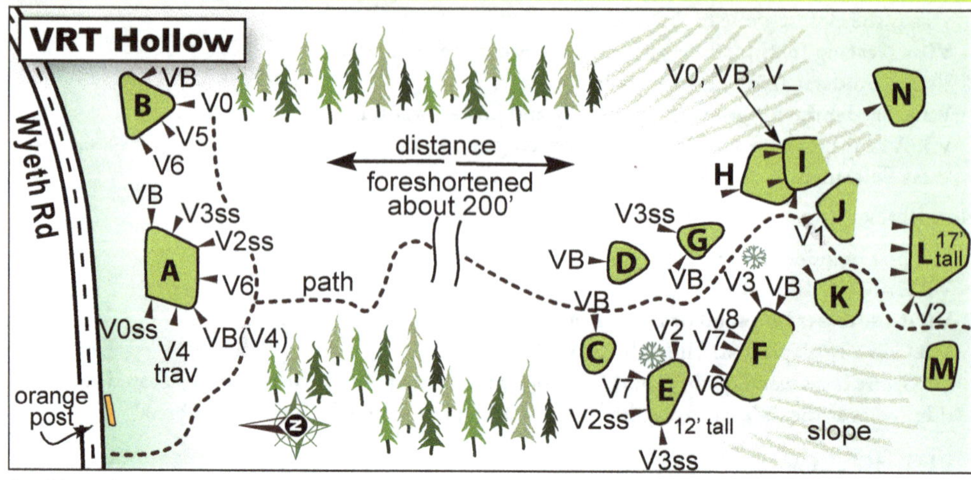

Said (nose), **V3ss Living Proof** (two pockets), **VB Lillooet**.

Ellenside Boulder (L to R) (#B)

V3 (V6ss) Right Hand of Power (far left), **V5 Crashing Down** (face), **V0 January** (nose), **VB Same For Everyone**.

The next boulders are in a cluster about 200' walk southward.

Boulder C: VB Seasons. And on....**Boulder D: VB __** (only one).

Molinos Boulder (#E) (12' tall) (beta L to R)

V2ss Easy Chair (left of tree), **V7 Save Me** (right of tree), **V2ss Good Thing** (SS low on jug), **V3ss Rain On Me** (at west nose).

Beauty Boulder (L to R) (#F)

VB La Bruga (flat face), **V3ss Indian Summer** (outer), **V8 First One to Fire** (direct), **V7 A Gringo Like Me** (start same, exit right), **V6ss Sheeps Ass**.

Boulder G: V3ss Pound a Week Rise, VB Devil Away (knobs).

Boulder I (flat faced slab): **VB Mary** (L), **V0 Cantares** (R), **V_ __**.

Boulder J: V1ss Crooked Grin.

Tenure Boulder (L) 18' tall (beta L to R)

V0 __, **V1 Rubber Rodeo** (center), **V1 Bone Pile**, **V2 Sister Sara** (far right nose).

LABYRINTH

An isolated cluster of mossy boulders surprisingly close to I-84 freeway. Park on shoulder of Wyeth Road east of Cascade Boulders parking spot. Some non-path off-trail minor brush thrashing a fair distance (and down a long forested slope) to reach the secluded spot. Or approach by parking along the freeway and hiking uphill (the shortest approach) to the cluster. The locale and lush green moss tends to keep most people at bay, though with boulders up to 12' diameter it has some utilitarian value (minimally explored). GPS UTM 10t 592075 5060888.

EASTERN COLUMBIA GORGE

HORSETHIEF BUTTE

The popular Horsethief Butte offers an ideal respite from the liberal amounts of western Oregon rain where you can often find sunny weather crag climbing by the Columbia River.

For rock climbers it offers a tremendous variety of short boulder problems within a series of corridors in the inner portion of the butte. This site offers an effective means to practice and enhance the basic concepts of rock climbing and rappeling. The natural open atmosphere of the inner butte offers easy communication from instructor to climber.

Brief History of the Area

The Butte is a prominent feature within the Columbia Hills State Park and is a popular site for climbing as well as hiking. The nearby lake was formed when The Dalles Dam was built.

For centuries local American Indians lived near the Butte. The ease of access to the river also provided excellent opportunity for them to catch some of the seasonal migration of salmon for food and for barter. Celilo Falls was the heart of a long established trading region that sustained a thriving community of native Indians from the Wisham, Cloud and Lishkam tribes. The Lewis and Clark expedition camped at a village during their journey west in 1805-1806. Salmon caught near the Celilo Falls provided an important source for trade and barter with other indigenous native tribes of the region. Excellent remnants of native Indian petroglyphs such as *she who watches* provide visitors with archeological insight of ancient tribal customs.

Visitor considerations and state park regulations

✦ Horsethief Butte has several areas signed as 'no climbing' for cultural resource protection. Columbia Hills State Park has archeological sites including Horsethief Butte which are protected by State and Federal laws. Disturbance and/or removal of any artifact, pictograph, or petroglyph is prohibited.

✦ Expect windy conditions.

✦ Beware of the occasional rattlesnake. Frequent visitor foot traffic tends to keep most rattlesnakes at a distance.

✦ Poison Oak grows along the base of several walls. This thick short shrub has seasonal glossy leaves which grow in groups of three per branch and have small white berries.

✦ Ticks are common in the Spring and Fall seasons. Ticks are quite small so be certain to inspect frequently for ticks if you visit here. There is a plethora of bouldering problems far beyond what this section could possibly convey, but this in-depth treatise strives to detail the greater portion of the well traveled climbs found at the Butte.

Most of the beta within this particular section includes dual grades. First is the bouldering V-scale grade, listed as if you are going to treat the problem as a bouldering event. Immediately followed by the standard YDS grade (5.9, etc) as if you are going

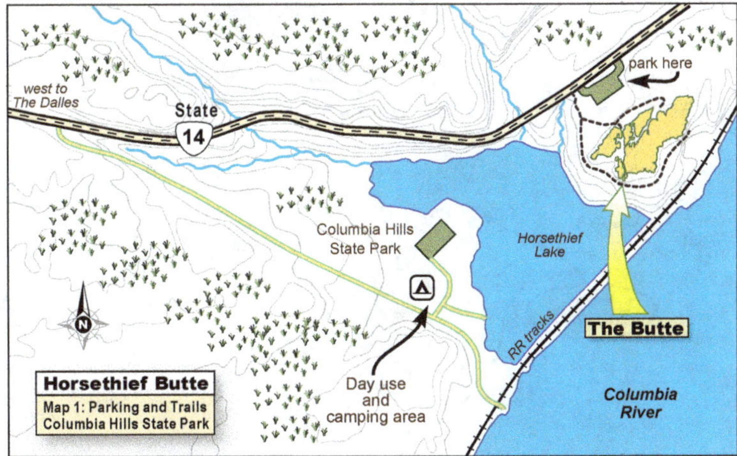

to lead (or top-rope) the problem. Many problems here are hi-ball. A few routes are generally only viable as top-rope or lead routes. Many of the problems here have at one time or another been solo bouldered (even though many do have substantial height risk issues). Horsethief Butte is ideal for, and often utilized for, both types (bouldering or climbing) of recreation activity. For the boulderer it's a nice all-year place to carefully learn some hi-ball technique on often easy climbing terrain. Just beware that certain landings need well padded.

Directions

Directions from Oregon: From exit #87 at The Dalles drive north across the Columbia River bridge on U.S. 197 for 3½ miles, then east on Washington State 14 for 2¾ miles to Columbia Hills State Park. The Butte is located east of the lake at Mile Post 85. Park along the highway shoulder immediately across a small bridge. Hike on the path south to the butte and enter either via the west side trail or at the 'Entrance Cracks' gap in the wall. Camping (closed from Nov. thru March) is available at the developed facility on the west side of the 90-acre Horsethief lake. Climb safely and enjoy your visit!

ENTRANCE CRACKS

1. OW & Hand Crack VB (5.9) ★★

Left of the left prow are several climbs in the shaded portion of the bluff. Both begin up the same crack using edges and steps. From the midway stance, embark up *left* in a wide offwidth crack using a small hidden edge in the offwidth which leads to better edges at the top. The *right* jam crack is closer to the arête. Ascend the lower crack to the midway stance, then embark up right into a jam crack which forces you to use the arête more than the crack. There are several more thin optional climbs just to the left of these two climbs that are fairly difficult.

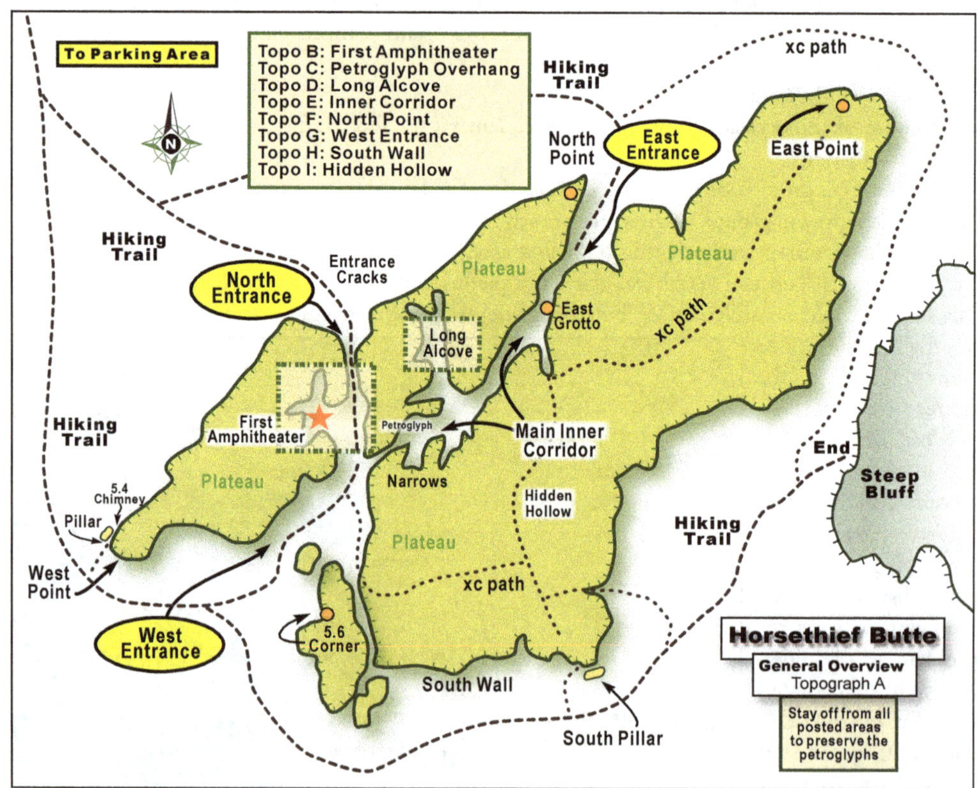

2.   Jam Crack VB (5.9)   ★★

Great hand and fist jam climb. Start initially in the Left Entrance Crack and punch out left to a short vertical jam crack.

3.   Left Entrance Crack V1 (5.10+)   ★★★

This is the left major corner system. Ascend the steep tricky corner by smearing delicately on smooth sloped holds using the thin crack where possible. No such thing as a free lunch.

4.   Arête V5 (5.12)

Between the two Entrance Crack routes is a technical minor arête top-rope.

5.   Right Entrance Crack V0 (5.10-)   ★★★

This is the right most (and best) of two classic corner systems known as the Entrance Cracks. Involves long reaches, technical smears, and powerful layback moves using a jam crack. On the right face of this entrance crack is another minor seam that branches up right at about 5.9.

THE PASSAGEWAY

These two under-age minors are together on the east wall of the Passageway just as it opens into the First Amphitheater.

6.   Face V0 (5.10-)

A short smooth face ending on a ledge.

7.   Arête V1 (5.10+)

Another short problem next to the previous.

The next two steep lines are found on the west wall of The Passageway.

8.   Corner VB (5.8)   ★

Layback up the pillar and stem the corner.

9.   Corner VB (5.7)   ★

Climb up a crack in a corner with a long reach to finish.

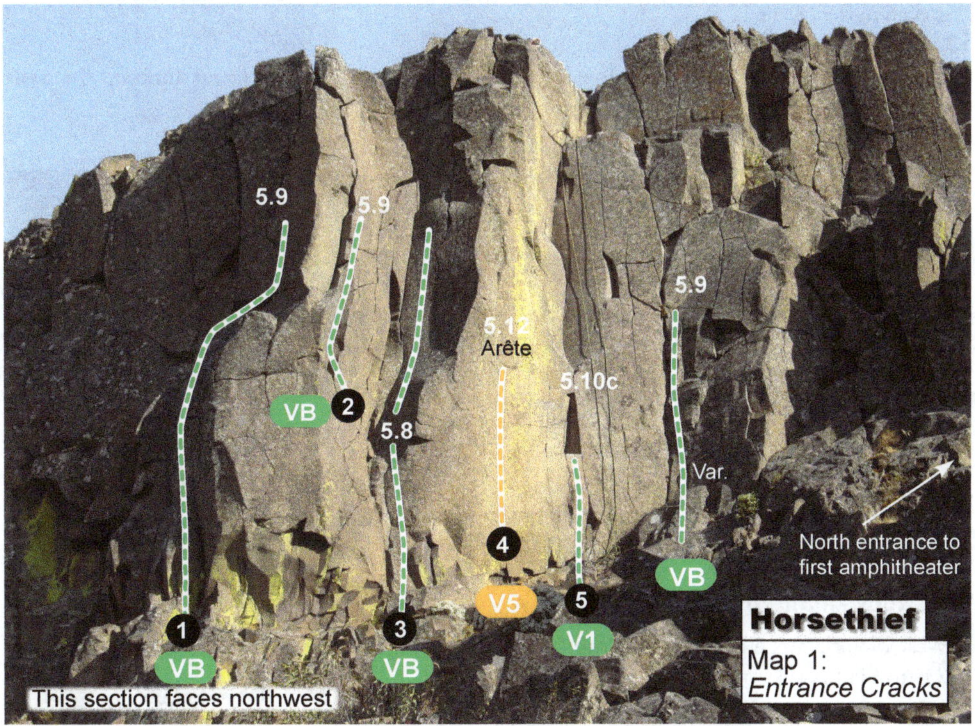

FIRST AMPHITHEATER

The following string begins on the west side of the Passageway and curls around the initial buttress counter-clockwise into the First Main Amphitheater. Two nooks (north tree nook and west nook) provide a great series of problems.

Wide Buttress

10. Groove V0 (5.10-)
Right side of the buttress.

11. Smooth Dihedral VB (5.7)
In the middle of the buttress climb up a dihedral corner using jams and stemming.

12. Discontinuous Cracks V0 (5.10-)
Broken cracks on left most side of buttress.

Tree Nook

A tiny nook with a small tree tucked in the corner.

13. Face VB (5.9) ★
Deep in the Tree Nook on the left side before the small tree is a tall face. Climb up the well-featured and cracked patina face to a tricky finish.

14. Crack-Prow V1 (5.10+)
In the same Tree Nook left of the tall face is a crack/prow. You can jam or bear hug this.

Half Nook

15. Thin Crack V1 (5.10+)
A stubby. Use the right diagonal crack on a smooth slab.

16. Green Slab VB
This is the outermost nose of a low angle slab.

17. Prow V1 (5.10+)
Climb the left side of the prow to a mantle.

18. Overhang V1 (5.10c)
Start on a left trending seam. Climb up to a jug and mantle.

West Nook - Right routes

West Nook offers a great punchy thin traverse all the way to Half Nook.

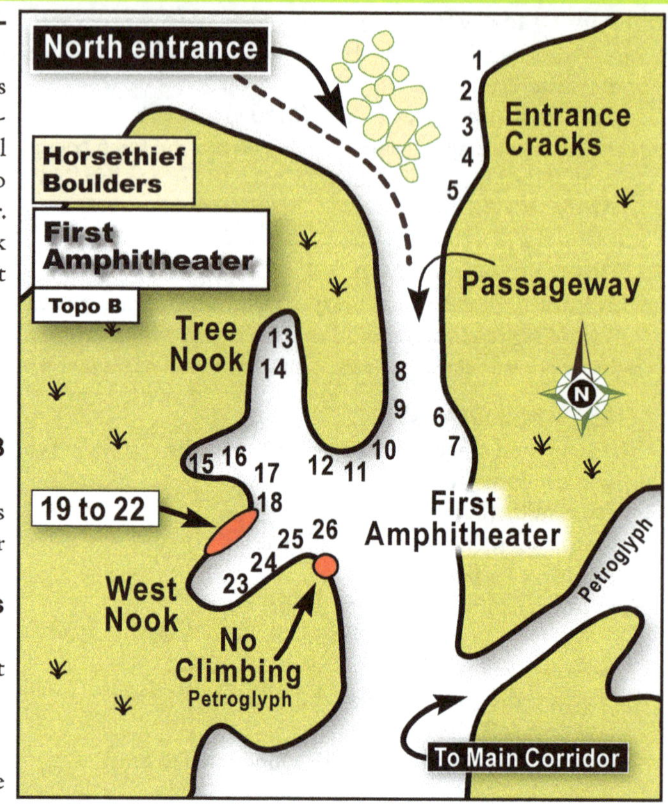

19. Flake VB (5.8)

A great warm up flake climb.

20. Crack Seam V1 (5.10+) ★★★

This classic line (and the next one) are the central feature of the West Nook. They offer complexity, steepness, and quality great for bouldering or for a top-rope.

21. Corner V2 to V4 (5.11- / 5.12) ★★★

Stellar V2 thin crack corner that is much harder than it looks. Using rules staying in the crack will make it V3. Traversing in from the far left then up the corner crack is V4.

22. Face V7 (5.13-)

Climb the thin face left of the corner using just the small holds on the face.

West Nook - Left routes

23. Low Angle Face VB

This is on the south side of the West Nook. Climb up on jug holds.

24. Face V0 (5.10-)

Climb up through the missing block.

25. Crack System V2 (5.11-)

Start on the jug and climb up the shallow crack to a flake.

26. Arête (CLOSED)

This is the outer buttress with posted off-limits signs informing visitors of the aboriginal petroglyph graffiti.

INNER CORRIDOR

From the First Main Amphitheater walk through a small opening in the cliff scarp (The Narrows). This quickly opens up into the Main Inner Corridor or Grotto. On your immediate left is the Petroglyph Overhang and just beyond (also on the left) is the Sunny Patina. A smidge beyond on the left is the Long Alcove. If you continue walking directly east all the way through this Main Inner Corridor you will pass the Long Wall and exit out the East Entrance to the North Point.

THE NARROWS & PETROGLYPH OVERHANG (TOPO C)

The first five problems are located on the right (south) wall in The Narrows just as you are entering the Main Corridor across from the 'off-limits' sign on the opposite side of the corridor.

27. Thin Crack V1 (5.10+)

Jam the crack in the

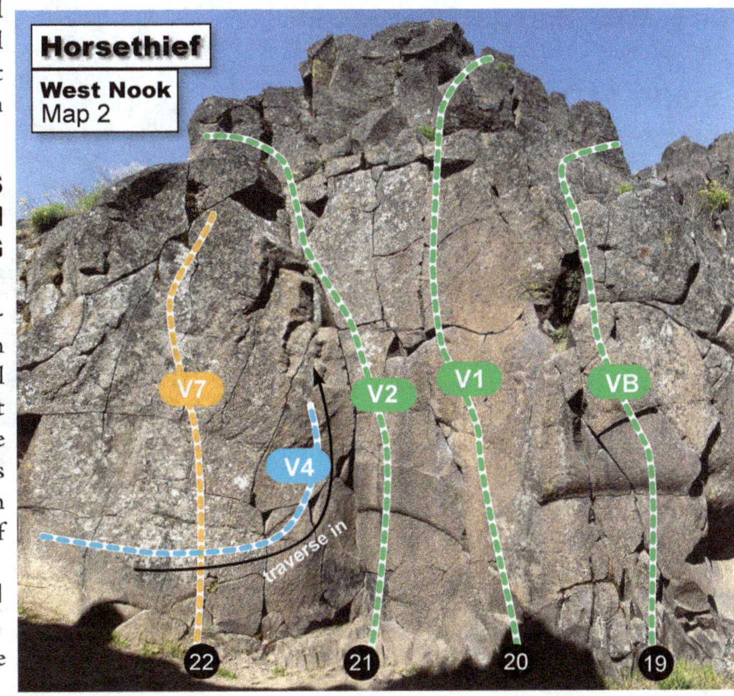

corner.

28. Steep Face V0 (5.10-)
Climb up on fractured jugs.

29. Bulging Prow V2 (5.11-)
A minor prow.

30. Tall Face V3 (5.11+) ★
A very committing tall boulder problem.

31. Tall Arête V4 (5.12-) ★★
A difficult line with tenuous pinches and smears on the lower half of a tall arête. Lock into each sequence, hold the balance, then slap for the rounded sloper.
Traverse Challenge

32. Narrows Traverse V3 (5.11+)
Traverse from before #27 passing the tall arête #31.

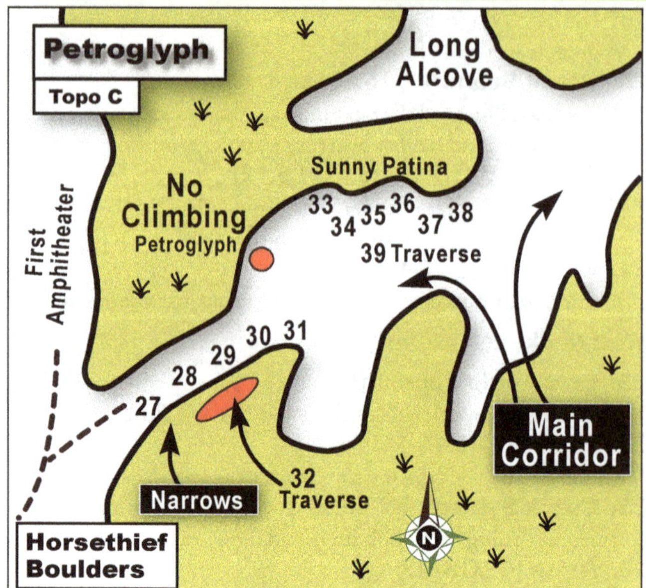

Petroglyph Overhang (CLOSED)

This is an overhanging inner scoop on the north side of the inner corridor at the narrows. There are posted off-limits signs informing visitors of the aboriginal petroglyphs.

SUNNY PATINA

After you admire the off-limits petroglyphs wander a few yards east to a great little sunny kink where this fine selection of favorites can be found. Definitely fire up the triangular shaped pocket climb called Arrow Point. In the distant past this line had a small block wedged in the triangle pocket with two ¼" bolts and a slice of metal holding it in place. Now days we all just enjoy the nature of the line without all that old hardware.

33. Arête VB
Short and juggy and a little loose on top.

34. Face V1 (5.10+) ★
A bump problem over a slight hang on a nose. A bit loose at top.

35. Arrowhead V2 (5.11-) ★★★
Certainly one of the best line face climbs at the Butte. Start left of the corner and balance up using the triangular arrow-like feature with your left hand. Power through a series of wild face crimper moves past the triangle, and to slightly loose jug holds at the top. Eliminates are possible also.

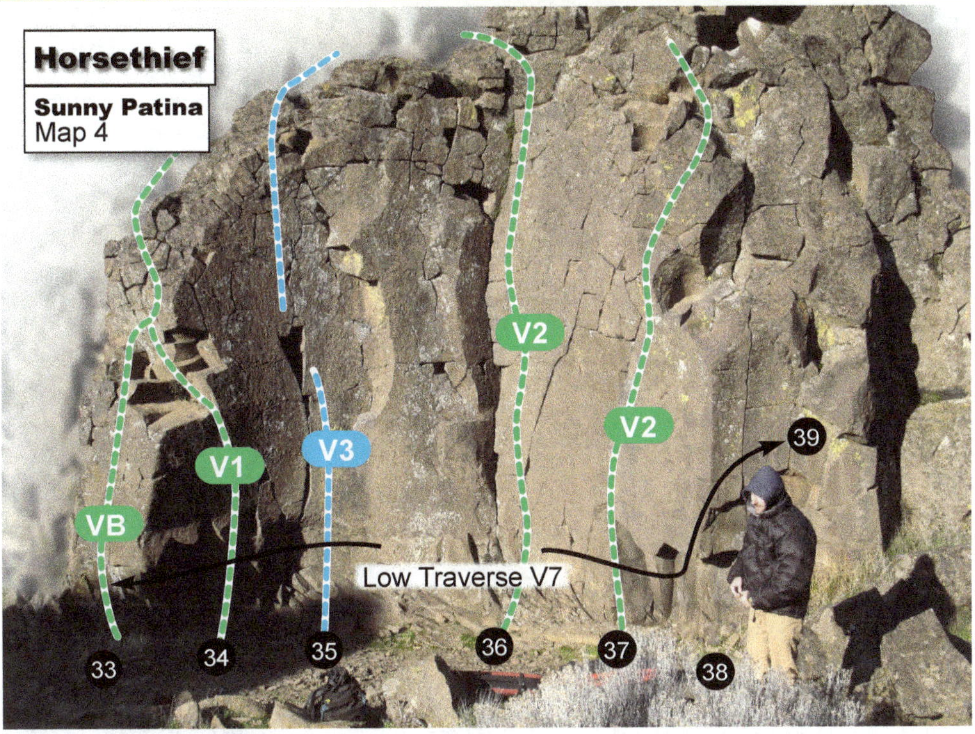

36. Cool Corner V0 (5.10-) ★ ★ ★

A classic stemming problem in the corner.

37. Thin Crack V1 to V2 (5.10+/5.11-) ★

Two thin cracks power up away from the corner. Using both thin cracks work up rightward and trick your way onto the slopers above. Eliminates bumps up grade.

38. Arête V3 (5.11+)

Sit start at hidden undercling and ends with a mantle finish.

The **Triangle of Pain V5** rules on this same arête: sit start to jug undercling, left crimp, triangle crimp in middle of face, left arête, mono-pocket right of the arête, and top to a mantle.

Traverse Challenge

39. Low Traverse V7 (5.13-)

Start on #33 and traverse right staying low to finish on top block 6' right of route #38. It is about V4 if you start and end high, and V7 if you start and end low.

THE LONG ALCOVE (TOPO D)

Walking east along the Main Inner Corridor (or Grotto) past the Petroglyph Overhang you will find a Long Alcove running left (north). This long alcove splits into two directions; the longer portion continuing north while the Veranda cuts back hard west to a very popular cul-de-sac.

Veranda

The Veranda is a stellar slice on the immediate left in the Long Alcove. This north facing and very flat smooth face has become one of

Jerad on a V4, the *Narrows*

the most popular spots to power up. The tick-list of problems here and the quality of the rock (smooth and slippery) combine to provide a string of favorites that will keep you jumping. The first problem starts on the very nose while the remainder is on the flat, steep, north-facing shaded aspect.

40. Outer Buttress V1 (5.10+) ★

Crimps and stemming lead to jugs and a nice finish. Variations (V2-V3) exist.

41. Arête to Corner V1 (5.10+) ★

Smear up ramp using a seam, palm the minor arête onto a tiny perch, then finish up a small inside corner.

42. Thin Crack V2 (5.11-) ★★★

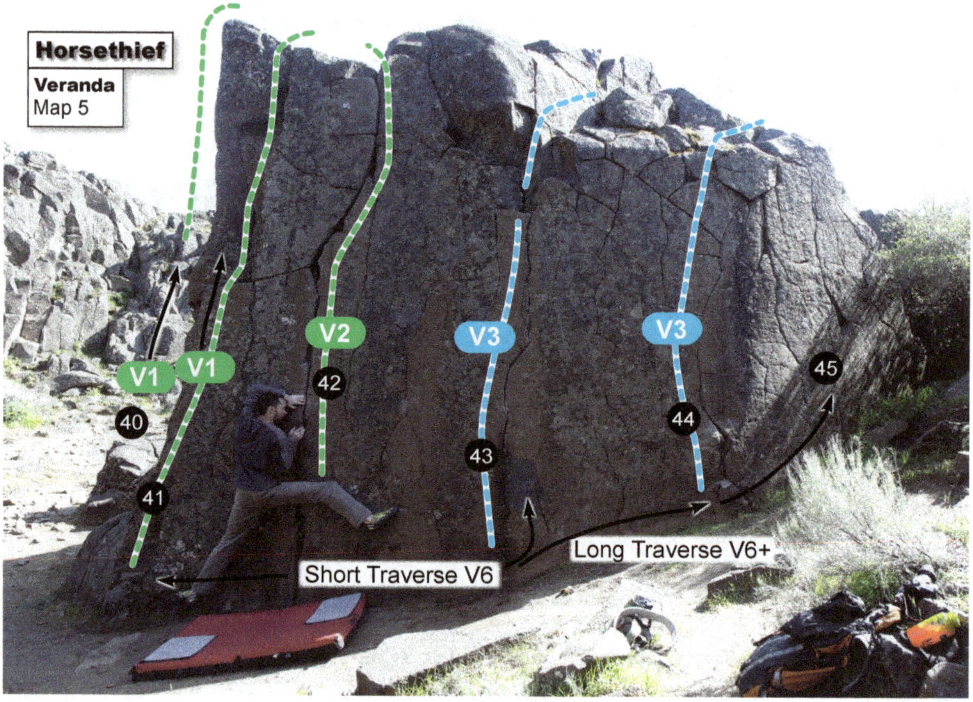

Classic boulder problem, and polished from plenty of use. One of the most well-known Horsethief

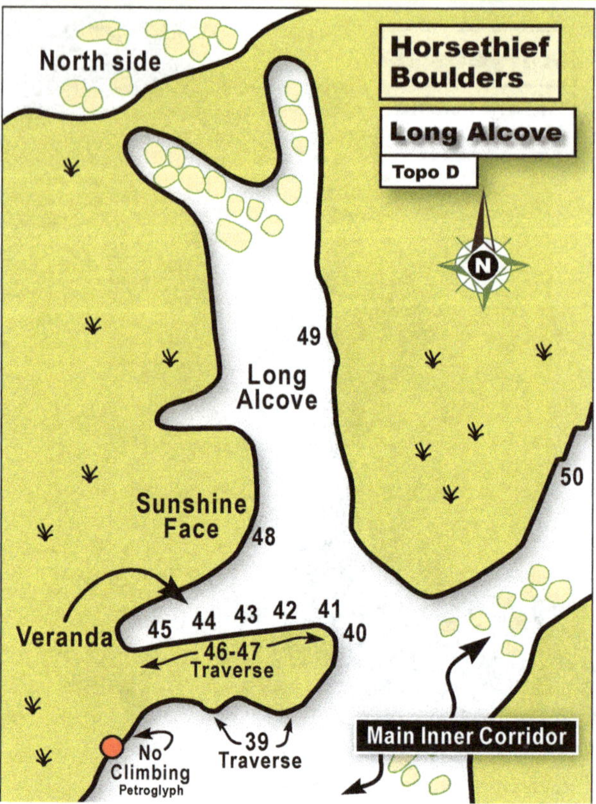

problems.

43. Thin Face V3 (5.11+) ★ ★ ★

Start on lowest holds 5' up for V3. A Horsethief test-piece.

44. Face V3 (5.11+) ★

Avoid the good jug on the right or it will be easier still.

45. Face V0 (5.10-)

Right most very short problem. The finishing block seems kind of sketchy. Traverse Challenge

46. Long Traverse V7 (5.13-)

Start on Arête (#41) and traverse low for the full length of wall, ending on the top of down climb rocks after Face (#45) and ends at the bush.

47. Short Traverse V6 (5.12+)

Start on Thin Crack (#41) and traverse right to Face (#43) and finish up to the top on that route.

Sunshine Face on left side of Long Alcove

In the Long Alcove is this sunny slice of rock which faces southeast and offers several top-rope problems of moderate difficulty on a nice wide and tall section of wall.

48. Main Face VB (5.6 to 5.9) ★

Plenty of variables on a steep face quite suitable for top-rope climbing. Even has a few V2-V4 eliminate problems if it catches your eye just right.

East Face of Long Alcove

Walk deeper into this Long Alcove until you are surrounded by poison oak bushes. On your left (west) side of the long alcove is a viable narrow minor arête with a thin left crack and edge-like features. On the right (east) side of the long alcove several fine long lead or top-rope climbs are available with plenty of variations, so do not feel limited to the only over-aged hillbilly listed below.

49. Crack Corner VB (5.7) ★

The obvious tall crack and corner climb (multiple exits) on east wall of the Long Alcove.

EAST HALF OF INNER CORRIDOR

Walk further east along the Main Corridor beyond the Long Alcove.

The Classic Arête is located on the sunny north side at a kink, while the ever popular Long Wall is on the shaded south side of the Corridor. At the far east end of the Main Corridor you will see the East Grotto Face, while beyond is the East Exit/entrance that quickly leads over to the North Point.

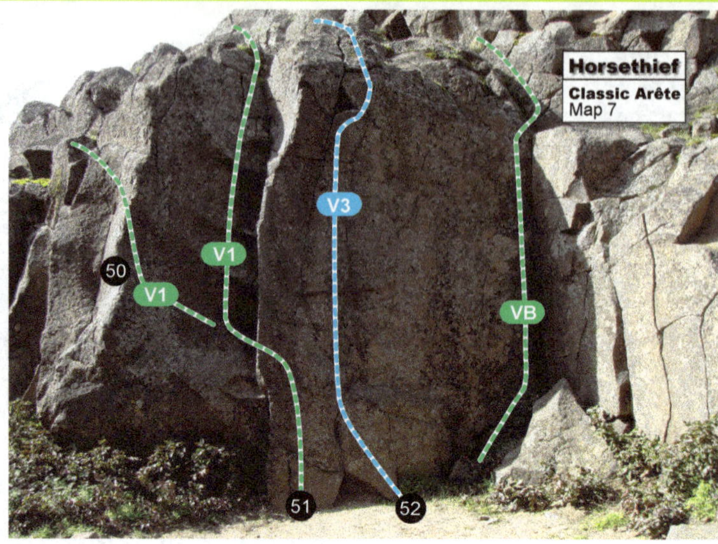

The Classic Arête

The next three problems are on a stellar sunny steep flat face with a prominent crisp short arête. Working the arête is one of the finest problems at the Butte. I never knew that V1 could be so fun till I tried this one. Nice sandy landing.

50. Dull Prow V1 (5.10+)

A minor round prow as a left exit.

51. Sharp Arête V1 (5.10+)   ★ ★ ★

Use the sharp arête and gingerly slide up left into the inside corner, and then dance up on intricate small edges to the large incut hold at the top. Classic Horsethief boulder problem.

52. Seam Only V3 (5.11+)   ★ ★

Avoid arête on the left at this grade. Involves a long lock-off to a mono-pocket, and then to a jug hold (wobbles but still there).

LONG WALL (TOPO E)

The Long Wall is one of the most popular sections of wall at the Butte for top-rope climbing. This portion of wall faces north and on hot days stays shaded while offering a plethora of fine problems, including one of the best traverses at the Butte.

Many of the rock climbs along the Long Wall offer numerous variables, so rather than attempting to solve every idiosyncratic nuance…just get the rope out and set up a top-rope and have at it.

53. Face to Mantle V2 (5.11-)

Immediately south of the Long Alcove on the shaded Long Wall. Down climb off right immediately after the mantle.

54. Thin Crack VB (5.8)   ★

The striking thin crack with good pure jamming, but is short lived.

55. Green Slab VB (5.6 to 5.9)

A long green slab with many variations; some are harder while some are easier.

Low Traverse at the *Sunny Patina*

56. Short Overhang V1 (V3ss)

Start sitting, do overhang, and end on ledge…or stand and make it V1 fun.

57. Corner to Ledge VB (5.7) ★

Climb the shallow inside corner to an awkward move getting on the big flat ledge, then waltz up the right face to top out.

58. Face to Groove VB (5.8) ★★

Great line! Climb the steep face on good holds to finish up a lower angled groove.

59. Steep Face V0 (5.10-) ★★★

Super classic line. Start at the thin crack and climb up an awkward face past missing blocks.

60. Face to Groove VB (5.7) ★★

Climb up the enjoyable well-feature face that has lots of cracks and holds until it eases in difficulty in the groove to the top. Beware of a loose thin flake up high.

61. Face VB (5.8) ★

Steep face with sequential holds.

62. Thin Block VB (5.7) ★

Grab the long thin block and climb up to a big edge and finish on the lower angle rock.

63. Groove VB (5.5)

A moderate groove on good rock at the far left end of Long Wall prior to the uphill scramble. Traverse Challenge

64. Long Wall Traverse V3 to V6 ★★★

A totally stellar boulder traverse can be done along the Long Wall in either direction. Start just west of Corner to Ledge #57 and continue to Groove #63. About V6 if staying low for the entire traverse. Or pick a shorter distance for a fun V3.

East Grotto Face

A nice sunny slab. The rounded slab formation is less than vertical and has many cracks and seams crisscrossing the face at angles.

65. Face VB to V0 (5.7 to 5.10-) ★

Nice blocky climbing on a wide rounded face with a corner in the middle of the wall.

NORTH POINT (TOPO F)

The following routes are quite tall (rope stuff) and are located at a sharp prow of rock facing out over the East Entrance. Most climbers reach this locale by walking through the entire inner main corridor. This info is just for reference and not intended that you should solo this stuff.

66. Old Bolt V1 (5.10)

Cruises up a smooth vertical face (several old ¼" bolts studs) past an upside down triangle roof feature on a flat patina face. Once you power past the triangle into the thin jam crack to a stance, continue up easy steps in a corner to the top. Somewhat loose at the top. About 30' left of this line is a nice short VB (5.9) jug haul boulder problem on a flat face.

67. North Point Crack V0 (5.10b) ★

Climb a steep crack to a stance, and then climb a smear move into a corner system immediately left of the arête.

68. North Point Arête V3 (5.11c)
★

Start at the North Crack and launch up right (2 bolts) on a smooth face, and then power out (3 bolts) the severely overhung arête to the top.

WEST ENTRANCE (TOPO G)

There are several options near the West Entrance that are good for learning technique.

69. West Chimney VB (5.4)

The West Chimney is found at the very tip of the West Point, and is a nice chimney smack between the main wall and a large obvious isolated pillar. Stem the chimney to the top of the pillar, and then launch up the nice series of steps and ledges to the tip of West Point. Once you top out on the tip you can easily descend southward down a boulder field slope. Or you can continue up another short steep step onto the main upper plateau and walk east to descend into the First Amphitheater.

70. Tall Corner VB (5.6)

A fairly well-used corner climb is available to your immediate south as you are hiking up the slope of the West Entrance.

SOUTH WALL (TOPO H)

To reach the South Wall river face hike past the Western Entrance south eastward around the Butte until you can see an obvious isolated pillar separate from the main massif. Scramble up a boulder slope to the base of the west-facing slot formed by this isolated pillar. These two climbs are on the main wall just to the left of the slot.

To set up a top-rope anchor walk east past the pillar to a steep ravine that accesses the top of this bluff. Or walk south across the plateau from the Main Inner Corridor to the top of the formation above the isolated Pillar.

71. Corner and Roof V0 (5.10a)

A good long climb and best done as a top-rope. Climb a steep corner and power out the overhang directly to the top.

72. Face and Prow VB (5.9)

Begin by powering up left using the prow and nearby features and continue to the top.

HIDDEN HOLLOW (TOPO

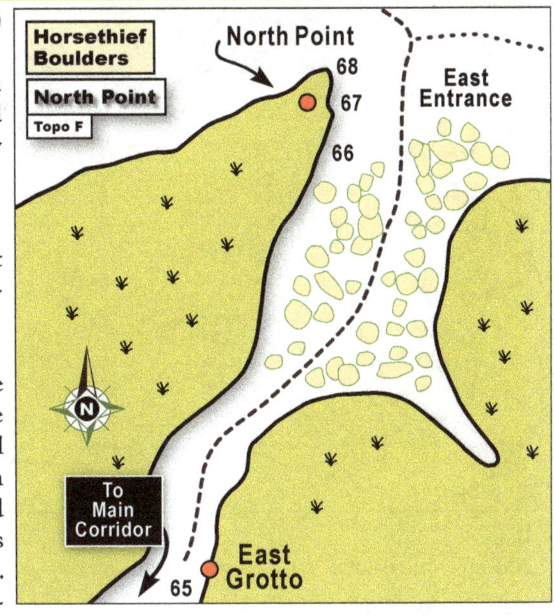

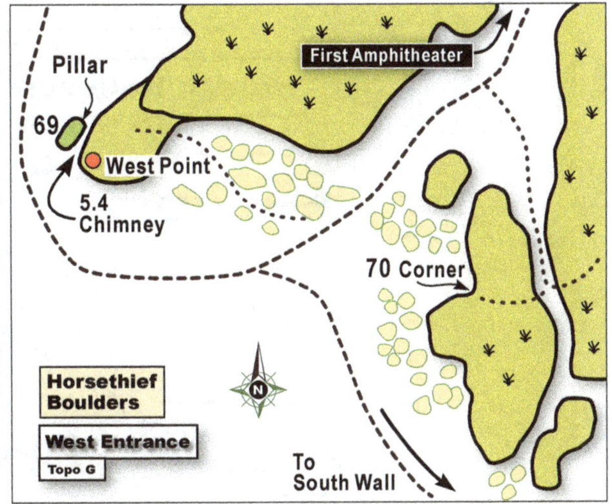

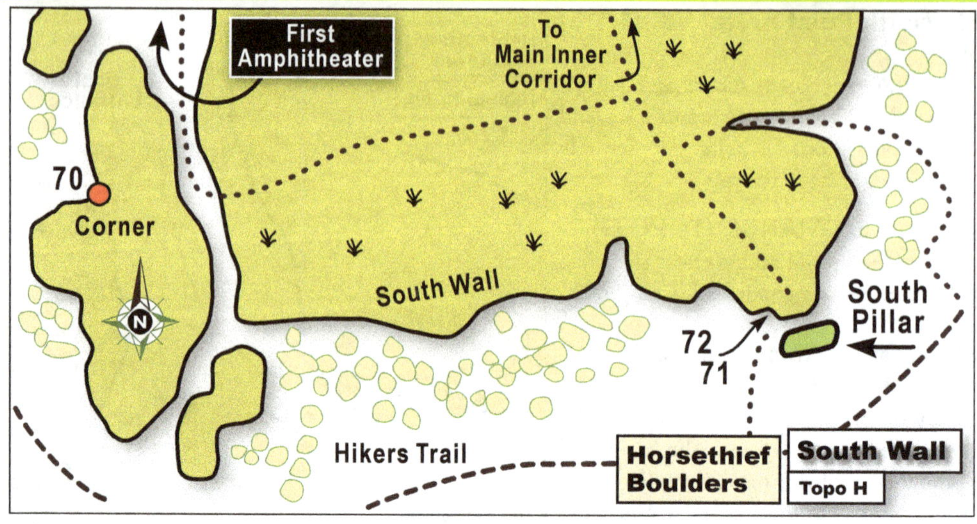

I)

A minor contrivance in the great blue on a rock plateau south of the main inner corridor.

South side of Hidden Hollow.

73. Face V0

Numerous thin cracks and edges crisscross at angles on a nice flat face.

74. Outer Edge V1

Makes use of the outer left edge of the same flat face.

North side of Hidden Hollow

75. Arête V6 ★

A round knob overhang with a sharp edge on the lower left. Sit start the bulge arête. Incut holds are better on the upper part.

76. Bulge V3

At the east end of the Hidden Hollow. Sit start climb the overhang using the arête.

77. Face V2

A short spit at the west end of the Hidden Hollow. Avoid the low corner on the right.

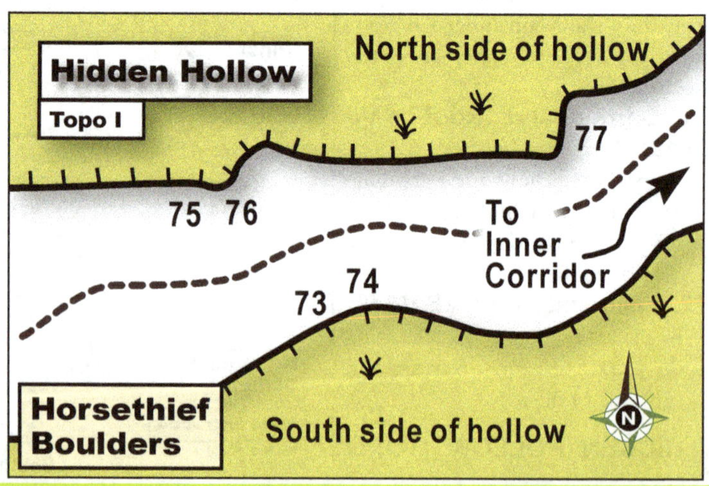

MT HOOD BOULDERING AREAS (SOUTHERN)

This section details bouldering sites on the southern slopes and valleys of Mt Hood, sites that are generally found along the US Highway 26 corridor (and up to White River on Hwy 35).

TIMBERLINE BOULDERS

Timberline Boulders offer a extensive quality string of high-altitude dacite and andesite boulders scattered widely across the south-facing alpine slope on Mt Hood. The greatest concentration of boulders is found between the 6000' to 7100' elevation, in a rough square mile northwest from Timberline Lodge and west of the Magic Mile Chairlift. Several other prominent stones exist east, and north, of Silcox Hut. The boulders range from little spit balls to large behemoths up to 24' tall, with the greatest concentration of lines ranging from VB-V4 (and a tiny score up to V6). The seasonal weather elements have fiercely and abrasively scoured the rock surface, thus keeping virtually all the boulders spotless of moss. Some of the larger stones remain above the snow pack year-round, and tend to have some black colored lichen growing on top portion of the block. The vivid high-altitude scenery of jet blue skies and strata-cumulus clouds combined with twisted clusters of mountain hemlock and alpine whitebark pine create a visually appealing, photographic destination.

History: The site has seen brief exploration by a few Lodge employees who scrambled on a few stones. Spread over a dozen years Mr O combined many day hikes with visits to all of the boulders, tapping various lines a little bit at a time. By about 2011 he had literally sent about 90% of all known problems at this site. Additional stout sends were established by Mr A in about 2011.

Season

The optimal season to access this area is from late June through late October. The sunshine and steady breezes tend to dry out the boulders very quickly, so even on an overcast day you may find bouldering feasible. Bring adequate clothing if the weather is cold. A light crashpad, or even a small satellite crashpad may be suitable if you plan to walk to the further destinations, because it is over one mile distance to reach the furthest boulders. Many boulder problems are tall, so expect committing lines with careful assessment. A typical daily tour usually yields 20-30 lines before the sharp weather-resistant phenocryst crystals gradually peal your finger pads raw. Several likely bouldering choices to aim for are Stormin' Normin, Blacktop, Zelda, or Zig boulders.

Directions

From Portland drive east on US Hwy 26 to Government Camp, then drive up Timberline Road to the parking lot at Timberline Lodge. The area is virtually treeless above the lodge, so getting visual bearings on certain large stones is relatively easy. Most of the time you will be in a big triangular zone above Pacific Crest Trail (PCT), west of the Magic Mile Chairlift (unless you went to Silcox), and east of Little Zigzag Canyon (unless you went all the way to Zippora). There is one north-south trail just west of the Stormin' Normin Chairlift that a lot of day hiker's use, and this can be a valuable access tool, if need.

To start, walk north from the lodge, initially on a generic trail till you locate the junction of the Magic Mile Chairlift dirt maintenance road and the PCT Skyline trail. Once you are here...there are several logical tour direction choices.

1.) Hike up the Magic Mile Chairlift (MMC) dirt access road a short distance to Zephyr Boulder, and onward up the road to Zeppelin and Zola Boulders, all generally near various chairlift

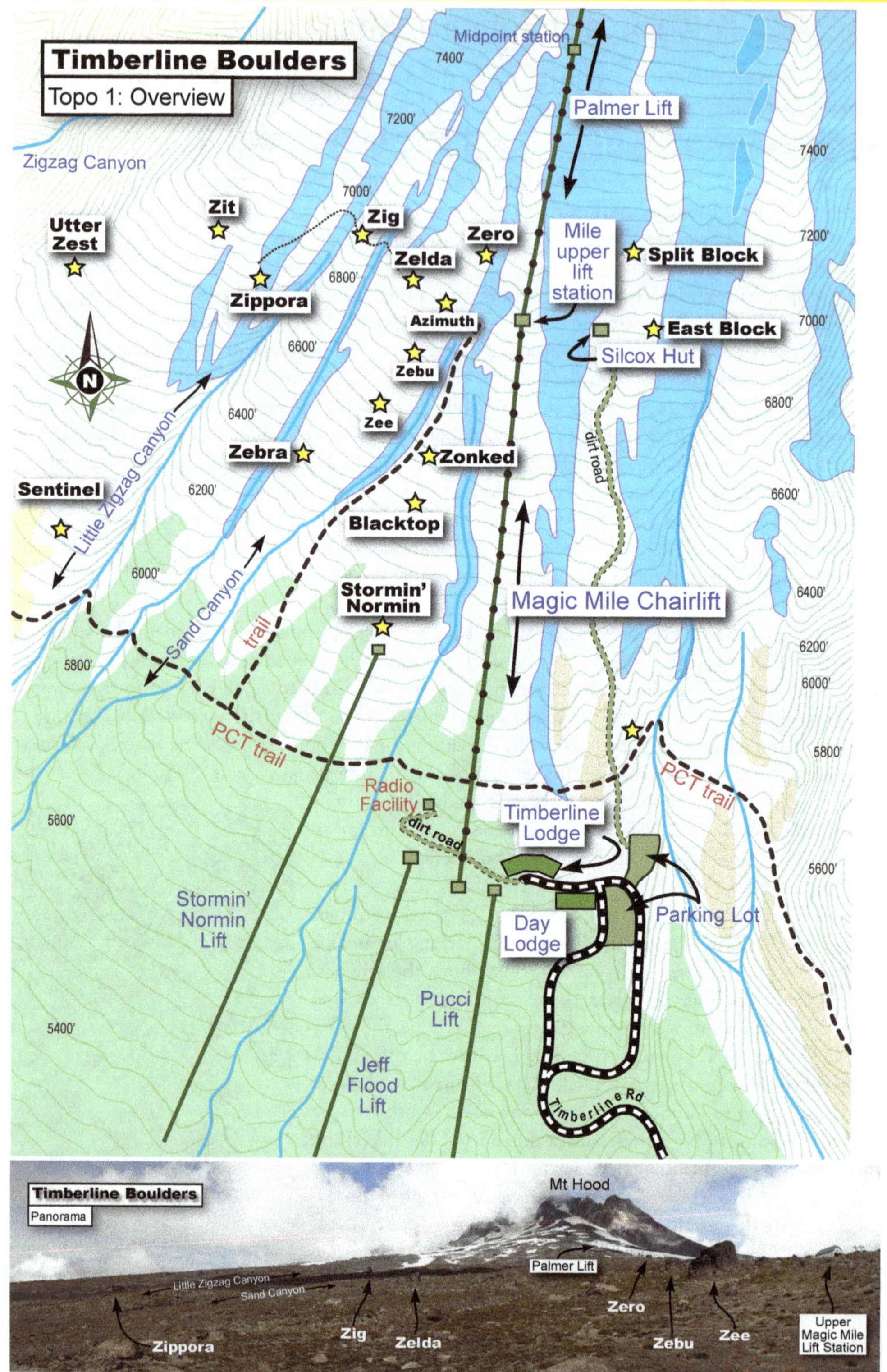
Timberline Boulders
Topo 1: Overview
Zigzag Canyon
Midpoint station
7400'
7200'
7000'
Palmer Lift
7400'
Zit
Zig
Zero
Utter Zest
Zelda
Split Block
7200'
Mile upper lift station
Zippora
6800'
Azimuth
East Block
7000'
Silcox Hut
6600'
Zebu
dirt road
6800'
6400'
Zee
N
Zebra
Zonked
6200'
6600'
Sentinel
Little Zigzag Canyon
Blacktop
6400'
6000'
Magic Mile Chairlift
Sand Canyon
trail
Stormin' Normin
6200'
6000'
5800'
PCT trail
PCT trail
5800'
Radio Facility
Timberline Lodge
5600'
dirt road
Parking Lot
Stormin' Normin Lift
Day Lodge
5600'
Pucci Lift
Jeff Flood Lift
5400'
Timberline Rd
Timberline Boulders
Panorama
Mt Hood
Palmer Lift
Little Zigzag Canyon
Sand Canyon
Zero
Zippora
Zig
Zelda
Zebu
Zee
Upper Magic Mile Lift Station

pole sets.

2.) Take PCT Skyline trail west a short distance, then follow this uphill to the upper lift station of Stormin' Normin Chairlift (SNC). A few yards above this upper lift station is the the Stormin' Normin Boulder, an obvious introductory stone, followed by Blacktop further uphill, then Black Gold, Zonked, etc. From Blacktop Boulder aim uphill (passing Black Gold, and Zonked) northwest to Zelda. From Zelda aim northwest across Sand Canyon to Zig Boulder, then across Little Zigzag Canyon and downhill 400' to a side branch where the low sitting Zippora Boulders. These two canyons are steep sloped when crossing them at a lower elevation, but still feasible if you want to do it.

Several 'way-out-there' options exist beyond Zippora Boulders, which are Zit Boulder, Utter Zest Boulder, and the south most oddity Sentinel Boulder, if you are so inclined. Most other stones in that region are low angle or too short. You can descend from Sentinel downhill several hundred feet to the PCT (Skyline) trail and hike back to the east directly to Timberline Lodge.

Stormin' Normin String

Stormin' Normin Boulder

Stormin' Normin is the lowest of the string of boulders at this section. Start here first, and then hike uphill to the next boulder in the string. There are several good problems on this short stone, which are considered to be the entrance exam for TLB. This string starts immediately above the upper chairlift station called Stormin' Normin. You can reach here by walking on the dirt road from Timberline Lodge west and slightly uphill to this site.

V1 First Run. Waltz up the minor groove on left.

V1 (V2ss) Stormin' Normin. Start on the jugs below the arête, and power up the hung prow to the top nose. Exit variants exist.

V2 Infinite Light. Low start same as Stormin' Normin, then climb up exiting via the right seam onto the slab to the right.

V4ss Thundercloud. On the eastside, slither onto the smooth slab rightward.

Razor Stone

A minor 10' tall stone about 80' directly west of the Stormin' Normin' Chairlift upper station in a main snow channel. The surficial texture has sharp as blades crystals that make sending anything on this unit a delicate matter. About six lines (L to R): **VB** face, **VB** crack, **V0** face, **V0** prow, **VB** corner crack, **V0**, **V0**. Nothing special here.

Lightning Bolt Boulder

A minor slump located a few yards north of the

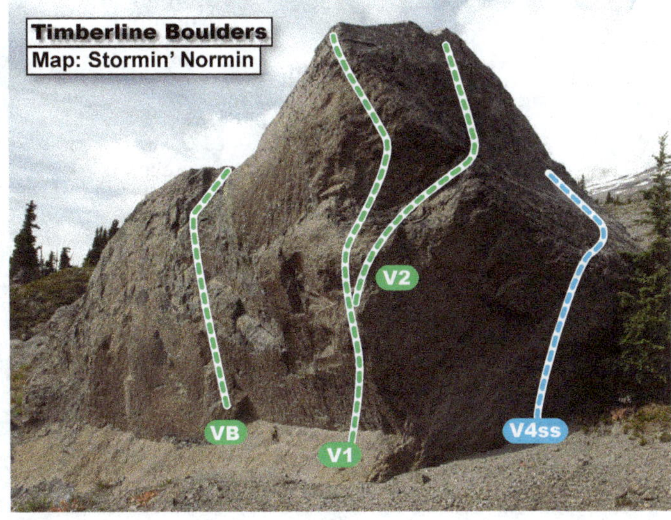

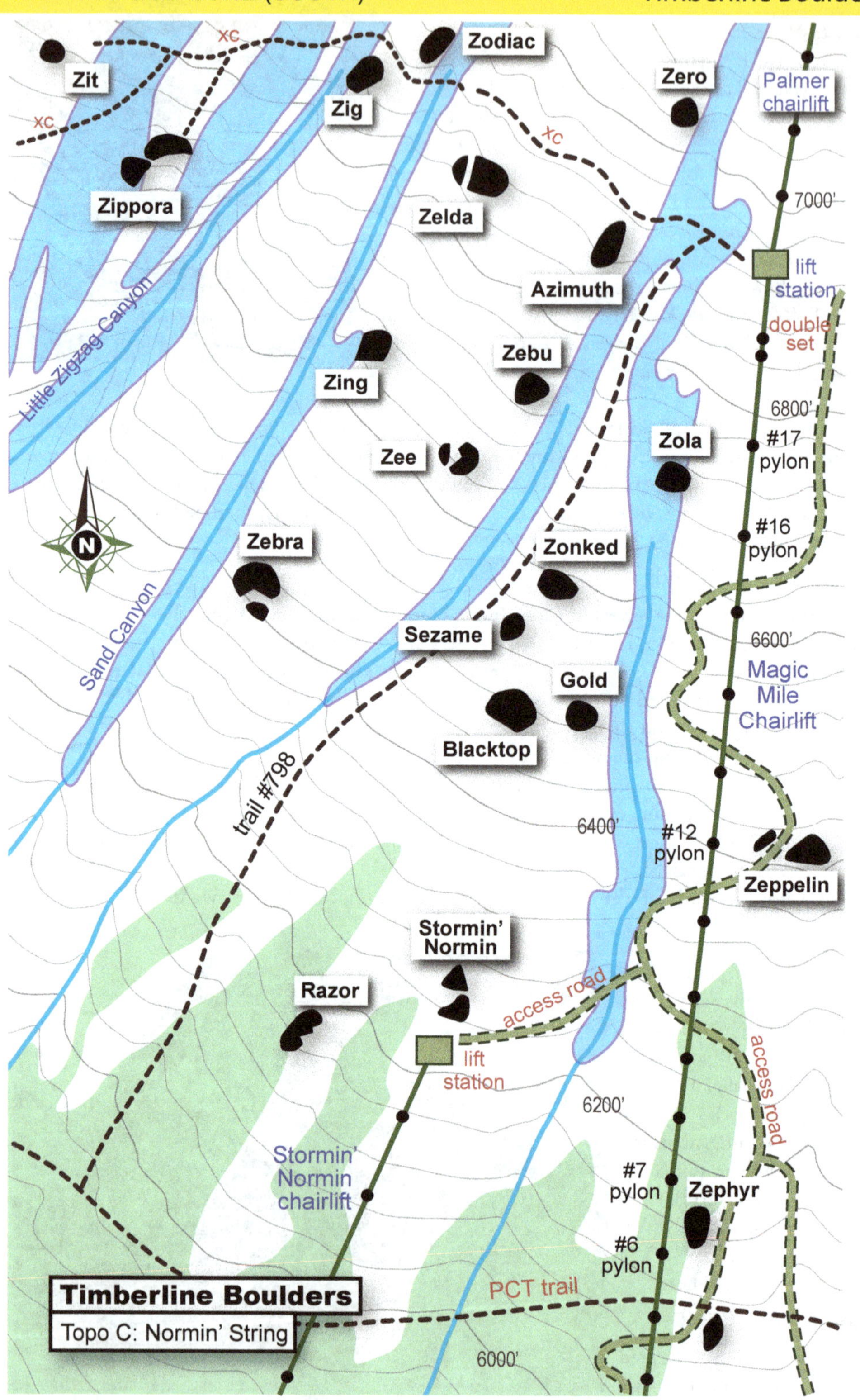
Zit
xc
xc
Zippora
Little Zigzag Canyon
Zig
Zodiac
Zelda
Azimuth
Zero
Palmer chairlift
7000'
lift station
double set
6800'
#17 pylon
#16 pylon
Zebu
Zing
Zola
Zee
Zebra
N
Sand Canyon
Zonked
Sezame
Gold
Blacktop
6600'
Magic Mile Chairlift
6400'
#12 pylon
Zeppelin
trail #798
Stormin' Normin
Razor
access road
lift station
Stormin' Normin chairlift
6200'
#7 pylon
access road
Zephyr
#6 pylon
Timberline Boulders
Topo C: Normin' String
PCT trail
6000'

main Stormin' Normin boulder.

V4ss Lightning Bolt.
V2ss Stuck Like Glue.
VBss Free Ride.

Beaver Estate Boulder

A short distance below Blacktop Boulder, this one is a large SE facing vertical stone (10' tall by 20' long)) with a big rodent nest at the base.

V0 South Side.
V3 Beaver Estate.
V2 Lil' Bro.
V4 Scat.

Blacktop Behemoth Boulder

Blacktop is a classic 16' tall monster and is part of the Stormin' Normin string of boulders. It's a good place to view the other boulders from the top of this monster so as to coordinate your direction of travel.

V0 Sunrise. Facing west-*ish*. Power up the initial steep face on slopers and run up the black lichen holds to the top.

V0 Sunset. The 2" wide curved rail. Start up the low angle slab on the left side of the monolith. Dance up the obvious curving rail and exit up left onto the black lichen slopers near the top.

V_ Black Lichen. Tall slab loaded with black lichen (project).

V0 White Knight. A fun line, start on the low angle slab. Aim up right onto the top of a tiny rock knob, then directly up to the top on good holds.

V1 Blacktop. The classic line with tech moves that keep you on edge to the top.

V1 Bones. A minor balance on the right most flat section of face.

Black Gold Boulder

This one sits about 40' to the east of Blacktop.

VB There are 2-3 of these other than the 3 following power lines listed below.

V2ss Vermiculite. Sit start on the east most side

V6 Black Gold. Crux necessitates palming onto smooth sloped slab on south side of block.

V1 Spring Flower. Ascend a seam on the SW side of the block

Sezame Street Boulder

A minor block in between Blacktop and Zonked, with eight slab VB's (some stubby SS).

Zonked Boulder

Zonked Boulder is about 300' uphill from Blacktop and is identified by the graffiti on it. Though

On Stormin' Normin' boulder

about 13' high, route scrounging is limited.

V3ss Zoned Out. Thin seam on left side at hung prow.

VB Blackhole of Anti-Knowledge. The obvious crack.

V0 Agent of Influence. A slightly hung break in the rock.

VB Zonked. A minor stubby prow on the right near graffiti.

One Stripe Zebra Boulder

One Stripe Zebra is a quality 14' tall splitter finger crack on a southeast facing vertical face and goes at **V1** with sharp jams, a hollow block at the top, and tricky mantle. No other logical options here.

Zelda Boulder ⚠

Big Zelda is a classic 24' tall broken-in-half double chunk monster block. The south face is a tall aspect with popular lines. The east face overhangs substantially. The second smaller west block (2.5' gap) is a bit crumbly in places. Zelda's main stone is 24' tall composed of good rock, and an overhung east face. The first 3 problems are on the West Block of Zelda:

V3 Zurich. Small Roof on west side

V0 Zip. Nice basic crack or face. Several variants all about the same.

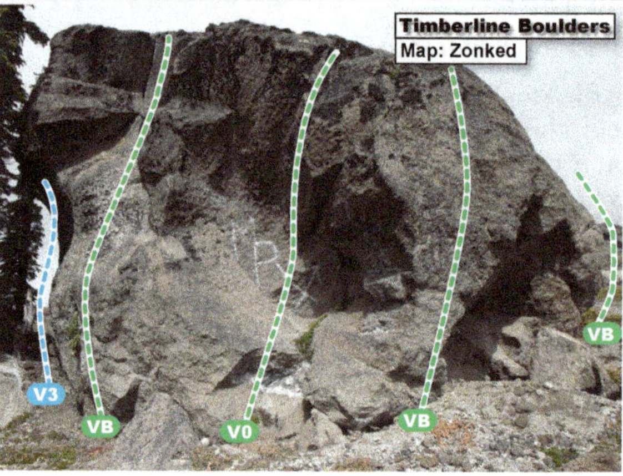

V1 Zap. Full south face using right hand on the arête prow and fluted holds.

VB Zelda. This is the classic line on Zelda. Dance up the initial moves to a tiny stance, then move up leftward following the slight groove. Starts powerful, stays steep, and has a rounded top out.

V1 Zelda Direct. A minor direct can be made using semi-hollow holds.

VB Zenith. Another classic line. Start same as Zelda but move up right to next groove then up to top.

V2 Zion. Technical line. Start at a minor roof and triangle pocket above lip, then use side-pulls and aim left till you can join Zenith to top up.

V2 Zealot. Starts same as Zion but over all four obvious small lips directly to the top.

V2+ Zircon. Variant start up past the initial two small lips, merges with left line.

V3 Zither. Ascends a steep overhung (hollow rock) crack to sloped face.

V3 Full Zelda Traverse (would be harder if using east face).

Zodiac Boulder

This stone (10' tall by 30' long) sits just uphill from Zelda on the west edge of a lesser arm of Sand Canyon, immediately above the east-west hiker's path. The beta, beginning with the north-

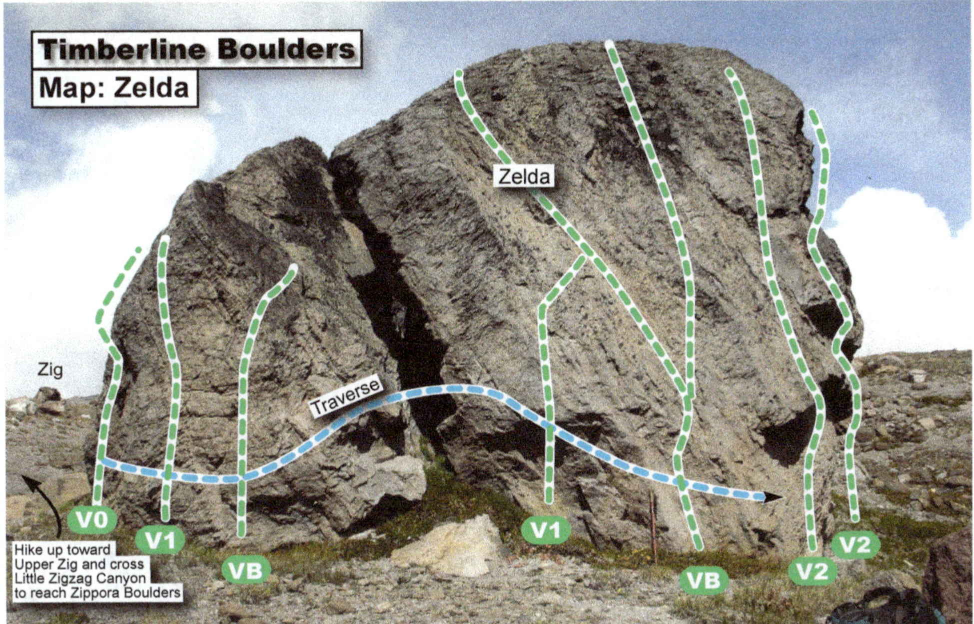

most line going counterclockwise is as follows. This stone is a bit flakey in places.

V3 Zodiac. A quality smooth andesite sequence on low overhung sidepulls, launch for the top jug, and mantle crux.

V3 Celestial Dreams. Start on the VB, traverse left to join the V3 line, then mantle up.

VB west groove.

VB SW nose.

VB east groove.

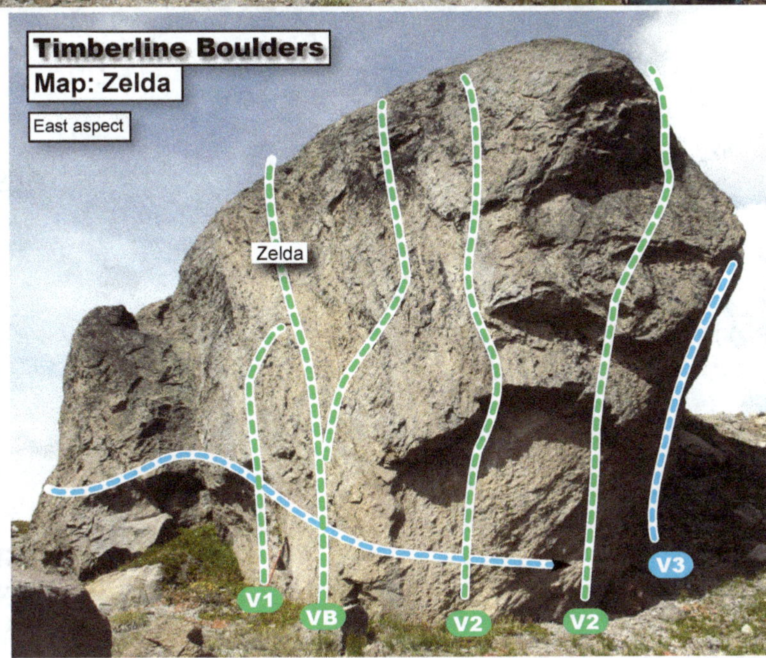

Zing Boulder

This is an 11' tall loner stone located about 250' downhill and slightly west-ish of Zelda Stone. A quality stone with a rounded rib that starts as a rounded overhang.

V2 Zing Arête. Standing start, high wide foot edges over a bulge to get established on the arête.

V3 Zing Face. A very smooth almost featureless slope on the right side.

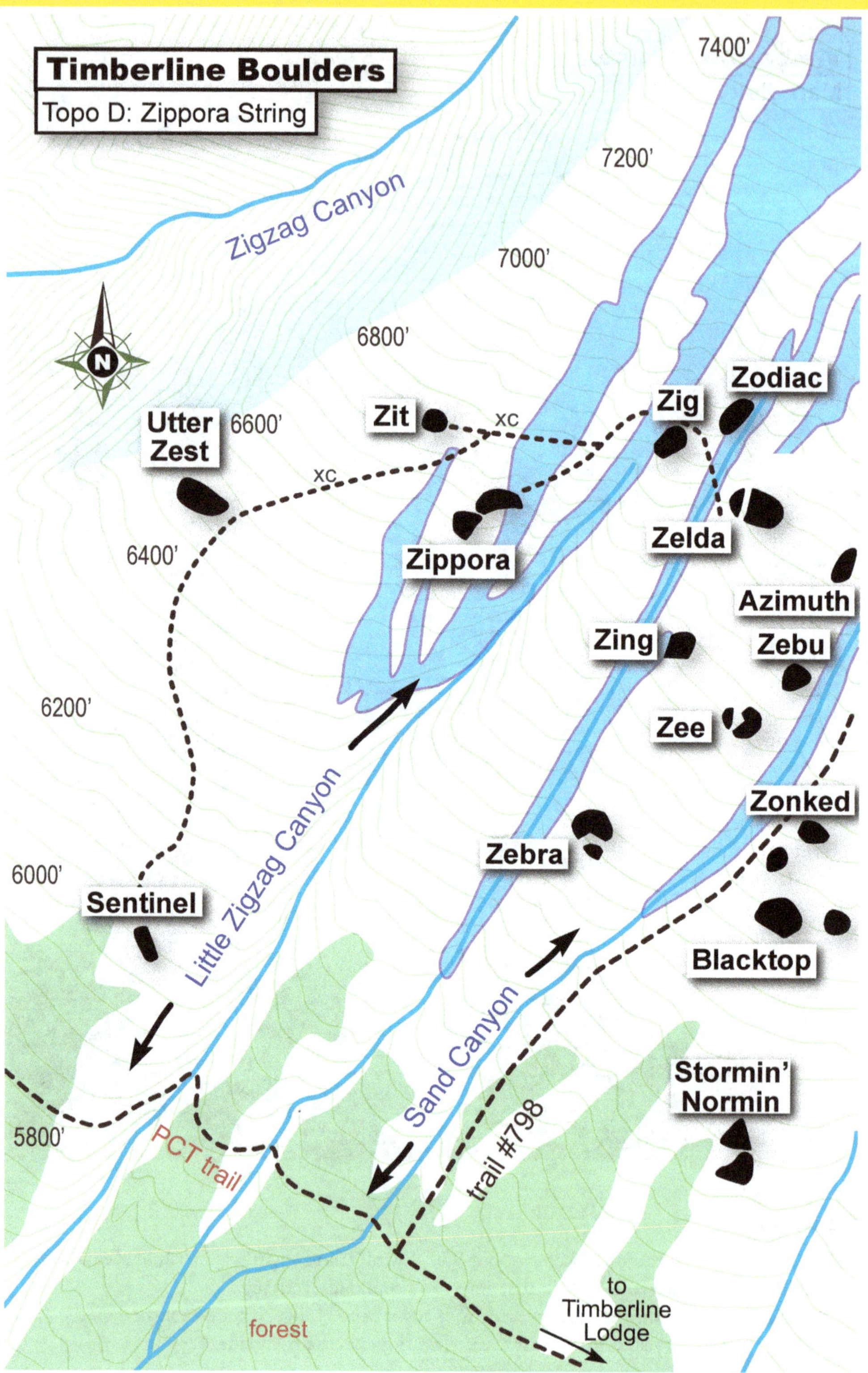
Timberline Boulders
Topo D: Zippora String
7400'
7200'
7000'
Zigzag Canyon
6800'
N
Utter Zest
6600'
Zit
xc
Zig
Zodiac
xc
Zelda
Zippora
6400'
Azimuth
Zing
Zebu
6200'
Zee
Little Zigzag Canyon
Zonked
Zebra
6000'
Sentinel
Blacktop
Sand Canyon
trail #798
Stormin' Normin
5800'
PCT trail
to
Timberline
Lodge
forest

Zig Boulder

Zig Boulder is overhung on the west and east sides, and has a possible traverse. This is reached by continuing west on the faint path (which extends west from the Mile Lift Station) just uphill from Zelda. Zig Boulder is perched on the east edge of Little Zigzag Canyon.

VB Zig Arête. Fun basic run.

V2 Zillion is an elusive delicate balancy face that starts with a high right step.

V3 Calm before the Storm. Two high steps, then onto a long smooth lichen covered slab.

V4 (?) High Roof. The big overhung roof on the east side.

V2ss Z-Crack. Obvious east low starter.

V3 Double Aught. East Low Lip

V4 Zoroaster. Thin crimps angling up left (briefly) on west side in minor overhung nook.

V2+ (V3ss) Pacific Pearl. Cool line on west side in overhung nook on round nose. Start on tiny crimps, dyno to jug, then mantle up.

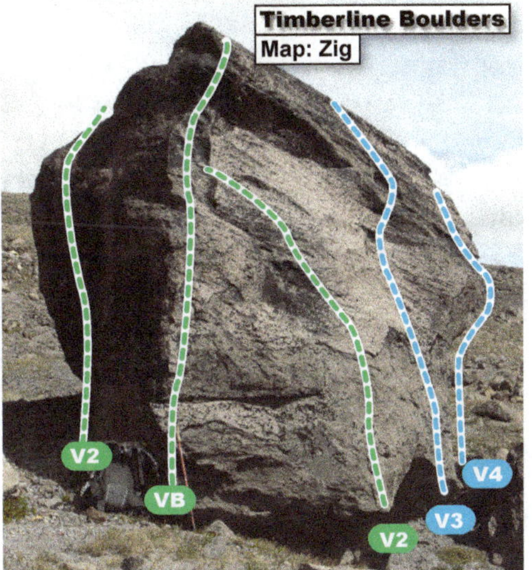

Zippora Boulders ⚠

Zippora Boulders cluster has several superb bouldering problems. The stone offers powerful, quality, 14' tall hi-ball problems on steep and overhanging rock. Get there by hiking west from Upper Zig Boulder across the Zigzag Canyon, then descend about 200' downhill to the Zippora cluster. Core lines face southeast. Site is located in a small side branch of the main canyon. The lower boulder offers smooth crisp features with a super overhung east side. The upper boulder is rough textured with a steep southeast aspect.

VB Zippora. A quality fun face. At the arête base move up left onto face using small edges.

V2 Zahara. Superb arête with slightly hung power crimps.

V4 Izadora. A cool upside down crimps power line (project).

V0 Nth Degree. A great awakening. Start under overhang on crack underclings, move up right into hung scoop, then up left to better crack holds.

V2 Weapons Grade Stupidity. A steep series of crimps on the tallest section.

VB Secular myopia. Minor problem with a hollow block to start, mostly large holds.

Zit Boulder

Zit Boulder is visible further west as you cross the Little Zigzag canyon near Zig boulder. It is like a little round bump out west-ish and appears to be big, but in reality is just a short 8' tall rock

with a flat smooth south side.

V0ss One Zit. Aim up left starting with right hand on incut in center face.

V1ss Two Zits. Aim up right starting with left hand on center face incut and right hand in the triangle incut pocket.

Utter Zest Boulder

Utter Zest Boulder can be found by hiking way out west from Zippora. Utter Zest is actually a cluster of four large boulders (uppermost east boulder) on the rounded ridge crest overlooking Big Zigzag Canyon. It offers a hard traverse line about 60' long at **V3**. Rock is rough textured, generally good for bouldering, and has minor hollowness on the rail. The traverse is a cruise combining considerable sustained effort. Start this traverse on the right by using the slopers to palm down going left, sliding down past the crux, along the low hand rail 4' off the ground, then up to the cooling off stance, then finish up the incut jugs on the far upper left, and top out on the boulder.

Sentinel Boulder

Sentinel Boulder is a serious looking oddity about 300' above the PCT Skyline trail and immediately west of the Little Zigzag Canyon. It offers 3-4 stout potential boulder problems. It stands tall (which is unusual) and provides a northeast face that is quite

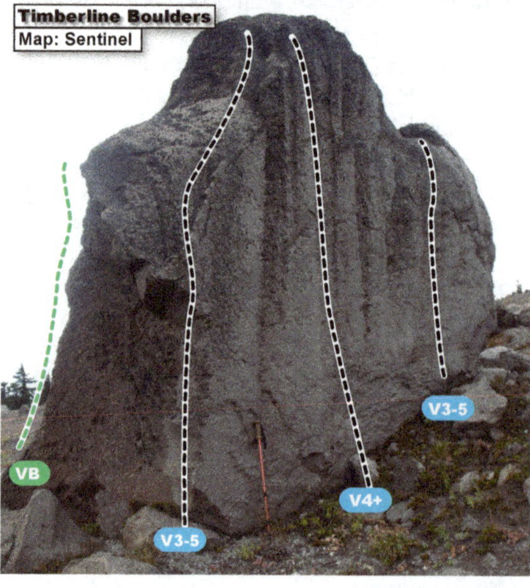

flat and smooth.

Zero Boulder

Zero Boulder is a highly visible round boulder on a prominent knoll 2 pylons up and northwest of the upper Magic Mile chairlift station about 200'. It is immediately west of a deep snow filled ravine used by skiers. The out of bounds ski signs run downhill along that same knoll.

VB Afterglow. Can jog up left onto the rib to top out.

V3 Zero. Power up the center of the east face on nothing and finish on nothing slopers.

V0 Roman Nose. On prow, several tight moves to a series of slopers to finish.

VB Jug Haul. A west side, slightly hung series of jugs.

Magic Mile String

The following boulders are located by walking from north of Timberline Lodge up a trail to the PCT trail, then continue walking up the dirt maintenance road (used by the lodge employees). There is not much else along the Mile Chairlift access road, because most of the blocks are generally too small.

Zephyr Boulder

This block is located 80' downhill from pole set #7. Excellent rock, 11' tall, broken in three pieces, and is a good introductory block for the area. About 200' above the PCT trail, located between pole set #6 and #7 on the Mile Chairlift.

V0ss Czarina. Sit start and use both edges of this narrow center block.

V1ss Czar. Start under the minor angled lip and pop up right, then use the left arête to top up. Good line.

V2 Zephyr. Techy, balancy on a slight overhang, then up to a rounded easier top out. High quality.

VB Aztlan. Fun slabby face, a basic introductory standing start problem.

VB Zin. Standing start with pinches and small edges.

Zeppelin Boulder

Continue walking up the access road (from Zephyr) to a set of two boulders next to the road, and about 200' east of pole set #12. The east block is the largest and is about 11' tall and rounds off nicely for the upper portion. Composed of andesite with prominent cut surfaces and edges.

V1 Zorro. Start low, and pop for the horn jug, then upward as it rounds out.

V1 Zulu. Start low in the overhung scoop on the south face, and work up left on positive edges. Cool line.

V1 Zeus. Start low in the same overhung scoop, but go directly up to the top. Cool line.

Zola Boulder

Continue to walk up the access road and aim for a prominent block 200' west and halfway between pole set #16 and pole set #17. The rock has a prominent crack on its south face slab. Height is 11' tall, with a 75° slab on the south face.

VB Delta. The basic obviously easy jam crack.

VB Omega. Cool delicate face problem on the south slab. Start on arête, move up left to face.

V3 Gamma. Climb the arête using very thin tech edges and tiny features.

V2 Alpha. Standing start using good side pulls. Power up and over the minor bulge. Cool line.

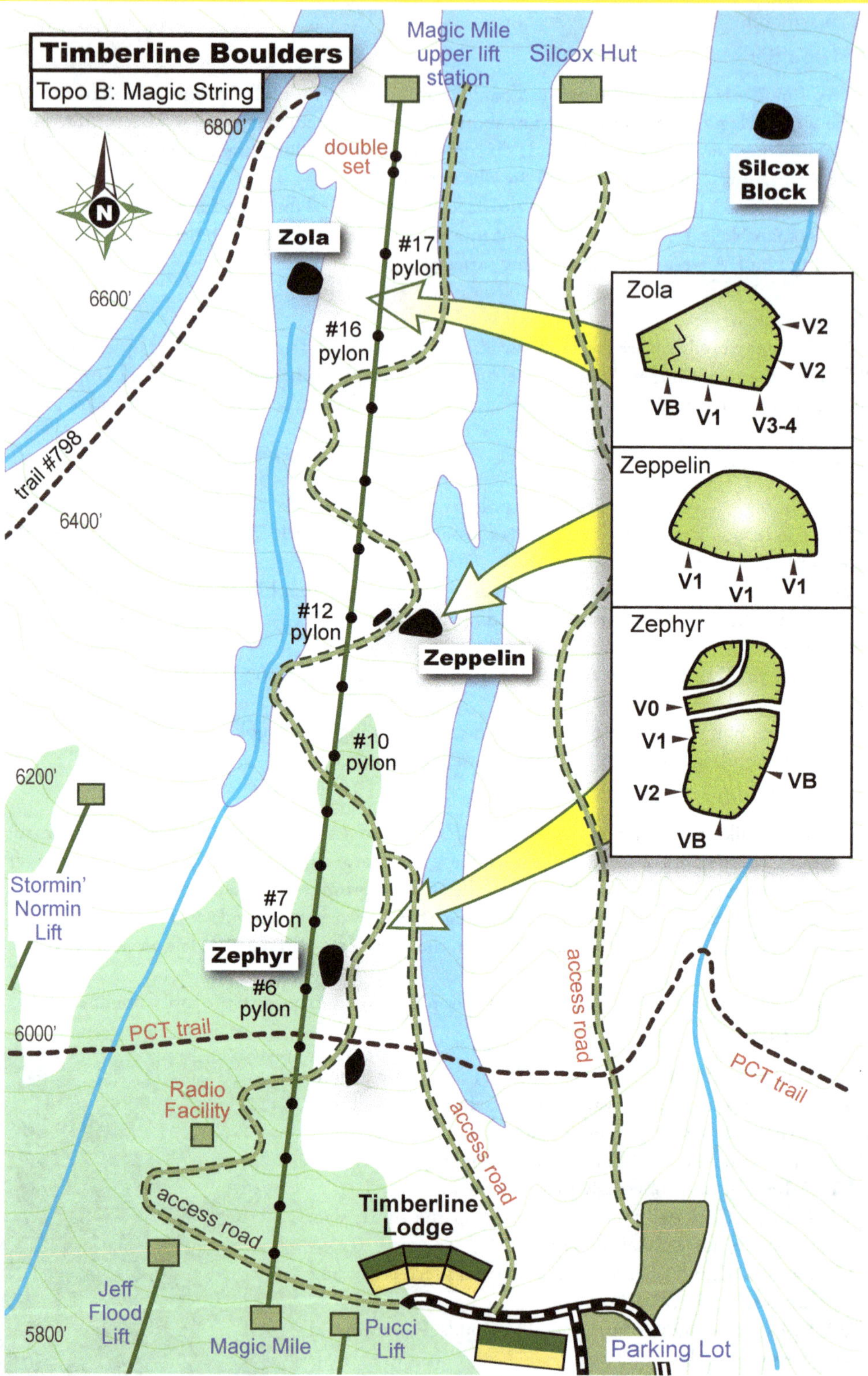
Timberline Boulders
Topo B: Magic String
6800'
N
6600'
6400'
trail #798
6200'
Stormin'
Normin
Lift
6000'
PCT trail
Radio
Facility
access road
Jeff
Flood
Lift
5800'
Magic Mile
Magic Mile
upper lift
station
Silcox Hut
Silcox
Block
Zola
double set
#17
pylon
#16
pylon
#12
pylon
#10
pylon
Zeppelin
#7
pylon
Zephyr
#6
pylon
Pucci
Lift
Timberline
Lodge
access road
access road
PCT trail
Parking Lot
Zola
V2
V2
VB   V1   V3-4
Zeppelin
V1   V1   V1
Zephyr
V0
V1
V2
VB
VB

V2 Zeta. Sit start and pop for jug and a jug (detached but solid block). Cool line.

Azimuth Boulder

Azimuth Stone is a flat laying (9′ tall by 20′ long by 15′ wide) stone difficult to distinguish from a distance, composed of grainy dacite rock. All routes overhang as starting move, except the VB. Located west of the ski boundary signs, west of the initial snow ravine. Located 200′ west of chairlift, and 100′ below the rough horizontal hiker's path that runs west from the chairlift building. Beta is from the north aspect counterclockwise (most are on west side). All routes opening move bulge except the VB.

V2 Azimuth. Sends up the rounded bulge

V1 Heady Aroma. Up overhung center scoop into low angle scoop.

V0 Coffee n' Cream. Minor stuff.

VB Gingerbread Eggnog Machiato. Incuts and steps on west side.

V0 Black Brew. A good line that starts low on left on overhang, run jugs to top.

V1 Java Jive. Start low on overhang, and move up left.

V1 Coffee Culture. Start low on overhang, and move up right.

Two traverses (**V4**), start at VB, go opposite directions.

Zebu Boulder

A boulder about 11′ tall on east side with three minor problems. Located directly west of Zola.

VB Zebu. Jugs on rounded SE nose.

V0 Coffee n' Cream. On scoop on center east face.

VB on jugs on uphill line.

Zee Boulder

A seemingly inconsequential block until you see the alcove on the west side. Has just one stout line 13′ tall.

V4ss Zen Master. Sit start and power up a thin finger locks crack that starts as a full overhang, and punch past the lip and cruise up right on better edges to the top.

Black Pearl Boulder

If you like to hike, then continue up along the west side of the Palmer Chairlift to the 3rd pole set down from the Palmer Mid-point lift house, and 300′ west of the lift. An overhung 40′ long west facing boulder with a flat lip running the entire length of the west aspect, small at both ends, and 11′ tall in the center. Difficult to see due to its flat top. All lines are full mantle exits.

V_ (?) ____ a vertical tips seam on the upper left section of overhung west face.

V1 Black Pearl is the center flake rail. Start low on obvious center flake, run rail up left, mantle out.

VB Hubris Greed & Ignorance. The basic fat jug run on right.

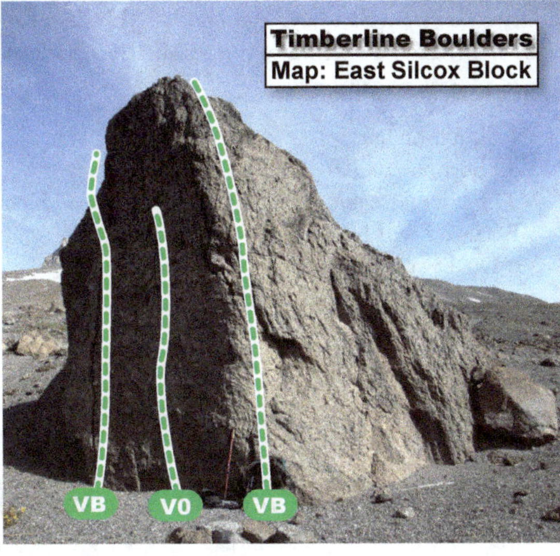

V3 Pearl Hunter. Run the entire 35' long lip traverse from right to left.

The following boulders are located east of the top lift station of the Magic Mile chairlift in the vicinity of the Silcox Hut.

Silcox Boulder ⚠

Silcox Boulder is located about 300' east of the Silcox Hut at the same elevation. Highly visible from all angles and located near a major snow ravine.

VB The Nose. The basic rounded nose with plenty of holds.

V0 Lichen. A steep lichen covered face just left of the nose.

V0 Detached Flake. Yup a detached flake.

Split Block Boulder

Split Block Boulder is to the north of Silcox Hut (about 300' uphill) at the level of the Palmer Chairlift at the 3rd pylon. A low **Split Traverse (V2)** exists on the W-S-E side. The rock is split in half east-to-west (encompasses 30' diameter).

SANDY RIVER BOULDERS

Along the ever popular Ramona Falls trail you will find several boulders near the hikers trail. These are erratic stones swept into their present location by floods long ago. Most stones are slick-as-snot basalt, well smoothed from tumbling, and chemical weathering, and are scattered in three sections along a distance of ½ mile (the first and biggest stone is a mere 300' walk) on flat sandy terrain. The rocks are basaltic (micro-crystalline plagioclase in deep black-gray matrix), and generally smooth with limited holds or smears, divots or crimps. Good flat landings, single crashpad viable site, some minor problems (VB-V4+ potential), some mossy aspects, though very limited total problems (less than 25). There are a few more stones alongside the river, but tend to get shifted by the river flows. All problems are well done.

Directions

Drive east from Sandy, Oregon on U.S. Hwy 26 to Zigzag, then drive north on NF18, turning right on NF1825 and drive to the Sandy River trailhead #797 (see diagram).

Split Block (11' tall)

- **V3** Shorty on left
- **V3** Short face on left
- **V3** Quality nose just left of off-width (on small block).
- **VB** The off-width between both blocks.
- **V0** Quality rib with pocket (on right big block).
- **V_** (?) Face left of tree (maybe not).

Triangle Stone (11' tall)

V0 South rib, **V3** East face, **V0** East ramp, **V1** Rib left of tree, **V1** Rib right of tree, **V3** North face, **VB** Low angle rib.
See diagram for more info.

ENOLA BOULDERS

Large andesite stones on a steep north-facing talus slope at the 3,000'

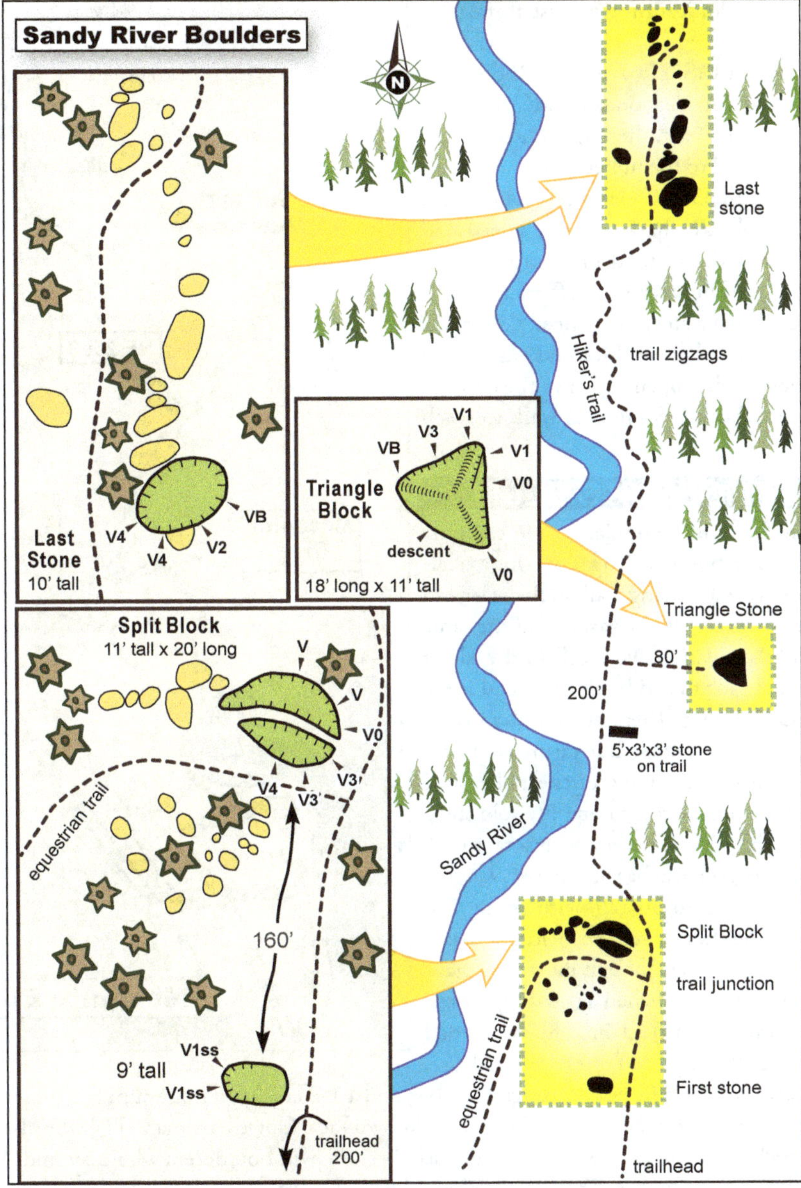

elevation near the popular rock climbing site called Enola (aka The Swinery). Potential problems range from VB-V9, for a total of perhaps 65+ lines, with moss and lichen. The cluster is a single, very compact zone, offering an array of pocket face lines, prows, overhangs, and numerous huge blocks (12'-18' diameter and up to 17' tall). A cool shaded environs, viable even on hot summer days with seasonal access ranging from May-October. Most stones have landed in ideal positions, lending to natural stances and ledges for easy padding with 1-2 crashpads. Extra pointers: site is generally untapped (or minimally explored) as of 2015. Due to its north-facing aspect the site is limited to mid-summer dry season, because the steep north-facing aspect of the talus slope tends to stay moist. Stout potential problems, luxurious growth of moss, and a very moist north facing slope will likely limit future interest at the site.

Directions

Drive east on U.S. Hwy 26 past Rhododendron 1¼ mile, turn left onto Road 27. Follow the paved portion east, then up west on a very rough gravel road to the upper west-most bend in the road at the 3,000' elevation (total of 2.3 miles from highway). Park on a small dead-end spur road in a thick stand of fir trees. From the forested parking area walk off-trail directly north, then down a steep (may need a short 20' hand line) wooded slope. Descend east of the north facing bluff. It opens up onto the boulder field. Expect about 7-8 minutes walk to reach the site.

EAST MOSQUITO BLUFF

Trillium Lake is a popular scenic camping and hiking area, but it is also known for a quality secluded rock climbing wall on the west end of Mosquito Butte. On the east end of the same butte (3,800' elevation) you will find a short wall conducive for mixed bouldering and some minor lead climbing. There are about a dozen existing problems to date, but future room for about 30+ problems (some of the taller stuff is rope terrain unless you commonly solo steep 30' stuff). The rock is a very grainy textured, well-weathered, vertical basalt outcrop, ranging in height from 12' to 30' tall, with some VB-V3 to date. The shorter section yields a feasible string of boulder lines, though most lines have some minor moss or lichen growth (particularly the corners). Tucked in a forest shaded setting the 200' long bluff sees minimal use.

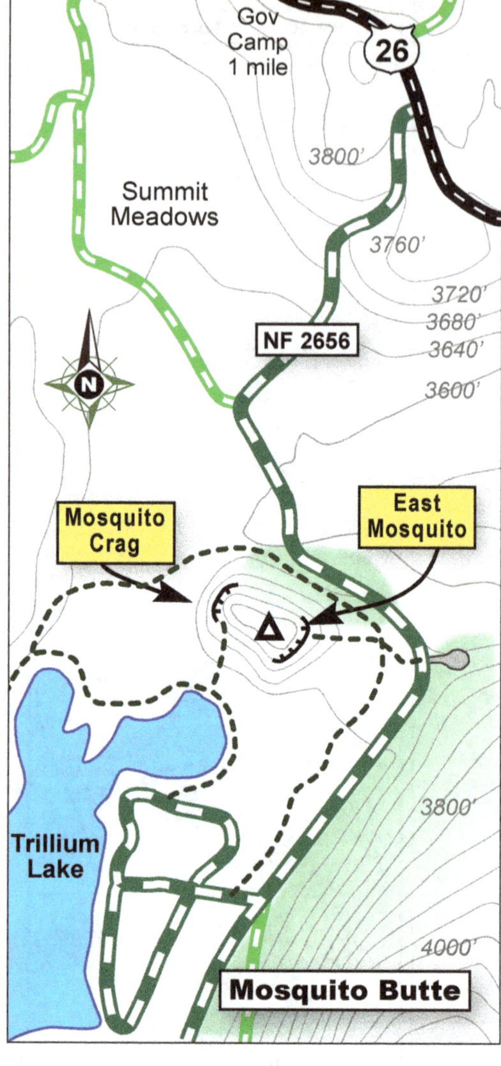

Seasonal access from mid-May through October, and a 1-2 crashpad minimum recommended site.

History: the site was tapped initially by well-known local Govie hardman [JT] who also utilized a nearby rock climbing wall. Stout raw lines still beckon avid boulderers who may find this small bluff worthy to tap further. The northernmost lines are tapped. Most of the V-ratings south of Antfarm are merely raw estimates.

Directions

Drive Trillium Lake road NF 2656 for ¾ mile south from U.S. Hwy 26. Park at the east end of the butte, and walk cross-country westward a few hundred feet to the butte (you will cross a hike/bike trail that circles the lake and butte). Beta is north to south (R to L).

North End

V3 _fj_ right side of overhung prow.

V3 _fj_ face and arête on left side of prow.

V0 _fj_ face to big edges and crack at top.

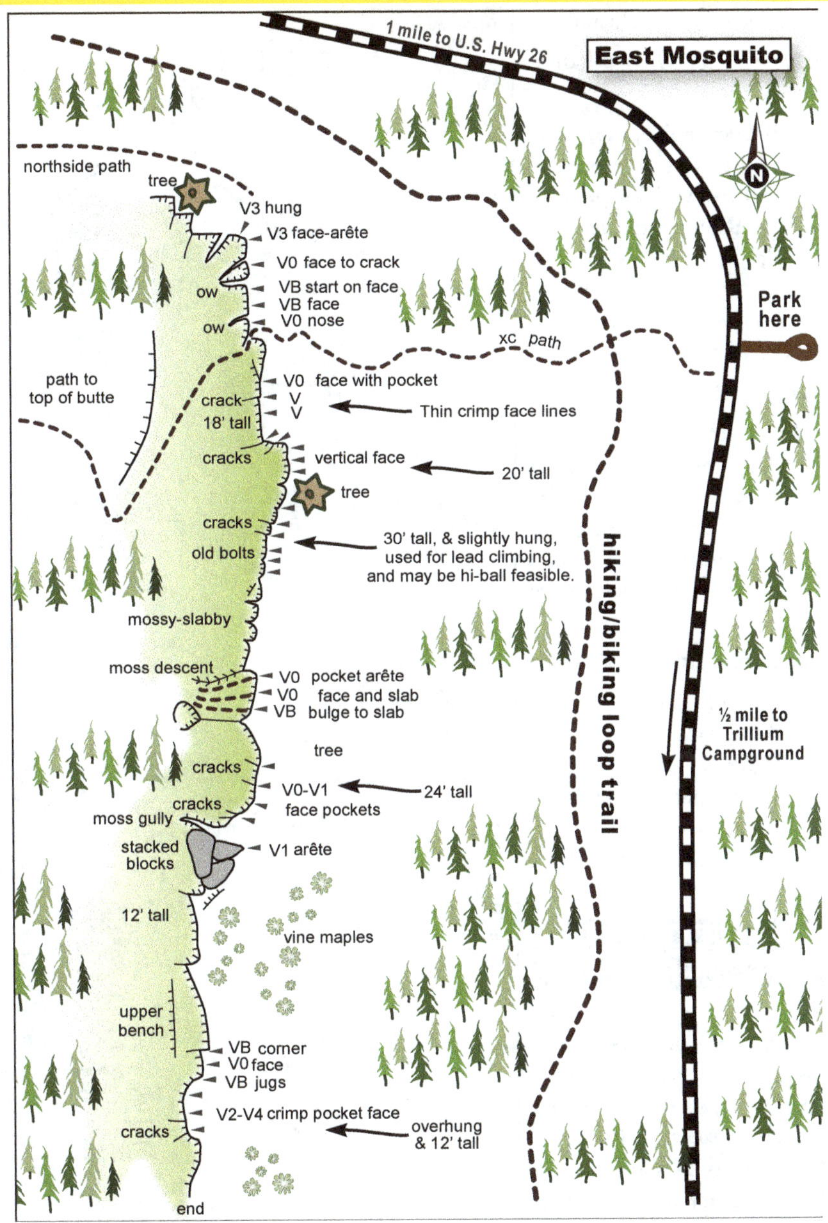

VB _ƒ_ face and merge with slot.

VB _ƒ_ gully

VB _ƒ_ nose

The cross-country path cuts up several steep steps here onto the knoll.

V0 Ant Farm. Start on giant pocket, reach to lip face edges, finish.

V2 (?) ⌒⌒ thin face and crack.

V4 (?) ⚠ tall slightly hung flat crimpy face.

Southward is a very tall section that may yield about 11 lead climbs (some old bolts exist). Then a brief gap to next cluster.

Tall 16' slab with a bulge along the base.

V0 Pocket Pretense tackles the vertical rounded nose prow with big pockets.
VB Riplets tackles the bulge then a thin slab.
VB Double Deception. Get over the initial bulge then cruise the slab.

Large tree

South of the tree is a 24' tall section that may yield 3-4 lead climbs or maybe hi-ball solo bouldering.

Then pass a stacked blocks section that may yield more bold stuff.

South end nook (12' tall)

VB moss corner
V0 thin face
VB jugs on face
V2-4 (?) pocket crimps on overhung face.
V2-4 (?) pocket face.
V_ (?) crack.

MUD RIDGE BOUL-DERS

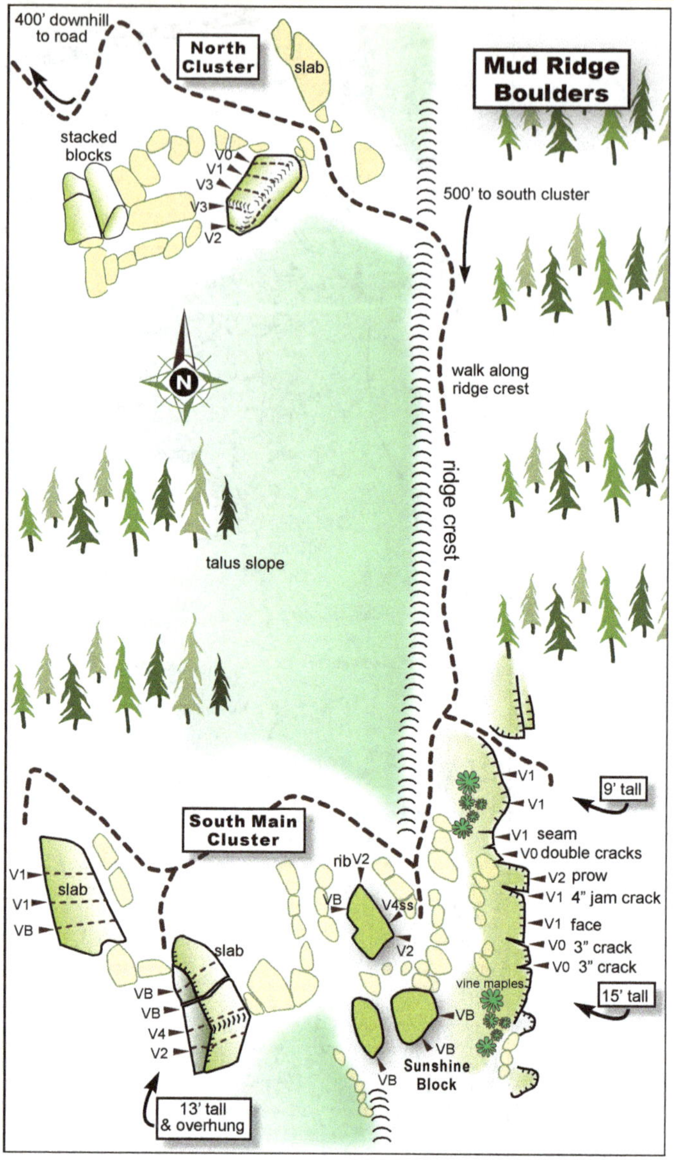

Nothing to write home about, but if you are utterly desperate, it exists. About 20 possible lines on weathered textured black basaltic rock, lichen exists on most aspects (some lichen removal), light surface textural grain for friction, all perched on a minor wooded knoll at the 3,800' elevation. A few of the problems are reasonable, some are not. Minimally explored to date (first by Mr O).

Directions

Drive the Trillium Lake road NF 2656, then drive south 1 mile on Mud Creek Road (prior to reaching the quarry) and park when you see a minor rock slope on the east side of road. Walk uphill angling rightward, off-trail scrambling up a steep slope from road to the knoll, then proceed south 200' to the south end cluster. See diagram for some of the beta.

WHITE RIVER BOULDERS

An idyllic scenic setting in an open pine tree lightly forested sandy flat area (where x-country skiers frequently tour) you will find two boulders that would interest a beginner VB-V3 boulderer. A scenic hike along the river on a closed gravel road, then up a brief slope to the pine tree flats. The first stone is the largest and offers a 360° circuit (plus variations). The stone surface is well textured with crimps, holds, smears, but surprisingly steep to overhung on the lower 2'-4' on the east and north side (beta list shows standing starts, though all lines offer sit start feasibility). Scenic area with quality photo ops and views of Mt Hood.

Where is the second smaller stone? Walk further up the trail till you reach the power line, then walk west 100' to the second minor 8' tall moss-free andesite stone with rounded crimps, a short stout rail run, and several basic lines. Seasonal access is June to early November.

Directions

Drive U.S. Hwy 26 east past Government Camp, then on Hwy 35 to the White River parking lot on the north side of the road. Walk north on a gated dirt road. Hiking distance is about ¾ mile from parking lot.

Pine Tree Boulder (11' tall)

VB Descent on west side.

V0 Face on west side.

V1 Round bulge

V2 Hung nose

V3 Overhang pullup.

V1 Thin face on east side.

V1 Foot knob start on east side.

V2+ss Stout overhang.

V3+ss Super hung, power over lip.

V3+ss Start under lip, power over lip.

Powerline Boulder (8' tall)

VBss Descent, **V0ss** East nose, **V0ss** Smears right of east nose, **V3ss** Side pull on arête then mantle, **V4ss** Start low on right, run rail up left, top out.

BOULDER MTN BOULDERS

Quality andesite bouldering in a scenic High Cascade Mtns forested setting just off the road at Bluebox Pass on US Highway 26. The name 'Boulder Mtn' is a bit of a misnomer; the site has far more trees and its the trees that keep you from seeing the next stone cluster (but overview maps do help). All things considered, whether its Bluebox, Boulder, Stone, or Tree Mtn, it's still a unique aesthetic destination worth visiting by any veteran of the game.

Boulder Mtn has three primary boulder talus fields, while the remainder of the stones (albeit some good gems) lay thoroughly scattered in open forested terrain. Some boulders tend to be fairly isolated from the next batch, making the hunt for them a bit more adventurous perhaps than the

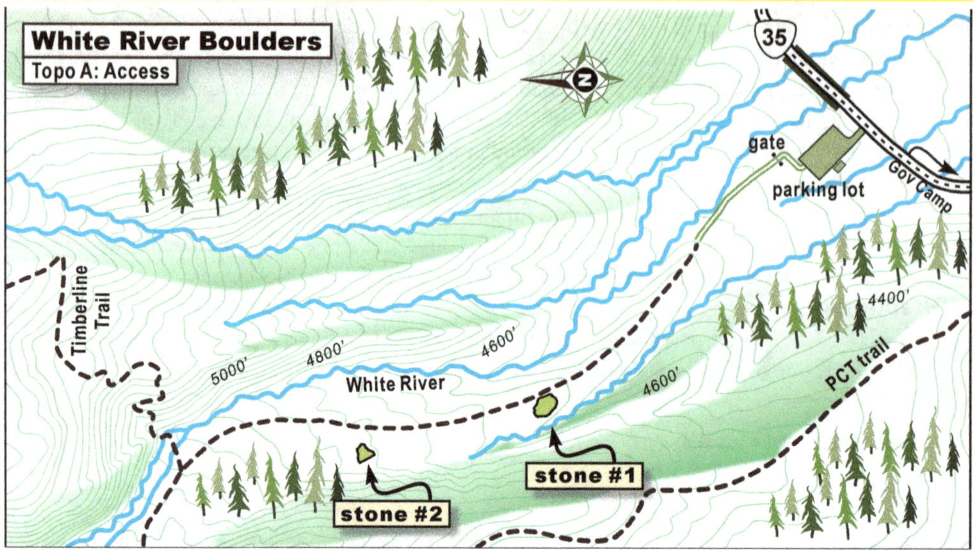

average person might willingly endure. Initially, focus where the raw meat is well-aged by sending lines in the primary boulder fields like the stellar Northwest Cluster (aka Lost City One), or perhaps the Southwest Cluster (Lost City Two). The entire Stone Mtn Bouldering zone will likely eventually yield 200+ boulder problems after its more thoroughly tapped. Due to sporadic route sending anticipate moss or lichen growth on certain problems for a while.

By far the best quality string of boulders is the extensive Northwest Cluster with its panoramic views of Mt Hood. This spot offers a fine quality set of beasts ranging in height from 8'-12' tall in an idyllic open forest sunny setting wrapping along the edge of a large talus field. This extensive cluster has minimal tumbling, thus most of the crimps and features are still well formed. This cluster should eventually yield about 80+ problems.

The eastern Bluebox String offers some very well-rounded stones on a southeasterly facing slope surrounded by an open forest. Some are so well tumbled stones to be almost bowling ball round, but scattered along the lower perimeter of the talus field zone is a string of big blocks which range from 8'-12' (one pocket riddled fin reaches 15' tall). The rock offers numerous gaseous air pockets, dishes, and scoops 2"-6" in diameter. The Bluebox String (VB-V6+) may eventually yield a limited 20-30+ problems.

Seasonal access to this entire bouldering haven is viable from late-May through October (longer if snow free at 4,100' elev).

General History

The quality Northwest Cluster [Lost City] and numerous other isolated quaility stones in the area were tagged by Mr Holzman, Mr Cousins, Mr Krossen (and numerous others) starting in about 2011. The Bluebox Group was first explored and various V's were tagged by Mr O in about 2011. This entire site is now seeing considerable influential by multiple teams of locals. The overall expansion of the range of clean problems at the site will involve a greater array of dedicated locals scattered over several more years.

Directions

Drive U.S. Hwy 26 to Government Camp, then seven more miles south to Bluebox Pass (Frog Lake). Turn west onto NF 2660, then immediately northwest onto a rough gravel logging road. Drive for ¼ mile to the switchback, and park at a wide pullout at the edge of an open forested area.

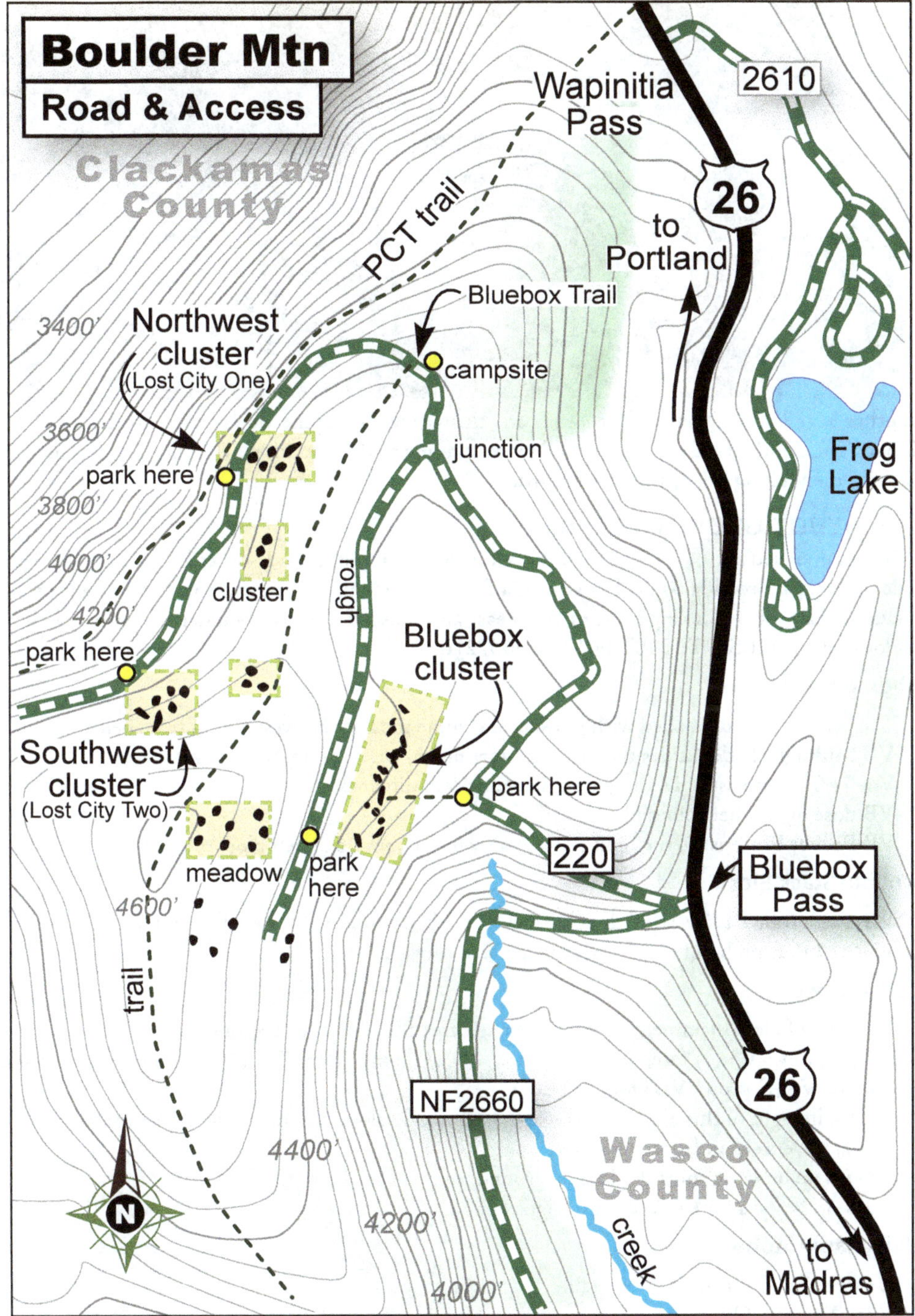

Walk horizontally west (best to have GPS or map) for 200' to the boulder field. Future road access is not assured, but if it gets a closure berm, the walk is short.

To reach the popular Northwest String drive up the same gravel road, but continue past the first switchback uphill till it levels off and it curls westerly to a 'Y' intersection. Go right, and drive for

another ¼ mile till you encounter a roadside cluster with sweeping views to the northwest of Mt Hood. The Southwest String is reached by continuing to drive south on this old road for another ¼ mile, then hiking briefly uphill eastward.

BLUEBOX GROUP (TOPO A)

This minor cluster of boulders can be accessed from gravel roads on either the east or west side (see map). Broad talus field of stones, a few low grade problems, and some stones with well-rounded features. The string is facing southeast and most of the large boulders are situated along its lower flank. GPS UTM 10T 601408 5007216.

Midnight Fin

The giant 16' tall fin loaded with pockets and some moss, at far west end of talus field.
VB Midnight Ride tackles the east side starting low on arête fin. Several VB's.
V4-5 (?) to the east of Midnight Fin is a rounded rail block.
VB nose of another round block nearby.
VB Pocket Pretense is the Split Block, using mega pockets on left block.

Double Stack Block

VB Contrivance is a vertical double-stacker block, one on top of the other with nice holds.
VB is a brief combo of blocks that make a slab n' crack.

East Alcove

A cluster of blocks jammed together offering short SS vertical or overhung lines.
V4 (?) prow, **V5** (?) face, **V2** (?) corner, **V7** (?) hung arête, **V3** (?) hung prow-corner-slot combo, **V3** (?) prow, **VB** blunt arête.
Just to the right of this alcove is a traverse, and just up slope are some minor SS problems.
V4 (?) traverse rounded low traverse.
V3-4ss up on hung short flat face to a round top.
V0 short vertical nose next door to right.

Vine Maple Stone

A single 2' wide prow about 11' tall.
V2ss Treason. Quality run, face crimps, lip, small backside sloper pocket, hi-step, done.

Northend Nook

A minor alcove with a brief pack of potential lines.

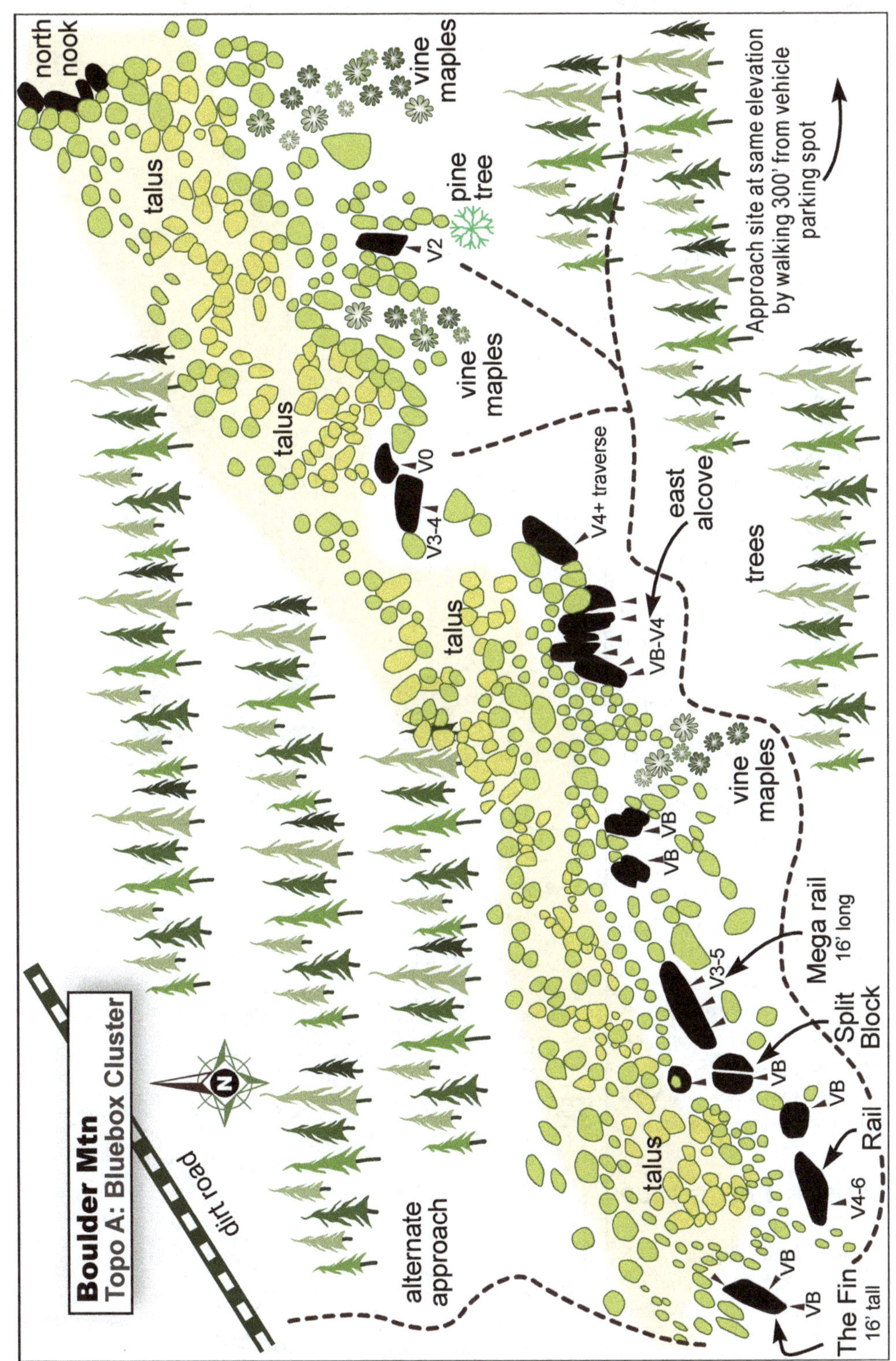
Boulder Mtn
Topo A: Bluebox Cluster
N
dirt road
alternate approach
north nook
talus
talus
talus
talus
talus
talus
vine maples
vine maples
vine maples
pine tree
trees
east alcove
V2
V0
V3-4
V4+ traverse
VB-V4
VB VB
VB
V3-5
Mega rail 16' long
Split Block
VB
VB
VB
Rail
The Fin 16' tall
V4-6
VB
VB
Approach site at same elevation by walking 300' from vehicle parking spot

LOST CITY (NW CLUSTER)

Certainly the best cluster of boulders to tap into on your first visit. Convenient parking spots, and zero approach time to get to the first stone (touching the roadside). The talus slope trends uphill away from the road in a sickle shape northward for several hundred feet. Access the problems by walking on either side of the talus field. Anticipate some moss or lichen on various problems during the initial exploratory years. GPS UTM 10T 601107 5008056.

TOPO B & C

Roadside Stone has some basic fun stuff (VB-V2).

Twin Boulders is a set of blocks with fine lines from VB-V5.

Pyramid Block is a tall split block that has VB-V1 (some SS). A double-stacked stone just to the east offers V4ss.

Nook #1 has V0 to V7 and some projects.

Nook #2 V0-V1, and on nearby stones V0-V4.

Nook #3 has V0 to V5 (potential V9+ project) and some SS lines.

Additional nearby stones yield V1 to V5 and some future projects.

South Nook has VB to V6ss on a series of 5-6 stones.

NORTH END GROUP (TOPO D)

North End Group yields the greatest (close radius) concentration of problems (VB to V7+) easily over 30+

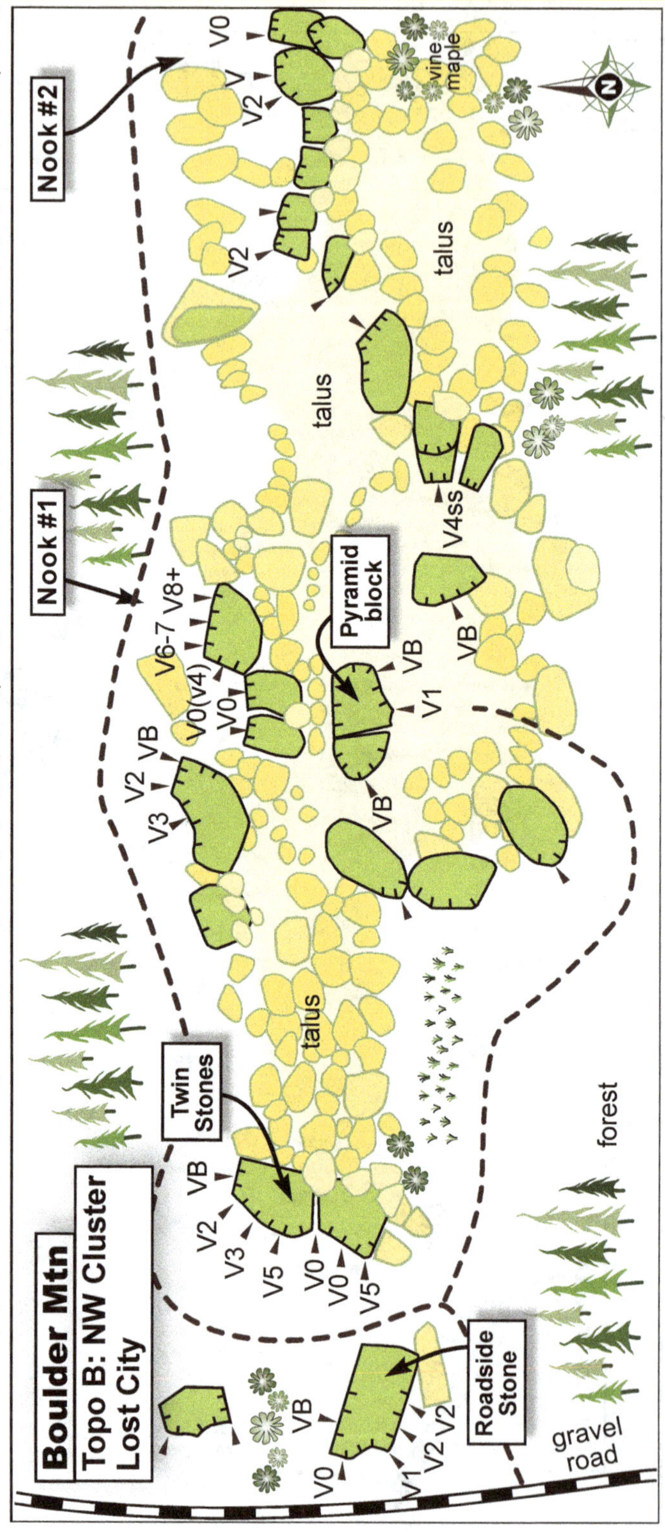

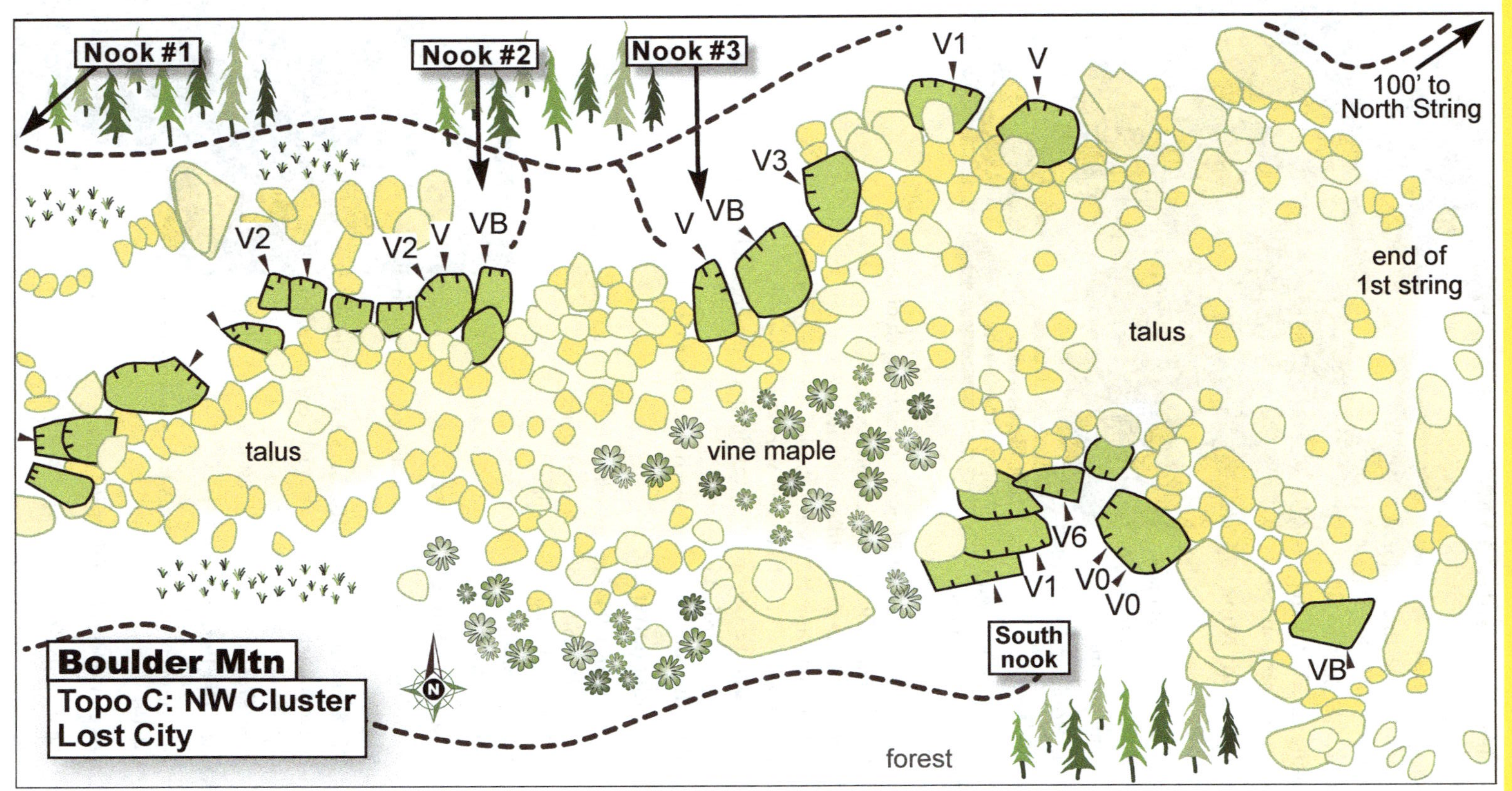
Nook #1
Nook #2
Nook #3
V1
V
100' to North String
V3
V VB
V2
V2 V VB
end of 1st string
talus
talus
vine maple
V6
V1
V0 V0
V0
N
South nook
VB
forest
Boulder Mtn
Topo C: NW Cluster
Lost City

problems on nearly 20 boulders, something for everyone. This is the utter north end of this major talus field (Northwest Cluster). Beta as follows using the A-Z letter sequence as seen on topo.

North End Nook #4 (letter A)

V-5+ to V-imaginable. Some are tapped, yet some still free.

Fire Boulder in Nook #5 (letter B)

A cool stone with a tight squeeze nook on its south aspect.

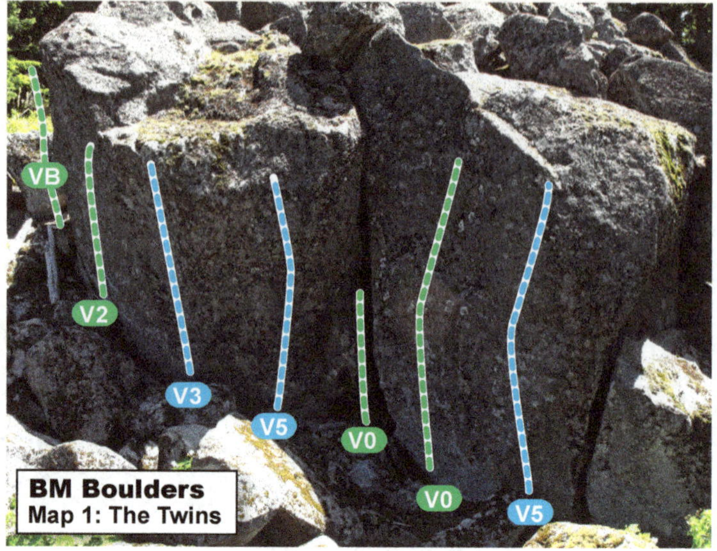

V2ss Fire in the Hole. Low on right in depth of nook.

V0ss Burn Baby Burn. Start on knob.

V0ss Straddle the Saddle. Obviously.

V2 (V4ss) Riptide. Pocket and left on crimp, working right, then traversing using top lip till knob then up. The classic line on this stone by either start.

V5ss Aquifer. Crimps up to tiny incut then merge right all way to route #2 knob.

V5ss _____. Project next left.

V2ss Illusion. On other stone behind you to south.

Fin Boulder (letter C)

The obvious tall skinny fin with a futuristic line awaiting.

V7-9+ The Fin. Project on west point.

VB Westside one move stepper.

V2ss [?] South side brief moves.

VB Gettin' off.

Monkey King Boulder (letter D)

A few basic entertaining lines on block just north of The Fin.

VB Slithering Sycophantic Slootballs. Run the horizontal left trending slab crack (on west side) to point then up big pockets.

V0ss Wussification. Short east face.

XX Boulder (letter E)

Two problems on a vertical face, ranking about **V4-V5.**

Three Dominoes Boulders (F)

The obvious flat vertical west facing stones (R to L).

VB Domino. The right outer point.

VB Domino Right Crack.

V1 Liberal Lemmings. A few short face moves.

VB Domino Left Crack.

V3 Domino Effect. The leftmost outer point.

North Point Boulder (Letter H)

Overhung on its north aspect and yielding three lines.

V4+ ___ left rib direct.

V0-1 ___ middle mantle.

V2-3 ___ Start on right and traverse left to merge and mantle over.

Fun Times Boulder (Letter K)

Basic VB's, but also has two very brief SS under the weather lines (*see topo*).

Excel Boulder (letter L)

A superb stone with several high quality lines. Located on east side of north point, and its a left leaning beast with a vertical south aspect with a string of SS.

V0ss ______ On far lower right, make a single move, then prance up low angle fat rib.

V0ss ______ alternate start onto the same rib above.

V3ss ______. Low and up slight hung face on crimps in center of face.

V3ss ______. On far left. Crimp up slight hung rounded face.

V5ss Reason To Be. Indeed a cool line. Start low on right, run entire slightly hung face up leftward to merge with previous line and top out.

Greek Goddess Boulder (letter M)

Mostly fun runs, but one problem has some SS spice to it (*see topo*). L to R:

VB, VB, VB, and **V2-3 (V3+ss)** on its hung east aspect.

The following are several other miscel-laneous boulder clusters at this site that might interest you.

SW Cluster

Drive the dirt road south till you get near the dead-end turn-around. Just before reach-

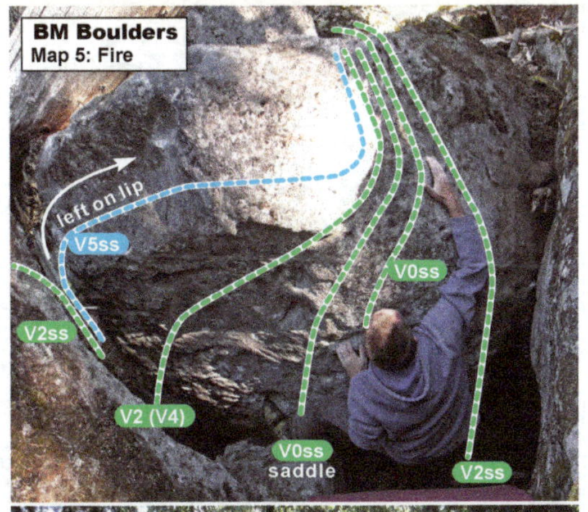

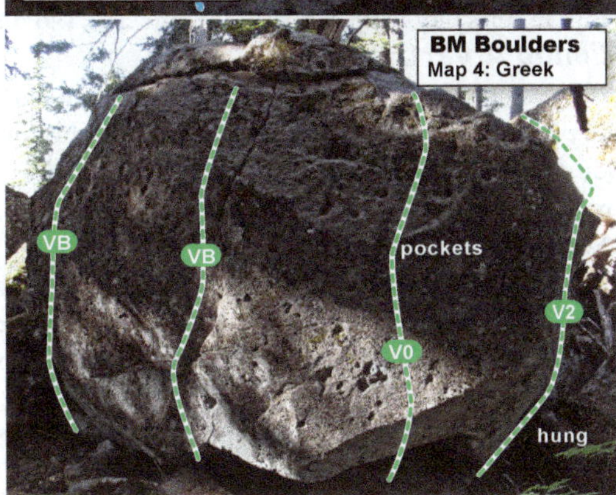

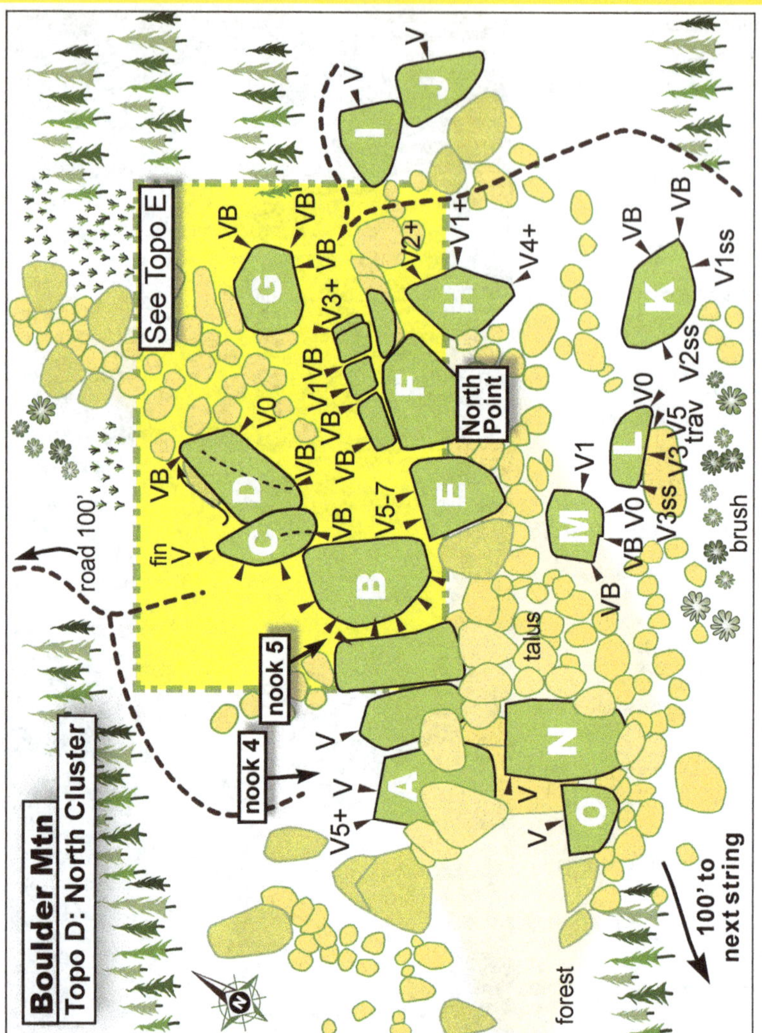

ing it, you will see a talus slope reaching down nearly to the road on your left (east). Park here. Walk uphill to the upper portion of the talus slope where you will find the primary large stones. Problems range in difficulty from VB to V7 (some SS). No diagram. GPS UTM 10T 600779 5007433.

Rimtop Area

If you opt to visit this tiny spot, its actually fairly close to the main Northwest Cluster. From the parking spot for that cluster, just walk south for 300', then hike uphill 200' to a small string of boulders facing west in a old logged zone (partially regrown). Or approach it by hiking the Bluebox trail (takes you longer). Problems range in difficulty V0 to V5 (very few total).

Woodlands Area

Generally reached by hiking the Bluebox trail south. Near a second logged zone, and just west a short distance from the hikers trail. A woodlands area cluster of about 10 stones with roughly 20+ problems. Problems range in difficulty VB to V7 (some SS).

South Meadow

Approach via the other road. From the 'Y' just east of the campsite (at the Bluebox trailhead), drive south on a very poor (AWD recommended) road for about ½ mile until the road opens onto a logged zone (with new regrowth). This is the southernmost logged zone. Park here, and hike briefly uphill along the northern edge of the logged zone looking for various boulders scattered broadly between the road and the hiking trail to the west at the top of the knoll. The problems range in difficulty VB to V7 (SS is common), yet many of the boulders are quite low and sit starts are the name of the game.

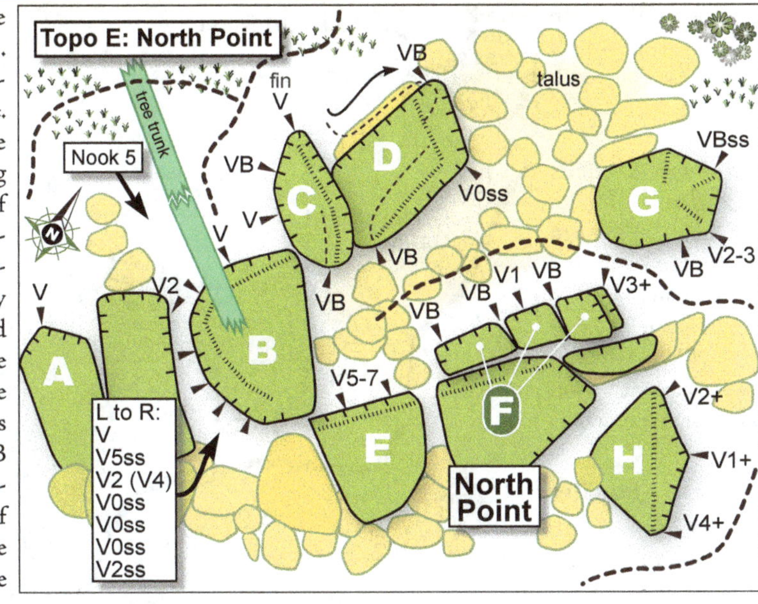

But a few gems to beckon. Expect to find 12-15 boulders with perhaps 20+ problems.

BENNETT BOULDERS

A fine quality, very compact andesitic bouldering area hidden in the back country of the Mt Hood National Forest. At the perfect altitude where moss or lichen are minimized, this tiny site provides an enjoyable days workout for any serious boulderer. Were it located anywhere else (on a paved road) it would surely be a mega hit for locals.

At the core spot, the tallest stone is about 13' tall, while the girth on a few are roughly 20' diameter. Generally moss free andesite rock with a lightly aged surface factor, yielding great friction on small sandpaper surface textured granules. Site has several classic lines, and about 40 problems total. Only 1-2 crashpads are needed.

The site is well tapped (except a few extreme V's), most grades are VB to V7, but several viable projects likely punch V7-9ish). Being at the 5400' elevation it's snow covered during winter months. General access is viable from July to October.

Other nearby boulder options: Brief boulders scattered above the road (just below a small cliff) Or, a small orange tinted vertical flat face exists at the *Terrible Traverse* (see map) may provide some VB-V0 brief entertainment.

Now the stickler...getting there. The gravel road is not maintained, thus its a AWD or 4WD only road (high clearance) and a slow careful drive on a road that has some narrow sections (at *Terrible Traverse*). Alternative? Yes....and far more enjoyable. Rack up your mountain bike on the top of your vehicle and your ready to go. The road is fairly level (with minor inclines).

Directions

Drive US Hwy 26 east of Gov Camp, then east on Highway 35 to Bennett Pass. Exit here, and turn into a large paved parking area with a rest room. Drive south on Bennett Pass road, which is a good gravel road for 1.7 miles to a junction. Park here (especially if its a low city car). The 'S' curves section is just ahead. Get on your bike, latch your crashpad on your back (and water), and south you go. At .7 miles you reach *Terrible Traverse* at a notch. (several VB-V0 on west side). At 2.25 miles you reach the 'T' junction of Bennett Pass and Bonney Meadows road. Continue south briefly on Bonney road (the talus slope becomes obvious immediately on your left (east). Stash your bike, and descend a 100' down slope to the main cluster (at the south end of the talus slope).

Mileage: 1.7 miles good gravel, 2.4 miles bad non-maintained road; total is 4.1 miles to site.

Elevation gain/loss: 4765' at (mtn bike) parking spot; 5372' at the bouldering site.

Bennett Boulder

Its the real reason you came here. Tall, hi-ball, and all quality lines from VB to V-hard.

V0 left face onto left rib.

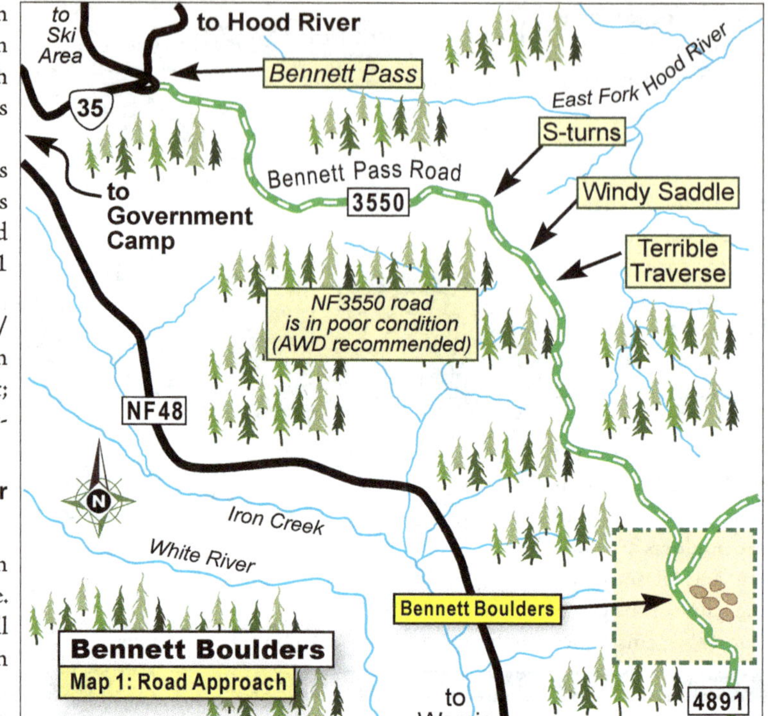

V6-9 face (starts almost same as previous but stays on face.

V6-9 thin seam on face.

V4-8 dimples to sloped small rails.

V3 Bennett Classic is the double sloped rails. The reason to be.

V3+ offers a variant busting up right from same start as previous.

VB is the basic right arête.

And the other nearby boulders:

Fin Boulder: A classic **V4ss**, but also some great easier stuff **VB-V0**, mostly SS.

Roof Boulder: The other great reason to visit here. Several classic lines, all SS, on a 45° overhung north aspect, with almost 11' of 'out-the-roof' crimp climbing.

Roadside Boulder: Mostly VB to V0 (SS) but has one nice low V2 rail.

Split Boulder: Offers several simple one move **VB-V0** lines.

Prow Boulder: Fun basic momentary things all **VB**.

Fun Boulder: Virtually all **VB** and nice for a warmup.

HUNCHBACK BOULDERS

The Hunchback Boulders are nestled quietly in a tantalizing tall Douglas fir forest which invites boulderer's to experience a little andesite bouldering near the elusive mega wall known as the Hunckback Wall. A gentle forest breeze generally keeps the place at a comfortable temperature even on hot summer days. This is a place where the sounds of nature predominate.

The problems range from VB to V8 (to date), are generally limited in totality mainly because there are only three boulders. The largest is of behemoth size (30' x 18') with a serious overhang on two aspects. The ultra cool main mega-stone has about 15 lines (one aspect is a superb 30' long traverse with a 45° undercut). Both nearby smaller stones have been tapped as well. Just 1-2 crash-

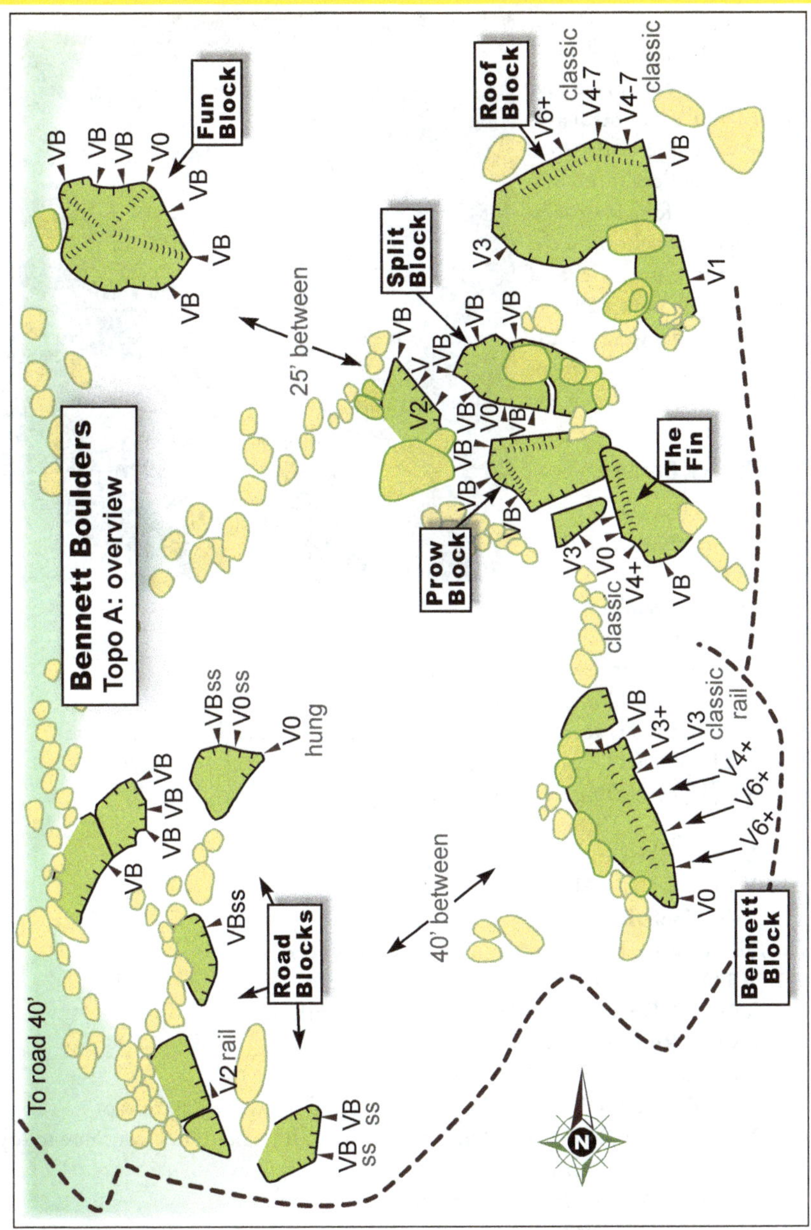

pads recommended, no ticks, no poison oak, cell reception (yes), low altitude (2600'), season from May-Oct, and sometimes accessible even into the winter months (if its dry).

The site has a convenient proximity to Portland (1-hour drive) with paved road access to the parking spot. A 25-minute steep uphill grunt on a narrow path gets you to the boulders, though due to the stout uphill grunt hike from the road it may keep some individuals at bay.

History: First tap by Mr O (2016); the punchy V's were tapped by Abbott/Anglin team.

Directions:

Drive east on U.S. Hwy 26 from Sandy, Oregon till you reach Welches. Turn south at the Subway store onto Salmon River Road (NF2618). Continue about 9/10 mile south passing a guardrail on the right, a small rotten roadside bluff on the left, and a deeply cut ravine also on the left. Park immediately on the west side of the road at a minor pullout. Step into the dry ravine for a few yards, then angle up right onto the south slope into a grove of cedar trees. A faint path begins there and zigzags gently uphill, and gradually steepens for the remainder of the uphill hike.

Hunchback Boulder ⚠

Starting on the south aspect. Beta from L to R (lower to upper):

1. **VB Imperialism**. The basic getdown.
2. **VB Liquid Desire** face variation.
3. **VB Royalty**. Crimps on slab.
4. **V7 Circuit Traverse**. The long uphill stellar traverse (lower ½ is done).
5. **V2 Exploited Class**. Lip mantle.
6. **V2 (V_ss) Ruling Class**. Hole mantle.
7. **V_ss [?] _____** (project).
8. **V3 (V_ss) Lemming Lore**. Hung crimp pull.
9. **V4 (V_ss) The Abyss**. Hung prow.
10. **VB Noob**. Fat dirty slot.

The following are on the overhung west aspect (R to L):

1. **V3 Of Noble Birth**. Jug start. Rightmost line.
2. **V5ss ONB Extension**. The SS extension of the above.
3. **V5 Bell Ringer**. High start.
4. **V6 Bell Ringer**. Standing start.
5. **V7ss Bell Ringer**. The full low traverse going right, then up to top.
6. **V7ss Acceptable Losses**. Dyno straight up to high hold then continue to top.
7. **V7-9 [?] ______** (project).
8. **V5 Quasi Moto**. High jug start, up and out right.
9. **V__ ______** (project).
10. **V__ ______** (project).
11. **V8 Full Moto**. Thin moves right to jug, then up right and out.
12. **V__ ______** (project).
13. **V0ss Megalonia**. Leftmost line. Layback and mantle over.

Quasimodo Boulder

A few yards SW of the big boulder. To date (L to R):
VB short flat face, **VB** outer steps, **V_** (?) hung power, **V5 Ex Libris**. (rightmost hung power

line [SS is +]).

Esmeralda Boulder

Located about 100' north along trail. To date (R to L): **V2 Zeno's** (rounded face/rib), **V2 Esmeralda** (seam to slab), **V_** (?) seam on face, **V_** (?) (leftmost blank face).

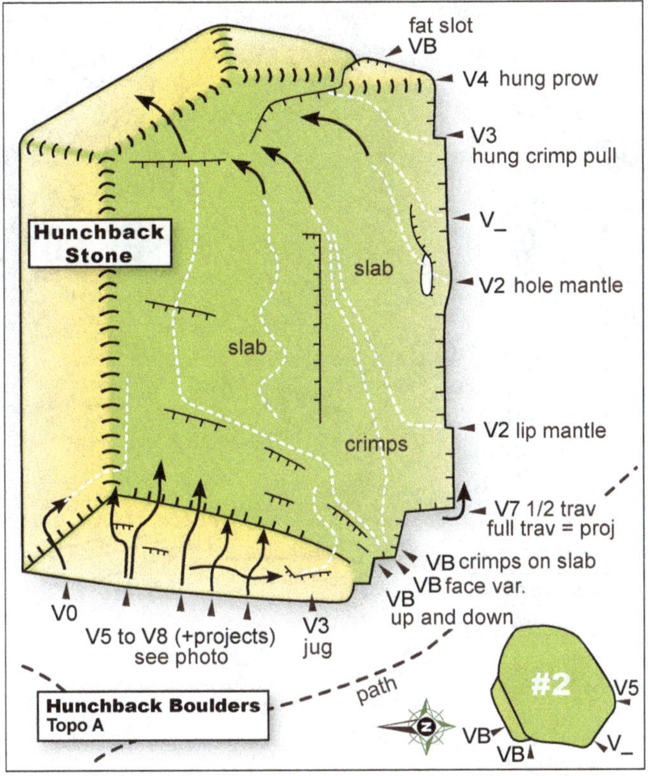

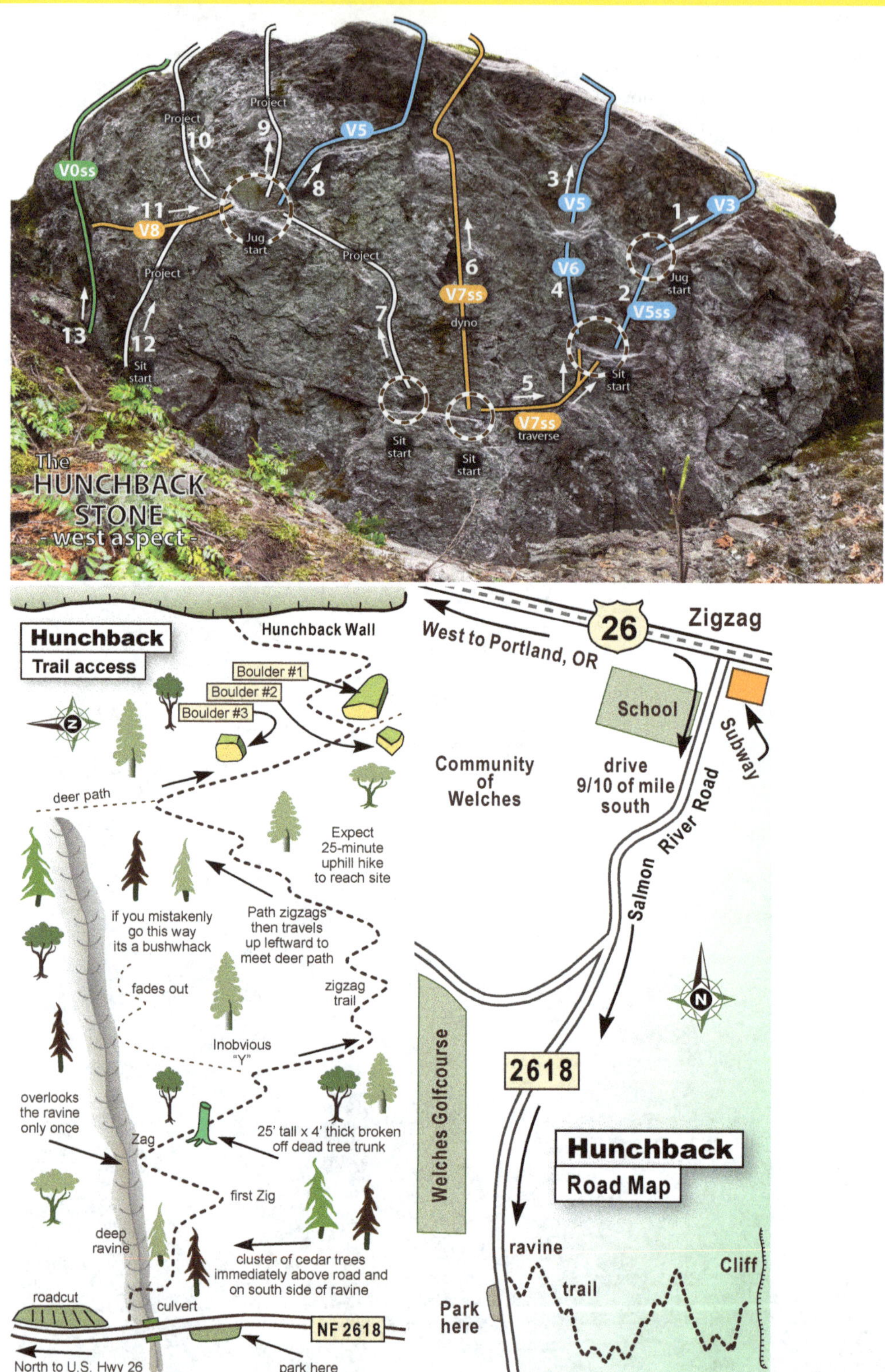
V0ss
Project
10
Project
9
V5
V0ss
11
V8
8
Jug start
Project
13
12
Sit start
Project
7
6
V7ss
dyno
5
V7ss traverse
Sit start
Sit start
3
V5
1
V3
4
V6
2
V5ss
Jug start
Sit start
The HUNCHBACK STONE
- west aspect -
Hunchback
Trail access
Hunchback Wall
Boulder #1
Boulder #2
Boulder #3
deer path
Expect 25-minute uphill hike to reach site
if you mistakenly go this way its a bushwhack
Path zigzags then travels up leftward to meet deer path
fades out
zigzag trail
Inobvious "Y"
overlooks the ravine only once
Zag
25' tall x 4' thick broken off dead tree trunk
first Zig
deep ravine
roadcut
culvert
cluster of cedar trees immediately above road and on south side of ravine
NF 2618
North to U.S. Hwy 26
park here
26
Zigzag
West to Portland, OR
School
Subway
Community of Welches
drive 9/10 of mile south
Salmon River Road
2618
Welches Golfcourse
Hunchback
Road Map
N
ravine
trail
Cliff
Park here

MT HOOD BOULDERING AREAS (NORTHERN)

This section details bouldering sites in the Hood River valleys, on both the Hood Fork and the West Fork river drainages, essentially areas found on the northern slopes or valleys of Mt Hood.

COOPER SPUR BOULDERS

For those who relish the invigorating nature of high-altitude bouldering, the stellar Cooper Spur Boulders provide a scenic, quality bouldering site just a short hike from the Cooper Spur trailhead (5,800') on the windswept northeastern alpine slopes of Mt Hood. The Cooper Spur Boulders are an idyllic little wonderland of rock, scoured impeccably clean by wind, snow and rain. The alpine scenery around the Cooper Spur Stone Shelter is a captivating, photographic blend of whitebark pine trees, numerous andesite and dacite boulders, jet blue sky, and the rugged north face of Mt Hood as a backdrop.

The 1.1 mile uphill hike begins at the Cloud Cap parking site, nestled in a hemlock forest. Just beyond the wilderness signage post, the hikers trail splits into several directions. The right trail fork goes up to Eliot Glacier along a windswept moraine ridge crest. This right trail fork also leads to the Eliot Cluster, a set of three boulders in a compact locale protected from the winds, a mere ¼ mile from the trailhead. The left trail fork is the primary trail (#600 Timberline trail) that leads up to the junction with the Tilly Jane trail (#600a) at the Cooper Spur stone shelter. From the stone shelter, the hikers trail braids uphill through the very midst of a vast cluster of boulders. There are a number of camping spots at the base of some boulders, some of which may be in use (more likely on weekends). Also, en route to the stone hut, but ¼ mile from the trailhead you will encounter an impressively large boulder 20' wide and 15' tall.

The Stone Hut Cluster of boulders begins near the metal roofed Cooper Spur stone shelter, and continues uphill for about 300' (from 6,800' to 7,100'). The entire area is littered with small stones (2'-6'), but of the larger 25 stones you will find 75+ boulder problems (VB-V5), with heights ranging from 9' to 12' (a few reach 14') tall.

The Eliot Cluster is a set of three stellar andesite stones (about 12' tall) with overhanging aspects, and a total of 17 problems (VB-V4) and several traverse lines. These stones are very likely to have been climbed upon eons ago. Historical bouldering data is non-existent. High altitude day hikers (and various mountaineers) who naturally boulder/scramble a bit are very likely to be first on many basic lines. Mr O did a virtual complete send of the entire site in approximately 2009.

The surface texture nuances of the stones show considerable weathering from rain, wind, and snow. This has softened the typical sharpness of the crystalline phenocrysts. With a softened textured surface friendly to bouldering, it is quite feasible to climb 40+ problems in one outing with-

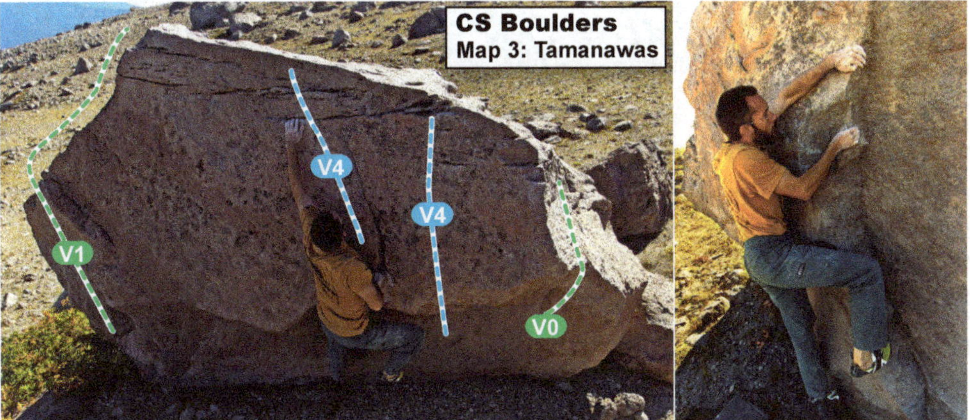

On Tilly Jane Boulder

out wearing the fingertip pads thin. This weathering factor creates a challenge though, by giving the surface a slick greasy feel (less noticeable on shaded aspects). Expect cool morning temperatures (colder in October), so plan your trip according to your V-fix favorites. Rock surficial variances range from low jug rails, a plethora of traverses, some pockety features, glassy slopers, rounded crimpers; all the typical variables that entice, yet situated at the 6700' elevation in full sunlight. One crashpad is recommended for this site. The vast majority of the problems are short, and the landings gravelly or sandy.

Brief summer seasonal access is from about July 15th (or when the road opens to the Cooper Spur trailhead) until late October or early November. Check with the Forest Service to determine if the gates have been closed at the end of the season. Very warm daytime temperatures may occur in July-August, but you can attain colder sending conditions from mid-September onward. If a 2½ hour drive from Portland may seem excessive, if so, consider car-camping at the trailhead, or in the general vicinity. The nearest town with some amenities is Parkdale (about 15 miles), and Hood River (about 30 miles) to the north. The Northwest Forest Pass is required when parking at this site. The graveled portion of the road is 9.5 miles from the ski area (paved up to the ski center) to the trailhead (good 2WD vehicle road).

THE ELIOT CLUSTER

From the parking site, walk up the trail past the registration sign (past the Tilly Jane trail) to a "Y" in the trail. The left trail is #600, but let's take the right trail to the Eliot Cluster of boulders. It ascends up a steep sandy slope, enters a small grove of trees, and shortly reaches the first large boulder alongside the

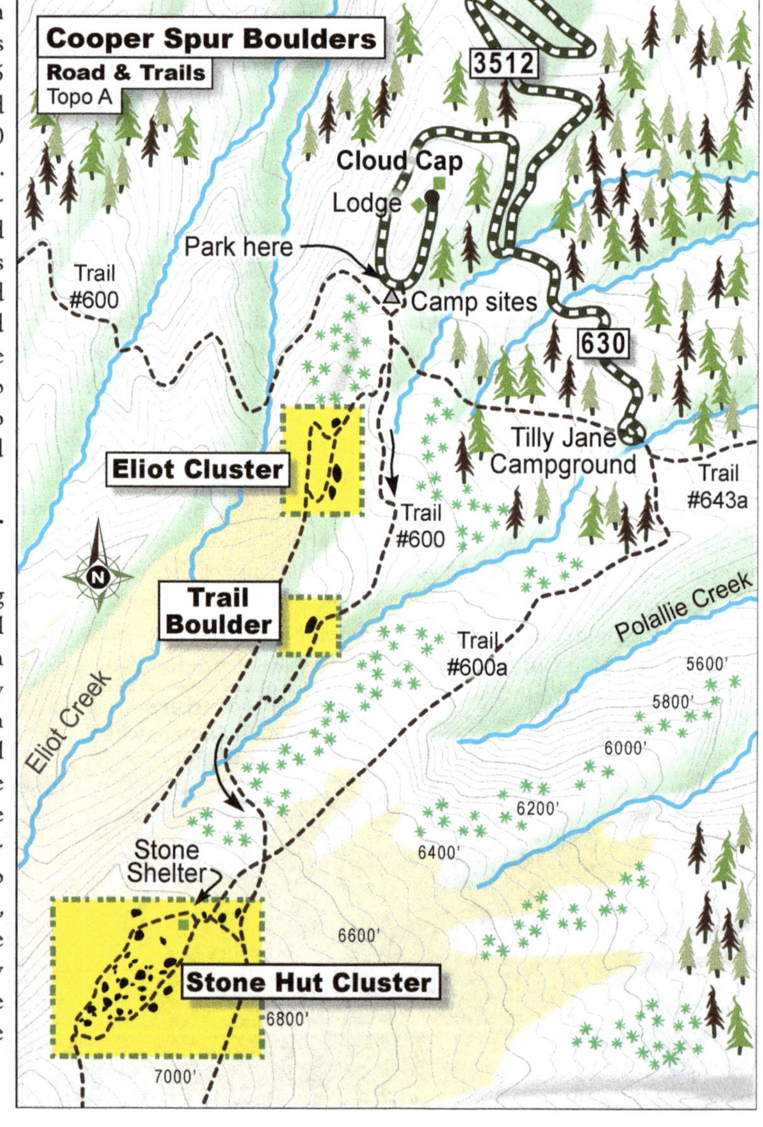

trail.

Barrett Boulder

A 12' tall (on the long side) block. Most of the lines are great on perfect stone.

V1 East Rib. Tackle the rib starting low on the right and angling up left to top.

V3 North Rib. Initial smear low on the right, crimp the rib, power the tricky moves onto a steep slab. Techy and committing moves. Ultra-classic.

V2 West Rib. Great moves with small edges and smears on the tallest section of stone.

V1 Shorty face on south.

Walk southward up the trail 50' and when it splits, go left, and walk 150' to reach two more massive stones.

Eliot Boulder (at Cooper Spur)

The largest andesite stone in this cluster (25' long by 12' tall).

Beta is counter clockwise:

V0 North slope.

V1 NW Face is an overhung start with rounded features for palming onto the slab.

V2 West Face Direct. Use crimps and slaps to make a direct run up over the rounded lip. Great line.

V2 West Ramp. Start low on the right using rounded slopers, and waltz your feet up the obvious ramp leftward to top up. Classic line on this block.

VB South down climb

V1/V2ss SS mantle up left, or up right (2 var).

V4-5ss a possible stout line on the smooth overhung central east face.

V3 East Point is a superb delicate set up with a high right foot on a small wafer edge to start.

V2 Corner groove that is surprisingly stouter than it appears.

V2 North Nose starts on rounded feature and moves up right to top up.

Wy'east Boulder

This stone is 12' tall, and offers several high quality lines.

V3 Northwest Face is a classic. Start low on small holds with your right foot down on the obvious sloper foot hold. Slap up and catch the better edges, then keep pulling over the lip to the slab top out.

On Tamanawas Boulder

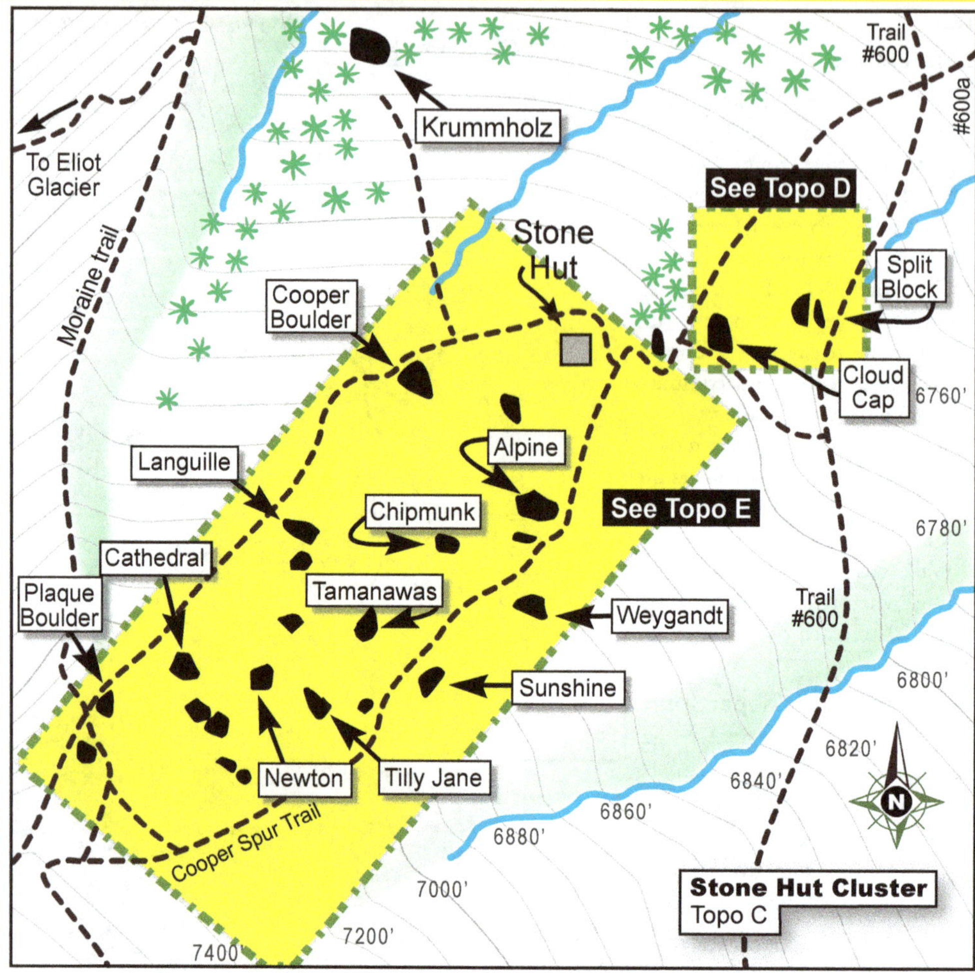

V2 North Fin is an ultra classic. Start on the east side and pinch and smear your way up.

V2 East Face has a short side pull maneuver.

We're all done here, so going back to #600 trail, start hiking uphill toward the hut. En route to the hut, but about ¼ mile up the trail you will encounter a massive 20' wide by 15' tall stone, with a shockingly steep overhanging aspect (5 potential problems over V5?, including a traverse).

Stone Hut Cluster

Continue up trail #600 until it junctions with the Tilly Jane trail #600a. Another 150' on the main trail you will encounter the first large stones.

Split Block Boulder

A nicely cleaved minor stone 11' tall with some minor warmup lines.

VB Perky Sidekick. Traverse the entire rim from right to left on the larger stone.

V0 Default Braggadocio. Center right face.

V1 Perpetual Pandaemonium. Center left face, thin feet smears to catch inset rock knob.

V0 Just Chill. The other boulder rail starting low on the right.

Cloud Cap Boulder

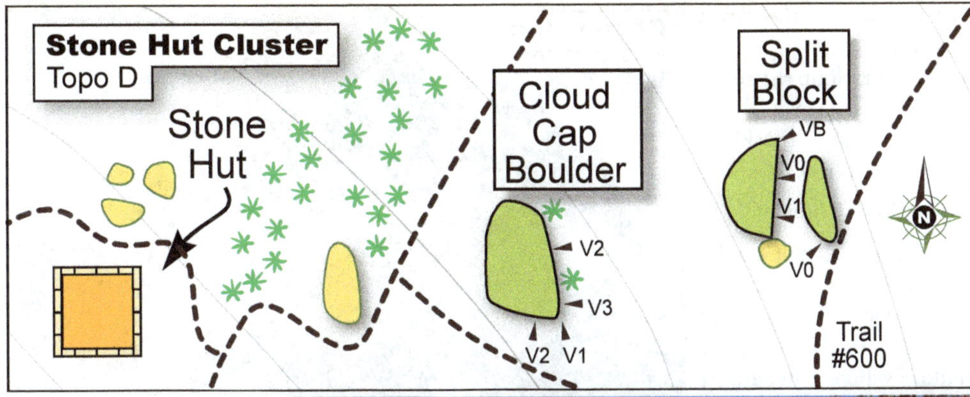

The prominent large stone located between #600 trail and the trail leading up to the stone hut. Several Whitebark pine trees grow along its northeast side.

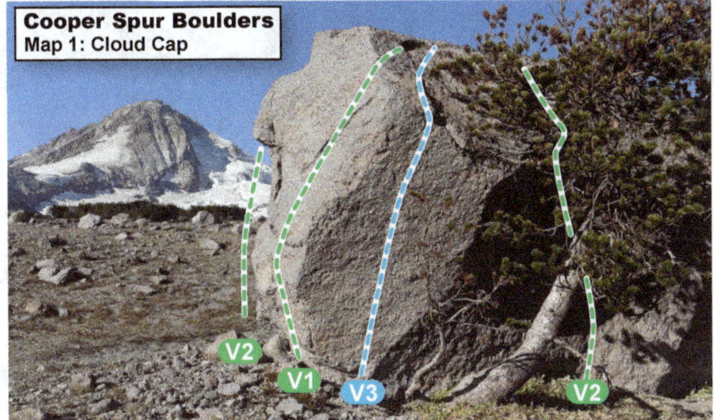

V2 Drunken Sailor is a sit start using the obvious low jug hold, feet under the overhang. Aim up the minor corner.

V1 (V3ss) Ocean Blue is the fine quality east nose using various small edges.

V3 Buzzsaw Politics is a challenging techy flat face just left of the pine tree.

V2ss Xenophobia is face to a crack between the two pine trees.

Coordinate your bearings at the stone hut shelter with the diagram. Three trails lead away from this location; the one you arrived on, a trail leading west, and a trail continuing south toward Cooper Spur. A minor fin block exists immediately northeast of the stone hut (VB-V2). Our initial destination is Cooper Boulder, the obvious large stone one-hundred feet from the hut along the west trail.

Cooper Boulder

An 11' tall by 18' wide block with 360° of quality problems on excellent rock with overhanging starts on most lines.

V0ss Cooper Classic is an cool overhung SS upside-down jug run on the SE side.

V1ss Cooper's Folly tackles the overhung east face.

V2ss Noble Savage. Tackle the overhung face.

V0 Jackanape Whippersnapper. NE arête.

V0 Solipsistic Sloth. Minor face.

VB nothing face.

V1 Champagne Campaign. West nose.

V0 Udder Codswallop. Smears on a steep face, then reaching up left.

V1 Myopic Pink Unicorns. Transcend up left on delicate face moves to a deep corner (avoid the easy holds on the down climb).

VB down climb the south nose.

The east side of this block offer great low traverses.

Krummholz Boulder

A superb 12' tall by 18' wide stone of impeccable quality rock. Though not visible, from the Cooper Boulder hike northwest downhill for about 150' into the cluster of stunted white-bark pine trees. Beta R to L:

VB East face basic.

V0 Topaz is a hueco.

VB Down climb.

V1 Agatized is great. Merely grab the large knob and continue up to the top using more knobs and pockets.

V1 Amber is a classic. Start on north side, smear and pinch the arête.

V3 Turquoise is the steep north face.

From the stone hut, walk south uphill on the Cooper Spur trail. Approximately 100' up the trail on the immediate right is the famous Alpine Boulder, perhaps the finest massive block in the upper park (12' tall by 24' long). Beta counter clockwise starting with B on SE side.

Alpine Boulder

Beta is clockwise, south side first:

VB Down climb.

V1 Turning Point. Dance up into the scoop.

V2 Unobtainium. Stellar line that tackles the rounded rib.

V5 Asteroid Wrangling. Wide flat overhung face with sit start using long reaches on crimps. The ultra classic test-piece at CSB. Faces the sunshine but can be slick as glass if the sunshine is baking it on a warm day.

V2 Grand Alliance is a leaning arête line that starts low on great holds and moves up to reach a big pocket, then up the arête rightward (Rules: stay on the overhung side of the rock).

VB Down climb.

V3 Let's Get Cirrus. Start on the obvious knob, run the rail edges up left and top out on problem to the left.

V3ss Olive Branch. Start low and send the crimps up the overhang and top up.

V5ss Vision Within. Crimps on overhung scoop.

V2ss Merchants of Deception. Pocketed fin with numerous holds on the overhung aspect (and a terrific line).

V3 Snowjob. North scoop is a delicate smooth face with a single high starting hold.

From the Alpine Boulder, walk uphill along the trail. Within 50' is a minor shorty block to the west that has two feasible lines on pockets and a crack. Just uphill and to the immediate east of the

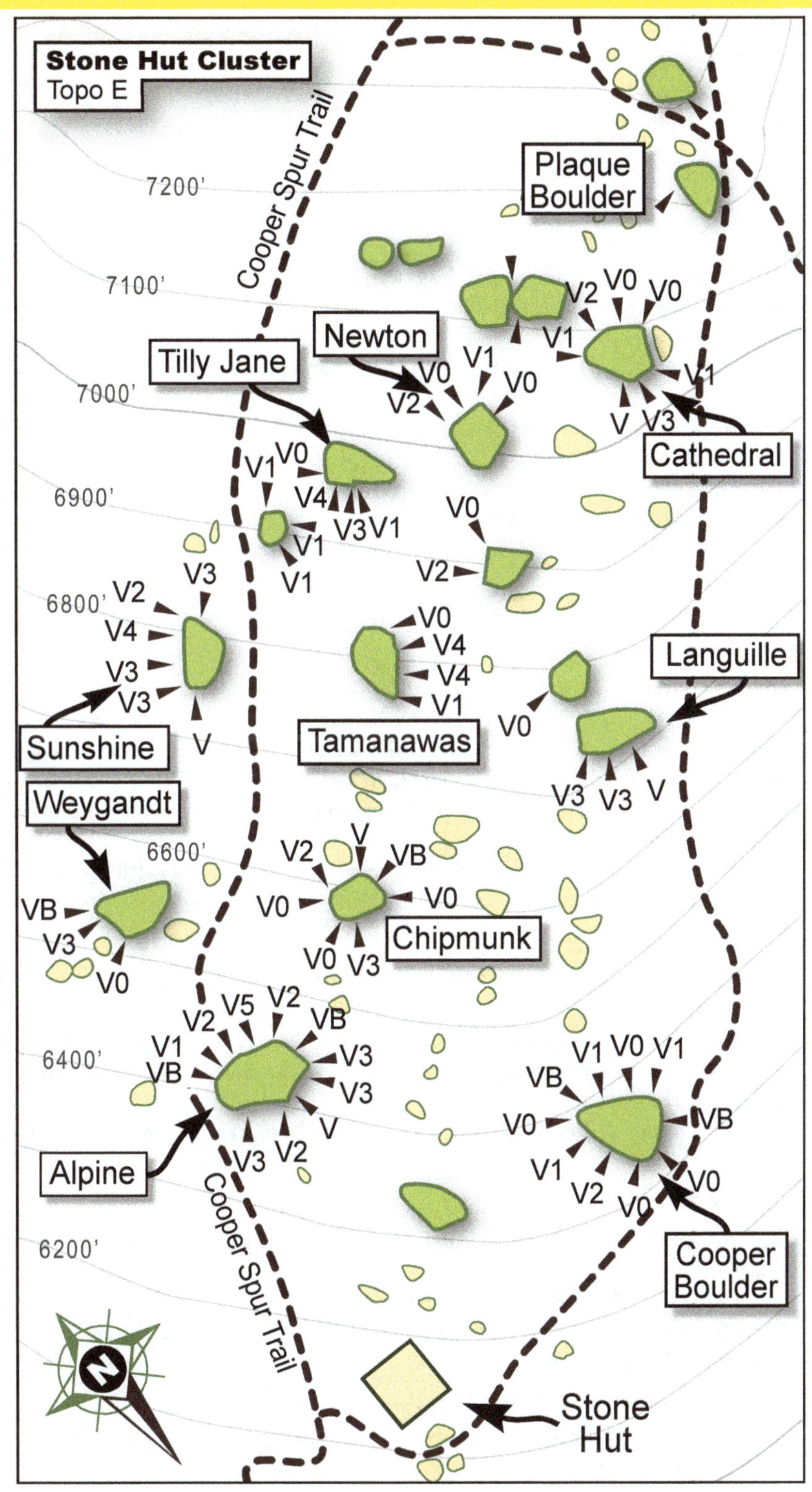
Stone Hut Cluster
Topo E
Cooper Spur Trail
7200'
7100'
7000'
6900'
6800'
6600'
6400'
6200'
Plaque Boulder
Newton
Tilly Jane
V2 V0 V0
V1
V1
V0 V1 V0
V2
V1
V0
V4
V3 V1
V1
V1
V0
Cathedral
V1
V V3
V0
V2
Languille
V3
V2
V4
V3
V3
V
Sunshine
Weygandt
V0
V4
V4
V1
Tamanawas
V0
V3 V3 V
VB
V3
V0
V
V2
VB
V0
V0
Chipmunk
V0 V3
V2
V5
V2
V2
VB
V1
VB
V3
V3
V1 V0 V1
VB
V0
VB
V
V3 V2
V0
V1
V2 V0
Alpine
Cooper Boulder
Cooper Spur Trail
6200'
N
Stone Hut

trail is the Weygandt Boulder (11' tall), a cluster of three blocks, one of which is large enough to warrant interest.

Weygandt Boulder

V0 Natural Regress. Layback seam is a good set of balance moves up a seam.

V3 Multipolarity. Mono pocket face is a delicate quality line.

VB Thingamabob. East arête is simple.

Chipmunk Boulder

Chipmunk Boulder is a set of two boulders, one of which has good power lines.

V0 Seamingly Cirrus. Stellar line that sends east slab face prancing up using rounded texture of the seam.

V2ss Utopian. East Face starts low on the left and moves up using a series of small divots and merges into the seam.

V5 Deep State. Round rail starts between the two boulders. Cruise up right on round rail using the overhung portion of the face.

VB down climb.

V0 Illiquidaceaous. West nose.

V3 Pretzel Logic. North Rail runs the north side sloping rail up right across face and top out on West Nose.

V0 Borealis. Step up left onto the slab.

Tamanawas Boulder

One of the ultra cool stones with a very flat west face that overhangs a little and a lot.

V1ss Jane's Arête is one of the best arêtes here. Climb mostly on the west side of arête.

V4ss Go Crack. Start low on the vertical crack on jug, smear on small foot edges under the big overhang. Leap for the flat hold way up high and left. Reset, match, and finish. Wow!

V4ss Go Bust. Using left hand on pinch jug, and slap up right to catch the arête, then catch the better flat edge, and finish.

V0 (V3ss) Illusion & Fallacy. SS on slopers, move up left, and catch the layback corner crack, layback up one move to top.

Languille Boulder

Immediately west of Tamanawas about 40'. Its a combo, a larger and a smaller block, both of which offer lines.

V3 Fresh Crow. Start with feet in the obvious pockets and move directly up the face.

V3 Flesch 'n Fisshe Alle Raughe. Tackles the rounded north nose straight on.

V5 (?) ___ Thin face.

V0 The Circuit. The other block is a short 7' tall boulder that is totally flat on top, so traverse the entire stone.

Minor Block

Approximately 50' southwest uphill from Tamanawas Boulder is this minor block with a flat east face to it.

V0ss Rocksters & Hucksters. Left fin from SS.

V2ss Reef & Riptide. Right rail using a right foot heel hook, run the entire rail up left and top up on the other line. Cool line!

Sunshine Boulder (10' tall x 18' length)

On the east side of the trail is this low stone offering well overhung SS style cool traversing.

V3ss Mere Mortal (V0ss if up only). Start SS on jugs left of Alpenglow, run jug rail to the very overhung nose, then over it.

V2ss Alpenglow. SS on incut jugs underneath powering over the most overhung part of the nose.

V4ss Thought Czar. East face crimps.

V3ss Broken Arrow. On NE face on tiny crimps, bump to catch tooth (side pull).

V3ss North Point a delicate matter on thin smears and crimps.

V5ss (?) North Side.

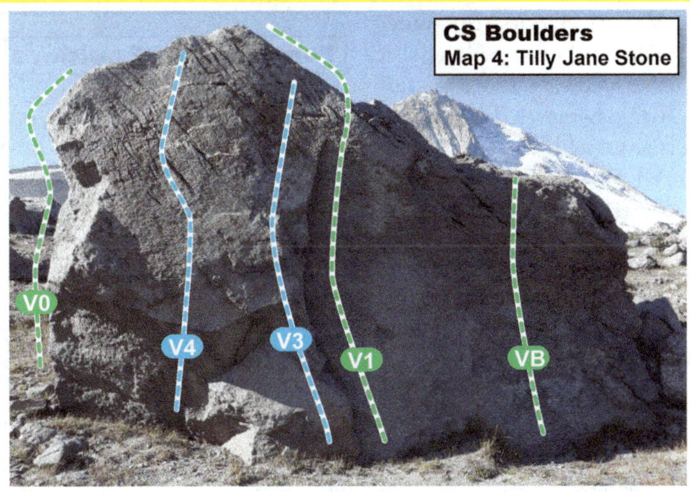

Tilly Jane Boulder

One of the ultra classic stones here, though visually small-*ish* when compared to the other monsters, the north face aspect has several choice lines that are simply beyond the edge of doubt. Located immediately west of the trail past another round unnamed block (has three short sit start V1-V2 lines on 8′ tall round block). Tilly Jane is readily identifiable by the vertical right-facing ramp on its north aspect.

V1 (V3ss) Tilly Jane is the reason to be. The initial method is to smear the foot inside the ramp, left hand pinching the outer edge of the ramp, catch lip, run lip left. Cool! Now move it up a notch to V3ss (the outer edge). SS on the outer left side of the same vertical ramp (right pinch), move delicately up to catch top rail, run left to tag the summit. Yeowza!

V4 Jane's Folly is the superb flat face on this block. Starts with a slight overhang for the feet, and powers up a series of sloped crimp holds on the face.

V0 Willful Blindness. East face using portion closer to the rounded rib. SS bumps it.

Newton Boulder (10′ tall)

A unique block that seems minor until you reach the uphill side and spot the high quality SS arête. Beta from (R to L) east to west:

V2ss Fig Newton. Foot in low pocket on right, power up left over rounded east nose.

V0ss Agent Provacateur. Several variants on low face.

V1ss Sir Newton. Ultra short arête SS on smaller holds, bump up using arête and prominent flat holds to top up.

V0ss Passions Forged in Fetters. Low using jugs, run short jug rail on west side.

Cathedral Boulder

Located uphill southwest of Newton Boulder 100′. It is the obvious black lichen covered 14′ stone. This large stone offers a nearly 360° set of problems to climb, though some will need a bit of dusting off the gnarly black lichen first if you need that one special hold.

V_ (?) Just right of the pine tree on the black lichen covered north face is a potential line.

Tymun on Jane's Folly V4

V3 (?) Tackles the outer side overhung north side of the following problem. Initial easy moves (black lichen masks holds).

V1 Figaro's Folly. Start between two large stones on upside down face where it calved off. Move up left on smears, limited crimps, casual reach over upper lip, dance up left over the top.

V0ss Campfire is a SS oddity one mover.

V0 Huckypuk. Tackle the face into a groovy dish on south side.

V2 Gothic Cathedral. Rounded delicate face, yet quality movement.

V1ss Bishop. Using slopers, bump up to slopers, finish with slopers.

A short distance southeast uphill from Cathedral Boulder is a double set of boulders that offer some minor SS problems (VB to V0). Nearby is the Plaque Boulder, which has an obvious steep glassy smooth aspect, and is the general upper limit of interest in this wonderland of rock boulders. Bring a camera to capture a scenic moment in time.

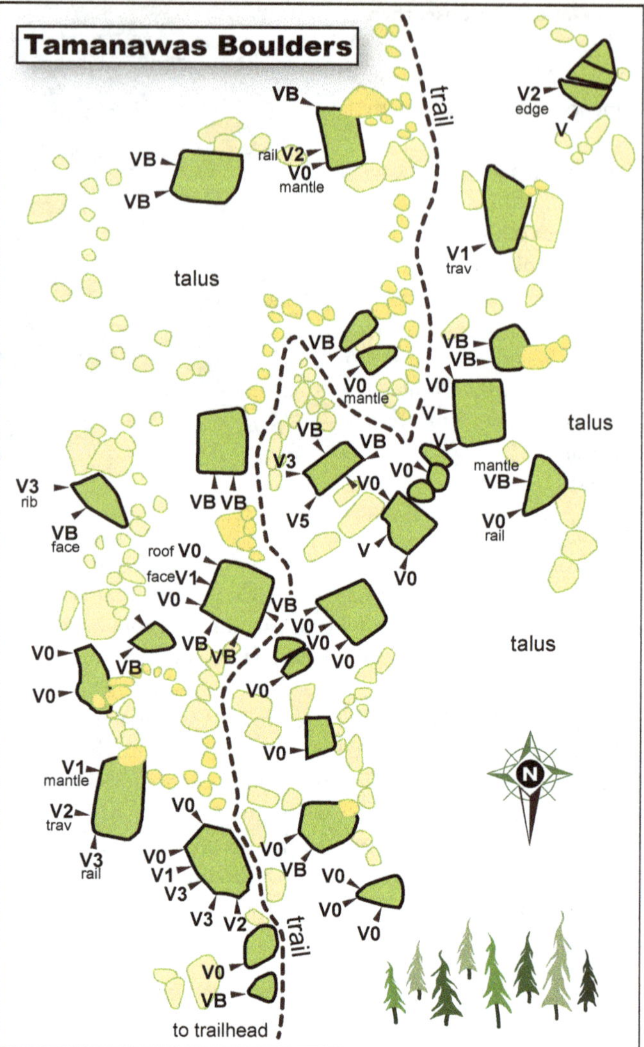

TAMANAWAS BOULDERS

A minor site of limited appeal because of the small number of problems and awkward landings all accumulated from a recent massive collapsed cliff. The site is creekside so it has well moderated cool temperatures even on a hot day in summer. The popular hikers trail travels right through the boulder field. The entire talus field is of recent history, in that the entire boulder field originated from a very recent collapse from a tall cliff band just uphill. Some of the rock is still very fractured so caution is wise. Most grades range from VB-V3 (up to V5), but has seen only minimal exploratory bouldering to date. Potential for about 30 problems.

Rock composition is dark basalt with tiny quartz crystal mineral (1-2mm) and black feldspar (1mm) infrequently distributed throughout the matrix. Surface nuances reveal plenty of crimps and smooth aspects all slightly slick feeling. Crashpads recommended (1-2). Boulder height range from short to hi-ball lines (9'-13'. The setting is a scenic mixed alder, cottonwood, hemlock and fir forest environ next to a refreshing cold stream.

Seasonal access is viable from mid-May through October, and is located at the 3,300' elevation. The site is just prior to Tamanawas Falls on the Tamanawas Falls trail #650, which starts immediately north of Sherwood Campground on Highway 35, about 20 minutes south of Hood River, Oregon. Hike distance is about 1.4 miles to the site. A few minor stones exist along the hiking trail, but are generally small VB oriented. See diagram for beta (some landings are ⌂).

ELIOT BOULDERS

A quality site and a relatively new block party arrival, created after late Fall season heavy rain storm flash flood conditions abruptly stripped the site of all trees and brush for several miles along Eliot Creek, ripping out a concrete bridge in the process. The clean sweep gave boulderers a wide open (until the trees regrow) sunny area with a string of fun andesite gems, from a mega monster stone (18' tall and 360° circuit of problems) to many smaller 8'-12' tall boulders that comprise a total of 90+ feasible boulder problems. Most landings are naturally groomed flat. Summer days can be warm (choose Spring or Fall season [or cloudy days] if V-power is your game. Existing lines range from VB-V5 (potential V7+). At present (2017) the site is void of trees (and moss), but anticipate by roughly the year 2030 considerable brush growth and trees will be reestablished in the area making the stones a bit more challenging to locate. Cell phone reception is good. Site is a 1-2 crashpad minimum recommendation.

Andesite rock type nuances are tumbled and rounded edges, light sandpaper-like crystalline surface texture, techy powerful footwork friction smears that utilize tiny nuances, small crimps, slopers, and palm slapping festivities on dicey steep lines. Some stones have a greasy slippery feel (some are basaltic) due to the flash flood tumbling action. The ultimate gem is certainly the massive Eliot Boulder, a must-do for anyone touring the site.

This site was barely explored (on Eliot Block) on a few problems in about 2009 by a few locals. An extensive site analysis was attained by Mr O who tapped 50% of the lines in one day, followed immediately after by Mr A who tapped an additional string of stout lines.

There are several minor boulders to the north of the gravel road (NF2810) where it crosses the creek. A short hike on sandy creek channels gets you there. But quality (some crumbly stuff), quantity (3-4 viable stones), girth and orientation are the limiting factors.

Directions

Drive south from Hood River 12 miles on Hwy 35 and turn SW onto Hwy 281 (Hood River Hwy) driving 1½ miles to Parkdale. From the center of town (at the general store) drive south on Clear Creek Road for 2¾ miles, then turn right onto NF2810 and drive 2¼ miles till it crosses Eliot Creek. Park just west of the bridge at a wide pullout. Walk south ¼ mile to reach the primary area, the Eliot Boulder being the furthest stone in the group. Paved roads to the site (its a primary road to Lawrence Lake).

Boulderphobia Stone

Boulderphobia is the first prominent stone 300' south from the road, located near the creek.

VB north side descent next to tree.

V1ss hung face.

V4ss Pillage the Village. Pockets (on west side).

V4ss Head above Water. Crimps on nose.

V0 Spendthrift. Rounded short nose.

V0 Race to the Bottom Short face.

On Grey Wolf (Fenrir)

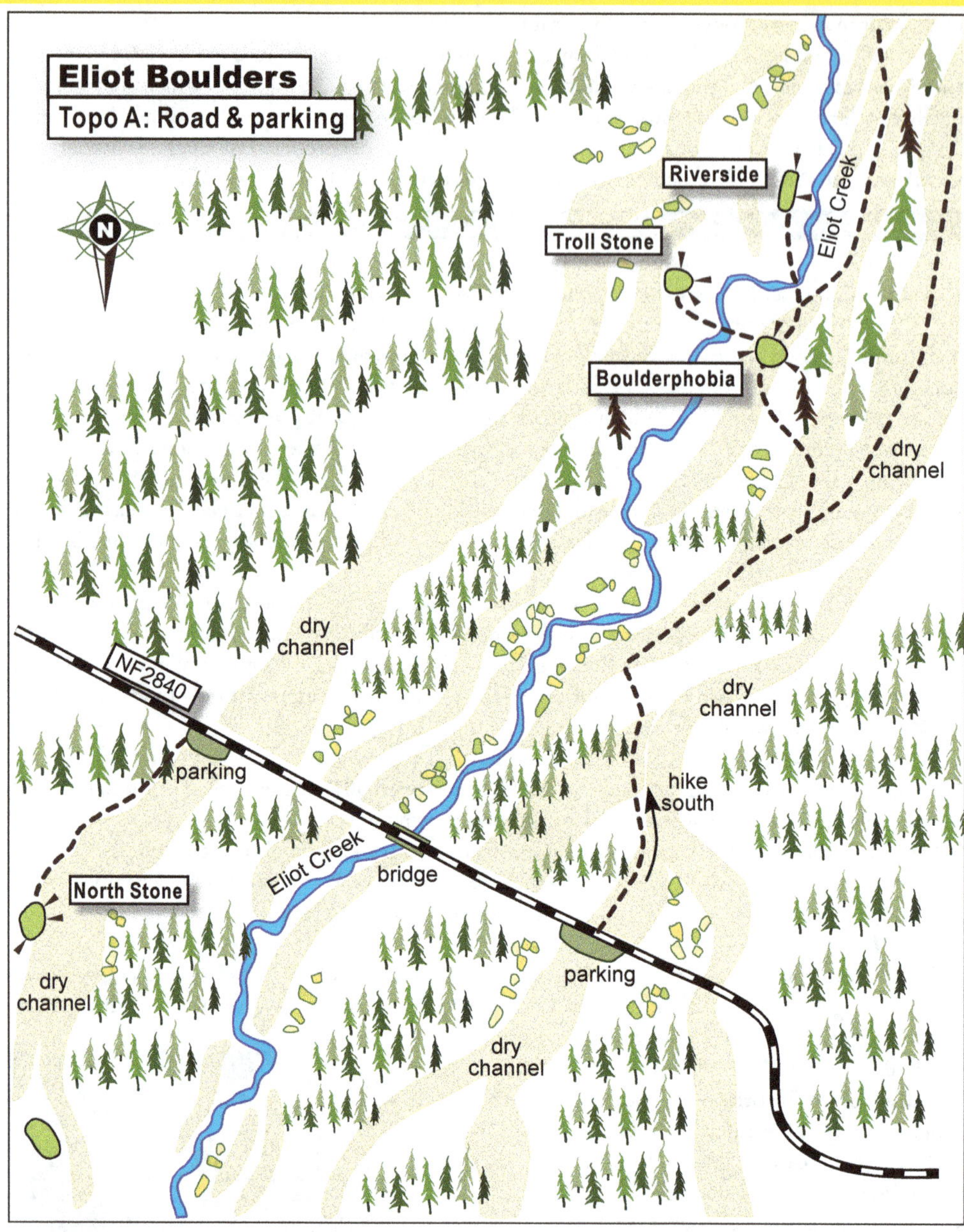

V4 Monkey Business. A short face with nothing to start, gastons to rounded top.

V2 (V3ss) One Arm Monkey is the classic on this stone. Left hand uses pockets.

V4 Blowout. East face.

V2 Washout. Slight groove near top.

Troll Stone

A slabby 12′ tall andesite stone directly east across the creek from Boulderphobia.

VB Million & Change (north side slab), **V0 Demagogues** (crimps on west), **VB**, and **VB**.

Riverside Stone

A narrow profile 11' tall stone just south of Boulderphobia beside the creek. **V0 Art of Deceit** (crimp face to left prow), **VB Street Anarchy** (crimps on center west face), **VB Hillbilly Bonehead** (corner), **V0 Tipping Point** (hung south point).

Skag Stone

A minor 8' tall stone with **V0 Pink Bunnies & Buttercups**, **VB**, and **VB**.

Minor set of stones

A 9' tall stone: **V1 Just Fools** (slab).
Unknown Stone: (V_?).
Unknown Stone: (V_?).

Tumbler Stone

A 9' tall stone with hung east prow. Will eventually tumble because it sits precariously on a small stone in a low sandy area (L to R): **V2ss Dippy Loopy Fringe Goofball** (south side), **V3ss Not One Iota**, **V4ss** (?) east hung prow, **VB Iota** (north side minor) with variants.

Fenrir Stone (aka Wolf) 10' tall

V3 Wolf (cool overhung rail).
V2 Mutato Nomime (thin smears).
VB Droolius Caesar (east face).
VB Particularly Stupid (north slab).

Minor set of stones

Trolltind Stone: V0 Shrouded in Secrecy, V0 Cultural Cross-pollinator.
Unknown Stone: V4ss (?).
Unknown Stone: V6-8ss (?) superhung prow, and a **VB** line.
Valhalla Stone: (11' tall) round stone that has a **V3 Midnight Poker Game** (high crimps on west side), and the rest are **VB, VB,** and **VB** all on east side, all well done.
Unknown Stone: a low SS ground scraper sloper-fest V7-8ss (?).
Ovest Stone: VB, and **VB.**
Fitzroy Stone: Large flat stone with a minor circuit traverse: **VB** north, **VB** arête, **V0 Till the Nadir is Reached** is the south side (traverse included), and no cookies.
Romsdal Stone: A 10' tall big fat stone with rounded slightly hung aspects on most sides. Beta L to R: **V4ss Need for Speed** (south), **V3ss Useful idiots** (south), **VB, VB, VB, V3ss Whirlwind of Change** (north nook).
Norsk Stone: A brief slick basalt unit. **V0ss Hollow Dreams** (south prow face), and **VB.**

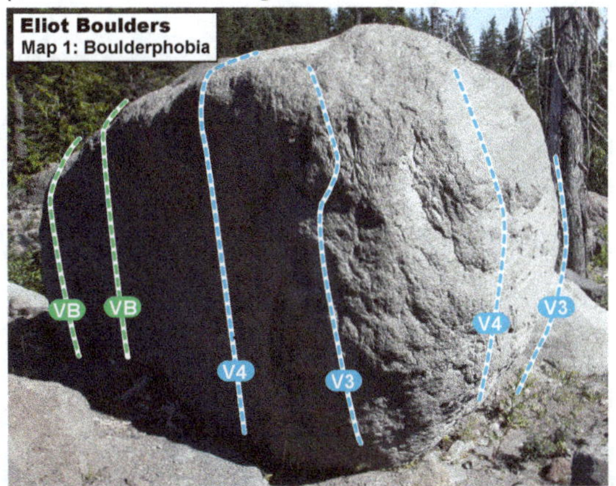

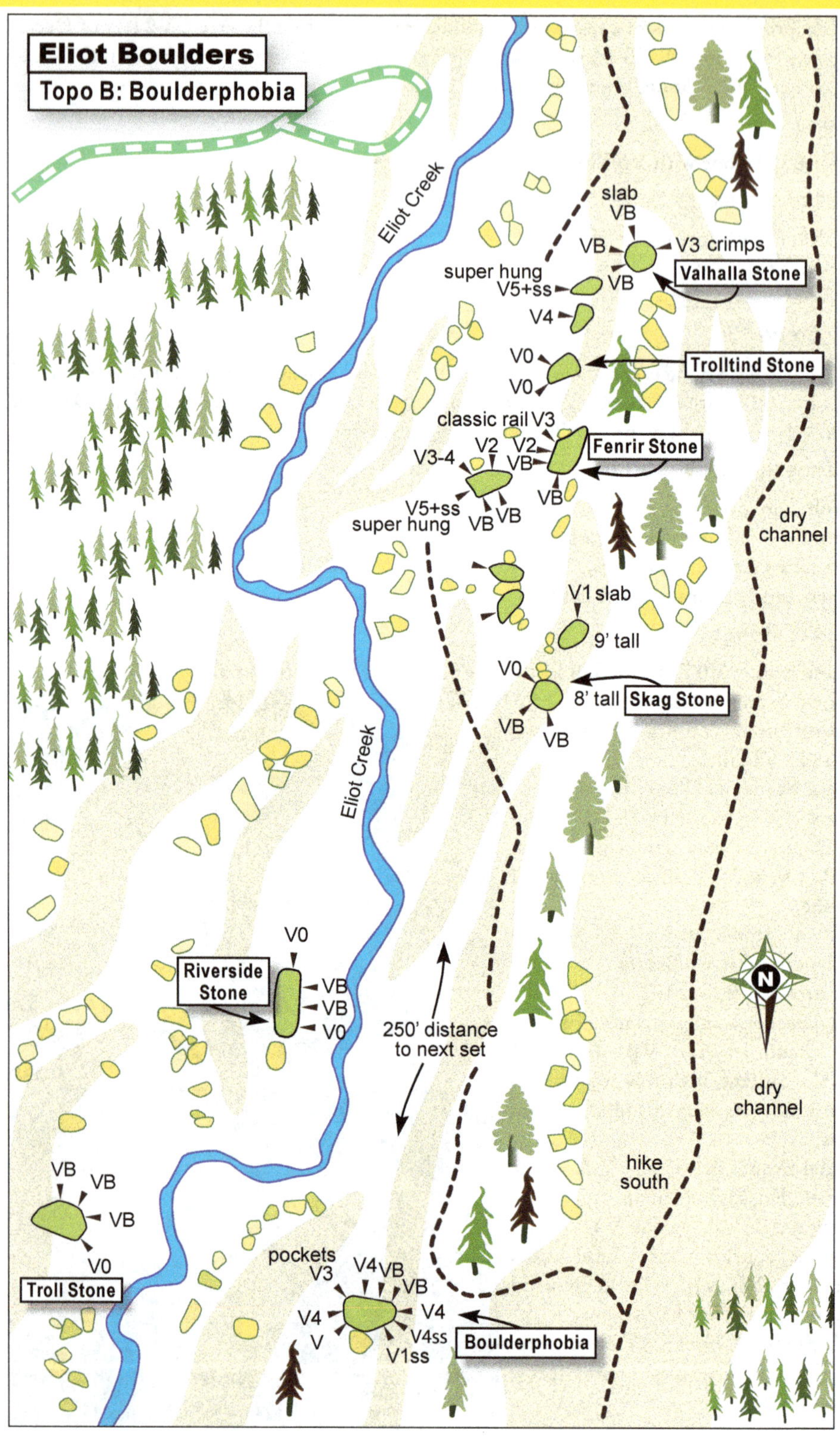
Eliot Boulders
Topo B: Boulderphobia
Eliot Creek
slab
VB
VB
V3 crimps
Valhalla Stone
super hung
V5+ss
VB
V4
V0
V0
Trolltind Stone
classic rail V3
V2
V2
Fenrir Stone
V3-4
VB
VB
V5+ss
VB
VB
super hung
V1 slab
9' tall
V0
8' tall
Skag Stone
VB
VB
dry
channel
Eliot Creek
V0
Riverside
Stone
VB
VB
V0
250' distance
to next set
N
dry
channel
hike
south
VB
VB
VB
V0
Troll Stone
pockets
V3
V4
VB
VB
V4
V4
V
V4ss
V1ss
Boulderphobia

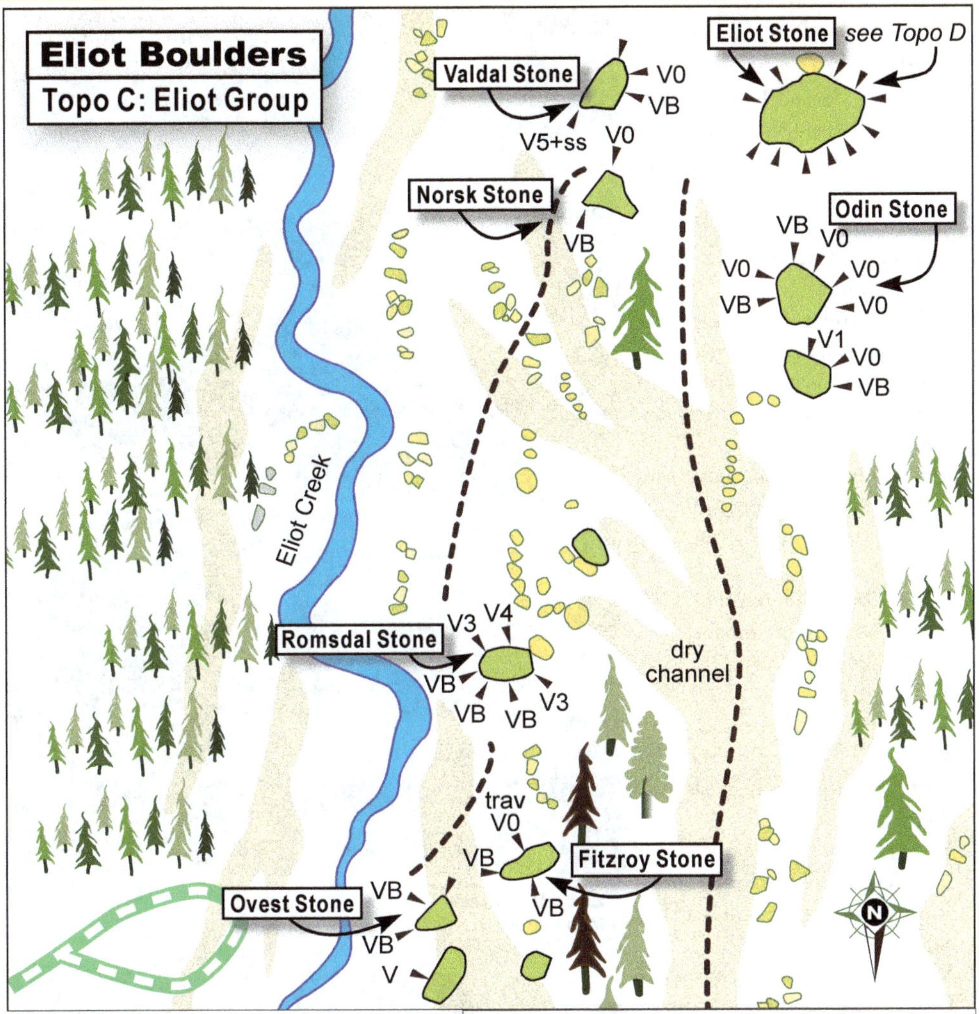

Eliot Boulders
Topo C: Eliot Group

Valdal Stone

A 8' tall long laying stone just east of the giant Eliot Stone. Beta: **V5ss+** (?) super hung prow, **VB Mere Stone's Throw** (crimps), **V0 Parsiminous Pipsqueak** (crimps), and **V_** (?) south.

Odin Stone & Kongen Stone

Two 8' tall fat low laying stones just north of Eliot Stone (beta L to R). Stone One (aka **Odin stone**): V0 Fracked, V0 Problem Child, V0 Iron Fist, VB Devil in the Details, V0 Living a Lie, VB Tribute & Bribary. .....and on Stone Two (aka **Kongen stone**): VB Duopic Antidote, V0 Essence of Power, V1 Essence of Truth. No free

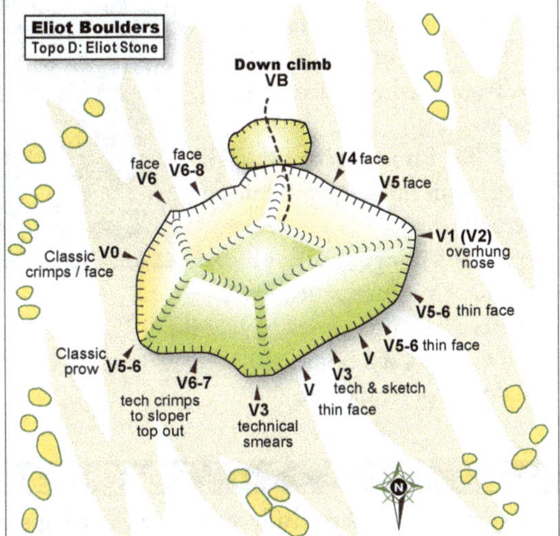

cookies.

Eliot Boulder

Eliot Boulder is the mega-gem 18' tall beast with 360° circuit and at least 12 viable problems, maybe a few more. Any traverse would be V-insane, if feasible at all. Beta is clockwise starting with the south face descent line.

VB Get Down. Ascent / descent using a smaller steppingstone.

V4 Dyno. Catch good hold, mantle to top. Start lower ups the V.

V5ss Day of Reckoning. Line up a tough compression sequence and dyno for jug, then mantle.

V1 (V2ss) Maelstrom. Cool west nose, finish as a mantle.

V5-6 potential

V5-6 potential

V_ (?) maybe, maybe not.

V3 Rules for Fools. Standing start with thin tech holds, and sketchy top out.

V_ (?) maybe, maybe not.

V3 Yggdrasil. North prow starts at odd side pull, catch a sloper, sketchy mantle.

V6-7 (?) Royal Standard. Crimps and sequential moves reaching up left to catch the lip; palm mantle onto slick slab. Hiball on northeast aspect (project).

V4 (?) Eliot Arête. ⚠ The mega gem hi-ball prow, but few actually do it.

V0 The Viking. East face hi-ball classic. Crimp crux sequence to stance, then a fat jug up high at top.

V6 Crimp City. Southeast.

V6-8 (?) potential (SE).

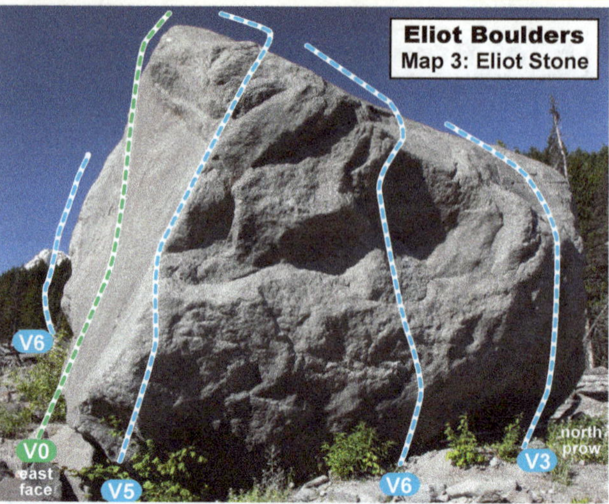

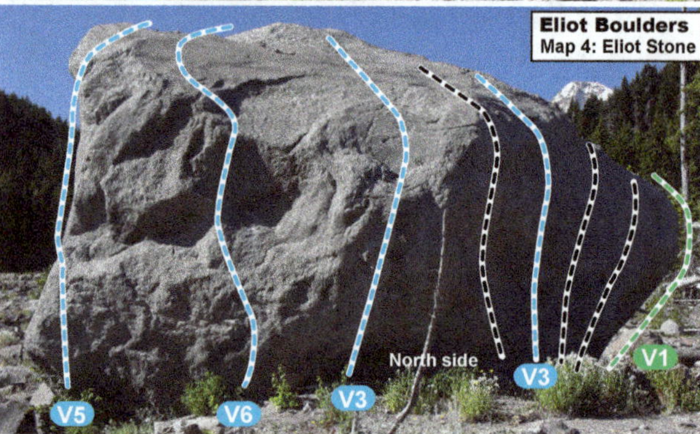

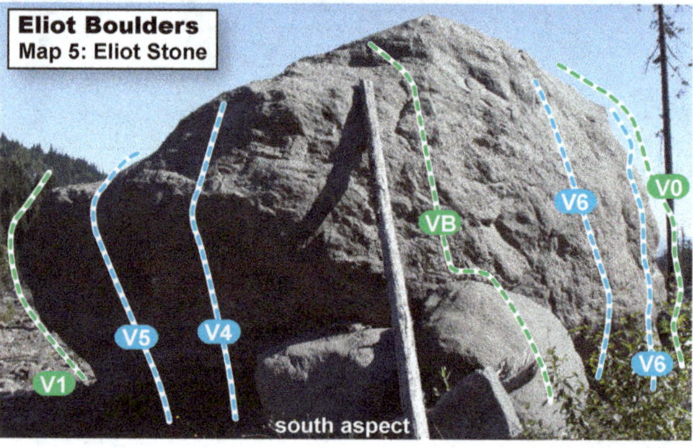

LOLO BOULDERS

A small site, very roadside accessible (first big stone is 20' from the asphalt) with a southwest

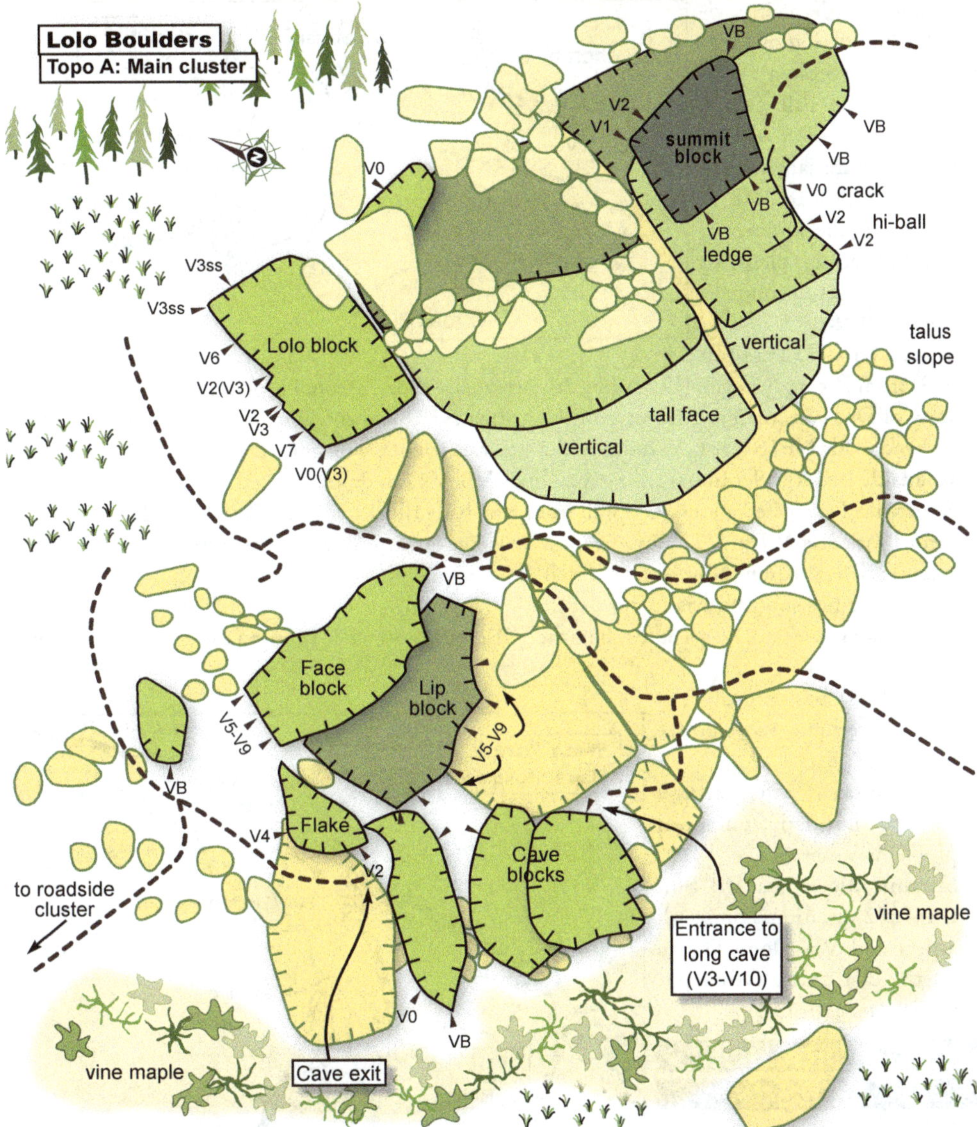

facing aspect, perched high on a forested ridge overlooking the upper West Fork Hood River basin. Accessible from mid-May through October, but quite hot on non-breezy days in summer. Bouldering is limited in scope to about 40+ problems, some very stout (V6-V9+) candidates, but plenty of VB-V4 lines do exist. Some persistent minor moss, and some welded lichen (which gives some holds a slick feel), but surface features offer numerous crimps and smears. The site has several quality problems, a 12' roof under a big block, all on stones that range in height from 8'-9' (up to 15' hi-ball lines on a few stones). A minimum of 1-2 crashpads is recommended. Oddly enough, cell reception does exist here.

The rock composition is a gray matrix loaded with minute (1-3mm) gaseous pockets, basaltic-andesitic but lacking prominent crystals, with noticeable surface texture enhanced or etched from weathering processes. Good quality rock at moderate altitude. The main formation is about 100' tall, though little of it is viable for bouldering or toperoping (oddly broken). Ideal for Spring or Fall season bouldering. *General history*: This site was initially tapped (many VB-V6) by Mr A and Mr O in the summer of 2013, yet there are plenty of stout V-lines yet to conquer.

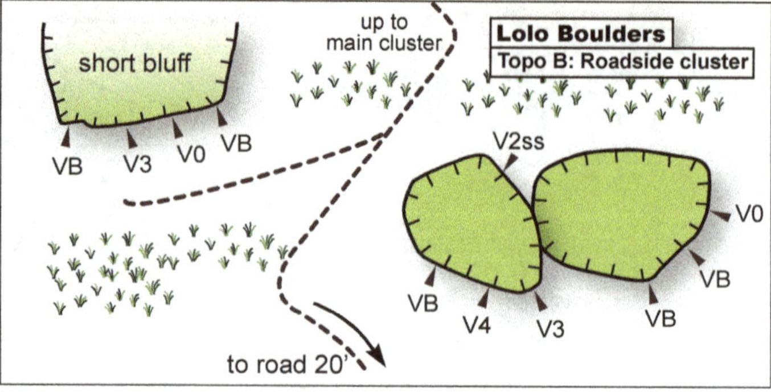

Directions

Drive over Lolo Pass (on NF18) from Zigzag, Oregon (U.S. Hwy 26 corridor). Or drive from Hood River via the tiny community of Dee Flat, then southwest on NF13, then NF18. At the junction of NF16 go uphill on this paved road (NF16) for 6.25 miles to the site. See overview diagram for general beta.

Roadside Blocks offer fine working man lines **VB-V4** (all done).

Short Bluff is located about 20' uphill from Roadside Blocks. It has **VB to V3** (all done).

Lolo Block has **V0 to V7**, some SS problems, on quality short face aspects, and some classic lines (such as the hung SS prow). All well done.

Face Block has short futuristic short stuff.

The Flake has V0 to V3+ (other than the VB), most notable is running the entire rib startingdown in the hole.

Lip Block has mostly untapped overhung short power lines (V3-V8).

Cave Blocks offer several enticing futuristic untapped problems V-hard.

Summit Block has **VB Sun Dance** (2 variations) on south aspect and **VB Moon Dance** on the east point. Other potential exists (hi-ball).

WEST FORK BOULDERS

Situated on the outskirts of the idyllic Hood River valley in a rain-shadow zone of the Cascade Mountain range, this site offers good bouldering for folks seeking sunnier climes. Good paved road access the entire distance (via I-84, then through Dee Flat)

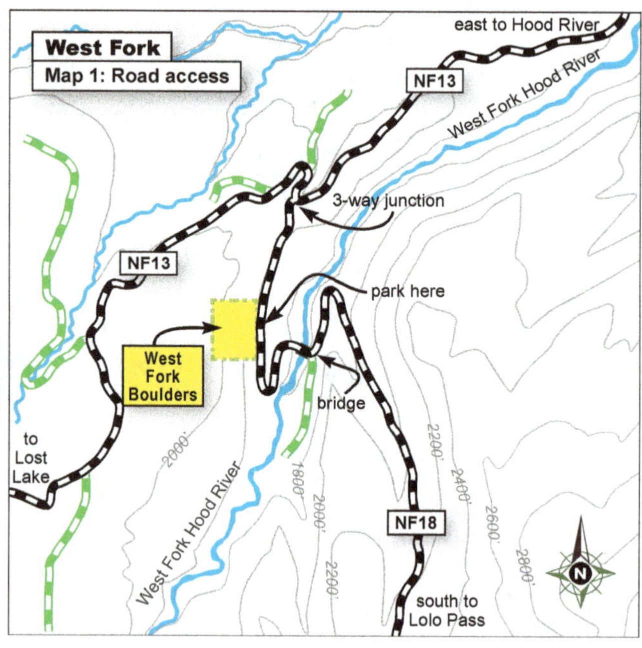

to the site, and a mere 200' walk to the first boulder. The entire boulder field is quite extensive (¼ mile long), yet there are a limited number of giant stones worth sending (all the best stuff is packed at the North Cluster).

Season ranges from mid-May through October (possibly longer), is often dry, and is a scorcher in mid-summer due to its sunny south-easterly aspect. Generally protected from the brunt of the rainstorms, its elevation (1,900') may have showers on high percentage days, but a 5%-40% rain forecast west of Cascade Mtn range is unlikely to effect the West Fork site.

Broad sweeping scenic views of the valley and Mt Hood yield great photo qualities. The andesite stones have a dark phenocryst matrix, but a remarkable subtle gritty texture that provides effective hand or foot smear friction. Rock textural nuances are unique edges, waves, and jugs to suit your scream (most existing lines have refined landings). Size of stones are massive (11'-25' diameter) though the tallest stone is only about 16'. Several stones of-

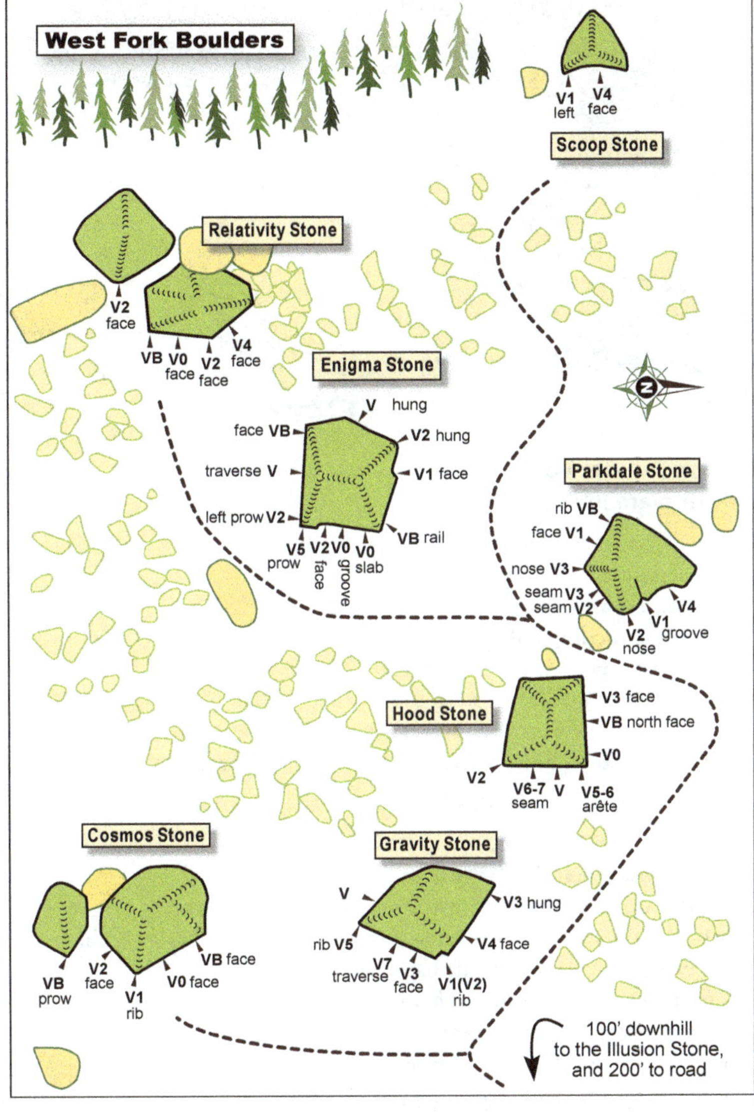

fer 360° worth of problems. Bring 1-2 crashpads minimum. No cell phone reception beyond Dee Flat. Walking upon the talus field requires agility on the rocky slope. Car camping options exist nearby.

History: Tapped primarily by Mr A and Mr O, though a few other persons did a few meaty lines (on Illusion, Hood and Scoop Stone).

Directions

Drive time from Portland is about 1.5 hours (approach via Lolo Pass is feasible). Take I-84 to exit #62 at Hood River, then drive south on 12th Street zigzagging south into the country on State Hwy #281 (Dee Hwy). At about 8 miles, turn right, cross the river bridge, and drive through Dee, continuing on NF13 (this splits so take the [left] south main road) to the junction of NF18 (Lolo Pass road). Turn south onto NF18 and drive ½ mile. The boulders are plainly visible above

West Fork Boulders
Topo B: Illusion Stone
Most problems overhang
at the base of this
17' long x 13' tall stone

the road. Park along the roadside below the boulder site.

Illusion Dweller Boulder (14' tall, 18' diameter)

This is the noble giant stone closest to the road.
VB descent on SW side.
V0 one move and mantle on south aspect.
V3-4 runs a crimp rail up right.
V3-4 east aspect crimp rail traverses left to arête.
V_ (?) over bulge and up steep slab.
V5 (?) north prow, just get over bulge.
V7ss Rip Tide. The lip traverse, starts low and runs left to north prow.

Gravity Boulder (18' long, 11' tall)

Beta is from right to left.
V3 Gravitational Pull hung nose.
V4 Rip Cord. Overhung move then up to the top point.
V1 (V2ss) Gravity. Starts at the east corner at a small foot notch.
V3 Newton. Mantle over the hang onto the face.
V6 Sir Isaac. Run entire rail left then up the arête.
V5 Gravitron. Tackle the arête.
V_ (?) thin short face on uphill side.

Enigma Boulder (12' x 12' stone)

Beta starts at descent, then counter clock-wise.
VB descent on uphill side.
VB Conspiracy. Short problem nice holds.
V5 Lupus Non Mordet. Traverse the thin face leftward.
V2ss Enigma Arête. SS using overhanging arête for right hand, small side crimp for left hand, punch up to catch the arête, and finish to top.
V5ss Algorithm. Tackle the arête by SS underneath, up and over the entire hang.
V3ss Filthy Rich. Face up a minor scoop, reaching for arête soon.
V0 Cyber Warfare. Tackle the slab with a slight kink on it.
V0 Cryptic Void. Dicey, hi-ball, that uses only the slab from the lowest point to the top.
VB Cryptanalysis. Fun rib to jugs using arête.

V1ss Rain Shadow. Overhung a few punchy moves to easier top out.
V2ss Rain Dance. Underneath SS then out to the lip and over it.
V_ss (?) one more next to descent line.

Hood Boulder (16' tall)

V3ss Lux Aeterna. Thin techy line (rightmost line)
VB Sheer Wishful Dreams. Basic face on north aspect
V0 __fz__. Nothing dance up onto slab.
V5-6 (?) ___ on lower east side overhang, power up arête.
V5 (V6-7+) (?) ___ Classic east face using thin seam crimps on overhang.
V2 ___ left arête one move, and run slab to top.
Several other variants exist on this stone.

Parkdale Boulder (14' tall)

Beta is from R to L.
V4 Cherry Jubilee is the cut loose swinger line out and over the overhang.
V1 Know your Enemy. The overhung groove on east face.
V2 Apple Turnover. The slightly overhung east nose with good small edges.
V2 Grapes of Wrath. Use tiny tips seam, reach up right to rail, and top out.
V3 Fine Wine. Start with tiny seam, but work up left on thin vertical terrain.
V3 Stark Reality. Sharp nose past a hollow flake to top rail.
V3 Ascendant Power. Thin center face.
V1 Creampuff. Short thin face just right of rib.

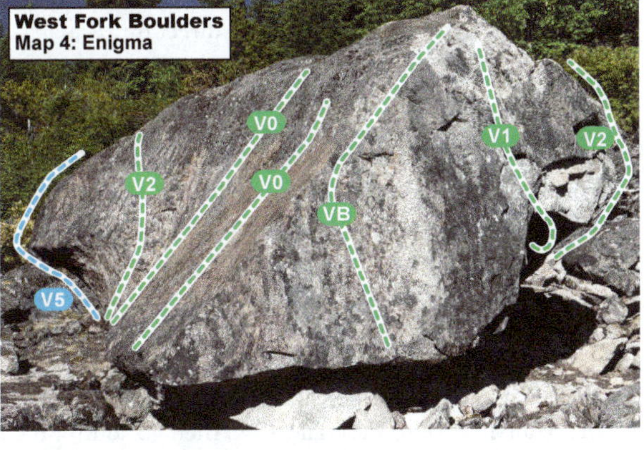

VB Cookies. Ascend a short vertical rib.

Cosmos Boulder (11' tall)

VB Shark Hunter. Basic face on right, starting low.
V0 Slaves. The center thin face.
V2ss Marathon Man. Pinch arête, then step onto ramp, then straight up.
V2ss Bondage. Bulge and pockets on face.
VBss Lipstick Ranch is a short jug run on a double stacked block to the left.

Relativity Boulder (11' tall)

V4 Brimming with Bile. Overhung tricky reach, mantle over bulge onto slab (this is the rightmost line).
V2 Cosmic Waltz. Crimp delicate balance move up and catch the incut on arête, then dash to top.
V0 Minor Waltz. Balance moves on face.
VB Minor Waltz. Steps on left.
V2 Another Nothing. Thin shorty on nearby block to the left.

Scoop Boulder (11' tall)

Way uphill behind the Parkdale Boulder is this loner stone.

V4ss _______. Crimps on overhung scoop, reach up right to round rail, then mantle over onto slab and finish up center rib. A direct up may boost the V-grade.
V1ss _______. Crimps over the left rail.

PINN BOULDERS

Pinnacle Trail Boulders (aka Pinn Boulders) is located alongside a hiker's trail on the northern slope of Mt Hood. A seldom visited minor site. Only a dozen or so stones are large enough to tap, yielding as a whole perhaps 25+ boulder problems. Site has two talus fields (East and West Talus), VB-V4 is common, some V5-8 likely, and the boulders range in height from 8-11' tall. Rock type is platey smooth fine-grained basalt with numerous crimp features, and often black lichen. The site was privy to a recent forest fire that zapped that entire region crisp, so it has no tree canopy to keep it cool (you get full sunshine). One crashpad suitable site.

Directions: Drive to Parkdale, OR, then go south on Clear Creek road for 2.7 miles, then SW on Laurence Lake road (4.2 miles). From the campground junction drive uphill south on NF2840 gravel road for 2.8 miles. Park at roads end. Hike trail #630 for 1.1 miles to reach the East Talus Cluster (after crossing a minor stream). Walk trail 350' more to the West Talus Cluster.

History: possible locals exploratory bouldering. Mr O tapped many lines VB-V4 in about 2016 on various boulders (and at North Point).

King Cool Boulder

V0 Tangibility (north nose), **V0 King Cool** (west nose), V5-8 (?)_____ (face), **V1 Logobabble**

(southeast face).

Burn Boulder

V1ss (V4ss+) Hypocrites (cool SS going left to point up).

Blaze Boulder

V1 Tinkered (NE), **V1 Tampered** (north), **V1 Tainted** (west), **V1 Tango** (west), **V0 Taco** (west).

North Point

V3 Razor, V1 Razorblade half traverse, **V0 Switchblade** (center), but **V3-5 Full Razorblade** full traverse beckons (project).

DEE FLAT BOULDERS

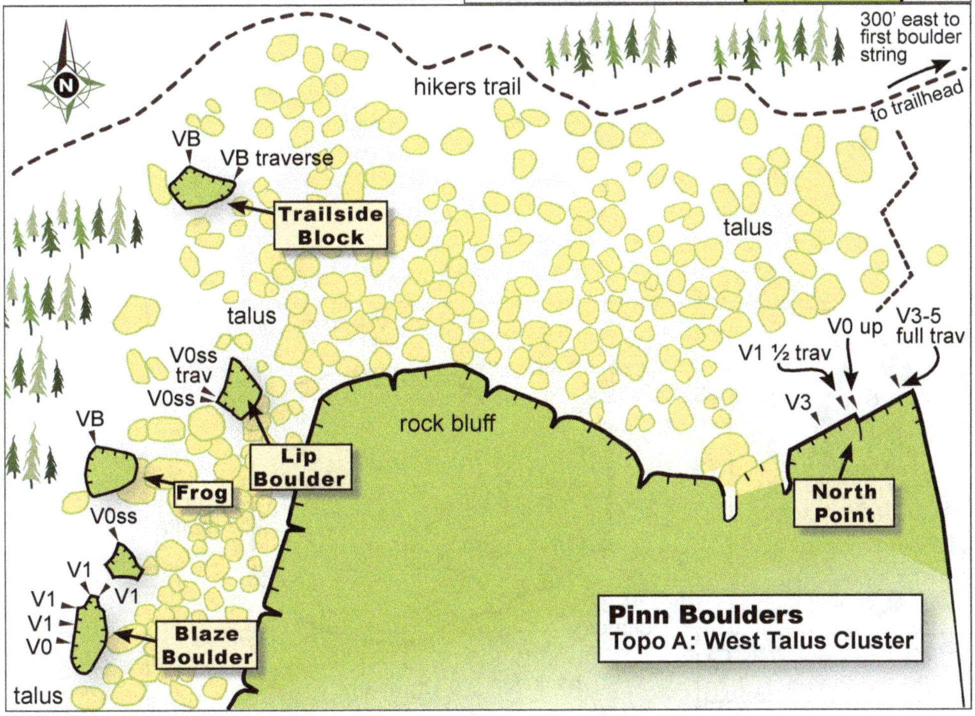

Not a particularly fancy musical tune, nor a unique site, but it has suitable andesite stones (12' girth on the big mother). Generally about 3-4 main stones immediately alongside a gravel road. Hot (too hot?) in summer, better in spring or fall season, VB-V4 is feasible, some brief SS lines, but as a whole perhaps 20+ viable problems (only the Dee Block is tapped at present). Brief entertaining stuff if you like low grade problems, and if you live

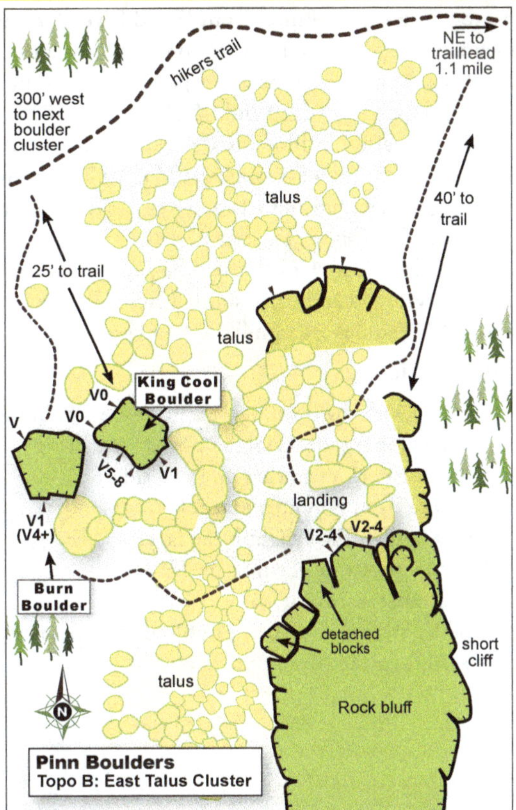

nearby. About 20 minutes from Hood River. Crashpad recommended (one), cell phone reception (yes), low altitude site, season from April-November, and possible year-round. **History:** Site was tapped by Mr O and Mr A in about 2016.

Directions: From Hood River drive south on 12th street on State Road 281 (aka Dee highway) for 10.2 miles to a junction. Turn right downhill onto Lost Lake Road, cross bridge, turn right onto Punchbowl Road, and drive 1.3 miles (to West Fork River bridge). Just .1 mile after the bridge, turn left on Green Point gravel road and drive south 1 mile. Two stones are on the left and 1-3 stones are uphill on the right.

Dee Boulder

Starting with the obvious west nose (beta going clockwise):
V0 Change Agent. Cool flat nosed west prow.
V0 D'form. Brief smears on NW side.
VB Dee Best. Fun north face slab.
V4 D'fender. East slight hung face.
V3ss D'interlude. Crimps on SE rib.
V0 Chubster. Minor one mover.
VB We Wuz Robbed. Enjoyable south side dash.
V3ss D'ception. Brief crimps on SW side.

Tymun on D'form V0 (Dee Boulders)

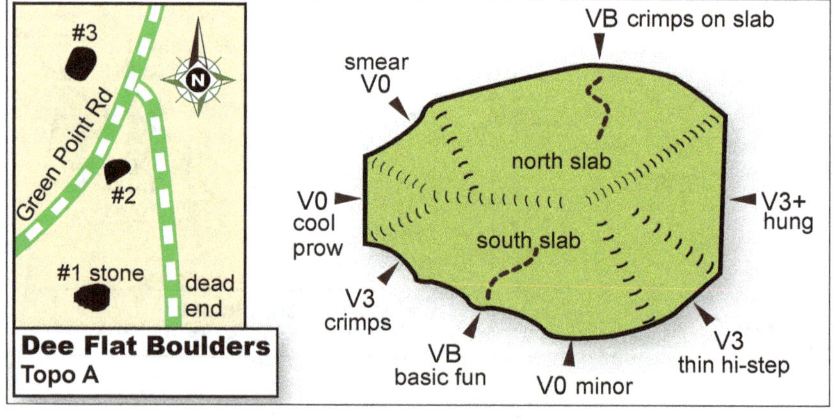

LOST LAKE BOULDERS

An extensive bouldering site that offers a substantial concentration of recreation opportunities, certain to become northwest Oregon's biggest bouldering site with a potential for over 1000 problems in a broad area where you can park your vehicle in one location and boulder all day. In terms of quality and quantity this highly rated site offers a great variety of bouldering problems at all levels (VB-V10 and higher), many basic fun runs VB-V3, desperate hi-ball powerhouse lines, and super overhung lines, all in a beautiful forested setting.

Many stones range from 9' to 14' tall with plenty of taller stones that reach about 25' tall. Some horizontal boulders stretch to 35' long, yielding a surprising number of problems on just one stone (10+ lines) and excellent long traverses.

The full extent of the boulder field (roughly 932,800 sq ft) covers an area from an initial bluff (near Buck Peak) above the road, down a gentle slope for a thousand feet northward. On hot days you will find delving into several of the cooler pits (15° cooler) agreeable. A single crashpad will suffice for the short lines, but 2-4 crashpads are optimal if you plan to tackle any of the really big beasts. Some of the formations (e.g. Tall Wall) easily qualify as roped climbing terrain. Of surface nuance features (ribs, rails, arêtes, overhangs, traverses) LLB has it all. The stone is composed of sticky textured andesite rock with minor amounts of moss/lichen.

The LLB bouldering site is situated about one mile from Lost Lake which has good camping and fishing options, great for multi-day camping trips, with paved road access to the site. A hikers trail meanders down hill between the middle and lower north talus fields giving convenient access to those sections. Most of the talus fields are challenging to negotiate because of angular blocky landings and pits (not exactly kid friendly).

The Upper South Talus Field is the most popular because of two easy access paths and the concentrated quantity of problems. The Middle Talus Field has the least quantity of problems (but one of the best boulders [Full House]. The Lower North Talus Field is the furthest from the road, the most time consuming to get to, and its talus field is a bit trickier to negotiate.

Camping options

The Lost Lake Resort and campground is about one mile up the road, and its a quality and popular lakeside camping facility (that means you can attach your camper unit to your pickup, rack up a canoe, bring a mountain bike, and stay for a week if you want to mix it all into the outing). The lake is Day Use/Overnight accessible, and has a general store, 148 campsites, a public boat launch, lodge rooms for rent, RV's spaces, etc. The store has plenty of basic amenities from Groceries, Beer/Wine, Fishing Tackle & License, Prepared Foods, etc. Wow! Let's go camping. The Lost Lake Resort web link is www.lostlakeresort.org.

Attractions / Detractions

Multiple pads are needed for tall lines; site elevation is 3,000' with snow in winter months, and summer can get quite hot mid-day in July-Aug. Seasonal access from mid-May to late October. The nearest town (Hood River) is about 35 minutes drive, so having an ankle twister here would be a slow process to see a doctor. LLB site is not granite (nor does it compete with granite quality) and the stones do have considerable moss or lichen. No cell phone service (well not exactly). If you drive about 1.5 miles west of Lost Lake resort on NF13 road you can attain spotty cell tower reception to the tower all the way down in Parkdale.

History

The site was likely explored minimally on several roadside stones by unknown locals (probably hikers). The site attained some activity in 2013 when a local tagged a string of new problems in one day. The site really kicked into high gear during the summer of 2014. Various associates and other teams stepped up to the plate early in summer of 2014 to tag a smart string of cutting edge problems. By the following year new problems reached into the elusive V10+ range. Within short time a broad array of folks from Portland to Bend were catching the wave at LLB.

Certain parts of LLB are well tapped (the Upper Talus), but the bouldering refinement phase as a whole (especially for the North Talus) will take years to fully tap (including the VB stuff).

The rock compositional structure has a strong surficial texture, definitive gray groundmass of miocene tertiary Andesite rock with a mineral matrix ranging from plagioclase platy feldspar, hornblende, pyroxine, biotite, and a considerable imprint of platy hexagonally shaped quartz (3-4mm in size). The unusual size of certain crystal minerals (e.g. quartz)

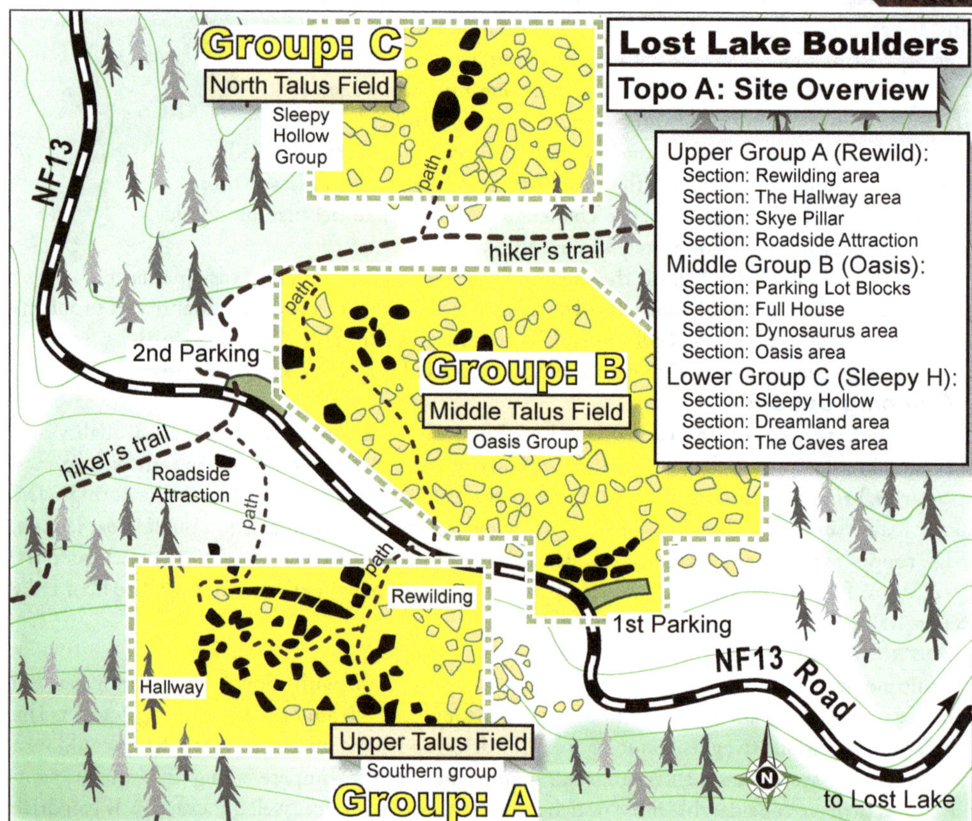

provides considerable friction-*ability* for smears and power crimps. Many boulders show parallel jointing resulting in giant cleaved cubes and prominent rectangular shapes.

Directions

Drive time from Portland is two hours. Take I-84 to exit #62 at Hood River, then drive south on 12th Street zigzagging south into the country on State Hwy #281 (Dee Hwy). At about 8 miles, turn right (at the old lumber mill site), cross a river, and drive through

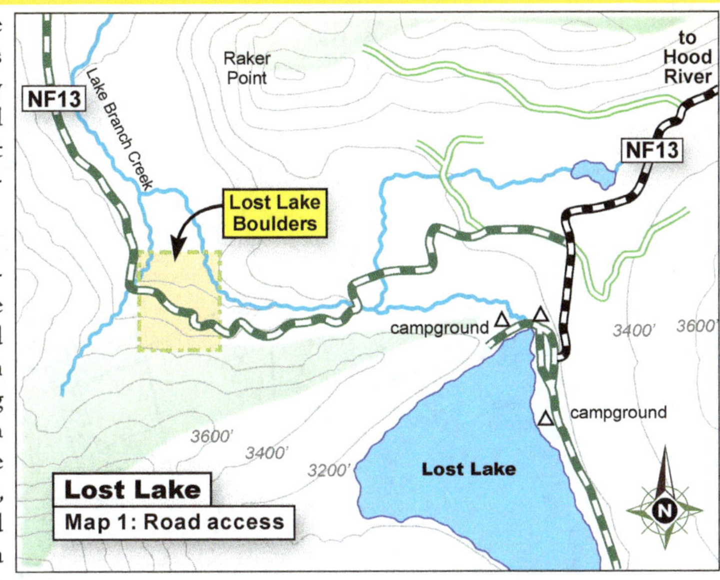

Dee, continuing on NF13 (this splits so take the left south main road) and drive NF13 (past the junction of NF18 Lolo Pass road) to Lost Lake. When you reach the 3-way road junction at

Lost Lake, turn right and drive the narrow paved NF13 road one mile west to the bouldering site. If you opt to drive the Lake Branch Road, it is less maintained, but still navigable.

Coordinates for the LLB bouldering site: GPS UTM 10t 590476 5038887, elevation 3,000'.

The beta and map tour is seperated into three major sections (South Upper Talus, Middle Talus zone, and North Talus). Those broad areas are more commonly called Rewilding area, Oasis area, and Sleepy Hollow area. Our diagrams will detail an entire group first (striving to give a sort of guided tour of each zone) fol-

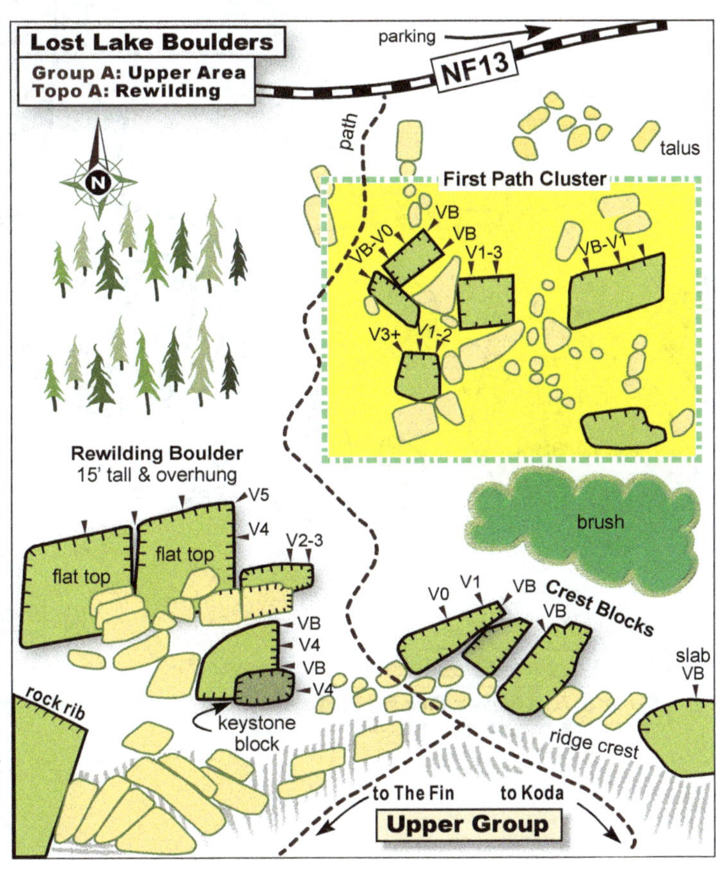

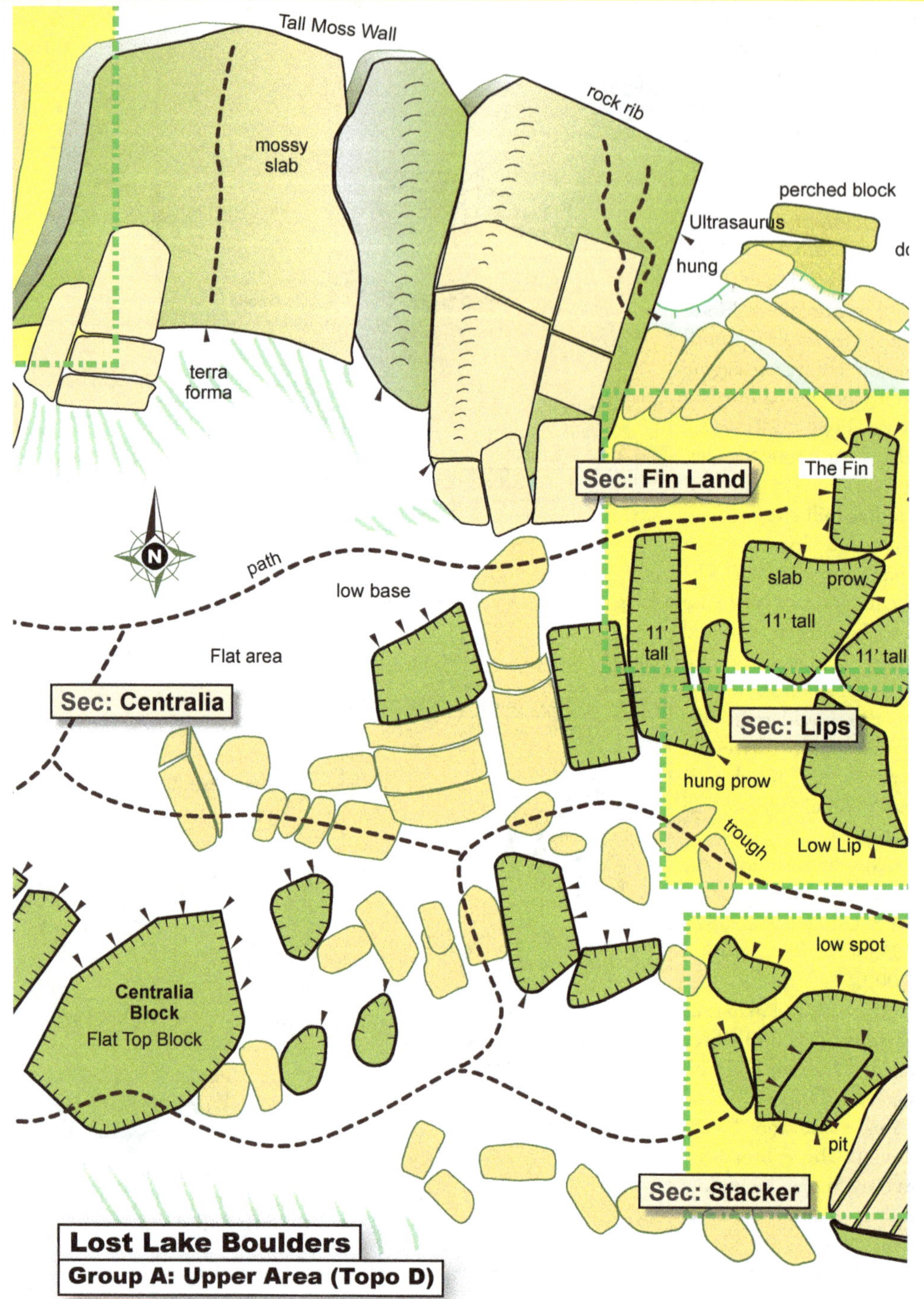

Lost Lake Boulders
Group A: Upper Area (Topo D)

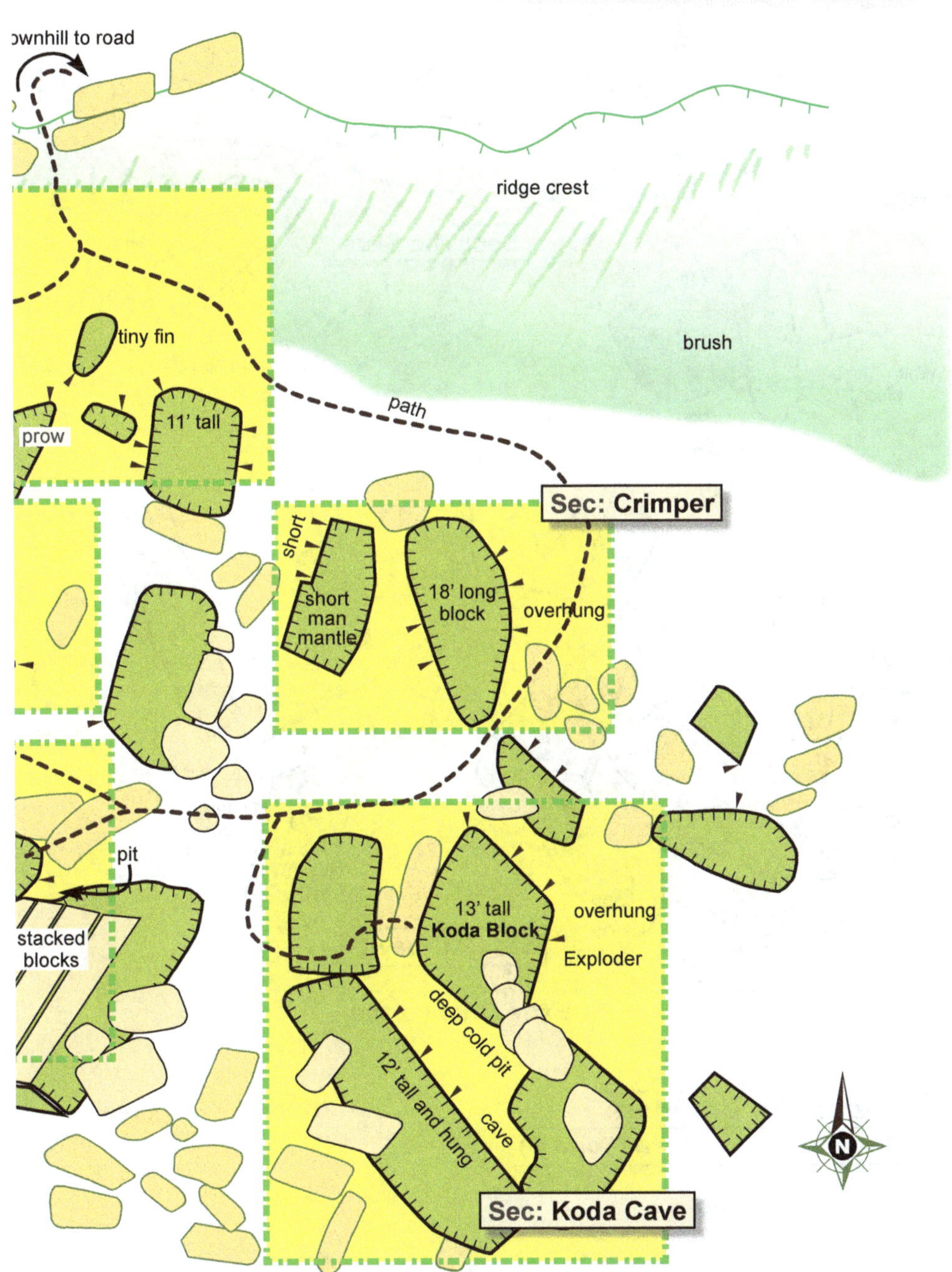
Lost Lake Boulders
Group A: Upper Area (Topo E)
ownhill to road
ridge crest
brush
tiny fin
prow
11' tall
path
Sec: Crimper
short
short man mantle
18' long block
overhung
pit
stacked blocks
13' tall
Koda Block
overhung
Exploder
deep cold pit
12' tall and hung
cave
Sec: Koda Cave
N

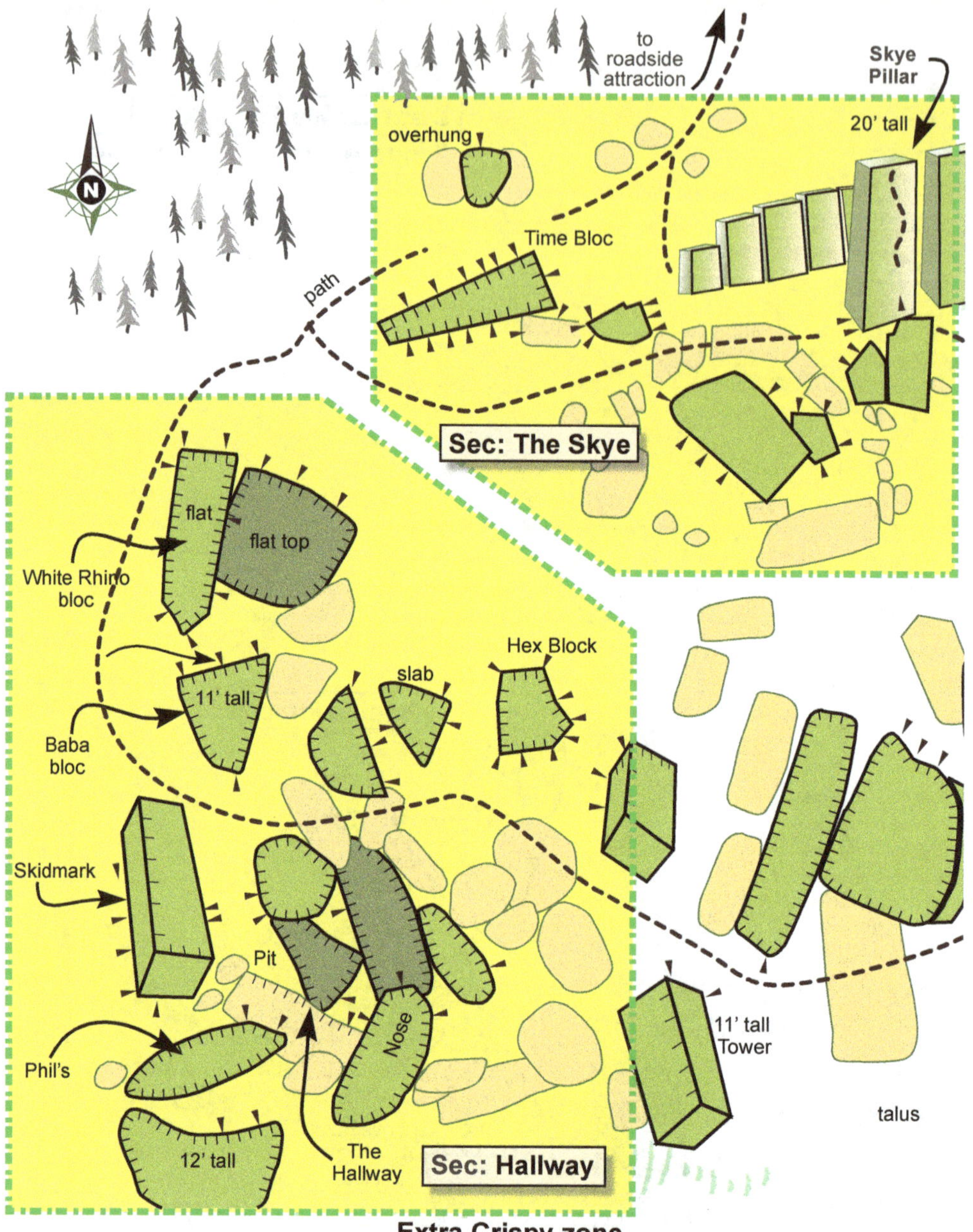

Lost Lake Boulders

Group A: Upper Area (Topo B)

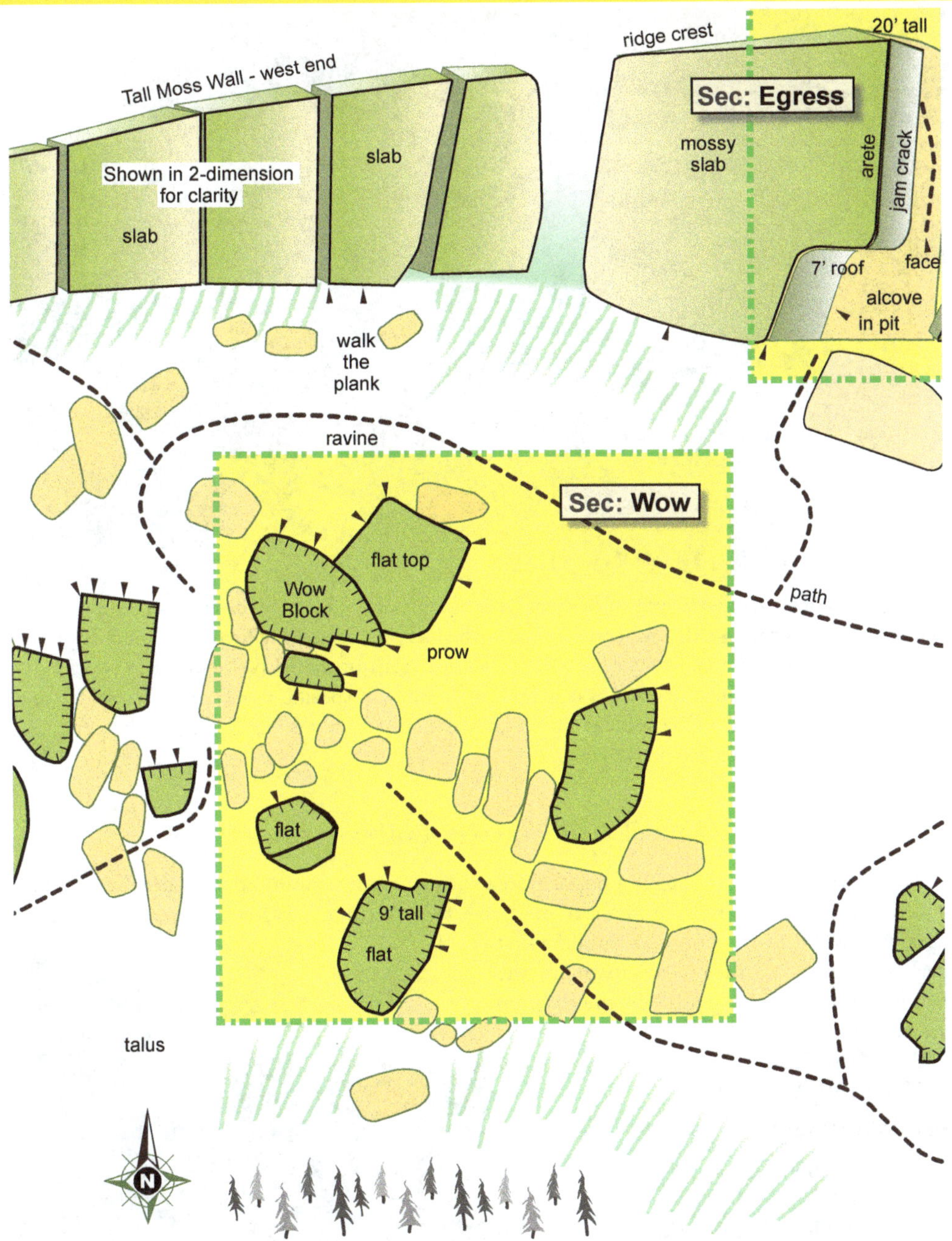

Lost Lake Boulders

Group A: Upper Area (Topo C)

lowing a sort of path of least resistance through the tangle of boulders. So don't expect our analysis and map designs that we detail herein to jive with "Joebob's" idea. Our highly detailed diagrams are very specifically effective visual overview representations of the LLB site utilizing concise at-the-site creatively designed maps. These diagrams are not GE specific, nor intended to match any space-based photography. The boulder shapes shown on the diagrams may not always be exact; the diagrams are not science, but artistry.

Upper Talus Field (aka Rewilding)

The Rewilding Area (UTF) is a popular area with a unique concentration of problems. It has a plethora of unique lines from minor to moderate, to powerful crimp-fests, to sketchy hi-ball af-fairs. Access this by walking west from the first parking spot for 200' then go up a path into the Rewilding Area. Some grades on the diagram are mere raw estimates.

First Path Cluster has five stones that can yield some VB-V4.

Rewilding Boulder

Rewilding Boulder has a tall north and east face aspect. Beta L to R:

V5ss Rewilding start on sloper and move up right.

V4 Extinct Species the hung arête.

And several more lines (done?).

Keystone Block

VB basic right nose.

V4 Endangered Species. Can smear in from

left or right to center of face then up.

VB Chubsteroni. Offwidth, exit right.

V4 Diving Board goes up left face and mantles over upper stone.

Nearby **Crest Boulders** yield VB-V1 minor stuff (most are done).

At the ridgecrest to the immediate west a few yards is Ultrasaurus, stuck on a slight overhung section of the utter east end of Tall Moss Wall.

Ultrasaurus ⚠

V7 Ultrasaurus is a powerful crimp line on a slight hung face.

V1-3 ____ several other lines exist down left on the less steep slab face aspect.

FIN BOULDER SECTION

Common spot to warmup on various minor prows on the end of a cluster of stones.

The Fin

Left to Right (NE around to west):

VBss Head Fake (basic NE face).

V3 Where the Sidewalks. North side.

V4 Light in the Attic. Direct up slightly hung nose on crimps.

V3 Ziggurat. Crimps on flat west face.

V1 Cover your Eyes. Lip traverse.

Tiny Fin

V2ss Archaeopteryx. SS little minor.
Two other nearby tall parallel blocks yield:

V3 Creeper. Prow on next block.

V1 Dorito. Prow on other block.

V_. Flat face on east side.

CRIMPER SECTION

Crimper Boulder

The east face of this boulder yields several power lines mostly SS on a low but long east facing aspect.

V9ss ____. Powerful hung crimps.

Immediately south of Crimper Block is a briefly hung stone with a V7ss.

To its east is a minor north facing block with a brief crack line (**V2 Archosaur**).

Koda Boulder

VBss Yixian. Basic north nose.

V_ potential on overhang.

V9ss Exploder. Hung east face with dyno or long reach to lip, and mantle.

Koda Cave

V2 Kibbles. Left slight overhang on jugs.
V1 Bow Wow. The center on jugs.
V0 Wo-of. The right face on jugs.

STACKER SECTION

Stacked Boulders

Starting with the upper smaller stone sitting on the big lower stone:

VB-V0 all around (well done), and north point is **V3 Tar & Feather.**

Lower main stone:

V3ss __ northeast deep pit has nice upside down jug run.

Lower main stones north face (all lines start in a low trough):

V7ss __ thin crimps on left (left of wide slot).

V2ss Gondwana. Straight up the round nose (just right of wide slot).

V2ss Pangaea. Crimps on right face trending up left merging onto same round nose.

LIPS SECTION

There are two main stones in this section. Both yield very overhang super low SS problems with quality powerful entertainment (V3-4ss).

CENTRALIA SECTION

Centralia Stone

A brief set of VB-V1+ lines wrap the north side of this stone. Other nearby stones (6-8ea) can yield a minor assortment of problems VB-V2ss.

WOW SECTION

A section with two half-worthy boulders of interest. Other nearby stones (including the big flat one Wow Block is sitting on) offer viable VB-V3 potential (some well done).

Wow Boulder 〰

V4ss Off My Tip. The right hung arête then over lip.

V5ss Get Swifty. The inner hung corner and over sloped lip.

Half Pint Block (just to left)

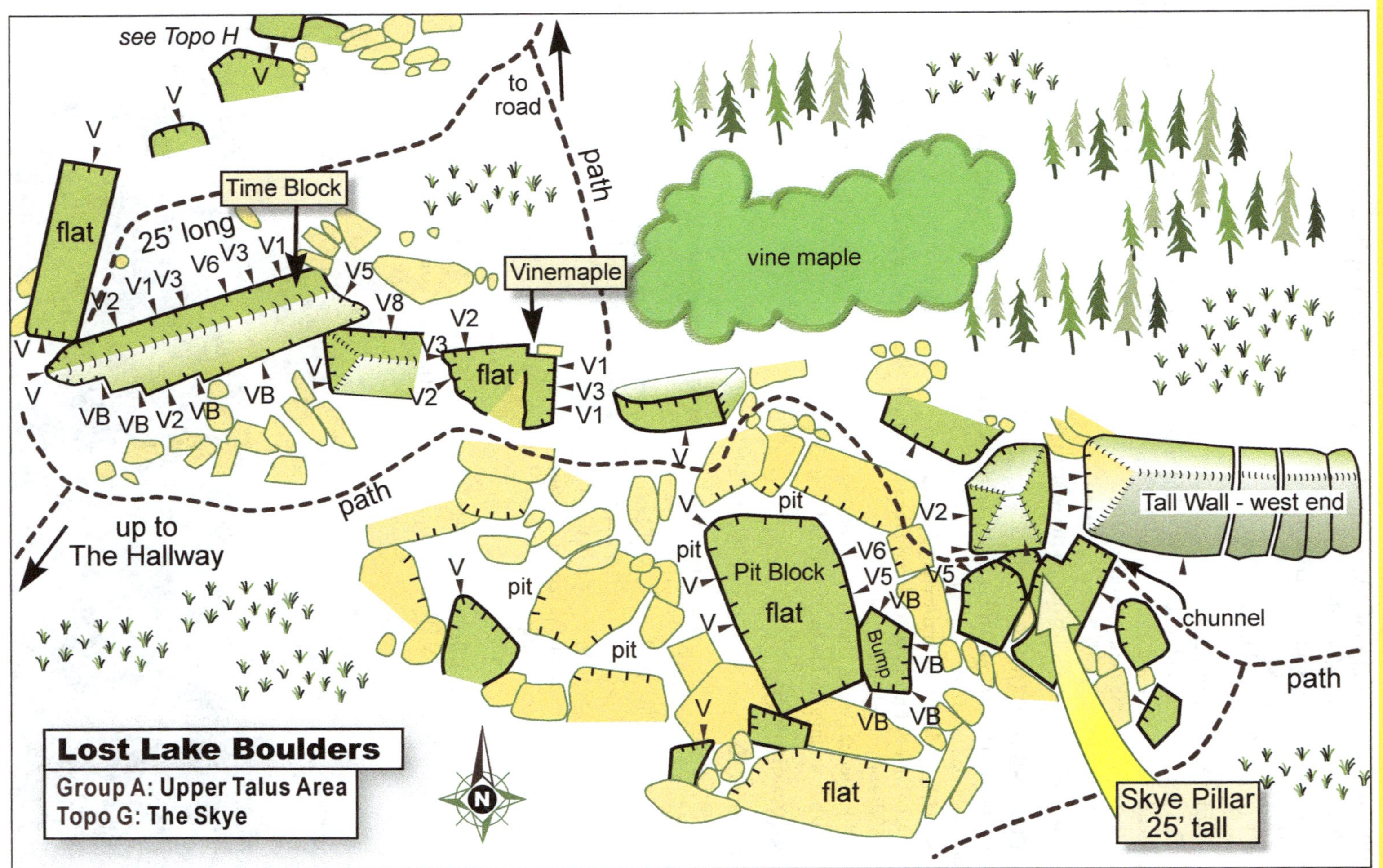

see Topo H
to road
path
vine maple
Time Block
flat
25' long
Vinemaple
flat
path
up to
The Hallway
path
Tall Wall - west end
chunnel
path
Pit Block
flat
Bump
flat
pit
pit
pit
pit
V
V
V
V1
V3
V6
V3
V1
V2
V5
V8
V2
V3
V2
V1
V3
V1
VB
VB
VB
V2
VB
VB
V
V2
V6
V5
V5
VB
VB
VB
V
V
N
Lost Lake Boulders
Group A: Upper Talus Area
Topo G: The Skye
Skye Pillar
25' tall

This is the tiny boulder (aka Warmup) immediately south of Wow Boulder.

V0ss Troodonts. Left south face crimps.

V1ss Fossil. Right south face crimps.

V1 __ east tall aspect.

V1 (?) __ taller still, down low right.

TALL MOSS WALL ⚠

This is a moss rich tall south-facing slab that runs for several hundred feet from Ultrasarus (at east end) to the Skye Pillar (at west end). The wall is all hi-ball, but a few lines do get etched into existance even on the mossy sections.

V0 Terra Firma. A slab line on the eastern portion.

VB Walk the Plank. Slab line on the western portion.

EGRESS SECTION ⚠

Located at a large alcove with a superb vertical east facing aspect. Many crashpads recommended for this hi-ball stuff.

V3 [?] ___ climbs the entire crack system.

V3ss Point of Egress. Start deep in the pit and runs crimps and edges up the hung face (just up out of the pit). Its all underground.

V8 Prince of Persia. Climb up out of the [same] pit onto the right face, then into a hi-ball crack to finish (standing start at horizontal hold gets V5).

SKYE SECTION

Skye Pillar ⚠

A 30' tall pillar with a prominent vertical west aspect. This is located at the far west end of the Tall Moss Wall.

VB Paleontology. The basic south face slab to the summit of the pillar.

V2 Phoenix. The noble west face line (variations may exist). Hi-ball on sloping rails and good holds that exits right at mid-height onto south face then to top.

V_ (?). _____. Immediately right of Phoenix.

V5 For the Never. A short crack on next block to right of Skye Pillar.

The Chunnel

The cavernous section behind Skye Pillar exists because a big stone abutts against the pillar, and the end of the Tall Moss Wall leaving a gapping chasm. This crawl zone yields a string of viable V0-

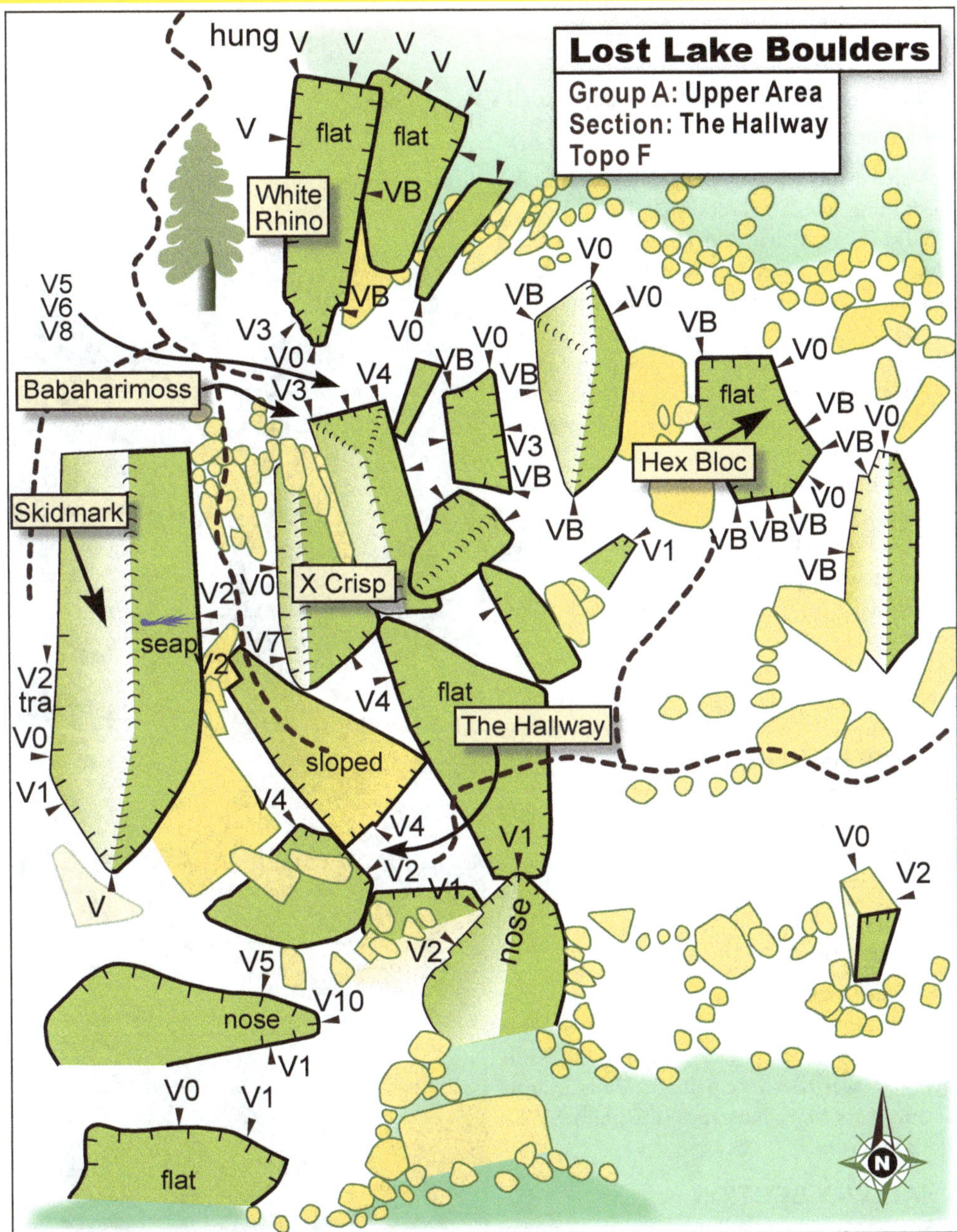

V4+ potential lines, some can top out, some not.

Pit Boulder

Cool stone in a low pit and hung on east, north and west aspects.

V5 Where The Wild Things Roam.

V6 Seek and Destroy.

V_ (?) ____.

V_ (?) ____.

V_ (?) ___.

Bump Boulder

Leans up against the Pit Block and yields all VB's (all done).

Time Warp Boulder

A stellar fun 35' long global ballistic missile with a fat string of quality problems, especially its north hung aspect. All totally cool.

V1ss Time Warp. On far left go up hung edges to lip & over. Also can start on sloped two-hander, bump left into the same route.

V3ss Anchors Away. Near previous fat sloper, start on crimps and cruise up over lip.

V6ss Born Free. Start low on right on crimps (near next route), move up left to join previous lines exit moves over the lip.

V3ss Enlightenment. The center rail straight up hung face.

V1ss Tattoo. On right start on incut rail jugs, punch up over lip.

V2ss (?) ______. A crimp shorty tucked low on far right.

V5ss Block Party. East flat face.

South side of this long block has a string of five slab lines, L to R, nothing special. **VB Bad Odor, VB Dysfunction, V2 Reactionary, VB Grin Weaper, VB Masochist.**

A boulder abutting next to the south side of the Time Block yields:

V8 Slaytonian Physics. Blank north slab.

V_ (?) ___. west end.

Vinemaple Boulder

Six lines total, all short nice stuff. Starting at the east face (R-L): **V1ss Manu Forte, V3ss Manu Propria** (center face), **V1ss Manu Militari;** and near the west point is **V2ss Manus Unum, V3ss Mare Nostrum** (the point), **V2ss Mare Liberum.**

HALLWAY SECTION

An extensive, concentrated pack of stones with crisp edges, lots of power, and some basic fun stuff. Starting at the north part on....

White Rhino Boulder

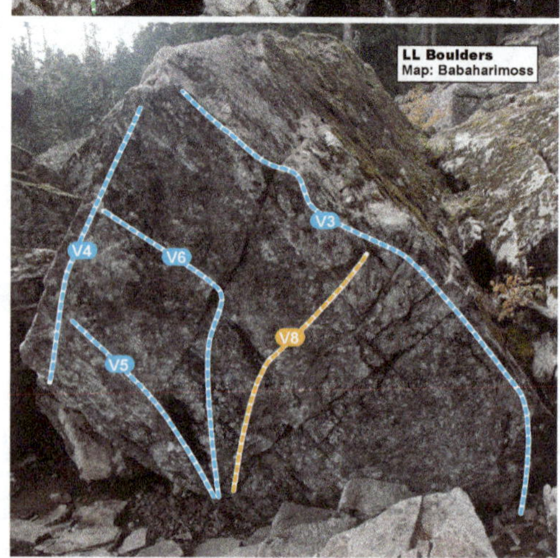

North aspect:

V_ (?) White Rhino (project).

V_ (?) WR Face.

South aspect:

V3ss Time n' Time Again. Traverse left to right and over prow.

V1ss True Vitt. Over hung prow.

VB-V0 the east face and minor traverse.

Black Rhino Boulder

This is the shorter flat topped unit immediately right (east) of White Rhino. It has some potential from V3-V5+.

Baba Boulder

Superb quality lines on a triangle shaped slightly hung north end of a large block.

V4 Babaharimoss. Left arête.

V5ss Morning Yoga. Start center, bust left to arête.

V6ss Gyoza. Center face directly up.

V8ss The Struggle Within. Center to right arête.

V3 Struggle Bus. Run the right arête to top point.

Skidmark Boulder

A long beast with problems on the west, south and east aspect.

V2 Skidmark Trav (west).

V0ss Sanity Gasp.

V1ss __ left of prow.

V3ss (?) __ south prow.

V2 Spineless Jellyfish. The eastside slab water seepage.

V2 Skidmark. Alternate.

X Crispy Boulder

V0ss Quality Time. Left face.

V7ss Extra Crispy. Start in pit on roof edge, go up left on slopers, then up right along rails and up to top. V3 standing.

V_ (?) Fade to Black. Inside un-

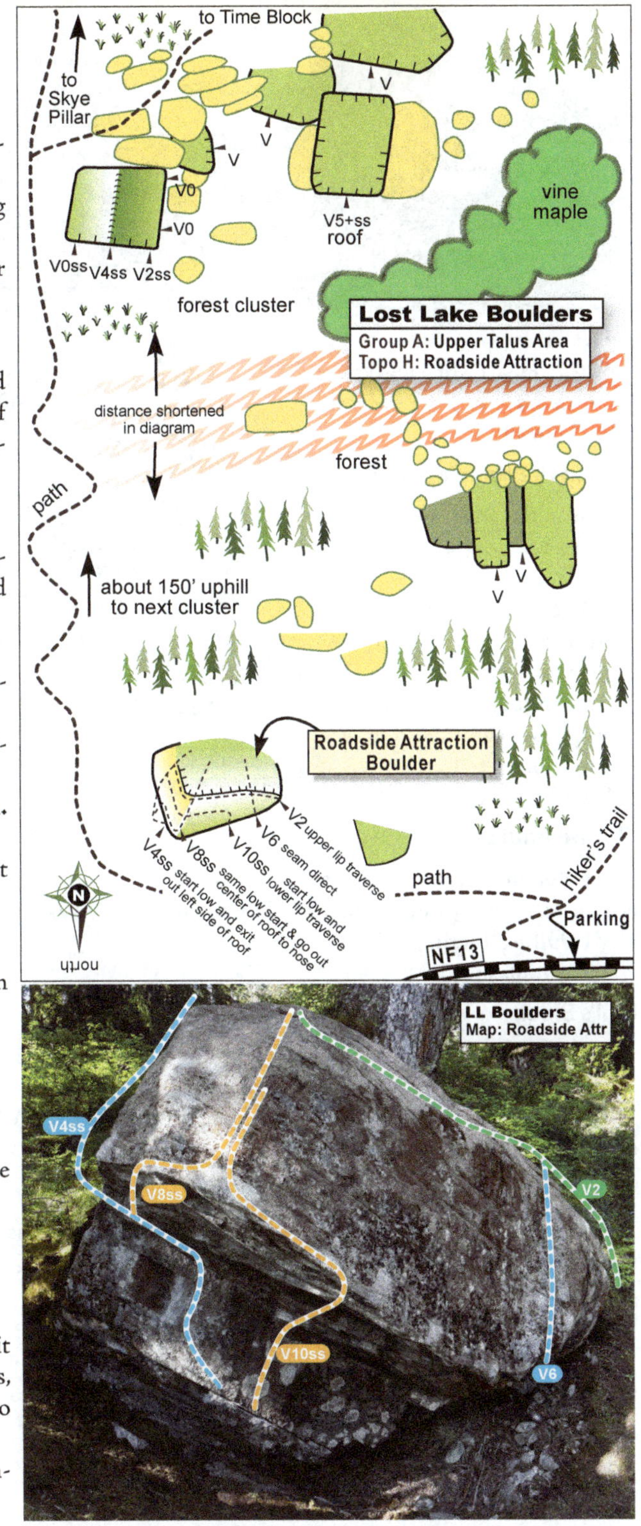

der backside.

V4ss Heart of Darkness. Deep in pit but power out the other hung block.

Kids in the Hallway Boulder

One of the great cool places to visit at LLB. Beta starts on north wall of tunnel-like hall:

V4 Kids in the Hallway. Start in hall, move right to arête onto outside face, then up top.

And on south aspect of hall:

V4 Cross the Hall. On west end of hall.

V2 (?) ___. Slot project?

Throne Boulder

V1 Bubble Arête. Short outer nose starts from atop another block (up east of Hallway)

V1 Pulling Teeth.

V2 Whiplash.

Phil's Block

Uphill south of Skidmark Block is a jutting hung prow: **V5 Al dante**, and **V10 Lasagna**, and **V0 Shortest Straw** (upside of the jutting prow).

The next (and last) uphill block: **V1 Spagettios** (Tall face), **V0 Pine Line.**

Hex Boulder

Hex Boulder is a flat topped unit with 8 total SS lines.

VBss (SW nose) **Presstitutes, VBss Regurtitation, VBss Blood, V0ss Greed, VBss** (SE nose) **Freedom, VBss Humid, V0ss** (NE nose) **Rites, VBss** (NW nose) **Ingrained Idiocy.** And a south lip traverse.

Nearby stones yield a few more V lines, most are well done.

Just east of Baba Blocks north aspect is a minor stone with a very brief flat east face. Two lines are VB (done), and center of flat face is **V3ss Double Tap.**

The minor pyramid-like stone offers short slabby VB's (done).

A tall-ish 'tower' east of 'throne' block has a V0 and V2.

Roadside Attraction Boulder

At the western parking spot walk briefly up the hiker's trail, then cut left to this classic big stone. The super hung roof offers quality power lines. The base flake broke off and the starts for certain routes are stouter.

V4ss Get Lost. Left end of crack, go left to lip, mantle up.

V8ss Lost & Found. Same as previous but at lip move right to nose, then up to top.

V10ss Roadside Attraction. Start under roof in middle at crack, go out to lip, run lip leftward to nose, then up to top.

V6 Mother Hucker. Far right. High edges in seam, and dyno.

V2 Not Lost. Traverse entire lip R to L.

MIDDLE TALUS GROUP

OASIS AREA

This large talus field lay north of the road, but certain amounts of it yield only scattered low SS problems. The better concentration lay along its northern reach just as it trends off near the hikers trail. So, from House Boulder in a grand arcing sweep eastward will get you some cool packaged gems. The overview diagram has two guided tours (the white and the black letter tours), and each focus on a specific concentrated zone.

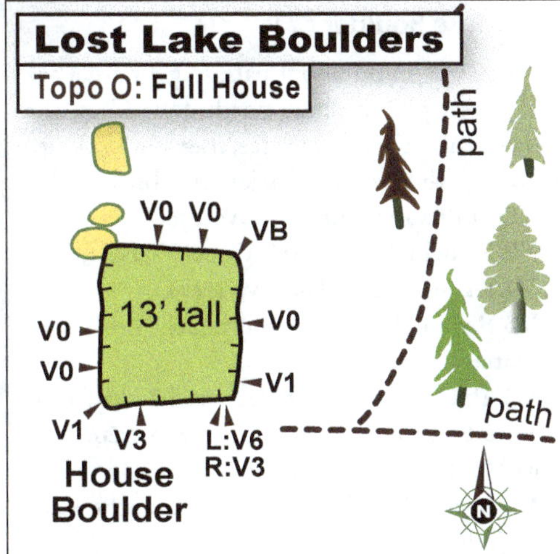

Parking Lot Boulders

This minor area has about 9-10 stones with about 20 total problems (most are SS). The biggest stones are listed below (west to east).

Squirrel Boulder

V0 (V3ss) White Squirrel east face of this stone.
Distraction Block is a minor block east of Squirrel Boulder; it has very brief VB-V0ss stuff.

Mindbender Boulder

This is a smaller stone just west of Foxglove.
V2ss Bender. Left on arête, right on sloper (V0-1 var).
V5ss Dr Mindbender. Start all on the sloper (mentioned above).

Foxglove Boulder

V1ss Wild Lily. Center west face.

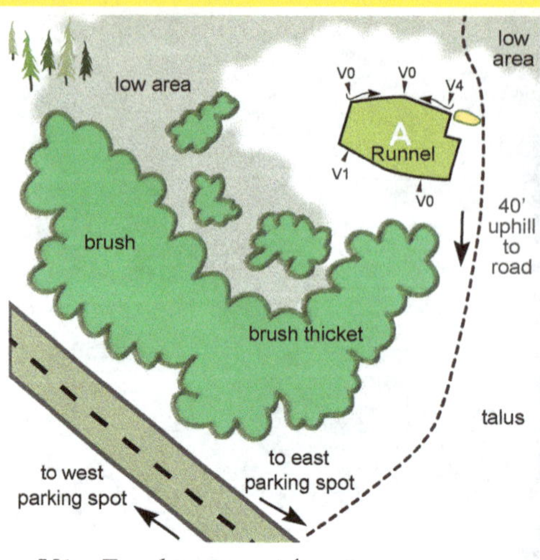

V1ss Foxglove uses right arête.

Full House Boulder ⌂

There is a round-about path to get here. Park at the west pullout; hike north dowhill on the hiker's trail for a few minutes, then cut back up-hill on a path that loops back to this big boulder.

V0 Stairway to Kevin's. West face.

V0 Knockin' on Kevin's Door. West face.

V1 Kevin's Gate. The SW arête.

V3 Raven. The classic south face (just left of center).

V3 Poe Arête. South face, right side, near arête. Start on face, transition onto arête. And its V6 if taking midway split left.

V1 Yard Bird. The SE arête using the east side entirely.

V0 The Plate. East face crimps.

VB Bull Run. NE blunt arête.

V0 __ north face slab (small edges).

V0 __ north face steep slab with crimps.

DYNOSAURUS CLUSTER

This is a concentrated zone of boulders about 100' east of Full House Boulder in the utter west edge of the Oasis talus zone (Middle Talus Field) which is below the paved road. This section is de-scribed as if you are descending from the road downhill 50' to the first large stone. This is the *white letter tour* (*see diagram*).

Runnel Boulder (A) has on its north side: **V0ss Runnel Arête** low on right traversing lip leftward to center, **V0** jug to lip mantle, and **V4ss Runnel In The Jungle** seam crimps traverse starts on far left.

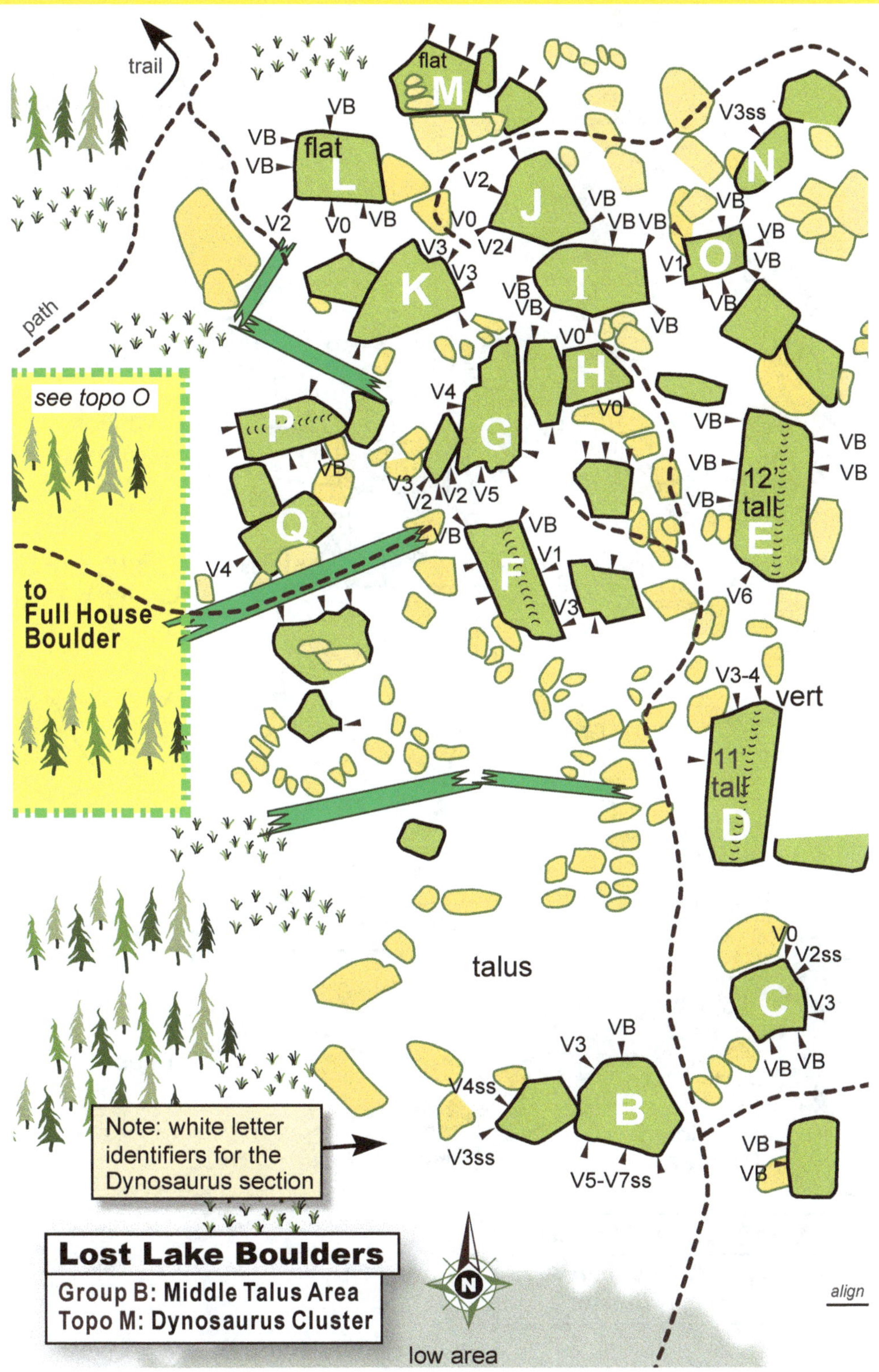

Lost Lake Boulders
Group B: Middle Talus Area
Topo M: Dynosaurus Cluster

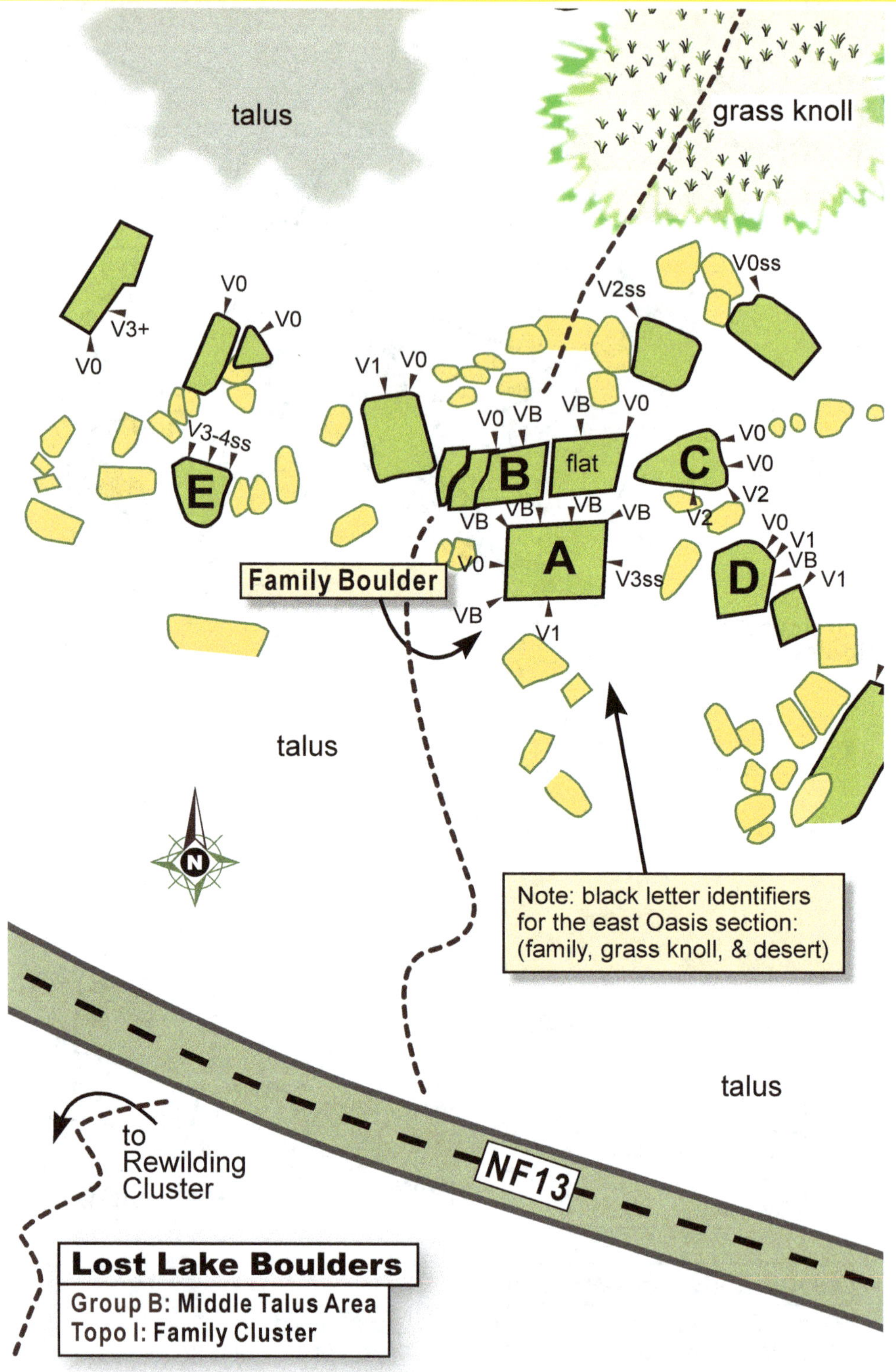

talus
grass knoll
V0ss
V2ss
V0
V0
V3+
V0
V1
V0
V0
VB
VB
V0
V3-4ss
E
B
flat
C
V0
V0
V2
V2
VB
VB
VB
VB
VB
A
V3ss
V0
V1
VB
D
V1
Family Boulder
V0
VB
V1
talus
N
Note: black letter identifiers
for the east Oasis section:
(family, grass knoll, & desert)
talus
to
Rewilding
Cluster
NF 13
Lost Lake Boulders
Group B: Middle Talus Area
Topo I: Family Cluster

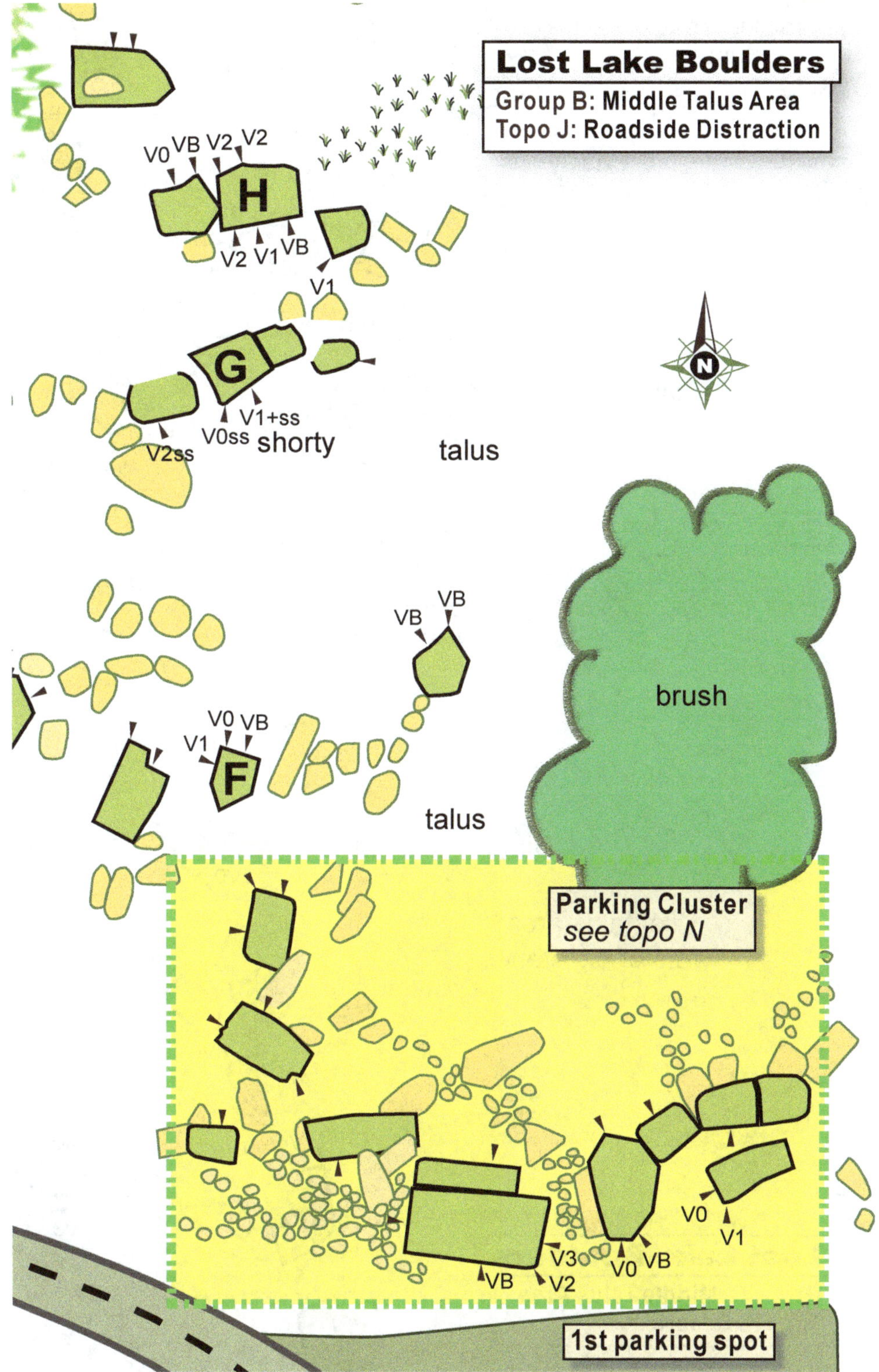
Lost Lake Boulders
Group B: Middle Talus Area
Topo J: Roadside Distraction
N
V0 VB V2 V2
H
V2 V1 VB
V1
G
V1+ss
V0ss shorty
V2ss
talus
VB VB
brush
V0 VB
V1
F
talus
Parking Cluster
see topo N
V0
V1
V3
VB V2 V0 VB
1st parking spot

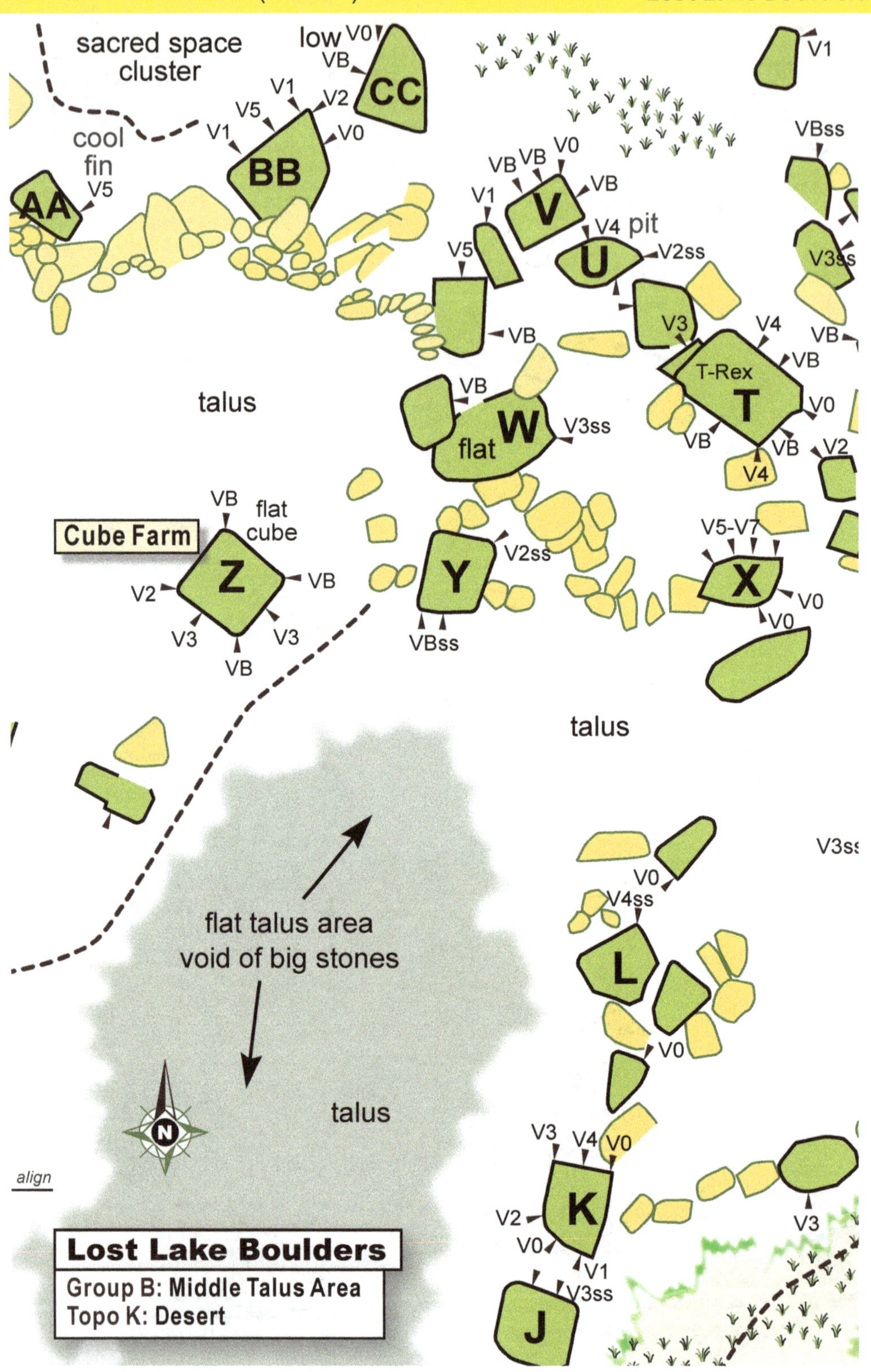
sacred space cluster
low V0
VB
cool fin
V5
V1
V5
V1
V2
V0
CC
BB
AA
V1
VBss
VB VB V0
VB
VB
V1
V4 pit
V2ss
V5
V3ss
V
U
V3
V4
VB
T-Rex
VB
T
V0
VB
VB
V3ss
VB
V2
flat
W
V4
Cube Farm
VB
flat cube
VB
V5-V7
V2
Z
VB
V0
V3
V3
V2ss
X
V0
VB
V3ss
Y
VBss
talus
talus
V3ss
V0
V4ss
flat talus area
void of big stones
L
V0
N
align
talus
V3 V4 V0
Lost Lake Boulders
V2
Group B: Middle Talus Area
V0
K
Topo K: Desert
V1
V3ss
J

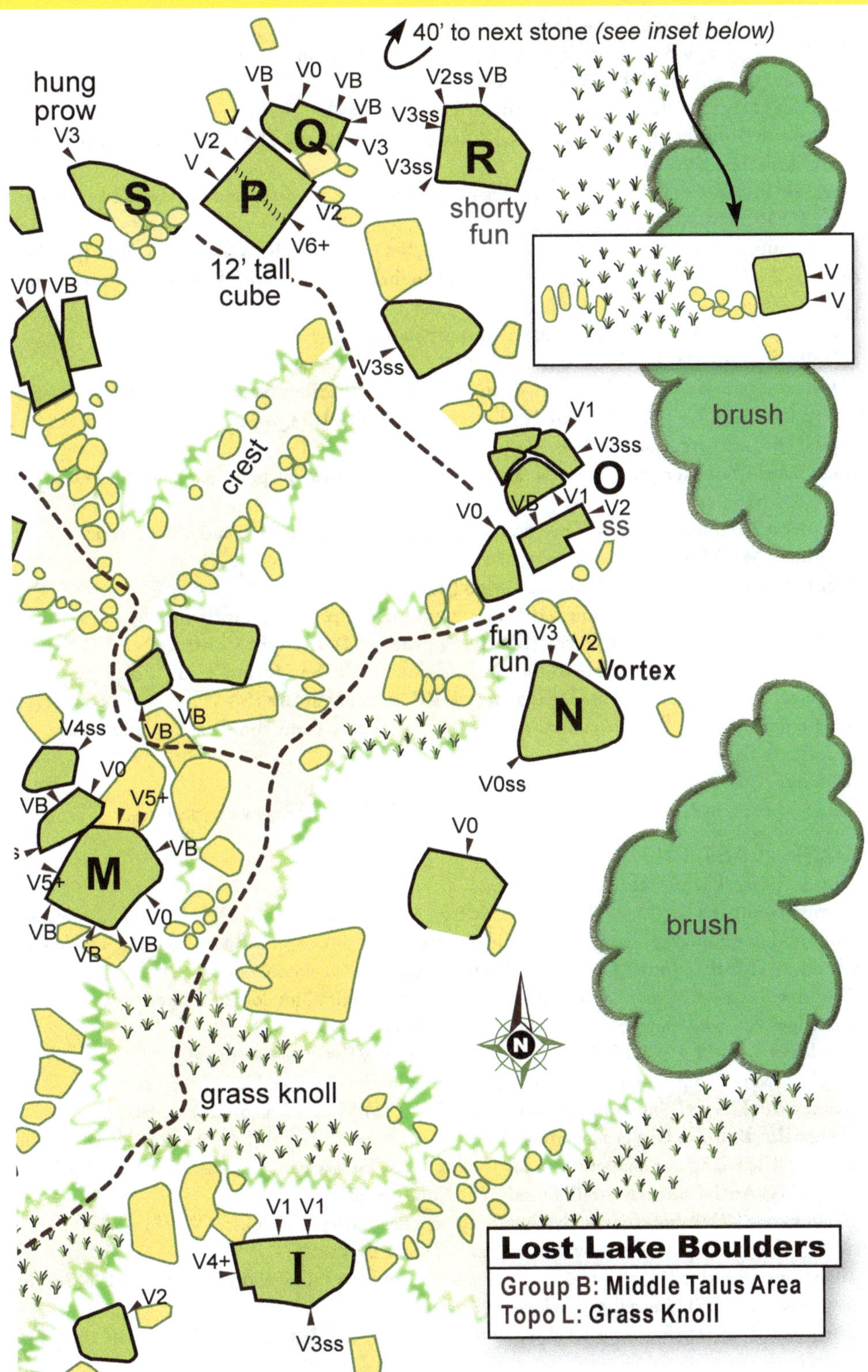
40' to next stone (see inset below)
hung prow
V3
VB
V0
VB
VB
VB
V2ss VB
V3ss
V2
V
V3
V3ss
Q
S
P
R
shorty fun
V2
V6+
12' tall, cube
V0
V
crest
V0 VB
V3ss
V1
V3ss
O
V0
VB
V1
V2 ss
brush
fun run
V3
V2
Vortex
N
V0ss
V0
VB
VB
V4ss
V0
V5+
VB
VB
V5+
M
V0
VB
VB
VB
grass knoll
brush
N
V0
V1 V1
V4+
I
V2
V3ss

Lost Lake Boulders
Group B: Middle Talus Area
Topo L: Grass Knoll

On south side: **V1 Jungle Arete**, and **V0 Jungle Juice**.

Boulder (B) has VB to V3ss (**V3ss Caught Inside**) on a main stone (+ futuristic SS).

Boulder (C) can yield VB-V3 (some SS).

Boulder (D) can yield V3+ on vertical north nose of this long boulder.

Megasaur Boulder (E) All VB's on all sides of slab are done. The south overhang provides a quality **V5ss The Bitter End** power line.

Jurassic Boulder (F) VB's on most sides of slab are done. The well manicured flat vertical east face is **V1 Rust Spot**. Possible SS additions.

Dynosaurus Boulder (G) has good SS lines, these are L to R: **V3ss Bona Fide** (use both prows), **V2ss Caveat Emptor** (prow only), **V2ss Inebrians** (right face), **V5ss Dynosaurus** (hung face with offset corner).

Permian Boulder (H) has one **V0ss Dinosaur** shorty crimp run.

Neolith Boulder (I) has VB-V0 (all well done).

Mother Earth Boulder (J). A superb stone with a cool scallop-shaped overhanging scoop on the west face (R to L): **V2 Jack of all Trades** (hung and fun), **V0 Queen of Hearts** (nose), and **V2 Royce Rolls** (pockets to slopers).

Lost World Boulder (K) has a cool overhung east aspect in a low pit: **V3 The Pit & Pendulum**, and the **V3 Sleeper**.

Mesozoic Boulder (L) short VB's (done), and **V2ss Friends** (prow), and **V0ss Affair**.

Boulder (M). Minor north side options.

Boulder (N). One low line **V3ss Iter Legis** (done).

Triassic Boulder (O) has eight VB-V1ss all around entire stone, mostly fun warmup stuff on a short boulder. **V1 Brink of Decay** (SW hung prow), **VB Thought Control** (N), **VB Erudite Thumbsuckers** (N), **VB Double Standard** (NE point), **VB Smidgeonette of Idiocy** (east face), **VB Idiot Proof** (SE point), **VB Get Down** (S), **VB Street Warfare** (S).

Paleozoic Boulder (P). West face can yield V4ss (**Tales from the Crypt**) while most other aspects get VB (some done).

Boulder (Q). A short west aspect may yield.

Most other stones in this Dynosaurus pack tend to be low and may yield SS lines.

OASIS (EAST TALUS SECTION)

This is the *black* letter string (see diagram).

Family Boulder [Boulder A] has VB to V1 on a large stone with angled slabs on all sides. My family and I developed this entire boulder. The problems names are: **Billy Joe, SusyQ, Uncle Bob, Auntie May, Mother Jones, Go Daddy, Sweet Sister,** & **Mother-in-law**.

Boulder B is a set of very flat low laying stones with potential for some SS lines.

Boulders C, D, E. Can yield SS problems VBss-V4ss+.

Boulders F, G, H, I, J, K, L. Can yield a good pack of VBss-V4ss potential.

Boulder M is a single large stone (and several small units) can yield VBss-V5+ss.

Vortex Boulder (N) has primarily one nice **V2 (V3ss) Vortex** line on its east face.

Forest Rat Boulder (O) is a group of three minor stones (all small). All are mainly brief shorty problems. The triangular shaped ultra low-ball is **V2ss Forest Rat**. On the NE block: **V1 Toxic Waste, V3ss Anti-Counter-Intelligentsia, V1 Environerd**.

Stonehenge (P). A big stone with something on a flat vertical south face (V6+?) with an undercut start. North aspect yields several lines and **V2 Cool Breeze**.

Bluestone Boulder (Q). All five are brief minor problems (all well done). The **V3 Lip Service** (left at nose), and **V0 Guerrilla Warfare** (NE nose slab).

Grimples Boulder (R). Four brief SS lines on low stone. **V3ss Yes No** (right to left along lip),

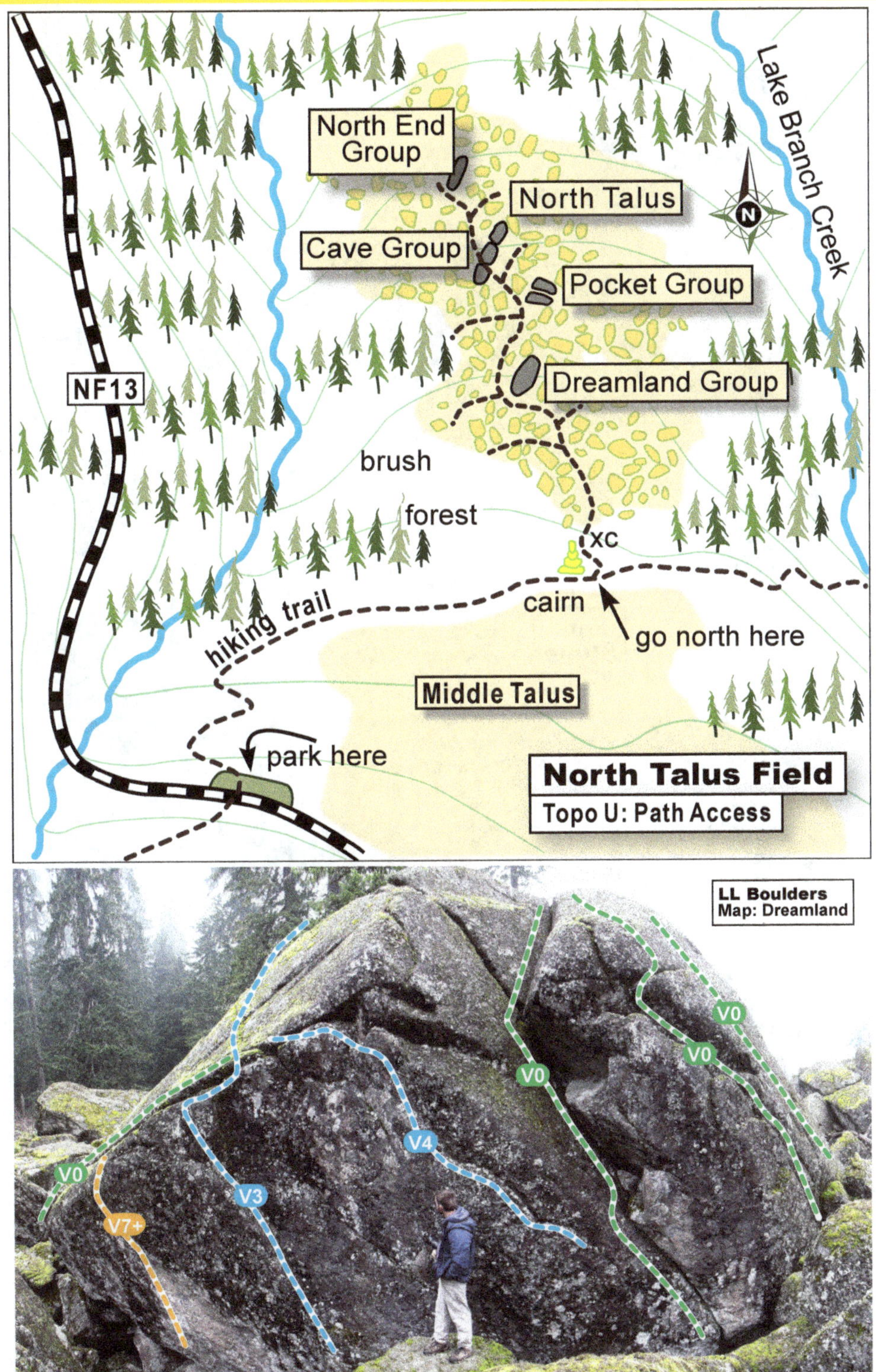
North End
Group
North Talus
Cave Group
Pocket Group
Dreamland Group
NF13
Lake Branch Creek
N
brush
forest
xc
cairn
go north here
hiking trail
Middle Talus
park here
North Talus Field
Topo U: Path Access
LL Boulders
Map: Dreamland
V0
V0
V0
V4
V3
V0
V7+

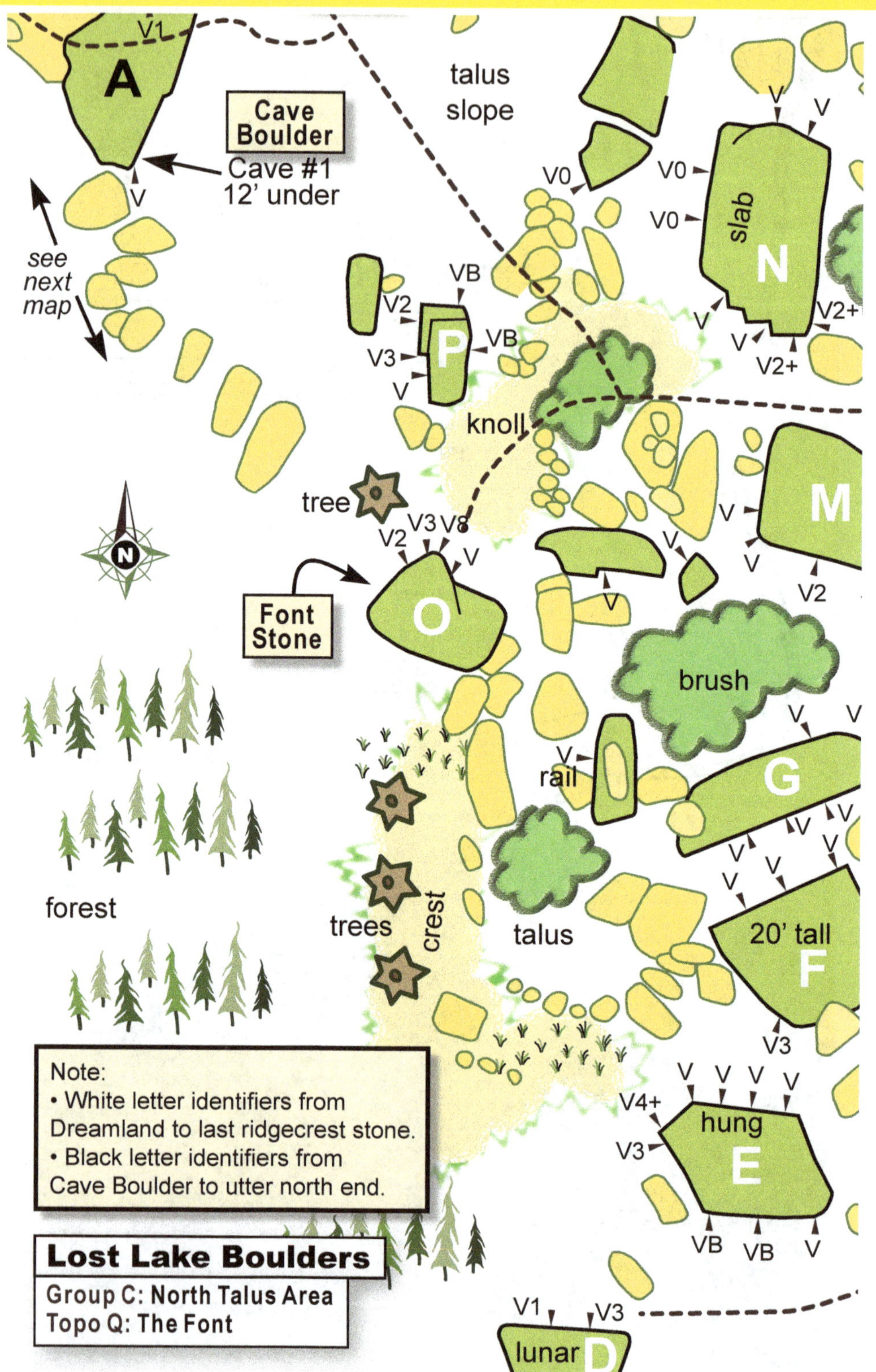
V1
A
Cave Boulder
Cave #1
12' under
V
see next map
talus slope
V0
V0
V0
V0
slab
N
V2+
V2+
V
VB
V2
VB
V3
P
V
N
knoll
tree
V3 V8
V2
V
M
V2
Font Stone
O
V
V
brush
rail
V
G
V
V
V
V
V
V
V
V
V
forest
trees
crest
talus
20' tall
F
V3
V
V
V
V
V4+
hung
V3
E
VB   VB   V
V1   V3
lunar D
N
Note:
• White letter identifiers from
Dreamland to last ridgecrest stone.
• Black letter identifiers from
Cave Boulder to utter north end.
Lost Lake Boulders
Group C: North Talus Area
Topo Q: The Font

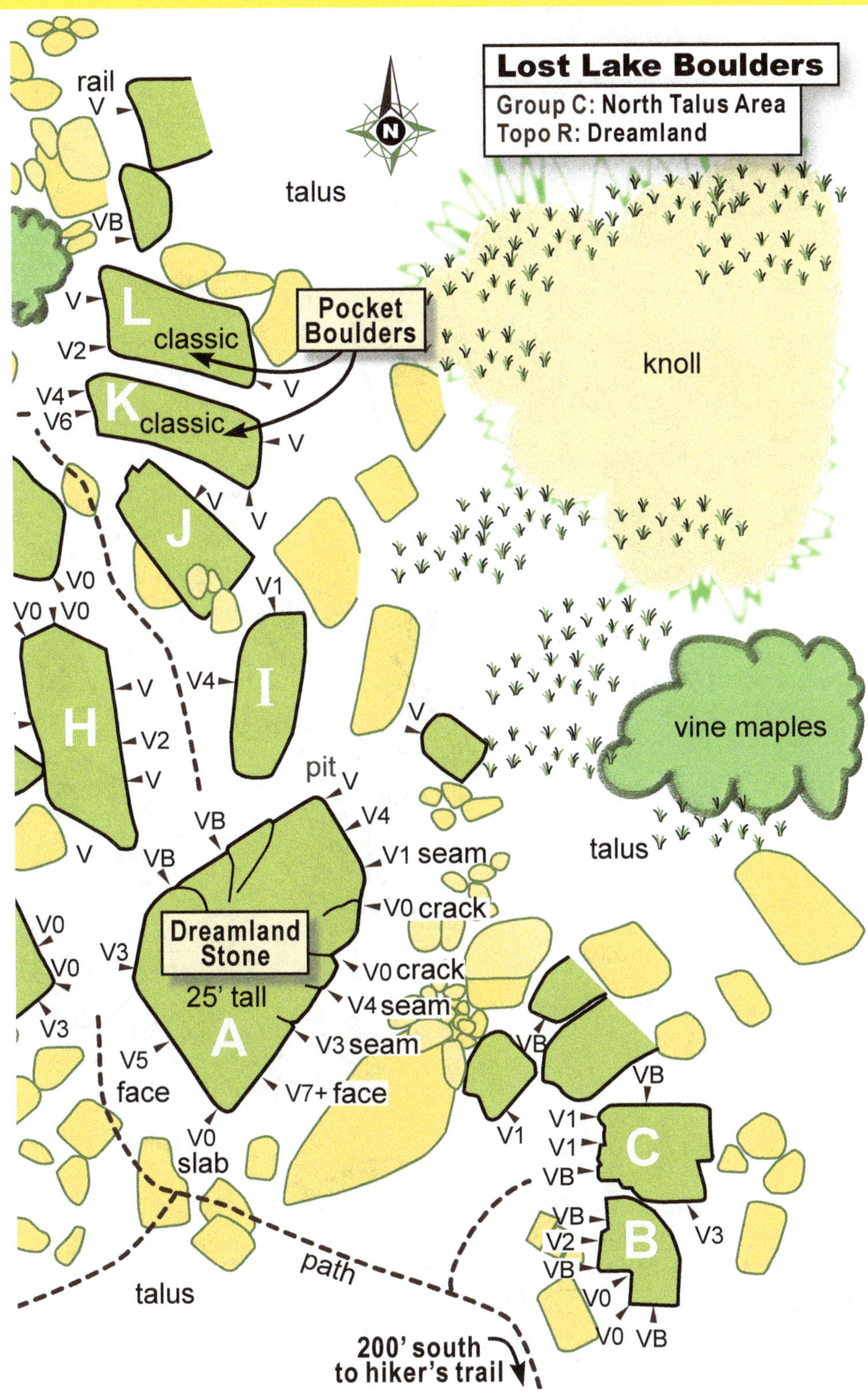
rail
V
talus
Lost Lake Boulders
Group C: North Talus Area
Topo R: Dreamland
N
knoll
L
classic
V
V2
Pocket
Boulders
V4
V6
K
classic
V
V
J
V
V
V0
V1
V0
V0
V4
I
H
V
V2
V
vine maples
V
pit
V
V4
VB
V1 seam
talus
V
VB
V0 crack
V0
Dreamland
Stone
V3
V0 crack
V0
V4 seam
V3 seam
A
25' tall
VB
V3
V5
face
V7+ face
V1
VB
V0
slab
VB
C
V1
V1
VB
VB
V3
V2
B
VB
talus
path
V0
V0
VB
200' south
to hiker's trail

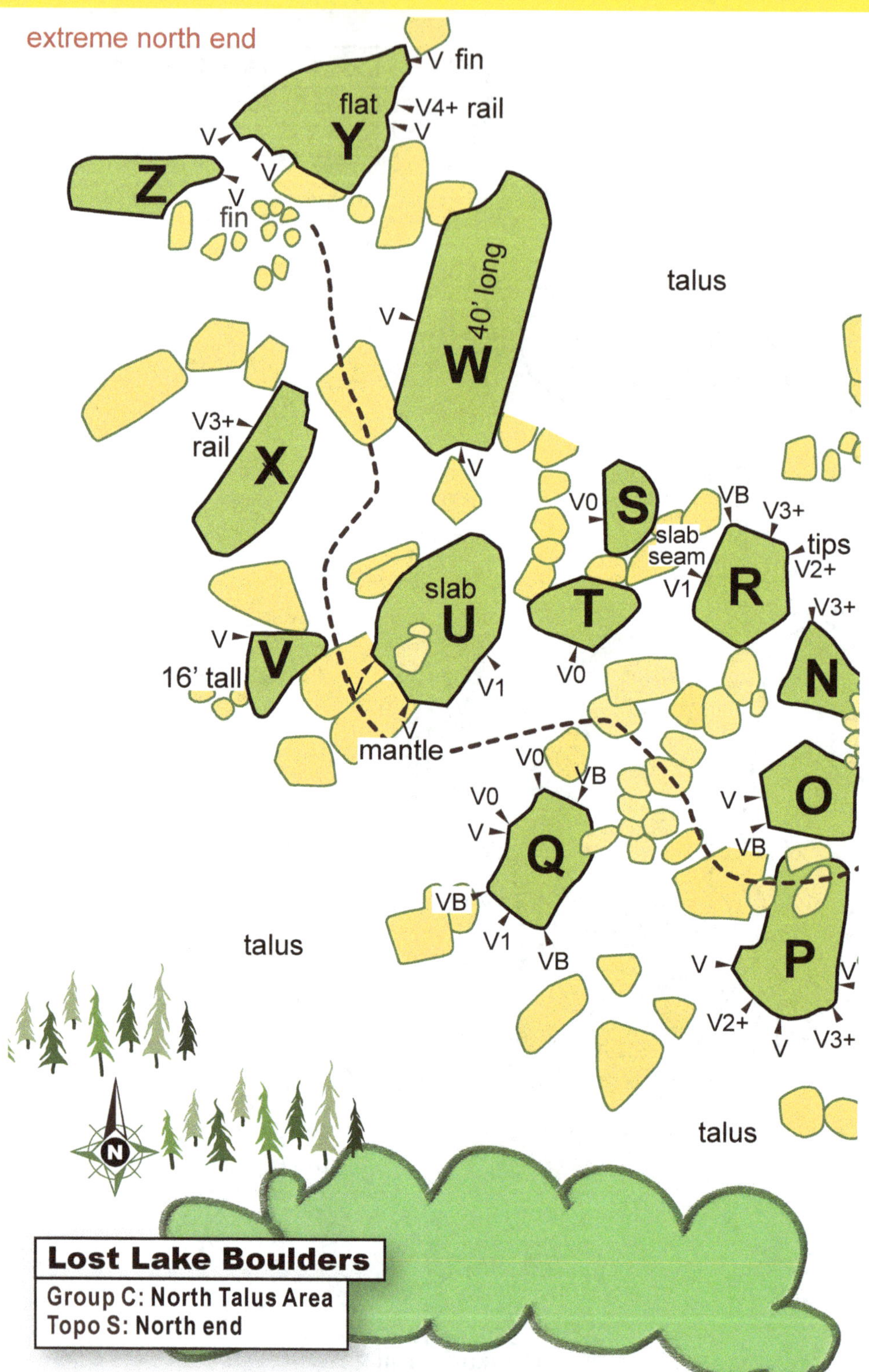

extreme north end
V fin
flat
Y
V4+ rail
V
V
Z
V
V
fin
40' long
W
V
talus
V3+
rail
X
V0
S
VB
V3+
slab
seam
tips
V2+
V1
slab
U
T
R
V3+
16' tall
V
V
V0
N
V1
V
mantle
V0
V0
VB
V
V
O
V
V0
V
Q
VB
VB
VB
P
V
V
V1
VB
V2+
V
V3+
talus
N
talus
Lost Lake Boulders
Group C: North Talus Area
Topo S: North end

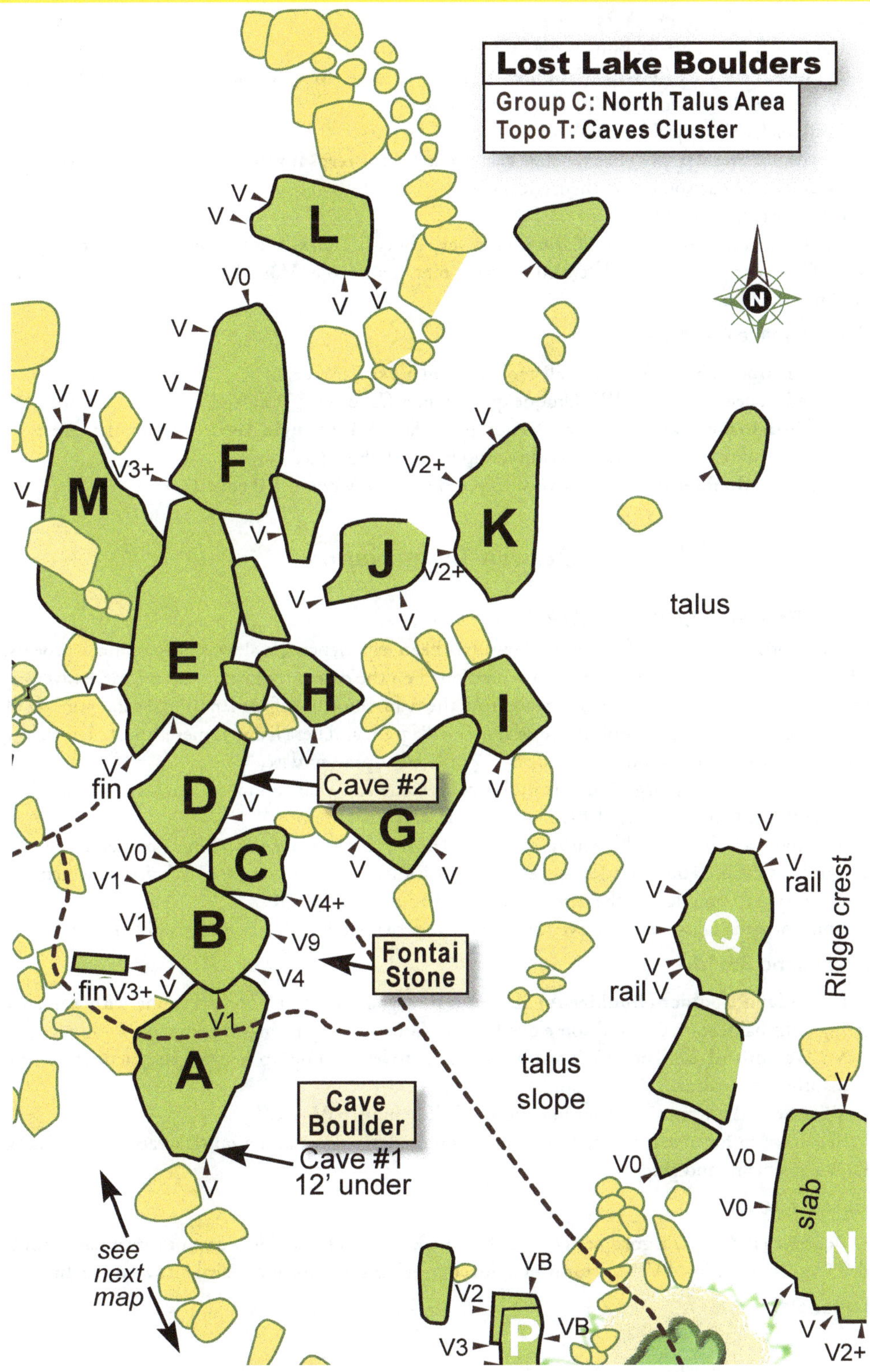
Lost Lake Boulders
Group C: North Talus Area
Topo T: Caves Cluster
N
L
V
V
V
V0
V
F
V
V
M
V
V
V3+
V
V
J
K
V
V2+
V2+
talus
V
E
H
I
V
Cave #2
D
V
G
V
fin
V
V0
C
V4+
V1
V
V
rail
V1
B
V9
Fontai
Stone
Q
V
V
rail V
fin V3+ V
V4
talus
slope
V1
A
V0
V0
Ridge crest
Cave
Boulder
Cave #1
12' under
V
V0
see
next
map
slab
N
VB
V2
P
VB
V3
V
V2+

V3ss Yes But (center up), **V2ss Grimples**, **VBss**.

Boulder S is a powerful hung prow (**V3 Jet Stream**).

Tyranosaurus Rex (T-Rex) [**Boulder T**] is a very large stone but sits in a trough. A V3ss line on north side. All other lines VB-V0 are well done.

Boulder U, V can yield VBss-V5ss on five small stones.

Pterosaur Boulder (W) has one low east point **V4ss Pterosaur** underneath (w/variants).

Boulder (X) has some wild theoretical stuff.

Boulder (Y) something.

Cube Farm Boulder (Z) is a flat top unit, very short SS lines. **V2ss Typo** (west point mantle), **V3ss Cube Farm** transitions leftward to west point, mantle out. **V3ss Thin Veneer** (south point). All lines well done.

Sacred Space Cluster

Cleaver Boulder (AA) is a 11' tall cool hung fin **V5ss Cleaver**.

Sacred Space Boulder (BB). Unique quality lines (L to R): **V0 False Promise** (east face), **V2 Sacred Space** (north arête), then on vertical north face, **V1 Triangle Arete** (start on flat face & go up left onto arete), **V5 Triange Face** direct up face, **V1** short face move.

Stegosaur Boulder (CC). Short west face and traverse **VB** and **V0** next door.

NORTH TALUS GROUP

SLEEPY HOLLOW GROUP

The North Talus Zone (Sleepy Hollow) has been experiencing a slower development process. Though some known grades/names are mentioned on the diagram most grades are mere raw estimates. This talus field is the furthest walk from the road, thus the refinement of the total number of routes will likely entail years of future effort. The diagram and beta listed is merely partial, focusing on some of the major boulders that are being utilized at present date.

There are some very large boulders in this zone, some very well-rounded stones, several cave-like crawls under big blocks, long slabs, some hi-balls, and much more.

Two tours are described here in this section. The first tour details the white letter sequence (the Dreamland zone). The second tour details the black letter sequence (the Cave's zone), which is a fine selection of boulders at the uttermost north end of the LLB site.

This northern talus zone will eventually yield approximately 250+ boulder problems.

Dreamland Boulder

Dreamland Boulder (Boulder A) ⚠ ⌂ is a megalithic classic monster stone with a quality string of hi-balls, some SS, and some overhung options, ranging from VB casual to V8+ insane.

V3 Dreamland. ⚠ The east face seam slanting up left. Crimp up to catch the incut crack rail, mantle, then waltz up slab to top.

V5ss Scared Kittens is a stout line on the slightly hung SW face.

See diagram for a general analysis of new potential problems and a quick wrap-up of existing known problems and grades.

Gossip Cluster

Boulder (B & C) is a great selection of four major stones located just east of Dreamland Boulder. Grades range from VB-V1 for over a dozen problems. All are at an ideal no sweat height.

Lunar Slab

EASTSIDE CASCADE MTNS AREAS

The Eastside Cascades bouldering section, encompassing five primary watershed valley systems, is a broad region (about 15 miles x 20 miles long) on the forested east-facing slopes of the High Cascade Mtn Range. Located a dozen miles east of Mt Hood, this zone is a virtual playground bouldering world, modestly utilized, yet holding a vast quantity and variety of bouldering bluffs and boulders (tapped and untapped) that hold both uniqueness and quality, often with easy access, thus more than enough incentive for you to step into the game over there. It ranges from generally Fifteen-Mile creek southward to Badger creek (within the Barlow Ranger District).

The only limitations are driving distance (if you are driving from Portland), winter snow (3-5,000' elev is common), and summertime baking heat. But Oregon being a moderate temperate climate, it's easy to pick cool overcast days in July and dash here for the good opportunities.

This particular regions bouldering is underestimated in scope (intensity and potential) but it certainly offers sufficient diversity. Locals from Hood River to Dufur have in small ways tapped the long established obvious spots such as Bulo Point (a really tiny fraction this region has to offer). Browsing through this chapter will certainly spike your interest in the plethora of arsenal at your doorstep in the Barlow eastside region.

Many of the sites are compact with a concentrated string of problems, and though some sites are limited in scope its often easy to drive to the site next door in a few minutes time. This region has it all, from hi-ball skyscraper problems, super overhung beasts, crimp-fests, VB jug runs, house-sized 35' long boulders, and small bluff outcrops. Why reign in your horse when this little region has so much variety, including great outdoor car-camping in a pine tree forest setting. Take a mountain bike and add to your adventurous weekend mix.

This section begins with sites in the headwaters of the Fifteenmile Creek valley (The Meadow, etc), then works eastward along the primary paved roads (culminating at boulders near Eightmile creek), followed by the Bulo Point area, then Jordan Valley sites and southward to Badger Creek Valley and sites near there. The region is bordered by several primary roads; NF 44 (north end), Highway 35 (west end), NF 27 [aka N South Road] (east end), and NF 48 (south end) road.

The primary paved road in this valley is the (NF44) Dufur Mill Road, which if followed eastward will junction with Highway 197 at Dufur, Oregon, which then leads directly into The Dalles, Oregon. Depending on your bouldering destination goal the eastern driving approach can be a bit more efficient.

Site titles (i.e. Campfire Boulders) described in this section correlate to bouldering, but in this region many sites are actual bluff outcrop formations (with some actual detached boulders). This region may be of limited interest to certain Portlander's because of the long drive, but it offers good options for May-June and Sept-Oct bouldering if you are seeking sunny and dry outdoor locales.

FIFTEEN-MILE CREEK VALLEY BOULDERING SITES

THE MEADOW

The Meadow site has been utilized by climber's and boulderer's since the '80s. It's an extensive

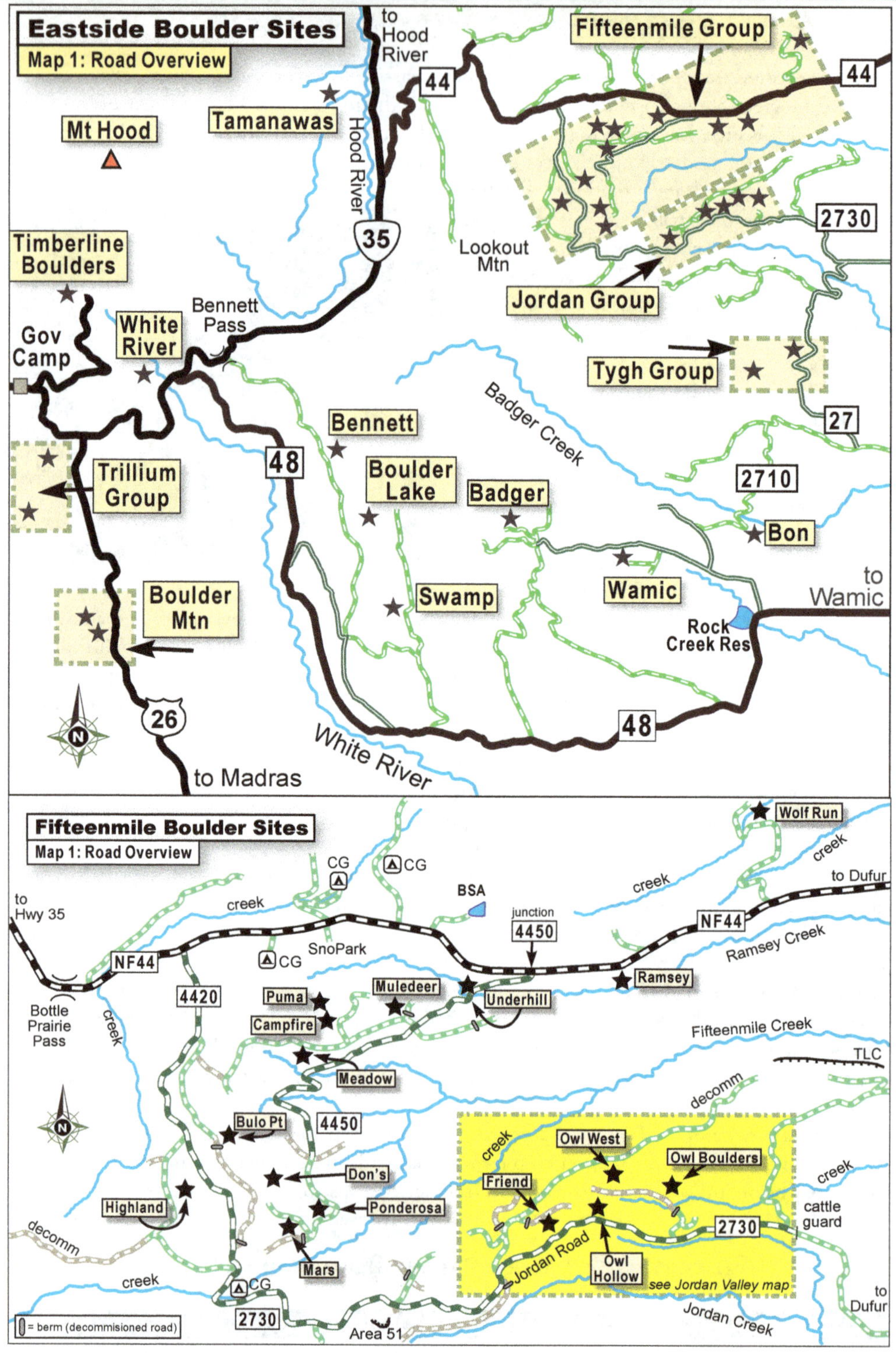
Eastside Boulder Sites
Map 1: Road Overview
to Hood River
Fifteenmile Group
44
44
Mt Hood
Tamanawas
35
Hood River
2730
Lookout Mtn
Timberline Boulders
Jordan Group
Bennett Pass
White River
Gov Camp
Tygh Group
27
Bennett
Badger Creek
Trillium Group
48
Boulder Lake
Badger
2710
Boulder Mtn
Swamp
Wamic
Bon
26
Rock Creek Res
to Wamic
White River
48
to Madras

Fifteenmile Boulder Sites
Map 1: Road Overview
Wolf Run
CG
CG
creek
BSA
creek
to Dufur
to Hwy 35
junction
4450
NF44
NF44
Ramsey Creek
SnoPark
CG
Muledeer
Ramsey
Bottle Prairie Pass
4420
Puma
Underhill
Fifteenmile Creek
Campfire
creek
TLC
Meadow
decomm
Bulo Pt
4450
Owl West
Owl Boulders
Don's
creek
Friend
Highland
Ponderosa
2730
cattle guard
decomm
Jordan Road
Owl Hollow
to Dufur
creek
Mars
see Jordan Valley map
CG
Jordan Creek
= berm (decommisioned road)
2730
Area 51

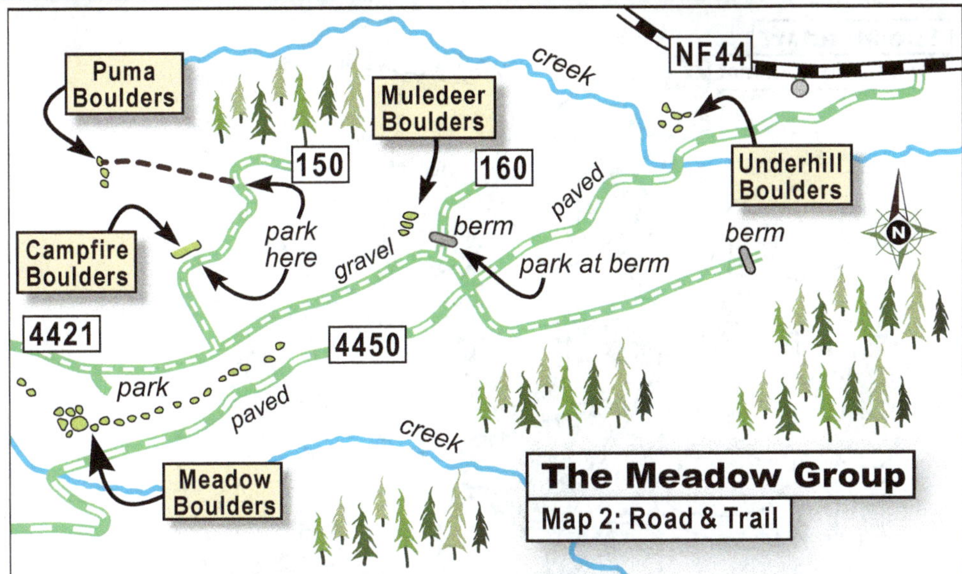

area, somewhat less frequented than Bulo, yet it offers characteristic similarities to Bulo Point bouldering. There are several short 25'-30' tall rock bluff scarps in an open forested area (most have seen some degree of minor climbing 5.7 – 5.10 range), and a vast array of short 10'-12' tall outcrops with numerous problems. Rock type and textural aspects are identical to Bulo Point. The common sections are described here, but there is plenty of untapped rock. The stones course-grained gritty porphyritic matrix has its  limitations (mostly VB-V5 ratings). Thus the Meadow is not high on a power boulderers 'to do' list. The headwaters of both Fifteen Mile Creek and Ramsey Creek have lengthy strings of bouldering feasible formations, all in a lightly wooded pine and fir tree environment conducive for reasonable cross-country travel searching for select bouldering opportunities. 1-2 crashpads should suffice.

History: The site has been long utilized by both Hood River-ites and Portlander's for minor climbing, top-roping, or bouldering.

Directions

To reach the Meadows drive south of Hood River on Hwy 35, then east on NF 44, then south on NF 4450 for 1.2 miles to a 4-way junction, then right (west) on gravel road NF 4421 for 1 mile. Park on the left at a pullout. GPS UTM 10T 620951 5026882, elevation 3,950'.

First Contact ⚠

First Contact has a short vertical east face. Grades range from VB-V4+ (and some SS). The common line is **V2 Smoove**, a sketchy hi-ball on a rounded NE nose of the easternmost stone.

Second Contact

Second Contact Boulder has VB-V3ss on a short south-facing slab.

Passageway

The **Passageway** has steep aspects on the immediate left VB-V2 (**see next**).

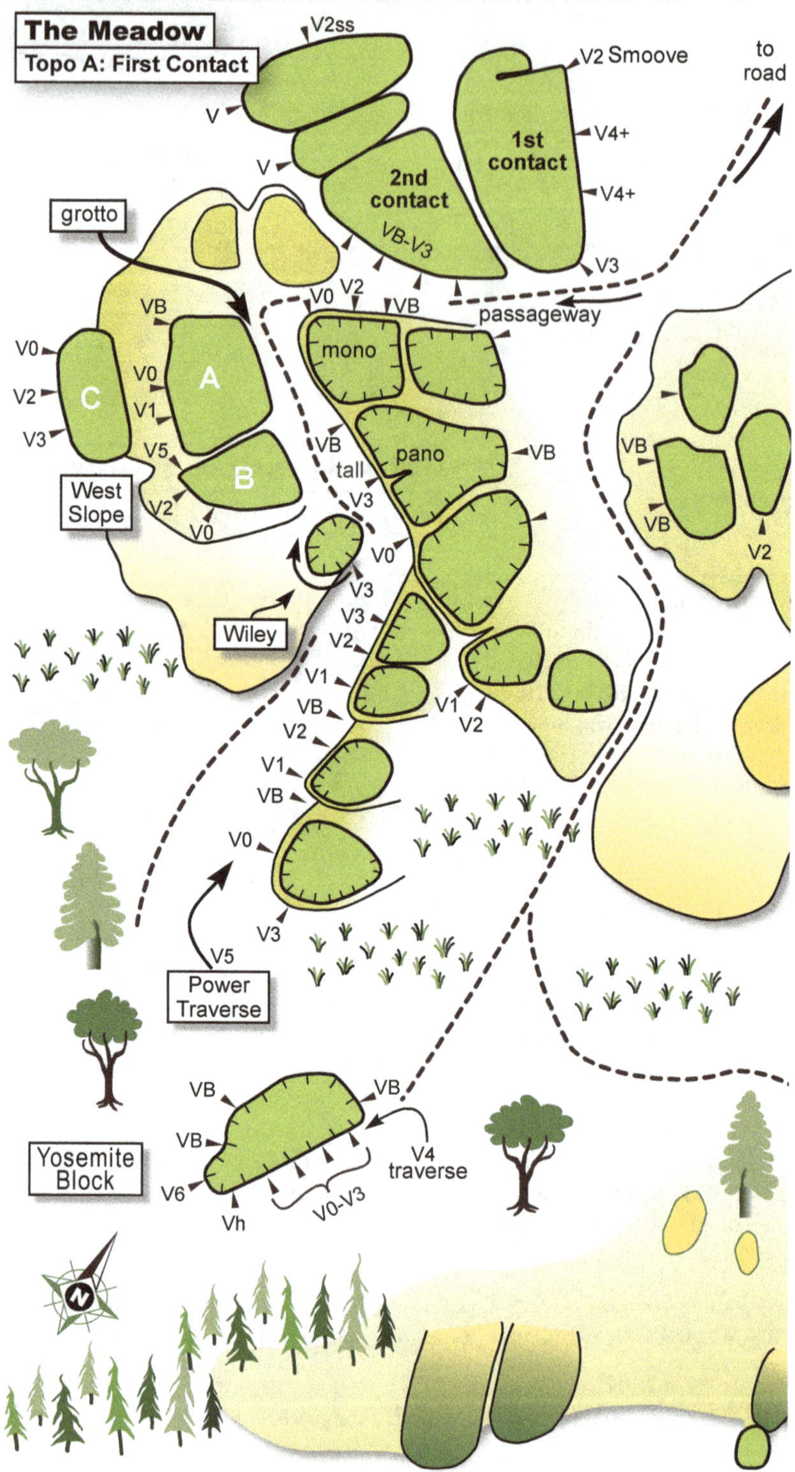
The Meadow
Topo A: First Contact
V2ss
V2 Smoove
to road
V
V
grotto
1st contact
V4+
V4+
2nd contact
VB-V3
V3
passageway
VB
V0 V2 VB
VB
V0
VB
mono
V2
VB
VB
V2
A
V1
VB
tall
pano
VB
V5
V3
B
V3
VB
V2
V0
V0
V3
V3
Wiley
V2
V1
VB
V1
V2
V2
V1
VB
V1
VB
V0
V3
V5
Power
Traverse
VB
VB
VB
VB
V4 traverse
Yosemite
Block
V6
V0-V3
Vh
West Slope
V0
V2
V3
C
V0

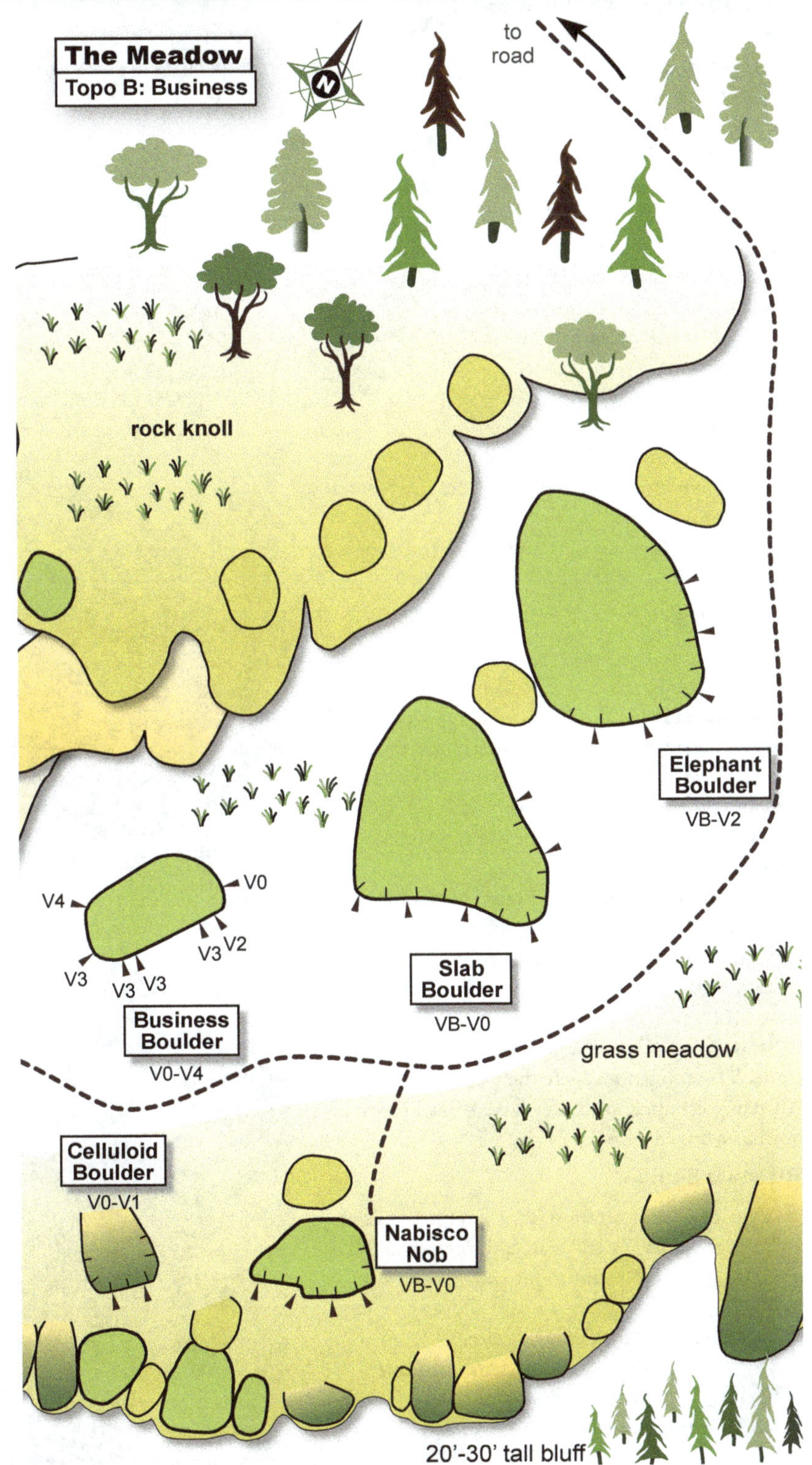
The Meadow
Topo B: Business
N
to road
rock knoll
Elephant Boulder
VB-V2
V4
V0
V3 V2
V3
V3 V3
Slab Boulder
VB-V0
Business Boulder
V0-V4
grass meadow
Celluloid Boulder
V0-V1
Nabisco Nob
VB-V0
20'-30' tall bluff

V2 The Mono. On the west-most rounded prow next to a tall pine tree.

V2 Onramp & Offramp. Two lines that traverse in from either right or left, then up.

V0 brief round prow.

Some other nearby boulders are:

Panorama Boulder. The west aspect has 3-4 problems (VB-V3) on a hi-ball steep face (brief overhung lip at top).

Wiley Coyote boulder is the round bowling ball shaped stone with a circuit traverse and several ways to mantle over the pig (V0-V3ss). A precarious looking round block.

V0ss The Ottoman. A minor round block traverse about 25' east of the Passageway.

Powerhouse

Powerhouse is a sloped zone that offers numerous stout overhung problems, and also the classic **Powerhouse Traverse (V5)**, a long uphill trending traverse. Start at bush (lowest right end of block string), traverse leftward uphill to the uppermost boulder where it meets the next bluff. Most vertical lines on this aspect range from VB-V3 with the grooves being the easiest.

West Slope boulders (Slabs of Doom) are a group of three stones (some hi-ball).

Stone B ⚠ has **V4 Dave's Problem** a cool tricky hi-ball. Plus several other devious lines on the outer west slab.

Stone C ⚠ ⌂ is the west aspect of an overhung stone. **V0** on jug, move left then up slot. **V2 Rocket Air** using crimpers in center face. **V3ss Havoc Harbor** has a crux at the lip.

Yosemite Boulder

A quality short stone with a circuit of problems including a short V4 traverse. Skipping the 3 VB's...

V1ss _____. On round right end.

V1 _____. Face right of next.

V1 Water Streak. Center of face.

V1 _____. Move up right into previous line.

V_ (?) _____. Something skinny here.

V6 Yosemite Sam. Unique west nose.

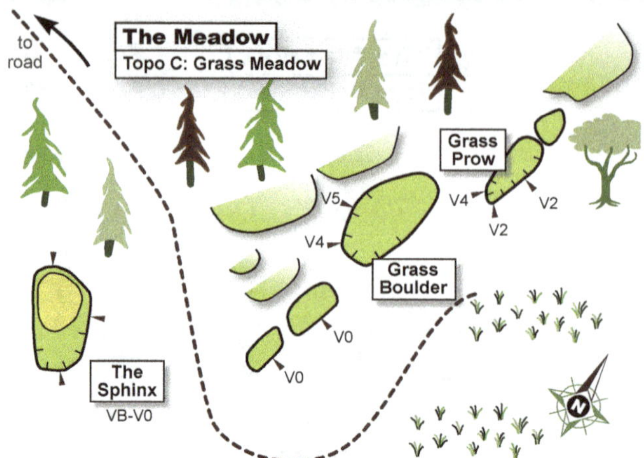

Business Boulder

Business Boulder. Nice problems (some SS) tapped long long ago by Jason, etc (beta R to L).

V0 the outer nose (east side).

V2 Business Casual (go up right).

V3 Business (same but go up left).

V3ss Commute (traverse right into previous).

V3ss Scrub Fest (direct up near tree).

V3 Branch Manager (west side).

V4 Back Office (shorty on west side).

Some other nearby boulders (*see topo*) **are:**

The **Celluloid Boulder** is a short vertical south face prow with several problems V0-V1 (all well done).

The **Nabisco Nob** boulder has four basic problems (3 **VB's** & **V0 Nabisco**) all well done.

Slab Boulder is a minor steep slab with a slight hanging lip (grades range VB-V0), all well done.

Elephant Boulder ⚠ is a really big stone with various problems all around it, ranging from VB-V1+ (mostly hi-ball).

Sphinx Boulder is a short plug with 2-3 VB-V0 problems.

Grass Boulder has several SS lines on three small stones.

Grass Prow wild overhung options (V2-V4) all well done.

A nearby extensive bluff

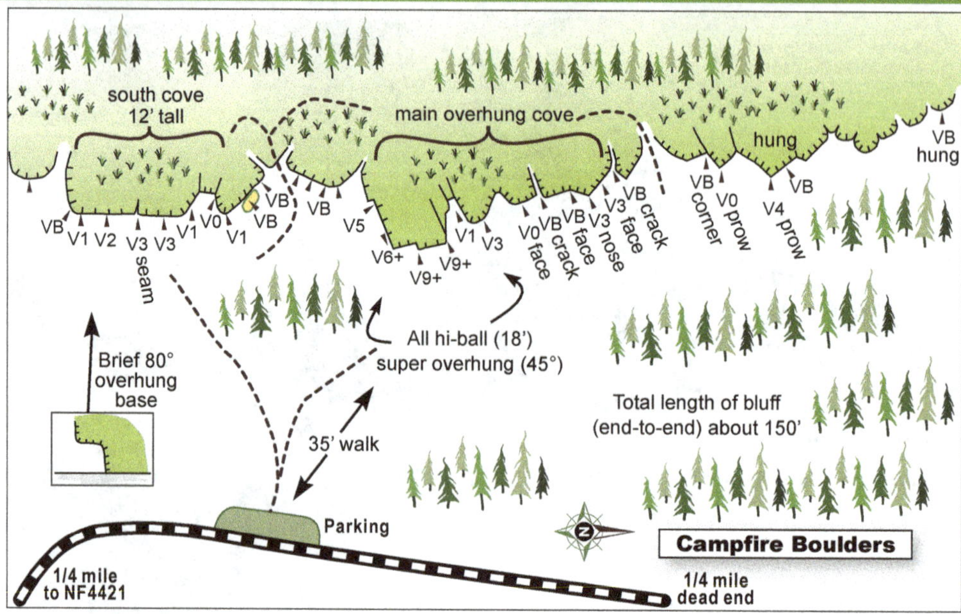

yields various bouldering options for about ½ mile northeastward. Various problems exist along its upper meadow slopes (no diagram).

RAMSEY CREEK BOULDERING SITES

This extensive creek valley is a secondary drainage of Fifteen-mile Creek valley offering potential bouldering at a number of scattered locations along the upper creek system. Some of the sites are in the uppermost portion of the creek (Campfire Boulders and Puma Boulders), some are seldom used (those I will skip), some are used for rock climbing (skipped as well), while some are available near NF44 road (the Underhill String and Wolf Run on Eightmile Creek).

CAMPFIRE BOULDERS

A quality bouldering site with a fascinating string of short and hi-ball power problems on a brief rock bluff formation. Basaltic-andesitic rock composition with a plethora of crimps and holds best suited for skilled boulderers. Most problems are technical, some are extreme due to the nature of the overhanging bluff. Crimp loaded features even on the overhangs. The alcove bluff overhangs about 45°. There are about 25 problems on three very brief sections of bluff. Total width of the site is about 150'

long. Located at the headwaters of Ramsey Creek.

Directions

Drive NF 44 (Dufur Mill Road) east, then turn south on NF 4450 for 1.2 miles, then west on NF 4421 for about .9 mile, then west on another gravel road for ¼ mile where it descends slightly in a dip and curls right. Park on the left in front of the bluff (35' from road).

GPS UTM 10T 621399 5027455, elevation 3,900'.

South End Bluff (beta L to R)

VBss Sawing Wood. Nose on left.

V1ss Brazilian Beauty. Slight groove up onto same nose.

V2ss Extinction. Hung dicey crimps to slight scooped dish up high (aim for it).

V3ss Infinity. Classic! Climb up hung crimps to a flared seam.

V3ss Masochism. Hung dicey crimpfest.

V1 Alligator Alley. Flakey roof to jug, then mantle with diligence.

V0 False Defector. Fat crack.

V2 Oobi Oobi. Prow full on mantle.

VB's on right.

Intro Slab. Has 4 minor VB's.

Campfire Alcove

V5ss Rocksters n' Roadsters. Hung left face on crimps, dyno to jug, go up, exit left.

V6ss Wild Wild West. ⚠ The ultra classic reason to be. From deep under it, power out entire left superhung arête on small crimps to outer lip, then up (hi-ball). Top out gets +.

V9ss+ (?) ⚠ SS straight out entire center roof, then up (hi-ball).

V9ss+ (?) ⚠ SS straight out a seam to lip, then up vertical face (hi-ball).

V1+ (?) ⚠ hi-ball hung slot.

V3 (?) the prow right of the slot.

Section right side of main alcove:

V0 Peach Blossom (minor face).

VB fat crack.

VB Black Tortoise (face).

V3 Too Little Too Late (nose).

V3 3rd Graders with Flyswatters (face).

VB Character Assassin (crack).

North End Minors

VB Ballyhoo. A corner.

V0 Fashionista. Basic prow.

V4 Fashionetta. Big prow.

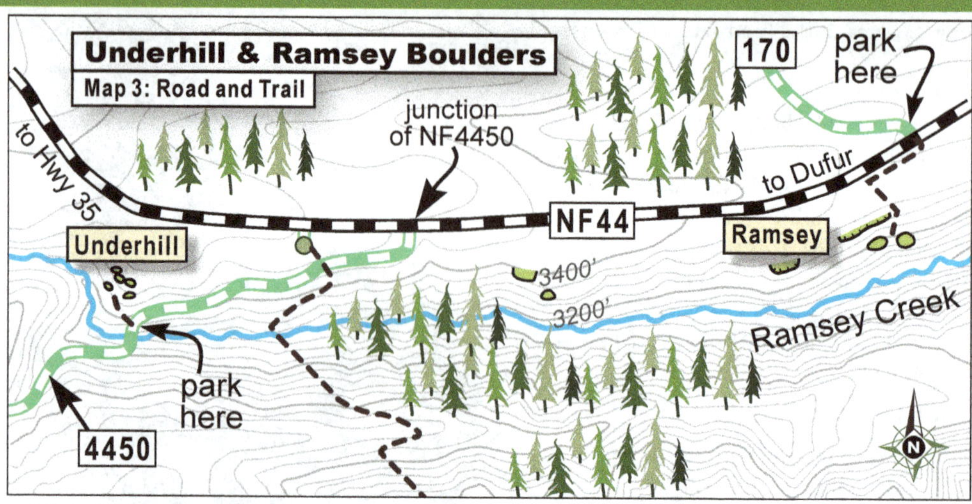

VB Dog Eat Dog. Fun face.
VBss North Pole. Brief line way up at utter north end.

PUMA BOULDERS

A minor cluster of stones with a brief string of problems at a site encompassing a space 150' long. Composed of well weathered basaltic-andesitic rock, offering some nice crimpy vertical aspects up to 12' tall on rounded stones. An open ponderosa forest with easy approach. Drive ¼ mile further north of Campfire Boulders on same dirt road and park when directly east of site where the road loops briefly west. Located at the headwaters of Ramsey Creek. Anticipate about 15+ viable lines VB-V4. **History:** Mr O tapped an initial first selection of problems here (2011?).

Directions

Drive NF 44 (Dufur Mill Road) east, then turn south on NF 4450 for 1.2 miles, then west on NF 4421 for about .9 mile, then west on another gravel road for ½ mile. This will pass the Campfire Boulders. Park at a point directly east of the Puma Boulders. Walk a flat slope west for 900' to the site. GPS UTM 10T 621187 5027794, elevation 3,980'.

MULEDEER BOULDERS

Brief rounded outcrop formation very close to a gravel road. Brief spat of bouldering entertainment (VB-V2) on about 15 total problems (some hi-ball). Minor surface lichen. Nothing special. See diagram.

Directions

Drive NF 44 (Dufur Mill Road) east, then turn south on NF 4450 for 1.3 miles, then west on NF 4421 for about 1/10 mile and park immediately at a road berm on your right. The bluff is visible 100' directly west. GPS UTM 10T 622326 5027532, elevation 3,760'.

UNDERHILL BOULDERS

Near a trailhead called Underhill Site there are several viable bouldering zones located next to the primary paved roads (NF 4450 and NF 44) of which two sites are described here (**Underhill West** and **Ramsey Boulders**). The other 'central' Underhill area along this same road may yield 15+ problems (untapped).

Underhill West Boulders is a little minor spot on a south-facing forested slope with short hung problems and some bold hi-ball lines. Stones range from 8'-12' tall (up to 17' on the upper giant), and some SS. Rock composition mirrors the Meadow/Bulo Point rock characteristics. Minimally tapped site, but expect to tap about 20+ problems.

Directions

Drive NF 44 (Dufur Mill Road) east, then turn south on NF 4450 driving for .7 mile parking at a pullout berm next to Ramsey Creek. Hike uphill west for 200' on a faint deer path to the site. GPS UTM 10T 623352 5027973, elevation 3,450' (Underhill west).

RAMSEY BOUL-DERS

Ramsey Boulders is a worthy tiny spot for those seeking late season dry weather bouldering options. A minor site, but the brief number of problems packs a lil' punch of power from VB-V4+ (eventually). A short 14' overhung rock bluff beckons. Two isolated large boulders about 60' below the bluff on an open sunshine slope are fun. Minimally tapped site. Rock composition mirrors **The Meadow** with medium grit surface, some distinct flake crimps and some roundness of each formation for the top out.

Directions

Drive NF 44 (Dufur Mill Road) east, then turn north on NF 170 and park here. Walk back west along the paved road ¼ mile, then south 500' (open forest) descending slightly to a minor bluff formation. **Note:** wide roadside pullouts on NF 44 are limited. The eastmost outcrop immediately south of NF170 does not yield any

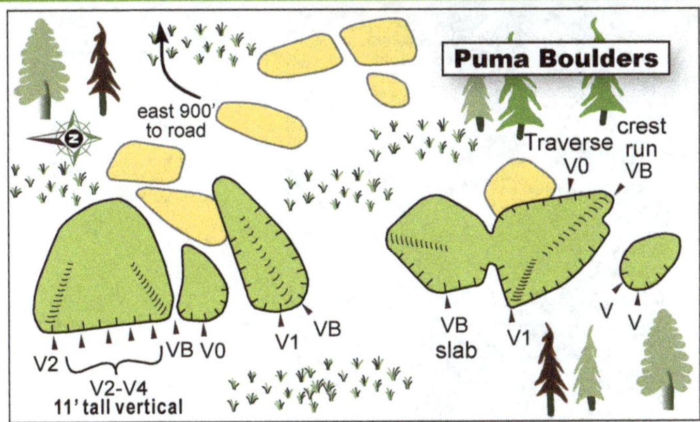

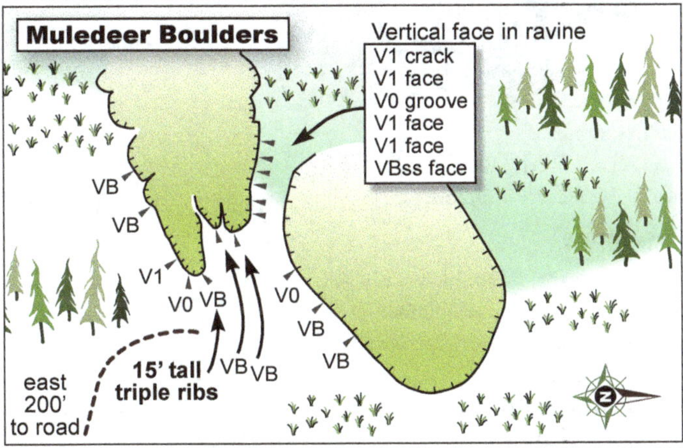

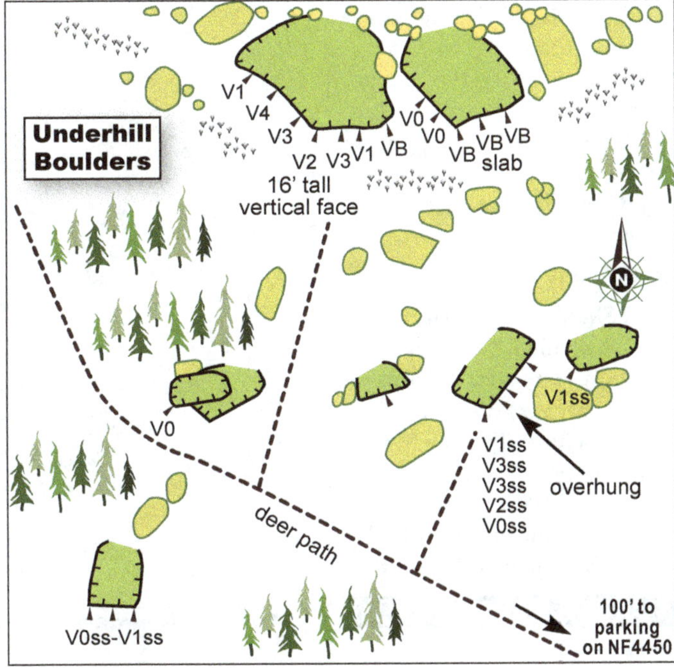

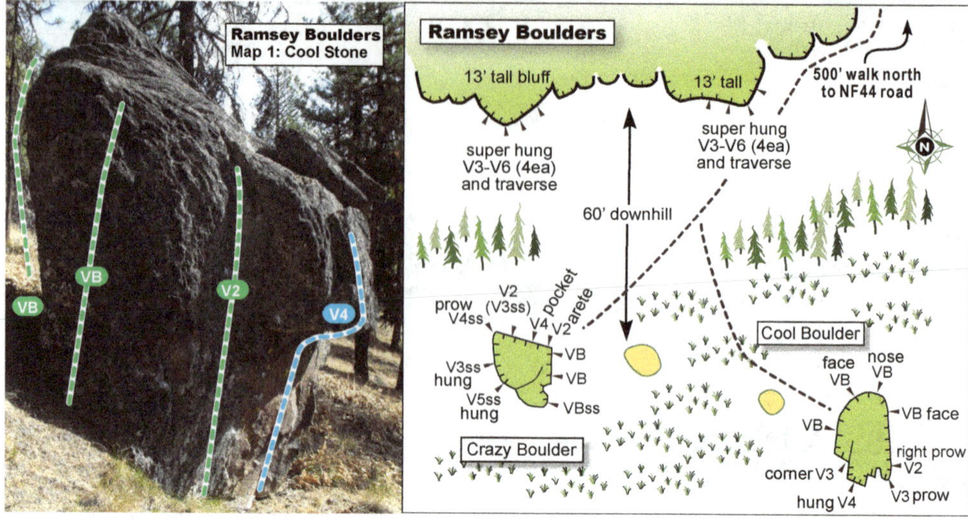

quality stone.

GPS UTM 10T 625893 5028216, elevation 3,260'.

Cool Stone

This is a brief boulder with a quality string of fun problems.

VB Intellectual Jungle. North side descent.

VB Brain Blindfolds. West face left of groove.

V2 Herds of Saurians. The corner groove.

V4 Status Quo. The cool jutting out overhung roof.

V1-2 Kleptocrat. SE prow w/ variants.

VB Due Diligence. East face crimps.

Crazy Stone

V2 Skunked. NE arête.

V3-4 Shafted. Giant gas pocket, bust up to arête (V3), or direct above pocket (V4).

V2 (V3ss) Funny Money. (Face).

V4ss (?) NW low prow.

V3ss (?) Hung low belly lip. Plus some minor other stuff.

WOLF RUN BOUL-

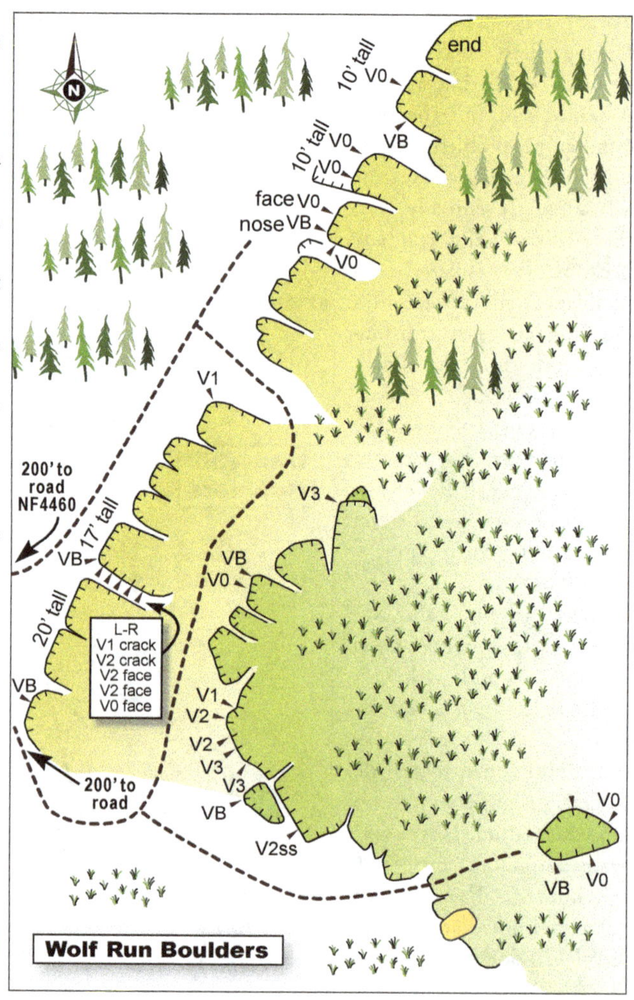

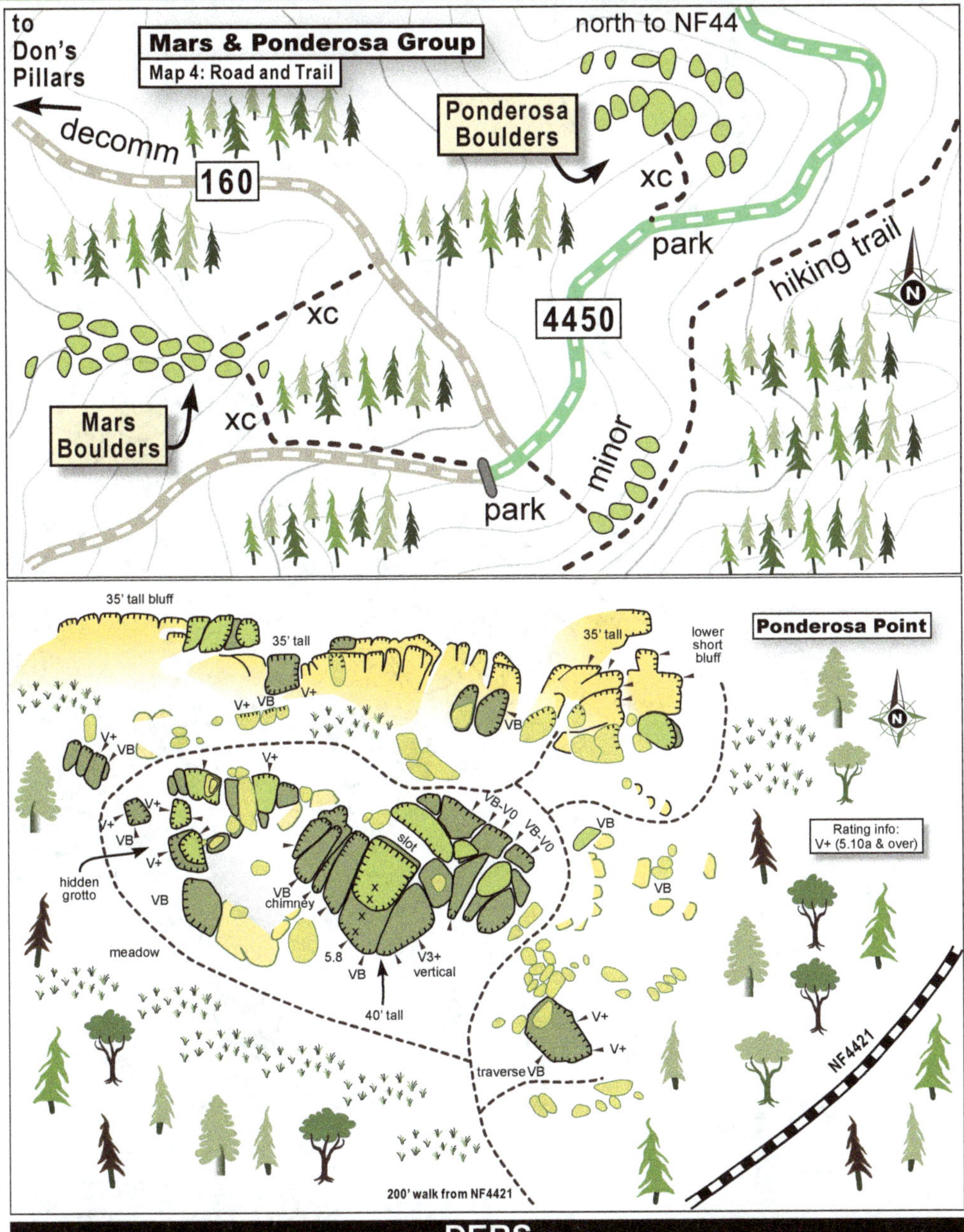

A minor boorish site, infrequently used (more commonly populated by cattle), but offering sunny bouldering on minor well-rounded short rock bluff formations wrapping around a minor knoll in an open ponderosa forest setting. Typical grainy rock surface texture of basaltic-andesitic origins, ranging in difficulty from VB-V3, about 25+ problems. Some moss/lichen on north aspects. Convenient location. Expect cow pies. Minimally tapped site.

Directions

From Hwy 35 drive east on NF 44. Turn north on gravel road NF 4460. Drive 2 miles northward till you reach a 'Y' intersection with a cluster of boulders located just east of the road. Park and

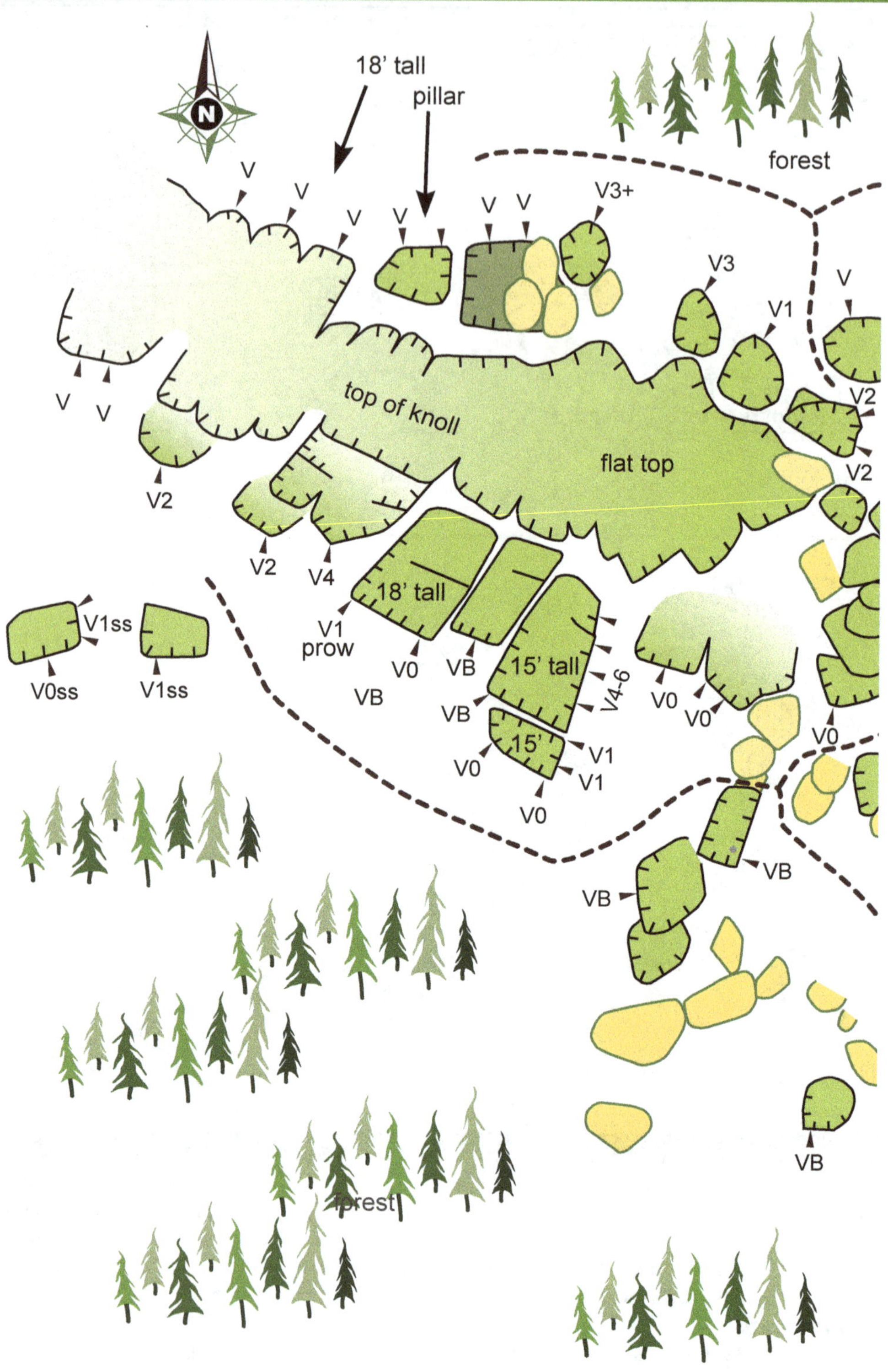
N
18' tall
pillar
forest
V
V
V
V
V
V
V3+
V3
V1
V
V2
V2
top of knoll
flat top
V
V
V2
V2
V2
V4
V1ss
V1ss
V0ss
V1ss
18' tall
V1
prow
V0
VB
VB
15' tall
V4-6
V0
V0
V0
V0
VB
VB
15'
V1
V0
V1
V0
VB
VB
VB
forest

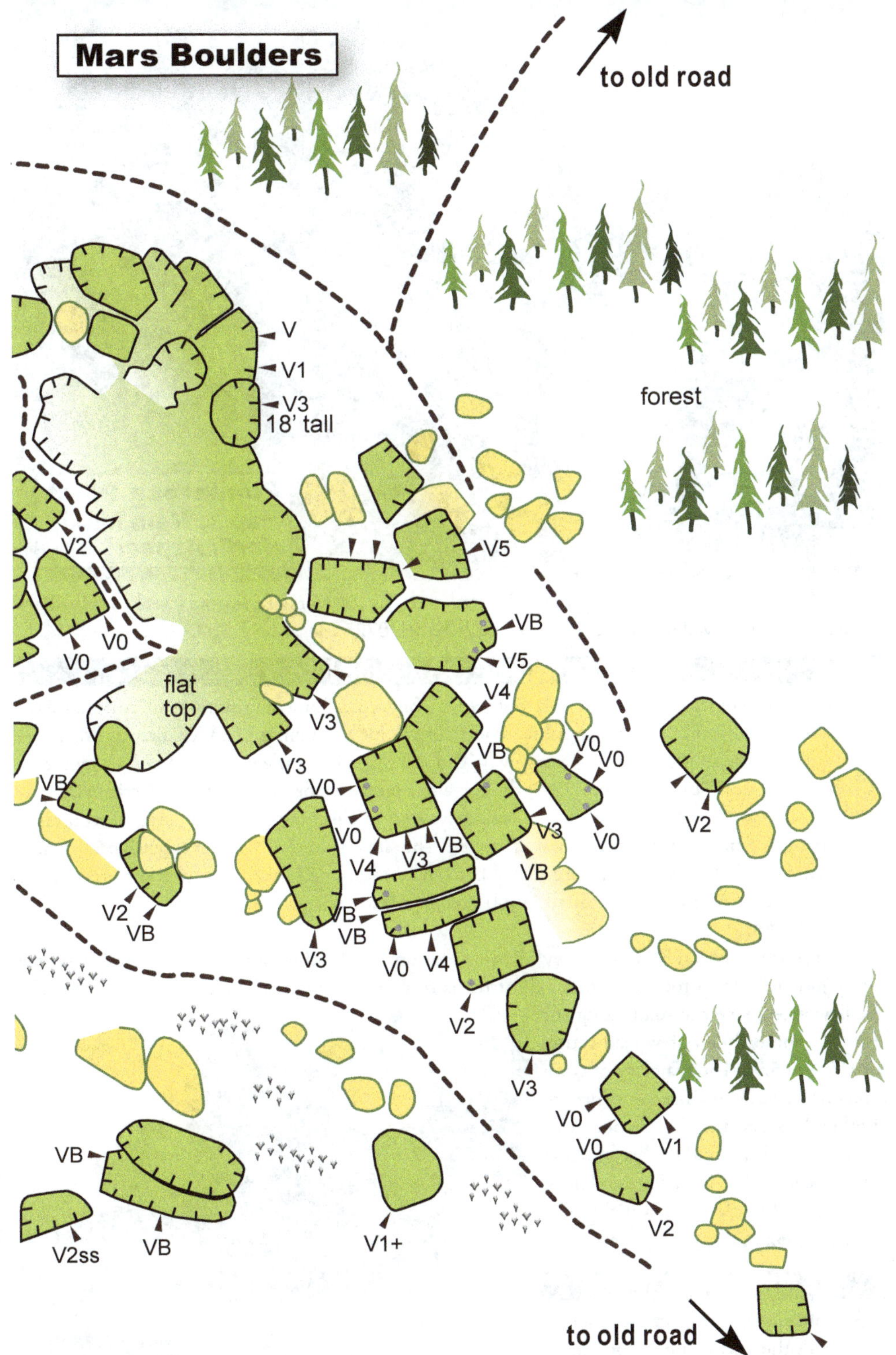
Mars Boulders
to old road
forest
V
V1
V3
18' tall
V2
V0
V0
flat top
V5
VB
V5
V4
V3
V3
VB
V0
V0
VB
V3
V0
V0
V0
VB
V4
V3
VB
V3
VB
V2
V2
VB
V3
VB
VB
V3
V0
V4
V2
V2
V3
V0
V0
V1
V2
VB
V2ss
VB
V1+
to old road

walk 200' east to the cluster. This group is located at the headwaters of Hessian Creek, a subsidiary of Eightmile Creek valley. GPS UTM 10T 627610 5030725, elevation 2,800'.

PONDEROSA POINT

Further south of the Meadow bouldering area is Ponderosa Point, a minor 45' tall rock knoll offering a nice variety of bouldering options. Ponderosa Point has a unique hidden alcove with a narrow shoulder wide subtle entrance passageway. The vast majority of the nameless boulder problems (VB-V4) were done long ago (pre-2008) though a few punchier, or hi-ball lines may still exist. The tall north-facing 35' tall bluff is generally conducive to lead climbing. Most problems surrounding the main massif and nearby blocks are well tapped. The site is suited to basic level bouldering (most grades land VB-V4). See diagram for visual beta (none described here in written form though if popularity increases it will be included in subsequent editions).

Directions:

Drive south of Hood River on Hwy 35, then east on NF 44, then south on NF 4450 (past the 4-way junction) for a total of 3 miles till it turns to gravel, then continue for ¾ mile more. The site is visible above the road along the crest of a minor hill. A few lead routes exist(5.4 to 5.9). The majority of common lines have been sent in one form or another. **History**: the site has been well utilized as early as (and probably earlier than) the late '80s (Don & friends) for climbing and bouldering. GPS UTM 621180 5024383, elevation 4,350'.

MARS BOULDERS

An unusually compact bouldering site where the entire site encompasses

The Pillars, Fifteenmile Ck Valley

an area no larger than about 250' x 250'. In a space that small is packed a fistful of boulders offering at least 100 possible problems on south-facing and north-facing blocks wrapping a minor bluff formation with easy access in an open forest setting. The quality problems have nuance and texture similar to heavy sandpaper (more like Bulo Point sandpaper) on basaltic-andesitic rock.

The site is a nest of tumbled blocks with narrow nooks and wide slots between the stones. High quality boulders from VB-V6 (perhaps a bit higher), numerous SS problems, taller lines, and a host of hi-ball lines up to 25' tall, some on free standing pillars and pedestals. Overhung problems, crimp-fests on rounded weathered features, as well as crispy crimps depending on how the block is situated. Minor lichen/moss on shaded aspects.

Recommended crashpads (1-2). Limited seasonal access generally from June through October, situated on a slight knoll with sunny aspects. Some tapped lines exist already, yet plenty of untapped lines still exist. The site is located near a tributary of Fifteenmile Creek on a wooded knoll below Marion Point. The site was initially explored by Mr O (and Mr A) who established the very first problems here. The beta section will be expanded in subsequent editions (when a longer list of boulder problems are tapped).

Pro/Con: at the very end of a National Forest road that is not being presently maintained. May need some off-trail familiarity via GPS, isolated forested locale in the upper reaches of the Fifteenmile Creek watershed.

Directions

Drive NF 44 (east from Hwy 35) toward Dufur, then south on NF 4450 all the way till the paved section ends, and continue on the gravel portion another mile (passing Ponderosa Point). At the road end park at a road berm (another bermed road continues NW). Walk southwest on a decommissioned road for about 250' to a rock blocking part of the old

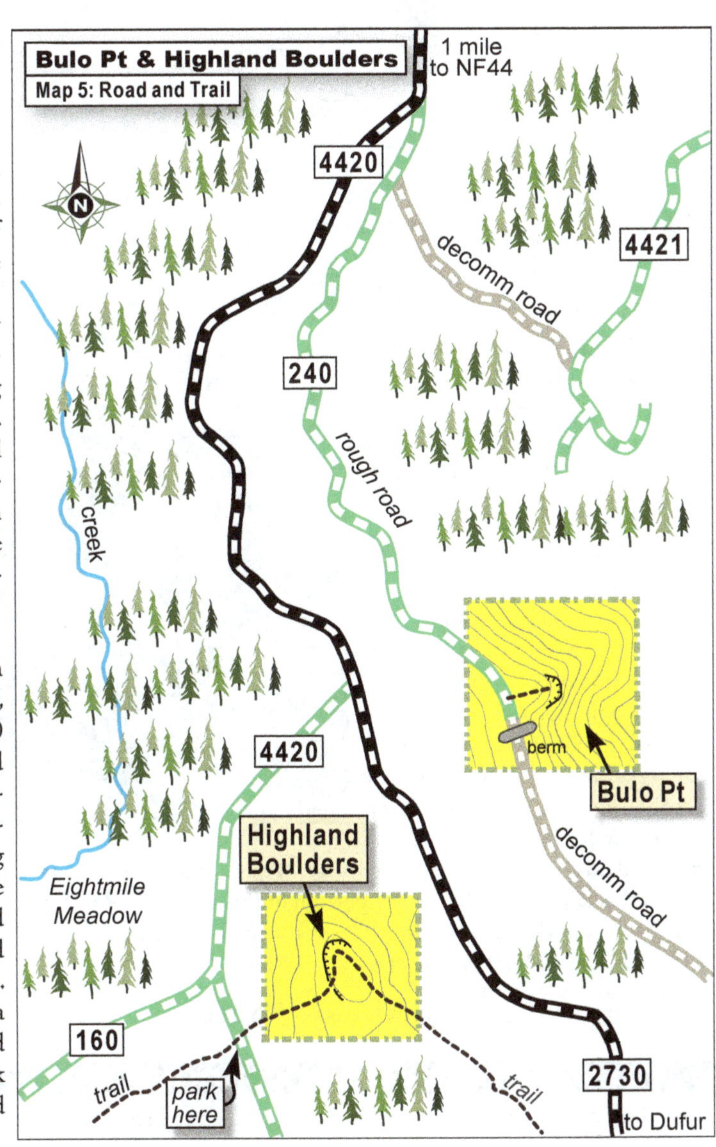

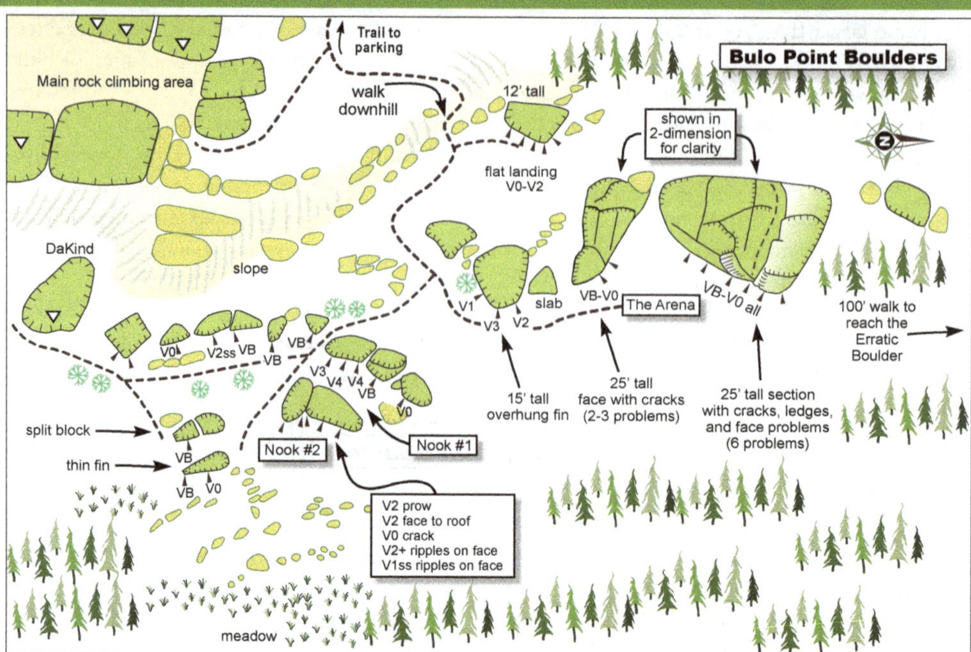

road. Walk right uphill using part of the 4-wheel path, then about 200' of open forest to a minor rock knoll. Old logging roads exist on the NE/SE side of the knoll so its generally easy to locate. GPS UTM 10T 620641 5024078, elevation 4,500'.

THE PILLARS

Basaltic rock formations located on a scenic open gravel slope surrounded by a pine tree forest, the outcrop is a mass of odd rock fins and rock boulders of variable rock size. Though isolated it has good potential for bouldering and is a virtual duplicate of Bulo Point with a potential for minor rock climbing. Don G. and friends explored and

scrambled on a variety of these outcrops way back in the late '80s (as well as numerous other locations in this upper valley). The last portion of this road (NF 4450) is decommissioned (berm) yet some AWD vehicles have continued using the road to reach the site. No diagram (just photo). GPS UTM 10T 620454 5024979, elevation 4,480'.

ROAD 4420 BOULDERING SITES

BULO POINT BOULDERS

The boulders at Bulo Point are short slices of eroded rock outcrops, some quite small (9'-15')

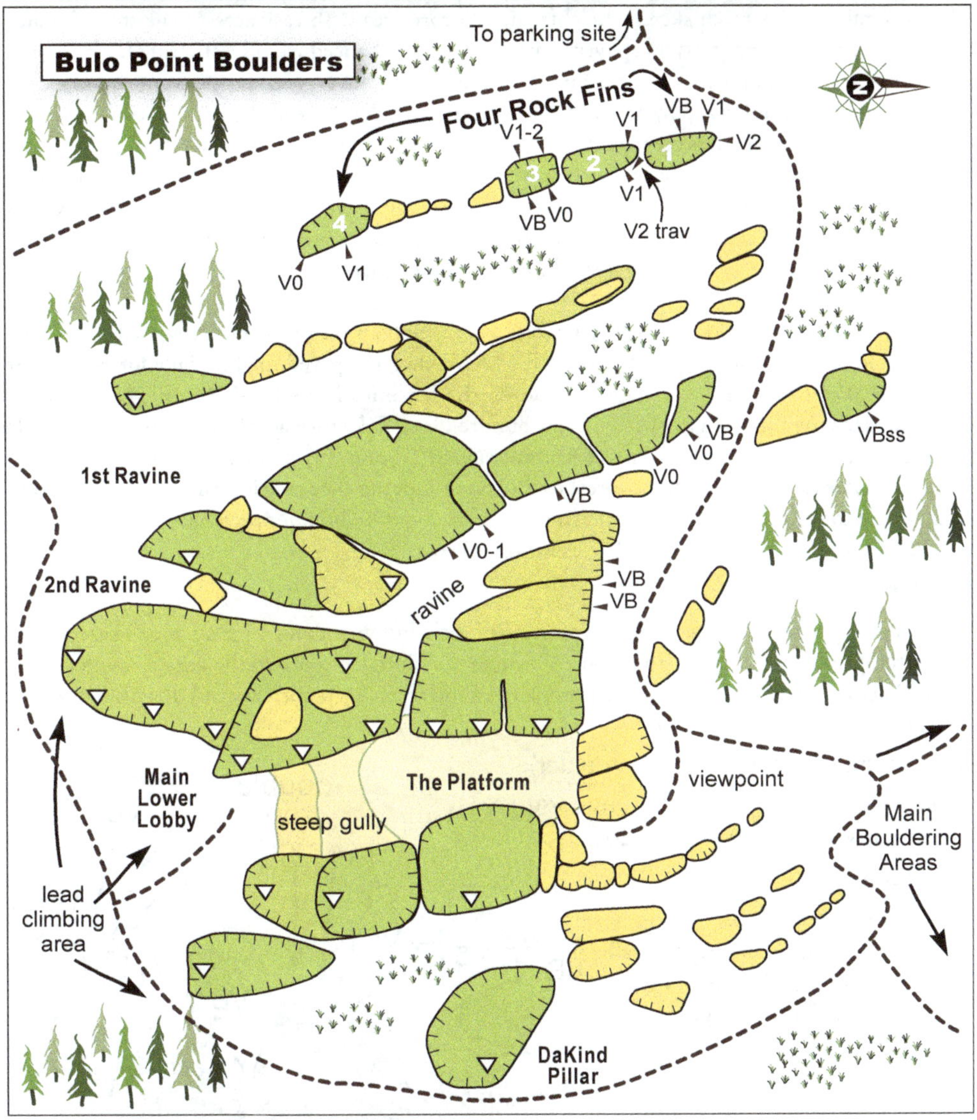

Bulo Point Boulders
To parking site
Four Rock Fins
V1-2
VB V1
V1
V2
3
2
1
VB V0
V1
V2 trav
4
V0 V1
VBss
1st Ravine
VB
V0
V0
VB
2nd Ravine
V0-1
ravine
VB
VB
Main Lower Lobby
The Platform
viewpoint
Main Bouldering Areas
steep gully
lead climbing area
DaKind Pillar

V2
V1
VB
fin #1
V1
fin #2
V1
V2
fin #3
fin #4
Bulo Pt Boulders
Map: Four Fins

while several sections reach sketchy heights, all in a core area with easy access. The stone is composed of course-grained gritty porphyritic matrix, partly enhanced from weathering factors, good for smears and friction, but a bit raw for crack jams. In all, its a good escape from the madding crowds, yet is well-known locally as a lead climbing site, too. The base of the boulder problems generally see less activity and less erosion. Avoid camping at Bulo Point (there are plenty of other places nearby). The site is accessible from late May to late October. The site is nestled in the sunny ponderosa pine covered eastside crest of the Cascade mountains overlooking the Fifteen Mile Creek watershed west of the small town of Dufur. **History:** a diverse array of Hood River-*ites*, Dufur-*ites*, and Portlander's scattered over 40+ years have utilized the place.

Directions

To visit Bulo Point, drive south from Hood River, Oregon on Hwy 35. Drive east on NF 44 for 8¼ miles and turn south (right) onto NF 4420. Follow the paved road initially for ¾ mile. At the Dufur Watershed sign take a gravel road on the left onto NF 4421-240, which is a narrow dirt road. This road splits again within a few hundred feet. Take the right fork and drive for 1 mile to Bulo Point. Park at the roads end (decommissioned beyond this point), and walk east down a footpath that leads out through the forest to the top of the crag. The crag is a one minute walk from your vehicle to the bluff top viewpoint. The site offers about 40 boulder problems VB-V6.

GPS UTM 10T 619520 5025515, elevation 4,730'.

Four Fins

Where the path splits are a set of four prominent rock fins with about 12 problems. These are the first outcrops you see walking from your vehicle to the bluff. En route to the viewpoint (just past the fins) are a spat of VB-V0 fun short problems. From the viewpoint, descend downhill north to the first flat landing to a single stone.

First Landing (Fountaine Bleau Boulder)

On a single boulder (L to R): **V0ss, V0ss, V1ss** (classic starts on low jug), **V0ss, V2ss.**

The Arena ⚠

Descend downhill briefly again en route to the **Arena**, stopping at a tall **Overhung Fin** (**V1** left side, **V3** hung nose of fin, **V2** right side). A few yards directly to the west is the Are-

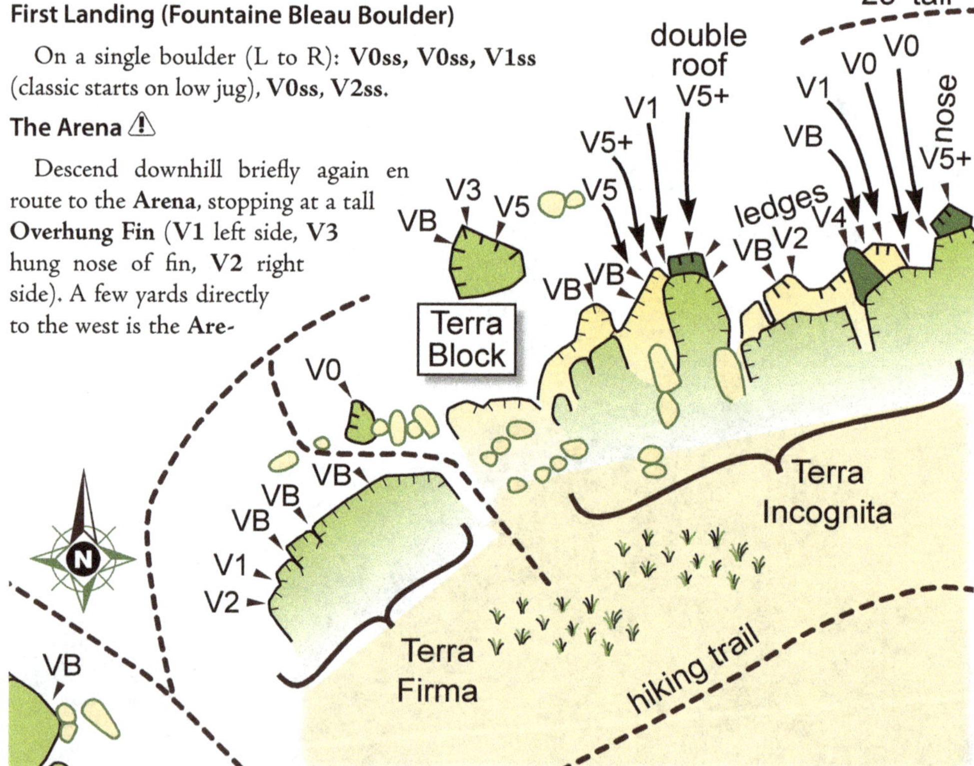

na alcove (with some hi-ball VB-V0). About a 100' bushwack walk directly past the main Arena northwestward you will reach the **Erratic Boulder** (*not shown on diagram*), but the beta is **V5ss Erratic** (left side, low on horizontal, dyno to lip from left sloper, mantle), **V2** crack, **V6** right arête.

Highland Boulders
Map 6: Terra Block
V3
VB
V5
on
left

Nook #1 and Nook #2

The prime reason to be here! Just a bit further down the path brings you to Nook #1 and Nook #2. Here you will find about nine excellent problems on quality Bulo Point stone.

Nook #1: V3 The Egg (left side), **V4 Dyno** (jug in center of face and dyno), **V4ss** Right Side. (on low edge, avoid foot block), **V5** traverse L to R.

Nook #2: V2ss Prow, **V2** face to roof, **V0**

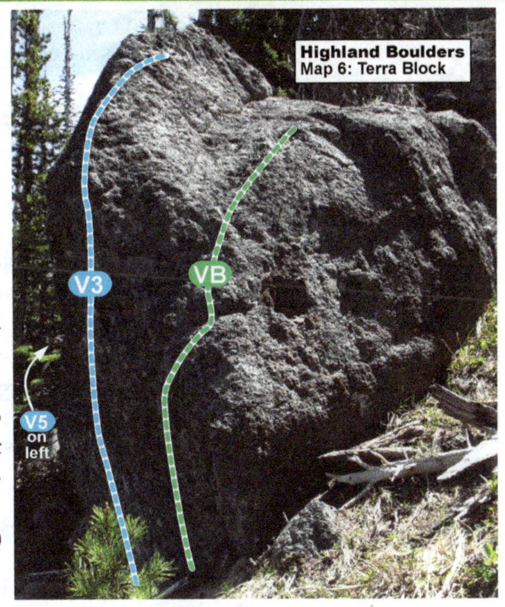

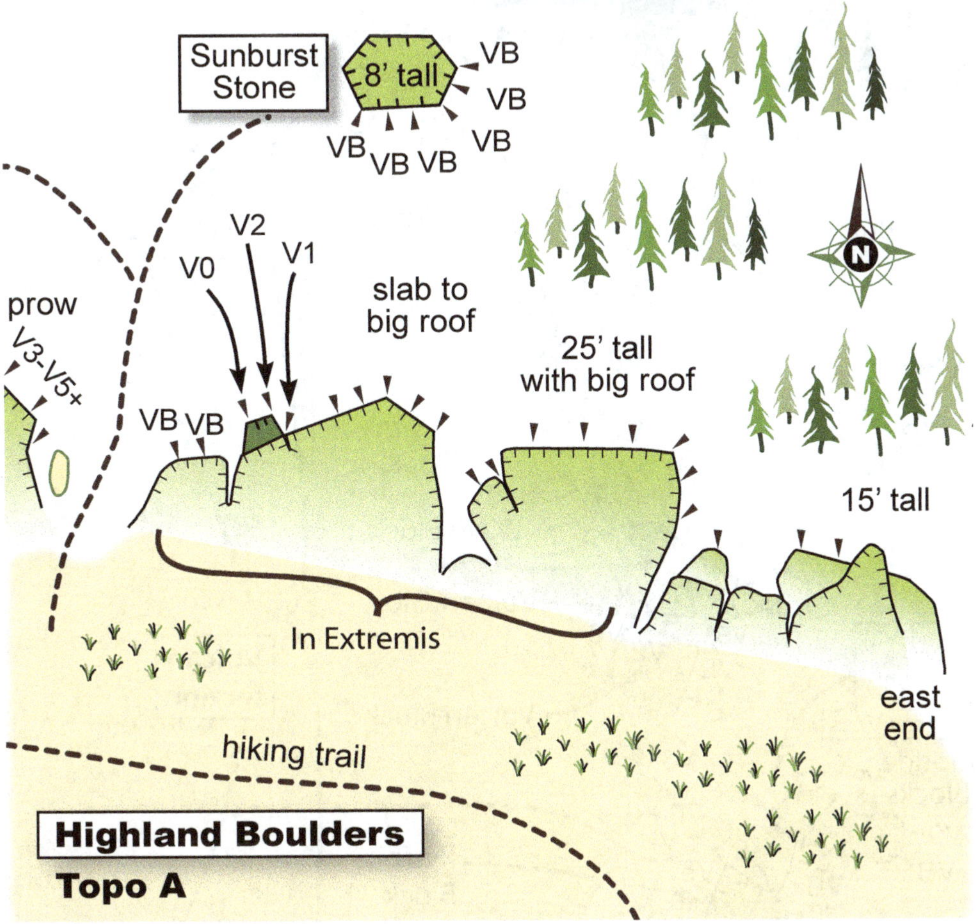
Sunburst
Stone
8' tall
VB
VB
VB
VB
VB VB
V2
V0
V1
prow
V3-V5+
VB VB
slab to
big roof
25' tall
with big roof
15' tall
N
In Extremis
east
end
hiking trail
Highland Boulders
Topo A

crack, **V2** face, **V1ss** right face low on jug.

Just south of both nooks (toward DaKind outcrop) are some minor short VBss-V2ss blocks that see minimal use.

HIGHLAND BOULDERS

Scenic pine tree forested bluff and boulders all wrapped around the north and west side of Eightmile Point. Certainly one of the better bouldering sites in the Bulo region. Many stone outcrops are the ideal height for bouldering (minus the 25' hi-ball stuff at the east end), and there is plenty of it (nearly 170+ problems, ranging from VB-V6+ (minimal moss or lichen). Compact site shaped like a 'C' wrapped around the knoll, spread over an area about 700' in length. Crashpads recommended (1-2).

Composed of weathered andesite, grainy large quartz minerals (2-3mm) with numerous

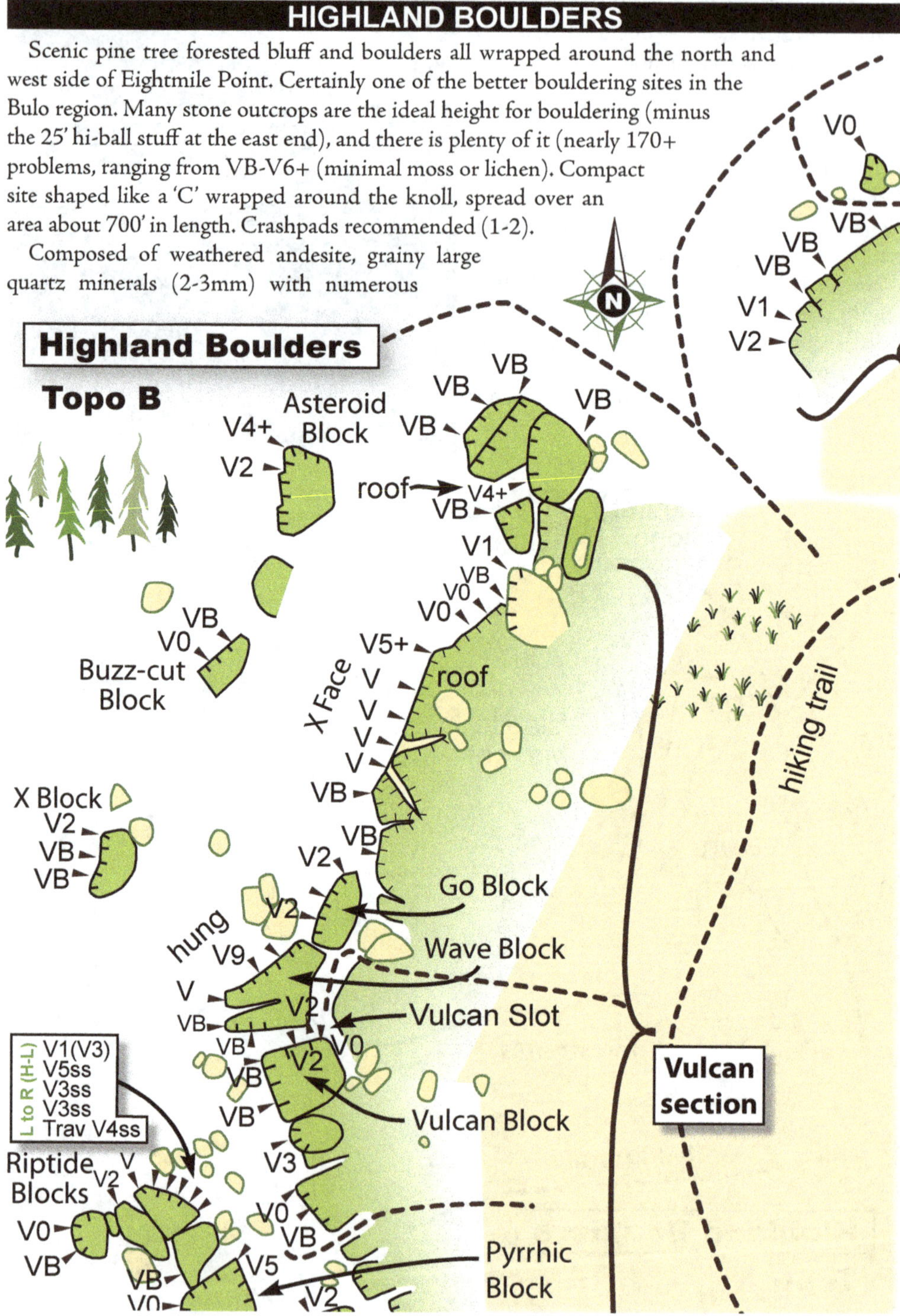

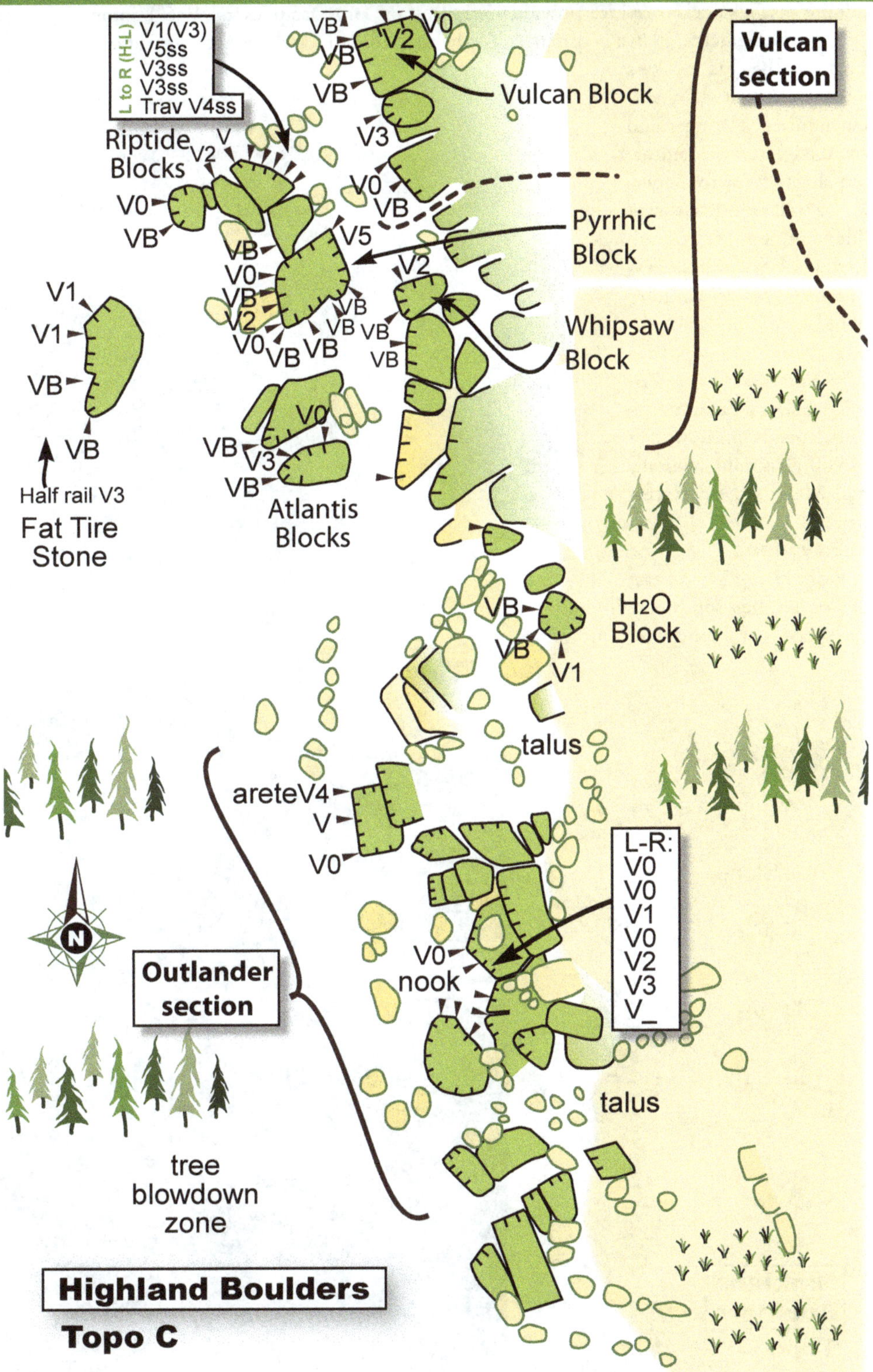
V1(V3)
V5ss
V3ss
V3ss
Trav V4ss
L to R (H-L)
Riptide Blocks
V
V2
V0
VB
V1
V1
VB
VB
Half rail V3
Fat Tire Stone
VB
V0
VB
V2
V0
VB VB
VB
V5
VB
V3
V0
VB
V2
VB
V0
V2
VB VB
VB
VB VB
VB
Atlantis Blocks
V0
V3
VB
VB
V0
VB
Vulcan Block
V3
V0
VB
Pyrrhic Block
V2
Whipsaw Block
Vulcan section
H2O Block
VB
VB
V1
talus
arete V4
V
V0
L-R:
V0
V0
V1
V0
V2
V3
V_
V0
nook
talus
N
Outlander section
tree blowdown zone
Highland Boulders
Topo C

minute gaseous pockets (which provide friction), some large gas pockets (1"-6"), some edges softened by the elements, all in a gray matrix. As the rock eroded (or cleaved) the textural rock nuances

such as the gas pockets were accentuated, yielding numerous crimps and small edges, crimpy smearfest shorty lines, to moderate, as well as hi-ball rocket lines, in essense superb friction-*ability*. **History:** Some minimal exploratory bouldering likely since the 90's. Mr O has tapped a substantial number of VB-V5 problems. Seasonal access depends on snow melt (4,900' elevation) generally mid-May until late October.

Directions

From Hwy 35 drive east of NF 44, then south on NF 4420 for 2.1 miles. Turn southwest onto gravel

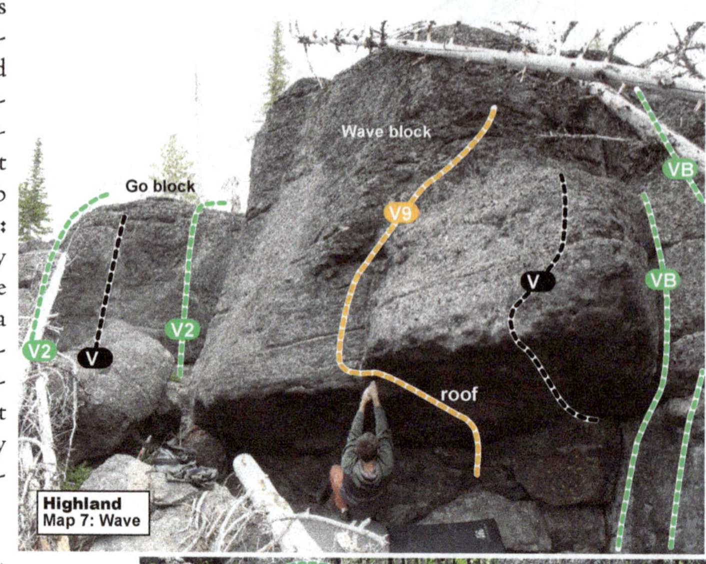

NF 4420 (the paved road south changes to NF 2730 road) and drive on gravel road NF 4420 for .7 mile, and park where trails #450 & #456 cross the road. Walk east about 800′ to the Eightmile Point knoll. GPS UTM 10T 618950 5024860, elevation 5,250′

Beta for the Highland Boulders is described starting at the outer NE end of the knoll (*see diagram*) at the tall hi-ball section called **In Extremis**, and culminating at the minor south end cluster of stones (just south of the hiker's trail).

IN EXTREMIS ⚠

The **In Extremis** section is the furthest NE part of the horseshoe shaped rock knoll. This section has potential up to V6+ (some of the short low V's are done). The height of much of the bluff here is risky hi-ball stuff.

Sunburst Stone is an isolated block about 50′ north of the bluff. Its quite short and flat offering only VB's.

TERRA INCOGNITA

Terra Incognita section yields similar hi-ball problems, but virtually all the VB-V2 problems are well done.

Terra Block

Terra Block has several nice lines VB-V5.

VB Night Flare, V3 Bermuda, V5 ___.

TERRA FIRMA

Terra Firma section has VB-V2 probmems, and all well done.

VULCAN ZONE

The Vulcan Zone is the best highlight of this site, filled with unique routes of all levels on cool rock formations and boulders. Numerous untapped lines on X-Face to Wave Block (left of the OW nose near Vulcan Slot).

Buzz-cut Block VBss-V0ss minor face

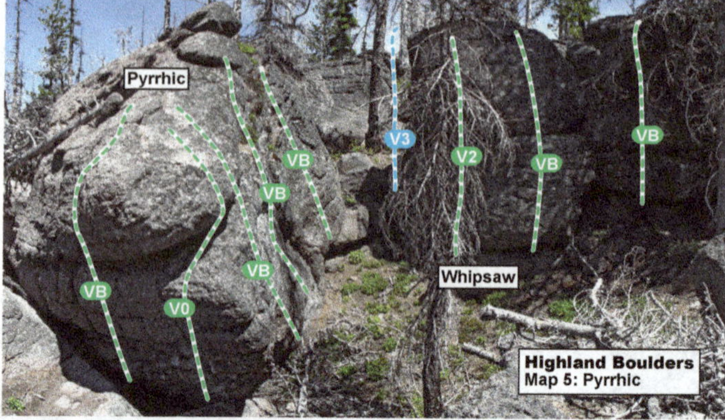

X-Block VB-V2 great stuff, especially the **V2ss Xaxia** problem.

The **X-Factor Face** is a nice section with extensive potential.

Go Block

Has two interesting **V2**'s (**Goji Berry** and **LingoJingo**). The cool Wave Block roof is stellar (**V9 Ex Libris**), and **VB Tidal Bore** is at the OW to the right.

Vulcan Block

A narrow slot access yields shorty lines. On the **Vulcan Block** (L to R): **V0 White Buffalo, V3 Without a Cause, VB, VB, V3 One Move Hillbilly** on west face.

Riptide Boulder

Riptide Blocks is a cool set of 3 boulders (mostly SS lines) from L to R (Hi-Lo) starting on the north aspect:

V4ss Riptide Traverse (see dots on diagram) is a classic. Then, the standard SS up lines which are all cool and worthy (first four):

V1ss Liberal Gene, V5ss Reactionary, V3ss Chaos, V3ss Lost Cause. Then two untapped lines. Then **V2ss New World** (NW end of #2 block), and west side of #3 block: **V0 Squatters**

Rights, and **VB** minor.

Pyrrhic Block

Beta R to L (south side first):
VB, & **VB** (south aspect), **VB Elusive Genius** (W hung face), **V0 Delusion Allusion** (SW prow), **V2 __** (reach pinch)**, VB __** (get down), **V0 __** (basic run), **VBss __** (low fun it on inbetween block).
V5ss Pyrrhic Victory (powerful NE nose).

Whipsaw Block

V3 Buzzsaw Politics (north), **V3 Whipsaw** (at point), **VB** (on west), **VB** (next block).

Fat Tire Block

Fat Tire Block the V1's are nice, and the traverse is interesting (beta L to R).
V1 Myopic Dissonance, V1 Torn Assunder, VB, VB, V3 Poverty Clinic (traverse), all done.

Atlantis Block

A set of two stones, mostly ultra low minor stuff VBss-V3ss (?).

H₂O Boulder

H₂O Boulder is an isolated basic stone: **VBss Water-water**, and **V1ss Visionaire.**

THE OUTLANDER

An independent group of stones offering a smattering of problems. A considerable amount of dead fallen trees conjest this section, but most problems are doable anyway.

The Arête

V4 Locus Classicus. Super cool arête.
V4+ Shorty face.
V0 Americana. Right flat face at point.

The Alcove

V0ss Unintelligentsia. Low moving right to point then mantle up, (use hung upper block lip too).
V0 Aberdeen Angus. Face at thin seam and crimps; catch jug and go.
V1 Rawhide. Short angled moves going up right from large pocket.
V0 Saddle Up. Crack and all.
V2 Shoot First Ask Later. Crimps to rounded top.
V3ss Livin' in a Lawless Time. Low on nose, work up left into previous.

Trailside Boulder

Trailside Stone is the first newcomer you meet on the way in. Its well done, and all worthy lines. **VB, V3 Trade Wind** (cool corner), **V2 Fuzzy Politics** (prow), **VB.**

SOUTH END

The unattractive **South End** section (south of the trail) has a few VB-V2ss short problems on minor boulders. Just cookie crumbs (some well done).

HIGH PRAIRIE BLOCK

Nothing special to write home about, but if your out hiking with your beloved esposa (with rock shoes and chalk bag) make a brief circuit of the big boulder. There is only one big stone so don't get fat dreams expecting something major from a utter minor.

A minor 25' long by 15' tall conglomerate breccia stone with a dozen lines (VB-V3ss, overhung potential to V5ss), all on a single stone utilizing very knobby textured features. Scenic hike, minimal elevation gain on a trail (5500' level) near the summit of Lookout Mtn. Drive from Hood River on U.S. Hwy 35, east on NF 44, then south on NF 4410 to Lookout Mtn Trail (#439). Hike the Loop Trail for ¾ mile till you encounter a big single stone.

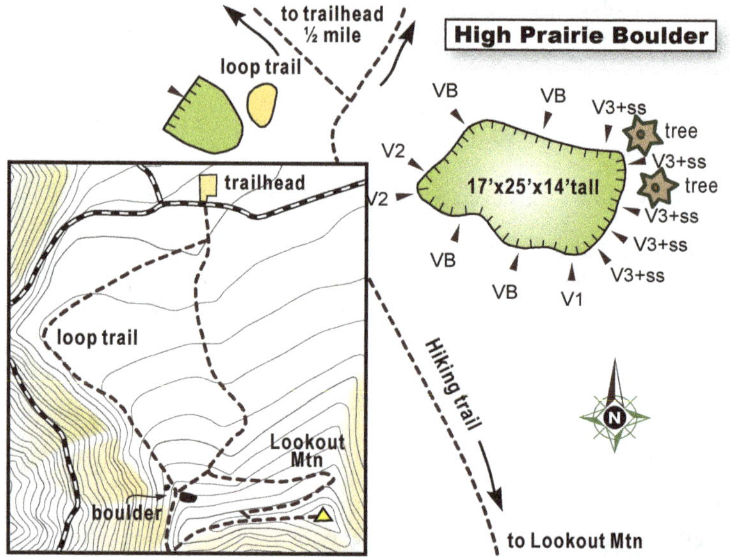

JORDAN VALLEY, TYGH VALLEY & BADGER VALLEY

Deep within the headwaters of Jordan Creek are several bouldering sites, some quite minor in scope, but other sites are quite extensive, so lengthy that it would take even a dedicated boulderer years to tap the potential problems that await. This watershed extends downhill eastward in a valley south of Fifteenmile Creek valley (where Bulo Point exists). The primary paved road in this valley is the (NF 2730) Cold Springs Road / Jordan Creek Road / Friend Road (each becomes the next eastwardly) which if followed eastward will junction with Highway 197, which leads directly to The Dalles, Oregon. Depending on your bouldering destination goal the eastern approach is a bit more efficient (though longer).

This valley may be of limited interest to certain Portland-er's because of the long drive (about 2¼ hours). But, it offers good options for May-June and Sept-Oct bouldering if you are seeking sunny and dry outdoor locales.

Geological rock structure characteristics change from Area51 crag eastward. Above, and to the north, the sites tend to offer finer-grained grit textural nuances (similar to Bulo Point). As you embark down into the Jordan Valley the rock textural nuances gradually change. From less gritty (near Friend Boulders) to considerably grittier (near Owl Wall), likely because each is a different lava flow, and may involve various subtle erosional weathering factors. The rock is basaltic-andesitic, usually gray (or darker gray) with some quartz minerals (2-5mm depending on zone) scattered

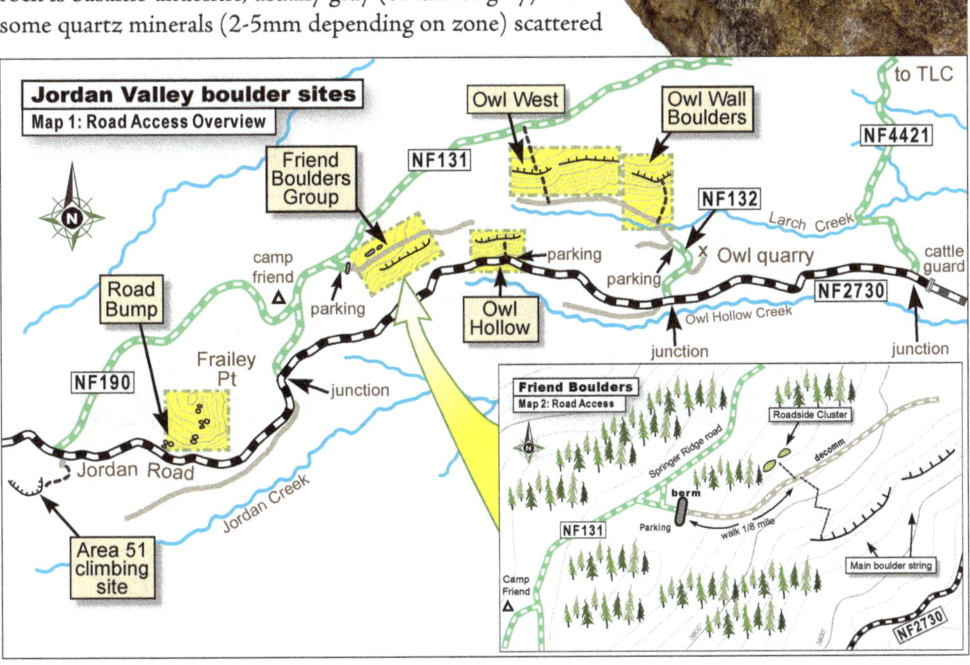

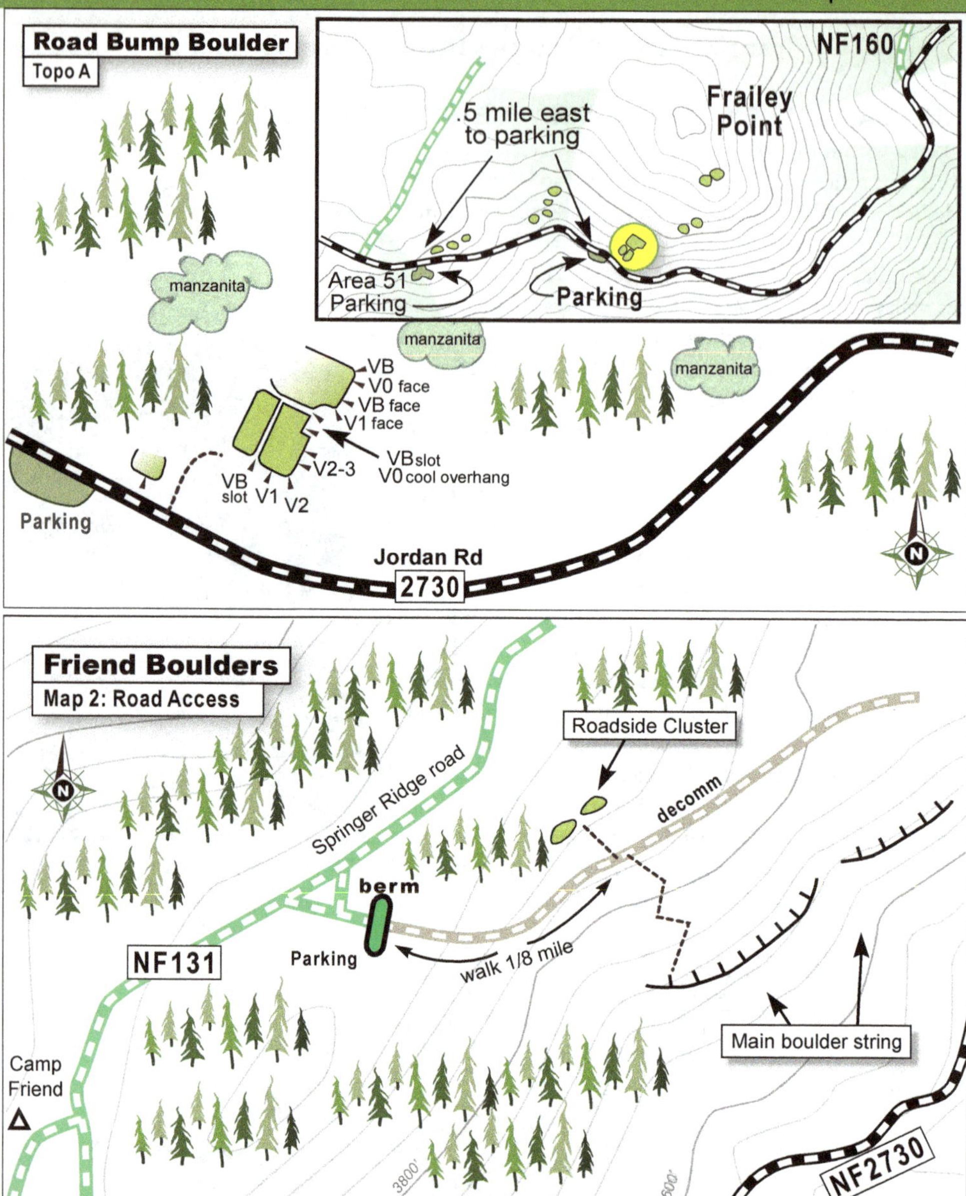

broadly in the matrix, and occasional small gaseous pockets (1-4"), again depending on the zone.

ROAD BUMP BOULDER

One large road scum boulder to provide entertaining sends on about a dozen problems VB-V4ss (9'-18' tall). The site is very accessible (and plainly visible from the road 50' uphill), merely a ½ mile east of the Area 51 rock climbing parking spot (see diagram). The lower main area has three main large stones (the upper areas closer to Frailey Point have yet to be explored). Directions: see map/diagram. Road Scum Boulder is the main broken cluster (beta R to L). **History**: The site was tapped by Mr O.

VB The Move at north end.

V0 Breathing Fire. Two small pockets on face.

VB Lard Belly. Minor face.

V1 Flaming Pompous Blowhard. From slot, go up right on face to prow, finish on crack.

VB Kissing the Ass of Evil. And its the big fat _slot_ brother.

V0 Road Scum. Best run here. From slot move left on crimps to jug, swing, going up for a cool send.

V2-3 ___ several directs on face.

V2 Dimbulbs. Over nose.

V1 Impious. Traverse up right.

VB Fatuous Facts. South slot.

FRIEND BOULDERS

Friend Boulders is a minor bouldering site with a scattered string of about 50 viable future problems (VB-V4) on brief outcrops of a minor south-facing bluff formation. Infrequently used, but offers convenient access, suitable for early spring or late fall season bouldering. The bluff height varies substantially, from low 10'-12' problems, to hi-ball stuff up to 35' (avoid). The bluff

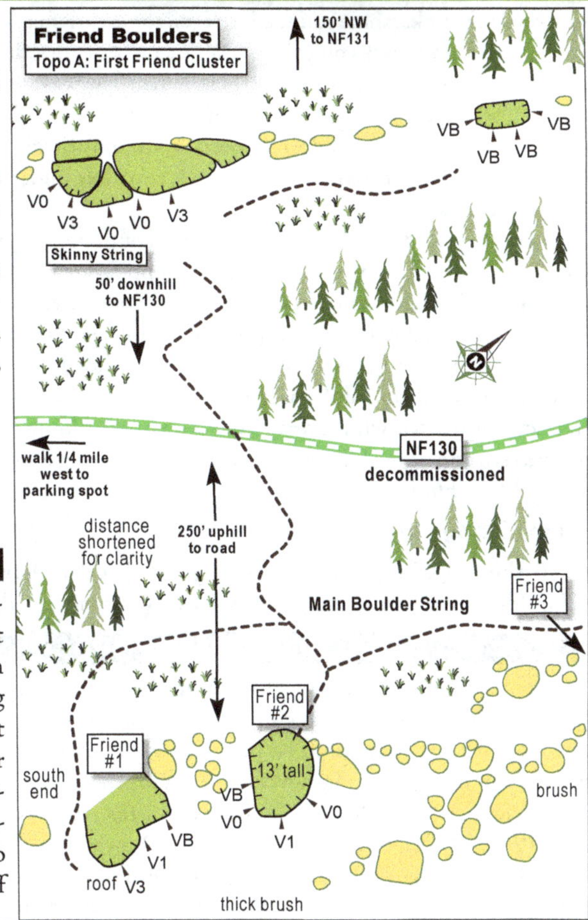

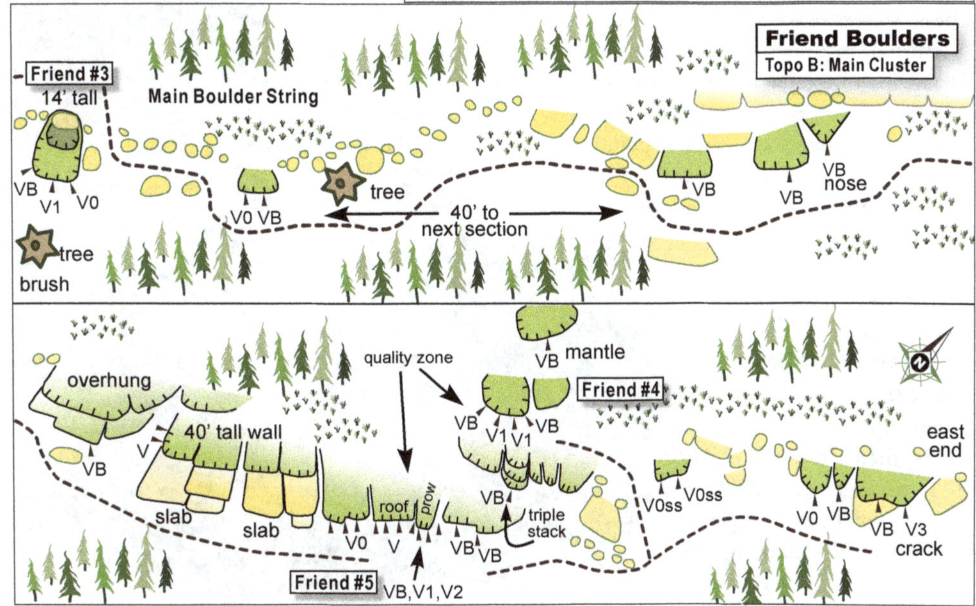

outcrops in chunks, some rounded aspects, some rock fins, some block-cut with vertical crimp runs, edges, seams, and cracks on gritty basaltic-andesitic rock. Its south-facing open sloped pine tree aspect can get hotter than a stove-top in summer. The seasonal time frame to visit here is spring or fall (May-June, Sept-Oct). Minor exploratory bouldering to date. GPS UTM 10T 624670 5024308 elevation 3,750' (at west end). **History**: The Skinny String (and a brief selection of other V's) were tapped by Mr O, but to date the full site is relatively under-utilized.

Directions

From Hwy 35 drive east on NF 44, then south on NF 4420 till it becomes NF 2730. En route you will pass the parking spot for Area51 climbing area (continue about two miles east past Area51 parking spot). This mainline paved road is Jordan Creek Road (NF 2730). Turn north onto (NF 160) Springer Ridge Road and drive for .6 mile as it becomes NF 130 and then turn right onto a dead-end road berm (NF 130) Camp Friend Road. Walk over the berm on the old NF 130 as it gently descends downhill east for about .3 mile. On your left (50' uphill) you will see two free standing formations with several VB-V3 on it (the Skinny String cluster). Directly downhill 250' is the western end of the FB group. The main bouldering outcrop string extends eastward for perhaps 400' in brief chunks.

Skinny String Cluster

V0 Skinny (left aspect), **V3 G-string** (nose), **V0 Welfare Queen** (face), **V0 Shinbone** (crack), **V3 Soldier of Fortune** (hung). All VB's are done on the other nearby block.

OWL HOLLOW BLUFF

A minor little site with a spat of about 25+ problems on a south-facing bluff formation that outcrops in brief chunks at its east end, then becomes an actual taller bluff on its west end. Due to its sunny aspect the site can be a scorching hot zone in summer, so seasonally useful in May-June or Sept-Oct. The boulder problems range in height from short (9'-11') to hi-ball (VB-V4) up to 15'-20' on some of the east outcrops. Crimps, jugs and slopers are common holds. A minor seldom visited site, but if your in the area, and you have already toured all the other places, take a hit.

Textural rock surface nuances are rounded well-weathered shapes, lots of small horizontal crimps, steep faces, cracks, and off-widths, on basaltic-andesitic rock identical to Bulo Point. Technically speaking, the site is a bluff formation (no rolled boulders), yet its low stuff is viable for bouldering. Visual beta diagram only. **History**: site has minor lower V's exploratory bouldering to date. No detailed beta at present (but a number of V's were tagged by Mr O).

Directions (from the west)

From Hwy 35 drive east on NF 44, then south on NF 4420 till it becomes NF 2730. En route you will pass the parking spot for Area51 climbing area. This mainline paved road is

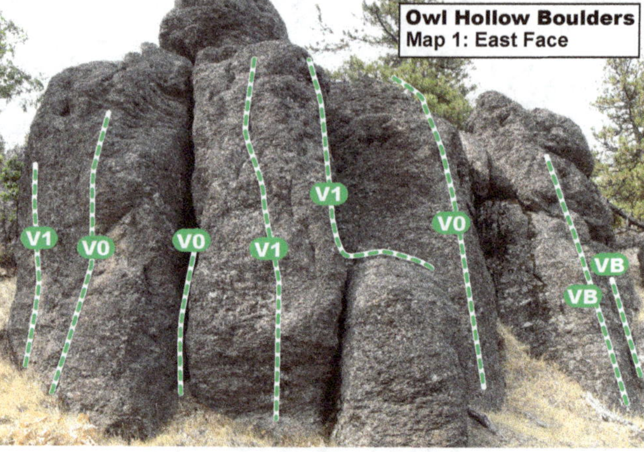

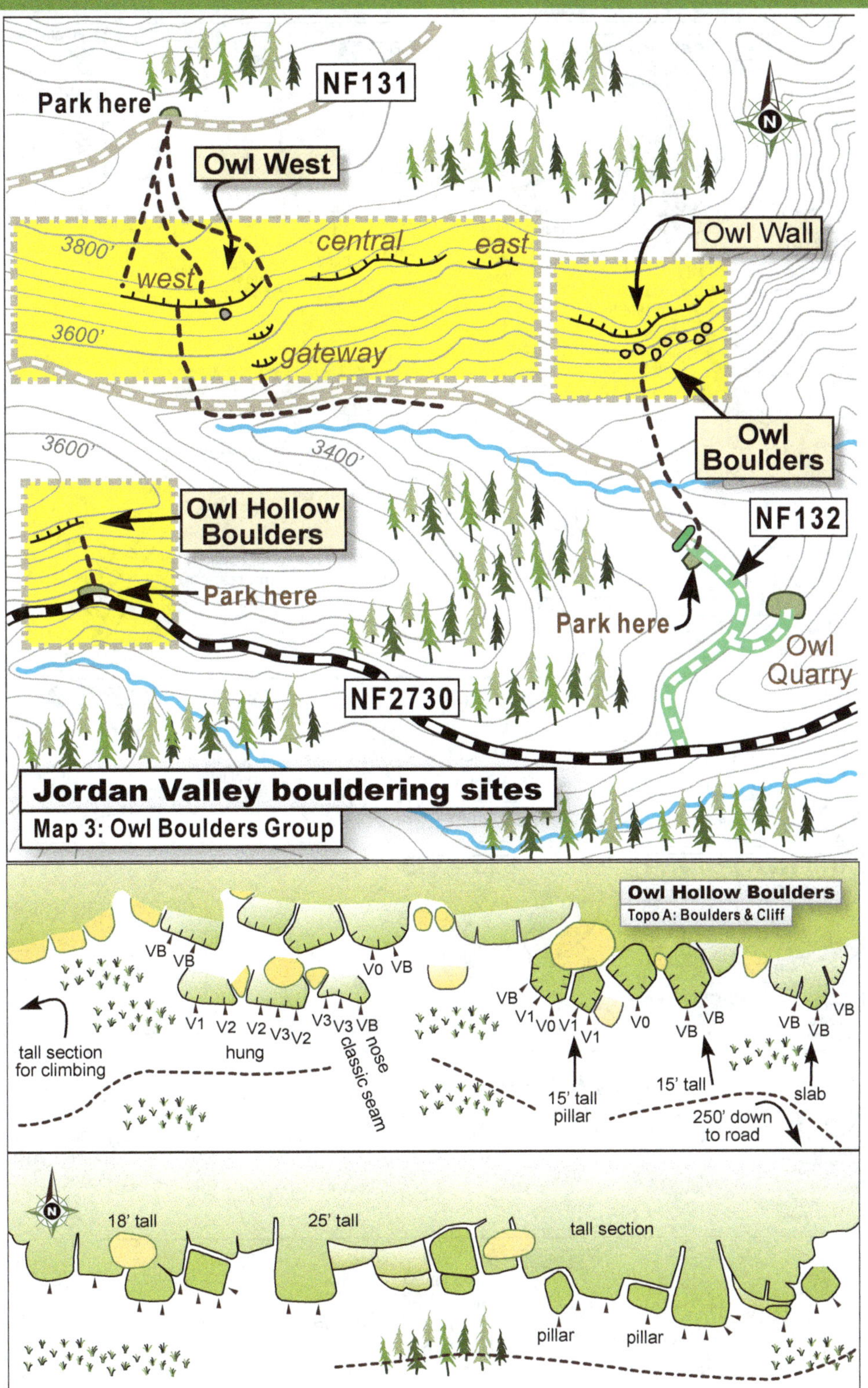
NF131
Park here
Owl West
3800'
central
east
west
3600'
gateway
N
Owl Wall
Owl Boulders
3600'
3400'
Owl Hollow Boulders
Park here
NF132
Park here
Owl Quarry
NF2730
Jordan Valley bouldering sites
Map 3: Owl Boulders Group
Owl Hollow Boulders
Topo A: Boulders & Cliff
VB VB
V0 VB
VB
V1 V2 V2 V3 V2
V3 V3 VB
hung
nose
classic seam
V1 V0 V1 V1
V0
VB VB
VB VB
VB
tall section for climbing
15' tall pillar
15' tall
slab
250' down to road
N
18' tall
25' tall
tall section
pillar
pillar

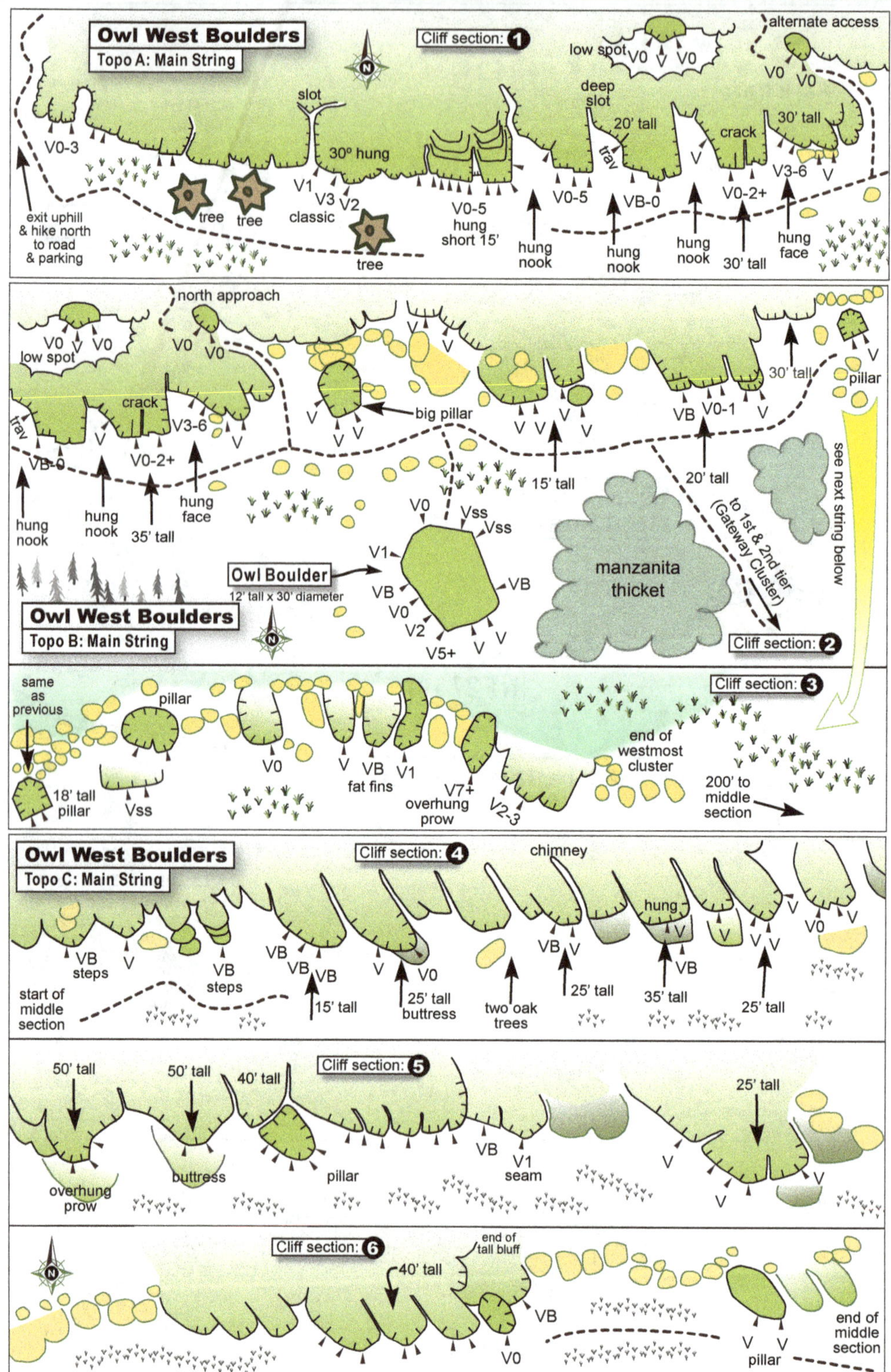
Owl West Boulders
Topo A: Main String
Cliff section: 1
N
slot
low spot
V0 V0
alternate access
V0 V0
deep slot
30' tall
20' tall
crack
V0-3
30° hung
V1
V3 V2
classic
trav
V
V3-6
V
V0-5
hung short 15'
V0-5
V0-5
VB-0
V0-2+
exit uphill & hike north to road & parking
tree
tree
tree
hung nook
hung nook
hung nook
30' tall
hung face

north approach
V0 V0
low spot
V0 V0
V
V
V
30' tall
V
pillar
trav
crack
V3-6
VB-0
V0-2+
V
V
big pillar
V
V
V
V
V
VB V0-1 V
15' tall
20' tall
hung nook
hung nook
35' tall
hung face
V0
Vss Vss
V1
VB VB
V0
V2
V5+
V
Owl Boulder
12' tall x 30' diameter
Owl West Boulders
Topo B: Main String
N
manzanita thicket
to 1st & 2nd tier (Gateway Cluster)
Cliff section: 2
see next string below

same as previous
pillar
Cliff section: 3
V0
V VB V1
fat fins
V7+ overhung prow
V2-3
end of westmost cluster
18' tall pillar
Vss
200' to middle section

Owl West Boulders
Topo C: Main String
Cliff section: 4
chimney
hung
V
V
V0
V
V
VB V
VB steps
V
VB steps
VB
VB VB
V
V0
25' tall buttress
two oak trees
VB V
25' tall
VB
35' tall
25' tall
start of middle section
15' tall

50' tall
50' tall
40' tall
Cliff section: 5
25' tall
VB
V1 seam
V
V
overhung prow
buttress
pillar
V

N
Cliff section: 6
end of tall bluff
40' tall
VB
V
V
V0
pillar
end of middle section

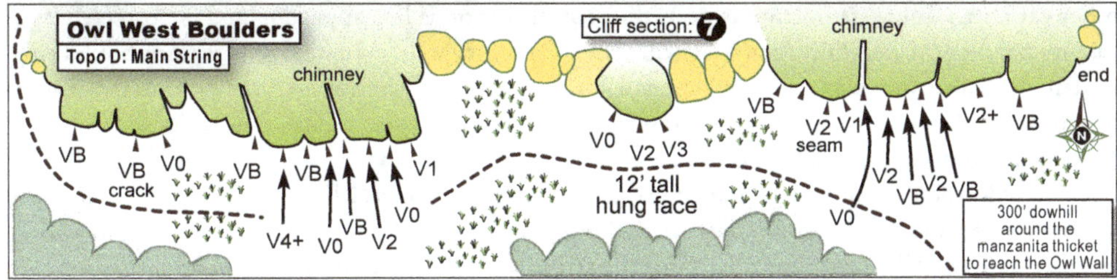

Jordan Creek Road (NF 2730). Park alongside this road at a wide spot (about 1.2 miles east of NF 160). This parking spot is about 1 mile west of the NF 132 Owl Quarry road. Hike uphill for 300' north to the site. Parking spot is 1.2 miles east from the T-junction with graveled Springer Ridge Road (NF 160); the parking spot is .8 mile west of the quarry access road (NF 130).

On maps NF 2730 is also listed as Jordan Creek Road. A brief one mile section west of the cattleguard is called Camp Friend Road until it reaches the quarry, then becomes Jordan Road. The parking spot is 2.0 miles west of the cattle guard (a USFS sign here states you're entering managed lands). GPS UTM 10T 625386 5024475 elevation 3,550'.

OWL WEST BOULDERS

An extensive cliff scarp bouldering site encompassing one mile of terrain (west to east), overlooking the small Larch creek valley. It eventually connects with Owl Quarry Wall & Boulders at its east end. Reaching the west portion of the bouldering outcrop is challenging, but luckily, two parking spots give several approach options that gain access to all the bouldering goals.

These outcrops (and boulders) tend to be slightly finer-grained grit rock texture of andesitic origins, but extra niceties such as knobs, crimps, seams, cracks, incuts, jugs, pockets, and lots of

other variables. The west portion is best; the central section is less appealing and is protected by a vast manzanita thicket. Future grades will range from VB-V7+. Minimal exploratory bouldering to date. Excellent for early spring or late fall season (May or October). A total potential estimate of future problems of the entire mile estate may yield over 150+ problems. Due to its south-facing aspect mid-summer hot days are generally not viable. Most landings are natural pine needle duff in a pine tree forested setting, so 1-2 crashpads is generally sufficient. Minor moss on a few sections. The entire site was briefly explored by Mr O [and later by Mr A] in about 2014 who tagged a wide number of lower V's along the entire one mile string, including the stellar Owl Boulder.

Directions

Drive paved Jordan Creek Road (NF 2730), then go northeast on gravel Springer Ridge Road (NF 160) for about 1.5 miles and park at a wide spot. Walk directly south 900' (open pine tree forest) to the bluff formation. Descend any reasonable slope to the base and coordinate via the diagram. Luckily the manzanita tangle does not encroach at the very base of the bluff, nor effect the giant Owl Boulder. GPS UTM 10T 625653 5024975 elevation 3,712' (Owl West upper end).

Owl Boulder

Owl Boulder (*CCW*): **VB** (descent), **V_ss**, **V_ss**, **V0 Ambient Noise** (north point), **V1 Biological Warfare**, **VB Old Rivalries**, **V0 Mandan Bride**, **V2 American Eagle**, **V3 Jet Lag**, **V5+**.

OWL WALL BOULDERS

This site offers some small wart-sized blocks and giant mega hi-ball boulders (up to 20' tall) scattered below the Owl Wall (aka Quarry Wall). Future grades will range from VB-V9+ on mostly crimp heavy features. Excellent for early spring or late fall season (May or October). The boulders beneath the Owl Wall may yield perhaps 60+ problems total (not including the cavernous maw at the base of the cliff). Due to its south-facing aspect mid-summer hot days are generally not viable.

Rock textural nuances tend to be quite gritty (grains up to ¼"), with friction attainable on all surfaces. Several extra benefits for this area are two super overhung sections of the cliff scarp that provide superb bouldering traverses, one on a 20' deep cavernous beast, the other on a juttingly overhung orange colored slice of cliff, all with nice flat landings.

Most landings are natural pine needle duff in a pine tree forested setting, so 1-2 crashpads is generally sufficient. Minor moss on a few sections. Avoid the really tall stuff and you will find a plethora of lines 8'-18' tall. Expect ticks in spring time. **History:** the Owl Wall Boulders has seen only minimal exploratory bouldering to date by a few local boulderers. As a whole the site has numerous quality future problems yet to be tapped. If the site becomes popular in the future a more concise database will be expanded in future editions (*see topo for visual*).

Directions

To reach the main Quarry Wall Boulders, from Hwy 35 drive east on NF 44, then south on NF 4420 till it becomes NF 2730 (Jordan Road). En route you will pass the parking spot for Area51 climbing area. This mainline paved road is Jordan Creek Road (NF 2730). About 2 miles east of the Springer Ridge Road (NF 160) graveled junction, turn north onto Owl Quarry road (NF 130), and drive up this for 1/3 mile to its very end (passing Owl Quarry on your right). Park at a berm on NF 130. To the north you will see the Quarry Wall. Walk past the road decommission berms on the old log road for 500' crossing Larch creek. Cut north directly to the cliff on a faint path for 500' more. The boulders are scattered along the base of the Quarry Wall. GPS UTM 10T 626581 5024919 elevation 3,430'.

TYGH CREEK BOULDERS

A brief cluster of stones in a dry semi-arid oak tree environment offering a smattering of 25+ problems. Some more bouldering problems can be tapped on a short bluff outcrop, from which the

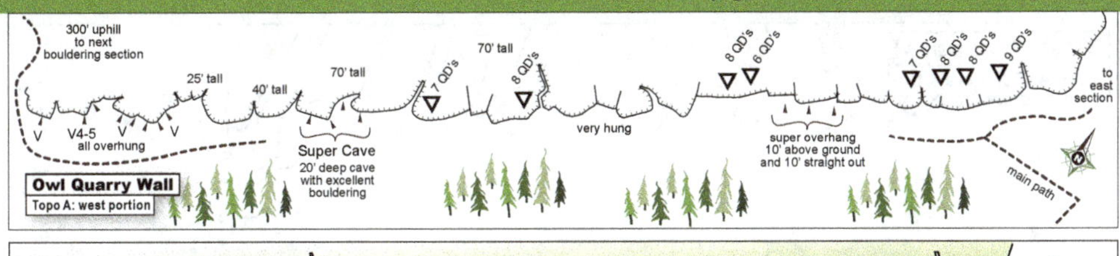
300' uphill to next bouldering section
25' tall
40' tall
70' tall
70' tall
7 QD's
8 QD's
8 QD's
6 QD's
7 QD's
8 QD's
8 QD's
9 QD's
to east section
V
V4-5 all overhung
V
V
Super Cave 20' deep cave with excellent bouldering
very hung
super overhang 10' above ground and 10' straight out
main path
Owl Quarry Wall
Topo A: west portion

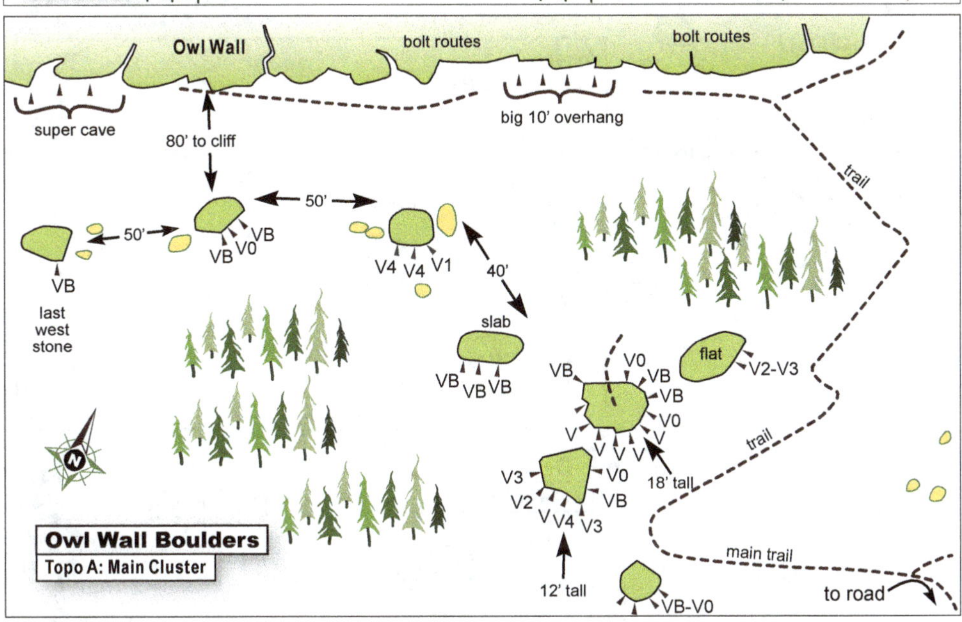
Owl Wall
bolt routes
bolt routes
super cave
80' to cliff
big 10' overhang
trail
50'
50'
VB
VB V0
VB
V4 V4 V1
40'
VB
last west stone
slab
VB VB VB
VB
V0
flat
V2-V3
VB
V0
V
V V V
trail
V3
V0
V2
VB
V V4 V3
18' tall
main trail
Owl Wall Boulders
Topo A: Main Cluster
12' tall
VB-V0
to road
N

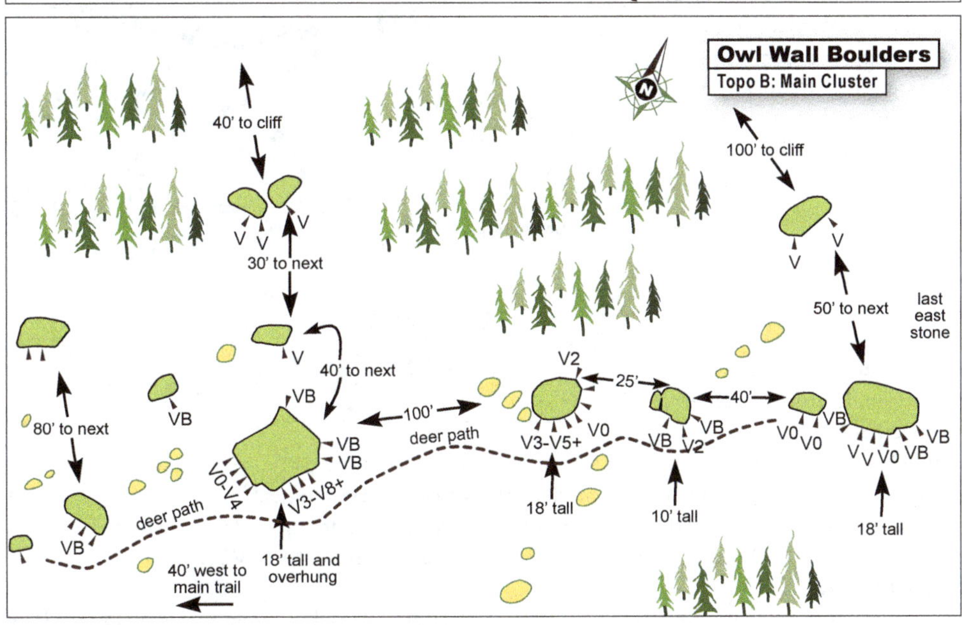
Owl Wall Boulders
Topo B: Main Cluster
N
40' to cliff
100' to cliff
V V V
V
30' to next
50' to next
last east stone
V
VB
V2
80' to next
VB
40' to next
VB
100'
deer path
25'
V3-V5+
V0
40'
VB
V0 V0
VB
V
V V0 VB
V0-V4
V3-V8+
deer path
18' tall
VB V2
10' tall
18' tall
VB
18' tall and overhung
40' west to main trail

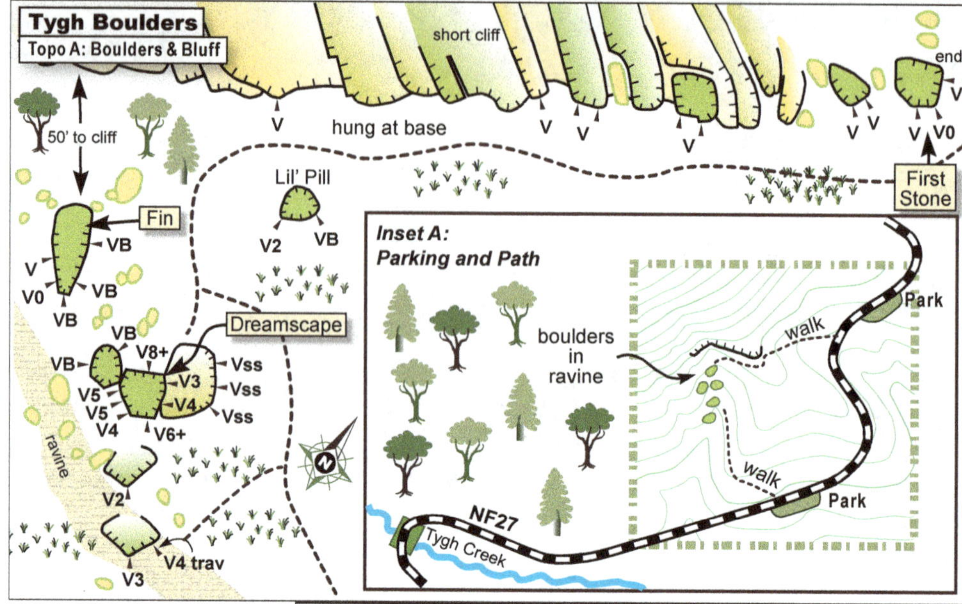

stones originated and tumbled into the minor ravine. The south-facing site aspect is conducive to early spring or fall season (May-June or Sept-Oct) bouldering. Convenient paved road access, and a 5-minute uphill hike up a gentle slope make the site readily viable.

Rock composition is basaltic with minimal crystalline mineral matrix. Surface nuances are some crisp cut aspects, some rounded blocks, limited softened crimps, most aspects offering power lines. Textural minute undulating variances offer viable edging. Mini-

mal lichen/moss. Most landings are natural duff/dirt. Deer (and cattle) paths crisscross the area so approach is by using one of those paths. Expect ticks in springtime. Crashpads recommended (1ea). Ratings range from VB-V7+. Minimal exploratory bouldering to date. **History:** Explored initially by Mr O in about 2014 who ventured up a brief selection of VB-V5's.

Directions

Navigate onto Jordan Creek Road (NF 2730) either by approaching from the west (Hwy 35) or east (Hwy 97). Drive south on NF 27 (aka N. South Road) for 5.1 miles and just prior to reaching the actual Tygh Creek bridge, you will park at 1-2 spots alongside the paved road. Hike uphill from either parking spot. Walk uphill from south for 930' to the boulders (or 630' from the east to reach the east bluff).

GPS UTM 10T 628243 5019153 (ravine boulders) elevation 2,800' at boulders.

Dreamscape Block: cool stone! Virtually every line is worth the time.

V3 Dreamscape is the diligent east face. And V4, V6+ (south), V4, V5, V5, V8+ (north).

The Fin: minor one-move SS lines (all done).

Lil' Pill: minor SS lines (all done).

First Stone: entry level VB-*ish* stuff.

BALL POINT BOULDERS

A unique, rarely visited, compact cluster of

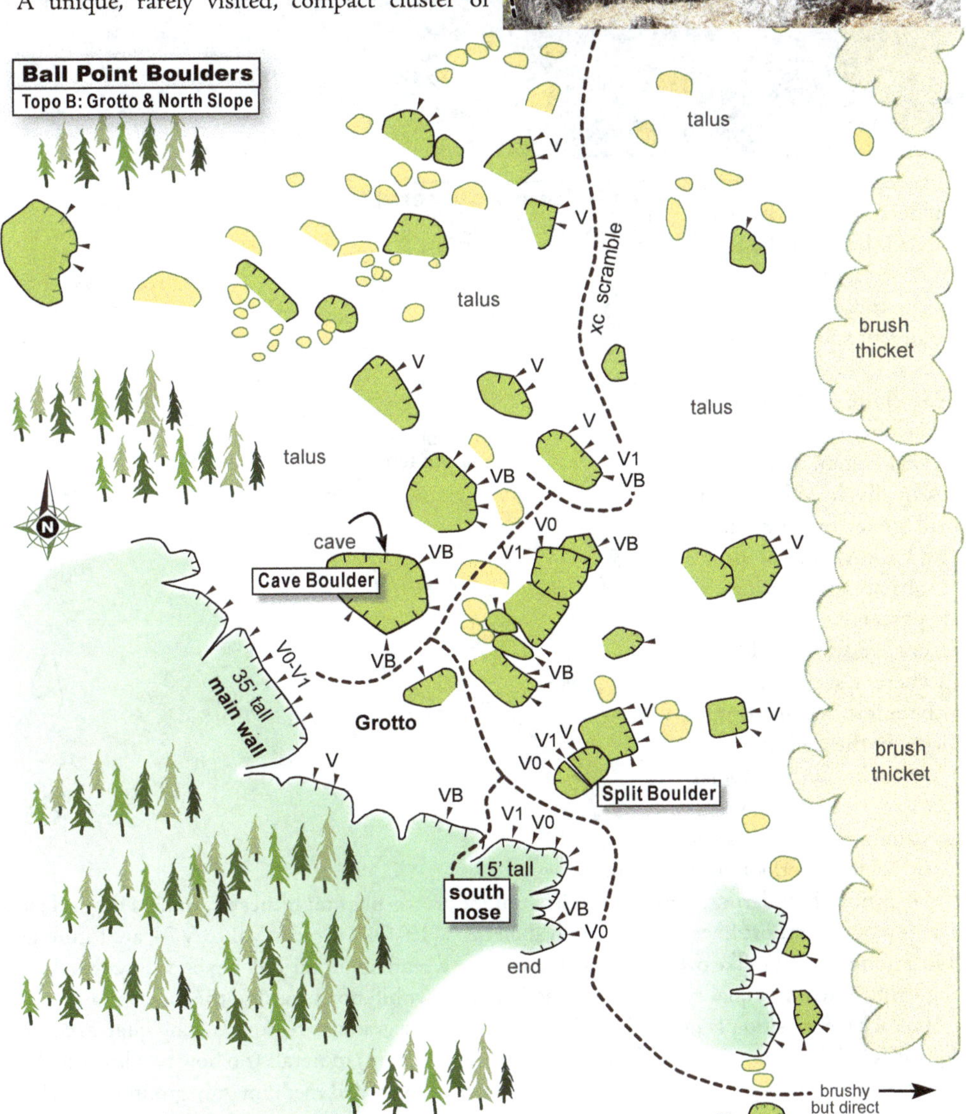

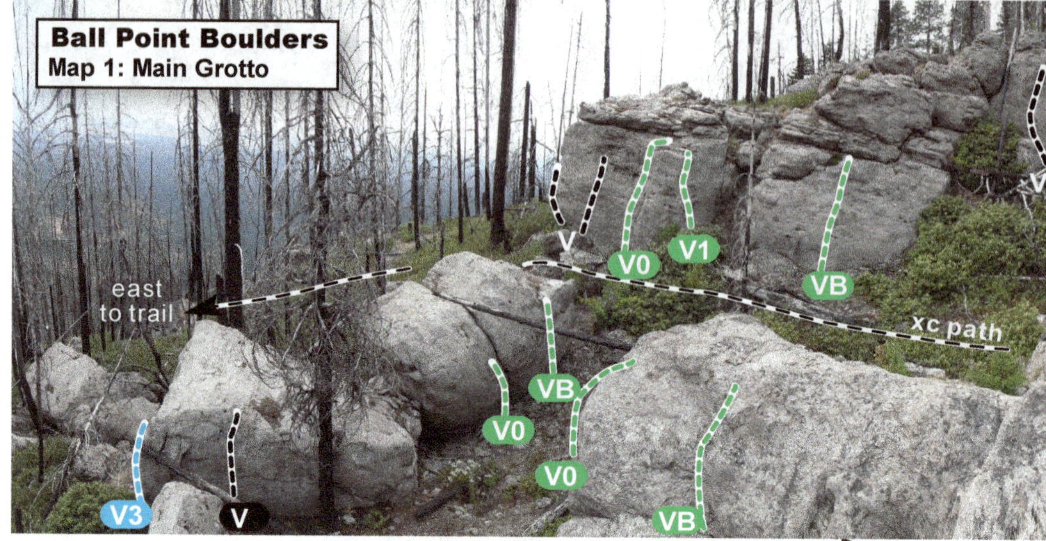

light colored andesitic big boulders wrapped by a minor rock bluff perched high on an isolated butte near a hiking trail. This outback bouldering site is located on the east facing slopes of Ball Point Butte with sweeping scenic panoramic views of the arid eastern slopes overlooking Tygh Valley. From small stones to giant beasts, from basic VB's to stout V's on substantial overhangs, so many seemingly beckoning reasons, and were it located anywhere else (other than in the midst of a manzanita thicket in the back-country) it would be fairly popular. Views are stellar with sweeping panorama of the entire eastside slopes overlooking Tygh Valley.

The primary bouldering core is tucked in a unique grotto-like amphitheater, and is a mega cluster of stones offering short lines (9'-12') and hi-ball lines (15'-24'). Grades VB to V7+ are future feasible, a number of ape-like overhangs exist, including a bluff about 35' tall. Beyond the core group a long string of massive quality stones are distributed downhill northward to the hiker's trail.

The rock composition is noticeably silicic andesite, very granular texture lacking quartz, strands of plentiful pink (4-5mm) mineral, black and opaque (2-3mm) minerals (no flow banding), including a variety of sharp gas pockets (1"-10") in a roughly congealed medium gray groundmass yielding great friction (but gnarly sharp cracks). The unweathered surfaces tend to be the most textured.

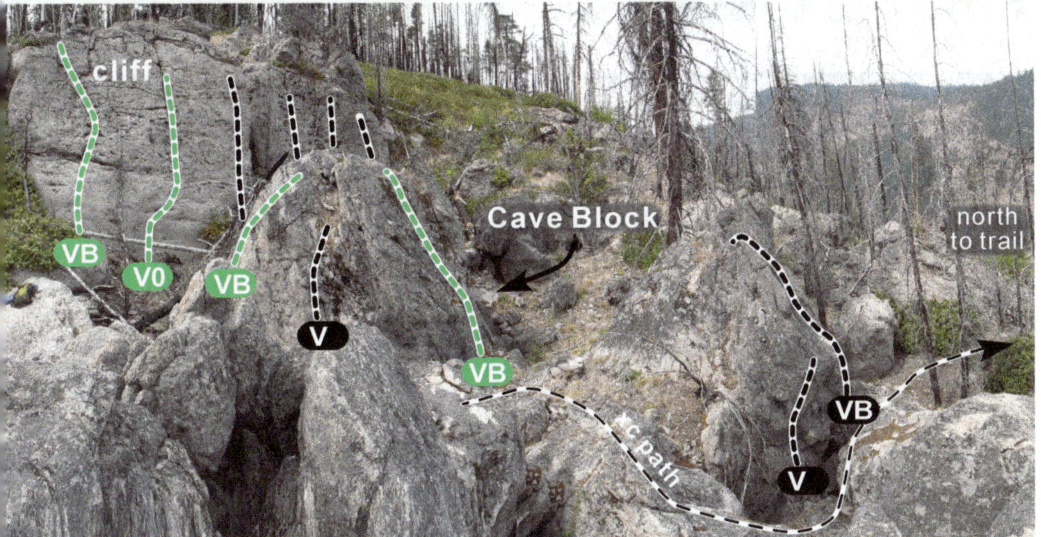

The area also has some light-gray rhyodacite or rhyolite formations.

The future total potential V-grade yield might exceed 100+ problems covering an estate perhaps 900' square. No moss/lichen growth at this time. Most overhung aspects have small detached flakes that drop off leaving clean surfaces underneath. A recent forest fire burned this area (2002 ?) leaving all dead tree trunks (full sunshine), yet the snowbrush and some thorny bushes have regrown quickly (3'-5'). **History:** Mr O briefly explored a number of lower V's (30+) at the site in about 2014. No specific beta list at this time, but if the site becomes popular an expanded beta list will be included in subsequent editions.

Pro/Con: the manzanita thicket is quite difficult to navigate (and will likely keep 99% of all boulderer's at bay). Good hiking shoes and wearing long pants is obligatory. Crashpad recommended minimum (1-2). Best to go in teams (its in the backcountry where the bear and cougar can eat ya). The site is plainly visible from the road and trail.

Season: visit only in spring or fall season (May-June or Sept-Oct) as mid-summer heat would be unmitigating so coordinate a visit based on the weather pattern.

Directions

Navigate onto Jordan Creek Road either by approaching from the west (Hwy 35) or east (Hwy 197). Drive south on NF 27 (aka N. South Road) for 7.3 miles. Park at Ball Point Trailhead (#468). Hike a gentle uphill trail for 1.3 miles (1,100' elevation gain). The initial one mile trail (#468) gently gains elevation (in full sunshine) along a dry rounded lightly forested oak tree environs. The trail ascends up below the eastern slope of the site, then wraps northward around the butte. Its better to hike uphill on the trail to the north slope, then tread up from the north slope to reach each boulder cluster (rather than tackling the manzanita tangle directly up from the east) because the northern approach has a bit less brush thicket to navigate.

Driving from the east: Drive from The Dalles south on Hwy 197 past Dufur, and in about 1 mile turn west on Dufur Gap Road. Drive 4.5 miles on this. Turn right on Friend Road and continue 8.7 miles. Turn south on the N. South Road (NF 27)

and drive 7.1 miles to the Ball Point trailhead (#468). GPS UTM 10T 626540 5018427 elevation 3,770'.

ROYAL BONN BOULDERS

Within a few miles on Rock Creek Reservoir is this minor north-facing rock bluff of variable height, some of which is conducive to bouldering. Convenient access and roadside camping in a semi-arid oak tree and pine tree forested environment make this region worthy for escaping from those endless early spring rains so common on the west side of the Cascades. The Royal Bonn Boulders is only minimally explored to date, with future ratings from VB-V5 likely, and nearby formations should yield additional problems. The rock composition is andesitic-basalt, well rounded slopers and crimp features on a short rock bluff with friction-friendly surface grit, involving technical often reachy movement. Hot in summer (best in spring or fall season). Most landings are duff (1-2 crashpads are sufficient). Minor surface lichen. Manzanita/snowbrush tangle along the top (between dirt road and bluff) may limit access to certain zones. **History:** minimal exploratory bouldering to date (first by Mr O who tagged a variety of V's).

Directions

Drive Hwy 35 to the White River crossing, then go southeast on NF 48 road to Rock Creek Reservoir. From Rock Creek Reservoir drive west on paved Wamic Mill Road (NF 4810) for 2 miles, then north on NF 4811 for 1.2 miles, then east on NF 2710 for 1.2 miles to the site near Bonnie Campground. Park at the top of the bluff and walk east along a 4WD dirt road called Dodson Road to access each particular bouldering spot.

Note: the main gravel road NF 2710 continues down across Badger Creek (past the campground), then north to the junction with NF 27 (N. South Road) which continues north to Friend

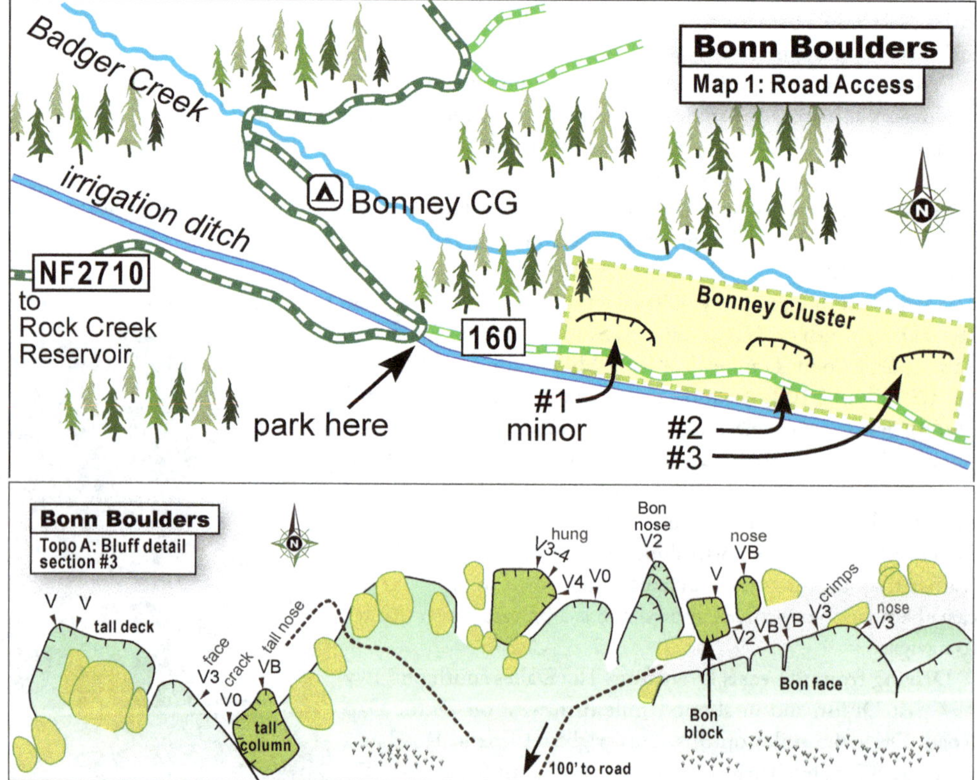

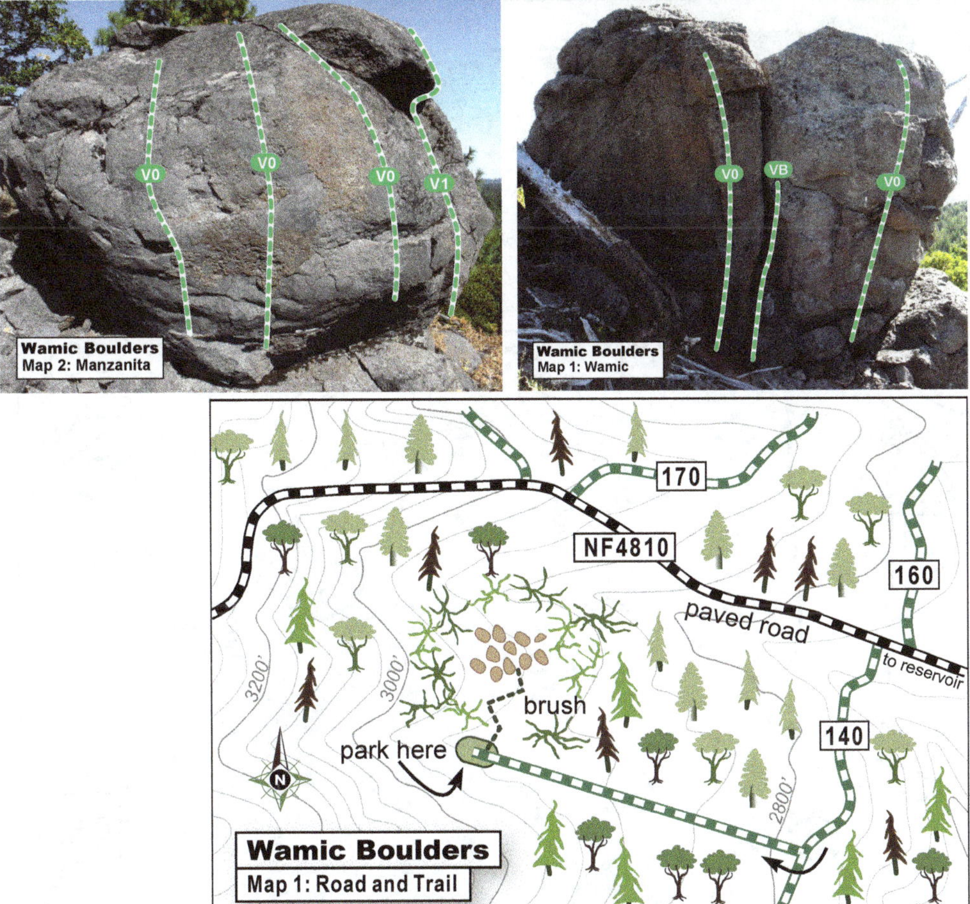

Road. This entire road network is driveable with a 2WD vehicle.

GPS UTM 10T 627345 5012204 elevation 2,375'.

Section Three (beta east to west):

Bonn Face ⌒⌒: V3 round nose / face. **V3 Zane Grey Classic** tech crimps on a steep face. **VB Stinkin' Bluebelly Boulderer** is a crack line. **VB Robbers Roost** face line.

Bonn Block: **V2 Death by Slow Draw** east prow, **V_(?)** north prow, **VB Cutthroat's** is next block east; has lower outer nose.

Bonn Nose: **V2ss Draw!** is a low odd prow with a very flat west aspect (start at pocket).

Hung stone: can yield **V0-V4+** (mostly SS).

Tall Column: **VB Get It Right Between The Eyes** is a rounded nose tall fun run.

Tall Deck ⌒⌒: can yield hi-ball **V0-V4+**.

WAMIC BOULDERS

A few miles west of Rock Creek Reservoir in cattle country is this secluded boulder-studded rock knoll, tucked in a pine and oak tree forest, and wrapped by an entanglement of manzanita brush (the knoll itself is brush free and in full sunshine). The rock type is basaltic with some plagioclase crystalline minerals (opaque 1-5mm and olivine 1-5mm) in a dark matrix. Considerable minute 1mm gas pockets throughout the matrix, noticeable little eroded surface scoops, all of which increases the friction-ability. Rock surface is quite clean (due to altitude and full sunshine),

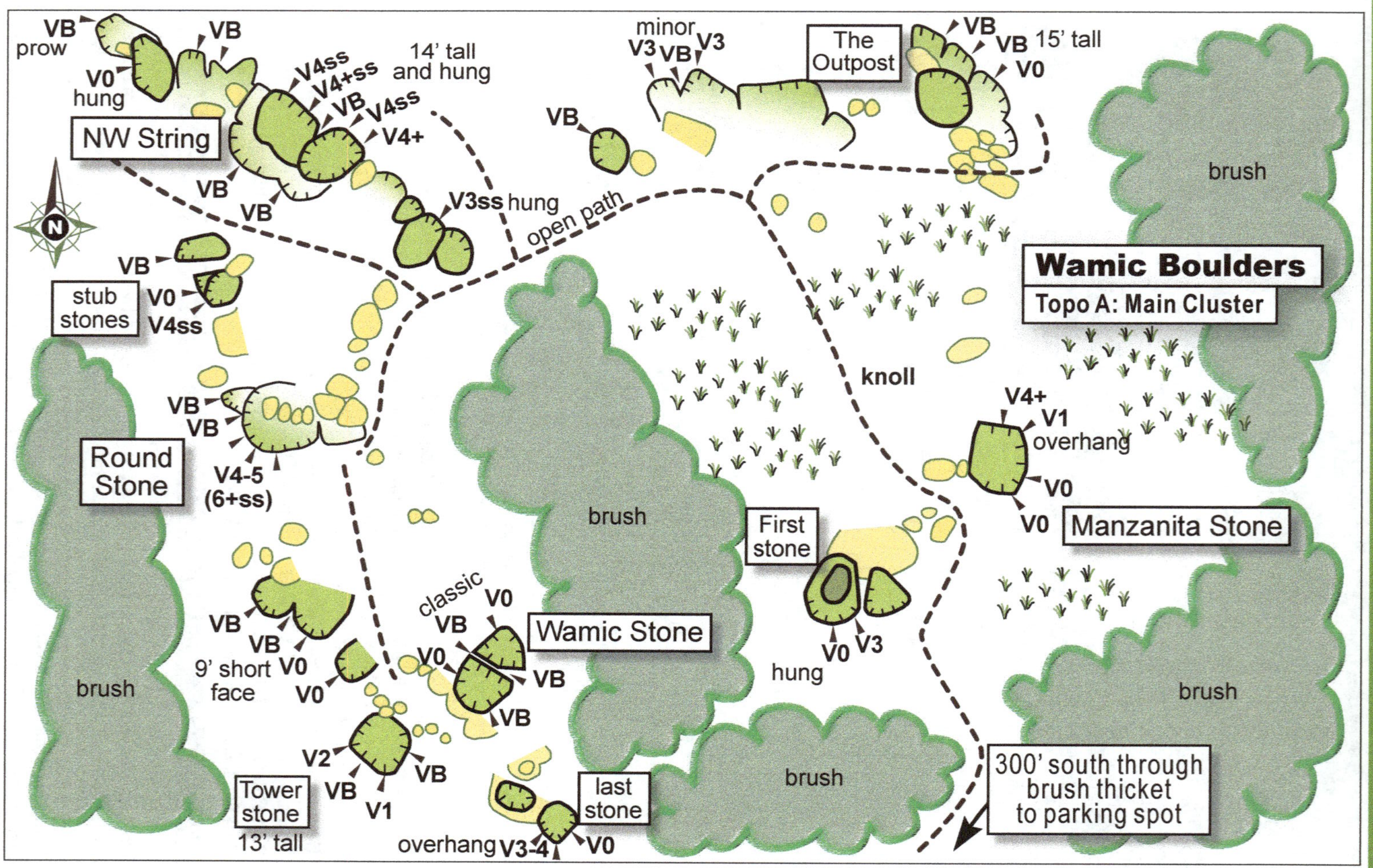

Wamic Boulders
Topo A: Main Cluster
brush
brush
brush
brush
VB
prow
V0
hung
NW String
V4ss
V4+ss
VB
V4ss
V4+
VB
VB
VB
stub stones
V0
V4ss
V3ss hung
open path
14' tall and hung
minor
V3 VB V3
The Outpost
VB
VB
VB 15' tall
V0
VB
knoll
Wamic Boulders
Topo A: Main Cluster
V4+
V1
overhang
V0
V0
Manzanita Stone
Round Stone
VB
VB
V4-5 (6+ss)
brush
classic V0
VB
V0
VB
Wamic Stone
First stone
V0 V3
hung
VB
VB
9' short face
V0
V0
VB
V2
VB
V1
Tower stone
13' tall
VB
last stone
V0
overhang V3-4
V0
brush
300' south through brush thicket to parking spot

light red-brown patina, numerous undulations and crimps, short lines (11-12') and hi-ball lines (15'+), and some stout overhung problems ranging in grade difficulty from VB-V6+. No moss/lichen. Seasonally best in spring or fall (May-June or Sept-Oct). **History:** The site was first tapped initially by Mr O (in 2014?). **Pro/Con:** long pants are recommended to negotiate the brush tanglefest. Possible ticks in spring season.

Directions

Drive Hwy 35 to White River crossing, then southeast on NF 48 road to Rock Creek Reservoir. From Rock Creek Reservoir drive west on paved Wamic Mill Road (NF 4810) for 3.3 miles. Drive south on an unmarked old dirt road ¼ mile to a 4-way junction, then west ½ mile to a cul-de-sac. Park here. Walk north uphill for 300' (60' elevation gain) to the top of a knoll. The manzanita is very thick between the road and the boulders (wear long pants to plow through it). A deer path zigzags through most of the tangle. GPS UTM 10T 621831 5011273, elevation 3,080'.

First Stone: it can yield V0-V3.

Manzanita Stone: V0 Sons of the Soil, V0 Dystopian Discontents, V1 Manzanita, V4+.

The Outpost: can yield VB-V3, some tall, some mossy, some squat.

NW String: East overhang stout V's. Fun VB-V0's west aspect (VB-V3 all well done). **V3ss Poison** (SE overhang), **V0 Denial & Deception** (NW hung point).

Stub Stones: two lil' minors. **VBss Boredumb, V0ss Naked Greed, V4ss Pure Greed.**

Round Stone: round hung block. **VB Highway Robbery, VB Circus Act, V4-5** (?).

Wamic Stone: total fun all aspects. **V0 Voiceless Subjects** (north point), **VB Wamic Classic** (west face), **V0 Slow Draw** (south), **VB Steroid Queen, VB Empire of Liberty** (east).

Tower Stone ⌒: VB to V2 (some untapped) has a tall outer aspect.

Last Stone: V0 Fashion Show, V3ss+ low super hung.

BADGER BOULDERS

A very extensive ultra-classic bouldering site nestled on a minor knoll situated alongside an infrequently used hiking trail. Top quality bouldering site with many fine boulders and outcrops

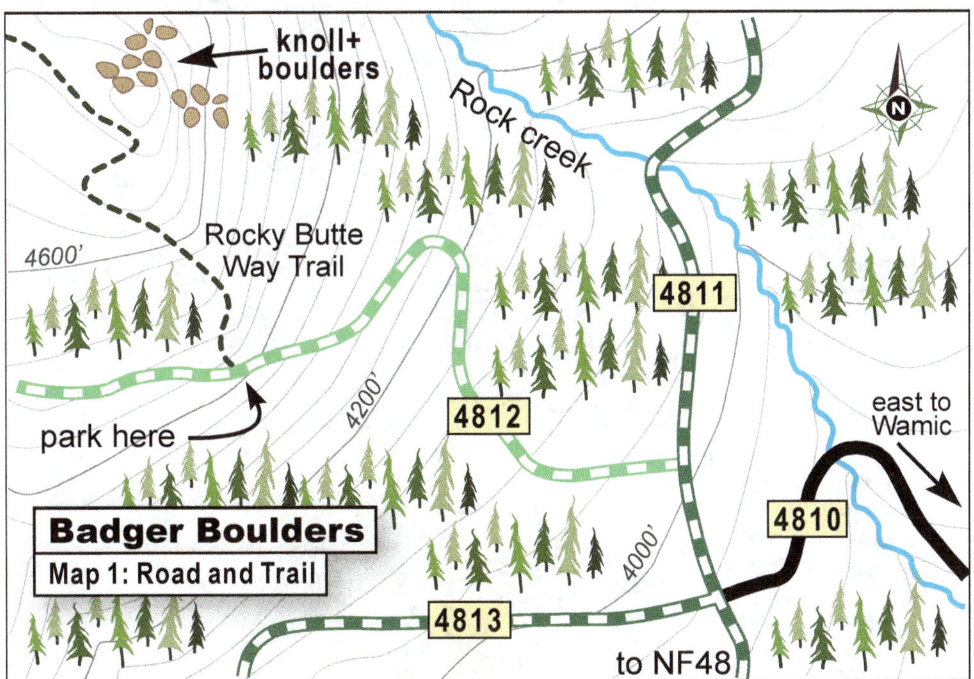

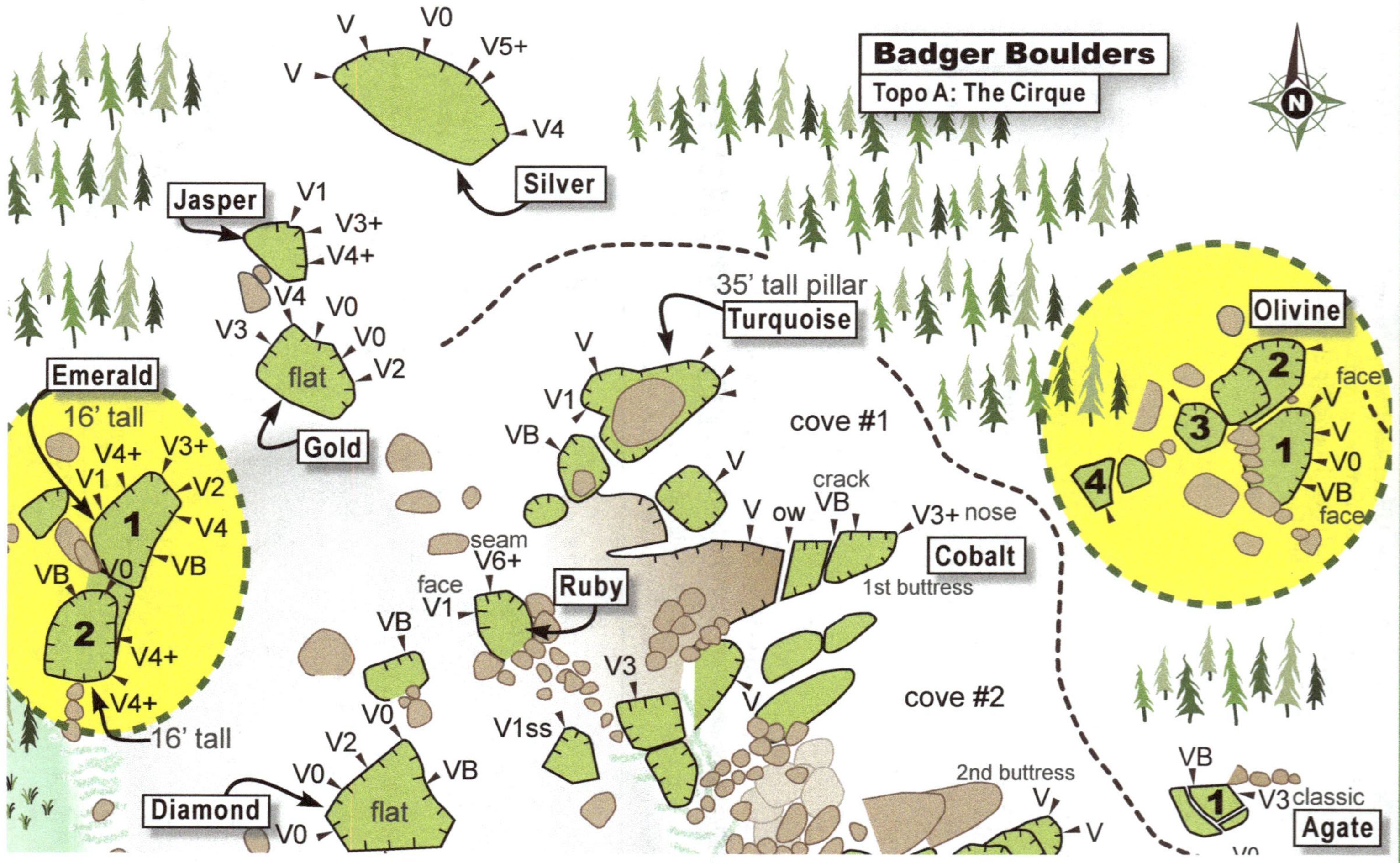

Badger Boulders
Topo A: The Cirque
N
V
V0
V5+
V
V4
Silver
Jasper
V1
V3+
V4+
V4
V3
V0
V0
V2
flat
Gold
Emerald
16' tall
V4+
V3+
V1
V2
1
V4
VB
V0
VB
2
V4+
V4+
16' tall
35' tall pillar
Turquoise
V
V1
VB
cove #1
V
seam
V6+
face
V1
Ruby
VB
V3
V1ss
crack
VB
V
ow
V3+ nose
Cobalt
1st buttress
V
cove #2
2nd buttress
V
V
Diamond
V2
V0
V0
VB
flat
V0
Olivine
2
face
V
V
V0
3
1
VB
face
4
VB
1
V3 classic
Agate
V0

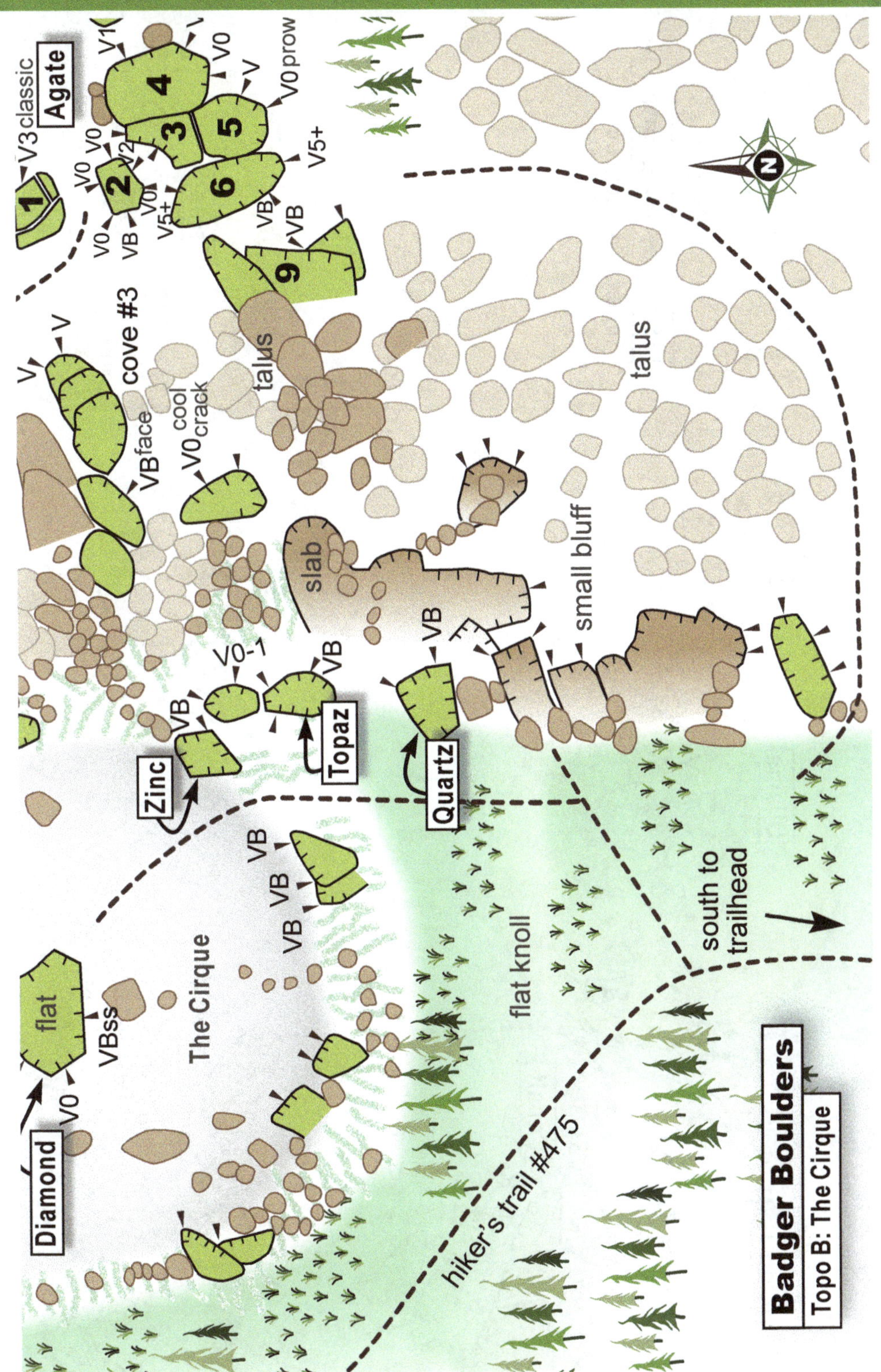

Agate
V3 classic
V1
V1
V0
4
V0
V0 prow
V0 V0
3
5
V
2
V2
V0
6
V5+
V0 V5+ V5+
V0 VB VB
VB VB
VB
9
V
V
cove #3
VB face
cool
V0 crack
talus
slab
talus
talus
small bluff
V0-1
VB
VB
VB
Zinc
VB
Topaz
VB
Quartz
south to trailhead
flat knoll
hiker's trail #475
The Cirque
VB
VB VB
VB
flat
VBss
V0
Diamond
N
Badger Boulders
Topo B: The Cirque

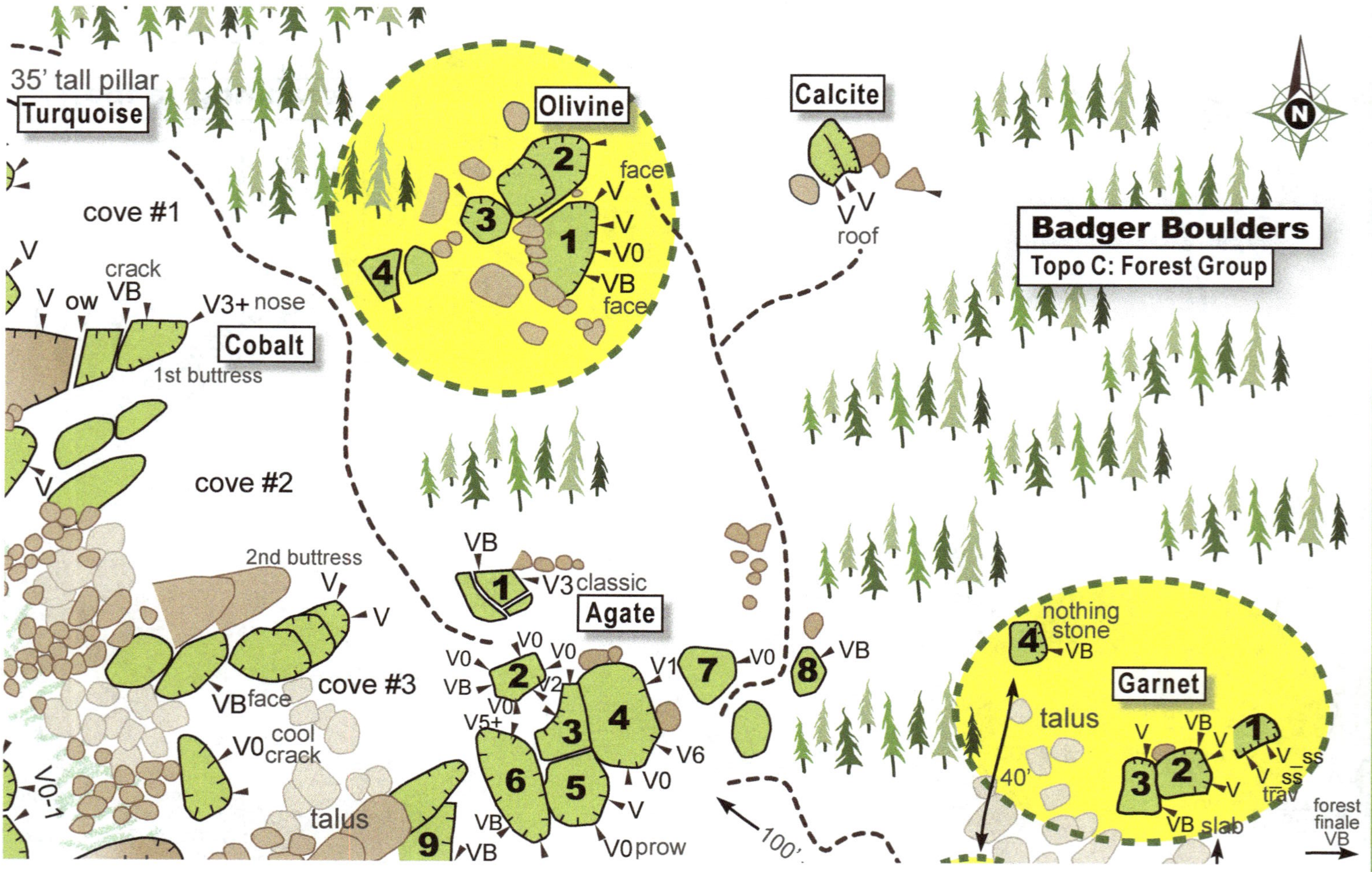
N
Badger Boulders
Topo C: Forest Group
35' tall pillar
Turquoise
cove #1
V
V ow
crack
VB
V3+ nose
Cobalt
1st buttress
cove #2
V
2nd buttress
V
V
VB face
cove #3
V0 cool
crack
V0-1
talus
Olivine
2
3
1
4
face
V
V
V0
VB
face
Calcite
V
V
roof
VB
1
V3 classic
Agate
V0 V0
V0
VB
2
V2
V0
V5+
3
4
V1
7
V0
8
VB
6
5
V6
V0
V
VB
VB
9
V0 prow
100'
Garnet
nothing
stone
VB
4
talus
V
VB
V
1
V ss
V ss
trav
V
40'
3
2
VB slab
forest
finale
VB

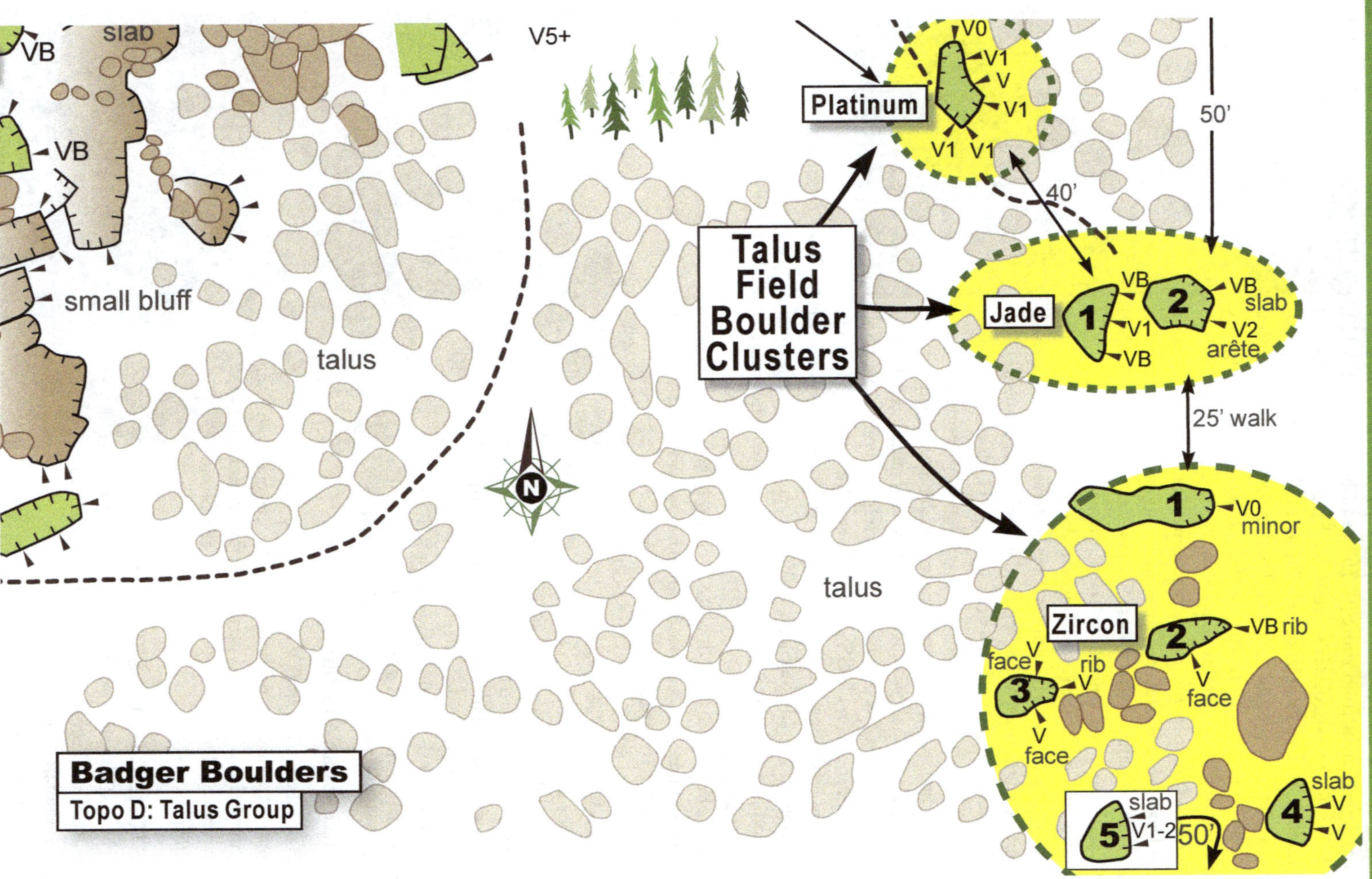

VB
slab
V5+
Platinum
V0 V1 V V1
V1 V1
50'
40'
Talus Field Boulder Clusters
VB VB slab
Jade 1 2 V2 arête
V1 VB
25' walk
small bluff
talus
N
talus
1 V0 minor
Zircon 2 VB rib
face V rib V face
3 V
V face
slab
4 V V
slab
5 V1-2 50'
Badger Boulders
Topo D: Talus Group

ranging in height from short (9'-15') to hi-ball status (17'-35'). The broad stone cirque is surrounded by perched rock fins and outcrops. Badger Boulders site will eventually yield 130+ problems (in the cirque and the east talus slope), plus another several dozen future lines along the trailside string. Most landings are natural duff, but the talus clusters are stony. Located in a mixed hemlock and fir tree forested environment at high altitude with moderate summer temperatures (dry enough to limit mosquitoes) and quality scenic views. Seasonal access from late May-Oct (late snow-pack may hinder early access).

Andesite rock type (evenly dispersed 1-2mm crystalline minerals in a gray matrix) with weather softened textural nuances (crimps, edges, tiny gas pockets, and micro surficial indents), features more pronounced on overhung aspects, all yielding a fine-grained sandpaper feel for quality friction bouldering. Minimal moss/lichen. Rock structural analysis yields porphyritic olivine bearing plagioclase phenocryst matrix that emanated from a large shield volcano lava flow at Grasshopper Point. The knoll site is referenced on USGS maps as Rocky Butte Point. **History:** This site was tapped initially by Mr O 2012-2016 [and by Mr A]. They conquered a very wide selection of V-grade problems (50%+) over several years. Crashpad recommended minimum (1-3). Additional site beta will be included in future editions as the development phase is expanded.

Directions

Drive Hwy 35 to the White River crossing, then go southeast on NF 48 road to Rock Creek Reservoir. From Rock Creek Reservoir drive west on paved Wamic Mill Road (NF 4810) for about 6.8 miles. When you reach a 4-way junction (Grasshopper Road & NF 4813) turn north and drive an ⅛ mile. Turn left (west) on NF 4813 and drive for about ½ mile to the trailhead (#475). Hike uphill northward for ¼ mile to the site. The site is broken into three sections: a trail-side fin cluster (not detailed here), the north cirque, and the east talus field. Total elevation gain from road to site is about 200'. Gravel approach roads to reach the trailhead are 2WD friendly. GPS UTM 10T 617460 5012085 elevation 4,780'.

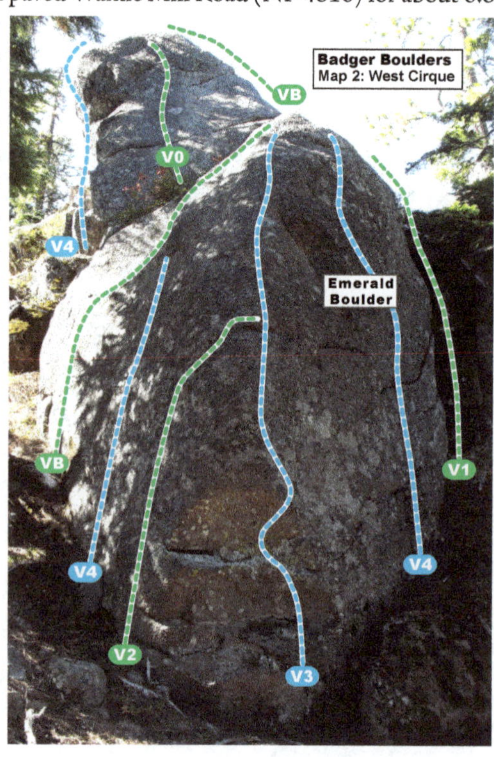

Quartz, Topaz, and Zinc Boulder

Basic short intro stuff VB-V1 (all well done) on four stones (nothing special). Several minor short VB's also exist on a few stones wrapping along the upper edge of the Stone Cirque.

STONE CIRQUE SECTION

The first place you are likely to start your tour is the Stone Cirque. From the Diamond Boulder to the Silver Boulder there's certainly something worthy enough here to spike your egocentrism. It's fairly convenient to walk downhill around the Turquoise Pillar to reach the superb Agate Cluster, and further to the Platinum Boulder (and its nearby options) on the lower talus.

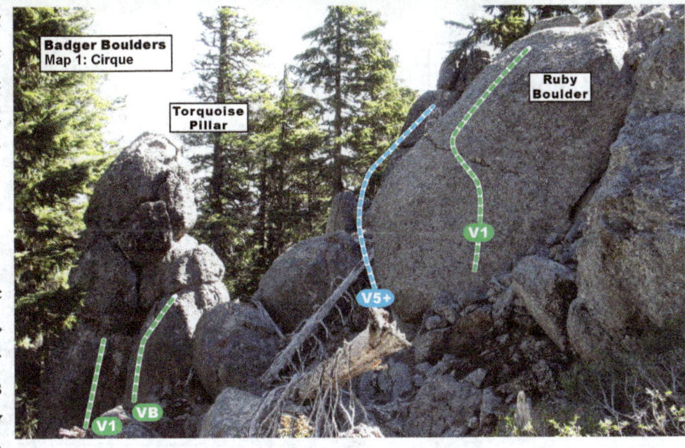

Diamond Boulder

Low squat fat pig in the center of the Stone Cirque. **VB Get Down** (east descent), **VBss** (south), **V0ss Bugaboo Under Every Bed** (SW point), **V0ss Grilled to a Carbon Copy** (NW face), **V2ss Jackals & Jackasses** (NW face), **V0ss Diamond Prow** (north point).

Ruby Boulder ᗰ

V1 Infinity & Beyond (west face), **V6+ (?)** thin hung seam (north side).

Emerald Boulder ⚠ ᗰ

Dual set of hi-ball blocks, one above the other. Lower block string L to R: **VB Agents of Change** (east side), **V4 Diktat** (thin face), **V2 Warmonger** (alternate to nose), **V3 Firebrand** (nose full on), **V5+** (thin face), **V1 Yak Manure** (uphill far right). The upper boulder string: **V4+** (east face), **V4+** (east face), **VB Down** (descent), **V0** (outer slab).

Gold Boulder

All SS (R to L from west): **V3ss Contempt of Silence** (west), **V4ss Barbarian** (north point), **V0ss Pig Market** (NE), **V0ss Weather Warfare** (NE), **V2ss Alien** (east).

Jasper Boulder

About three short untapped SS options (V1ss-V4ss+).

Silver Boulder

One large boulder (east face L to R). **V4 Bajillion** (SE hung nose), **V5+ & V5+** (east face), **V0 Square Circles** (hi-step onto slab 2-ways), **V_ss** (N), **V_ss** (N).

Turquoise Pillar ⚠

An actual pillar (about 35' tall), double stacked, a bit spooky to top out, but most of the problems wrapping around the units base can be done. **V1ss Formula One** (west side nook), and **VB**

Turquoise Pillar to summit. Minimum 5-6 possible lines.

LOWER FOREST SECTION

Cobalt (First Buttress) ⚠

A buttress of partly detached stones. Some potential north side lines (VB-V_+), and a potential hi-ball pronounced east prow (V3+). Minumum 6+ lines.

Second Buttress ⚠

Offers some potential hi-ball stuff. Just beyond in Cove #3 (up high) is **V0 Cool Crack** (short crack on rounded block).

Olivine Boulder Cluster: Has about 6-7 possible VB-V4+ lines (none yet tapped).

Calcite Boulder Cluster: Two possible short V_ overhung problems. Project.

Agate Boulder Cluster

A set of nine boulders in this tightly-packed high quality cluster.

Stone 1: V3ss Velocity (classic east prow), **VBss Bah Humbug** (north shorty).

Stone 2 (Circuit Stone): VB (west), **V0 Too Sane** (NW), **V0 Too Stoopid** (north), **V0 Circuit Jerk** (east), **V2ss Geko Dancer** (SE), **V0ss Cowabunga** (south).

Stone 3: has two possible shorties (VB-V2).

Stone 4: V0ss Humdrum (south side onto slab), **V6ss Li'l Brother** (SE face), **V1 (V6ss) Li'l Sister** (east end low onto slab).

Stone 5: V0ss Power n' Politics (minor south face), **V6ss+(?)** (possible).

Stone 6: V6+(?) hung bulge on big beast, **VB Lux et Lex** (west face).

Stone 7 & Stone 8: V0 and **VB**.

Stone 9: Has a left slanting **VB** crack.

TALUS FIELD SECTION

Platinum Boulder

Ultra-classic boulder and a great reason to be here! Beta from Right to Left (north prow first):
V0 Sybaritic Abandon (north nose), **V1 Claws & Paws** (east face), **V6-8 (?)** (east face skin-

ny) , **V0 No Man's Sky** (classic arête), **V0 Empyrean Dreams** (other cool south arête), **V0 WTFudge** (variation face), **VB Get Down** (west).

Garnet Boulder Cluster

A cluster of three stones (and one isolated unit).

Stone 1 (Garnet): several low SS lines (and a traverse), both look cool. Project.

Stone 2: **VB** to **V_ss**, about three possible.

Stone 3: **VB Dodo** (slab), but a **V_ss** (north side) awaits.

Stone 4 (Nothing Boulder): **VB Nothing Man** (tall east face).

Jade Boulder Cluster

This is two closely oriented stones, both offering unique quality lines. Several more stones exist in the forest below the talus field (some are tapped).

Stone 1 (Jade): The upper stone. **VBss daVinci** (start on right, go along rail, mantle at notch), **V1ss Vitruvian Man** (from VBss run lip & face leftward, exit on leftmost high point over lip), **VBss Scapegoat** (left rib).

Stone 2: Has entertaining stuff. **VB Ideological Fogbank** (slab), and tricky **V2 (V4) Velociraptor** (arête), or the harder variant using high leftmost aspect to exit up over.

Zircon Boulder Cluster

The Zircon string is four closely oriented stones (and one isolated unit).

Stone 1: **V0 Baja Burrito** (minor slab move).

Stone 2: **VB Barking Mad** (rib), and **V2(?)** __ (south face).

Stone 3: Quality stone with some stout shorties. **V_** (north), **V_** (east

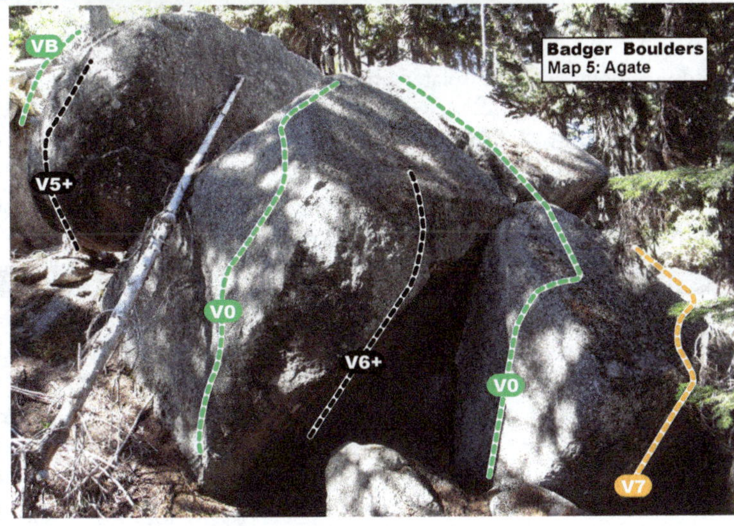

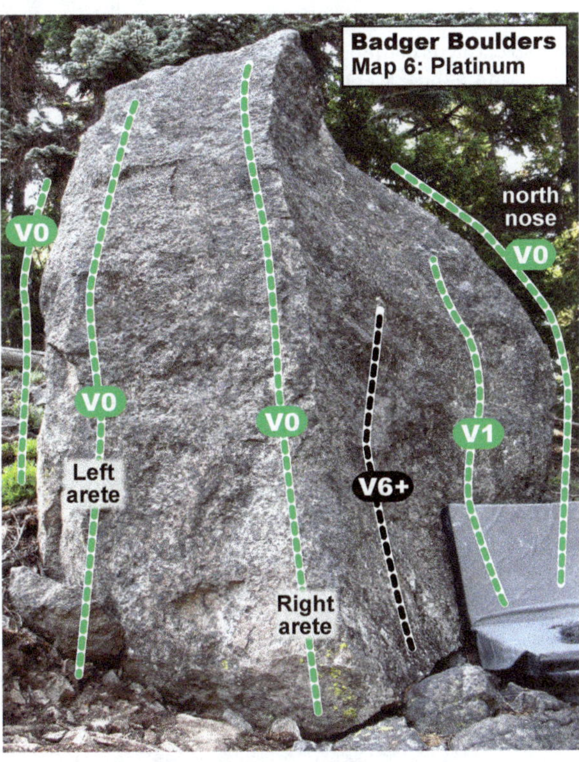

rib), **V_** (south).

Stone 4: Several slabby V's on a stone at the edge of the forest.

Stone 5: Southernmost isolated unit (two possible very short **V_ss** lines).

The **east-facing bluff** ⌂ (overlooking the east talus field) certainly has a plethora of futuristic options(mostly hi-ball). The **Trailside Fin Cluster**, though not included in this beta list or diagram, does offer a fairly extensive string of potential future options, extending for several hundred feet SE downhill away from the main bouldering zones. In a few short years all this will be thoroughly tapped and included in subsequent editions of this guidebook.

BOULDER LAKE BOULDERS

A minor little site in a beautiful scenic setting, primarily of interest as a family outing to the lake (mixed with some bouldering, fishing or camping). A very short hike ¼ mile with nice camping options around the lake in a pine / fir tree environs.

Bouldering is limited in scope here to about 25 problems, though scrounging about may yield a few more problems. The boulders tumbled from a nearby cliff scarp, so crimps and edges are slightly softened, as well as weathered by the elements. One crashpad will suffice as most of the problems are short (8'-11'), Most lines are lower grades (VBss-V3ss), often SS. Rock type is basaltic with smooth friction (no moss, minimal lichens). The rock structure is composed of single tone gray groundmass lacking any obvious crystalline structure, uniform structured texture, medium gray basaltic rock with reasonable friction on fresh cut surfaces, yet quickly attains a softened surficially weathered texture.

Directions

Drive US Hwy 26 to Government Camp, then east on US Hwy 35 to White River bridge. Turn southeast onto NF 48 road, and drive for about 10 miles. Go north on NF 4880 (Boulder Lake sign) and drive 5 miles (passing Swamp Creek Boulders) to trailhead #463.

Lake Front Boulder Cluster: Three stones (one big fat flat unit), all fun basic **VB** stuff, sort of free lake frontage property type of bouldering (some SS).

Native Stone: VB-V0 (**V0 Native Soul** traverse is nice).

Indian Stone: V0 Indian Summer

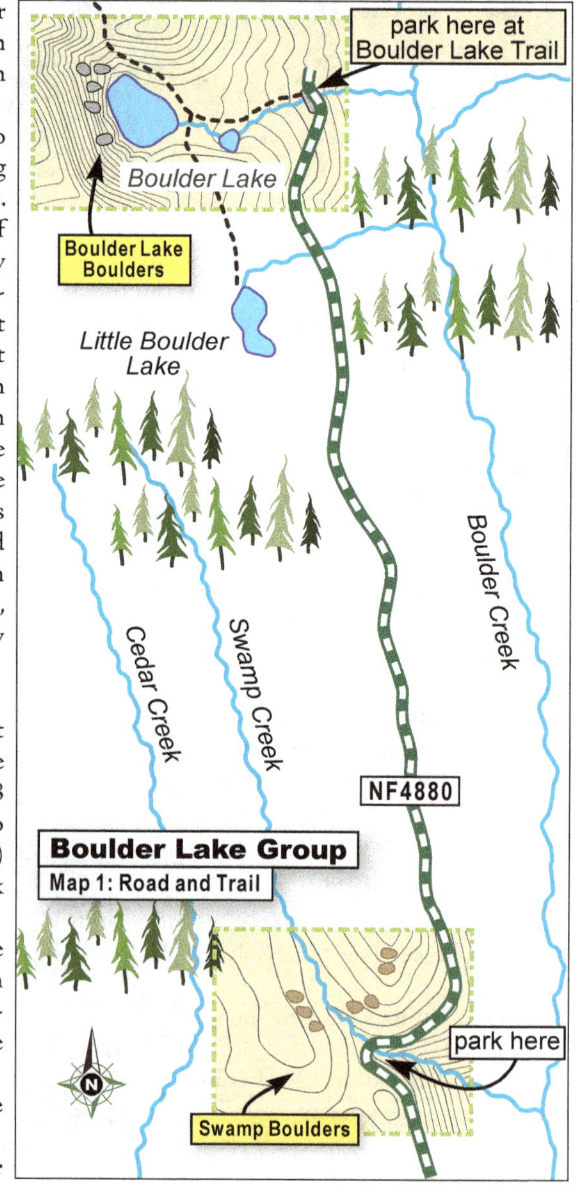

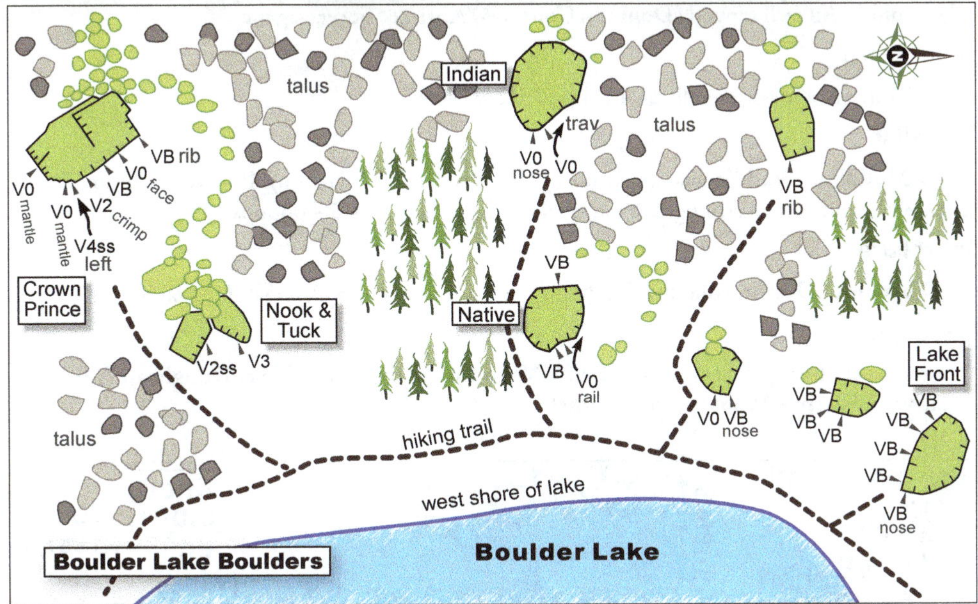

(nose), and **V0 Feather** (traverse right) is nice.

Nook & Tuck Stone: low belly scrapers yielding **V2ss and V3ss.**

Crown Prince Boulder

The only really big stone (wider than taller) offering mostly SS problems, some decent. The beta is from left to right: **V0ss Anarchic Scum** (mantle on left aspect), **V0ss Ignominous Befuddling** (mantle), **V4ss Crown Prince Traverse** (traverse left low), **V2ss Strategic Alliance** (crimp), **VB Skulduggery** (center slab), **V0 Loggerhead** (right slab face), **VB Scrapheap of History** (N point).

SWAMP BOULDERS

A brief roadside bouldering spot that you pass en route to Boulder Lake Boulders. All problems can be sent in a short session. A general max total of about 20 short VB-V5+ problems (often SS) on boulders and parts of a bluff. The textural nuances range from crimps to slopers on a strong friction-friendly grit surface where the crystals and gray matrix have been mildly softened and weather scoured clean. The Spring Cluster and Knoll Stone is OK. Seldom utilized site. The rock structure has prominent phenocrysts up to 3-4mm in a medium gray groundmass. Weather scoured rock features (on certain aspects) yields minimal surficial softening, retaining a fair degree of rough surficial friction, consistently positive for smears. **History:** unknown, but many of the VB-V4 problems were tapped by Mr O.

Directions

Located on the immediate west side of the gravel road at Swamp Creek on gravel road NF4880 (*see directions to Boulder Lake Boulders*).

Spring Cluster

Beta described left to right: **V0 Leaning Brave, VB Bubble of Denial, V4 Venomous Sting, V3 Sword & Shield, VB Five O'Clock Shadow** (rightmost).

Knoll Stone

All ultra-low one-move problems. **VB-V0 (V1-2ss) Double-Counteragent.** Were it any bigger it'd be...uhhh. All well tapped (**Double-, Counter-, Anti-, & Secret-agent**).

South Scarp

The **South Scarp** is generally avoided (tall and broken).

Tall Pillar

VB Muddling Muddlehead (east nose), **V0 Proverbial Lightning Rod** (face). Immediately south of the pillar an overhung face may yield some punchy **V4-5+** options.

Short Face

V0 Vector of Dezinformatsiya (up point over block), and **V3 (?)** short hung face.

North End

Some basic short problems. **VBss Sam's Virtuoso Performance, VBss Dungheap, VBss Banana, V0ss Warp & Woof** (northernmost).

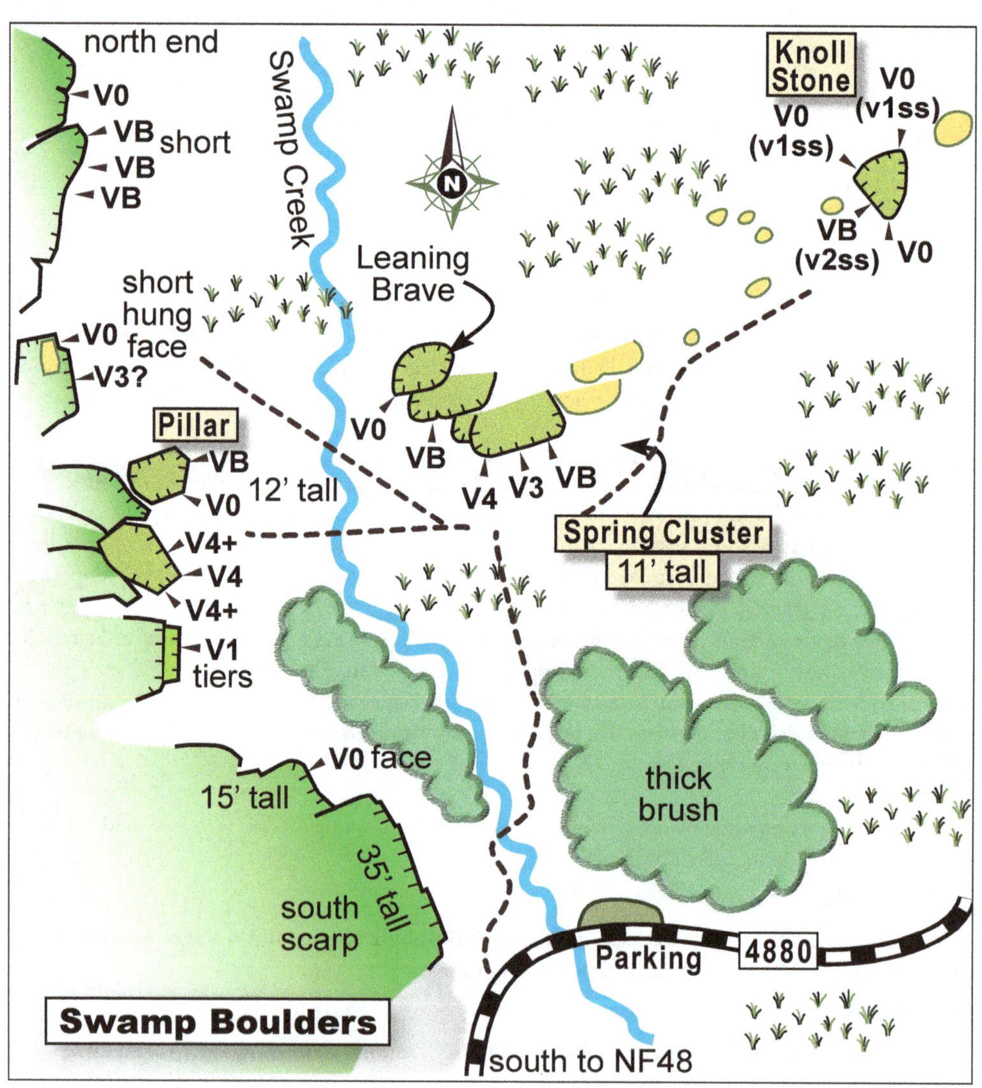

CLACKAMAS RIVER AREAS

HIGH ROCK BOULDERS

A stellar bouldering site located near High Rocks summit on the upper Clackamas River, this high-altitude site is encapsulated in a beautiful misty vine maple and conifer forest ridge top scene. The South Cluster offers low V-grade problems, but its the primary North Talus Cluster (not visible from the road) where the real gems are packed. The site yields quality andesite problems of every degree, from vertical crimp scum-fests, slab smears, rail traverse runs, to dicey thin techy hi-ball problems, all in a very concentrated area at the edge of a fir forest. The andesite rock structure consists of numerous tiny medium-to-dark crystalline phenocrysts in a gray matrix, yielding superb fine grained quality stone surficial features perfect for bouldering.

Seasonal accessibility exists for 5½ months from June-October. The boulders range from 8' to 25' tall. Most landings are naturally easy to pad. Many VB-V6 problems available (up to V9+) with about 90 problems feasible above the road. Many stones are scoured naturally clean by the elements (minimal lichen/moss). The north slope cluster is excellent on hot days, and the site is accessible by 2-wheel drive city type vehicles. A mega stone with an 15' long overhung belly underside found here is a rare commodity for this region. Overall, HRB is a superb site in a back-country setting, minus the crowds.

History: The majority of lines at this site were tapped by Mr O and Mr A (2011-2017).

Directions

Drive Hwy 224 south of Estacada continuing on NF 46 to Ripplebrook Ranger Station, then go east on NF 57 for six miles, then turn north on NF 58 and drive uphill to High Rocks peak. Continue past this peak on NF 4610 for another 1½ miles, taking the gradually descending gravel road (headwaters of Linney Creek) northeastward. Paved road to within ½ mile of the site. GPS UTM 10T 587117 5002980, elevation 4,410'.

SOUTH TALUS GROUP

Located 100' directly above the first pullout parking spot on a prominent east facing talus field. Mostly low-grade easy

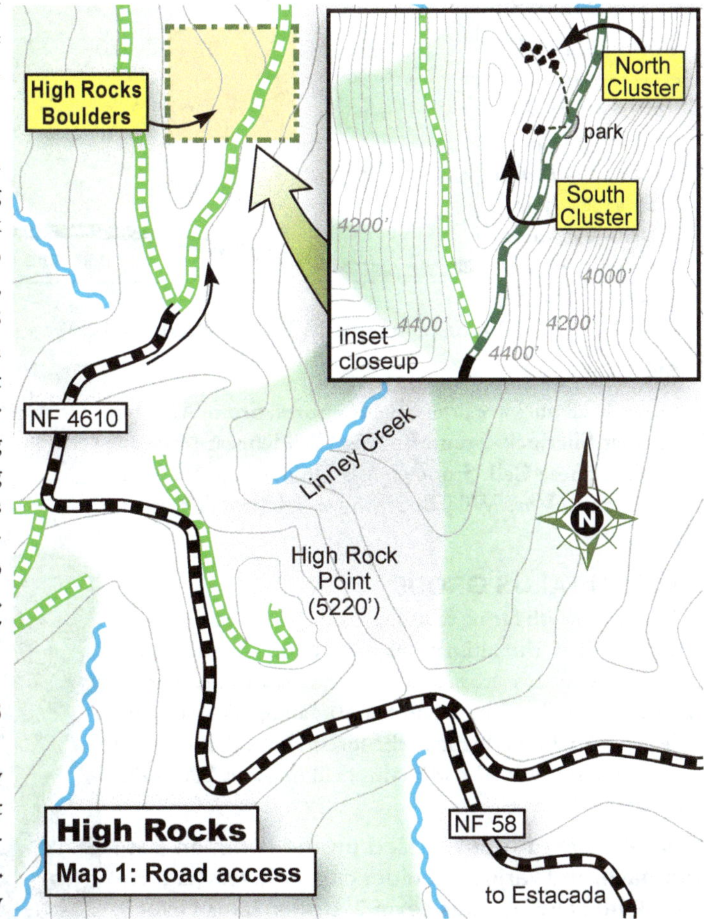

problems, including a few cool lines.

High Rock Slab (L to R):

V0ss Torpedo (left face), **V0ss Wish Me Dead** (left face), **V0 Bubbleheads** (face), **VB High Rock Arête** long low angle arête, **V0 Sunburst** (cool seam on long slab), **V0 Magic Fairy Dust** (smears on slab), **VB Unicorn Poop** (far right minor).

Split Stone (L to R):

VB Bulldust, VB Horse Feathers (just right of slot), **VB Fairy Faarts, V1ss Feeble Brains** (east point), **V2ss Cockamamie, V4ss Hocuspocus** (mantle),

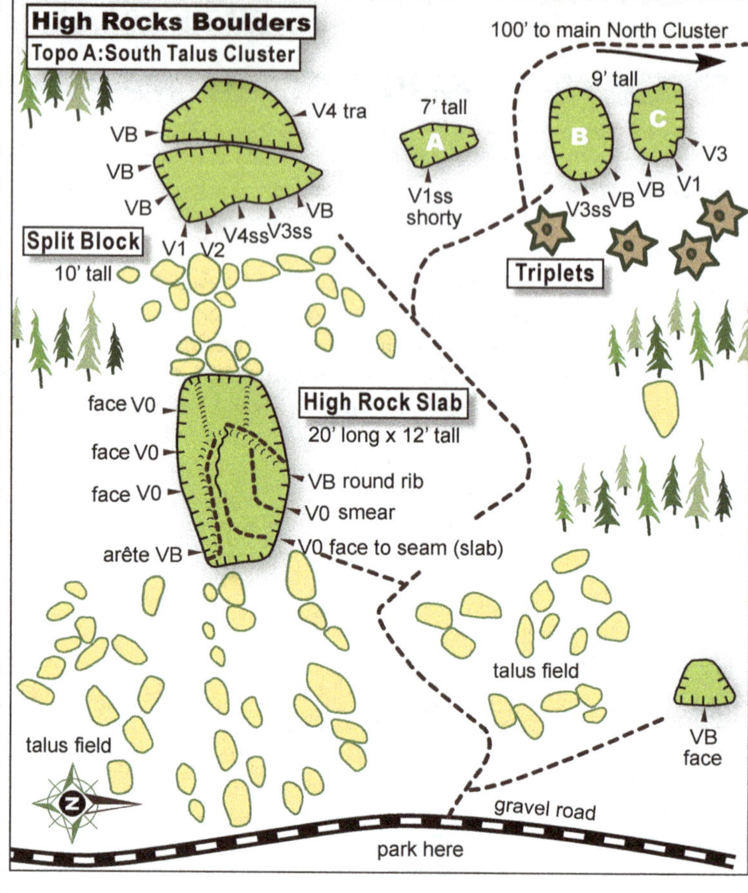

V3ss Airy Fairy Promises (mantle), **VB Boorish,** and **V4ss Woo** traverse.

Triplet Stones

Virtually all lines are brief SS adventures. **Stone A: V1ss No Schist Sherlock. Stone B: V3ss Wildebeest** (traverse left), **VB Cancer Cell. Stone C: VB Douchebag, V1 Banshee Blizzard, V3ss Wild Boar** (move right uphill & mantle).

NORTH TALUS GROUP

This large north facing talus field is the true heart of bouldering at HRB, the ultimate place to be to experience the best of the best this site has to offer. It is best to drive north past the first pullout about another 400' and park at a minor wide spot. A faint path enters the forest above the road and takes you to this valued north talus field in about 200' walking distance.

This self-guided tour is based on the common path approach, and various boulder cluster levels (e.g. Entrace Path Level 1, Talus Level 2, Upper Talus Level 3,

At High Rocks Boulders

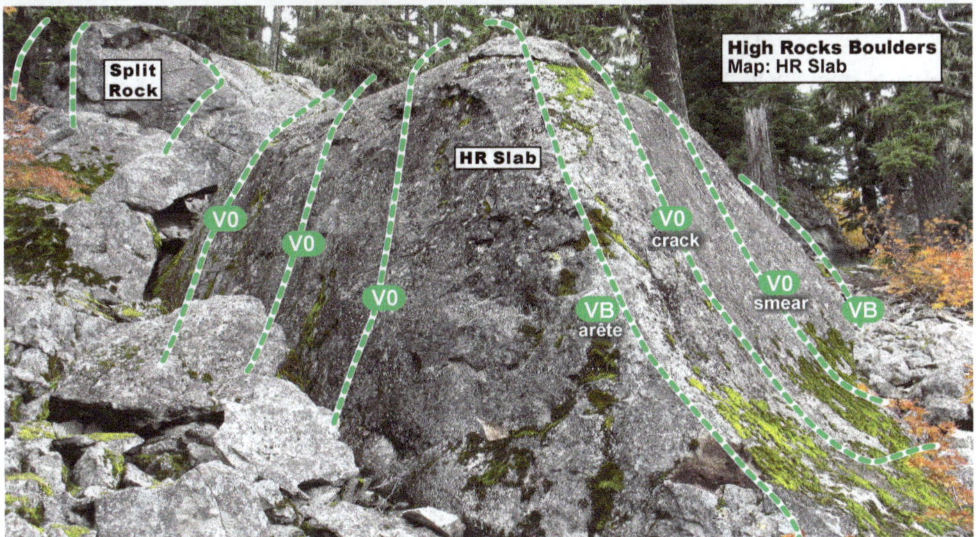

Forest Clusters Level 4). Each cluster is naturally stacked on the talus slope.

Entrance Path Group (Level One)

Solar Boulder

Ultra-classic boulder. This massive boulder has a series of superb problems and traverses. The beta is from L to R starting at the north side traverse.

V0ss Gran Minimum. North side traverse (SS leftmost hung point) going to far right.

V0 (V5ss) Lux Libertas. The standing is basic, but the SS puts fire to the message. SS runs the entire seam from low left to high right.

V6ss Lux Aeterna. Low power cling crimp start, entering into seam and firing up right.

....And for the variables on the famous westside traverse:

V2ss Half Baked (simple mantle over).

V2ss Nothing Burger (the ½ traverse starting L to R ending at point).

V2ss Horny Toad Mantle (mantle the point).

V2ss Half Burger (the other ½ traverse starting at point going right to exit).

V4 Gran Maxima. The ultra-classic full traverse problem at HRB. This cool traverse will bring out the arrogant pride in just about everyone.

V5ss Lux et Veritas. Jugs out SE underside onto skinny exit crimp.

V_ss Underworld. The underside is a rare gem, with partial eliminates, and full power problems on a 75⁰ overhang, several exits options, all combined to give Oregon one of the best high-

At High Rocks Boulders

end boulder problems. A few eliminate grades seem to range from about V6/7, V11, and possibly even V13/14 for the entire underworld power run.

Szechuan Boulder

Some minor lines, and some potential husky stuff on north aspect. Beta L to R:

VB Lux Virtus, **VB Lux Orbis**, **V0 Lux Sit** (flake on nose), **V4 Lux et Tenebris** (right side short nose), **V__** (hung face), **V__** (hung face).

Cryptic Boulder

Cool minor north aspect. Beta L to R starting on vert north side:

V3 Myrmidons (left rib), **V2 Sesquipedalian Tergiversation** (face), **VB Wackadoodle** (short nose), **V3ss Greed is my Creed** (odd seam scum).

Knight Boulder

A vertical 12' tall north aspect and short west side. Beta R to L.

V0ss The Exemplar. West side low and long reach.

VBss Ignorant Bliss. The short point.

V0 Elixir of Exotica. Start in north side pit, obvious flake block, power up into previous.

V3 Good Knight. The center north face.

V0ss Rumor Control. SS low left, bump up rail running across all lines.

Blackout Boulder

Blackout Boulder has several cool punchy tall lines on a flat face. Beta L to R:

VB Certified Old Faart. Far left steps at OW.

V5 RPM Riot. Superb left power face trends up right using leaning rib [+ alt left exit].

V4 Unhinged. Powerful hi reach to catch flake.

VB Bird Brains. Minor far right.

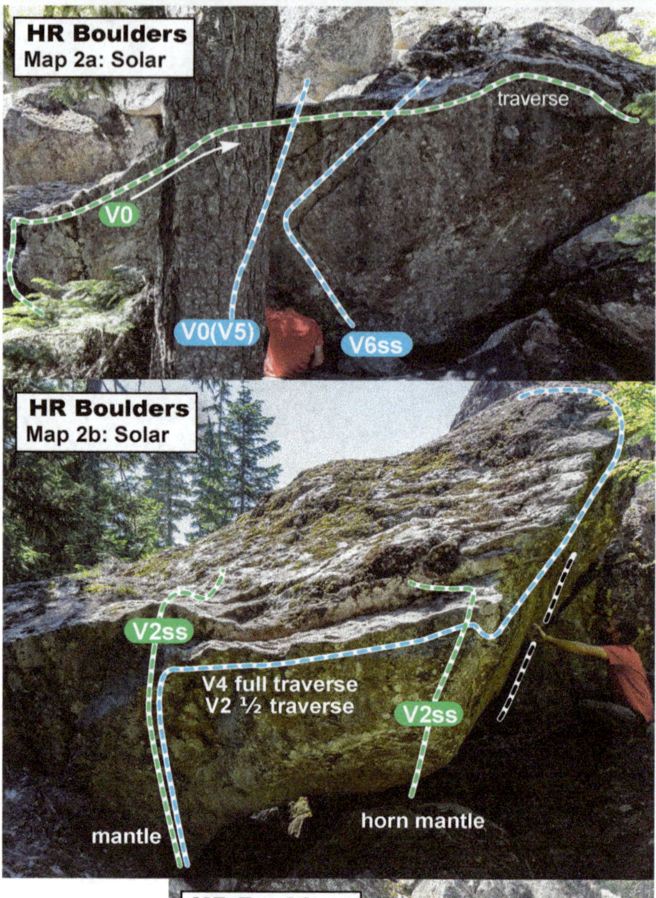

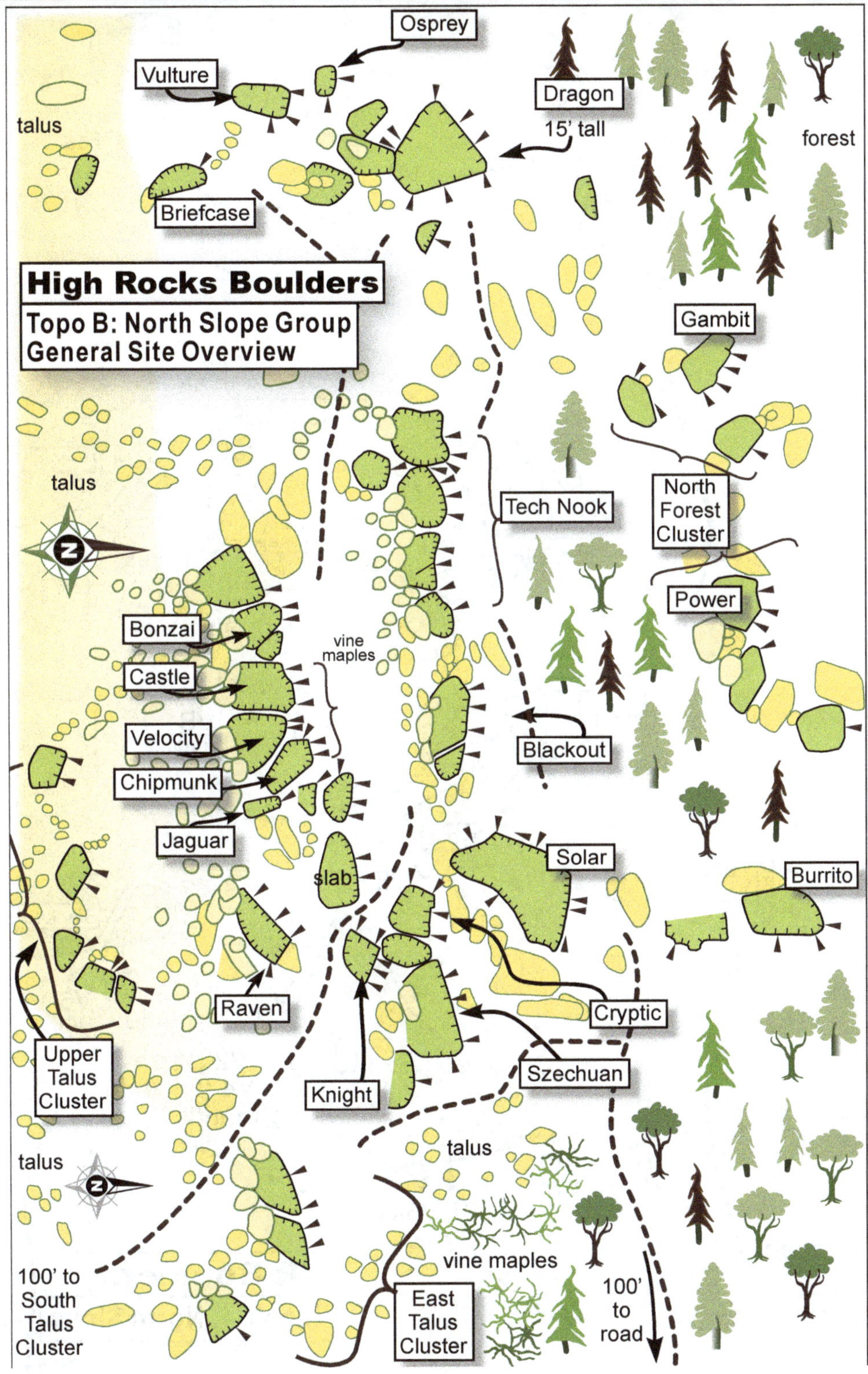
Osprey
Vulture
Briefcase
Dragon
15' tall
forest
talus
High Rocks Boulders
Topo B: North Slope Group
General Site Overview
Gambit
talus
Bonzai
Castle
Velocity
Chipmunk
Jaguar
vine maples
Tech Nook
North Forest Cluster
Power
Blackout
slab
Solar
Burrito
Raven
Cryptic
Upper Talus Cluster
Szechuan
Knight
100' to South Talus Cluster
talus
talus
vine maples
East Talus Cluster
100' to road

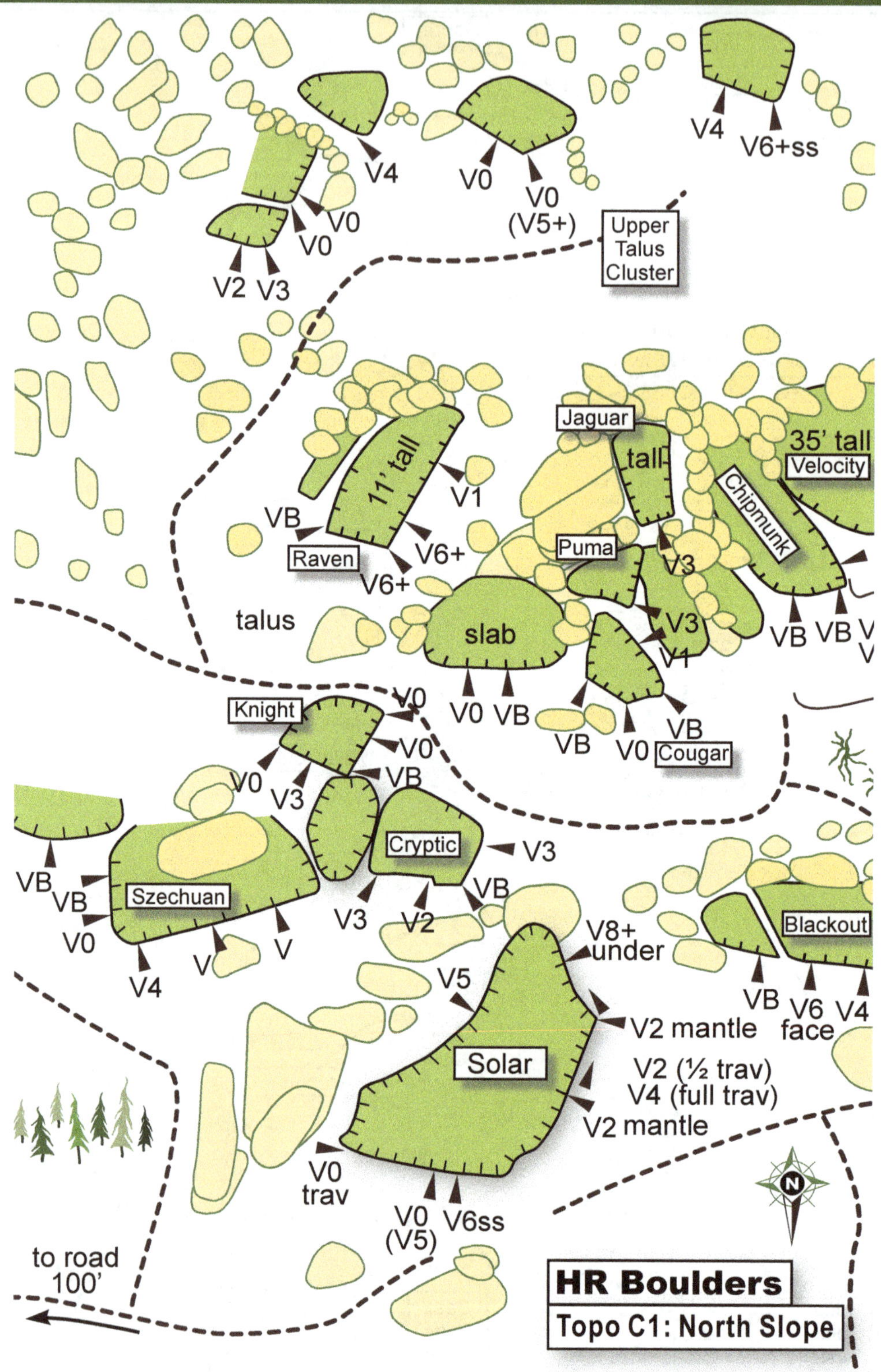
V4
V6+ss
V4
V0
V0
(V5+)
V0
V0
V0
V2 V3
Upper
Talus
Cluster
Jaguar
35' tall
Velocity
tall
11' tall
V1
Chipmunk
VB
Puma
V3
Raven
V6+
V3
V6+
V1
talus
slab
V3
V0 VB
VB VB V
V
V0
VB
V0
Knight
V0
Cougar
V0
VB
V3
VB
Cryptic
V3
VB VB
V3 V2
Szechuan
VB
V8+
under
Blackout
V0
V V
V5
VB V6 V4
V4
Solar
face
V2 mantle
V2 (½ trav)
V4 (full trav)
V2 mantle
V0
trav
V0
(V5)
V6ss
N
HR Boulders
Topo C1: North Slope
to road
100'

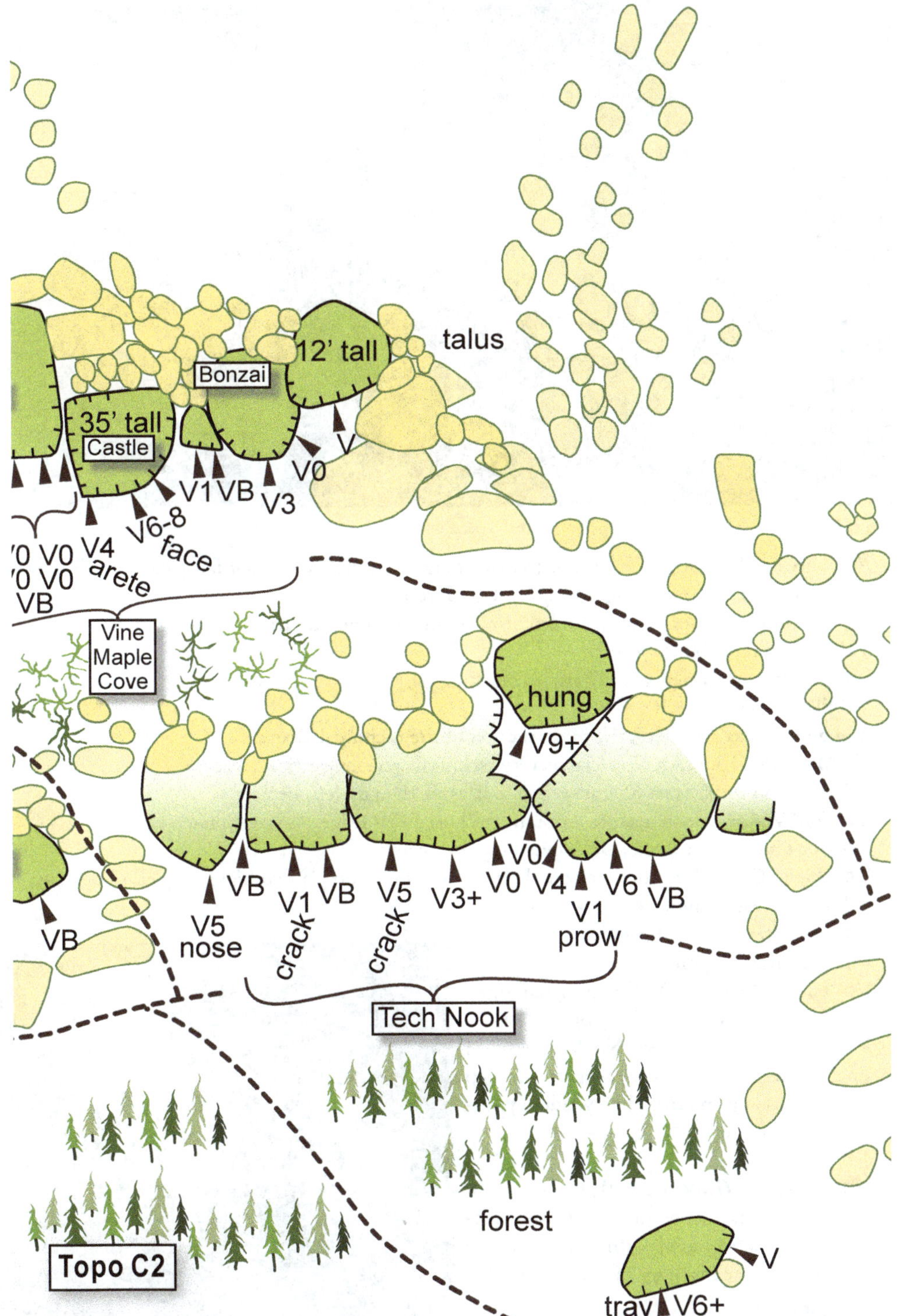

talus
12' tall
Bonzai
35' tall
Castle
V
V0
V1 VB V3
V6-8 face
V0 V0 V4 arete
V0 V0
VB
Vine Maple Cove
hung
V9+
VB
V5 nose
VB
V1 crack
VB
V5 crack
V3+
V0
V0 V4 V6 VB
V1 prow
Tech Nook
forest
Topo C2
V
trav V6+

Tech Nook

A quality north facing nook with fir trees shading the stones, keeping it fairly cool on a hot day. Most of the routes are overhung (about 5°). Beta L to R.

V5 Thermodynamics (short rounded prow on single stone). It's the 2nd Law.

VB Banana Republic (corner).

V1ss Know your Enemy (brief angled crack).

VB SkulQuackery (minor steps).

....**and on the next boulders, the main section of the technical alcove:**

V5 Magnum Opus. An ultra-classic very technical crack on vertical face.

V4 (?) Muon Flux. Start on undercling to flat rail, then up left. Project.

V0 Cold Water. Fun run using foot ramp to horizontal ledge, and continue.

V0 Don't mess with Texas. Deep overhung slot corner.

V4 Magna Carta. Start on horizontal crimps and move up via two highly angled sloped small rails one for each hand.

V1 Magister Dixit. Rounded prow nose with plentiful sidepulls.

V6 Patria Nostra. Overhung flared open book corner with powerful top out.

V7+ ____. Above the Tech Nook fat slot is a single stone (overhung north aspect with deep pit). A hidden gem crimp line yielding probable V7+ss project.

Upper Talus (Level Two)

Extensive string of boulders. This tour captures all the beta beginning with a minor cluster of stones on the far east edge of the talus field.

Eastmost Cluster

High Rocks Boulders

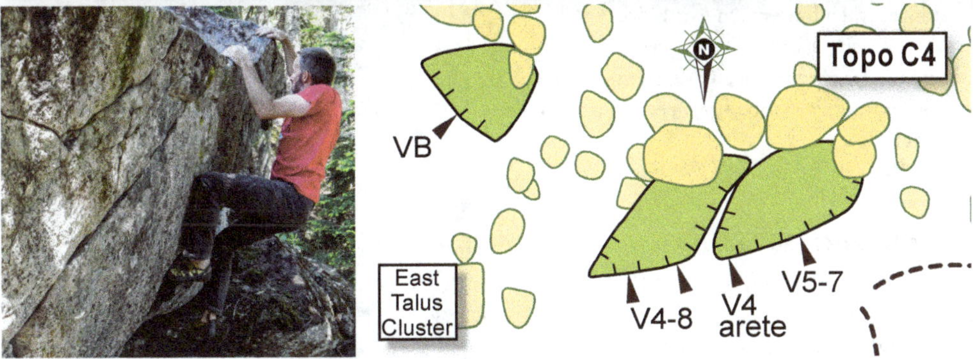

Eastmost Cluster (two main units) all short options. Beta L to R. **Stone #1:** **VB** (isolated slab block), **Stone #2: V4-8ss** (hung beast), **Stone #3** (rightmost): **V4ss Crash of Rhinos** (short leaning arête), **V5-7ss Till the Rivets Began to Pop** (flat face) project.

Raven Boulder

VB The Raven is the easy jug run up out of a slot up the east side.
V6+ (?) M-Direct. Overhung power line on north side merging right (project).
V6 (?) Masterpiece. Hung power line with crimps and dyno to lip (project).
V1ss Impish Imbroglio. Fun hung jugs line.

Minor Moss Slab

VB (Rambunctious Sister), and V0 (Pork Barrel). Several minor slab lines.

Cougar Boulder

VB Guns & Butter. Left side, tall with small crimps/slopers.
V0 Mood Music. Center up right.
VB Sweet Bippy. The rib on right.
V1ss Mala Fide. Short face in a tight slot.

Puma Boulder

V3 Undoing. A hung ships prow with exhuberant moves getting it all done.

Jaguar Boulder ⛰

V3 Rare Earth. Superb quality flat face utilizing the left palmy arête.

Vine Maple Alcove

This cove is wrapped by colorful vine maple shrubs (with naturally flat landings).

Chipmunk Boulder

VB Udder Madness. Smears and crimps on left outer face.
VB Chipmunk is the prow like a ladder.
V0 Razzle-dazzle. Start at the prow, but traverse right on face then up.

Velocity Boulder (30' tall) ⚠

V0 Unlimit. Left face on crimps (long reach), mid-way

High Rocks Boulders

stance, and a long reach exit hold.

V0 Velocity. Right face on crimps, catch large soft hold on right near OW, then long reach to crimps, midway sloped stance, and odd finalé at final bulge.

VB Ragged Edge. Fat OW between both major stones.

Castle Boulder (30' tall) ⚠

One of the best boulders at HRB, but no free lunch on this one baby.

V4 Light Years. Superb slightly hung prow for 15' (crux), then delicate smears 15' to top.

V6-7 (?) definitely a trademark line on right face (project).

V6-7 (?) another stunning power line (project). Between Castle Boulder and Bonzai Boulder is a minor brief tiny unit. **V1 Oxymoronosis** (left), and **VB Mud to the Gunwales** (right).

Bonzai Boulder

V3 Little Bonzai. Left face angling up right on minute crimps, merge into next line.

V0 Bonzai. Standard crimp line on the right reaching up left catching a hold at bonzai tree.

V_ ___ Future hung face on next boulder.

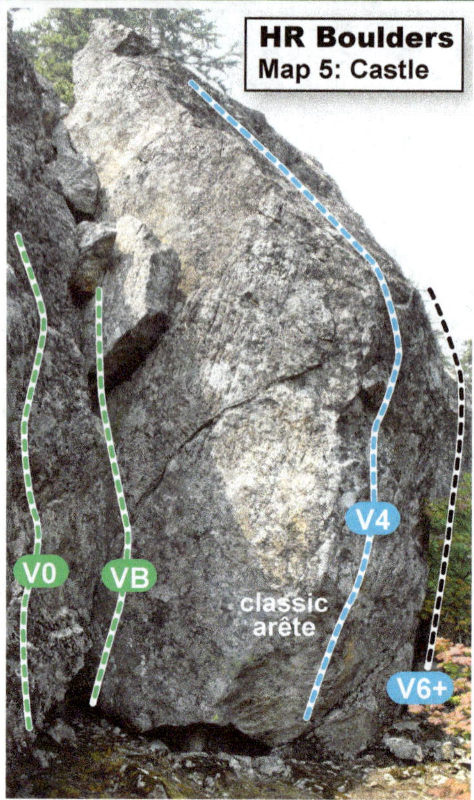

Uppermost Talus Cluster (Level Three)

This is a string of five boulders located on the uppermost portion of the north slope talus field, all with short problems that provide enticing quality. Beta L to R, beginning on the lowest leftmost stone, ending with the highest stone on the right.

Stone A (leftmost): **V2 Sunburst of Perception.** Center flat face, exiting up left, **V3 Semantic Leap.** Starts same as previous, moves right and up round nose.
Stone B: V0ss Echo Chamber. Traverse right and over lip

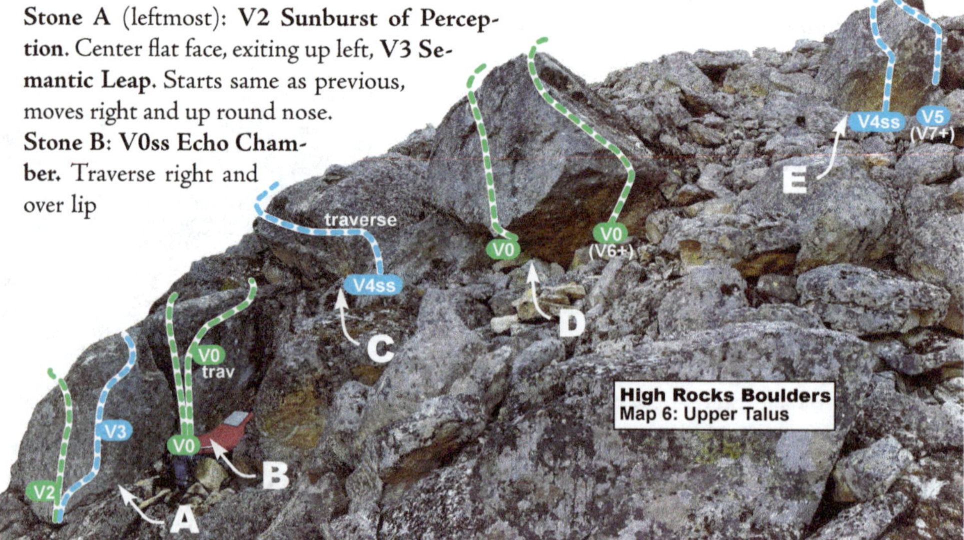

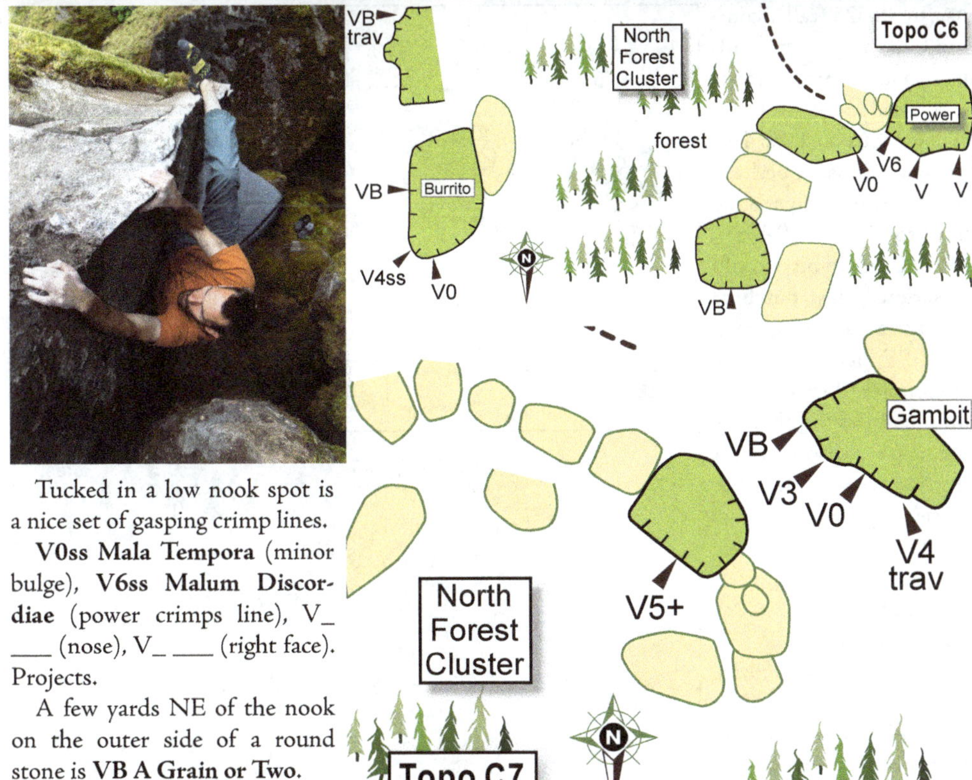

Tucked in a low nook spot is a nice set of gasping crimp lines.

V0ss Mala Tempora (minor bulge), **V6ss Malum Discordiae** (power crimps line), **V_ ___** (nose), **V_ ___** (right face). Projects.

A few yards NE of the nook on the outer side of a round stone is **VB A Grain or Two.**

Gambit Boulder

Subtly deceptive problems on a minor stone aspect. Palm-fest stuff. Beta L to R.

VBss Dumpster Divin' (basic on left).

V3ss Brobdingnagian Contrivance. Open pinch left hand, and go up short nose.

V0ss Granolahead (mantle).

V4ss Gambit. Punchy traverse from right to left.

Empyrean Boulder

Minor stone (not shown in diagram) just 12' south of Gamit Boulder.

V4ss (?) Empyrean. Full traverse left to right. Project.

V4ss (?) Chiaroscuro Desert Sky. Power undercling, up over. Project.

LEMITI BOULDERS

Mosquitoes in the high country are not bad – they are oppressive! So, if you are into adventure bouldering, you might eventually chalk it onto your list. This minor knoll of boulders has a few nice problems, yet some dubious rock to avoid, and it takes a watchful eye to see the difference here. The approach is a short jaunt from the road in a forest setting with minimal elevation gain (100'). The rock composition is Quaternary basalt (Qb4) breccia, some of it well formed. A variety of about 30 short problems 9'-15' tall (and higher), with a rough surface texture with tiny pockets, intrusive knobs, and scattered translucent ¼" plagioclase crystals in a black matrix. Moss/lichens on north aspects. Crashpads (1-2) recommended. The site is not very appealing.

The West String of boulders (closer to the road) is the better product verging to andesite rock fins (up to 25' tall), composed of a gray groundmass with various tones of embedded crystals and small gaseous pockets. This string comprises perhaps 20 possible problems to tap (short to hi-ball) VB-V6.

Pro/Con: you could get seriously lost out here without a compass, map and GPS; its an obscure backcountry locale, mosquito madness in July-Aug, long snow season, 4,500' elevation, high clearance vehicle suggested. **History:** Various lower V-grade problems at this site initially tapped by Mr O (2012?).

Directions:

From Estacada drive Clackamas River Road (NF 46) to NF 4690 junction. Drive east on paved road NF4690 for 8 miles (turns to gravel) to a T-junction with Skyline Road. South is Olallie Lake. Turn left (north) and drive a very rough road 1.75 miles and park on NF-031. Take a GPS/compass bearing. Hike ESE in a forest for 400' till you encounter the West String of boulders (which is about 200' long). Continue to follow this string eastward for another 400' till you reach a rock knoll. Total distance road to knoll (1000'). **Note:** Oregon Skyline Road is the north-south mainline dirt road from T-Lake to Olallie Lake. GPS UTM 10T 595716 4972691, eleva-

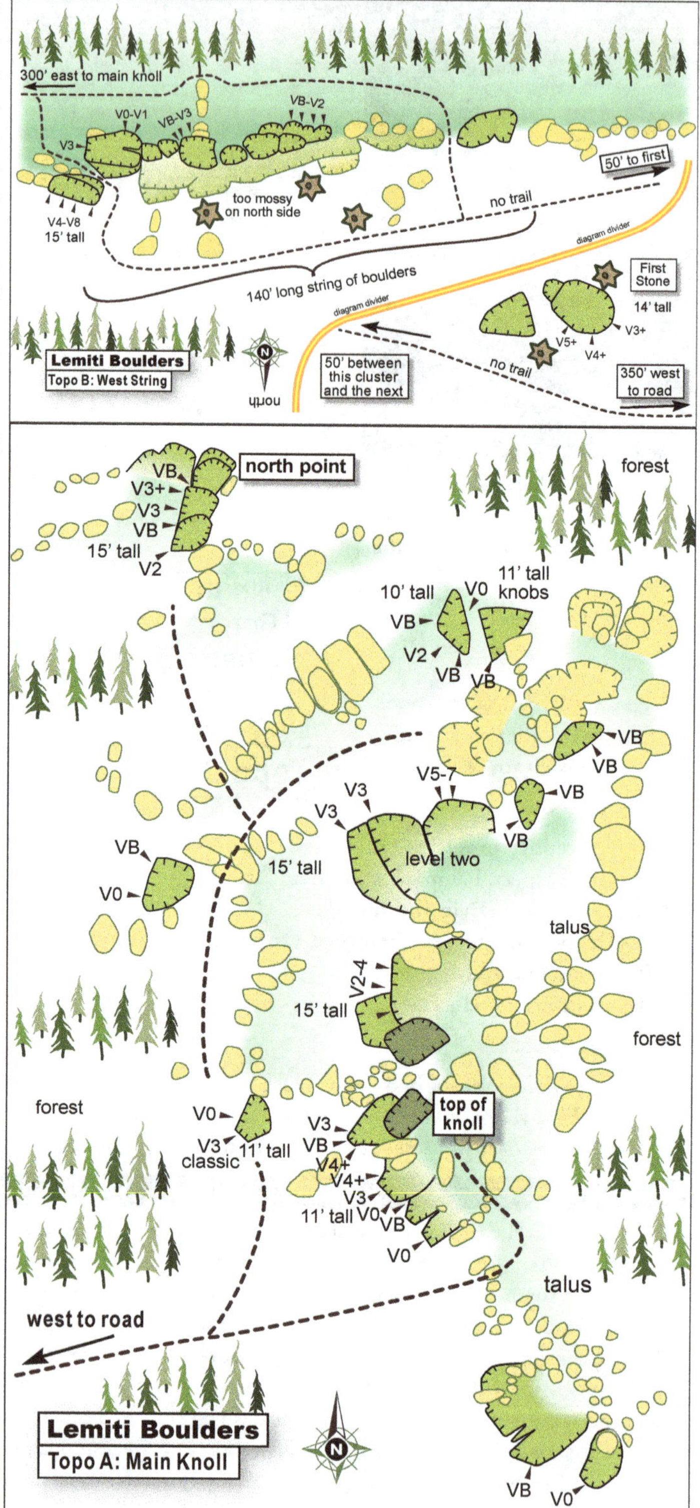

tion 4,480'.

OLALLIE LAKE BOULDERS

A superb scenic region typically favored by fishermen, hikers, or campers, but also ideal for adventurous boulderer's who are enthralled hunting for quality basaltic-andesite outcrops and boulders scattered broadly throughout this zone. Primarily a summer destination, high-altitude area with superb quality bouldering opportunities, where an outing can be combined with an overnight camping trip. Very extensive area originally deposited as lava flows, now visible as short rock bluffs, where numerous large stones tumbled onto broad talus slopes. Stones range in size from 8'-20' diameter. The rock nuances are light grain textural phenocryst matrix qualities great for grip and friction-ability, a rock surface well weathered by the elements, providing ideal on-sight sending conditions for bouldering. The high altitude locale (5,000') eliminates most moss or lichen growth.

Many common bouldering spots are detailed in this section, but the entire region will take many years to fully tap. The area is crisscrossed by hiking trails, while the forest is thinly covered pine and fir tree forest with minimal brush (huckleberry bushes, etc), so off-trail travel is reasonable. If planning to wander further afield take a map, compass, and have some sixth sense GPS familiarity. Climate is variable from breezy, overcast rain, or hot sunny days, and will include the droning sound of a billion mosquitoes in July-August.

Lower Lake Campground and parking site offers a stellar string of huge tumbled blocks in a shaded north-facing aspect that is conducive for sending on hot days.

The Gold Bluff alongside trail #725 is a short 9'-17' tall, extensive south-facing formation with easy access, and a plethora of bouldering options. Beware that numerous lines are easy to start, but often the top-outs define the crux (rounded, down-sloping, spacey top-outs). This is back-country adventure bouldering, and any injury would not be a fast rescue. A 1-2 crashpad minimum recommendation site. Many VB-V4's have been done, while the harder listed V's on the diagrams are hypothetical and could easily be dimensionally harder.

History: This site was extensively tapped by Mr O and Mr A from 2011-2017 sending a wide variety of modest V-grades. Clusters of boulders are plentiful further afield so you likely will find new untapped boulders for many years ahead.

Directions

A long 3-hour drive from Portland. Drive Hwy 224 through Estacada, then continue on NF 46 to the junction of NF 4690, then drive this east to the junction with NF 4220 (Skyline Road), then go south 5 miles (rough gravel road) to Olallie Lake. A small general store at the lake offers some amenities, and there are quality camping, cabins (check their website), and yurt rentals available, too. Road access to the lake begins on July 20th, and is open until the late-Fall season when fresh snowfall blocks access.

GPS UTM 10T 595304 4962792, elevation 5,054' (at Gold Bluff Boulders).
GPS UTM 10T 595091 4963962, elevation 4,840' (at Camp Boulder).

LOWER CAMPGROUND

Camp Boulder

The Camp Boulder (11' tall) is 50' south of the the camping area in talus field #1. Beta L to R: **VBss Foo** (basic jugs on east face), **V4ss Camp Classic** (north face crimps to lip), and **V4ss Fine Wine** (crimps on right over lip). This stone cluster is located in the first talus field and tends to stay cooler. Other possible minor SS boulder problems exist on nearby blocks.

From Camp Boulder (talus field #1) walk westward 100' to reach talus field #2. Two blocks on the left talus offer VB-V3 (all done). A short vertical 15' tall bluff with two fun jug lines (**VB Life's Journey, VB No Other Way**) ⌒⌒ exist on the left prow, and a V4+(?) ⌒⌒ super hung powerline

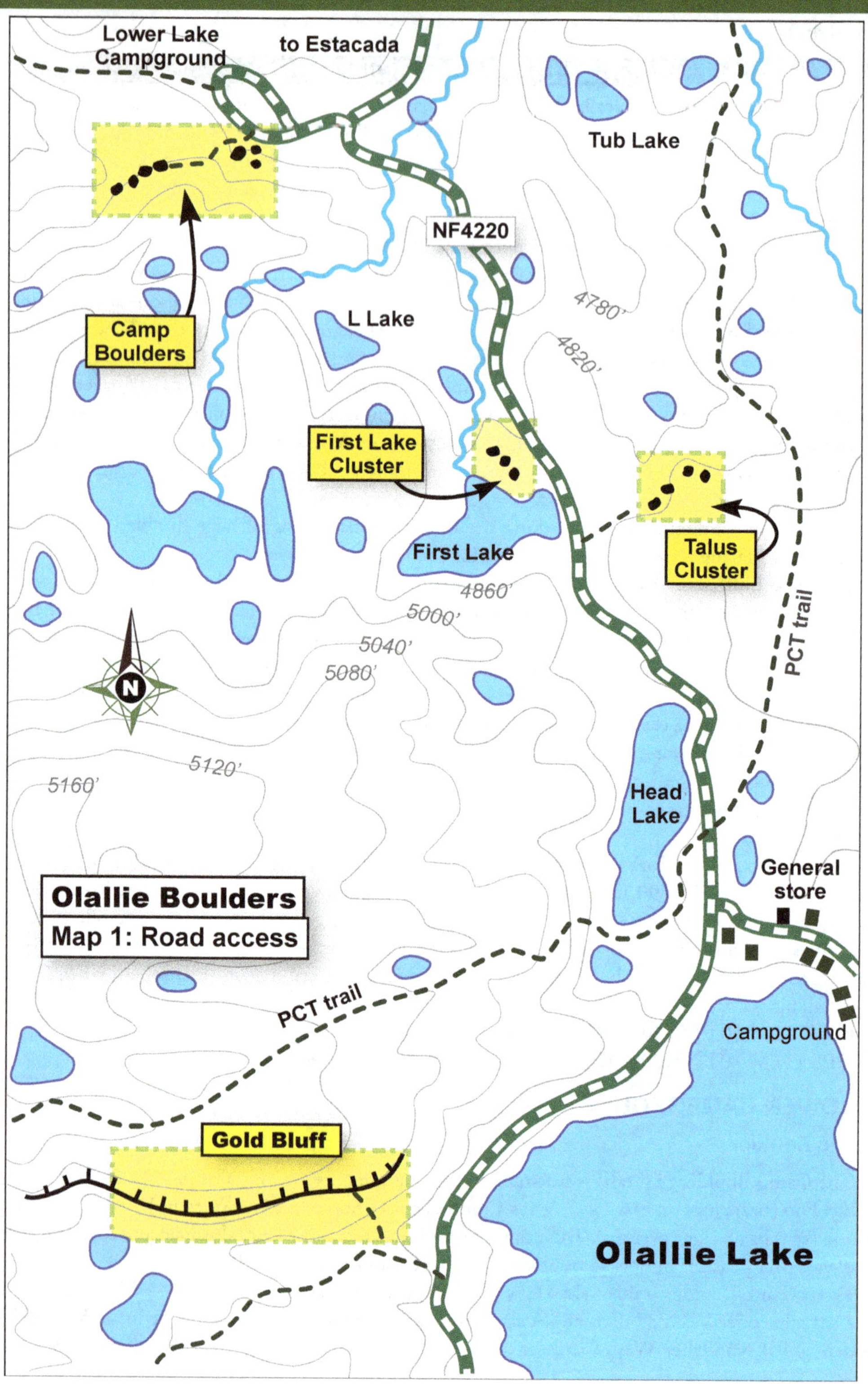
Lower Lake
Campground
to Estacada
Tub Lake
NF4220
4780'
4820'
Camp
Boulders
L Lake
First Lake
Cluster
Talus
Cluster
First Lake
4860'
5000'
5040'
5080'
PCT trail
N
5120'
5160'
Head
Lake
General
store
Olallie Boulders
Map 1: Road access
PCT trail
Campground
Gold Bluff
Olallie Lake

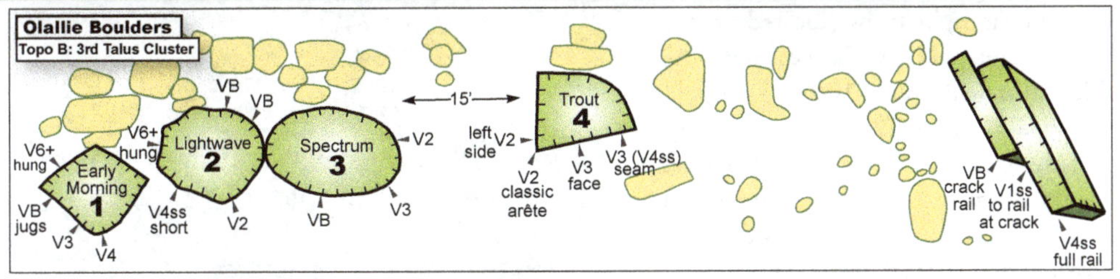
Olallie Boulders
Topo B: 3rd Talus Cluster
VB
VB
VB
V6+
hung
V6+
hung
Lightwave
2
Spectrum
3
V2
left
side
V2
Trout
4
V3 (V4ss)
seam
Early
Morning
1
VB
jugs
V4ss
short
V2
V2
V3
V2
classic
arête
V3
face
VB
V3
V4
VB
V3
VB
crack
rail
V1ss
to rail
at crack
V4ss
full rail

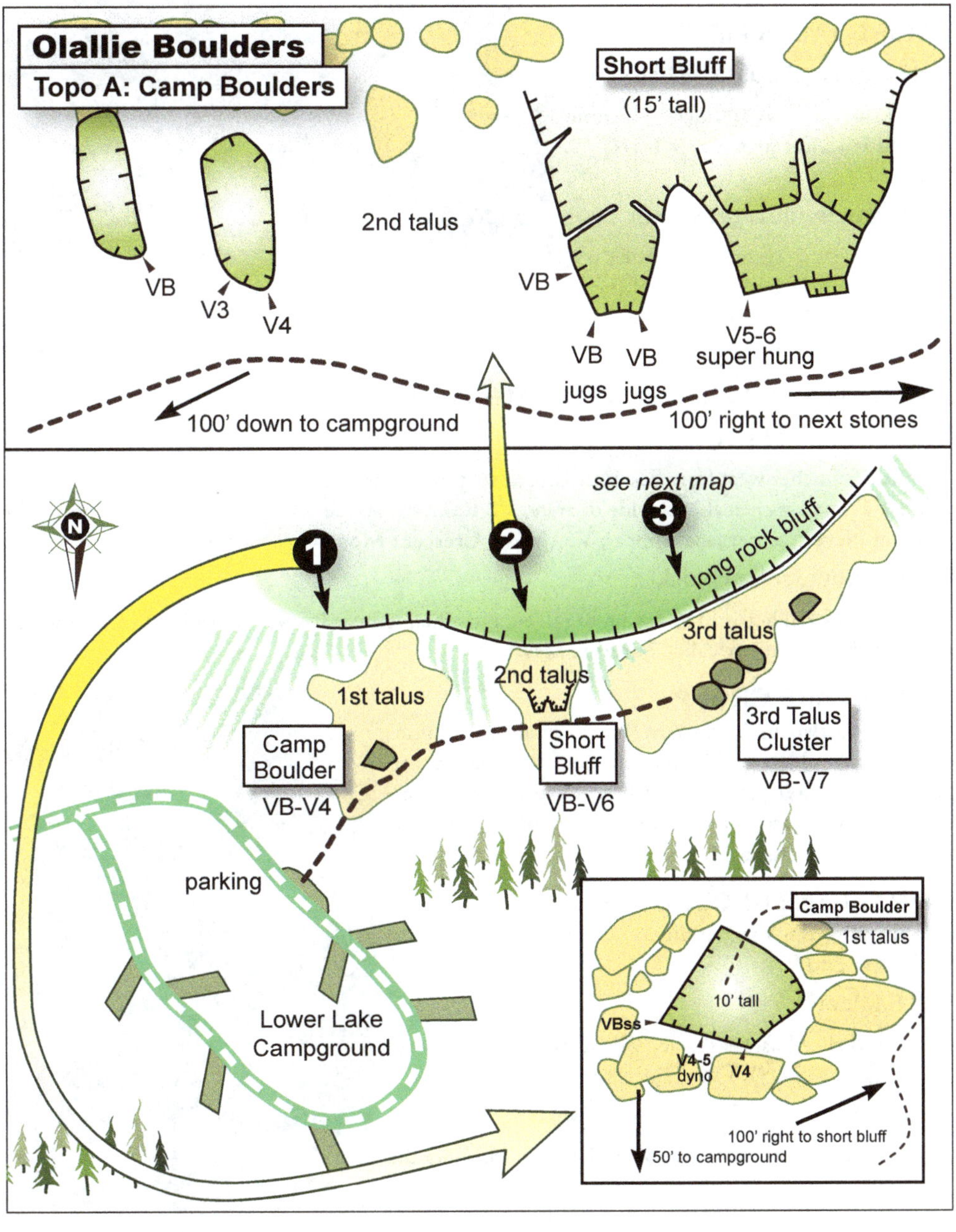

Olallie Boulders
Topo A: Camp Boulders

Short Bluff
(15' tall)

2nd talus

VB

VB
V3
V4

VB

VB
jugs
VB
jugs
V5-6
super hung

100' down to campground
100' right to next stones

N

see next map
3
long rock bluff

1
2
3

3rd talus

2nd talus

1st talus

Camp
Boulder
VB-V4

Short
Bluff
VB-V6

3rd Talus
Cluster
VB-V7

parking

Lower Lake
Campground

Camp Boulder
1st talus

10' tall

VBss

V4-5
dyno
V4

100' right to short bluff
50' to campground

exist on the right prow (located on the second talus field). Walk west onto the third talus field, and in 100' you will find four quality stones, and a rail-*ish* thuggish thingamabob boulder further west on the same talus. There are several superb classic lines here. VB-V6ss, and possibly harder stuff. Most landings are feasible with 1-2 crashpads.

Olallie Boulders
Map 4: Trout Block

THIRD TALUS FIELD

Early Morning Boulder (#1 stone)

V6+ss (?) __, **VB Early Morning Light** is a short jugs run. V3ss (?) __. V4ss (?) __.

Lightwave Boulder (#2 stone)

V6+ss (?) __ hung face, **V4ss** __ hung face, **V2 Polished Jewel** (face), VBss face, VBss face.

Spectrum Boulder (#3 stone)

VB Dogbite, V3 Pole of Cold, V2 Blue Monsoon (face).

Trout Boulder (#4 stone)

Walk 15' further west from Spectrum Stone to Trout Boulder.
V2ss Trout uses just the left side of arête, **V2 Rainbow Arête** is the classic left sharp prow, **V3 Never Never** (center face crimps), **V3 (V4ss) Crescent Moon** (right seam).

Paradox Boulder (rail block)

VBss crack rail leftward, **V1ss** up to rail at crack then leftward, **V4ss (Paradox Lies)** is the full rail from the toe. All are called **Paradox Lies**.

FIRST LAKE GROUP

There are two main clusters (and several other minor clusters) of boulders in this area. The beta describes the minor **Knoll Cluster** just north of First Lake, and the **Armstrong Cluster** east of the gravel road wrapping along the north edge of a talus field.

FIRST LAKE KNOLL CLUSTER

Walk 50' from the parking spot northwest to a rock knoll. Beta L to R.

Slab Boulder

VB Red Bird basic east slab, **V0 Universal Law** (center east slab), **V2ss** (?), **V2ss** (?).

The Knoll

Knoll starting on left wrapping rightward around the

rock knoll.

V3 Technorati is hung classic face with mantle. **V3 Noble Cause** is classic crimps on next block. **VB Boorish** minor face.

Seam Boulder (split by a thin seam)

V5ss (?) left of seam, **V4ss** (?) seam, **V0ss Atavistic Taboo** (at point). **VB Thumbscrews** (left-right prow either way). **V0ss Crime of the Century** (slot). **VB Political Pandemonium** (it's a pocket line on a minor point on west side).

Circuit Boulder

A minor low flat topped boulder just north of knoll.

V0ss Circuit (low from pit), **VBss Gluton** (at point), **VBss Free Cocaine** (west side), **V0ss Antihistory** (north nose), **V2ss Two2Much** (NE aspect), **VBss Rabbit Hole** (east side).

ARMSTRONG CLUSTER

Five primary boulders worth delving upon. A short hike on the other side of a knoll just east of the gravel road. Go Lance!

Boulder A: **V0ss Illusion, V0ss Delusion.** Two minor face lines.

Boulder B: **V0ss Boorish** minor.

Boulder C: **V3 Going Contrary** (right face), **V2 Fantasy** (the nose), **V0 Dysfunction** (crack on left).

Armstrong Boulder (D): **V3ss Dynasty** , **V0ss Donkey Sweat**, **V5+** (?) **Fine Wine** just right

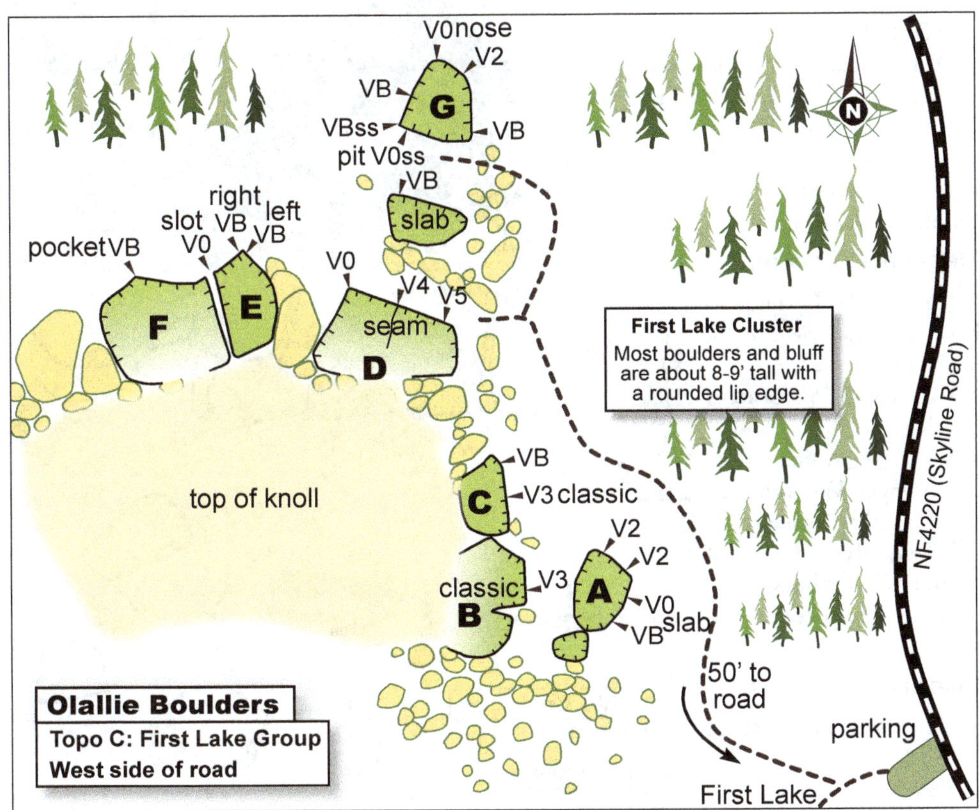

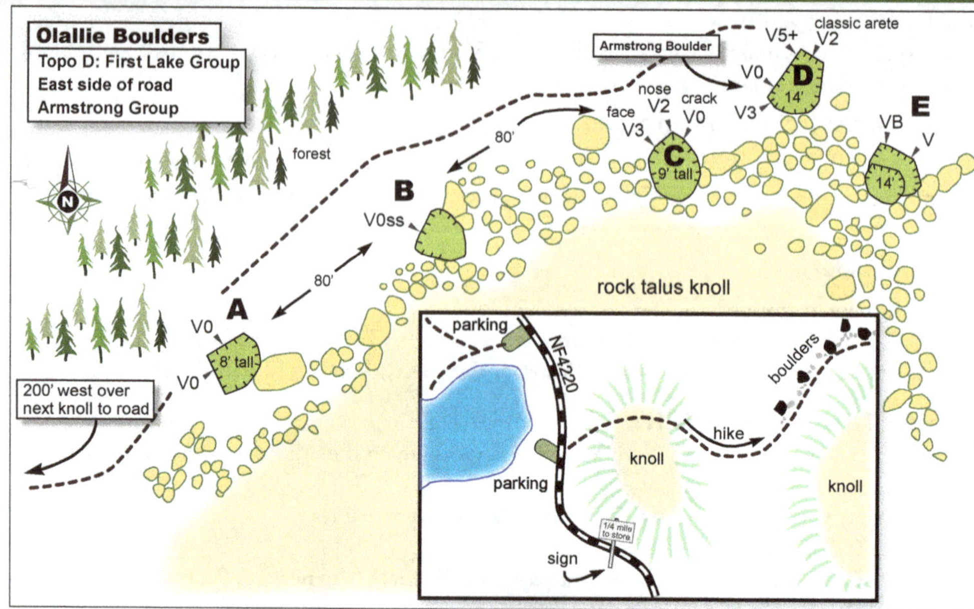

of point (project), **V2 Mind Mist** (cool long
smear slab transitioning to right and up rib).

Boulder E: minor dubious stuff.

GOLD BLUFF

Olallie Gold Bluff begins near the road
at trail #725, and culminates at the Aspen
Block (see diagram for beta). Three minor
approach boulders with VB-V2 (ss) are usually bypassed for the better quality lines on
the bluff.

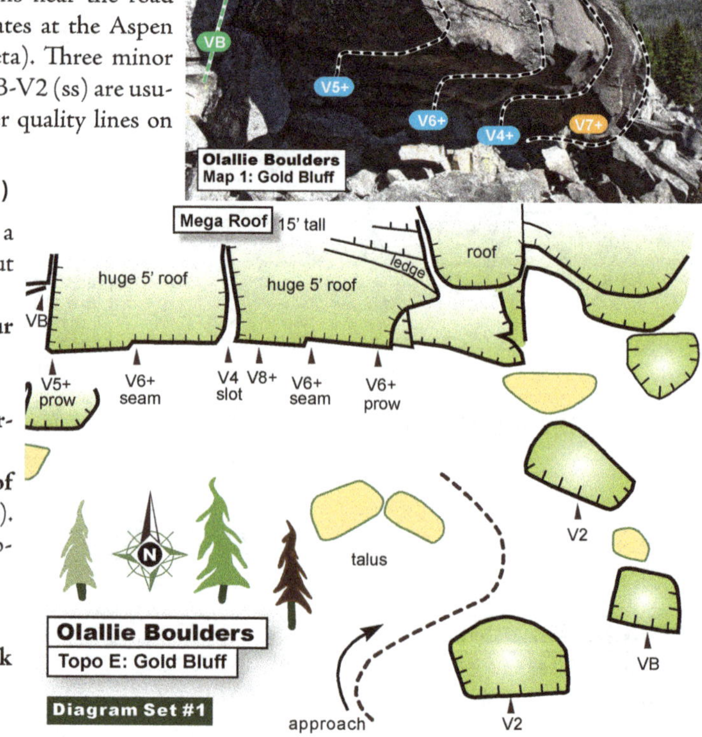

Mega Roof (Diagram #1)

V4 to **V7+** (?) under a
huge roof (can yield about
5-6 problems) ⋀⋀.

VB Agent Provocateur
(fat slot).

V5 (?) ___ seam.

**VB Foggy Vaporous Ar-
senal** (another fat slot)

**V3+ss Red Barrel of
Monkeys** (short hung nose).

To the left is a descent op-
tion.

Gold Face (Diagram #2)

V2 Blankety Blank
(crack).

V5 (?) ___ seam.

V2 Olallie Jam Meister (cool jam crack).

Diagram set #3

VB Snowflakes (basic 2" jam crack).

V3 Unalienable Right (tips seam).

VB Scapegoat (minor step corner).

V1 Olallie Jollie (thin seam).

V4 Olallie Gold (face only).

VB Spookfest (minor step corner).

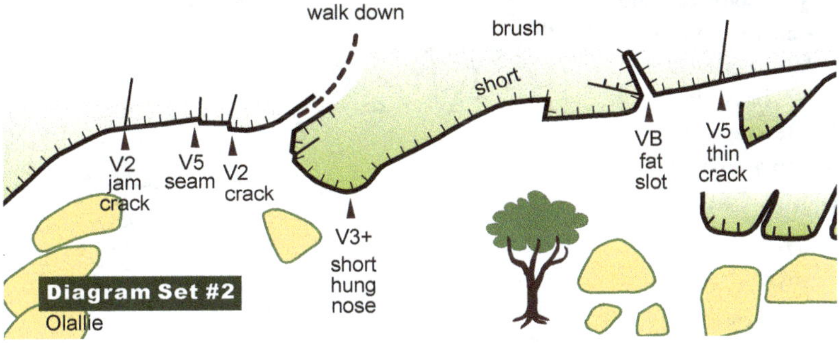

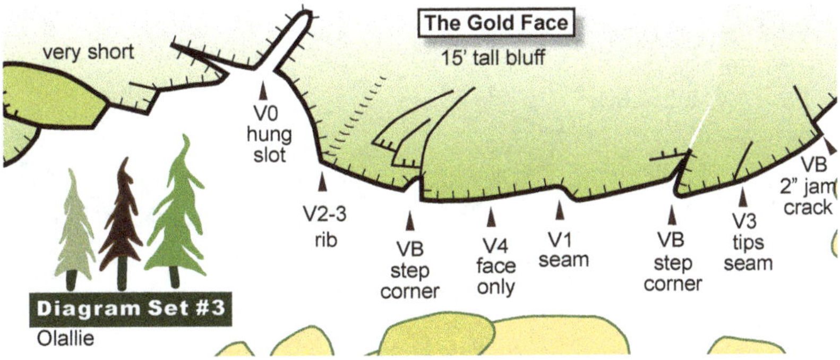

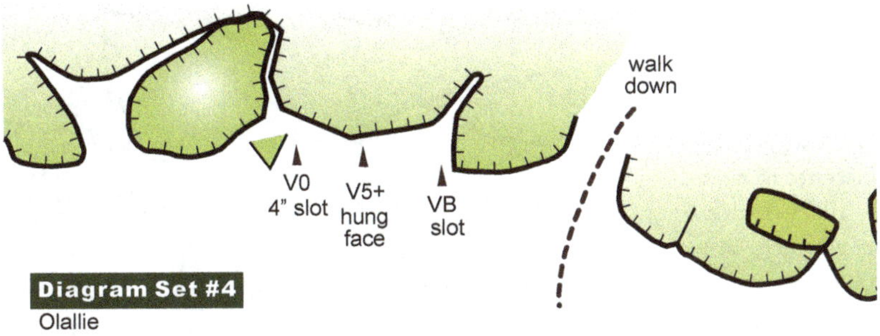

V2 Axe-Grinding (vertical rib).

V0 Nyet on your Life (hung fat slot).

Walk west a short distance to next...

Diagram #4

VB basic slot.

V5+ (?) hung face.

V0 Thorn of Conscience (a 4" slot).

Walk west a short distance to next...

Diagram #5

V1 Loot & Conquest face prow.

V0 basic fat slot.

VB basic slab.

Walk west a short distance to next...

Diagram #6

VB basic slot.

V0 Negative Falsehood (face).

VB Useful Idiots (a 4" fat crack).

V2-3 Head Fake (seam on face).

V4 Inkstain (arête).

Walk west a short distance to next...

Double Stack Boulders (Diagram #7)

VB Double Trouble (up over both stones).

VB Double Vision (face to left of doubler).

Walk west a short distance to next...

VB basic slab crack.

V3 ___ face on a nose.

V0 ___ vertical

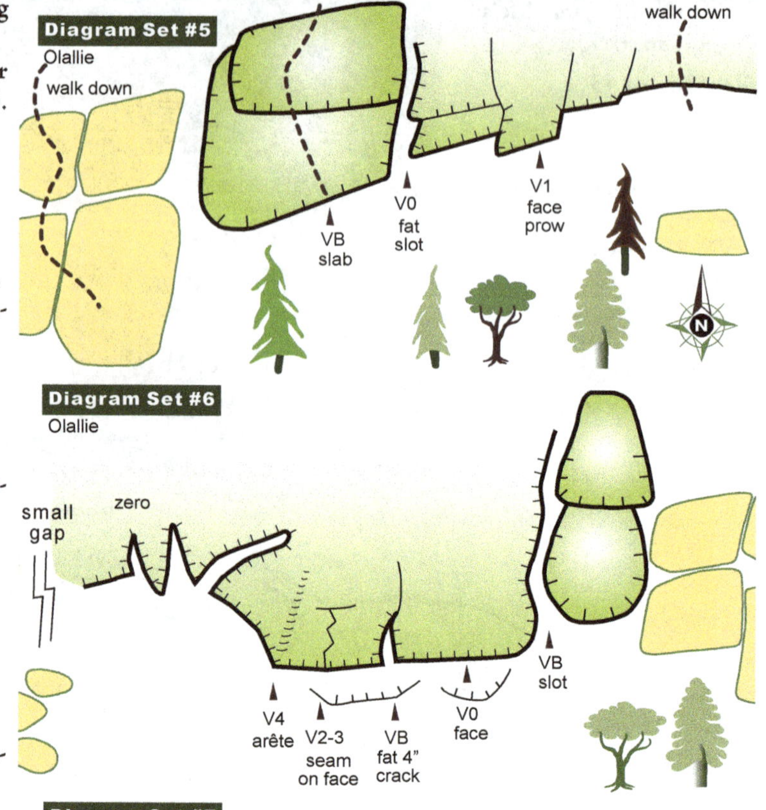

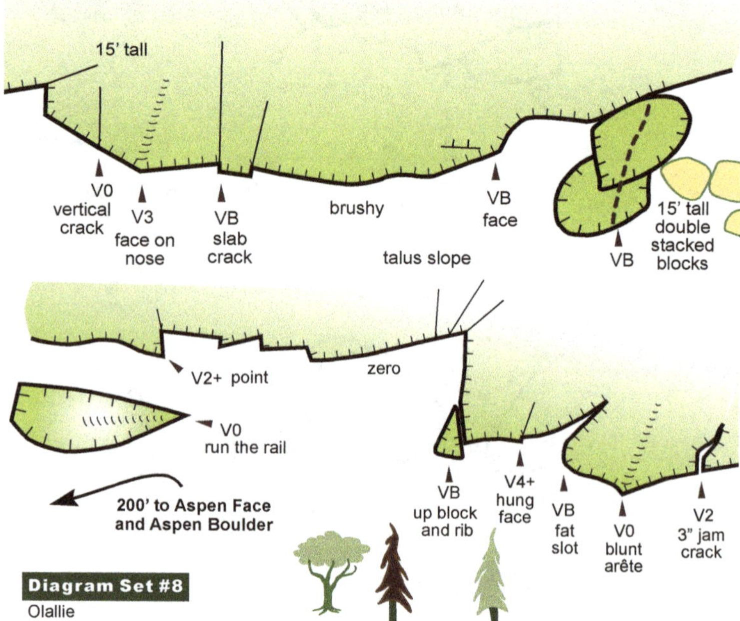

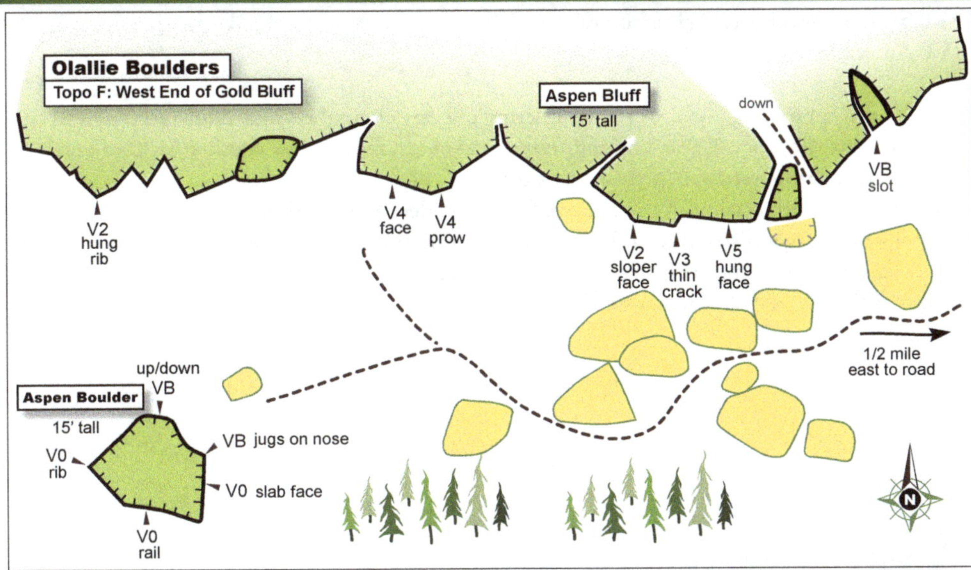

crack.

Diagram #8 ⌃⌃

V2 ____ a 3" jam crack.

V0 ____ a blunt arête.

VB basic fat slot.

V4+ (?) hung face.

VB a cruise up juggy holds on a block and rib.

Walk west a short distance to next...

Rail Block (Diagram #8)

V0 **The Rail** run on uphill side of block.

V2+ss ____ point on main bluff next to the Rail Block.

Walk 200′ westward to the Aspen Face and Aspen Boulder.

Aspen Face ⌃⌃

VB ____ slot
descent from bluff top.

V5 (?) ____ hung face.

V3 (?) ____ hung thin crack.

V2 (?) ____ sloper face.

Walk west a short distance to...

V4 (?) ____ prow.

V4 (?) ____ face.

Just 50′ downhill distance is the last boulder...

Aspen Boulder

VB **Bondage** (north descent).

VB **Sundial** (jugs on NE nose).

V0 **American Exceptionalism** (east slab face).

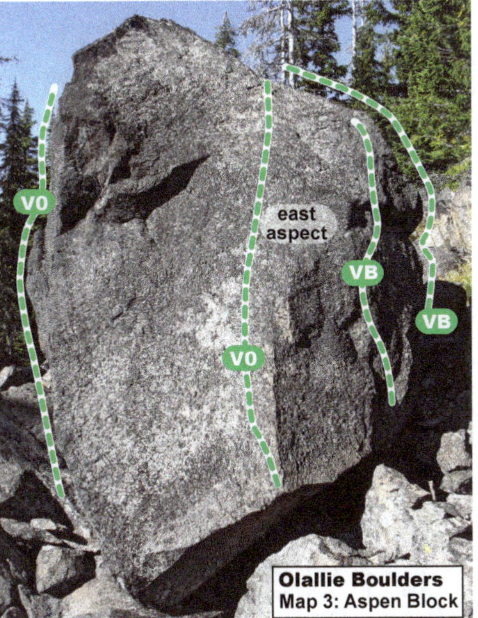

V0 Scaremongering (classic south rail).
V0 Autobahn (west rib).

This is the approximate end of the bouldering options along the Gold Bluff formation in this particular zone (its first 1000'). A brief forested gap is next, followed by another 2500' of potential futuristic bouldering outcrops further westward.

Due to the superb quality of the entire Olallie Boulders site certainly additional new boulders and problems will get discovered and tapped in the years ahead. Join the A-team as we continue to explore this fabulous zone. This detailed Olallie Boulders beta section will be expanded in future editions as the new data becomes available.

CENTRAL & SOUTHERN WILLAMETTE AREAS

DRUID STONES (MARYS PEAK)

The Druid Stones at Marys Peak host a quality string of bouldering options on excellent gabbro rock, a rock sill formation found on various summits in the central Oregon Coast range. The best selection is found at two main areas (the Druid Stones area and at Los Tres Nuevos area) near the radio towers on the west summit. The entire bouldering area consists of roughly 90+/- boulder problems (albeit some are very short). Several additional partially explored locales a bit lower down the mountain are New Wave Group, the 3500 Group, and the Pillar Boulders. If only there were more gabbro rock boulders at Marys Peak. The quantity discovered and tapped so far is limited in scope, yet perhaps more will be discovered in the future.

History: Various local groups and individuals (usually from Corvallis) explored portions of the brief pillars and road embankment cuts over a broad span of years, but no primary record remains, except for a few fixed bolts. One important person, Paul Waters (and associates), in recent years made an important contribution by sending and recording the full spectrum of boulder problems. It is due to his special efforts that this site has become a well known Corvallis bouldering site. Some of the popular classics are: **Cobra Commander V1, Pistol Grip V3, Snakecharmer V3ss, Pistol Whipped V3, Tech Nine V4,** and other problems.

Paul at Druid Stones

Directions

Drive west from Corvallis on state U.S. Hwy 20 to Philomath, then at the west end of town, turn southwest on Hwy 34 (a sign says "Marys Peak Recreation Area"). In about 7 miles the road becomes narrow and winds up to the Coast range pass. At the pass turn right onto Marys Peak Road. There is a day use recreation fee within upper portion of the corridor, beyond Connor's Camp (kiosk located there). GPS UTM 10T 454581 4928288, elevation 3,560' (at site).

The summarized beta listed below starts with the presumed boulder name, followed by the lowest and highest V-scale problems found on that particular block (not necessarily inclusive of all SS lines, nor projects), then the total estimated quantity of problems found on that block (shown in brackets). In other words, it's a short arm list,

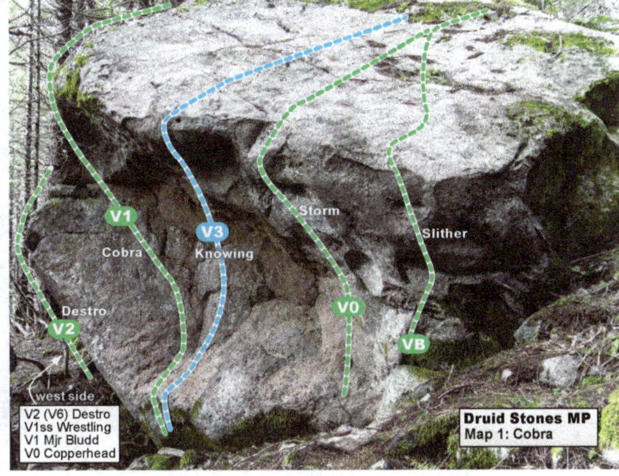

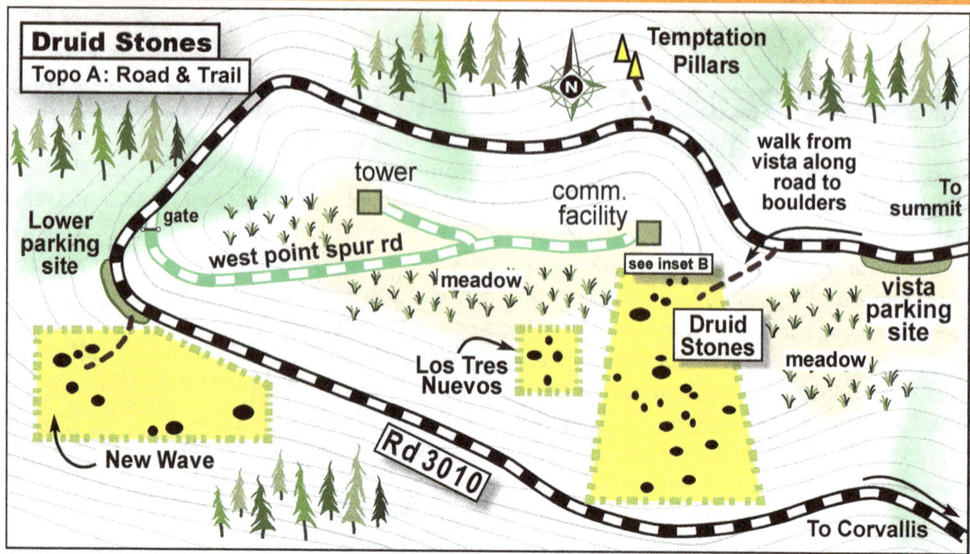

minus the details of each problem. The diagrams though will point you to each specific problem on a particular stone.

Druid Stones area:

1. **Medusa VB** [2 total problems]
2. **Rope de Dope VB-V1** [2 problems]
3. **Sublime VB-V2** [5 problems]
4. **Athena VB-V1** [4 problems]
5. **Cobra Commander V0-V3+** [8 problems]
6. **Norseman V0-V2** [7 problems]

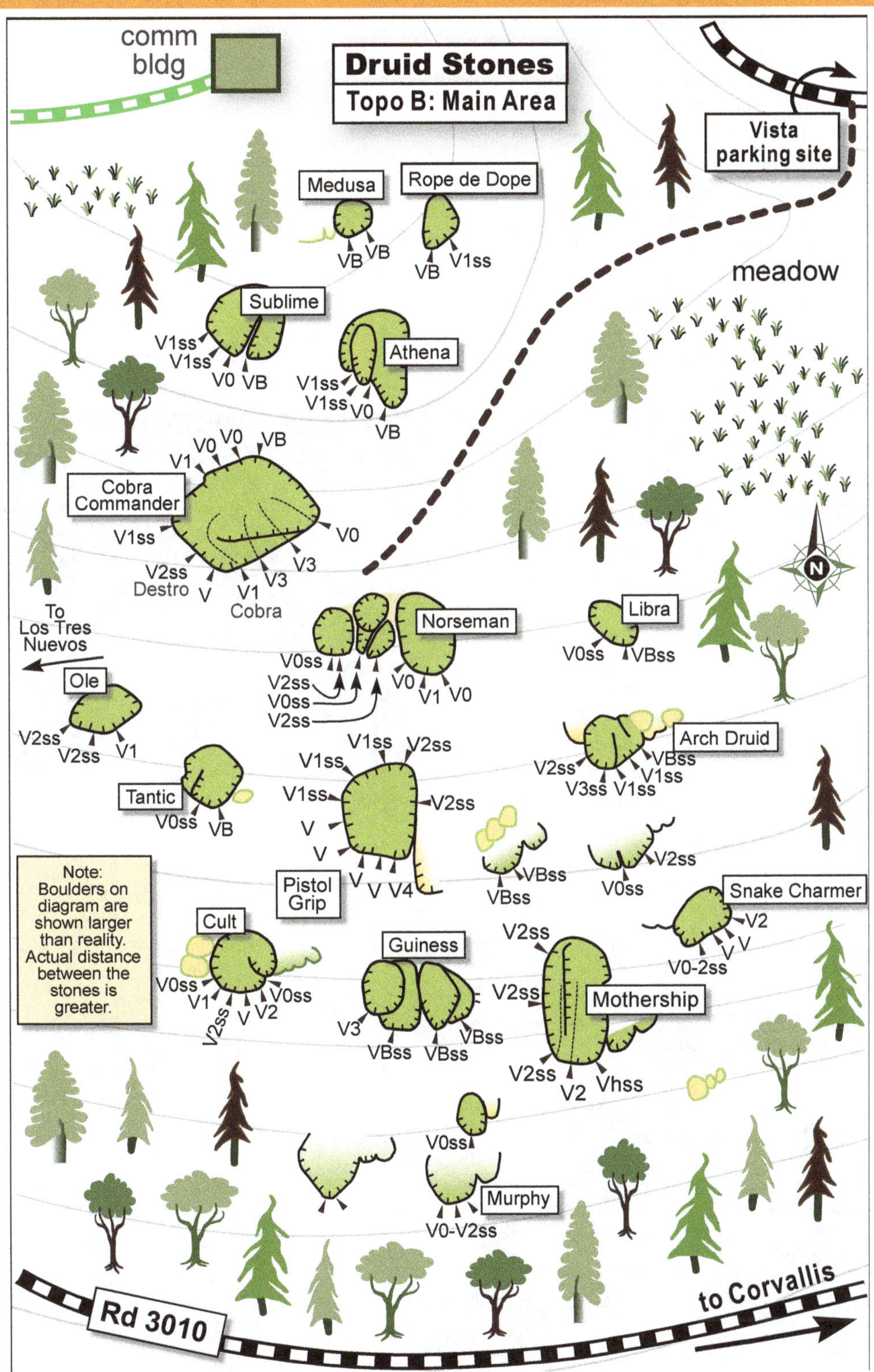
comm bldg
Druid Stones
Topo B: Main Area
Vista parking site
meadow
Medusa
Rope de Dope
VB VB
VB
V1ss
Sublime
V1ss
V1ss
V0 VB
Athena
V1ss
V1ss V0
VB
V0 V0 VB
V1
Cobra Commander
V1ss
V0
V2ss
Destro V
V1
Cobra
V3
V3
Norseman
V0ss
V2ss
V0ss
V2ss
V0
V1 V0
Libra
V0ss VBss
To Los Tres Nuevos
Ole
V2ss
V2ss V1
Arch Druid
V2ss VBss
V3ss V1ss
V1ss V2ss
V1ss
V1ss V2ss
V V2ss
Tantic
V0ss VB
V
V
V V4
Pistol Grip
VBss
VBss
V2ss
V0ss
Snake Charmer
V2
V V
V0-2ss
Note: Boulders on diagram are shown larger than reality. Actual distance between the stones is greater.
Cult
V0ss
V1 V0ss
V2ss V V2
Guiness
V2ss
V2ss
Mothership
V3
VBss
VBss VBss
V2ss Vhss
V2 V2
V0ss
Murphy
V0-V2ss
Rd 3010
to Corvallis
N

7. **Ole V1-V3** [4 problems]
8. **Libra VB-V2** [2 problems]
9. **Arch Druid VB-V3** [5 problems]
10. **Pistol Grip V1-V4** [10 problems]
11. **Tantric VB-V0** [2 problems]
12. **Mountaineer VB** [2 problems]
13. **Snake Charmer V0-V2** [6 problems]
14. **Mothership V1-V2** [4 problems]
15. **Guinness VB-V3** [2 problems]
16. **Cult V0-V2** [6 problems]
17. **Scotch on the Rocks V_(?)**
18. **Flopping Murphy V0-V2** [3 problems]

Los Tres Nuevos area:

19. **Sessions V0-V2** [3 problems]
20. **Anglin Memorial VB-V1** [6 problems]
21. **Japhy Ryder V1-V2** [5 problems]
22. **Cavalier V0-V2** [3 problems]

THE GARDEN BOULDERS

The Garden Boulders near Sweet Home, Oregon, though slightly less popular today, it is still a remarkable concentrated core pack of superb bouldering problems. The beastly size and scope of the boulders at the 'Enchanged Forest' still are utterly impressive even today, and if you reside mid-Willamette valley between Salem and Eugene you are very likely utilizing the place for your quality destination bouldering venue.

General history: the bouldering problems at

Paul W at the Garden Boulders

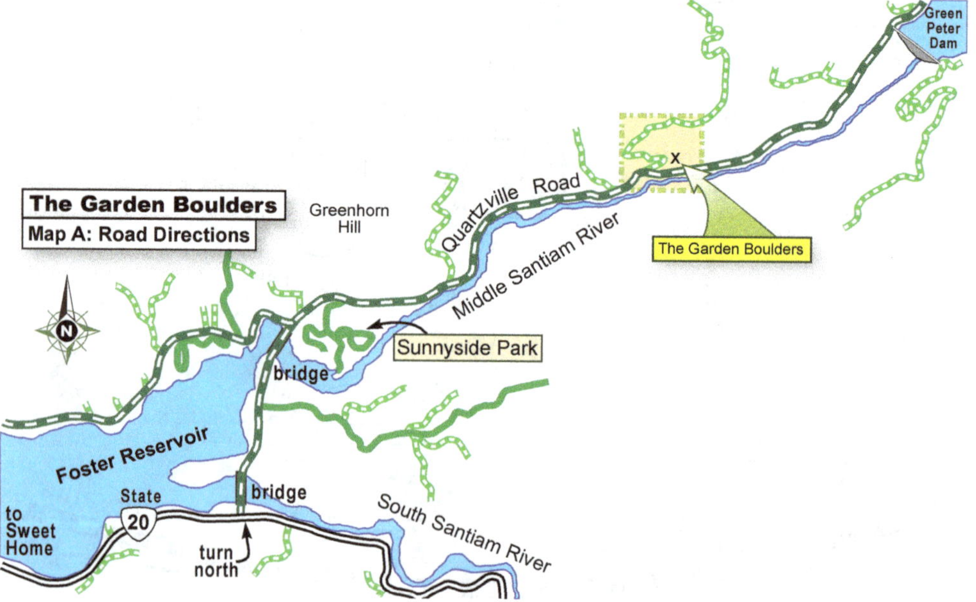

V0
V3
V1
V5
V8
V8
V5+
V5
Garden Boulders
Map 2: South String
Garden Boulders
Map 1: South String
V3
V3
V3
Garden Boulders
Map 3: The Ear
V5+
V8
V5
V4
VB
Garden Boulders
Map 4: Octernal
VB
V2
V4
V
traverse
direct
V3+
V6+
V7/9

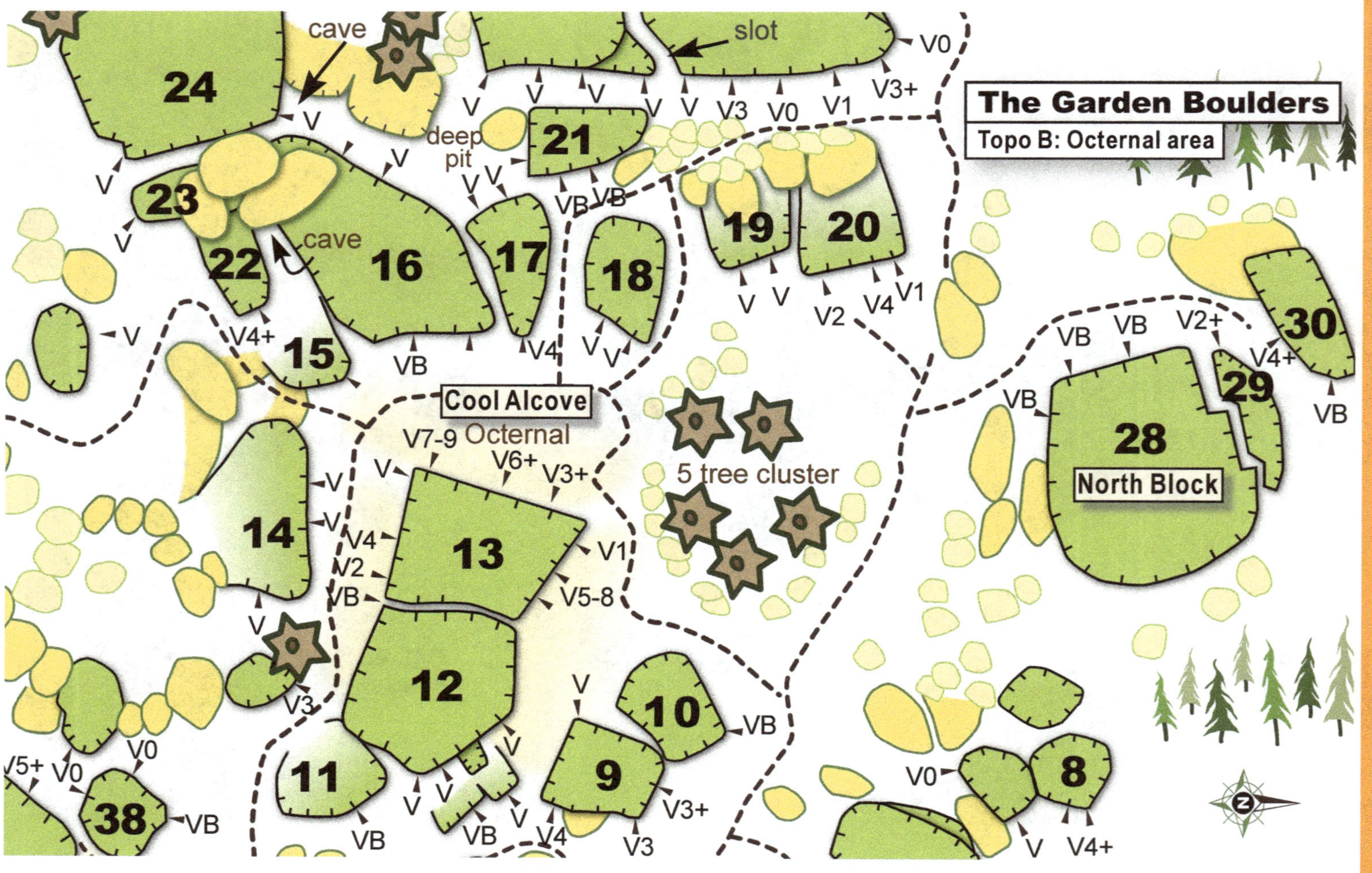

The Garden Boulders
Topo B: Octernal area
cave
slot
deep pit
cave
Cool Alcove
V7-9 Octernal
5 tree cluster
North Block
24
23
22
21
19
20
30
16
17
18
15
14
13
12
11
10
9
8
38
29
28
V0
V3+
V1
V0
V3
V
V
V
V
V4+
VB
VB
VB
VB
V4
V
V
V2
V4
V1
V6+
V3+
V
V4
V2
VB
V1
V5-8
VB
V3
V
V
VB
V4
V3
V3+
V0
V5+
V0
V0
V
V4+
VB
VB
VB
V2+
V4+

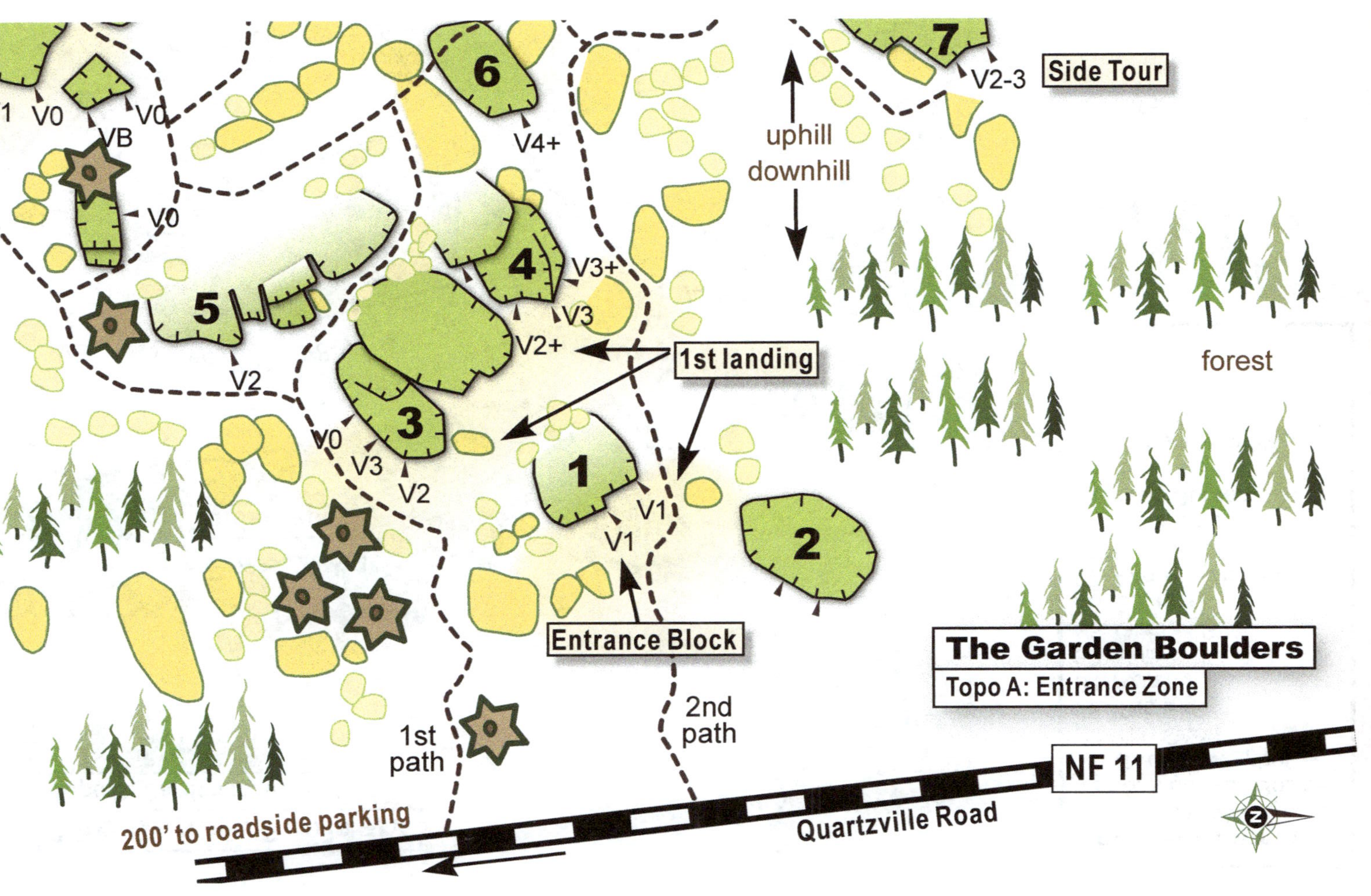
Side Tour
V2-3
uphill
downhill
forest
V1 V0 V0
VB
V0
6
V4+
5
4 V3+
V3
V2
V2+
3
V0
V3
V2
1st landing
1
V1
V1
2
Entrance Block
1st path
2nd path
The Garden Boulders
Topo A: Entrance Zone
200' to roadside parking
Quartzville Road
NF 11
N

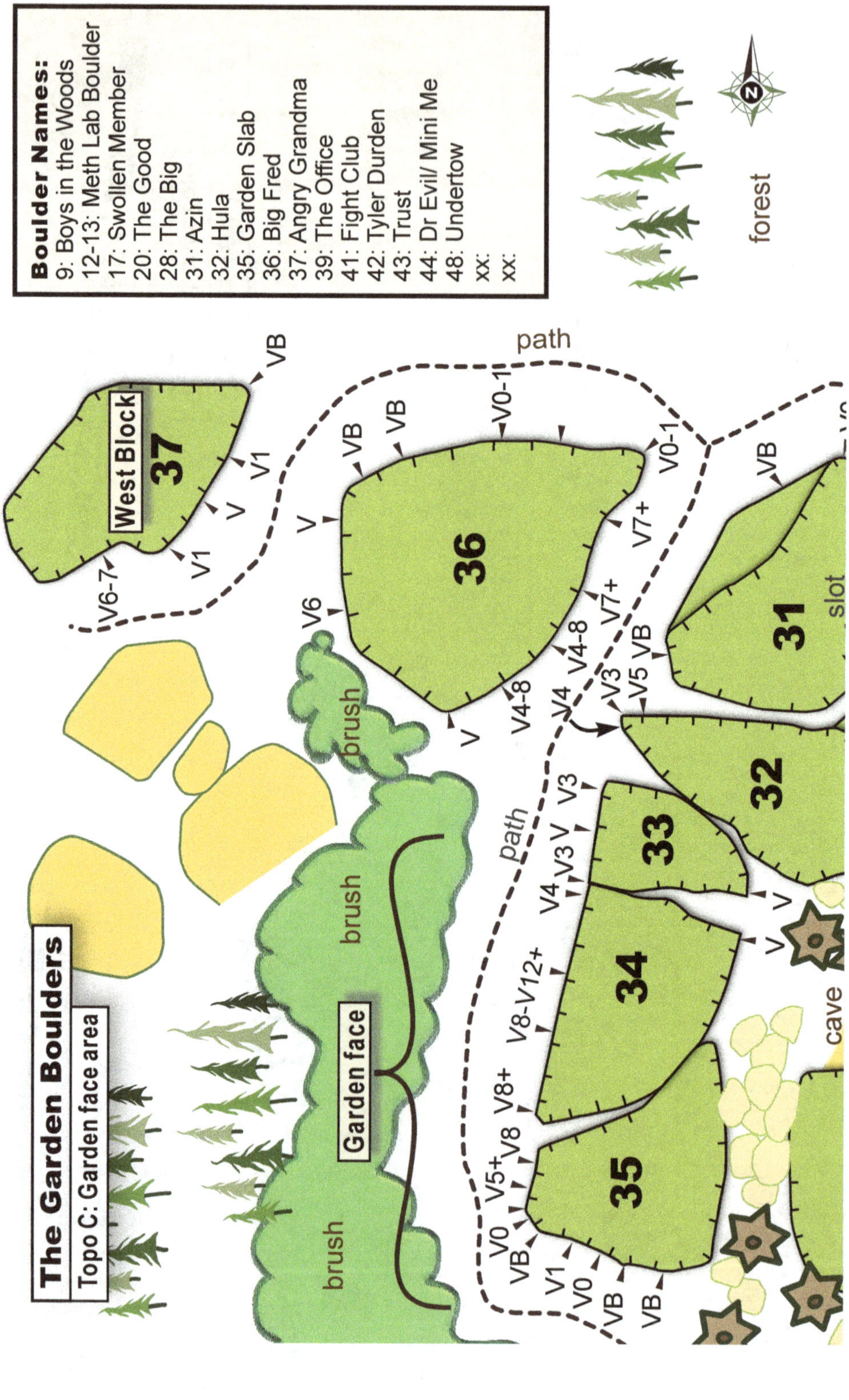

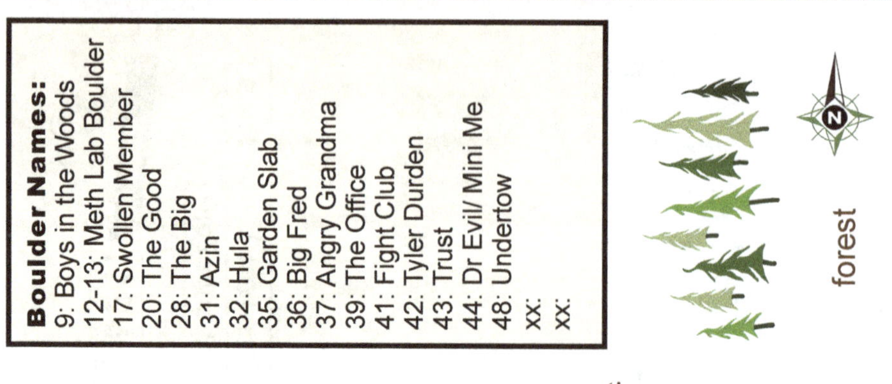

Boulder Names:
9: Boys in the Woods
12-13: Meth Lab Boulder
17: Swollen Member
20: The Good
28: The Big
31: Azin
32: Hula
35: Garden Slab
36: Big Fred
37: Angry Grandma
39: The Office
41: Fight Club
42: Tyler Durden
43: Trust
44: Dr Evil/ Mini Me
48: Undertow
xx:
xx:
forest

The Garden Boulders
Topo C: Garden face area
West Block
37
path
36
31
32
33
34
35
slot
cave
brush
brush
brush
brush
Garden face
path
VB
V1
V
V1
V6-7
V6
V
VB
VB
V0-1
V0-1
V7+
V7+
V4-8
V4-8
V4-8
V3
V5
VB
VB
V4
V3
V
V4 V3 V
V8-V12+
V8+
V8
V5+
V0
V1
V0
VB
VB
VB

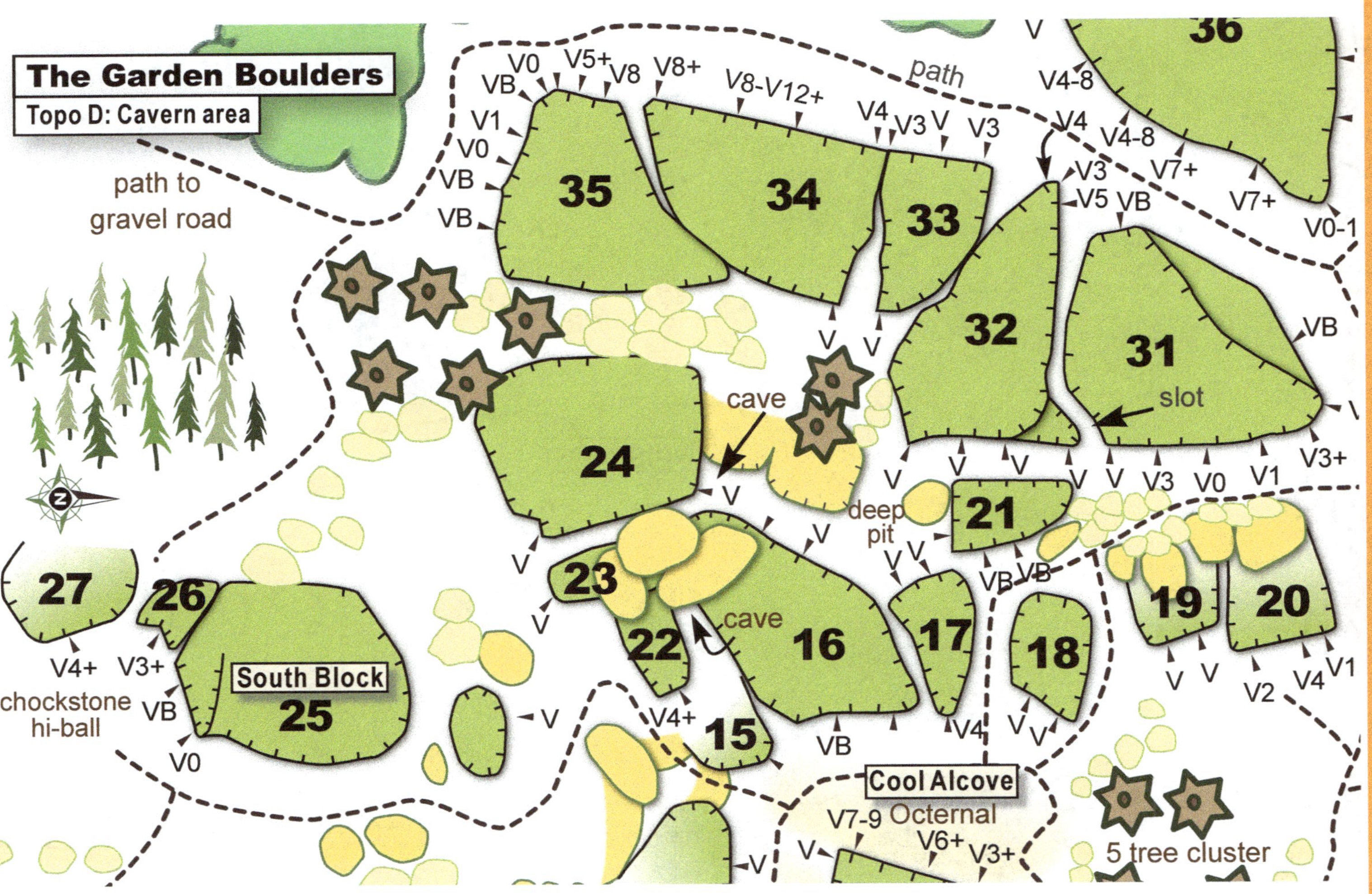

The Garden Boulders
Topo D: Cavern area
path to gravel road
path
slot
cave
cave
deep pit
South Block
Cool Alcove
V7-9 Octernal
V6+
V3+
5 tree cluster
chockstone
hi-ball
15
16
17
18
19
20
21
22
23
24
25
26
27
31
32
33
34
35
36
V0
VB
V5+ V8
V8+
V8-V12+
V4 V3 V
V3
V4
V4-8
V3
V5 VB
V7+
V7+
V4-8
V0-1
VB
V3+
V3
V0
V1
V1
VB VB
V4
V2
V4
V1
V4+
V3+
VB
V0
VB
V4+
V0
V1
V0
VB
VB

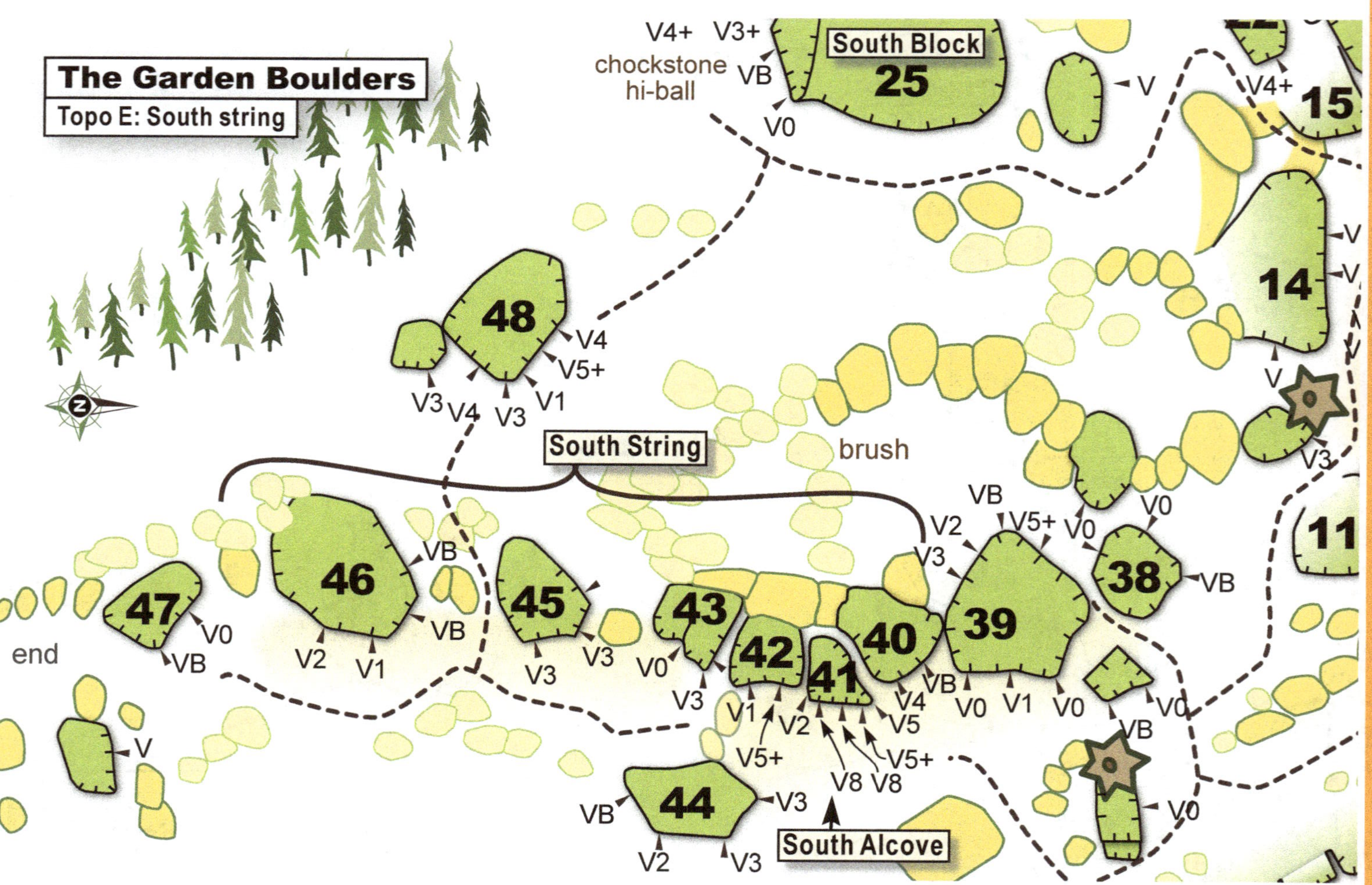
The Garden Boulders
Topo E: South string
South Block
25
V4+ V3+
chockstone VB
hi-ball
V0
V
V4+
15
14
V
V
V
V3
11
48
V4
V5+
V1
V3 V4 V3
South String
brush
VB
V5+ V0
V0
V2
V3
38
VB
V0
46
VB
VB
45
V3
V3
43
V0
V3
42
V1
V2
V5+
41
V8 V8
V5+
40
V4
V5
VB
V0
V1
V0
V0
VB
V0
39
47
V0
VB
end
V
44
VB
V3
V2 V3
South Alcove

The Garden have likely all seen an ascent or seen considerable projecting history over many years by different groups or local individuals. Various locals from Sweet Home to Eugene to Portland have been very active over several decades at this site, some of whom did not intermingle during those years (due mainly to generational gap or hometown origins). Some problems are serious hi-ball endeavors up to about 30' tall, but many boulders scratch the ceiling modestly from 8' to 17'.

The site is much more extensive than our diagram reflects (consult other locals if wanting to explore further afield). Bouldering grades vary from VB to V9+ on basaltic-andesitic rock. **Note**: the grades (if any) listed on the diagrams are mere non-representational estimates, and are not indicative of the actual real rating. Route locator pointers merely indicate a (non-absolute) [possible] V-problem.

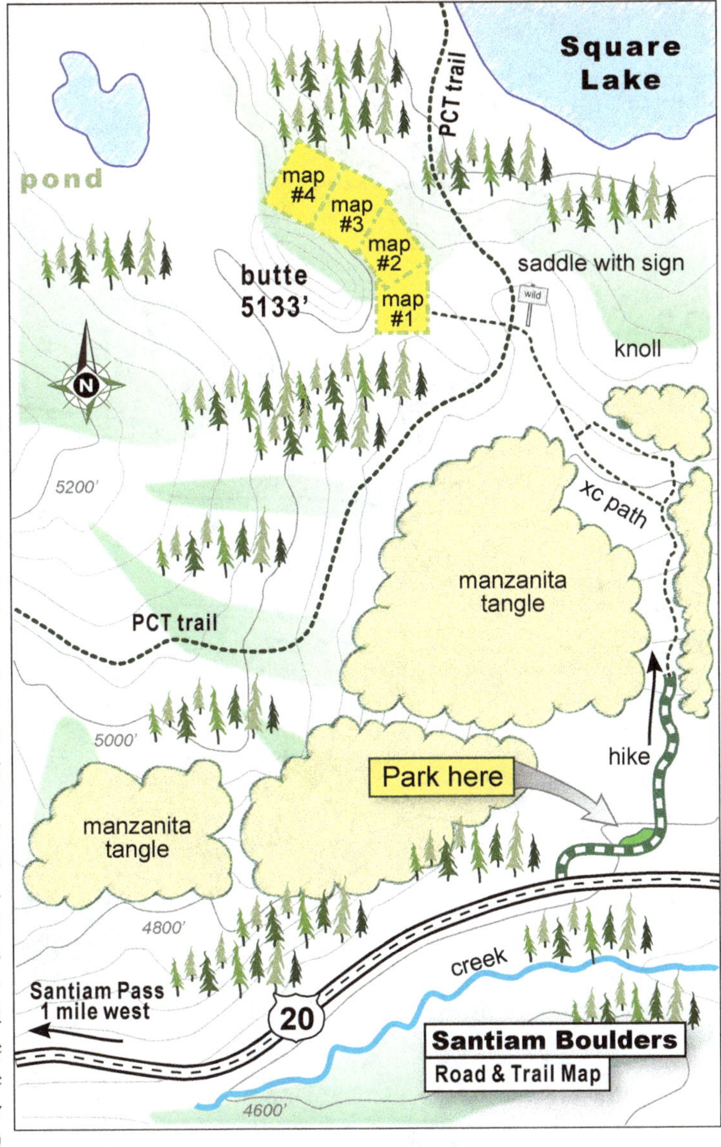

This set of diagrams primarily introduces you to the site and leaves you with the need to determine the actual grades of the problems (though many of the diagrams listed grades are within 1-2 degrees of accuracy). If you have time contact us and share your beta so as to make future editions of this book more concise.

Directions

Drive I-5 freeway to Albany, Oregon. Drive east on U.S. Hwy 20 for 28 miles to Sweet Home. When you are just east of town, turn north at the east end of the Foster Reservoir onto Quartzville Road. It immediately crosses a bridge over the east end of the reservoir. Drive for 3.4 miles and park at a wide spot on the right side of road. Walk further along the road for about 400', then enter a narrow path uphill into a grove of trees where you will meet a tightly packed cluster of mossy huge boulders. **Note**: Don't drive or park on the private logging road that cuts uphill near the parking

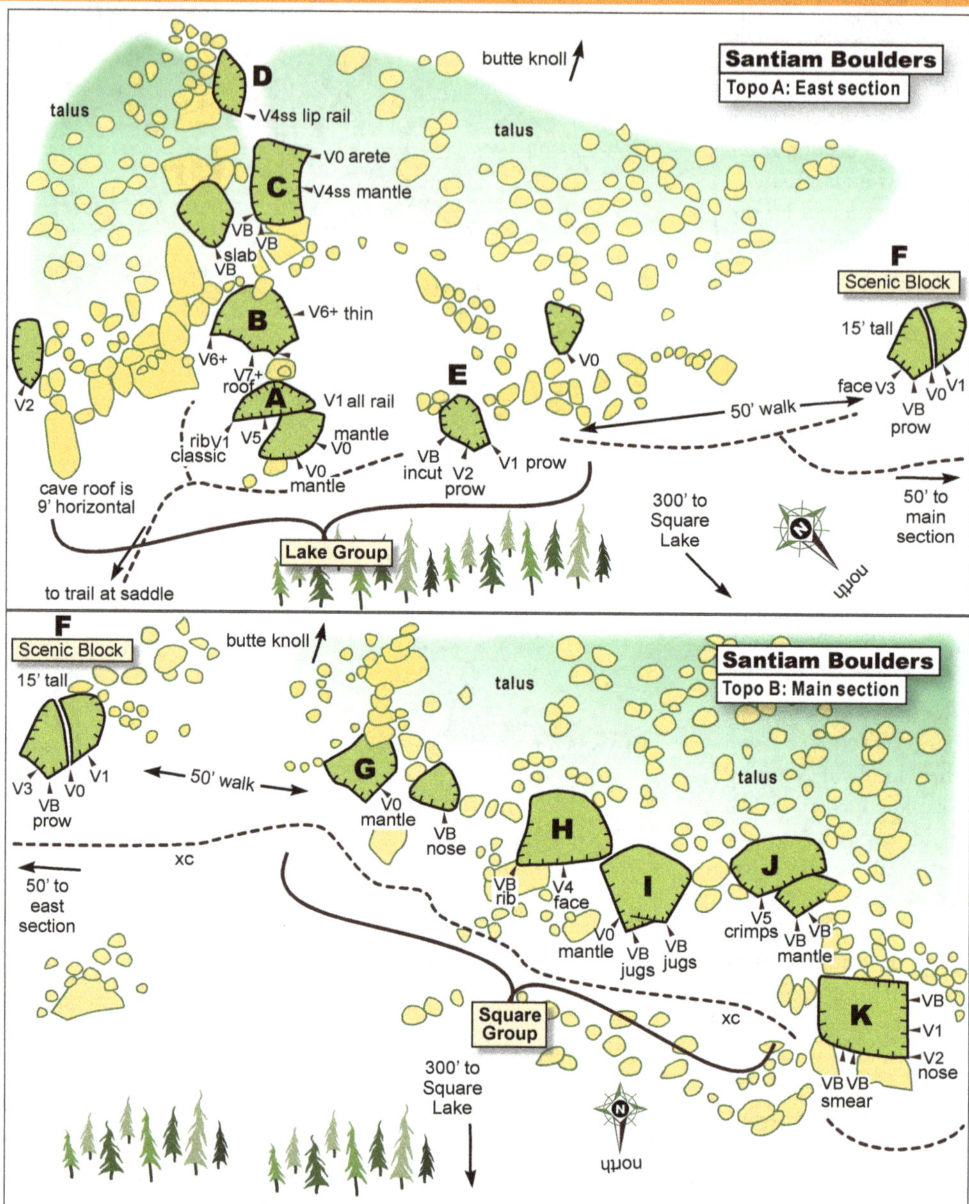

spot and site. If you perchance to drive past the bouldering site and end up at Green Peter Dam (you are 1.5 miles too far). GPS UTM 10T 533794 4920917, elevation 850'.

SANTIAM BOULDERS

A rare high-altitude northern Oregon bouldering site with a high quality pack of boulders. The site encompasses a broad string of large boulders wrapping around the north side of a prominent butte overlooking Square Lake, a small lake southeast of Three-Finger Jack peak. A plethora of grades range from VB-V5 (and likely to V8+) out of a total of roughly 90 problems. Boulders range in height from 8'-12' (up to 15' tall). Great bouldering, and superb scenery.

Many of the boulders lay in grassy duff soil so landings on many are natural (except on the actual talus slope). A recent forest fire swept this region burning all the trees, so the boulders are fully exposed to the sunshine and heat of summer (the site will reforest eventually). Moss and lichen free (for now), so step up and send. Seasonal access is feasible from June-October. Convenient easy access for day hike or camping nearby. Crashpad minimum (one will suffice). **History:** unknown, but Mr O thoroughly sent many (about 80%) V-grades at this site in about 2013.

Pro/Con: mosquitoes are very friendly during the summer till mid-August, but choose days with turbulance (clouds and wind) and the bugs will minimize.

Rock composition is basaltic, striated from glaciation, with a light brown surface patina and tiny aeration pockets. Unique weather etched rock surface nuances give it plenty of variety. Surficial weathering effects have increased the textural nuances by eroding the softer matrix revealing black feldspar and white/opaque crystal minerals (1mm), giving the overall exposed rock surface a rimples etched surface with contours, all tightly packed into a medium gray groundmass. Problems range from overhung crimps, steep slab smears, to lip mantles and more. Superb friction – an ultra light sandpaper feel of a type that your fingertips do not get raw from extended bouldering.

Directions

From Salem drive east on U.S. Hwy 20 to Santiam Pass. From the junction of NF 2690 (Hoodoo Ski Area / Big Lake road) you will continue east of the summit for about 2 miles. Turn north onto a narrow dirt road in a cluster of trees. Park here. Walk north uphill following the old road grade into a manzanita tangle. An undeveloped path continues through the tangle as it aims for the saddle between to minor knolls. When you reach the saddle another hikers trail crosses here and continues down to Square Lake. Walk just a few dozen yards on the hikers trail, then walk uphill cross-country northwest toward the north side of the large butte (knoll 5,133' elev). The first major stones are apparent from a distance. The eastern cluster of stones is mostly stout stuff, so traverse the slope horizontally to the north slope of the butte to reach the next main cluster of stones. Expect about 25 minutes to hike from road to site. Use a GPS

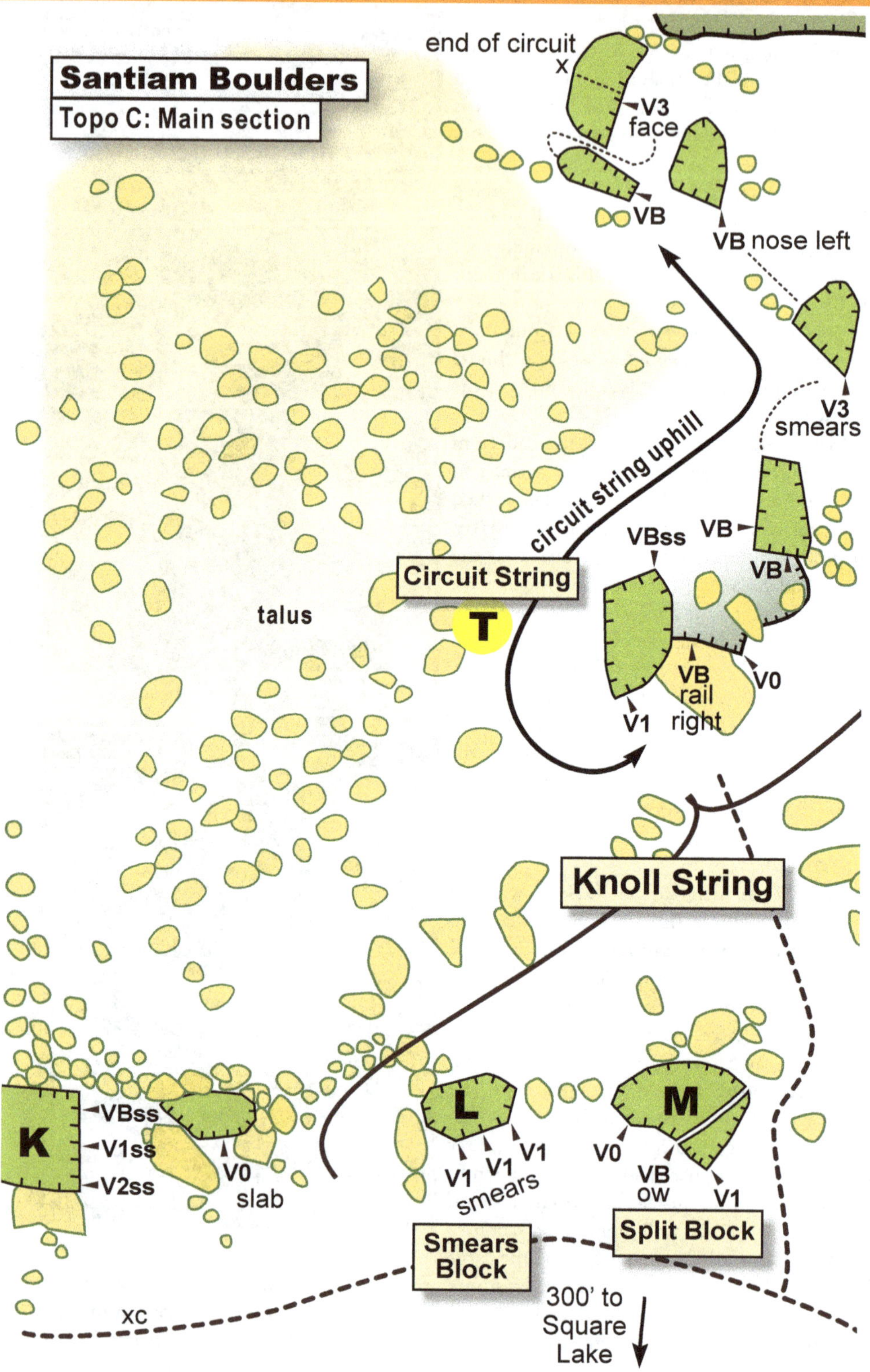
Santiam Boulders
Topo C: Main section
end of circuit
x
V3
face
VB
VB nose left
V3
smears
circuit string uphill
VBss
VB
VB
VB
Circuit String
T
talus
VB
rail
right
V0
V1
Knoll String
K
VBss
V1ss
V2ss
V0
slab
L
V1
V1
V1
smears
M
V0
VB
ow
V1
Split Block
Smears
Block
xc
300' to
Square
Lake

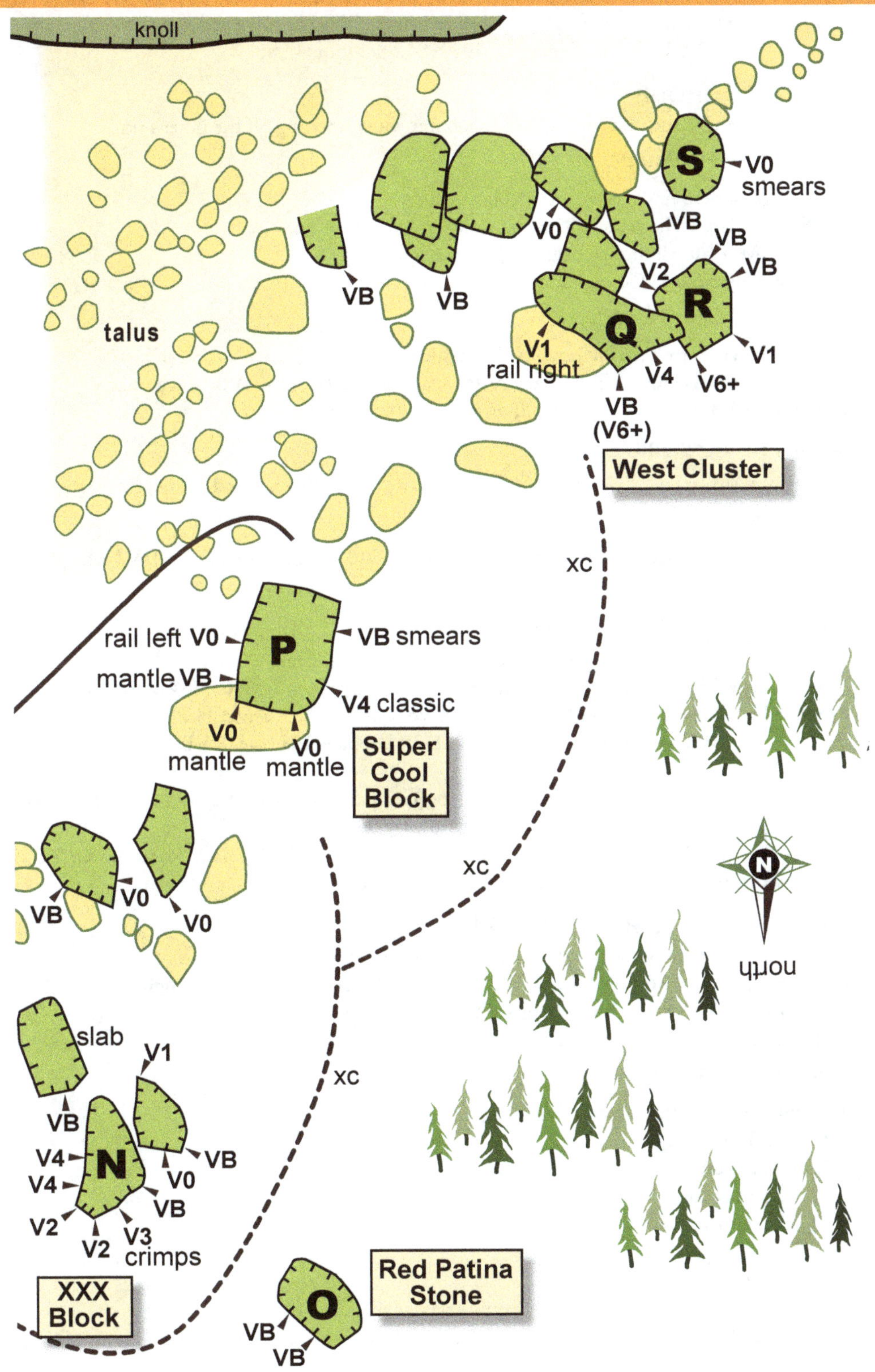

knoll
talus
S
V0 smears
V0
VB
VB
V2
VB
Q
R
V1
rail right
V4
V6+
V1
VB
(V6+)
West Cluster
xc
rail left V0
P
VB smears
mantle VB
V4 classic
V0
V0
mantle
V0
mantle
Super
Cool
Block
xc
N
north
VB
V0
V0
slab
V1
VB
V4
N
VB
V4
V0
V2
VB
V2
V3
crimps
XXX
Block
O
Red Patina
Stone
VB
VB
xc

unit if the manzanita thicket navigation is not your forte. Total distance from road to site is about ½ mile distance. GPS UTM 10T 593509 4920584, elevation 4,980'.

THE LAKE GROUP

The Lake String is the first section you encounter when stepping off the hiker's trail.

Boulder A (Flat Fin Boulder)

Has several superb lines on the rib/rail of the fin.

V1 Spin Meister. The classic rib run starting on left side of fin.

V1 Mere Mortal. All the rail beginning on the right.

V5ss Paradigm Shift. Center flat face on fin.

Boulder B (Wild Roof Boulder)

Boulder B: Very stout problems all tucked under a large roof (V5ss-V7ss+ [?]).

Boulder C: VB Tribute, VB Bribary, **V4ss Quagmiritis** (mantle), **V0 All against all.**

Boulder D: **V4ss Tech Titan** (lip rail traverse).

Boulder E (Little Pyramid)

VBss Buzz-cut (incut), **V2ss Double Helix** (prow), **V1ss Neutralized** (prow).

Boulder F (Scenic Boulder)

V3 Ideologic (left face), **VB Anti-Logic** (center rib), **V0 Flux of Time** (crack), **V1 Blacklisted** (right face).

THE SQUARE STRING GROUP

The Square String can be reached by walking west about 50' from the Scenic Boulder.

Boulder G: **V0 Full of Greenschist** (mantle), and nearby stone **VB Nabob Games** (nose).

Boulder H: **VB Scylla of Solidarity** (rib), **V4 Voodoo Science** (center face).

Boulder I: **V0ss Jewel Heist** (mantle), **VBss Dull Propaganda** (jugs), **VBss Dustbin of History** (jugs).

Boulder J: **V5ss Marguerita for my Seniorita** (crimps), and the next door stone **VBss State-of-the-Art Primitive** (mantle), **VBss Whackamole** (mantle).

Boulder K: **VBss Yurrong** (smear), **VBss All Lies** (smear), **V2ss Jingoistic Xenophobia** (nose), **V1ss Lowest Low** (shorty), **VBss Much Ballyhooed** (shorter still).

THE KNOLL NORTH SLOPE STRING

The Knoll String of boulders is the core zone where numerous classics exist.

Boulder L (Smears Stone): **V1ss Fat City, V1ss In Lean Times, V1ss Unlogic.**

Boulder M (Split Stone): **V0ss Political Detox** (left face), **VBss Nullified Vacuum** (offwidth), **V1ss Monsieur Sophisticate** (nose).

Boulder N (XXX Boulder)

This unique stone offers an enticing set of lines (beta L to R).

V4ss Iron Fist (left face).

V4ss Parabellum Paradigm (left face).

V2 Reality Vacuum (left nose).

V2 Ultimate Meaning (right nose).

V3 XXX (crimps).

VB Witch Hunt (west face).

Immediately west a few feet of XXX Boulder is a smaller boulder.

V0 Utopian Illusion (north face), **VB Maxim of Prudence** (north point), **V1 Flaming Pomp-**

ous **Blowhard** (south point).

And a **VB Boo** short slab a few feet south of Cool Stone.
Boulder O (Red Patina): VBss Knuckleheaded Nitpicker, VBss Wimpsville Stuff.

Boulder P (Super Cool Boulder)

This is the other superb boulder (beta L to R).
V0 Kangaroo Court (rail running left).
VB Twaddle (mantle).
V0 Doublespeak (mantle left point).
V0 Double Standard (mantle right point).
V4 Superspymaster (crimps face).
VB Bankrupt in Paradise (smears on west side).

WEST GROUP

The upper West String cluster of boulders are a tightly
packed core of 10 blocks (and several classic lines).

Boulder Q

Boulder Q is the flat unit perched on another stone.
V1ss Known Unknowns (rail going right).
VB (V5+ss) Whack-job. Step in mantle, or SS low up
onto point.
V4ss Blood Vengence (steep face).

Boulder R

Boulder R is a quality big stone.
V6+ (?) north hung point.

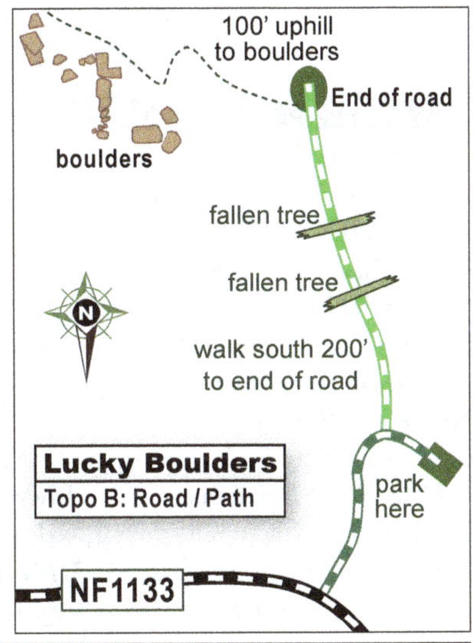

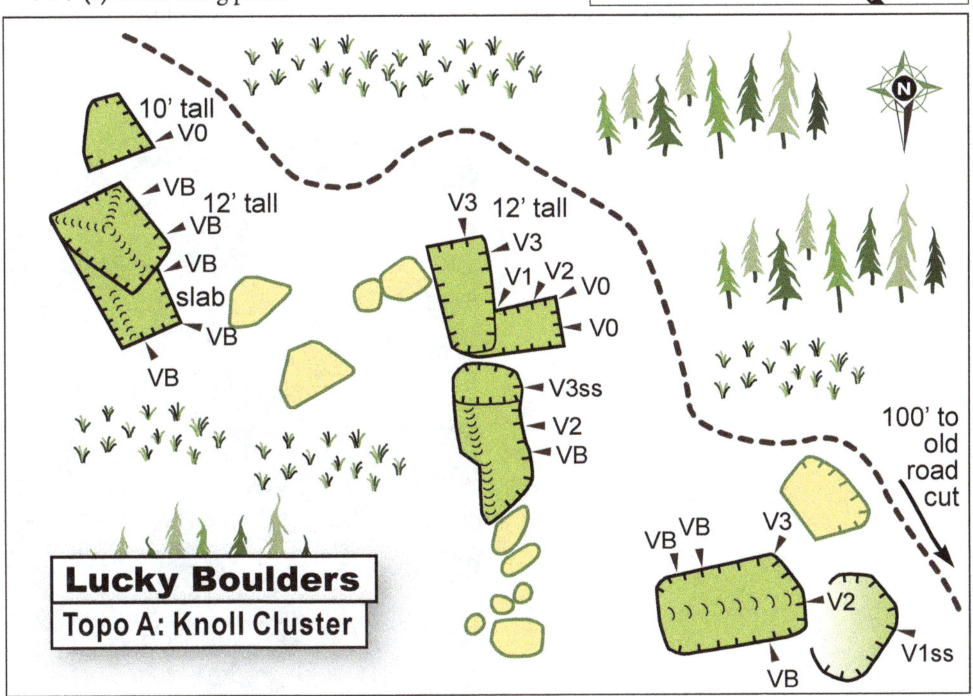

V1 Security Risk (west point prow).
VB Reef of Civil Ruin (wide face left).
VB Verwöhnt Brat (wide face right).
V2ss Cold Warrior (on upper backside).

Boulder S has minor **V0ss Slippery Slope** (short smears).
Lastly, several nearby short stones have a few random **VB-V0** options (all well done).

CIRCUIT STRING

Circuit String (T) goes up the talus field almost to the knoll as a rambling **Circuit Jerks** tour. Start on the lowest unit and run either the V1 or the VBss rail (rightward). Step up, then run the VB on next block, then V3 smear on next block and so on.

LUCKY BOULDERS

A scenic rocky prominence (and some boulders) juts up at the jet blue sky in the forested high-country south of Detroit Dam. Will it be popular? No, it has an unlucky location in the middle of nowhere. But with a camera in your pocket, chalkbag and rock shoes in a fanny pack, an adventure in your heart is just enough for an exploratory jaunt in the scenic old Cascade Range of western Oregon. This site has weathered andesite boulders (vertical and overhung aspects), yet overall is limited in scope (about 20+ lines). A brief hike up onto the backside of the rocky ridge crest knoll provides quality views of the region and photo opportunities of jagged short rock horns. **History:** Numerous V-grades were tapped by Mr O in about 2012. The rock cliff has seen exploratory rock climbing activity in the not too distant past.

Directions: Drive east on U.S. Hwy 22 from Salem to Detroit Dam, then cross the dam on NF 2212, driving this paved (then gravel) road for 15.7 miles (8 miles of it is gravel) to a 4-way junction. At the junction of NF 1155/NF 1133/NF 2212 drive east on NF 1133 for 4 miles to the site. Turn south onto a short old logging road for 200′ and park. Walk this south on an old roadbed for 900′ to its end, then cut uphill in open forest for 150′ to the boulders. GPS UTM 10T 566791 4938453, elevation 4,380′.

URBAN & OTHER MISCELLANEOUS AREAS

The following bouldering options are merely referential listings. Though several are important high status sites (specifically Carver and Sisters Boulders), the other miscellaneous areas are not necessarily intended to be something to consume your vitality. Each new year brings to the forefront an ever greater array of quality bouldering sites throughout this entire micro-region. Some of the following are only intended to offer you alternate fallback options, though some of the sites have certainly been utilized enjoyably by folks at one time or another in years past.

THE SCHWINGUS

A secluded obscure site on a very brief overhung rock scarp, with a limited quantity of fairly decent problems. Some risky landings, some suspect loose blocks, and occasional itinerant persons dwelling there, yet the problems offer a standard punchy set, combined with a set of eliminates. Seldom used these days because of a combination of unappealing factors.

Directions

Take exit #5 eastbound of I-84 (or exit #23 from I-205 at Sandy Blvd). Once you are one NE 82nd Avenue, drive north to Fremont Street. Turn east and drive approximately ½ mile until the road curves north to become 91st Avenue. Shortly the road curves east again and becomes Rocky Butte Way. Park alongside the paved road (near the college dorms, after passing the church domes. On the north side of road walk easterly on a prominent trail (that parallels the roads stone masonry retaining wall). As the trail nears the freeway it descends gradually to a zigzag where it turns back west. At this point a subsidiary trail branches off and aims directly to the freeway chain-link perimeter fence, then continues south alongside the fence for roughly 300 yards, then veers rightward to the slightly overhung bouldering cliff in a lightly forested setting. Beta is from L to R.

V0 to V3 Left Side. Multiple variations exist.

V7 Death Row. Undercling under roof, then straight up on slopers/edges to layback, ends on pointed jug.

V8 Tooth and Nail. Variant that begins on DR and ends on TN.

V7ss Incisor. SS at large tooth, send to horizontal crimp seam, catch an undercling under a roof, ending on jug 3' up right. Rules: avoid dihedral.

V5 Molar. Duplicates Incisor to horizontal crimp, then right hand gaston, & roof undercling.

V2ss Warm up. SS on low flat jug, and up corner to Incisor jug.

V6 Jungle Bunnies. Classic. Begin low on the Warm Up, traverse right using obvious sloper, then a square-ish hold, then dyno to the finishing jug. Rules: no other holds.

V4 Traverse the entire face in either direction.

V5 Low traverse (as it says) passing a small movable block.

V4ss Stone Jerks. Classic. SS in a rocky pit, first hold is a large hollow block, climb directly up

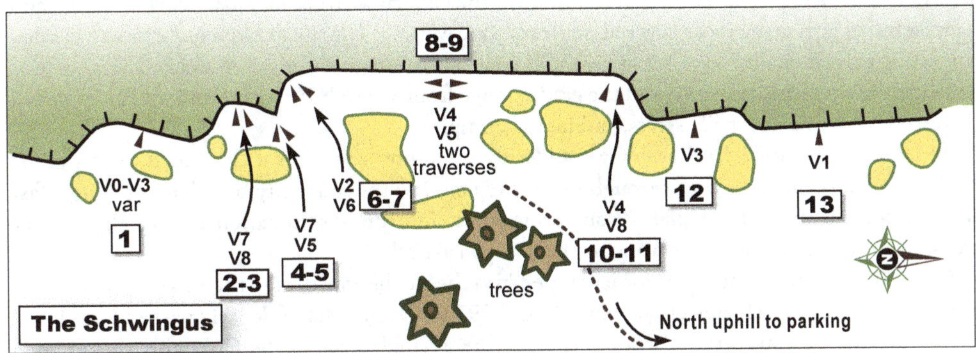

until difficulties force you right, then continue higher to a ledge; traverse right to descend.

V8 Congo. Cruise SJ, but instead of exiting right, bear up left using rock fin.

V3 Face. Begin on low roof, ascend directly up using various sized edges.

V1 Right Face. The warmup.

MAGMA ZONE

An obscure, north-facing basalt outcrop with a minor selection of easy to moderate lines, in an area that stays shaded and cool much of the year. Seldom used by locals today simply because there are better bouldering options elsewhere in the region.

Directions

Drive east on I-84, take exit #18, and park at Lewis & Clark State Park (Broughton Bluff). Walk past the rest facility onto a trail that travels east. Walk roughly one mile east from the parking site. You will pass a yellow lichen covered cliff, two big trail side stones, Dave's Wall, a minor deep ravine, then a minor ridge at the edge of a deep brushy ravine. Stop here; scramble up a faint path 160' to the short basalt bluff. Avoid topping out on the lines (considerable brush and moss). Most problems are still somewhat clean (up to the drop off point). Beta from R to L (see diagram).

The Zone Section

V1 Kindle, V1 Chaos Lace, V1 Chaos Left, V1 Morphing, V3 In the Zone (ascend a shallow arête), **V1 Ribbon of Axis, V1 Eye of the Cobra** (a quality face to the right of a prow), **V0 Steam Escape, V2 Magma Man** (the classic overhanging prow).

Phantom Phase Section

V3 Phantom Phase, V4 The Phantom (start PP, exit left at crimper and mono, avoid diagonal jug on right), **V2 Tiger Tightly.**

Lava Bomb Section

V2 Pure Bomb, V2ss Lava Burst (SS and move directly up on pockets), **V0 The Ramp, V0 Lava Blast, V3 Lava Bomb, V0 No Name, V2 Guide by Voice.**

Super Hive Section

V1 Sticky Stinger, V4 Super Hive (lip traverse right to left, end on ledge), **V5 Hive** (start at low point, move directly up on slopers), **V2 Buzz Diver, V2 Pinch Face, V2 The Mangler.**

CARVER BOULDERS

The Carver bouldering site is the original beginnings of quality bouldering in the Portland, Oregon region in the fog shrouded era of the late '80s and early '90s. After new indoor bouldering and climbing gyms began to successfully take root in Portland various eager individuals and small teams went in search of nearby outdoor bouldering opportunities. And behold, Carver, being a well-known rock climbing lead site at that time fit the pattern well, because just below the cliff band a forest full of lush green moss covered boulders were waiting. The site, though quite mossy, yields a fine string of high quality favorites many locals continue to enjoy sending even today. There are over 160 boulder problems available, and the grades range from VB to V10, with plenty of SS, some rail traverses, numerous low belly starts, and lots of crimping.

Today, the site is still a fair haven for bouldering, but it now competes with a much greater venue of destination bouldering sites throughout this region. For the inner city boulderer seeking a fast fix the place still offers viable quality bouldering entertainment. In summation, it's a locally popular site well known for its boulders being as short as you are tall.

General History: A variety of locals tapped into the site heavily during the 80's-90's first phase, and again during a brief later phase from about 1997-2001. Pockets of densely packed large boulders, from the Bonzai to the Carpet cluster, or the Triangle Face to the Columbia cluster were

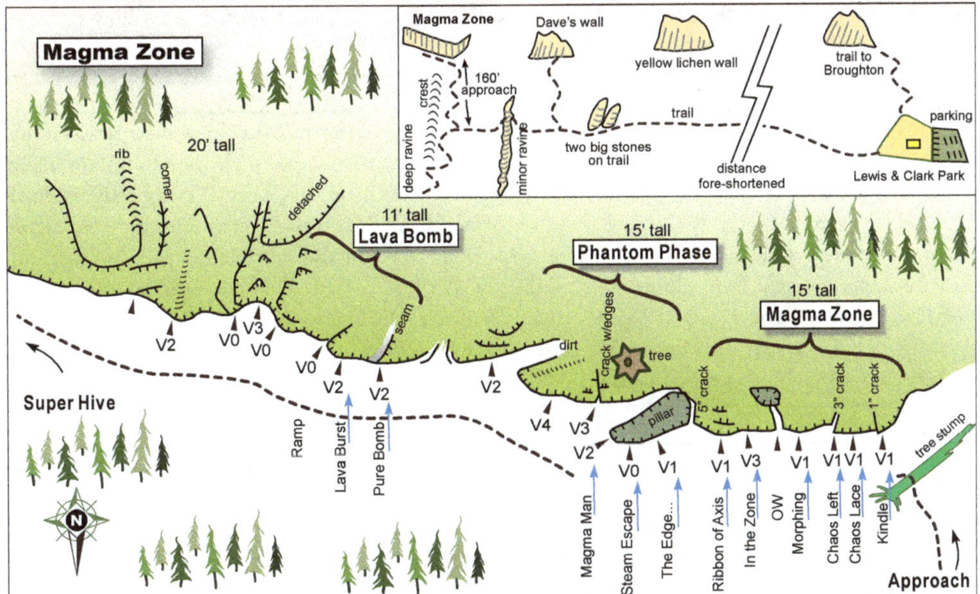

revealed and tapped over a busy 5-7 years timeframe. Notable locals such as G Lyon, J Bernert, A Coleman, M Pajunas, M Alfers, G Rall, T Abbott, M Slayton, A Burr, and many others were instrumental in bringing this place onto the bouldering circuit. Mr Abbott made the first digital (html) guide to Carver Boulders in

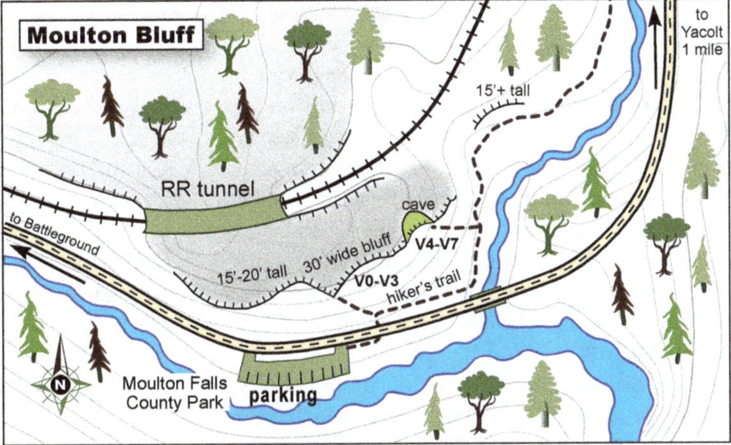

April 2001. Mr Bernet produced the first pamplet guide in 2002 ("Bouldering in Carver, Oregon"). Mr Williams produced a briefly sold Carver bouldering guide in 2012.

The entire Carver property (the cliff and boulders) is privately owned. To rock climb or boulder at Carver you are required to be a member of the CCC by signing a liability release waiver, and obeying all rules established by the owner concerning access to the site.

Visit the official Carver Climbing Club website (www.carverclimbingclub.org/) for more info and directions. Several local indoor sports gyms in Portland provide alternate ways to become a member of the CCC organization. Browse Spencer's web blog for a brief analysis of the bouldering (carverbouldering.blogspot.com/). Take the time to visit this little local gem bouldering site.

MOULTON BLUFF

Brief and utterly obscure bouldering potential (VB-V4) on scattered basaltic formations. A minor 5' tall cave-*like* formation offers V4-V6+ (12' deep x 20' width) power roof clinging, ground crashpad entertainment. Most options here are damp for 8-9 months of the year. Drive I-205 freeway into Vancouver, then State 503 north to Battleground, Washington, then follow signs to Moulton Falls State Park on the Lewis River near Yacolt, Washington.

THE WIND

A very, very tiny spot that is often windy with a south-facing full sunshine orientation. The minor outcrop formation is an overhung protrusion on a talus slope, with mostly hollow flake crimp handholds, that despite its profound overriding nuisances, has been infrequently utilized for bouldering by a few individuals desperate for anything dry in the winter months [*Hamilton Boulders anyone?*]. Located at the same level as Windy Slab (on the south slope of Wind Mtn in the Columbia Gorge). Park along the shoulder of Washington SR14 and scramble 150' up the steep talus slope to the bench at Windy Slab. From the slab walk west about 615' gaining elevation slightly as you near the minor bluff formation where the bouldering occurs. GPS UTM 10T 596622 5061865. No beta, no diagram.

SISTERS BOULDERS

Seeking a bouldering site that receives nearly 300 days of sunshine per year. Sisters Boulders could quite possibly be that kissing cousin. Situated a few miles northeast of Sisters, Oregon, this bluff formation is surprisingly appealing for bouldering, and for top-rope climbing on the taller formations. The horseshoe-shaped rock formation is studded with a number of 12'-24' tall bluff and seperate pillars. V-scale grades range from VB to V7+. Many problems involve intricate movement on steep vesicular (pocketed) aspects, overhung in places, and usually ending on a well-rounded knobby top. The tallest climbs are along the outer perimeter of the Front Gates section and at both ends of the Fortress formation. If your fingertips are well callused to withstand the gritty nature of the tuffaceous rock, you can solve the riddle on several dozen problems till your fingertips get raw. The formation is the end product of magmatic volcanism, which over time the surrounding soils eroded by decompositional weathering, leaving the more resistant bluff formation. The constituent textural minerals in the rock matrix give it a stout gritty surficial feel. The Sisters Boulders is a year-round viable bouldering site (weather dependent).

For concise beta to this unique little site enquire with Bend area locals (such as the *Central Oregon Bouldering* website). This brief section is included merely as an example to point you to the one of the many further afield bouldering options that do exist in Oregon state.

Directions

From Sisters, Oregon drive north on N Locust Street (which becomes Camp Polk Road, which becomes Wilt Road) for 8.1 miles total. Turn west on Blaze Lane and go 300', then north 300' on a cul-de-sac dirt road to the parking spot. **Note:** The Blaze Lane turnoff is about 3 miles past Hinkle Butte lookout access road. The primary paved road turns to gravel shortly after Hinkle Butte Road. Car camping is feasible in the area, but amenities are available only in town.

GPS UTM 10T 623515 4913960, elevation 2,920'.

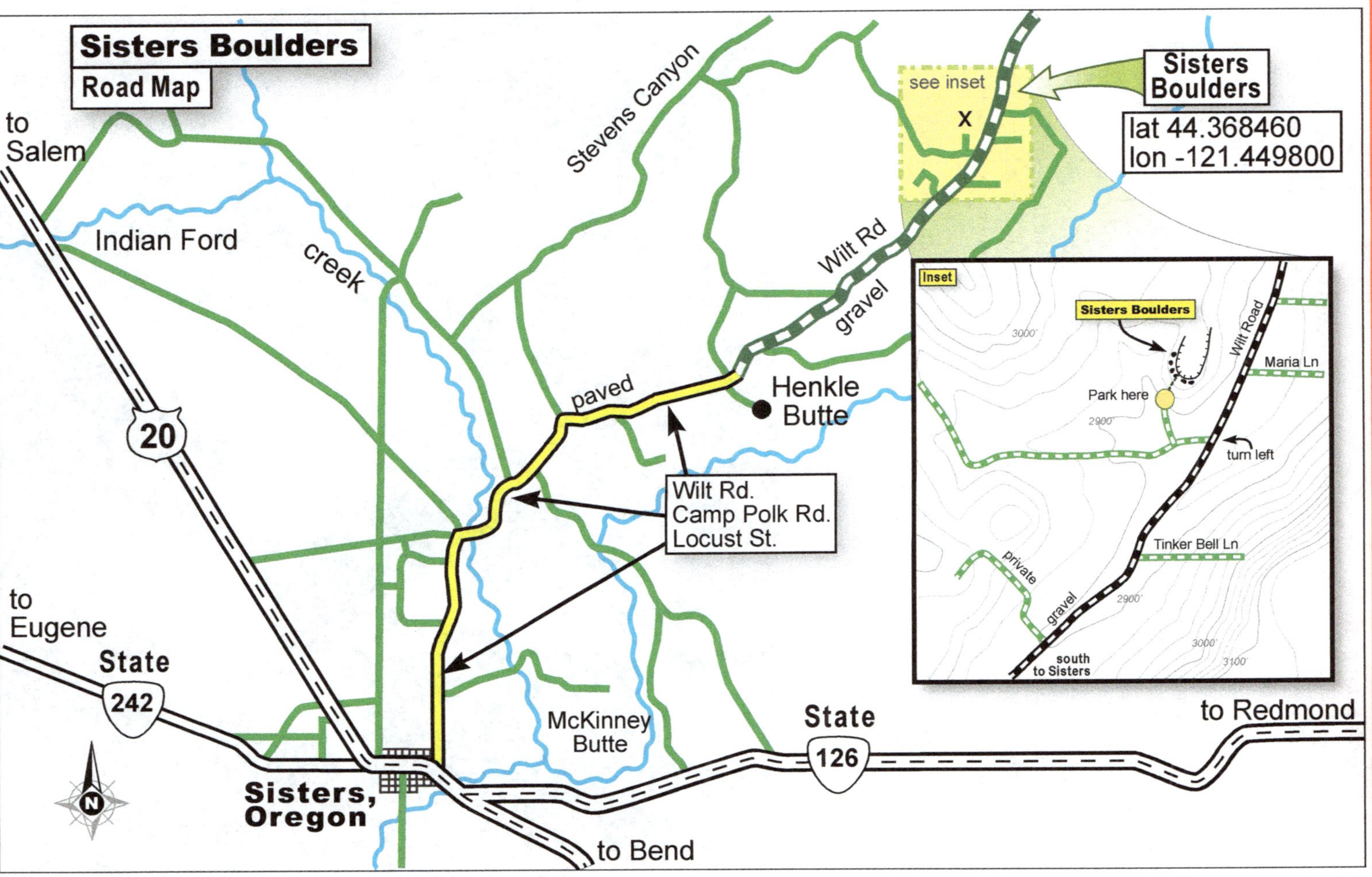
Sisters Boulders
Road Map
to Salem
Indian Ford
creek
Stevens Canyon
Wilt Rd
gravel
see inset
x
Sisters Boulders
lat 44.368460
lon -121.449800
Inset
3000'
Sisters Boulders
Park here
2900'
Wilt Road
Maria Ln
turn left
private
gravel
Tinker Bell Ln
2900'
3000'
3100'
south to Sisters
paved
Henkle Butte
Wilt Rd.
Camp Polk Rd.
Locust St.
20
to Eugene
State 242
N
Sisters, Oregon
McKinney Butte
State 126
to Redmond
to Bend

Guidebook Summation

In years past this general region (northern Oregon and southwest Washington) has *not* been known for its outdoor bouldering venue. But today the game has changed substantially due to an overwhelming interest in the sport of bouldering.

In one gigantic sweep the comprehensive legacy of this bouldering guidebook tackles that great information void, and covers in a wealth of detail many of the bouldering options found in this relatively minor micro-region of the USA. One notable and ultimately qualitative overriding feature of this unique book is its ability to bring to the forefront an impressive analysis of both the historical bouldering sites (and its related events), as well as many of the latest cool bouldering sites worth visiting (like LLB).

The 66+ bouldering sites described within this book are only a small fragment of the total viable sites still yet to tap in this region. This books fully loaded rocket list of endless bouldering options, found right here in this little corner of two Pacific Northwest states, all detailed right here in this notable guidebook, should keep you energetically pushing your maximum V-edge for many years ahead.

In the end this extensive guidebook treatise on bouldering will see dust settle on the comment, "There's just not much bouldering near Portland."

On a captivating sunny alpine day,
Sam powers a stellar problem at the
Alpenglow Boulders

CPSIA information can be obtained
at www.ICGtesting.com
Printed in the USA
BVHW061918300821
615370BV00003B/3